A New Jersey Anthology

A New Jersey Anthology

compiled and edited by

Maxine N. Lurie

Rutgers University Press
New Brunswick, New Jersey

First published in 1994 by the New Jersey Historical Commission
Newark, New Jersey

Reprinted 2002 by Rutgers University Press
New Brunswick, New Jersey

Copyright © 1994 by the New Jersey Historical Commission

Library of Congress Cataloging-in-Publication Data and British Library
Cataloging-in-Publication Data are available upon request.

ISBN 0-8135-3267-1

Manufactured in the United States of America

To my teachers,
David Leach and David S. Lovejoy

Contents

Preface

This book grew out of a perceived need among teachers (myself and others) for a selection of readings that could be used in courses either on New Jersey history or on United States history taught in New Jersey. With both functions in mind, it is designed to deal with general topics illustrated by specific and local (meaning state) examples. Although there is a wealth of materials available on aspects of New Jersey history, much is not always accessible; many important articles are either out of print or else are contained in scholarly journals of limited circulation. It is hoped that this book will both fill a need and encourage readers to explore the issues it raises in other publications. To assist such readers, the introduction contains footnotes to works that discuss various subjects of necessity only briefly mentioned. In addition, the headnote preceding each selection ends with a list of suggested readings, works of a general nature as well as works specifically on New Jersey.

The journal articles and book chapters included here were selected to cover New Jersey history both chronologically and thematically, from the colonial period to the 1980s. They represent the wide variety of contemporary historical studies, including works analytical or biographical in form, political or social in emphasis. Some illustrate historiographical trends; others deal with historical puzzles. The headnotes introduce readers to the issues and methods that have engaged historians, both in general and in relation to each specific event or figure in New Jersey history. The headnotes also ask questions in an attempt to prod readers to think about history, historians, and the particular place where they live.

Like most authors, I would like to thank a number of people. The manuscript has profited from several readings given it by my husband Jonathan Lurie as well as from the editorial assistance of Kathryn Grover. I have benefited from the cheerful help of many friends in Special Collections at Rutgers University Libraries and have enjoyed the encouragement given by Susan Schrepfer and Richard P. McCormick in the history department and by Robert Burnett when at the New Jersey Historical Society. Most appreciated has been the support of David, Deborah, and Daniel Lurie, all old enough to understand the work of their historian-parents.

Maxine N. Lurie
August 1993

Despite its industrial image, New Jersey has been largely rural throughout much of its history; areas of the state remain devoted to the production of fruits and vegetables. Blueberry picker on the Lower Bank, Burlington County, about 1960. Photograph courtesy the Augustine Collection, Special Collections, Rutgers University Libraries, New Brunswick, New Jersey.

Introduction

Although a relatively small state, only 4.8 million acres in area, New Jersey has a long and complex history. Its past is full of paradoxes and contradictions that make it a challenge to study and understand. Primarily an agricultural state for most of its history, New Jersey was also one of the earliest to turn to manufacturing and chemical research. Today, while continuing to call itself the "Garden State," it has both the highest population density in the country and the largest number of hazardous waste sites. Although seemingly paved from one end to another with cities that sprawl into adjacent suburbs, large areas remain devoted to horse farms, cornfields, orchards, nurseries, blueberry bushes, and cranberry bogs. For much of its past New Jersey has been conservative in politics, policies, and attitudes, but it has also been in the forefront of recent reform efforts and judicial decisions. Although an old state—the so-called "cockpit of the Revolution," with numerous historical markers to attest that designation—it has largely failed to develop an identity of its own.

Early on New Jersey was described as a "barrel tapped at both ends," caught between bigger, and better-known, New York and Pennsylvania.[1] It was a thoroughfare, "the corridor state," a place one traveled through by horse, train, and then car to get somewhere else. Even today the primary image for outsiders is of the New Jersey Turnpike lined with belching oil refineries. As such it has become the butt of national jokes and has been called, among other names, "the armpit of America."[2] The tendency for even New Jersey residents to identify with their neighbors has been symbolized by the lack, until very recently, of a television station broadcasting from within the state's borders. Former governor Thomas Kean's ad campaign "New Jersey and You, Great Together" was aimed, at least in part, at creating a positive image *and* personality for an entity more than three hundred years old.

History itself explains New Jersey's identity crisis. At an early point it was divided into an "east" and "west" (later transformed into "north" and "south"). Political disagreements followed these divisions. Also, from the beginning diversity characterized its development. The state ranges geographically from an extensive seashore, fertile plains, and "barren" pinelands to muted mountains.[3] From the colonial period on its population included a variety of ethnic and religious groups. One result of all this diversity has been much disagreement. Thomas Fleming suggests New Jersey's motto "might well be 'Divided we stand'" for, he notes, "few states have equalled the multiplicity and duration of New Jersey's internal quarrels."[4]

New Jersey has long had a dubious reputation for its politics and its "justice." In 1944 the *Elizabeth Daily Journal* observed that "few states have been so cursed with political gangsters as New Jersey." Notorious figures include Lord Cornbury in the eighteenth century and "Boss" Frank Hague in the twentieth, both frequently cited examples of corruption. There are numerous examples of election returns falsified by a varied of methods— ballot boxes being stuffed, polls remaining open for ten weeks in 1789, gerrymandered districts such as the "horseshoe" being created in Hudson County in 1871 and several odd shapes designed in 1992. To avoid detection, poll books have been burned, and even a judicial ruling obtained that ballot boxes could be opened but the contents not examined. New Jersey presented the first Congress with the first disputed federal election, not the state's last. In 1894 two senates tried to occupy the state house in Trenton simultaneously.[5]

All this political "skulduggery," and more, is a consequence of both the numerous divisions within the state and a long record of closely contested politics. Although political parties have come and gone in New Jersey, the balance within the state, whether between Federalists and Jeffersonian-Republicans, Jacksonian-Democrats and Whigs, or modern-day Democrats and Republicans, has generally been close. Voters have frequently changed their party choice from one election to the next. Their independent attitudes often have meant that the governor and the majority of the legislature came from different parties.[6]

New Jersey has also had a long history of opposition to taxes, in part a function of the rural, conservative nature of the state. In the colonial period government was financed through paper money, the interest earned by its loan serving in lieu of taxes.[7] During the nineteenth century the state obtained money first by granting a railroad monopoly and then by liberal incorporation laws—both in return for fees. Not until the 1970s, with status as a wealthy urban state long since reached, did New Jersey enact laws providing for sales and income taxes to support public services. As a result, the state lagged behind much of the rest of the country in funding educational facilities and other services. Residents still feel the effects of this slow development. Because of the long dearth of higher educational opportunities the state continues to send a disproportionately high number of students outside its borders to college and often loses their brainpower permanently as a consequence.

Where New Jersey has been in education, politics, and culture makes its present more comprehensible. Residents can be proud of some, though not all, of their state's history, and they should not sell it short. Their little state is complex and interesting.

◆ ◆ ◆ ◆ ◆ ◆

As elsewhere on the North American continent, Indians were the first inhabitants of New Jersey. Their population has been estimated at between eight and twelve thousand, most of them Lenni Lenapes, at the time of European contact. And, as elsewhere in early America, their numbers were decimated by the diseases brought by whites. The native American population of New Jersey, it is estimated, quickly dwindled to between twenty-four hundred and three thousand in 1700, to less than one thousand in 1763, and to fewer than two hundred by 1800. Those who did not succumb to illness were pushed out by land-hungry white settlers. They went first to West Jersey, then to Pennsylvania or New York, and ultimately to Oklahoma and Canada.[8] Although the first whites to make contact with this original native American population were probably French, Spanish, and English fishermen or traders, the earliest European settlers were Dutch and Swedes. In 1609 Henry Hudson explored both New Jersey's coast and the river that took his name. His efforts were followed up by the Dutch West Indies Company in 1621. The Dutch were primarily interested in establishing trading posts to obtain furs and concentrated their efforts more on the east side of the river. In addition, conflicts with native American inhabitants forced their eastward retreat to New Amsterdam in 1643 and 1655. As a result the Dutch were few in number and short on success: by 1660 their settlements in New Jersey consisted of isolated residents and the fortified hamlet of Bergen.

The Dutch were not the only newcomers to the region nor alone in having difficulties with the native population. In 1638, when the New Sweden Company established an outpost on the Delaware, Governor Johan Printz (known as "big belly" because he weighed more than four hundred pounds) wrote that he would like "a couple of hundred Soldiers" on hand "until we broke the necks of all of them in the river."[9] The soldiers were not forthcoming, and the Swedes, after several confrontations with the Dutch, surrendered their claims to the region in 1655. At that time, an estimated four hundred Swedes and four thousand Dutch populated the entire Delaware valley (not just New Jersey).[10]

Commercial rivals of the English in Europe and elsewhere, the Dutch did not retain their hegemony in America for long. Their colony provided a further source of conflict because it physically divided the northern and southern portions of the empire the British were building. As a result, in 1664 Charles II granted his brother, the Duke of York, a widespread American colony incorporating parts of present-day New York, New Jersey, and Maine. The Duke sent Richard Nicolls off as governor and head of a military expedition designed to intimidate the Dutch. It did, and the English flag was raised over New Amsterdam without a shot being fired.[11]

Scarcely had Nicolls left England when the Duke turned over the "most improvable part" of his dominions to George Carteret and Lord John Berkeley, two English noblemen who had remained loyal to the Stuarts during their exile at the time of the English civil wars. In the meantime Nicolls had granted two tracts of land in what would be called "Nova Caesarea" or "New Jersey." The first, Elizabeth-Town, went to a group of Puritans from Connecticut; the second, Monmouth, to a mixture of Quakers and Baptists from New England. In 1666 other Puritans purchased land from the Indians and established Newark. Because the new proprietors refused to recognize these titles, they proved a long-term source of contention in the colony.[12]

The proprietary period in New Jersey lasted from 1664 to 1702, a brief but confusing time. Rapid division and sale of proprietary shares created an ever-changing group of proprietors. Berkeley sold half the province to a group of Quakers headed by John Fenwick and Edward Byllynge in 1674. Carteret's portion went to another group of Quakers, including a number of Scottish investors, in 1682. As a result there were actually two New Jerseys, West and East, each with its own governor and legislature. First Berkeley and Carteret, and then the later proprietors of the two sections, provided "Concessions" and "Constitutions" which incorporated such important concepts as representative government (including consent to taxation), religious toleration, and trial by jury.[13] Despite these political concessions, designed to attract settlers to the province, relations between residents and proprietors were not always smooth. There was a "Revolution" in East Jersey in 1672, disorder in West Jersey in 1681, and a number of disturbances in both provinces in the late 1690s. As a consequence of their troubles in governing, and also because of challenges to their authority from England, the proprietors surrendered their political claims to the province (but not their title to the land) in 1702.

When New Jersey became a royal province in 1703 it contained about ten thousand residents, an ethnic mix of Indians, Dutch, Swedes, English, and Scots and a religious mix of Puritans, Quakers, Baptists, Presbyterians, and Anglicans, among others. The legacy of division into an east and west continued to have political ramifications even though there was once again a single "New Jersey." The diversity that would characterize the state into the present was already obvious and significant.

The royal period in New Jersey history divides into two portions, 1703–1738 and 1738–1776. Initially the colony shared its governor with New York and elected a separate legislature. The result was a series of governors who paid little attention to New Jersey, and that small amount usually bode no good—for most of them were more concerned with lining their own pockets than with the welfare of the colony. The first, Lord Cornbury, has been described as a greedy transvestite, a "detestable magot." He is alleged to have accepted first a bribe from the eastern proprietors and then the contents of a "blind tax" collected by their opponents. The "Ring" that surrounded him engaged in a large-scale land grab. A successor, William Burnet, accepted one thousand pounds for "incidentals" from the assembly and promptly signed a bill it desired. William Cosby appeared in the colony only once in four years and fought with its leading politicians. Only Robert Hunter stands out for his honesty, skill, and attempt to clean up politics. Bribery, disputed elections, and raucous disagreements thus early became part of New Jersey politics.[14]

In 1738 Lewis Morris was appointed the first separate royal governor of New Jersey. Although a native son, he proved no more responsive to New Jersey residents than his predecessors. The assembly wanted paper money; he wanted a higher salary. Neither would make concessions, and the colony's government was thus locked in a stalemate. Financial disagreements also plagued two of his successors. Both Jonathan Belcher and Francis Bernard tried to obtain support for England's efforts in the "Great War for Empire" only to have the assembly refuse, claiming "poverty." The aid that was given, after the French and Indians appeared to threaten the western frontier of the colony, came through deficit financing (paper money). At the end of the French and Indian Wars, New Jersey had the largest per capita debt of any colony.[15] Throughout this period New Jersey politicians divided into numerous factions that jockeyed for power both among themselves and with the royal governors around the issues of paper money, taxation, and ending the rioting (particularly between 1735 and 1755) caused by controversies over land titles. The result, as in other colonies, was to increase the power of the colonial assembly.[16]

Also significant in this period was the religious revival known in the American colonies as the Great Awakening. George Whitefield, the English minister who conducted revival meetings up and down the Atlantic coast, stopped and spoke in New Jersey several times. Similar efforts were led by such "native sons" as Gilbert Tennent among the Presbyterians and Theodore Frelinghuysen among members of the Dutch Reformed church.[17] In addition to conversions, the Awakening led to the splitting of churches by warring factions and to the creation of educational institutions such as the College of New Jersey (Princeton) in 1746 and Queens College (Rutgers) in 1766.

In the 1760s New Jersey, diverse in religion and population, had a primarily rural economy. The total population was approximately one hundred thousand; the largest "city," Elizabethtown, probably had fewer than one thousand residents. Although there were both rich and poor people, it was basically a middle-class society; Governor Belcher described it as the "best country I have seen for middling fortunes, and for people who have to live by the sweat of their brows." It was also a provincial community primarily concerned with local affairs. England was far away. Provincialism slowly lessened over the years until this small colony suddenly found itself caught in the center of the whirlwind known as the American Revolution.

In 1763, William Franklin, a young lawyer and the illegitimate son of Benjamin Franklin, was appointed governor of New Jersey. He was destined to be the last royal official to hold this position.[18] With the Great War for Empire ended, England moved to bring under control both its additional territory and the large debt it had acquired in the course of that conflict. Two measures passed by Parliament particularly affected New Jersey. The Currency Act restricted paper money issues used to finance the colonial government and its war debt. The Stamp Act imposed a direct tax on legal documents and other items.

Despite its rural conservative atmosphere, New Jersey did not entirely escape the furor raised by the Stamp Act throughout the

American colonies. Lawyers resolved to do no business requiring the stamps; William Coxe, the local stamp agent, could not rent a house for fear it would be destroyed. The assembly claimed that "all Taxes laid upon us without our Consent" were "a fundamental infringement of the Rights and privileges Secured to us as English Subjects and by Charter." New Jersey protested the stamp tax, but without urban crowds there were no riots comparable to those in Massachusetts, and without firebrands like Patrick Henry there were no radical statements such as those coming from Virginia.

An economic boycott of English goods helped induce Parliament to repeal the Stamp Act. But the principles behind American objections were not recognized in England, and the law was replaced in 1767 by the Townshend Acts which imposed taxes on lead, paper, paint, and tea. In protest, Americans resorted to nonimportation agreements. Along with other legislatures, New Jersey's petitioned the king. Again Parliament backed off. The acts were repealed, except for a symbolic tax on tea which became an issue after the passage of the Tea Act in 1773.

To ensure that the tax on tea would not be paid, Bostonians threw the leaves into the harbor. New Jersey radicals staged their own "tea party" by burning a shipment at Greenwich, while college students in Princeton vowed not to drink the brew. England responded with the Intollerable Acts, closing Boston Harbor and altering Massachusetts's governmental structure. Designed to divide the colonies, the policies had the opposite effect. Americans sent aid to Boston and also began to arm. While New Jerseyans participated in these colonial protests, the state was never in the vanguard of patriot activity. Small, provincial, conservative, lacking a newspaper of its own, it was more concerned with the robbery of the provincial treasury in 1768 and the ensuing controversy than with developments in the larger world around it.[19]

New Jersey thus moved slowly, hesitantly, towards revolution. After July 1774 two governments coexisted in the colony with a new Provincial Congress gradually siphoning authority from the old royal legislature. During this process Franklin not only held on to his position longer than any other royal governor but also used his influence to try to keep New Jersey in the empire. He almost succeeded. At one point in 1775 New Jersey's delegates from the Continental Congress returned to plead with the assembly not to break ranks; later, three representatives from other colonies were sent to ensure that New Jersey remained true to the "Common Cause."

In June 1776, fourteen months after fighting had begun at Lexington and Concord, the Provincial Congress finally ordered Franklin arrested and deported to Connecticut. New, more radical delegates were sent from New Jersey to the Continental Congress. Richard Stockton, Abraham Clark, John Witherspoon, John Hart, and Francis Hopkinson arrived in time to sign the Declaration of Independence. But New Jersey still hedged its bets. It wrote a Constitution referring to itself as a "colony" and stating that the document would be "null and void" if a reconciliation with the king should occur.

The constitution of 1776, written in haste as British forces landed on nearby Staten Island, reflected the times in other ways as well. It provided that a legislature, elected annually, would choose a governor. This official was further weakened by the lack of veto and appointment powers. Although including property qualifications to vote and hold office, the constitution granted the right to vote to "all inhabitants . . . of full age"—a provision that enabled some women and blacks to vote until 1807.[20] In spite of defects that soon became clear, the brief document served until 1844.

The first state governor elected under its terms was William Livingston, a wealthy New York Whig lawyer who had recently moved to New Jersey to enjoy a peaceful country existence. Instead he spent the wartime years with a price on his head constantly moving to avoid capture by the British. New Jersey had become a corridor through which the armies of both sides marched while local loyalist and patriot forces confronted one another in what frequently amounted to a nasty civil war.[21] In addition to numerous skirmishes, several major battles of the war were fought within the state—Trenton in 1776, Princeton in 1777, and Monmouth in 1778. The Continental Army spent three winters, two in Morristown (the winter of 1779–1780, when it snowed twenty-eight times, was reputed to be the worst of the century) and one in Middlebrook (now Bound Brook).

Caught between contending forces, disagreeing with neighbors and relatives, New Jerseyans chose different sides. A relatively high number of its citizens remained loyal to the crown, some serving with the British forces. William Franklin, after being "exchanged" and released from his Connecticut prison, headed the detested Board of Associated Loyalists in New York City. Southern and western New Jersey contained many Quaker pacifists who tried to remain neutral. Some residents shifted sides depending on whether American or British soldiers were standing on their doorstep. The Baroness von Riedesel, wife of the highest-ranking Hessian officer to serve the British in America, described three visits to the Van Horne Inn in Middlebrook. On the first the innkeeper's family announced their loyalty to the king; during the second, when American officers were present, they stayed up late singing, "God save great Washington! God damn the King"; on the third visit, they asked her to assure the king of their support. Other New Jerseyans were consistently and fiercely tied to the patriot cause, some paying for this with loss of property, imprisonment, and their lives. For all it was a difficult time—until the British sailed out of New York harbor in 1783.[22]

The war ended in New Jersey, at least officially. The peace treaty was received while Congress met in Princeton, and George Washington wrote his farewell address to the troops at Rocky Hill. The consequences of the war were few but dramatic in New Jersey—independence, public and private buildings in ruin, the removal of loyalists to England or Canada, and lowered property qualifications for voters. Because the state was still primarily rural and conservative, other changes came about more slowly.[23] Though glad that the "late unpleasant times" were over, New Jersey entered the Confederation period of the 1780s with economic problems of its own and fearful of the pitfalls it thought the national government faced under the Articles of Confederation. In 1778, before ratifying the Articles, the legislature questioned how the new government would handle western lands, as well as its ability to tax or to control state tariffs on trade. Increasingly concerned with these problems, in 1786 the state refused the national requisition for money. Similar sentiments led to the appointment of delegates to the Annapolis Convention later that year with instructions to work for change in the Articles, and then to the quick selection of representatives to the Philadelphia Convention.[24]

New Jersey played a significant role in the writing of the United States Constitution. Its delegation, through the efforts of William Paterson, proposed a "small state" plan, basing representation on states rather than population. The contingent stubbornly adhered to this proposal until a compromise was devised and was incorporated into the design of the senate.[25] When the document was completed it was sent on to the states for ratification, a process that was protracted and difficult in many places. But it was not in New Jersey. Because provisions of the new Constitution corrected the defects of the Articles to which New Jersey residents had previously objected, there was little debate over its contents. A convention ratified quickly and unanimously, making the state the third "pillar" in the new nation. To celebrate, the delegates retired to a local Trenton tavern, ate dinner, and drank thirteen toasts in honor of the occasion—the last to the United States and "liberty."

The unanimity of 1787 gave way to the disagreements of 1789 as diverse, closely contested politics returned to the state. In the first election, a wild, bitter affair, the divisions were primarily sectional and personal.[26] As the 1790s continued, issues came to resemble those debated throughout the country. Reflecting national concerns (particularly economic policies and foreign affairs), New Jersey residents divided into Federalists and Jeffersonian-Republicans.

Particularly divisive were the Jay Treaty of 1795, a copy of which was burned in Flemington because it was seen as favoring England, and the Alien and Sedition Acts of 1798, criticized for the restrictions they imposed on freedom of speech and the press. Under the terms of the latter a Newark man, Luther Baldwin, was tried and convicted of sedition because he said he wished that a cannon salute to visiting President John Adams had hit his posterior. Republican newspapers noted the fine of $150 for this "heinous" crime and concluded that "joking could be dangerous even in a free country."[27]

Until 1800 the Federalists dominated New Jersey politics. Afterward, except for a Federalist resurgence during the War of 1812, the Republicans controlled most political offices, although, as usual, New Jersey elections were close. Both sides created state political conventions, legislative caucuses, and party newspapers to build and keep support, all of which increased popular participation and stimulated greater public discussion of issues.[28]

The Jeffersonian-Republicans increased the size of the nation with the Louisiana Purchase and embroiled it in controversies with both England and France. In 1812 the United States again went to war with England over, among other issues, maritime rights. New Jersey, with a relatively small foreign trade and numerous Quakers, briefly returned the antiwar Federalists to power. The legislature condemned the war as "inexpedient, illtimed" and "dangerous," while the militia refused to serve outside the state's boundaries (as did the forces of many other states). Yet when the war ended with Andrew Jackson's spectacular victory at the Battle of New Orleans, many state residents felt a sense of pride in their nation (even though the larger conflict was actually a draw).[29]

A surge of nationalism and a decline of political opposition followed the war in the United States. The "Era of Good Feelings" was characterized by one-party politics as the Federalist party, because of its opposition to the war, declined precipitously. However, even in this period political disagreements in New Jersey did not entirely disappear; they just revolved again around older, local issues. Clearer divisions reappeared in the state and nation with the election of 1824 and the Jacksonian period it inaugurated.

In the meantime significant developments in transportation and industrialization took place in New Jersey. As the state linking New York and Pennsylvania, as well as North and South, New Jersey was particularly involved in what has been called the "transportation revolution," the rapid development of roads, steamboats, clipper ships, railroads, and canals after 1800.[30] From 1801 to 1829 the legislature chartered fifty-one companies to build and operate "turnpikes," privately constructed roads that charged tolls. New Jersey investors built and operated steamboats in competition with New York inventors who claimed a monopoly. Thomas Gibbons constructed and Cornelius Vanderbilt operated the *Bellona*, whose flag proclaiming "New Jersey must be free" defied authority from across the Hudson. In 1824 the United States Supreme Court ruled in *Gibbons v. Ogden* that only the federal government could regulate commerce; no state could grant a monopoly over interstate traffic. Colonel John Stevens built the first steam locomotive in the country and in an 1825 demonstration ran it around a circular tract in Hoboken at the speed of six miles per hour. He was later involved in the establishment of a railroad line that connected Philadelphia and New York. The canal "mania" that swept the country led to the construction of the Morris Canal in the northern portion of the state and the Delaware and Raritan Canal in the central part.[31] The consequences of these developments were profound. Canal barges transported coal from Pennsylvania mines and helped fuel industrialization. Railroads crisscrossed the state carrying tourists to the shore. Politics was also transformed. In 1830 the legislature chartered the Joint Companies (the Delaware and Raritan Canal and the Camden and Amboy Railroad). In return for a minimum payment of $30,000 a year to the state (sufficient then to cover most of the budget), the railroad received a monopoly of the route between New York and Pennsylvania.

The company also exercised a predominant influence in state and local politics; New Jersey was sometimes called the "state of Camden and Amboy." Despite critics who charged that the costs were high, the service poor, and the road unsafe, the monopoly continued until 1873. Two years earlier the lines had been leased to the Pennsylvania Railroad for 999 years, which meant that no longer could the company claim special privileges as a purely state institution. The Penn system used the tracks, operated the canal, and competed with other lines now also running through the state.

Along with changes in transportation came early industrialization. In 1791 the state chartered the Society for Useful Manufactures, which purchased the site of the Passaic River's Great Falls, the second largest waterfall in the eastern United States, as a source of waterpower. The company established Paterson as a center for manufacturing and, although an initial failure, by the mid-nineteenth century its mills were producing cotton and silk textiles, as well as various machines (including locomotives). From an early point, South Jersey manufactured iron and glass, Trenton companies made ceramics and other products; in the north, Newark became a center for leather goods and beer, Plainfield for hats, New Brunswick for rubber and wallpaper. Cities grew, the labor force changed, and by 1840 the state was no longer totally rural.

In New Jersey and elsewhere, animated politics returned with the election of 1824 and the subsequent creation of the "second party system." The election began as a four-way race between John Quincy Adams, Andrew Jackson, Henry Clay, and William Crawford. It ended with the House of Representatives electing Adams as president; Henry Clay was appointed his secretary of state. Adams had charges of "corrupt bargain" ringing in his ears while Jackson immediately began campaigning for 1828. Two parties (based on economic and political disagreements as well as personalities and patronage) eventually emerged from the political battles that followed, the Jacksonian-Democrats and the Whigs. Although complicated by the state's own diversity, the divisions within New Jersey reflected those in the nation as a whole but diverged on the question of banks and corporations. State elections were, as usual, close—so close that in 1838, in what was dubbed the "Broad Seal War," Whig delegates certified as victors by the governor (using the state seal) were challenged by Democratic opponents. A Democratic Congress refused to seat the Whigs. Once again, as in 1789, a New Jersey political brawl had spilled over to Washington.[32]

In addition to a revival of partisan politics, the Jacksonian era brought an increased interest in political and social reform. Some of the political developments typical of the period in other states had already occurred in New Jersey, including the broadening of the suffrage and the use of political conventions. Others, particularly constitutional change, came later to the state. Not until 1844, long after most of its neighbors, was the Revolutionary Constitution of 1776 replaced. Governor Daniel Haines viewed it as simply "incompatible with the present age." The legislature had spent an inordinate amount of time on special acts (most frequently to grant divorces) and on political appointments. The state lacked independent courts and had a weak governor who was not popularly elected. The Constitutional Convention revamped the original document, but compared to what other states chose to do the resultant reforms were modest. Under the new constitution, New Jersey elected governors every three years, but they could not serve consecutive terms and possessed a veto that could easily be overridden. Senators were elected for three-year terms, assemblymen for one. The constitution established a separate chancellor for courts of equity and a court of appeals, banned legislative divorces, made provisions for amendments, and included a Bill of Rights. Like its predecessor, it was a conservative document that, despite its defects, survived for a long time. Not until 1947 did New Jersey replace it.[33]

The Jacksonian period also spawned myriad social reforms. Fueled by economic changes, population growth, evangelical religion, and the development of humanitarianism, reformers, particularly in the North and Northwest, turned to remodeling society and its institutions. They were particularly interested in debtors, drunkards, prisoners, and the "insane" and promoted model communities, education, and abolition. But New Jersey's endemic conservatism inhibited reform, and its predominantly rural character made social problems less visible than they were in rapidly urbanizing places.

Still, reform in New Jersey in this period reflected the concerns of American society at large, and it increasingly involved the remodeling or creation of institutions. New Jersey renovated its prisons to provide a system of individual cells, then thought to be more conducive to rehabilitation. But one historian concluded that the resultant system of solitary confinement unfortunately created "more madmen than repentants."[34] "Madmen" themselves were the object of concern as Dorothea Dix and others lobbied the state legislature to create a mental asylum, eventually built in 1848.[35] Reformers hoped the new jail would prevent recidivism of convicts, while the asylum would cure the sick.

Other reformers worked to keep debtors out of state institutions altogether. An 1830 report on imprisonment for debt stated, "We know of nothing worse in the whole length and breadth of the land than in New Jersey." Legal revisions in 1844 made it no longer possible to imprison someone for owing as little as five dollars; no longer would half the jail population of the state consist of debtors unable to earn money to repay what they owed because of their incarceration.[36]

Other reformers attempted to improve schools; still others created utopian communities, models that would avoid the problems brought by industrialization, commercialism, and competition. In New Jersey they established the North American Phalanx in Red Bank in 1843. It lasted twelve years and spawned the shorter-lived Raritan Bay Union near Perth Amboy in 1853. Both communities attempted to build alternative methods of social organization and a more cooperative life. The Red Bank group combined farming and industry, private and communal life, so that all could work according to their "strengths and tastes." Disagreements over religion, the value of various trades, and the quality of intellectual life, however, weakened the organization. A fire compounded its problems, and the group disbanded in 1855.[37] These efforts paralleled such contemporaneous attempts elsewhere as the Shaker communities, Brook Farm in Massachusetts, and Robert Owens's New Harmony in Indiana. These experiments intrigued later reformers, including those who would attempt such projects in the 1960s.

On a practical level, though, neither utopian communities nor improved schools lasted beyond this period. By 1830 there were pauper schools for the poor and academies for the rich, but free public education was nonexistent in New Jersey. As other northern states created public schools, New Jersey failed to act. Appointed in 1848, the state's first superintendent of education wrote that a "merciful man . . . would not winter his horse" in existing district schoolhouses.[38] In 1855 the first normal school (or teachers' college, now Trenton State College), was established, but not until 1871 did state laws begin to provide truly "free" elementary schools.[39] In the 1990s the state and its courts still argue over how these institutions should be funded.

The fact that New Jersey moved slowly in some areas is shown dramatically in the length of time it took to abolish slavery in the state and the way this act was ultimately accomplished. Slaves in colonial New Jersey worked on farms, in the iron industry, and in private households. They were more prevalent in the eastern section than in the Quaker-dominated western region. Although the American Revolution increased abolitionist sentiment by adding a political commitment to natural rights to the currents of Quaker theology, the state did not pass a law for abolition until 1804. It was the last northern state to do so, and even then it was made "gradual" so that slavery was not totally abolished in the state until the Thirteenth Amendment was adopted in 1865.

Other northern states, such as New York and Pennsylvania, also provided for gradual emancipation, but the last slaves were freed in those states earlier than they were in New Jersey. Even so, freedom came quicker than William Griffith, president of the New Jersey Antislavery Society in 1804, anticipated: he predicted that it might take "a century" before slavery was "eradicated from our country." New Jersey's conservatism accounts for much of the delay the state's enslaved African Americans encountered. Slaves were property, and state politicians were unwilling to confiscate it in one fell swoop; instead, they freed the children of slaves born after 1804 as they came of age (twenty-five for males, twenty-one for females) on the grounds that they would then have repaid their masters, through their labor, for their initial investment. The freedmen, frequently described as "degraded" and "rejected," remained at the bottom of the economic and social heap, but their new status was still preferable. One former slave declared that he "wouldn't be a slave ag'in, not if you'd give me the best farm in the Jarsies."[40] New Jersey's conservative position on this issue is also apparent in its handling of fugitive slaves. While other northern states moved to block the application of federal fugitive slave laws within their boundaries by adopting personal liberty laws, New Jersey passed its own law to assist southerners in recovering their property. But an 1836 law required jury trials to prove that slaves were truly fugitives before they were returned to their southern owners.

Although a northern state, New Jersey has been called a "border state" because of its attitudes during the Civil War. Actually the state supported the war effort and even raised more troops when first asked than required. However, the Democratic party remained strong, and a considerable amount of sympathy existed for the South. The "Opposition Party" was slow to take the name

"Republican" and, though it objected to the extension of slavery in the West, it was not inclined to attack the institution in the South. New Jersey was the only free state not to give all its votes to Lincoln in 1860 and to vote for General George McClellan (then living in West Orange) in 1864. State Democrats divided: some thought the South should be free to secede, a few even that New Jersey should join the Confederacy, but most supported Lincoln's efforts to keep the Union together. When they dominated the legislature in 1863 the more radical Democrats pushed for the passage of "peace resolutions" and chose "Copperhead" Colonel James W. Wall United States senator to finish an uncompleted term. Newspaper editors in the state also divided. Some opposed the war and the draft, the Democratic *Newark Journal* going so far as to ask those who desired "to be butchered" in Mr. Lincoln's war to "step forward at once." These complex divisions, including the continuance in power of the Democratic party, also occurred in neighboring New York and Pennsylvania, while opposition to the draft led to rioting in New York City. But New Jersey met most of its commitments. In the end 88,305 New Jerseyans served the Union during the war, and 6,300 of these men died.[41]

In many ways New Jersey's ambivalence on the Civil War characterized the state through much of its history and reflected the state's endemic hesitancy to act. Its diverse population and its continued tendency to generate close and changing election results (now a consequence of divisions between Democrats and Republicans) also kept conflict alive in the state. When the Republicans won in 1865 Charles E. Elmer praised God that New Jersey residents had finally "returned from all manner of wickedness and declared themselves Loyal and true to the Union." But he spoke too soon: political controversy reemerged shortly afterward in the state's bifurcated response to Reconstruction.

Reconstruction was a seesaw process for the nation as a whole. The President contended with Congress for power, and the victorious North argued with the defeated South over the position of the states within the Union and of African Americans within American society. New Jersey's positions on these questions were complicated. First Democrats, then Republicans, then Democrats, then Republicans controlled the state legislature, the governor's office, or both. Between 1865 and 1870 the state both rejected and accepted the Thirteenth, Fourteenth, and Fifteenth Amendments. In addition to close elections, resulting in power shifting between parties, the state's actions reflected a residual support for states' rights and for the South, and a degree of long-standing racism that characterized most of the North and was not distinctive to New Jersey.[42]

Even as the country coped with Civil War, Reconstruction, and their aftermath, it moved on to other issues. In national politics Democrats and Republicans took positions on the tariff, civil service reforms, and prohibition, but New Jersey politicians did not always follow their party's platform. Not all New Jersey Democrats supported free trade; not all Republicans favored local option laws forbidding liquor sales. Contests were close as politicians tailored their appeals to various interests, and late nineteenth-century voters turned out in large numbers. Politics provided entertainment, recreation, and jobs. Generally Democrats were more successful in electing governors until the mid 1890s; then Republicans had the edge. The depression of 1893, dislike of William Jennings Bryan and his "free silver" platform, and the taint of corruption took their toll on the Democrats. Not until Woodrow Wilson ran for governor in 1910 would they return to power. By then election law reforms, modern advertising techniques, declining party loyalty, the development of motion pictures, and the rise of professional sports had combined to reduce the percentage of voters who went to the polls.[43]

The last third of the nineteenth century was marked by rapid and interconnected growth in industrialization, immigration, and urbanization. Alongside these developments emerged sometimes stark contrasts between rich and poor, management and labor, and morality and popular recreation. The contradictions and problems of the age generally were mirrored in New Jersey. And by 1900 the state had become even more diverse and complex.

In the 1870s New Jersey attracted new industries such as oil refineries and large-scale services such as insurance companies. Modern research laboratories whose inventions were designed, tested, and marketed by supporting companies appeared. Thomas Edison's facilities, first at Menlo Park and then at West Orange, were precursors to the seven hundred research laboratories of a century later; today New Jersey stands fourth in the nation in research and development spending. By the 1890s numerous chemical and pharmaceutical firms (along with polluted waterways) were also established.[44]

The "robber barons" of this age also devised new methods of organizing and conducting business. In addition to the light bulb, the phonograph, the motion picture, and new uses for oil products and steel, they invented the trust. In the 1890s, as New

Jersey discovered the value of such combinations as a new source of state revenue, it became the home of the trusts. Liberal laws encouraged national companies to incorporate in the state—for a fee. A single building in Jersey City contained "offices" for more than twelve hundred corporations; the seven largest companies in the country and 150 of the top 298 were chartered in the state in 1904. Not everyone found this state enterprise admirable. Lincoln Steffens, the noted Progressive reformer, called New Jersey the "Traitor State." The influence that the trusts exercised in state politics fed a growing interest in reform.[45]

The trusts, insurance companies, and later public utility corporations were not the only politically weighty entities in New Jersey. Railroad companies had been significant since before the Civil War, and afterward they proliferated; track mileage nationwide expanded tremendously. Within the "corridor state" routes leading towards New York City achieved ever greater significance. Tax exemptions for railroad property and methods of evaluating that property became an issue in state and local politics (particularly in Jersey City) from at least the 1880s to the 1940s.[46] In addition, rapidly growing cities awarded franchises for "traction companies" (trolley car lines) and for water, gas, and electric services. The opportunities for "honest graft" (and dishonest) multiplied.[47] In the 1890s speculators built race tracks, some legal, others not, and gambling became a significant interest as well. William E. Sackett, writing of the period, stated that it was "almost unheard of" for anyone opposed to the railroads to be elected in New Jersey, but the other "interests" exerted considerable influence as well.[48]

While some New Jerseyans became rich—indeed, very rich—at the same time others toiled long and hard for little pay. Brewers in Newark worked fourteen to eighteen hours a day, six days a week, and another six to eight hours on Sundays; they earned between $20 and $25 a month.[49] In 1886 they struck for shorter hours and better wages. Paterson, which became the scene of a nationally publicized strike in 1913, contained numerous textile mills where women and children worked as many as thirteen hours a day in unhealthy and sometimes dangerous conditions. At the same time silk manufacturer Catholina Lambert built a home, literally a castle, on the mountain overlooking the city and stocked it with paintings by such European masters as Rembrandt.[50] Other wealthy industrialists flocked to Morristown where they built "cottages" (resembling those of Newport, Rhode Island, erected in the same period) containing thirty rooms or more.[51] This took place at the same time that such cities as Newark literally packed residents like sardines into flimsy tenement houses lacking adequate ventilation and sanitation.[52] With such contrasts in lifestyle it is not surprising that Paterson alone experienced 137 strikes between 1881 and 1900. The period from 1870 to 1900 was one of frequent, and sometimes also bitter and violent, incidents of labor unrest in New Jersey, as in many other parts of the country.

The workers who labored in the Paterson mills, as had those who helped all of America industrialize, came from many different lands. In the early nineteenth century immigrants had arrived in large numbers from Ireland and Germany; the Irish built canals, while the Germans operated breweries. In the late nineteenth century they came from Poland, Italy, Russia, and other southern and eastern European countries. They worked in the fields in south Jersey as well as in factories in the north. Most flocked to the cities, where work was most plentiful. The size of this immigration and a sense of its impact can be gleaned from statistics in the 1910 census. Twenty-seven percent of the state's population was foreign-born, slightly lower than in New York but higher than in Pennsylvania. In Paterson, the foreign-born made up 36 percent of the population; in Passaic, they were 52 percent. The percentage of foreign-born in the United States as a whole was 16 percent at the time. New Jersey was unusually diverse before the Civil War, but by the early twentieth century its heterogeneity had entered another dimension. To some it had become "a virtual tower of Babel, a confusion of tongues and creeds." Distinctive ethnic neighborhoods arose, but the great variety of backgrounds, languages, and religions that resulted from this influx made the organization of labor unions complex and difficult. In addition, the large numbers of Catholics, particularly in such places as Jersey City, at times led older Protestant residents to political backlash.[53]

Although New Jersey's diversity was not new, the rate of expansion of its population, its degree of urbanization, and change in the nature of its agriculture were novel developments of the turn of the century. In the twenty-five years after 1890 the population almost doubled, reaching nearly three million by 1915. Farm acreage peaked in 1879. Afterward, the state became more urban than rural, and what its farmers grew changed. In the colonial period they had concentrated on beef, cattle, and wheat. Increasingly, dairy and chicken farming become more significant, then vegetables both for the market and new canning industry. The

Joseph Campbell Company began processing produce in 1869; it and tomatoes remain important in south Jersey. Cranberries and blueberries were raised in bogs and the pine barrens. Later, nurseries produced trees, shrubs, roses, and bedding plants when suburbs began to grow, especially after 1950.[54]

The late nineteenth century was also the time when popular forms of recreation and entertainment now taken for granted first developed. Football, baseball, horse racing, golf, tennis, and bicycling became increasingly available and affordable to spectators and participants of different classes.[55] Large numbers of tourists began to vacation at New Jersey lake and seashore resorts, made accessible in large part by railroads. Sloops and stagecoaches brought visitors to Cape May from Philadelphia after the War of 1812, but Long Branch did not become *the* vacation spot until 1869 when President Grant discovered its delights—and could arrive in a private railroad car. The rich and famous flocked there until the Democrat Grover Cleveland was elected in 1884; then the fickle wealthy took off for the newest faddish place. In the 1880s Lakewood had nearly one hundred hotels that helped entertain the well-to-do. The largest and best-known resort of the period was Atlantic City, but it tended to attract a crowd of middle- and working-class people who came for day-long excursions on railroad coaches. They walked on the boardwalk, waded in the water, rode the ferris wheel, ate saltwater taffy, and did the things visitors still do, except patronize legal casinos (unavailable before 1976).[56]

Even resorts, particularly Atlantic City, confronted problems by the late nineteenth century as the contradictions between Victorian values and practices became increasingly apparent. The gap between morality and reality symbolized larger problems in American society. Offended by political corruption, the stark differences between rich and poor, the growth of trusts, and the restrictions on economic opportunity this growth implied, reformers of the Progressive era sought changes. Motivated by faith in democracy, efficiency, progress, and the possibility of social justice, they proposed a whole series of reforms in government, education, the workplace, and neighborhoods. New Jersey, still conservative and slow to react, gradually joined in the collective din for change until, for a brief time while Woodrow Wilson was governor, the state actually stood in the forefront of the Progressive movement.

In New Jersey, as in some other states, Progressivism started on the local level as a reform movement within the Republican party called the "New Idea." Gradually, the Democratic party also issued calls for reform. Mark Fagan and George L. Record in Jersey City pushed for better schools, more public parks, honest and efficient government, and (particularly important in Jersey City) equal taxation for railroads.[57] They and others also sought restrictions on corporations, an end to "perpetual franchises," institution of the direct primary, and other limits on the powers of political "bosses." Women joined various civic clubs and pushed for such reforms as conservation of the Palisades, pure food and drug legislation, school improvements, the establishment of a women's college (Douglass College, now part of Rutgers University), and the right to vote. Some of them also helped organize settlement houses in urban areas designed to provide education and services particularly for immigrants. Efforts at reform moved on to the state level during the governorships of Franklin Murphy and John Franklin Fort, although their successes were limited; it was left to Woodrow Wilson to implement major changes.[58] For a brief time, New Jersey had a forceful governor able to muster enough legislative support for reform measures.

Wilson himself seemed an unlikely candidate for the role of Progressive reformer. Born in Virginia and the son of a Presbyterian minister, he had become a professor of political science and then president of Princeton University in 1902. His efforts to bring changes to that Ivy League institution ran into difficulties over the question of eating clubs (still a controversial issue) and the location of the graduate school. Seen as a conservative who could be controlled, he was the choice for governor of the Democratic party's political bosses in 1910, but at the outset of the campaign Wilson broke with the bosses, especially James Smith, Jr., of Newark, and appealed to reformers in both parties for support. As governor he proceeded to push actively for a series of laws embodying Progressive ideals. In short order the legislature enacted election reforms providing for direct primaries, banned corrupt practices by regulating campaign contributions, created a public utilities commission empowered to regulate the industry, and established workmen's compensation. Later additions were the "Seven Sister" acts designed to end New Jersey's role as a haven for corporations (repealed, however, in 1920 because they reduced state revenues). In 1912, when Republicans regained control of the state legislature, Wilson went on to campaign for and to win the presidency.[59]

As president Wilson carried Progressivism to the national level. While he was in office the world went to war, and the United

States, despite Wilson's urgings to remain neutral in "thought and deed," was drawn into the conflict. The large number of Germans in New Jersey meant that there was sympathy for the Axis cause at first, but the state went on to support the Allies and the war effort as a whole.

As elsewhere in the country patriotism was sometimes carried to an extreme. Reflecting the national xenophobia, residents changed the name of "German Valley" to "Long Valley," while Hamburg, Dresden, and Bismark streets in Newark became Wilson, London, and Pershing. The state commissioner of education assured the public that all teachers were loyal. But if they were not, they were expected to "at once resign and get out of the schools."[60]

During the war, New Jersey served as a center for wartime industrial production, as a major shipping point, and as a training ground for troops. The state manufactured munitions, chemicals, ships, and airplanes. Sixteen military complexes were established for training and assembling troops, the largest of them Camp Merritt in the north and Fort Dix in the south. Thirteen hundred buildings were constructed at Merritt, only to be abandoned after the war. Hoboken became a major point for the embarkation of soldiers; 40 percent of those who went to Europe passed through its port.[61] Some of these wartime enterprises had a lasting impact on the state as they increased its industrial base.

As the war came to an end the United States adopted Prohibition. The temperance movement, including an advocacy of total abstinence, had waxed and waned over the nineteenth century, but it attracted greater support during World War I when advocates argued that drinking was "foreign" (Germans drank beer) and an unproductive use of grain crops. Passage of the Eighteenth Amendment in 1917 divided Americans, and New Jersey residents, along ethnic, religious, and urban-rural lines. It was also not easily enforced, particularly in a state with such a long coastline. In 1929 James M. Doran, national administrator for the program, stated, "We regard New Jersey as one of the hardest spots to handle in the entire country." By 1933 the nation had given up trying to "handle" liquor by forbidding it, and Prohibition was repealed.[62]

Prohibition came to an end as the country struggled with the worst depression in its history. The stock market crash in 1929 was the symbolic beginning of a disastrous financial decline caused by imbalances in the world, as well as the American, economy. New Jersey, with its large industrial base, was particularly vulnerable. By 1932 the unemployment rate in the state was 30 percent. The national average was 25 percent, but in some industrial cities fully half of the laboring population was unemployed.

As local and state governments ran out of funds, they turned to the federal government which, after the election of Franklin D. Roosevelt in 1932, responded with the numerous initiatives of the "New Deal."[63] Designed to provide relief for those in need, to reform the economy so as to prevent a recurrence of depression, and to experiment with alternatives for the future, the New Deal was meant to "prime the pump," to put people to work so that they could earn money, spend it, and in the process revive the economy. A variety of "alphabet soup" agencies ran construction projects, operated theaters, and took surveys. New Jersey obtained new post offices, hospitals, stadiums (in Jersey City and at Rutgers), and schools. Conservationists created a national park at Jockey Hollow (near Morristown), site of the Continental Army's encampment during the American Revolution, and artists decorated the "old terminal" (then new) at Newark airport. Jersey City particularly benefited from this largess as the Democratic party funnelled projects for the state through Frank Hague in return for the votes his political machine turned out for Roosevelt. The enormous medical center built there was a monument to this collaboration.[64]

Another project in New Jersey was designed both to create work and serve as a model community. The New Deal created "greenbelt" cities across the nation to combine employment, the amenities of urban living, and the restful qualities of a rural landscape. Several were built outside Washington, D.C., Cincinnati, Ohio, and Milwaukee, Wisconsin; one, originally called Jersey Homesteads, was placed in south Jersey. The community initially attracted Jewish residents and socialists from New York City, mostly garment workers, who wished to live in a rural cooperative environment. Plans called for a self-contained community with a factory, a farm, and homes. Houses were little cinder-block affairs built quickly (though not inexpensively as intended). The manufacturing enterprise has long since been abandoned, but the town of Roosevelt, as it is now called, persists along with some of its original residents.[65] By 1938, although prosperity had not entirely returned to the nation or state, the New Deal began to run out of steam. Conservative Democrats and reviving Republicans blocked new programs and even rolled back some existing ones. More important were problems caused by the rise of Germany and Japan. With the outbreak of war in Europe in 1939, foreign affairs took more and more of the nation's attention. After Pearl Harbor the United States went to war without the divisions and doubts that had accompanied its entry into World War I.[66]

New Jersey's role in World War II was very similar to the one it played in the First World War. The state served primarily as a manufacturing center and a site for training troops. Factories turned out ships, airplanes, munitions, medical supplies, processed foods, and other goods in ever-increasing amounts.[67] Fort Dix, the Kilmer facility, and other installations in the state trained troops and prepared them for embarkation. Atlantic City hotels were used as hospitals. The naval station at Lakehurst sent blimps, and the Civil Air Patrol at Pomona sent airplanes, to look for German submarines off the Jersey coast. Before the war was over, more than two million men and women had been processed through New Jersey for service overseas. When the veterans returned they swamped Rutgers and other colleges to take advantage of the liberal educational provisions of the GI Bill of Rights.

The war years also saw a struggle in New Jersey over revisions of the state constitution. Elected on the Democratic ticket in 1940 as a prospective counterweight to Frank Hague and his "machine," Governor Charles Edison, son of the inventor, called for change in the document, then nearly one hundred years old.[68] It was difficult to amend, placed severe and antiquated limits on the power to borrow money, and had put in place a decentralized executive department whose ability to cope with modern problems was limited. In addition, the court system had become the "most complicated . . . in any English speaking state." Revising the constitution became a partisan political issue. Hague opposed it, rural county officials feared losing equal representation in the state senate, and the war proved a distraction. Both Edison and his successor in office, Walter Evans Edge, failed in their attempts to obtain a new document. Hague's opposition was decisive. He feared any changes that would increase the power of New Jersey's governors—undoubtedly at his expense.

But in 1947, as the nation moved on to the problems of postwar adjustment and the emerging "cold war," New Jersey acquired a new governor, Republican Alfred E. Driscoll. Determined to enact constitutional changes, he created bipartisan support for revisions and deliberately included representatives from as many of the diverse groups in New Jersey as possible. A special convention met for the summer in the Rutgers University Gymnasium and collectively wrote a document designed to modernize the government and satisfy previous critics, including Frank Hague.

The Constitution of 1947 unified the executive branch and simplified the court system. It provided for a strong governor to be elected to a four-year term. Governors could succeed themselves once and had significant veto powers. Provisions for collective bargaining, a Bill of Rights, and a first-in-the-nation antidiscrimination clause also became part of the revised constitution. The document was further altered in 1966 to meet the Supreme Court's standard of "one man one vote"; representation in the state senate became proportional to population rather than being set at three senators per county.[69] These constitutional changes were truly significant. Long regarded as politically backward, New Jersey became an example that other states studied. It emerged with an increasingly active governor and a model court system. Local and county governments (and their politicians) became less important; old-fashioned "boss" control, such as Hague had exercised, increasingly became a thing of the past. Attention began to focus more on Trenton, and gradually New Jersey became a modern state—able to shape a role for itself, and perhaps, finally, even an identity of its own.[70]

In the postwar period, the rapid expansion of suburbs, the related decline of cities, the increase in state services supplied to residents, changes in the economy, and a new wave of immigration all contributed to altering the state. New Jersey became more diverse, particularly in terms of population, than ever before. But it also became more homogenous as divisions between north and south and between rural and urban areas became less pronounced as suburbs and new industries filled the spaces between them.

"Suburbs" were not new to America, or to New Jersey, in the 1950s. But the number, size, and speed with which they grew were novel. The rapid growth was a consequence of the postwar population boom, extensive highway construction, and cheaper methods of mass producing "tract" houses. The New Jersey Turnpike was completed in 1953 and the Garden State Parkway a year later. Both opened regions of the state for settlement as they made it feasible for people to commute.[71] The later construction of such interstate routes as 78, 80, and 287 spread development further. By 1960 New Jersey was the most densely populated state in the nation; by 1980 70 percent of its people lived in the suburbs. There was a political impact as well: Republicans and Democrats spread more evenly throughout the state, and the number of registered "independents" increased.

As the suburbs grew, many of the cities declined. At first the exodus was led by those who wanted a house surrounded by a green lawn.[72] After the riots of the 1960s, in which twenty-three people died and damage to property exceeded $10 million, residents who feared remaining in Newark, Camden, Plainfield, and other cities plagued by violence and crime left in a stampede. Cities lost population; Camden declined from 124,000 in 1950 to 85,000 in 1988. They also lost revenues at a time when funds became more essential to support services to the largely poor population left behind.[73] Not until the mid-1980s did urban renewal begin to reverse the situation. The Gateway project in Newark, an aquarium in Camden, and a reconstructed downtown in New Brunswick have begun to revive those cities. But these changes have been slow, frequently controversial, and sometimes displaced poorer residents and older businesses.

A response to the increasing inequalities between wealthy suburbs and poor cities came in the New Jersey Supreme Court's Mt. Laurel decision, which prohibited suburbs from using zoning laws to exclude prospective poor or African-American residents. After several modifications and legislative action, the state now has an Affordable Housing Council which works out plans by which suburbs can either build low-income housing or contribute to its construction in cities.[74]

Since World War II, New Jersey industry has also changed. Much of it moved to the suburbs, and manufacturing, particularly "heavy" industries, declined. Electronics companies, pharmaceutical firms, communications headquarters, and various research facilities became a larger part of the industrial mix. Enormous office complexes, such as those on the Route 1 corridor, sprouted up as service industries grew more important. And, though it still displays the sign "Trenton makes, the world takes," the capital is now primarily a government center, housing state and federal office buildings and courthouses.

New Jersey's population not only grew but changed after the Second World War. The 1950s saw a large influx of Hungarians, the 1960s Cubans and South Americans, the 1970s Vietnamese, and the 1980s Asians. Entirely new ethnic differences and neighborhoods are visible. As the population, road mileage, and suburbs grew, so did the services provided by the state. Programs supported by Governor Richard J. Hughes in the 1960s reflected the Great Society initiatives of the Johnson administration. Additional parks, cultural and educational facilities, and an expanded Newark airport appeared. Rutgers grew from a small Ivy League institution into a major state university, state teachers' colleges became institutions with a wider mission, and new county colleges were built, some of them from scratch.

In 1945 New Jersey still had no statewide tax. To finance the new services provided in the years that followed the government ultimately turned to sales and income taxes. New Jersey had never willingly taxed much and did not begin to do so even as late as the 1960s without a political struggle. Only after 1976, when the state Supreme Court closed the schools because financing them solely through property taxes was held inherently unequal, did the legislature pass an income tax. Not all school districts are yet equal, but state government now has greater power to effect this outcome.

At the end of the 1980s, New Jersey was a very different place than it was even in 1945. Yet in some ways it has shown remarkable constancy over the last three hundred years. Its population is still diverse, the range of ethnic and religious groups wider than ever before. The contests between its political parties remain close, and though sectional differences are muted, they still exist. And New Jersey continues to develop a sense of identity. Former governor Kean's slogan, "New Jersey and You, Great Together" conveys a positive message whose meaning is not yet clear, and in this respect it encapsulates the complex, contradictory, paradoxical, and interesting aspects of New Jersey history since the seventeenth century.

Notes

1. This description of New Jersey is usually attributed to Benjamin Franklin.

2. Poking fun at New Jersey is not a new practice. It has apparently been done from the beginning. An example, clearly not the earliest, is the comment of about 1871 by Senator James W. Nye of Nevada, who declared that no one was "too degraded" for citizenship: "We have New Jersey, and all things considered, it has proven a success." Quoted in Eric Foner, *Reconstruction: America's Unfinished Revolution, 1863–1877* (New York, 1988), 497. For views of and from the turnpike, see Angus Gillespie and Michael Rockland, *Looking for America on the New Jersey Turnpike* (New Brunswick, N.J., 1989).

3. Charles A. Stanfield, *New Jersey: A Geography* (Westview, N.J., 1983); Frank Kelland and Marylin Kelland, *New Jersey: Garden or Suburb* (Dubuque, Iowa, 1978); Peter O. Wacker, *Land and People: A Cultural Geography of Preindustrial*

New Jersey; Origins and Settlement Patterns (New Brunswick, N.J., 1976).

4. Thomas Fleming, *New Jersey: A History* (New York, 1984), 3–4.

5. William Nelson, "Early Legislative Turmoils in New Jersey," *The American Magazine of History* (1905): 221–31; Richard P. McCormick, "New Jersey's First Congressional Election, 1789: A Case Study in Political Skulduggery," *William and Mary Quarterly* ser. 3, 6 (1949): 237–50; Richard P. McCormick, *The History of Voting in New Jersey* (New Brunswick, N.J., 1953); William E. Sackett, *Modern Battles of Trenton*, vol. 1 (Trenton, N.J., 1895); John D. Venable, *Out of the Shadow: The Story of Charles Edison* (East Orange, N.J., 1978), 167–68; John Reynolds, " 'The Silent Dollar:' Vote Buying in New Jersey," *New Jersey History* (hereafter cited as *NJH*) 98 (1980): 191–211; and Dayton David McKean, *The Boss: The Hague Machine in Action* (Boston, 1940).

6. Richard P. McCormick, "An Historical Overview," in *Politics in New Jersey*, ed. Alan Rosenthal and John Blydenburgh (New Brunswick, N.J., 1975), 1–30.

7. Donald L. Kemmerer, "A History of Paper Money in Colonial New Jersey, 1668–1775," *Proceedings of the New Jersey Historical Society* (hereafter cited as *Proc. NJHS*) 74 (1956): 107–44; Donald L. Kemmerer, "The Colonial Loan-Office System in New Jersey," *Journal of Political Economy* 47 (1931): 867–74; Frederick R. Black, "Provincial Taxation in Colonial New Jersey, 1704–1735," *NJH* 95 (1977): 21–47; and John W. Cadman, Jr., *The Corporation in New Jersey: Business and Politics, 1791–875* (Cambridge, Mass., 1949), 425–28, 440–41.

8. Herbert C. Kraft, *The Lenape: Archeology, History, and Ethnography* (Newark, N.J., 1986); Clinton A. Weslager, *The Delaware Indians: A History* (New Brunswick, N.J., 1972); Clinton A. Weslager, *The Delaware Indian Westward Migration: With the Texts of Two Manuscripts (1821–1822) Responding to General Lewis Cass's Inquiries About Lenape Culture and Language* (Wallingford, Pa., 1978).

9. Kraft, *The Lenape*, 201.

10. Clinton A. Weslager, *Dutch Explorers, Traders, and Settlers in the Delaware Valley, 1609–1664* (Philadelphia, 1961); Clinton A. Weslager, *The English on the Delaware: 1610–1682* (New Brunswick, N.J., 1967); Adrian C. Leiby, *The Early Dutch and Swedish Settlers of New Jersey* (Princeton, N.J., 1964); and Firth Haring Fabend, *A Dutch Family in the Middle Colonies, 1660–1800* (New Brunswick, N.J., 1991).

11. Richard P. McCormick, *New Jersey from Colony to State, 1609–1789* (Newark, N.J., 1981); John Pomfret, *Colonial New Jersey: A History* (New York, 1973); Wesley Frank Craven, *New Jersey and the English Colonization of North America* (Princeton, N.J., 1964).

12. John Pomfret, *The New Jersey Proprietors and their Lands* (Princeton, N.J., 1964); John Pomfret, *The Province of West New Jersey, 1609–1702* (Princeton, N.J., 1956); John Pomfret, *The Province of East New Jersey, 1609–1702: The Rebellious Proprietary* (Princeton, N.J., 1962).

13. Julian Boyd, *Fundamental Laws and Constitutions of New Jersey* (Princeton, N.J., 1964).

14. Marc Mappen, "The First Bribe," in *Jerseyana: The Underside of New Jersey History* (New Brunswick, N.J., 1992), 17–21; Mary Lou Lustig, *Robert Hunter 1666–1734: New York's Augustan Statesman* (Syracuse, N.Y., 1983).

15. Eugene R. Sheridan, *Lewis Morris, 1671–1746: A Study in Early American Politics* (Syracuse, N.Y., 1981).

16. Thomas L. Purvis, *Proprietors, Patronage, and Paper Money* (New Brunswick, N.J., 1987); Michael Batinsky, *New Jersey Assembly, 1738–1775* (Lanham, Md., 1987).

17. Milton J. Coalter, Jr., *Gilbert Tennent, Son of Thunder* (Westport, Conn., 1986); James Tanis, *Dutch Calvinist Pietism in the Middle Colonies: A Study in the Life and Theology of Theodorus Jacobus Frelinghuysen* (The Hague, 1967), 78–86; Randall Balmer, *A Perfect Babel of Confusion: Dutch Religion and English Culture in the Middle Colonies* (New York, 1989).

18. Larry R. Gerlach, *William Franklin: New Jersey's Last Royal Governor* (Trenton, N.J., 1975); Willard S. Randall, *A Little Revenge: Benjamin Franklin and His Son* (Boston, 1984); and Sheila Skemp, *William Franklin: Son of a Patriot, Servant of a King* (New York, 1990).

19. Larry R. Gerlach, *Prologue to Independence: New Jersey in the Coming of the American Revolution* (New Brunswick, N.J., 1976); Larry R. Gerlach, "Politics and Prerogatives: The Aftermath of the Robbery of the East Jersey Treasury in 1768," *NJH* 90 (1972): 133–68; Larry R. Gerlach, ed., *New Jersey in the American Revolution, 1763–1783: A Documentary History* (Trenton, N.J., 1975).

20. Charles R. Erdman, *The New Jersey Constitution of 1776* (Princeton, N.J., 1929); Edward Raymond Turner, "Women's Suffrage in New Jersey," *Smith College Studies in History* 1 (1916): 165–87; Marion Thompson Wright, "Negro Suffrage in New Jersey, 1776–1875," *Journal of Negro History* 33 (1948): 171–75; Irwin N. Gertzog, "Female Suffrage in New Jersey, 1790–1807," *Women and Politics* 10 (1990): 47–58.

21. Alfred Bill, *New Jersey and the Revolutionary War* (Princeton, N.J., 1964); Leonard Lundin, *Cockpit of the Revolution: The War of Independence in New Jersey* (Princeton, N.J., 1940); Adrian C. Leiby, *Revolutionary War in the Hacksensack Valley: The Jersey Dutch and the Neutral Ground* (New Brunswick, N.J., 1980).

22. Precise estimates of numbers of loyalists are difficult to make and depend on definitions (active or not, for example, or including neutrals or not). See A. V. D. Honeyman, "Concerning the New Jersey Loyalists in the Revolution," *Proc. NJHS* 51 (1933): 117–33; Ruth M. Keesey, "Loyalism in Bergen County, New Jersey," *William and Mary Quarterly* ser. 3, 18 (1961): 558–76; Paul H. Smith, "New Jersey Loyalists and the British 'Provincial' Corps in the War for Independence," *NJH* 87 (1969): 67–78; and C. C. Vermeule, "The Active Loyalists of New Jersey," *Proc. NJHS* 52 (1934): 87–95.

23. Gregory Evans Dowd, "Declarations of Dependence: War and Inequality in Revolutionary New Jersey, 1776–1815," *NJH* 103 (1985): 47–67.

24. Richard P. McCormick, "The Unanimous State," *Journal of Rutgers University Libraries* 23 (1958): 4–8; Richard P. McCormick, *Experiment in Independence: New Jersey in the Critical Period, 1781–1789* (New Brunswick, N.J., 1950); Mary R. Murrin, *To Save This State from Ruin: New Jersey and the Creation of the United States Constitution, 1776–1789* (Trenton, N.J., 1987).

25. Maxine N. Lurie, "The New Jersey Intellectuals and the United States Constitution," *Journal of Rutgers University Libraries* 49 (1987): 65–87; John E. O'Connor, *William Paterson: Lawyer and Statesman, 1745–1806* (New

Brunswick, N.J., 1979).

26. McCormick, "New Jersey's First Congressional Election," 237–50.

27. James M. Smith, "Sedition, Suppression, and Speech: A Comic Footnote on the Enforcement of the Sedition Law of 1798," *Quarterly Journal of Speech* 40 (1954): 284–87; James M. Smith, *Freedom's Fetters: The Alien and Sedition Laws and American Civil Liberties* (Ithaca, N.Y., 1956), 270–74.

28. Rudolph J. Pasler and Margaret C. Pasler, "Federalist Tenacity in Burlington County, 1810–1824," *NJH* 87 (1969): 197–210; Rudolph J. Pasler and Margaret C. Pasler, *The New Jersey Federalists* (Rutherford, N.J., 1975); Carl E. Prince, "Patronage and a Party Machine: New Jersey Democratic-Republican Activists, 1801–1816," *William and Mary Quarterly*, ser. 3, 21 (1964): 571–78; Carl Prince, *New Jersey's Jeffersonian Republicans: The Genesis of an Early Party Machine, 1789–1817* (Chapel Hill, N.C., 1967); Walter R. Fee, *The Transition from Aristocracy to Democracy in New Jersey, 1789–1829* (Somerville, N.J., 1933).

29. Peter D. Levine, "The New Jersey Federalist Party Convention of 1814," *Journal of Rutgers University Libraries* 33 (1969): 1–8; Harvey Strum, "New Jersey Politics and the War of 1812," *NJH* 105 (1987): 37–69.

30. George Rogers Taylor, *The Transportation Revolution, 1815–1860* (New York, 1962).

31. Wheaton J. Lane, *From Indian Trail to Iron Horse: Travel and Transportation in New Jersey, 1620–1860* (Princeton, N.J., 1959); Archibald D. Turnbull, *John Stevens: An American Record* (New York, 1928); Maurice Baxter, *The Steamboat Monopoly: Gibbons v. Ogden, 1824* (New York, 1972); George Dangerfield, "The Steamboat Case," in *Quarrels That Have Shaped the Constitution*, ed. John A. Garraty (New York, 1987), 57–69; Barbara N. Kalata, *A Hundred Years, a Hundred Miles: New Jersey's Morris Canal* (Morristown, N.J., 1983); Crawford Clark Madeira, *The Delaware and Raritan Canal: A History* (East Orange, N.J., 1941).

32. Richard P. McCormick, "Party Formation in the Jacksonian Era," *Proc. NJHS* 83 (1965): 161–73; Richard P. McCormick, *The Second American Party System: Party Formation in the Jacksonian Era* (Chapel Hill, N.C., 1966), 124–34; Herbert Ershkowitz, *The Origins of the Whig and Democratic Parties: New Jersey Politics, 1820–1837* (Washington, D.C., 1982); Peter D. Levine, "The Rise of Mass Parties and the Problem of Organization: New Jersey, 1829–1844," *NJH* 91 (1973): 91–107; Peter D. Levine, "The Behavior of State Legislative Parties in the Jacksonian Era: New Jersey, 1829–1844," *Journal of American History* 62 (1975): 591–607; Peter D. Levine, *The Behavior of State Legislative Parties in the Jacksonian Era: New Jersey, 1829–1844* (Rutherford, N.J., 1977); Michael J. Birkner and Herbert Ershkowitz, " 'Men and Measures': The Creation of the Second Party System in New Jersey," *NJH* 107 (1989): 41–59.

33. Peter D. Levine, "The Constitution of 1844: Constitutional Reform and Legislative Behavior in Nineteenth Century New Jersey," in *Development of the New Jersey Legislature from Colonial Times to the Present*, ed. William C. Wright (Trenton, N.J., 1976); John E. Bebout, *The Making of the New Jersey Constitution: Introduction to the Proceedings of the New Jersey State Constitutional Convention of 1844* (Trenton, N.J., 1945).

34. Quoted in Fleming, *New Jersey*, 114. See also James Leiby, *Charity and Correction in New Jersey* (New Brunswick, N.J., 1967), Chap. 2.

35. Frederick M. Herrmann, "The Political Origins of the New Jersey State Insane Asylum, 1837–1860," in *Jacksonian New Jersey*, ed. Paul A. Stellhorn (Trenton, N.J., 1979), 84–101; Leiby, *Charity and Correction*, Chap. 3.

36. Michael A. Lutzker, "Abolition of Imprisonment for Debt in New Jersey," *Proc. NJHS* 84 (1966): 1–29.

37. Herman Belz, "The North American Phalanx: Experiment in Socialism," *Proc. NJHS* 81 (1963): 215–47; George Kirchmann, "Why Did They Stay? Communal Life at the North American Phalanx," in *Planned and Utopian Experiments: Four New Jersey Towns*, ed. Paul A. Stellhorn (Trenton, N.J., 1980), 10–27; Jayme A. Sokolow, "Culture and Utopia: The Raritan Bay Union," *NJH* 94 (1976): 89–100; George Kirchmann, "Unsettled Utopias: The North American Phalanx and the Raritan Bay Union," *NJH* 97 (1979): 25–36; Maud H. Greene, "Raritan Bay Union, Eagleswood, New Jersey," *Proc. NJHS* 68 (1950): 1–20.

38. Fleming, *New Jersey*, 114.

39. Joel Schwartz, "The Education Machine: The Struggle for Public School Systems in New Jersey Before the Civil War," in *Jacksonian America*, ed. Paul A. Stellhorn (Trenton, N.J., 1979), 102–19; Nelson R. Burr, *Education in New Jersey, 1630–1871* (Princeton, N.J., 1942).

40. Simeon F. Moss, "The Persistence of Slavery and Involuntary Servitude in a Free State (1685–1866)," *Journal of Negro History* 35 (1950): 289–314; Giles R. Wright, *Afro-Americans in New Jersey: A Short History* (Trenton, N.J., 1989); Arthur Zilversmit, "Liberty and Property: New Jersey and the Abolition of Slavery," *NJH* 88 (1970): 215–26; Arthur Zilversmit, *The First Emancipation: The Abolition of Slavery in the North* (Chicago, 1967); David Brion Davis, *The Problem of Slavery in the Age of Revolution, 1770–1823* (Ithaca, N.Y., 1975).

41. Alan A. Siegel, *For the Glory of the Union: Myth, Reality, and the Media in Civil War New Jersey* (Rutherford, N.J., 1984); Charles M. Knapp, *New Jersey Politics during the Period of Civil War* (New York, 1924); William C. Wright, "New Jersey's Military Role in the Civil War Reconsidered," *NJH* 92 (1974): 197–210; Maurice Tandler, "The Political Front in Civil War New Jersey," *Proc. NJHS* 83 (1965): 223–33; Mark Lender, *One State in Arms: A Short Military History of New Jersey* (Trenton, N.J., 1991), 48–66; I also wish to thank William Gillette, who permitted me to read the manuscript of his forthcoming book on Civil War New Jersey.

42. Foner, *Reconstruction*; Larry A. Greene, "The Emancipation Proclamation in New Jersey and the Paranoid Style," *NJH* 91 (1973): 108–24; Jonathan Lurie, "Mr. Justice Bradley: A Reassessment," *Seton Hall Law Review* 16 (1986): 342–78; Leslie H. Fishel, Jr., "Northern Prejudice and Negro Suffrage, 1865–1870," *Journal of Negro History* 39 (1954): 8–26.

43. John F. Reynolds, *Testing Democracy: Electoral Behavior and Progressive Reform in New Jersey, 1880–1920* (Chapel Hill, N.C., 1988); Sackett, *Modern Battles of Trenton*.

44. Arthur C. Tressler and John R. Pierce, *The Research State: A History of Science in New Jersey* (Princeton, N.J., 1964); Paul Israel and Robert D. Friedel, *Edison's Electric Light: Biography of an Invention* (New Brunswick, N.J., 1986); Martin V. Melosi, *Thomas A. Edison* (New York, 1990).

45. Charles W. McCurdy, "The Knight and Sugar Decision of 1895 and the

Modernization of American Corporation Law, 1869–1903," *Business History Review* 53 (1979): 304–42; Christopher Grandy, "New Jersey Corporate Chartermongering, 1875–1929," *Journal of Economic History* 49 (1989): 677–92.

46. Hermann K. Platt, "Jersey City and the United Railroad Companies, 1868: A Case of Municipal Weakness," *NJH* 91 (1973): 249–65; Hermann K. Platt, "Railroad Rights and Tideland Policy: A Tug of War in Nineteenth-Century New Jersey," *NJH* 108 (1990): 35–57; Richard J. Connors, *A Cycle of Power: The Career of Jersey City Mayor Frank Hague* (Metuchen, N.J., 1971); Venable, *Out of the Shadow*; Eugene M. Tobin, "In Pursuit of Equal Taxation: Jersey City's Struggle Against Corporate Arrogance and Tax Dodging by the Railroad Trust," *American Journal of Economics and Sociology* 34 (1975): 213–24; Harley L. Lutz, *The Taxation of Railroads in New Jersey* (Princeton, N.J., 1940).

47. On "honest" and "dishonest" graft, see William L. Riordon, ed., *Plunkitt of Tammany Hall: A Series of Very Plain Talks on Very Practical Politics, Delivered by Ex-senator George Washington Plunkitt, the Tammany Philosopher, From His Rostrum—the New York County Court House Bootblack Stand* (New York, 1963), 3–6.

48. Sackett, *Modern Battles of Trenton*; Reynolds, *Testing Democracy*.

49. John T. Cunningham, *New Jersey: America's Main Road* (New York, 1966), 224.

50. Philip B. Scranton, ed., *Silk City: Studies on the Paterson Silk Industry, 1860–1940* (Newark, N.J., 1985); James D. Osborne, "Italian Immigrants and the Working Class in Paterson: The Strike of 1913 in Ethnic Perspective," in *New Jersey's Ethnic Heritage*, ed. Paul A. Stellhorn (Trenton, N.J., 1978), 10–34; Delight W. Dodyk, "Women's Work in the Paterson Silk Mills: A Study in Women's Industrial Experience in the Early Twentieth Century," in *Women in New Jersey History*, ed. Mary R. Murrin (Trenton, N.J., 1985), 11–28; Anne Huber Tripp, *The I.W.W. and the Paterson Silk Strike of 1913* (Urbana, Ill., 1987); Nancy Fogelson, "They Paved the Street with Silk: New Jersey Silk Workers, 1913–1924," *NJH* 97 (1979): 133–48; Robert H. Zeiger, "Robin Hood in the Silk City: The I.W.W. and the Paterson Silk Strike of 1913," *Proc. NJHS* 84 (1966): 182–95; Steve Golin, "Bimson's Mistake; Or, How the Paterson Police Helped to Spread the 1913 Strike," *NJH* 100 (1982): 57–86; Steve Golin, "The Paterson Pageant: Success or Failure?" *Socialist Review* 69 (1983): 45–78; Steve Golin, *The Fragile Bridge: Paterson Silk Strike, 1913* (Philadelphia, 1988); Martin Green, *New York, 1913: The Armory Show and the Paterson Silk Strike Pageant* (New York, 1988).

51. Marjorie Kaschewski, *The Quiet Millionaires: The Morris County That Was* (Morristown, N.J., 1970); John W. Rae and John W. Rae, Jr., *Morristown's Forgotten Past—"The Gilded Age": The Story of a New Jersey Town, Once a Society Center for the Nation's Wealthy* (Morristown, N.J., 1980).

52. Stuart Galishoff, *Newark, the Nation's Unhealthiest City, 1832–1895* (New Brunswick, N.J., 1988).

53. Rudolph Vecoli, *The People of New Jersey* (Princeton, N.J., 1965); the quote appears on 210. For an example of religion and related conflict see Samuel T. McSeveney, "Religious Conflict, Party Politics, and Public Policy in New Jersey, 1874–75," *NJH* 110 (1992): 18–44; Douglas V. Shaw, *The Making of an Immigrant City: Ethnic and Cultural Conflict in Jersey City, New Jersey, 1850–1877*

(New York, 1976).

54. Hubert G. Schmidt, *Agriculture in New Jersey: A Three-Hundred-Year History* (New Brunswick, N.J., 1973); Paul G. E. Clemens, *The Uses of Abundance: A History of New Jersey's Economy* (Trenton, N.J., 1992). Clemens summarizes changes in agriculture and industry over time.

55. John T. Cunningham, "Games People Played: Sports in New Jersey History," *NJH* 103 (1985): 1–31; Foster Rhea Dulles, *America Learns to Play* (New York, 1940); Donald J. Mrozek, *Sport and American Mentality, 1880–1910* (Knoxsville, Tenn., 1983).

56. John Brinckmann, *The Tuckerton Railroad: A Chronicle of Transport to the New Jersey Shore* (privately printed, 1973); Harold F. Wilson, *The Story of the Jersey Shore: A Social and Economic History of the Counties of Atlantic, Cape May, Monmouth and Ocean*, vols. 1 and 2 (New York, 1953); Charles E. Funnell, *By the Beautiful Sea: The Rise and High Times of That Great American Resort, Atlantic City* (New Brunswick, N.J., 1983).

57. Eugene M. Tobin, " 'Engines of Salvation' or 'Smoking Black Devils': Jersey City Reformers and the Railroads, 1902–1908," in *The Age of Urban Reform: New Perspectives on the Progressive Era*, ed. Michael H. Ebner and Eugene M. Tobin (London, 1977), 142–55; Eugene M. Tobin, "The Progressive as Politician: Jersey City, 1896–1907," *NJH* 91 (1973): 5–23.

58. Ransom E. Noble, *New Jersey Progressivism before Wilson* (Princeton, N.J., 1946); Michael H. Ebner, "Redefining the Success Ethic for Urban Reform Mayors: Fred R. Low of Passaic, 1908–1909," in *Age of Urban Reform*, 86–101; Joseph Lincoln Steffens, *Upbuilders* (New York, 1909), 3–93; John D. Buenker, "Urban, New-Stock Liberalism and Progressive Reform in New Jersey," *NJH* 87 (1969): 79–104; Eugene M. Tobin, "The Progressive as Humanitarian: Jersey City's Search for Social Justice, 1890–1917," *NJH* 93 (1975): 77–98; Eugene M. Tobin, "The Commission Plan in Jersey City, 1911–1917: The Ambiguity of Municipal Reform in the Progressive Era," in *Cities in the Garden State: Essays in the Urban and Suburban History of New Jersey*, ed. Joel Schwartz and Daniel Prosser (Dubuque, Iowa, 1977), 71–84; Ella Handen, "In Liberty's Shadow: Cornelia Bradford and Whittier House," *NJH* 100 (1982): 49–69; Ella Handen, "Social Service Stations: New Jersey Settlement Houses Founded in the Progressive Era," *NJH* 108 (1990): 1–29.

59. Arthur F. Link, *Wilson: The Road to the White House* (Princeton, N.J., 1947); David W. Hirst, *Woodrow Wilson, Reform Governor: A Documentary Narrative* (Princeton, N.J., 1965); Henry A. Turner, "Woodrow Wilson and the New Jersey Legislature," *Proc. NJHS* 74 (1956): 21–49.

60. Continuation of an emphasis on 100 percent Americanism and an intolerance for differences was reflected in the 1920s in the rise of the Ku Klux Klan. See Howard B. Furer, "The Perth Amboy Riots of 1923," *NJH* 87 (1969): 211–32; Mappen, "The Klan," in *Jerseyana*, 166–70; David M. Chalmers, *Hooded Americanism: The First Century of the Ku Klux Klan, 1865–1965* (New York, 1965), especially Chap. 35, "Methodists and Madness in the Garden State," 243–53.

61. Lender, *One State in Arms*, 75–82; Howard B. Furer, "Heaven, Hell, or Hoboken: The Effects of World War I on a New Jersey City," *NJH* 92 (1974): 147–69.

62. Quote in Cunningham, *New Jersey*, 288. J.C. Furnas, *The Life and Times of the Late Demon Rum* (New York, 1965); Norman H. Clark, *Deliver Us from Evil: An Interpretation of American Prohibition* (New York, 1976); Mappen, "Keeping New Jersey Sober," in *Jerseyana*, 176–79.

63. Richard A. Noble, "Paterson's Response to the Great Depression," *NJH* 96 (1978): 87–98; Clemens, *Uses of Abundance*, 79–85.

64. Connors, *Cycle of Power*; McKean, *The Boss*; George C. Rapport, *The Statesman and the Boss: A Study of American Political Leadership Exemplified by Woodrow Wilson and Frank Hague* (New York, 1961); Lyle W. Dorsett, "Frank Hague, Franklin Roosevelt and the Politics of the New Deal," *NJH* 94 (1976): 23–35; Mark S. Foster, "Frank Hague of Jersey City: 'The Boss' as Reformer," *NJH* 86 ·(1968): 106–17; Richard J. Connors, "Politics and Economics in Frank Hague's Jersey City," in *New Jersey since 1860: New Findings and Interpretations*, ed. William C. Wright (Trenton, N.J., 1972), 76–91; Hildreth York, "The New Deal Art Projects in New Jersey," *NJH* 98 (1980): 133–71.

65. Edwin Rosskam, *Roosevelt, New Jersey: Big Dreams in a Small Town and What Time Did to Them* (New York, 1972); Paul K. Conklin, *Tomorrow a New World: The New Deal Community Program* (Ithaca, N.Y., 1959); Joseph L. Arnold, *The New Deal in the Suburbs: A History of the Greenbelt Town Program, 1935–1954* (Columbus, Ohio, 1971).

66. Unlike World War I, German Americans did not sympathize with the homeland. See Mappen, "Swastikas in Sussex County," *Jerseyana*, 205–9; Martha Glaser, "The German-American Bund in New Jersey," *NJH* 92 (1974): 33–49.

67. The Kearney shipyards employed six thousand people in 1939, compared to forty thousand in 1942. For general background see Allan M. Winkler, *Home Front U.S.A.: America during World War II* (Arlington Heights, Ill., 1986); and, on New Jersey, Lender, *One State in Arms*, 82–96.

68. Dorsett, "Frank Hague"; Venable, *Out of the Shadow*, 164–215.

69. Richard J. Connors, *The Process of Constitutional Revision in New Jersey: 1940–1947* (New York, 1970); Venable, *Out of the Shadow*, Chap. 12; Alan Shank, *New Jersey Reapportionment Politics* (Rutherford, N.J., 1969); Vorhees E. Dunn Jr., "The Road to the 1947 New Jersey Constitution: Arthur T. Vanderbilt's Influence on Court Reform, 1930–47," *NJH* 104 (1986): 23–41.

70. Gerald M. Pomper, ed., *The Political State of New Jersey* (New Brunswick, N.J., 1986); Alan G. Tarr and Mary C. A. Porter, *State Supreme Courts in State and Nation* (Westport, Conn., 1988); Robert A. Carter, "Meese, Brennan and Jersey Judicial Activism," *New Jersey Lawyer* 120 (August 1987): 27–30.

71. John E. Bebout and Ronald J. Grele, *Where Cities Meet: The Urbanization of New Jersey* (Princeton, N.J., 1964), 52–77; Linda Keller Brown and Patricia Vasilenko, "Time, Space, and Suburbanities: The Social-Spatial Structure of Essex, Union, and Morris Counties in the Twentieth Century," in *Cities of the Garden State*, 85–108.

72. Philip Roth, *Goodbye Columbus* (New York, 1959). Although fiction, this novel offers a good description of the movement from Newark to the suburbs.

73. Barbara B. Jackson and Kenneth J. Jackson, "The Black Experience in Newark: The Growth of the Ghetto, 1870–1970," in *New Jersey since 1860*, 36–59; Judith F. Kovisars, "Trenton Up Against It: The Prescription for Urban Renewal

in the 1950s and 1960s," in *Cities of the Garden State*, 161–75; John T. Cumber, *A Social History of Economic Decline: Business, Politics, and Work in Trenton* (New Brunswick, N.J., 1989).

74. Jerome G. Rose and Robert E. Rothman, eds., *After Mt. Laurel: The New Suburban Zoning* (New Brunswick, N.J., 1977).

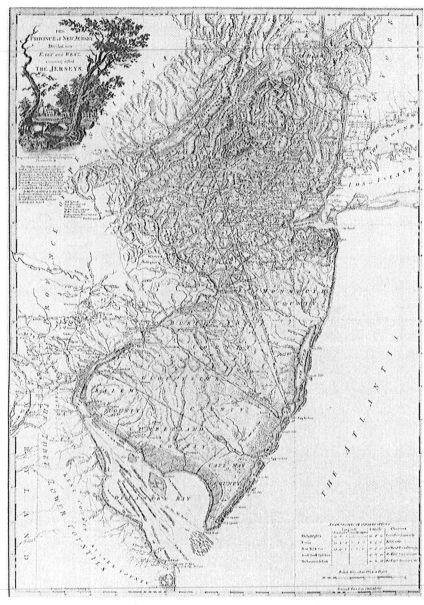

Although formally divided into East New Jersey and West New Jersey for only twenty-eight years, until 1702, the proprietors of each province retained title to the land and granted dividends in each into the nineteenth century. The two north-south lines on this 1778 map, engraved and published in London by William Faden, reflect earlier disputes over the boundary between the two Jerseys. Photograph courtesy New Jersey Historical Society.

1

Historians who study American colonial history have necessarily been concerned with establishing the sources of American institutions. Out of this interest has come a long-standing debate over whether the baggage settlers brought to the New World—political and social ideas as well as clothes, tools, and designs for houses—were more formative than the ways in which their new surroundings forced them to create institutions. In the nineteenth century historians from George Bancroft to the first professional, university-trained Ph.D.s of the 1870s and 1880s traced the origins of American political institutions to the Anglo-Saxons of England and their German Teutonic heritage. Later Frederick Jackson Turner countered these arguments by emphasizing instead the singular impact of the New World environment, particularly the "frontier," on American ideas, institutions, and attitudes.

This argument continues to concern colonial historians. David Grayson Allen's *In English Ways* (1982) argued that the experiences Englishmen brought with them to Massachusetts were most important for understanding the communities they created. According to Allen, these experiences, particularly political and agricultural practices, varied greatly among groups emigrating from different English regions and help explain some of the conflicts between settlers and settlements in that colony. England in the seventeenth century was changing rapidly, moving in stages from older communal farming arrangements to "modern" individualistic practices. Massachusetts settlers left England at a time of political conflict and Civil War, of disagreement over ideas and institutions.

Although the historical debate about the relative influences of culture and environment have mainly been argued from the examples of New England and Virginia, it has clear implications for the study of New Jersey history. What kinds of political institutions did Englishmen (or, for that matter, their predecessors, the Dutch and Swedes) establish in New Jersey? New Jersey was a proprietary colony; title to its government and land were granted by the king to individual "lords," not to a corporation as it had been in Massachusetts and Virginia. The proprietors determined the form of government and method of land distribution. What were the sources of the proprietors' ideology? What problems did they face in putting it into effect? The following article deals in part with the difficulties proprietors confronted in maintaining and exercising what they saw as their rightful political powers. Challenges to their political authority came from both English officials and residents of the colony, but why? Did conditions in New Jersey foster some of this opposition? Did these conditions make the very idea of proprietors somehow inappropriate or obsolete?

Another related issue occupying colonial historians is the idea of American "exceptionalism." The notion of this nation's singularity was central to Turner's frontier thesis. Louis Hartz in *The Liberal Tradition in America* (1955) argued that America was different from Europe because it had never gone through the feudal stage of development. As a result the country had a truncated political spectrum; the range from conservative to liberal was much shorter than in other countries. Americans, he concluded, are and have always been "liberals." If, as the following article suggests, colonial proprietors (New Jersey's included) represent a continuation of feudalism, then is it true that Americans escaped so completely this aspect of world history? Does New Jersey show us that the truth is somewhat more complicated than the Hartz thesis has alleged?

Hartz defined liberalism in reference to a Europe that had experienced a feudal past and socialist present, a conservative nobility opposed to change and a radical proletariat in favor of it. Americans instead were "born free"; they were liberals in the Lockean sense whose political divisions (compared to Europe's) were telescoped into a middle ground. Some American historians, seeing greater divergence than Hartz, have used the words "conservative," "liberal," and "radical" to describe political differences, interpretations of the Constitution, willingness to use government power, and support for change. But the definitions of these terms and how they have been used has changed over time. What "conservative" meant to Alexander Hamilton in 1790 is not the same as what it meant to Ronald Reagan in 1990. How would you define these terms?

Even those who, accepting Hartz's thesis, see America as a liberal society have sometimes disagreed on what being liberal means in the context of republican ideology. They have postulated a divergence between "classical" and "liberal" republicanism: classical republicanism looked to the past, emphasized the community or the family, and was satisfied with a subsistence economy; liberal republicanism looked to the future, stressed the individual, and rewarded competitive and acquisitive actions. Part of the historical debate centers on when Americans became individualistic capitalists driven by the desire for commercial success. Most historians suggest the move from an interest in communal self-sufficiency to an individualist interest in commercial markets took place between 1790 and 1820. How do these ideas apply to groups such as the Board of Proprietors of East Jersey who over two centuries evolved into a modern corporation?

The exceptional nature of the United States is claimed on the basis of comparative historical analysis. By examining several countries, or a number of American colonies, similarities and differences become apparent that help build a clear understanding of the singularity of a place. When New Jersey is examined from a comparative perspective, it appears in some ways "unique." What experiences peculiar to the colony made New Jersey unique in this period? At the same time New Jersey was part of the British empire and then the new United States. As such it shared ideas, institutions, and ethnic and religious groups with its neighbors. It also shared such experiences as royal control and the American Revolution. What events and issues specifically did New Jerseyans share with other settlers of the New World?

Suggested Readings

Allen, David Grayson. *In English Ways: The Movement of Societies and the Transferal of English Local Law and Custom to Massachusetts Bay in the Seventeenth Century*. New York, 1982.

Craven, Wesley Frank. *New Jersey and the English Colonization of North America*. Princeton, N.J., 1964.

Greene, Jack P. *Pursuits of Happiness: The Social Development of Early Modern British Colonies and the Formation of American Culture*. Chapel Hill, N.C., 1988.

Hartz, Louis. *The Liberal Tradition in America: An Interpretation of American Political Thought since the Revolution*. New York, 1955.

Hawke, David. *The Colonial Experience*. Indianapolis, 1966.

McCormick, Richard P. *New Jersey from Colony to State, 1609–1789*. 1964. Reprint. Princeton, N.J., 1981.

Pomfret, John. *The Province of West New Jersey, 1609–1702: A History of the Origins of an American Colony*. Princeton, N.J., 1956.

———. *The Province of East New Jersey, 1609–1702: The Rebellious Proprietary*. Princeton, N.J., 1962.

———. *Colonial New Jersey: A History*. New York, 1973.

Turner, Frederick Jackson. "The Significance of the Frontier in American History." In *Frontier and Section: Selected Essays*. Englewood

Cliffs, N.J., 1961. 37–62.

Ver Steeg, Clarence. *The Formative Years*. New York, 1964.

◆ ◆ ◆ ◆ ◆ ◆ ◆

New Jersey: The Unique Proprietary

Maxine N. Lurie

New Jersey, it has been suggested, has received little attention from historians because it was an "average" colony lacking in "distinctive characteristics."[1] Pausing only long enough to classify New Jersey as a "middle colony," many historians have then gone on to study its more interesting neighbors. But New Jersey has had an unusual and important political and legal history. In the colonial period it underwent a metamorphosis from a feudal institution to a corporation, a transformation unique in North America and one which prefigured modern business structures. Further distinctions also differentiate New Jersey from the other proprietary colonies it superficially resembled and show that it began and evolved in unique ways.[2]

The original English grant for the colony in 1663 came from the Duke of York, not the King. The question of whether the Duke had the same power to confer political control as he had to convey a land title to the early proprietors marked politics in New Jersey from its inception. The ultimate resolution of the question split control of the land from title to the government. Before the resolution, the difficulties the proprietors encountered in exercising governmental authority in the period to 1702 were compounded by a series of splits among the proprietors themselves. Although New Jersey was one of several multiple proprietorships, shares in it were fractionalized to an extraordinary degree, a fragmentation exacerbated by the way land was granted as dividends to these fractional holders. In addition, New Jersey was the only proprietary colony broken into two—East and West Jersey—with ownership of each half vested in differ-

Pennsylvania Magazine of History and Biography 111 (1987): 77–79.
Reprinted by permission of the Historical Society of Pennsylvania.

ent groups. The boards of proprietors created in the seventeenth century have survived to the present, but they changed from groups of feudal lords to the precursors of modern corporate boards.

New Jersey was initially part of the grant given to James, of York, by his brother Charles II on March 12, 1664.[3] Later that year, the Duke conveyed part of his territory to Sir George Carteret and Lord John Berkeley, two friends and supporters from the interregnum. Berkeley sold his half in 1674 to John Fenwick and Edward Byllynge, two Quakers whose involved affairs and subsequent disagreements complicated the colony's early history.[4] In 1676, Byllynge, the Quaker trustees handling the dispute between Fenwick and Byllynge, and Carteret signed a Quintpartite Agreement dividing the colony into East and West Jersey. George Carteret died in 1680; two years later, his widow sold what had by then become East Jersey to a consortium of twelve members, a group which soon doubled its membership. The twenty-four East Jersey proprietors were predominantly Quaker, and approximately half were Scots. In 1687 Byllynge's heirs sold his West Jersey shares to Dr. Daniel Coxe, an avid English speculator, and in 1691 Coxe sold most of his shares to the West Jersey Society, an investment company.

All of New Jersey's proprietors—from Berkeley and Carteret to the West Jersey Society—assumed that they had purchased the right to the government as well as the land of their colony.[5] But the original grant, a re-conveyance from the Duke of York, did not specifically mention powers of government. The proprietors' assumptions about their right to rule were early challenged by jealous colonial officials in New York. The Province of New York had lost some of its best lands and customs revenues to the newly established Jersey colony; New York officials worked aggressively in an attempt to squash an independent government in New Jersey.[6] The power issue was not completely resolved until the Jersey proprietors surrendered their charter on April 15, 1702.

Further confusing matters was the Dutch re-capture of New York and New Jersey, lasting from July 1673 until November 1674. When the Treaty of Westminster returned the land to Charles II, the King issued a confirmatory grant to the Duke. The Duke, in turn, issued to Carteret for East Jersey a brief release, which only mentioned the right to the soil; but no release for West Jersey was issued to Byllynge and Fenwick. It was not until 1680 that the Duke confirmed the sale of West Jersey to the Quakers.[7] The

Dutch reconquest and subsequent English regrants served to confuse further the situation because, once again, the new documents did not spell out the proprietors' rights in governing Jersey.

Still other problems emerged. Clashes between New York and New Jersey authorities, along with pressure on the Duke of York by his friend William Penn, led the Duke in 1680 to submit the legal questions around the Jersey colony to Sir William Jones, an eminent English lawyer, for his opinion. Jones found that New York officials did not have the authority to collect customs duties in New Jersey, inferring from this that New Jersey proprietors had the right to govern their colony. The Jones Decision clarified, for the moment at least, New Jersey's right to an independent government, but it did not resolve who could exercise this right in West Jersey.[8]

Acting upon the Jones Decision, the Duke—perhaps inadvertently—identified only Edward Byllynge by name in confirming the political rights of the West Jersey proprietors. Byllynge asserted sole right to the government. Resident proprietors disputed this claim but lost the argument before Quaker arbitrators in England in 1684. In 1687 Byllynge's heirs sold the right to the government to Dr. Daniel Coxe, who later sold it to the West Jersey Society. Thus, in West Jersey title to the land and title to the government were clearly separated. This did nothing to clarify political relationships among colonists, New York officials, or the English government. The disagreements and frequent transfers of political rights in West Jersey did not help the proprietors of either section who were trying to validate their claims to the government of the Jerseys in the 1690s.

Confusion expanded when the proprietors of both East and West Jersey agreed, under pressure, to surrender their governments to James II so that the province could be included in the Dominion of New England. With the Glorious Revolution, proprietary government returned to both East and West Jersey in 1692, but the political dissension remained.

After 1696 English officials deliberately contributed to a confused state of affairs by forcing the proprietors to surrender their governments to the Crown. They did this by refusing to grant approbation to proprietor-selected Governors (Jeremiah Basse, then Andrew Hamilton), approbation required under the Navigation Act of 1696. This led the colonists to challenge the legitimacy of those governors, a challenge that undermined the proprietors' authority and contributed to disorder and confusion in both Jerseys from 1698 to 1702. The Board of Trade evidently believed that approving the governors would recognize the proprietors' right to govern. This action was part of a campaign against all proprietary colonies in a concerted effort to tighten control over the empire as a whole. New Jersey, as the weakest colony, gave way first. Although some of the same questions were raised about Penn's right to govern Delaware (as part of Pennsylvania), he and his heirs ultimately withstood the challenges. In the end, the significant distinction is not that New Jersey relinquished power that Pennsylvania did not, but that threats to the New Jersey proprietors' right to govern surfaced first, lasted longest, and were most profound.

Much of the political disorder and confusion characterizing New Jersey under the proprietors was a direct consequence of the proprietors' questionable right to govern. Other proprietary colonies also experienced frequent political disputes and disorder. In spite of New Jersey's label as the "rebellious" colony,[9] several of the proprietary colonies were in constant uproar. Maryland was in almost perpetual turmoil during the seventeenth century. In 1681 Lord Culpeper, Governor of Virginia, wrote that his neighboring colony was "in torment" and "in very great danger of falling to pieces."[10] Writing about Virginia, Edmund Morgan referred to "lazy Englishmen."[11] They might also have been characterized as unruly and difficult to govern. There were rebellions in both North and South Carolina. New Yorkers refused to pay taxes and duties in the 1680s unless they had an assembly, while Penn's settlers gave him many difficult times. William Penn thought his settlers quarrelsome, wicked, "disingenuous," and "unsatiable."[12] These general complaints about the "nature" of English colonists were most pronounced in the proprietary colonies.[13]

In New Jersey, conflicts erupted in the 1670s over quitrents, and in the 1690s, in both East and West Jersey, over quitrents and the qualifications and approvals for the office of governor. Disputes over rents and land titles along the borders with New York (as well as between the two sections of New Jersey itself) punctuated the 1740s and 1750s. Aggravating the disagreements among proprietors and settlers were questions as to who really held the right to govern and boundary disputes which jeopardized land titles.

Other colonies witnessed political battles, unrest, and rebellions, but only New Jersey had two of its colonial governors literally dragged from their beds and carted off to prison in another colony (New York) for having had the audacity to govern.

Imprisonment was the fate of both Philip Carteret of East Jersey in 1675 and John Fenwick of West Jersey in 1677 and 1678. Carteret indignantly wrote that Sir Edmund Andros of New York had

> sent a Party of Soldiers to fetch me away Dead or alive, so that in the Dead Time of Night broke open my Doors and most barbarously and inhumanly and violently halled me out of my Bed, that I have not Words enough sufficiently to express the Cruelty of it; and Indeed I am so disabled by the Bruises and Hurts I then received, that I fear I shall hardly be a perfect Man again.[14]

John Fenwick founded the town of Salem and asserted his right, as a West Jersey proprietor, to govern the new settlement. As as a result, he complained,

> my house was beset, my door broken down, and my person seized on in the night time by armed men sent to execute a paper ordered from the Governor of New York, to whom I was sent prisoner in the depth of winter by sea—his order being to bring me in dead or alive—where he tried me, himself being judge, keeping me imprisoned for the space of two years and about three months.[15]

Only in New Jersey, too, can one find the governor of one colony seizing a ship, half of which was owned by the governor of another colony. Thus, Lord Richard Bellomont of New York seized the *Hester*, half of which Jeremiah Basse of East Jersey owned, in a dispute over the collection of customs duties. The dispute ultimately involved the question of the right to New Jersey's governments. It ended with the surrender when the proprietors agreed to give up their "pretended" rights to govern.[16]

New Jersey's cloudy political situation claimed another casualty. The Jersey proprietors—like those in Maryland, New York, Pennsylvania, and Carolina—planned that much of their population would be concentrated in cities, designating some of them centers for government and trade. The West Jersey proprietors hoped to make Burlington such a "chief city"; the East Jersey proprietors in 1682 declared their intention to build a "principal town" at Perth Amboy "which by reason of situation must in all probability be the most considerable for merchandise, trade and fishing, in those parts."[17] With the exception of Philadelphia, these planned, proprietary "cities" remained little more than villages throughout the colonial period.

This was especially the case in New Jersey, where even in 1797 there was "no town of very considerable trade, size, or importance."[18] Officials of the colony of New York—who sought to prevent the development of ports in neighboring New Jersey before 1700—were partially responsible for this state of affairs; so too was the tendency of the more fully developed cities of New York and Philadelphia to drain trade and commerce from the colony. But other reasons, unique to New Jersey, led to the failure of urban development. Colonial cities were ports, centers designated to receive imports and collect customs; New Jersey's ports fell victim to the proprietors' questionable rights to govern and to collect customs. By the time New Jersey became a royal province her cities could not compete successfully with firmly established ports to the north and south.

New Jersey proprietors were not unique in wanting to profit from their lands. But their extraordinarily long land tenure was unusual, and it had far reaching consequences for the colony and state. The Jersey proprietors obtained their grants or purchased their shares because they expected profit from land sales or rentals, from produce or rent from proprietary farms, and, on occasion, from trading or manufacturing enterprises. Although specific figures are relatively scarce, it seems clear that in New Jersey as elsewhere colonization proved to be an expensive outlay offering few immediate returns. Only shares kept until the second or third generation realized significant returns. As in Maryland and Pennsylvania, these long-range profits generally derived from increased land values as the colony grew and matured.

Early land sales and rentals did not produce much money for a number of reasons. "Sales" prices and rents were difficult to collect; proprietary agents often kept inaccurate records; and money itself was scarce.[19] In addition, the legal mechanisms for enforcing land contracts were inadequate. In some cases, the assemblies declined to create such procedures; in others, local juries refused to issue judgments. Zealous proprietors—like those in East Jersey—faced a hostile populace whose animosity increased with rent collection efforts. William Penn in 1707 advised James Logan, his agent, to "cherish or threaten tenants as they give occasion for either," but neither cherishing nor threatening availed much in Pennsylvania, New Jersey, or other proprietary colonies.[20]

Settlers also avoided land payments by squatting or by deliberately neglecting to take out proprietary titles and pay rents. In

East Jersey towns, some settlers claimed that titles from Indians (Newark) or titles obtained prior to the arrival of proprietary agents (Elizabethtown) were sufficient and that, under these titles, payments to the proprietors were not required. Boundary disputes served as another excuse for nonpayment; residents argued that these disputes "rendered them unsafe in paying their Quit rents."[21] New Jersey was not alone in these difficulties. Townspeople on Long Island insisted that Indian titles pre-dating the Duke of York's patent exempted them from his rents, while settlers in Pennsylvania and Maryland used boundary disputes to justify withholding payments.[22]

Nor was the problem of trying to obtain returns from land sales and rents restricted to the early years of settlement. Controversy over rents contributed to disorder in New Jersey in the 1740s and 1750s. Continued difficulties in collecting rents led the East Jersey proprietors to liquidate their holdings after the American Revolution.[23] James Parker, the most active member of the East Jersey Board of Proprietors in this period, complained that constant vigilance was necessary to obtain returns.[24] Again the New Jersey experience was not unusual; at the time of the Revolution arrears in Pennsylvania were enormous.[25]

In fact in East Jersey and elsewhere the proprietors' right to any rents was questioned. Thus Lewis Morris argued at one point that the proprietors' "quit rents are an unjust tax upon us and our heirs forever," while Maryland Protestants at the time of the Davyes-Pate uprising in 1676 maintained that they had transported themselves "into this Country, purchased the land from the Indians with loss of Estate and many hundred mens lives (yea thousands)," and had defended themselves, "whereby our land and possessions are become our Owne."[26]

The proprietors tried to increase their profits by other means. In Maryland, Carolina, Pennsylvania, and New Jersey they established farms and manors, to be run by themselves or their agents. Thus, six Scottish proprietors of East Jersey took joint title to some of their dividend lands, pooled resources, sent tenants to the colony, and waited for returns. But returns never materialized.[27] At other times proprietors sought profits by establishing trading posts to supply settlers with necessities. Maryland, Carolina, and Pennsylvania proprietors, as well as the Scottish proprietors of East Jersey, Dr. Daniel Coxe, and the West Jersey Society also, unsuccessfully, tried to profit from fishing, fur trading, and manufacturing.

In the early years expenses clearly outran returns. Expenses included fees for charters, land purchases from the Indians, and the transportation of settlers and supplies. Thus, George Carteret spent money to send approximately thirty colonists with Philip Carteret, the first governor; members of the West Jersey Society transported three men and a "few" families; some of the Scottish proprietors in East Jersey pooled their money to send ships and about 250 settlers to the colony.[28] They were evidently not reimbursed for their efforts, and they lost money. Much the same situation occurred in Pennsylvania, Maryland, and Carolina. This is why proprietors preferred that settlers come at their own expense whenever possible, and why they used headrights to entice them. They also tried to have large investors bring settlers with them at no cost to the proprietor. For example, in New Jersey Berkeley and Carteret granted to Major Nathaniel Kingsland and Captain William Sandford a tract of 15,300 acres in 1671, on condition they settle ten families "besides their own" within seven years.[29]

There were also expenditures for the costs of government and for defense. The proprietors tried to get the colonists to pay for these items, but with varying success. Even when the proprietors succeeded, it usually took them many years and a struggle with the colonial legislatures before the colonists accepted responsibility for these expenses. New Jersey, just prior to the division, and West Jersey, in 1693, passed taxes to meet some government expenses. But when they surrendered the province to the king in 1702, the East Jersey proprietors maintained that they had always underwritten the government. This is confirmed by the earlier statement by the assembly that "the planters and Inhabitants of this Province have been at Equal Charges with the proprietors in England, in that they have made all Highwayes, bridges, Landings and prisons, etc.," and would pay nothing more because "they were not willing to maintain a government against themselves."[30]

Yet an additional financial burden diminished the return on funds invested in New Jersey. Fractionalized ownership led to regular trading in proprietary shares; each transfer of title required that previous proprietors be bought out, leading to additional expenses and a drain on profits. Though difficult to document, these expenses must be taken into account before the profits of an individual proprietor can be calculated. Of the other proprietaries, only in Carolina did such transfers occur; but nowhere did the transfers happen with the frequency and cost of New Jersey. Berkeley sold West Jersey to Fenwick and Byllynge for

£1,000. Byllynge then sold ninety shares at £350 each. The widow of George Carteret sold East Jersey for £3,400. And the West Jersey Society bought 20 shares of West Jersey, two shares of East Jersey, and other New Jersey property from Dr. Daniel Coxe for £4,800.[31] The Society sold 1,600 shares of stock at a par value of £10 each. This process continued into the eighteenth century.

It should not come as a surprise that the Jersey proprietors profitted little, if at all, in the early years of their grants. The only returns to Berkeley and Carteret were the sales prices they received when they sold their respective halves. Subsequent proprietors of both East and West Jersey did not make money before 1702. The East Jersey proprietors had expected that they would realize over £500 sterling annually from rents alone. In 1696, however, total income from rents was nearer £200, enough to cover the governor's salary, but leaving nothing for the proprietors.[32] The West Jersey Society generally sold rather than rented land. By 1702, the Society had disposed of £6,000 worth of land, but the money (if any was indeed collected) was never returned to investors in England. Nor were there many remittances after 1702. Lewis Morris, who long served as agent for the Society, was dismissed in the 1730s for having failed to send funds to the proprietors.[33]

Over the long term, the Jersey proprietaries became profitable investments. Individual proprietors who held on into the eighteenth century, and even those who invested then, profitted from the sale of proprietary shares, from the sale of lands obtained as dividends, and perhaps even from rents. The same held true for the last proprietors of Maryland and Pennsylvania, who realized revenues from rents and land sales up to the Revolution and received some compensation for losses afterwards. Some in East Jersey thought the Revolution a close call and feared the same fate as Baltimore and the Penns.[34] But the New Jersey proprietors survived even the Revolution. Land dividends continued to be granted, both in East and West Jersey, into the nineteenth century. In addition, after 1800 the East Jersey Board declared the first cash dividend for proprietors and distributed money derived from the sale of United States government securities. In some ways, then, New Jersey had the most successful proprietors of all. Their very perseverence brought them into the era of the early American corporation.

The fragmentation of ownership in East and West Jersey—a

pattern which did not appear elsewhere—also moved the proprietary toward a corporate form. Although multiple ownership was in some ways a consequence of the long continuation of the proprietorship, it was a process that began early and from the outset had the momentum for continued fractionalization. Carolina was another multiple proprietorship, but one in which the number of shares never increased. In fact, the *Fundamental Constitutions of Carolina* was based on the fact that shares were not divisible; the frame of government assumed that there would always be eight "lords," with each responsible for a distinct area of government. Over the sixty-six years of the proprietorship, only forty individuals served in those roles; even though at the time of the surrender of the charter in 1729 only two of the original families remained.[35] At times some of the Carolina titles were in the hands of minors. Two shares were involved in litigation. The surrender itself took ten years, because ownership of one quarter of the province was unclear. But there always were eight shares.[36]

The East Jersey's *Fundamental Constitutions* was based, by contrast, on the expectation of increased fractionalization of holdings. The constitution provided for limits on the impact that this pattern of ownership would have on the government of the colony. To keep one proprietor from dominating the others, the constitution prohibited anyone from holding more than a one twenty-fourth interest. Likewise, to prevent proprietors from "squandering" their interest in the government, holders of less than a one ninety-sixth interest lost their political role.[37] These provisions controlling access to government recognized that an unlimited number of individuals could own shares in the land. As that possibility approached realization in the eighteenth century, the East Jersey proprietors restricted membership on its Board of Directors to those owning at least a quarter share (1/96th) in the proprietary. But there were no limits on how often a share could be subdivided; holders of even the smallest fraction were still entitled to land dividends. The same fractionalization of proprietary shares occurred in West Jersey, though title—first under Edward Byllynge, then under Dr. Daniel Coxe and the West Jersey Society—to the government there was kept intact. West Jersey differed, then, from East Jersey in denying fractional holders a say in government matters. But both East and West Jersey granted land dividends to holders of even the smallest fraction of a proprietary share.

The number of shareholders in East and West Jersey increased rapidly. East Jersey went from twelve to twenty-four to eighty-five shareholders in the 1680s alone, and the size of individual holdings dropped quickly to a twenty-fourth and then a forty-eighth share. By the eighteenth century, even a ten-thousandth share was recorded.[38] West Jersey went from two shareholders in 1674 to one hundred twenty by 1683, and from one hundred full shares to holdings of one sixty-fourth of one of those shares.[39] Splitting holdings further was the West Jersey Society, created in 1691. This holding company owned two shares of East Jersey, twenty shares of West Jersey, and parcels of land in New Jersey and Pennsylvania; speculators traded in the shares of the society.[40]

The fractionalization that contributed to the evolution of the New Jersey proprietorship had other consequences as well. Almost all of the original proprietors in each colony were economically or politically prominent and influential men. Many were involved in one way or another in more than one colonial enterprise. But as time passed and proprietary titles devolved upon others, the status of the proprietors as a group declined and with it their ability to protect their colonies. This pattern of development was true everywhere, but it was exacerbated in New Jersey.

Berkeley and Carteret, the original proprietors of New Jersey, were royalist supporters of the Crown during the exile years of the Civil War period, and they held significant government posts in the Restoration government.[41] Their Jersey holdings later went to men who lacked equivalent status and influence. Neither John Fenwick nor Edward Byllynge in West Jersey were politically prominent and influential, while the men who purchased the one hundred shares from them in later years were even less "weighty." In East Jersey the twelve proprietors included several Scottish lords (who later took the wrong side in the Glorious Revolution), but the group was mainly comprised of Quaker polemicists, tailors, and merchants. With the exception of William Penn, these men lacked influence at court. As the twelve proprietors became twenty-four, and then more, their individual status and influence further declined. At the time of the charter's surrender, only Penn stood out as significant.[42] This problem of diminished standing persisted into the eighteenth century, diluting the power and influence of the Jersey proprietors.

After 1674, New Jersey—begun as one colony—was in fact two, divided into an east and west, with each section owned by different proprietors. Carolina had been split north and south, because distance between the two early centers of settlement made one government impracticable. But both Carolinas belonged to a single group of proprietors. Similarly, Delaware and Pennsylvania were administered separately for political and religious reasons, although both were the property of the Penns. In New Jersey, the impact of this unusual division was felt long after the surrender of the charter reunited the two halves into a single royal colony. In fact, the political and economic consequences continued into and beyond the eighteenth century. As a result of the separation of New Jersey into eastern and western divisions there were two capitals, two treasurers, a sectionally balanced council, and an extraordinary political factionalization of the colony.

The West Jersey proprietors appointed Burlington as their capital; East Jersey proprietors selected Perth Amboy. The surrender agreement alternated governmental meetings between the two towns. From 1702 to 1776, alternate meeting places was customary practice, set aside only when royal governors argued that ill health or the press of business required the legislature to meet elsewhere.[43] When William Franklin, the last royal governor of New Jersey, pushed for the building of a formal governor's house, his request mentioned the need for two such residences.[44]

The situation changed with the Revolution. Both governor William Livingston and the legislature were forced to move about the state in an effort to avoid capture by the British. The government continued to wander after the war. Meeting thirty-five times in the period from 1776 to 1791, the legislature sat in Burlington, Perth Amboy, Princeton, and Trenton. The state considered each when attempting to locate a single, permanent capital.[45] In 1790 Tench Coxe wrote William Paterson that New Jersey should "soon . . . fix [its] Government in one place" in order to promote manufacturing and stability. Coxe argued for a site accessible to ocean-going ships, suggesting "Brunswick & its Vicinity" as the most suitable.[46] His selection was ignored; the next year the legislature choose Trenton, and for the first time since the 1670s New Jersey had one capital.

Even after reunification, the historic division of the colony multiplied the number of factions in New Jersey. In the period from 1703 to 1729, Governors Cornbury, Hunter, and Burnet contended with competing East Jersey factions led by Scottish proprietors, English proprietors, and Nicolls patentees as well as such West Jersey factions as the West Jersey Society, Quakers (who were often also resident West Jersey proprietors), and Anglicans (including the West Jersey proprietor Colonel Daniel Coxe). The political divisions continued into the 1780s and constituted the fundamental cleavage of the Confederation period. The Revolutionary War had heightened sectional antagonisms. East Jersey was more frequently affected by fighting, and West Jersey Quakers refused to help militarily or economically. Disagreements over the use of paper currency after 1783 also followed sectional lines. But the bitter fight between East and West Jersey proprietors over the boundary line between their sections—an issue kept constantly before the legislature from 1782 to 1786—most clearly continued and aggravated "the traditional internal split within the state."[47] The political impact continued into the next century, long surviving the formal division into East and West Jersey which lasted only from 1674 to 1702.

Perhaps the most enduring legacy of the proprietary period were the boards of proprietors established to handle business in both East and West Jersey. These associations have survived to the present. Both have evolved into modern corporations. In the process, the New Jersey proprietorship transformed itself from a feudal lordship to a capitalist company.

Of the five grants, proprietary in origin, for mainland colonies, two—Carolina and New Jersey—were "multiple" proprietorships. That is, the original grants for these colonies went to more than one individual. These multiple proprietorships exhibited some similarities. Proprietors in both colonies contributed money to the ventures and became, in effect, shareholders. Those who did not contribute monetarily were later held ineligible for returns. The Carolina proprietors agreed in 1663 to require periodic contributions of £25 each. At the end of three years, six of them had laid out £100 each; two never met their obligations.[48] Each proprietor in East Jersey was asked to put £300 into a common fund to meet the purchase price and initial expenses. Other assessments followed. And the 1725 agreement which reorganized the East Jersey Board of Proprietors required contributions towards common expenses. The West Jersey Society expected shareholders to pay up to £10 per share for expenses; in the first twenty-seven months assessments totaled £5 5s per share. Over the years, the Society collected £8,108 of the £9,200 to which it was entitled.[49]

The proprietors of East Jersey created a board to manage their affairs in 1685; West Jersey created a council to do the same in 1688. Both entities were formed in the colony; the entities themselves remained in America. In this regard, both differed from the board of directors for Carolina—and, for that matter, the West Jersey Society—which were located in England. The Jersey proprietors also differed from their Carolina counterparts in that they did not give up their lands with the surrender of their charters. The Jersey proprietaries persevered, surviving even the American Revolution.[50] As a result, the proprietors of New Jersey went from being feudal lords to being corporate stockholders, a status recognized in the late nineteenth century when the East Jersey Board of Proprietors convinced a state legislative committee that the Board was a corporation, even though it lacked a formal corporate charter. The Board argued successfully that the organization and operation of the Board predated the state.[51]

The survival of the New Jersey proprietors as a modern corporation is especially noteworthy because the beginnings of this transformation can be seen as early as the 1670s and 1680s. A similar process started in Carolina, but there the proprietorship did not survive to make the final transformation. According to John Pomfret, the "Carolina proprietorship, the prototype of New Jersey's, was . . . a feudal fief rather than a trading company, and it embodied the ideas of a landed nobleman rather than those of a London merchant."[52] Multiple proprietorships in their actual operations early on combined feudal fief and company. As feudal arrangements broke down, the New Jersey proprietorship ultimately became simply a company.

There is a connection between the nature of the New Jersey proprietorship and the political problems experienced by her proprietors. New Jersey started out with two feudal lords who sold their proprietorships to groups rather than individuals. These groups were not "lords" in the traditional sense of the term; nor were they partners nor, at least originally, corporations. A lord could have political power, but it was not as clear that a quasi-corporation (not yet a recognizable corporate body) could possess such authority. Thus the changing nature of the New Jersey proprietorship complicated the question of political control which was confused from the outset by the Duke of York's grant to Berkeley and Carteret. In this sense the dispute over political control in New Jersey is really symptomatic of a more fundamental change which was nothing less than the transformation from a feudalistic entity to a modern one.

Notes

An earlier version of this paper was presented before the Seminar for New Jersey Historians sponsored by The New Jersey Historical Commission and the Department of History, Princeton University. I would like to thank the New Jersey Historical Commission for a research grant, Rutgers University Libraries for research leave, Richard P. McCormick and John Murrin for pointing out things I had not considered, and Jonathan Lurie for reading drafts.

1. Richard P. McCormick, *New Jersey from Colony to State* (Newark, 1981), x. In contrast, John Pomfret (*Colonial New Jersey: A History* [New York,1973], xvi) pointed to New Jersey as "unique," citing as justification its divided proprietorship, the proprietors' ownership of the soil only, and the complex land system.

2. For a comparative discussion of the proprietary colonies, see Maxine Neustadt Lurie, "Proprietary Purposes in the Anglo American Colonies: Problems in the Transplantation of English Patterns of Social Organization," Ph.D. dissertation, University of Wisconsin, 1968.

3. This grant included territory that sprawled from Maine to New Jersey and incorporated Long Island, Martha's Vineyard, and Nantucket Island.

4. Byllynge was in bankruptcy and later claimed Fenwick's involvement was as a trustee to protect Byllynge, the real owner. William Penn arbitrated the dispute, and Quaker trustees were appointed to handle Byllynge's affairs. They divided the proprietorship into one hundred shares, awarding ninety to Byllynge and ten to Fenwick.

5. The Quakers said they had been "induced" to buy Berkeley's half by the "powers of government" included in the conveyance "because to all prudent men the government of any place is more inviting than the soil for what is good land without good laws." They wanted the government to "assure people of an easy and free and safe government" without which settlers would not come "for it would be madness to leave a free and good and improved country, to plant in a wilderness." Letter from the West Jersey Trustees to the Duke of York's Commissioners, 1680, quoted in John Clement, "William Penn and His Interest in West New Jersey," *Pennsylvania Magazine of History and Biography 5* (1881), 324; Samuel Smith, *History of New Jersey* (Burlington, NJ, 1765), 117–18.

6. See the discussion of the problems of John Fenwick and Peter Carteret which follows.

7. In 1683 he confirmed the sale from Carteret to the twenty-four proprietors.

8. This was not a definitive resolution of the question, because English officials later maintained that the Duke could not convey his political rights to another party.

9. John Pomfret, *The Province of East New Jersey, 1609–1702: The Rebellious Proprietary* (Princeton, 1962).

10. Quoted in Michael G. Hall et al., *The Glorious Revolution in America: Documents on the Colonial Crisis of 1689* (Chapel Hill, 1964), 143.

11. Edmund Morgan, *American Slavery, American Freedom: The Ordeal of Colo-*

nial Virginia (New York, 1975); chapter 3.

12. Penn to James Harrison, November 20, 1686, Papers of David Lloyd and others Relating to Pennsylvania (materials from the Pennsylvania Historical Society microfilmed and presented to the Wisconsin Historical Society by Roy Lokken); Penn to [?], April 8, 1704, ibid.; Penn to Logan, May 18, 1708, *Penn Logan Correspondence, Memoirs of the Historical Society of Pennsylvania,* (Philadelphia, 1872), 10, 271. (Hereafter cited as *Penn-Logan Correspondence.*)

13. Richard Dunn makes this clear by illustrating the difficult time both proprietary and royal governors experienced in the West Indies colonies. *Sugar and Slaves: The Rise of the Planter Class in the English West Indies, 1624–1713* (New York, 1972). Even within England it was difficult for authoritics to exercise their power in certain rural areas. See Robert W. Malcolmson, " 'A set of ungovernable people': the Kingswood colliers in the eighteenth century," in John Brewer and John Styles, eds., *An Ungovernable People, The English and Their Law in the Seventeenth and Eighteenth Centuries* (New Brunswick, NJ, 1980), 85–86. This may indicate that disorder and rebelliousness were endemic to the peripheral areas of the state and empire. That it was more characteristic in the proprietary colonies is shown by the fact that of eighteen "rebellions" in America between 1645 and 1760, thirteen occurred in the proprietaries, five in royal colonies, and none in the charter colonies. (For a list of the eighteen, see Richard M. Brown, "Violence and the American Revolution," in Stephen Kurtz and James H. Hutson, *Essays on the American Revolution* (New York, 1973) 85–86; the calculations are mine.) An 1701 pamphlet noted that "in some of the Proprieties, the Hands of the Government are so feeble, that they can not protect themselves against the Insolencies of the Common People, which makes them very subject to Anarchy and Confusion." Louis B. Wright, ed., *An Essay Upon the Government of the English Plantations on the Continent of America* (repr., San Marino, CA, 1945), 37.

14. In William A. Whitehead, ed., *Documents Relative to the Colonial History of State of New Jersey,* 1 (Newark, 1880), 316. (Hereafter cited as Whitehead, *Documents Relative to New Jersey.*) See also Edwin Hatfield, *History of Elizabeth, New Jersey* (New York, 1868), 189–95. Andros acted to prevent establishment of New Jersey's right to an independent government. He demanded that Carteret cease operating a separate government, and then he had Carteret tried in New York for resisting this order. The jury verdict found Carteret not guilty, but the court ordered him to desist anyway.

15. In Pomfret, *Province of West Jersey,* 84. Fenwick was tried in New York in 1677 but because his deeds to West Jersey were held in England by John Eldridge and Edmund Warner (to whom he had mortgaged his property), he could offer no proof of his position. He was fined by the court and required to give security for good behavior. He was arrested again in 1678 and held in New York. In 1683 William Penn bought out Fenwick's interests and claims; shortly afterwards New Jersey political rights were recognized as inhering in Edward Byllynge.

16. The dispute started in 1693 over the right of the New Jersey proprietors to create ports free from New York jurisdiction and customs collections. After 1696 East and West Jersey proprietors petitioned the Board of Trade to recognize New Jersey's rights to free ports. In 1697 the Board agreed there were no regulations against New Jersey ports. But later the same year Attorney General Sir Thomas Trevor and Solicitor General Sir John Hawles ruled that because the power to designate ports was not given to the Duke of York, he could not

have transferred this power to the New Jersey proprietors. The proprietors proposed a test case; the Board of Trade then moved to tie the right to ports to the right to the government. The proprietors feared they might lose such a test, refused the arrangement, and turned to devising an acceptable surrender agreement. In a final ironic development, the Hester Case, which served as the test the proprietors had decided to avoid, ended in Basse's favor. The Chief Justice stated he was not convinced New York had jurisdiction over New Jersey. But it was too late; the proprietors had already conceded.

17. *Brief account of the province of East-Jersey, in America, published by the present proprietors, for the information of all such persons who are or may be inclined to settle themselves, families and servants in that country* (Edinburgh, 1682), in Smith, *History of New Jersey*, 542.

18. Robert Proud, *History of Pennsylvania* (Philadelphia, 1797), 1, 166. In 1740, Lewis Morris wrote to the Duke of Newcastle that Perth Amboy and Burlington "are both Inconsiderable places and like to remain so, neither of them fit for the seat of government, nor so convenient scituated for that purpose as some others." William A Whitehead, ed., *The Papers of Lewis Morris, Governor of the Province of New Jersey, from 1738 to 1746* (New York, 1852), 121.

19. In the early years, proprietors often "sold" land and reserved a quitrent; in this case, the annual rents were lower than those on land which was simply rented.

20. Penn to Logan, 1707, *Penn-Logan Correspondence, 10*, 229.

21. Remonstrance of Assembly to Governor Gookin, May 7, 1709, *Minutes of the Provincial Council of Pennsylvania, Colonial Records of Pennsylvania 2* (Philadelphia, 1852), 455.

22. J.R. Brodhead, *History of the State of New York 1609–1691* (New York, 1871), 2, 71, 109; Alexander Flick, *History of the State of New York* (New York, 1933), 2, 85–86; J.M. Neil, "Long Island, 1640–1691: The Defeat of Town Autonomy," M.A. thesis, University of Wisconsin, 1963, 62–64, 70, 86; Jerome Reich, *Leisler's Rebellion: A Study of Democracy in New York 1664–1720* (Chicago, 1953), 13–14, 23.

For problems with rents in Pennsylvania and Maryland, see *Penn Logan Correspondence, 9*, 102, 262, 365–66; 10, 25, 50, 123, 303; *Papers Relating to the Provincial Affairs of Pennsylvania, Pennsylvania Archives s.2 v. 7* (1878), 65; Beverley W. Bond, *The Quit-rent System in the American Colonies* (New Haven, 1919), 161–62.

23. Gary Horowitz, "New Jersey Land Riots 1745–1755," Ph.D. dissertation, Ohio State University, 1966; Thomas L. Purvis, "Origins and Patterns of Agrarian Unrest in New Jersey, 1735 to 1754," *William and Mary Quarterly 39* (1982): 600–27; Introduction in Maxine N. Lurie and Joanne R. Walroth, eds., *The Minutes of the Board of Proprietors of the Eastern Division of New Jersey from 1764–1794*, v. 4 (Newark, 1985), xxi–xlii.

24. Parker wrote "Where ever I turn my Eyes as a Landlord or as a Proprietor of Lands in Common or unlocated the greatest Destruction presents itself and such a licentious Behaviour in the people in general that Really people who have not their Interests immediately under their Eyes have only but a very gloomy prospect." Letter to John Stevens, January 11, 1786, Stevens Family Papers, New Jersey Historical Society, MG 409, #272.

25. In 1779 this was estimated at L118,569 4s. 6 1/2d.; Bond, *Quitrent*, 161n.

26. "Letter of Lewis Morris to the people of Elizabethtown, July 13, 1698," *New Jersey Historical Commission Proceedings 14* (1877), 185; "Huy and Cry," (1676) in *Proceeedings of the Council of Maryland 5* (1887), 140. See also: *New York Post Boy*, June 9, 1746, Letter to Mr. Parker; the author attacked the proprietors' right to land, on the grounds that "No Man is naturally intitled to a greater Proportion of the Earth, than another," and stated that he who took vacant land and "bestowed his Labour on it" should have "the Fruits of his Industry." In William Nelson, ed., *Newspaper Extracts 1740–1750*, v. 2, *New Jersey Archives* 12 (Paterson, NJ, 1895), 308–9.

27. Ned Landsman, "The Scottish Proprietors and the Planning of East New Jersey," in Michael Zuckerman, ed., *Friends and Neighbors: Group Life in America's First Plural Society* (Philadelphia, 1982); Ned Landsman, *Scotland and Its First American Colony, 1683–1765* (Princeton, 1985), part II.

28. Wesley Frank Craven, *New Jersey and the English Colonization of North America* (Princeton, 1964), 48; Frederick Black, "The Last Lords Proprietors of West Jersey: The West Jersey Society, 1692–1702," Ph.D. dissertation, Rutgers University, 1964, 262–65; "Account of Shipment to East Jersey in August, 1683, by Some of the Proprietors," Whitehead, *Documents Relative to New Jersey 1*, 464–69; John Pomfret, "The Proprietors of the Province of East New Jersey, 1682–1702," *Pennsylvania Magazine of History and Biography 77* (1953), 261; John Pomfret, *The Province of East Jersey*, 197–98.

29. "Some Early New Jersey Patentees paying Quitrents," *New Jersey Historical Society Proceedings 48* (1930), 233.

30. October 29, 1686, *Journal of the Governor and Council of East Jersey* 13:169.

31. John Pomfret, *The New Jersey Proprietors and Their Lands* (Princeton, 1964), 25–26, 36–39, 73–74; Anthony Q. Keasbey, "Purchase of East New Jersey," *New Jersey Historical Society Proceedings 17* (1882), 24; William T. McClure, "The West Jersey Society, 1692–1736," *New Jersey Historical Society Proceedings* 74 (1956), 3–4.

32. Pomfret, *The Province of East Jersey*, 298–99; Pomfret, *The New Jersey Proprietors and Their Lands*, 51, 55–56. Andrew Hamilton wrote William Dockwra in 1688 about L950 raised by a group of East Jersey proprietors for investment in the colony. Hamilton observed that the money was "sunk and gone"; a note appended to the letter about twenty years later added that there was "nothing left for so much money but the bare land." Whitehead, *Documents Relative to New Jersey* (Newark, 1881), 2, 27–34.

33. Black, "Last Lords Proprietors," 56, 269; McClure, "The West Jersey Society, 1692–1736," 8; John Strassburger, " 'Our Unhappy Purchase': The West Jersey Society, Lewis Morris and Jersey Lands, 1703–36," *New Jersey History*, 98 (1980), 97–115.

34. Memo on Reasons why Books should be Returned, n.d., William Alexander Papers, NYHS, Box 43. At this point the proprietors feared the New Jersey legislature "in their present levelling mood [would] follow the example of Pennsylvania in taking possession of the whole." It is difficult to document the profits precisely, but occasional figures are suggestive. James Alexander, prominent East Jersey proprietor in the first half of the eighteenth century, died in 1756. His papers contain several lists of property obviously enumerated to facilitate division among his heirs. One group of lands, the Sussex lands, appears on a list showing that portion on which mortgages were held, as well as what was left to be sold. The whole is valued at L5439.9.5 procla-

mation money or L5892.15.2 New York money. "An Account of What Remains Due of the Sussex Lands for Rights Sold," n.d., Alexander Papers, NYHS, Box la.

35. William S. Powell, *The Proprietors of Carolina* (Raleigh, NC, 1963), 10; Kemp P. Battle, "The Lords Proprietors of Carolina," *North Carolina Booklet* 4 (1904) 5–37; Herbert R. Paschal, "Proprietary North Carolina: A Study in Colonial Government," Ph.D. dissertation, University of North Carolina, 1964, 98–114.

36. The two original families that remained were Colleton and Carteret, and Carteret kept his portion of the lands. Also the two shares which were disputed were claimed or held for more than one individual, but they were not divided the way New Jersey shares were.

37. This rule was violated by Arendt Sonmans who held more than one full share. The quotation is from *A Brief Account of the Province of East New Jersey in America: Published by the Scots Proprietors Having Interest there* (Edinburgh, 1683), 13; see also "Fundamental Constitutions of East Jersey," in Julian Boyd, ed., *Fundamental Laws and Constitutions of New Jersey* (Princeton, 1964).

38. Pomfret, *The Province of East Jersey*, appendix: "Transfers and Fractioning 1683–1702," 397–99. Many references to fractional holders appear in the four volumes of the *Minutes of the Board of Proprietors of the Eastern Division of New Jersey*, George Miller ed., vols. 1–3; Lurie and Walroth, eds., vol. 4.

39. Pomfret, *The Province of West Jersey*, 124, 285–89, gives one example of a conveyance that read "1/32 of 3/90 of 90/100."

40. The West Jersey Society remained in existence in England until 1923. McCormick, *From Colony to State*, 48.

41. John Berkeley had served during the Civil War in the Royal Army and then as secretary, treasurer, and financial manager for the Duke of York. He was rewarded for his services in 1658 by being made Baron Berkeley of Stratton on Cornwall. After the Restoration he served as a member of the Privy Council and as a commissioner of the Admiralty. In 1670 he was appointed a Lord Lieutenant of Ireland, and from 1675 to his death in 1678 he served as ambassador extraordinary to France.

As early as 1626 George Carteret had been appointed Governor of the Isle of Jersey and in 1640 treasurer of the Navy. During the Civil Wars he provided shelter in his province for Edward Hyde, Lord Clarendon, a favorite of Charles II, and also for the Duke of York. There is some evidence that in 1650 Charles tried to recompense him with the grant of an island near Virginia. After 1660, he served as a member of the Privy Council, Vice Chamberlain of the Household, Treasurer of the Navy, and Lord of the Admiralty.

Berkeley and Carteret were distinguished by the services they had rendered the Duke of York and the King, as well as by the fact that they both served with James in the Navy. These associations help explain their roles in the proprietorship of Carolina as well as that of New Jersey.

42. There is a list of proprietors, their holdings, and their occupations in Pomfret, *The Province of West Jersey*, Appendix: "The Proprietors of the One Hundred Shares of West New Jersey," 285–89; Pomfret, *The Province of East Jersey*, Appendix: "Transfers and Fractioning 1683–1702," 397–99; John Pomfret, "The Proprietors of the Province of West New Jersey, 1674–1702," *Pennsylvania Magazine of History and Biography* 75 (1951): 117–46; Pomfret, "The Proprietors of the Province of East New Jersey," 251–93.

43. The legislature met in Trenton in 1745 at the request of Governor Lewis Morris who noted that he had been ill and "reduced almost to a Skeleton." In 1752 Governor Belcher called the legislature to Elizabethtown as an "Extraordinary Necessity" because his physicians advised against a longer "Journey at this time of the year." Whitehead, *Documents Relative to New Jersey* (Newark, 1882), 6, 257; Frederick W. Ricord, ed., *Documents Relative to New Jersey, Journal of the Governor and Council* (Trenton, 1891), 4, 393, 398.

44. Correspondence between Franklin and the Lords of Trade, in Frederick W. Ricord and William Nelson, eds., *Documents Relative to New Jersey* (Newark, 1885), 9, 385–86, 396, 404.

45. Mary Alice Quigley and David E. Collier, *A Capitol Place: The Story of Trenton* (Woodland Hills, CA, 1984), 35. Twenty-two of the thirty-five times the legislature met in Trenton.

46. Tench Coxe to William Paterson, January 11, 1790, William Paterson Papers, Rutgers University Libraries, oversized. I thank Kenneth Bowling for pointing out this letter.

47. Richard P. McCormick, *Experiment in Independence: New Jersey in the Critical Period 1781–1789* (New Brunswick, 1950), 100, 135–57. McCormick quotes Noah Webster that "the jealousies between East and West Jersey . . . [are] almost az great az between the northern and suthern states" on the seat of government and any other matter.

48. First meeting of the Proprietors, May 25, 1663, in Langdon Cheves, ed., *The Shaftesbury Papers and other Records Relating to Carolina, Collections of The South Carolina Historical Society*, v. 5 (Charleston, SC, 1897), 5; Account 1663, CO5/286 Carolina Entry Book, May 1663–October 1697, 221ff (LC microfilm ACLS British MSS Project PRO Reel #1); *Carolina Lords Proprietors' Accounts of Disbursements and Receipts, 1663–1666, listing Fees in Passing ye Charter and Duplicate of Carolina* (Charleston, SC, 1963). Neither Sir William Berkeley nor Clarendon ever paid in any money.

49. *A Brief Account of the Province of East New Jersey in America*, (1683), 12; Instructions to Governor Laurie, July 20, 1683, Aaron Leaming and Jacob Spicer, eds., *The Grants, Concessions and Original Constitutions of the Province of New Jersey* (Philadelphia, 1881), 171–73; Agreement of the Proprietors about the land, 1684, Ibid., 186–87; Instructions to the Governor and Commission Land, July 3, 1685, Ibid., 211; Account of the Several Rates or Assessments laid upon the Proprietors of East Jersey, September 23, 1690, *Documents Relative to New Jersey* 2:37–40; Agreement of the Members of the West Jersey Society for the managing and improving of their lands, March 4, 1692, Ibid., 73–80; Accounts of the Disbursements by the Proprietors of East Jersey upon the Publick Affairs of the Province, Ibid., 202–5; George Miller, ed., *The Minutes of the Board of Proprietors of the Eastern Division of New Jersey* v. 1 (Perth Amboy, 1949), 49–50; Black, "Last Lords Proprietors," 1–2, 75–82, 102–11, 182.

50. Memo on Reasons why Books should be Returned, n.d., William Alexander Papers, NYHS, Box 43.

51. *Report of the Joint Committee to Investigate the Acts and Proceedings of the Board of Proprietors of East Jersey, Touching the Rights and Interests of the State, And of the Citizens Thereof* (Trenton, 1882), 39–40.

52. Pomfret, *Colonial New Jersey*, 22.

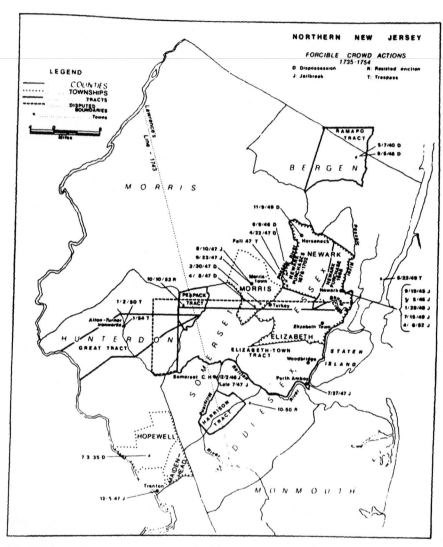

Forcible crowd actions in northern New Jersey, 1735–1754. Although such incidents spread from Ramapo to Trenton, they were centered in the Passaic Valley. Map courtesy William and Mary Quarterly.

2

By the early eighteenth century all the mainland American colonies had been settled. Unlike colonial historians who study the seventeenth century, historians of this period have been less interested in institutional foundations than in the origins of the American Revolution. Their interpretations of that central event have divided into two broad camps, the first emphasizing consensus and the second conflict.

Progressive historians of the early and mid-twentieth century tended to see behind the Revolutionary turmoil the clashing economic interests of different "classes." Thus the agrarian uprisings that took place in several colonies, New Jersey included, were interpreted as the result of conflict between wealthy landlords and poor farmers. Landlords wished to collect "quitrents," charges for the use of their land based on old feudal dues, from farmers who settled on the land and who, by improving it, built into the land whatever true value it possessed. In analyzing the land riots that disturbed New Jersey between 1735 and 1754, Thomas Purvis did not find them to have been motivated by a simple disagreement over the payment of rents. What, then, brought them on? What did problems over land titles have to do with the discontent in New Jersey? Were the riots in fact a battle between rich and poor?

Another historical question revolves around the nature of crowds. Historians and even participants in riots or "mob" actions have different perspectives on what gives rise to such events. Conservatives have deplored crowd action as the work of the "lower" orders, "the rabble," or of "outsiders" who instigate local trouble. Liberals and some radicals see in such disorders a justified uprising by heroic people, a legitimate response to some form of oppression.

In *The Crowd in the French Revolution* (1960) and later works, historian George Rudé sought to answer a number of questions, some of which Purvis also later addressed. How do crowds behave? How are they composed—that is, exactly who took part in these crowd actions? What groups in society did these crowds represent? Were crowd members in fact all members of the "lower orders"? What were the aims of the crowds, and did they succeed in obtaining their objectives? All of these questions can be asked of those who protested in New Jersey.

There are other issues as well. Does a crowd move spontaneously, or have its actions been planned ahead of time? Do its leaders come from the "mob" itself or from outside? If they are outsiders, are their concerns more ideological than local?

Rudé argued that preindustrial (eighteenth-century) European crowds had their own conceptions of justice and rarely killed anyone. In *From Resistance to Revolution* (1972), Pauline Maier applied Rudé's thesis to the events leading up to the American Revolution. She argued that American crowds tended to be extra-institutional, to act when there was no applicable law or when "normal channels of redress had proven inadequate." The Sons of Liberty before the Revolution were merchants and craftsmen who today might be referred to as "middle" class, but they acted violently against specific targets, usually in a limited and controlled fashion. How do Purvis's conclusions about crowds in colonial New Jersey compare with these analyses?

Before historians can study the members of a crowd and classify them in any way, they need to define their terms, set parameters for the groups they define, and find appropriate sources. Different terms and sources have been used over time. The classical divisions, articulated by Greek philosophers, are "plebeians," "aristocrats," and "monarchs." In the nineteenth century Karl Marx divided society into "proletariat," "bourgeoisie," and "nobility." Today, number-crunching economists rank individuals by quartiles and decatyles based on their incomes.

Eighteenth-century historians dealing with a preindustrial society usually use terms more flexibly—settling on "lower," "middle," and "upper" classes. Who is included in each group depends on income, property, occupation, education, and status (hence, colonial ministers, even when poor, are usually considered to have been upper class). While a modern historian can examine census records, income tax returns, and real estate valuations or insurance records, historians of eighteenth-century life study probate records (wills), tax lists, and inventories of estates. What terms and what sources does Purvis use?

Purvis's article raises questions the previous article also raised. The proprietors emerged as players in the agrarian unrest in eighteenth-century New Jersey because they retained title to their lands after they surrendered the government to the Crown. What political and economic role did the proprietors play in New Jersey at the time? What responsibility did their legal actions, judicial positions, and actions as government officials bear for the agrarian disturbances? In what ways did the complex land system used by the proprietors contribute to the discontent? What responsibility did the farmers share for what happened? How much of the conflict was a result of farmers' aggressiveness, and how much a consequence of New Jersey's unusual proprietary system?

Suggested Readings

Hoerder, Dirk. "Boston Leaders and Boston Crowds, 1765–1776." In *The American Revolution: Explorations in the History of American Radicalism*, edited by Alfred F. Young. Dekalb, Ill., 1976.

Horowitz, Gary S. "New Jersey Land Riots, 1745–1755." In *Economic and Social History of Colonial New Jersey*, edited by William C. Wright. Trenton, N.J., 1974. 24–33.

Kim, Sung Bok. *Landlord and Tenant in Colonial New York: Manorial Society, 1664–1775*. Chapel Hill, N.C., 1978.

Maier, Pauline. *From Resistance to Revolution: Colonial Radicals and the Development of American Opposition to Britain, 1765–1776.* New York, 1972.

Mark, Irving. *Agrarian Conflicts in Colonial New York, 1711–1775.* 1940. Rev. ed. Port Washington, N.Y., 1965.

Morgan, Edmund S., and Helen M. Morgan. *The Stamp Act Crisis: Prologue to Revolution.* 1953. Rev. ed. Chapel Hill, N.C., 1963.

Pomfret, John. *The New Jersey Proprietors and Their Lands.* Princeton, N.J., 1964.

Rudé, George. *The Crowd in the French Revolution.* Oxford, Eng., 1960.

_____ . *Wilkes and Liberty: A Social Study of 1763 to 1774.* Oxford, Eng., 1962.

_____ . *The Crowd in History: A Study of Popular Disturbances in France and England, 1730–1848.* 1964. Reprint. London, 1981.

_____ . *Ideology and Popular Protest.* New York, 1980.

◆ ◆ ◆ ◆ ◆ ◆

Origins and Patterns of Agrarian Unrest in New Jersey, 1735 to 1754

Thomas L. Purvis

On August 2, 1735, Gov. William Cosby of New Jersey called for the apprehension of a dozen or more men who had assaulted and dispossessed two families in Hopewell, Hunterdon County. Cosby's proclamation gave the following account of the affair:

> I have received Information upon Oath, that one *Duncan Oguillon* and one *John Collier*, were on the second Day of *July* last past, severally put into the Possession of the Dwelling Houses and Plantations . . . of *John Parks* and *Thomas Smith*, late of Hopewell in the County of *Hunterdon*, by *Daniel Coxe*, Esq: . . . And that in the Night between the Thursday and the Friday following, divers Persons unknown, to the number of Twelve or more, being all disguised, having their Faces besmear'd with Blacking, and armed with Clubs, and Sticks in their Hands, Did in an Insolent, Violent, and Riotous Manner, break into and enter the said respective Dwelling Houses, and did Assault, Beat, and Wound the said *Duncan Oguillon* and *John Collier*, and other Persons then in the said several Dwelling Houses; and them did with Force & Arms, violently amove and turn out of possession, Cursing, Swearing, and Threatning in a most outrageous manner, that they would Kill and Murder the said *Daniel Coxe* Esq: in Defiance of all Law and Government.[1]

Although an isolated occurrence in 1735, this event foreshadowed more extensive violence in the province. Between 1745 and 1754, at least twenty-three incidents of collective force or intimidation took place in six counties. Crowds resisted the enforcement of eviction notices, broke open jails, and assaulted officials. The hostility such as that vented on Duncan Oguillon and John Collier was repeated many times, as men armed with clubs turned neighbors out of their homes.

These disorders are among the least-studied civil disturbances

William and Mary Quarterly, ser. 3, 39 (1982): 600–627. Reprinted by permission of the author.

in colonial America. New Jersey's inability to solve fundamental problems of land ownership resulted in chronic litigation, political discord, and, finally, outbursts of public violence. The events that occurred between 1735 and 1754 provide an opportunity to examine the conditions necessary to spark such extreme resistance to constituted authority and to assess popular attitudes toward the use of force.

Although agrarian unrest in New Jersey has not received detailed attention from historians, several have studied it in connection with better-known rural disturbances elsewhere in the colonies. It has been generally believed that forcible resistance marked the final stage of spirited opposition to landlord domination, provoked by the attempts of a few individuals to monopolize access to vast tracts and then exact quitrents from settlers and inhabitants. Quitrents are held to have been particularly inflammatory, for they not only exploited small farmers but threatened the colony's freeholders by making land tenure, previously free of all obligations, conditional on payments to a rentier elite. New Jersey husbandmen were thus engaged in a class struggle. In the broadest interpretation, they were fighting a sinister effort to reshape America's social order along European lines.[2]

This article challenges this emphasis on landlord domination and quitrent obligations. By reviewing the claims of the principal defendants in proprietary lawsuits, it undertakes to distinguish between the land claims of settlers in different localities and then proceeds to identify the factors that most crucially determined the extent to which different groups became involved in public disorders. Previous treatments have largely ignored these matters, perhaps because they were obscured by the assumption that the principal cause of violence arose from efforts of great and greedy landowners to reduce yeoman freeholders to tenants. In fact, popular opposition to landed proprietors was more complex than historians have supposed and represents a response to pressures far more serious than the imposition of quitrents or even manorial obligations.

A thorough familiarity with the land titles being contested is essential to explaining agrarian unrest in New Jersey. Historians have correctly emphasized the importance of the Elizabeth-Town and Newark patents as catalysts of violence but without assessing the degree to which either area was affected. Furthermore, the attention given them has obscured important controversies elsewhere. It is misleading to characterize all groups contesting property titles as *rioters*, because their involvement in collective disorders varied greatly. A more precise term is *land claimant*, which will be generally employed here.

The most ambitious land claimants were the Elizabeth-Town Associates, elected representatives of freeholders who held rights in land divisions. Their title derived from an authorization to buy Indian lands, signed by the duke of York's acting governor, Richard Nicolls, on September 30, 1664. On October 28, 1664, four men acquired a tract bounded by the Raritan River, Arthur Kill, and Newark Bay, and extending north to the first major watercourse, either Bound Creek or the Passaic River. The western boundary was to lie twice the distance from the Raritan to the next major stream, which the associates maintained was the Passaic; if so, the tract contained approximately 400,000 acres.[3] Within a year eighty associates held rights to town allotments, and by the 1740s hundreds of freeholders could trace title to their land back to these eighty through inheritance or purchase.

When the transaction was authorized, events in England had already placed it in jeopardy. James, duke of York, had given possession of the region to John, Lord Berkeley and Sir George Carteret on June 24, 1664. He made this transfer while Nicolls was at sea, en route to the colony, and neglected to inform him of the conveyance until after the sale of the Elizabeth-Town tract in the fall. The purchasers discovered the change in ownership only when Philip Carteret arrived as governor in August 1665. Even so, Carteret's behavior seemed to validate the patent. He resided in the new town (named Elizabeth for Sir George's wife), and he acquired a share in the patent. The townsmen interpreted the governor's residence and personal investment as evidence that their title was secure and free of any obligations to George Carteret and Berkeley. Conflict nevertheless developed in 1670, when the two lords proprietors demanded quitrents and the settlers refused to pay.

George Carteret died in 1680, and in February 1681/2 the executors of his estate auctioned the northeast half of New Jersey to a partnership of English and Scottish Quakers, which soon became predominantly Scottish and non-Quaker. Most of the investors emigrated to East Jersey to establish estates and exercise their rights of governmental jurisdiction. The proprietors attempted, on the basis of York's prior transfer, to invalidate all grants made before Governor Carteret's arrival. Having control of the province's executive and judicial offices, they intimidated East Jersey residents into repatenting their land by threatening to impose civil restrictions and to confiscate the property of all who refused. The proprietors ultimately forced occupants of the Elizabeth-Town tract in Middlesex and Somerset counties to accept their claims but had little success in Essex and southern Morris counties.

Despite having signed proprietary deeds under duress—deeds that they considered unenforceable at law—Elizabeth-Town residents continued to resist. A decisive verdict resulted from an appeal by Jeffrey Jones, an Elizabeth-Town freeholder, to recover title to his land from James Fullerton, a grantee of the proprietors. The court of common pleas at Perth Amboy had found for Fullerton, but in 1697 the Privy Council reversed the decision and awarded possession to Jones. An affidavit sworn by Jones's lawyer, William Nicoll of New York, indicates the grounds for Council's action: "[T]he sole Dispute was, Whether Col Richard Nicholls, a governor under the King of *England*, in those Parts, might not grant License to any of the Subjects of *England*, to purchase Lands from the native *Pagans*? and if upon such License and Purchase, the *English* Subjects should gain a Property in the Lands so bought? all which was resolved in the Affirmative, and the Judgement given in the Contrary accordingly reversed."[4] The proprietors later denied that the decision established a precedent, asserting that it was given "for some Error in the Proceedings," but the record mentions no such technicality.[5] Later victories in East Jersey trials convinced most Elizabeth Townsmen that their titles were legally secure and would be sustained by local courts. Even if a favorable jury verdict were overturned by proprietary influence, *Fullerton v. Jones* encouraged them to believe that an appeal to England would reverse the action.

Common law, as well as equity, supported most of Elizabeth-Town's claims in Essex, Somerset, and Morris counties. The northern portion of Middlesex County ceased to be controversial after it was sold as two townships to settlers who eventually capitulated to the proprietors' demands. The Elizabeth-Town tract's northern and western boundaries were open to dispute because of imprecise language in the Indian deed.[6] Consequently, perhaps one-quarter of Elizabeth Township itself may have been left unprotected by the grant. After *Fullerton v. Jones*, the East Jersey proprietors tried to prove that the patent's true size was not 400,000 acres but a much smaller area. They contested titles selectively, arguing that even if the Nicolls patent were valid, it protected only lots occupied within about five miles of Elizabeth Town during the initial years of settlement, comprising approximately 20,000 acres.[7]

Historians have portrayed the struggle over the Elizabeth-Town tract as a legal offensive by aggressive proprietors against ill-prepared and vulnerable farmers. The opposite seems more accurate. The Board of East Jersey Proprietors revived as a functioning body in 1725 after a long period of inactivity. For a decade thereafter, it gave much less attention to the disputed claims with Elizabeth Town than to numerous other problems. It even requested suggestions from the Elizabeth-Town Associates for settling the controversy, expressing the "hearty inclination of the Proprietors to an amicable agreement with them."[8]

The Elizabeth-Town Associates, whose affairs were now directed by seven leading citizens elected for indefinite terms, meanwhile prepared an ambitious challenge to the proprietors. In 1735 the board received evidence that the associates were secretly surveying tracts for sale well beyond Elizabeth Township. The board's minutes leave no doubt of the proprietors' apprehension that "if some remedy be not speedily found to put a stop to those practices, it will prove hard if not impossible in time to contend with them."[9] Their forebodings were well founded. "Mr. [James] Alexander further acquainted this Board," recorded the minutes ruefully in 1741, "[of] the controversy with Elizabeth Town drawing into length and they gaining possession almost every day of the Proprietors land and swelling their pretensions to enormous bounds never before so much as dreamed of."[10]

The associates' activities galvanized the proprietors into taking forceful steps to combat them. They began drafting a comprehensive suit to annul the Elizabeth-Town title. Three lawyers, working simultaneously under proprietor James Alexander's supervision, required over four years to complete the massive Elizabeth-Town Bill in Chancery. When filed on April 17, 1745, it contained over 100,000 words of printed text, plus lengthy affidavits, many schedules of land transfers, and several maps. The bill was the most direct and formidable challenge leveled against the associates to that date.

The East Jersey proprietors also initiated numerous ejectment actions against grantees and lessees of the associates on the western half of the tract beyond Essex County. At the same time, they generally refrained from suing for lands within Elizabeth Township, even in localities that may have lain outside the grant's true boundaries. Their past success in similar cases had been limited, and it seemed more urgent to prevent the associates from gaining control of additional tracts of unsettled land. For example, when the Board of East Jersey Proprietors instituted suits against residents of Somerset County southwest of Turkey in Essex County, it exempted equally vulnerable landholders in Turkey itself.[11] While land on the periphery of the grant became increasingly entangled in court actions, few residents of Elizabeth Township had cause to worry about the prospect of suits. Rising tensions over disputed titles after 1735 thus developed from the litigation surrounding the associates' land transactions in Somerset, Morris, and Hunterdon counties, rather than property in Elizabeth Township proper.[12]

The situation was further complicated by the fact that a second set of land claimants, in Newark, defended title to all of that township. The title was based on the purchase in 1666, with Governor Carteret's approval, of approximately 20,000 acres enclosed by Newark Bay, the Passaic River, Bound Creek, and First Mountain. Not content with this area, Newarkers maintained that Carteret's patent was an unrestricted license to buy Indian lands bordering the original tract. Newark residents acquired over 50,000 acres in the years following 1678, concluding with the 13,500-acre Horseneck tract west of First Mountain in 1702.[13] Few of the surveys were recorded officially, and the Horseneck deed could not be produced in court because it had been destroyed in a fire.[14] These tracts were highly vulnerable to challenge. Unlike the Elizabeth-Town Associates, Newark claimants were notably reluctant to bring their western titles to trial.[15]

The text of Carteret's Newark license gives no evidence that it authorized multiple purchases; the document was certainly written to sanction only a single acquisition.[16] An earlier letter from the governor to the interpreters responsible for negotiating the sale also implicitly contradicts the Newark view by directing the translators and the Indian grantors "to View the said Land, and to put the Limitts."[17] While Newark spokesmen always contended that the Carteret patent validated later titles, they eventually devised highly unorthodox rationalizations to support their position, even speculating that the provincial government lacked jurisdiction to regulate any sales made by Indians.[18] Such reasoning not only contravened the colony's laws but implicitly denied the crown's power to dispose of the dominions ceded by the Dutch. Newark's undocumented titles and novel theories stood little chance of being upheld in court or upon any appeal to Great Britain.[19]

The Elizabeth-Town and Newark controversies were by no means the only important disputes, though they have received almost exclusive attention from historians of rural discontent in New Jersey. Extensive tracts of fertile land were contested, sometimes violently, in Bergen, Middlesex, Somerset, and Hunterdon counties. Claimants in these localities had bought lands directly from East or West Jersey proprietors, or made Indian purchases with the proprietors' approval, only to discover that their property was threatened by technical defects in the original conveyances. Inaccurate surveys and improperly maintained records created overlapping claims among the proprietors. The resulting confusion encouraged disgruntled proprietors to file ejectment suits against individuals holding deeds signed by speculative rivals. The suits made many honest freeholders feel insecure about their property and were a source of great outrage. By the 1740s, numerous Jersey farmers would have agreed with the following characterization of such practices. "It has always been supposed that a *just* and *honest* Purchase of, and from those who had Right and Property would secure the same unto the Purchaser, and it has always done so and been so Accounted of, save, in these Parts, and among such *Creatures* as the *Proprietors*."[20]

The land embroiled in such litigation eventually swelled to hundreds of thousands of acres. In 1709 Peter Sonmans authorized four men to negotiate an Indian purchase for the Ramapo tract on the New York border, which included at least 43,000 acres in New Jersey.[21] He held a commission as the East Jersey proprietors' agent and general attorney and was licensed to approve Indian sales, but his authority proceeded from a proprietary clique in London opposed by the dominant faction in the colony.[22] The latter group denied the legality of Sonmans's commission and sued to recover the Ramapo lands. Similar confusion surrounded Sonmans's approval of a 170,000-acre tract called New Britain northwest of Elizabeth Town.[23]

These contests raised serious doubts about the reliability of proprietary conveyances. So, too, did the activities of Dr. Jacob Arents who bought the rights to survey lands for himself in northern Essex County from the proprietors about 1740. He sold lots based on his entitlements to farmers in those areas but never registered the deeds on which they depended. The proprietors began suing his grantees for trespass shortly afterward, although the purchasers had acted in good faith and Arents had been the negligent party.[24]

Ownership of tens of thousands of acres in West Jersey was also in doubt. In 1692 the West Jersey Society, a proprietary organization of London investors, began discussions with Dr.

Daniel Coxe, formerly the colony's largest proprietor and land-holder, looking toward the purchase of three tracts: one of 30,000 acres (future Hopewell Township), another of 15,000 acres (future Maidenhead Township), and a third of 4,500 acres in the southern Jersey county of Salem. By 1694 the society decided not to conclude the transaction, yet it inexplicably advised its agents in New Jersey to begin selling lots on the same tracts. Within seven years the society alienated 12,000 acres in Hopewell and 1,800 acres in Maidenhead, while Coxe's representative disposed of another 2,000 acres in the latter township. Coxe's son Daniel began suing for recovery of all the lands after he arrived in the province in 1702, even the 2,000 acres sold by his father's agent; he was still pressing claims to 3,000 acres in Hopewell and virtually all of Maidenhead as late as 1737.[25] The Coxe family also sought possession of 7,540 acres west of Lawrence's Line on the Harrison tract, and it claimed parts of the Peapack tract and the West Jersey Society's Great Tract.[26] The West Jersey Society itself disputed title to another 13,400 acres on the Great Tract occupied by 97 settlers in Hunterdon County in 1735.[27]

All this confusion set the stage for conflict. Successive transfers of the colony from the duke of York to Carteret and Berkeley, and finally to several groups of bickering proprietors, gave rise to frequent challenges against the original patents. The unification of East and West Jersey in 1702 offered little opportunity to establish an efficient system of registering real estate because the granting of land remained in proprietary hands. The several boards of proprietors continued to authorize overlapping surveys, to lose deeds, and to omit the recording of important transactions. Whether negligence, ineptitude, or corruption were to blame, title to entire townships was sometimes left in doubt. "The tenures in the Western Division are soe doubtfull or precarious," wrote Gov. Robert Hunter in 1714, "that it must either remaine unpeopled, or the People be involved in unextricable Law Suites and Confusion."[28] Hunter's words would prove prophetic for East Jersey as well.

In retrospect it is obvious that even within each division no monolithic body of proprietors existed. Internal squabbling and inadequate record keeping underlay the disarray of titles. It proved impossible to determine the colony's east-west division line until 1743, because several proprietors refused to cooperate. Moreover, aggressive litigants such as James Alexander, Samuel Nevill, and John Coxe pressed inflammatory eviction suits independently of other proprietors.

Failure to guarantee secure tenure and repudiation of signed deeds brought widespread disrepute on the proprietors generally. Hapless freeholders victimized by the chaotic circumstances had little inclination to make careful distinctions; to them, the proprietary interest appeared united in predatory avarice. "[B]ecause of the general Outcry or dislike to those called the Proprietors," assembly leader Richard Smith noted in 1749, "they have, how justly I cant say gotten such a general Odium on their Name that the People wod not pay any Money to support their Schemes," adding that "it would but have been setting the Country by the Ears for [th]e Legislature to have attempted the raising of Money for that service."[29] That the proprietors deserved most of the opprobrium heaped on them should not obscure the responsibility borne by their antagonists for increasing tensions over property titles. The Elizabeth-Town Associates' sales and leases in Morris, Somerset, and Hunterdon counties, prior to confirmation of those titles in court, needlessly placed innocent purchasers in legal jeopardy. The culpability of Newark grantors in this regard was even greater. They sold quitclaims west of First Mountain to outsiders who probably did not realize the serious legal deficiencies of the Indian deeds on which their claims to the property depended. The highly dubious transactions of Elizabeth Town and Newark subjected growing numbers of people to the risk of being evicted and heightened the chances that the steady rise in litigation over landownership would explode into violence.

By 1745, possession of perhaps a half-million acres was in doubt, threatening the property of thousands of individuals. Previous accounts have stressed the importance of quitrents in precipitating agrarian disturbances because of their potential danger to the economic interests and status of the colony's freeholders. This view is of little use in explaining rural discontent, particularly in West Jersey where freehold tenure had always been customary. Quitrents were a minor consideration, even for the East Jersey proprietors, and hardly more than an annoyance for their opponents when compared to other legal liabilities. East Jersey proprietors had demanded annual quitrents from all landholders since 1670, but the rents proved impossible to collect because so many settlers believed them to be legally unwarranted. It is unlikely that the proprietors intended to enforce these obligations more rigorously after 1725, for such action would have been the least profitable way of capitalizing on landed wealth.

Quitrents varied from a halfpenny (sterling) per acre on undeveloped lands to twopence for meadows and improved acreage; moreover, once land had been patented, as were most of the disputed areas in East Jersey that were settled, the rents could not be raised.[30] By the early eighteenth century, these rates were far undervalued in relation to land prices. In 1707, for example, the proprietors collected rent in arrears for twenty-two years on 4,000 acres along Saddle River in Bergen County, and received the meager sum of £229 3s. 4d., current money (£139 sterling).[31] Had they been able to sell the land at rates as low as 10s. per acre, they could have realized £2,000, current money, and would have earned £120 (£73 sterling) yearly if lent out at legal interest. In contrast, annual quitrents on those same 4,000 acres yielded only about £10 8s., current money. By 1743, few quitrents had been collected for almost forty years, yet the arrears had reached only £10,000 (sterling), an approximate annual rate of £250.[32] By comparison, the proprietors spent £295, proclamation money, on the printing expenses alone of the Elizabeth-Town Bill in Chancery, and in 1764 they paid David Ogden £200, current money, for seven weeks' legal work.[33] The minuscule return on quitrents would thus have barely covered the costs of collection. East Jersey proprietors had recognized that quitrents were not only unremunerative but detrimental to their plans for peopling the province as early as 1695, when they proposed to permit purchasers to buy the quitrent rights to their land by adding twenty years' rent to the selling price.[34]

Negotiable leases, either long or short, offered better returns but had serious disadvantages. Leasing brought problems of rent arrearages, improper maintenance of fields or meadows, and destruction of valuable timber. Payments proved difficult to increase, despite rising real estate values. Proprietary records for tenants holding 4,000 acres at Ramapo show that payments remained constant at 1s., current money, per ten acres from 1740 to 1760.[35] The yearly rent on 4,000 acres was only £20 (£12 sterling). Leases, like quitrents, offered little opportunity for substantial gains. The only way to obtain high, immediate returns on land was to sell freehold titles in fee simple.

Peter Sonmans, James Alexander, and Andrew Johnston were among the wealthiest East Jersey proprietors. Income from land sales was far more important to them than quitrents or leases. None of the three can be described as engrossing land or refusing to convey deeds in fee simple. All alienated large amounts of freehold land and profited immensely. Sonmans, who held more proprietary shares than any other individual, sold lots recklessly from 1703 until his death in 1734. He conveyed at least 43,000 acres and received £10,895, current money, an average of £351 (£212 sterling) yearly.[36] Between 1721 and 1754 James Alexander disposed of 11,200 acres of unimproved land for £6,562, current money.[37] He obtained a yearly return of almost £200, current money (£121 sterling), a far greater sum than quitrents on uncleared land, about £38, proclamation (£23 sterling), would have produced. Even long leases at the rates paid by the Ramapo tenants would have earned Alexander only £56, current money (£34 sterling), annually.

A partnership of East Jersey proprietors owned the 25,000-acre Peapack tract in Somerset County. While managing the land between 1743 and 1763, Andrew Johnston kept a journal that shows that he encouraged individuals to buy rather than lease.[38] In 1753, for example, Johnston bluntly told one tenant to purchase his land within one year or be evicted, explaining that "we chose [sic] to sell and not to lease."[39] The only land withheld from sale was a plot designated as the "mine lot," evidently reserved for mineral excavations or a forge.[40] Many residents preferred to rent and had to be pressured into becoming freeholders. Johnston had to compel a tenant of the Elizabeth-Town Associates to buy his lot from the proprietors and abandon his lessee's status, an ironic reversal of the view that attributes agrarian unrest in New Jersey to the frustrated ambitions of would-be independent freeholders.[41]

Sonmans, Alexander, and Johnston sold immense quantities of land; more important, they conveyed fee simple titles with no quitrent obligations. Johnston's records of the conditions of Peapack land transfers make no mention of quitrents. Deeds signed by Sonmans and Alexander likewise exempted the grantees from such charges. Deeds frequently specified that a peppercorn or an ear of Indian corn be rendered yearly, if demanded personally by the grantor on the premises; but such stipulations only showed that proprietorship was becoming largely symbolic.[42] Samuel Nevill, heir of Peter Sonmans, considered quitrents so inconsequential that in 1737 he bargained away all proprietary rights to them in Woodbridge Township, a densely populated community of 23,040 acres in northern Middlesex County; he received in return clear title to 120 acres bordering his estate.[43] Sonmans, Alexander, Nevill, and the Peapack associates thus transferred over 100,000 acres free of quitrents.

If quitrents were inconsiderable, the question arises why the

East Jersey proprietors sought payment of them in the Elizabeth-Town Bill in Chancery.[44] The answer is that they had no alternative, because quitrent rates had been set by seventeenth-century patents forced on the defendants' ancestors. The proprietors could only sue for their recovery, plus legal interest. It is nevertheless evident that they pursued the arrearages in court as the best strategy for exploiting the lands more profitably.

The eastern proprietors' petition in Chancery demanded that the Elizabeth-Town Associates pay all back rents, with interest, from March 25, 1670. It moreover requested that grantees and lessees of the associates be permitted to sue for return of payments made for farms and tenements located wherever unpatented lands reverted to the proprietors, as in Somerset and Hunterdon counties.[45] A favorable decision would have forced the associates to pay an enormous sum (perhaps £15,000 sterling) while defending themselves against a swarm of lawsuits brought by their former grantees and tenants. These conditions would have overwhelmed the associates, since their primary financial resource had been the sale of disputed lands west of Essex County. That the proprietors intended this result is indicated by the petition's further request that if the associates failed to pay, they should be compelled to "avoid and quit the Possession of the said Lands, to be enjoyed by your orators and their Fellow Proprietors for the Rents, Issues, and Profits thereof."[46] In effect, the proprietors were willing to forgo £15,000 in back rents and interest (which had always been uncollectible) in return for undisputed possession of the Elizabeth-Town tract. They conservatively estimated land values at £1–3 per acre, making title to several hundred thousand acres more than sufficient to offset the lost quitrents. The "Clinker Lots" by themselves, comprising 17,000 acres in southern Elizabeth Township long demanded by the proprietors, were certainly worth £3 per acre, or £51,000, because of the improvements made by the owners since the properties were surveyed and occupied about 1700.

Had the East Jersey proprietors won control of Elizabeth-Town's lands, what would they have done with them? The Peapack tract's history offers the best indication of their intentions. The proprietors systematically surveyed Peapack for settlement, just like any other group of land speculators. They preferred to sell, but also rented to men who were unable or unwilling to buy. By selling to all who desired a freehold estate and by leasing to others, the proprietors maximized their income. Significantly, deeds in Peapack did not demand quitrents. The annual payments were low in relation to the land's market value, and insisting on quitrents would have deterred settlement at Peapack because many parts of the province were still sparsely occupied and lots in nearby West Jersey were routinely disposed of in fee simple. When quitrents interfered with land sales, they became expendable.

Many disputed tracts had been settled early and were well populated. Such areas promised exceptional profits to the proprietors if title could be established. Values were high and rising, largely because of improvements made by owners. Sales of property already improved by generations of industrious farmers brought enormous revenues. Not only were prices at a premium in well-settled regions, but the purchasers were already present. All that was required was to force those whose possession had been voided to buy back their former homes. These persons would be understandably reluctant to abandon their farms; they could be expected to sign mortgages or agree to lease until they had saved the standard first payment of one-third the property's value.

Several East and West Jersey proprietors attempted to exploit the highly inflammatory strategy just described. Landholders in the Harrison and Ramapo tracts and several townships of Hunterdon County endured years of expensive litigation intended to coerce them into repurchasing their property, after technical errors were discovered in the original deeds given by earlier proprietors.[47] When the Horseneck claimants in western Newark Township lost their farms in arbitration, they had to sign new mortgages on their former homes or leave.[48]

Proprietary ambitions threatened a prospect far worse than land monopolization or landlord domination, for thousands of families feared, with good reason, the loss of lands that had been inherited or bought in good faith. Since real estate and fixed improvements comprised most of a farmer's wealth, this loss would mean impoverishment, eviction, and the sacrifice of a life's work. The poignancy of the situation was best expressed in a petition to the king from distressed farmers on the Harrison tract who pleaded, "[W]e do further beseech your Majesty to provide such Effectual Means as will wholly put it out of the Power of the Proprietors and other Great Men, to sell lands to the poor Labouring People, and receive their Pay for it, and when the Lands are cleared and made Valuable then to Sue for them again, and compel the People to buy them the Second time, or undoe them with many and Expensive Law Suits."[49]

Who were the "poor Labouring People" whose dilemma was described in the petition? Some conclusions can be drawn about the social standing of land claimants from the limited evidence that survives. Ninety-seven settlers on the Great Tract in Hunterdon County were forced to accept West Jersey Society titles in 1735; the average individual holding was 138 acres, approximately the size of a typical farm in southeastern Pennsylvania.[50] A 1774 map of the disputed Horseneck tract prepared by a proprietary surveyor reveals a median holding of 86 acres, larger than most East Jersey freeholds at that time.[51] Of 120 individuals identified at land disturbances whose residences could be located, probate records exist for 56, including 39 with inventories or bequests. Almost half of the inventories or bequests were made before 1770; their values varied from £16 to £2,246, with a median of £203. The typical inventory probated in New Jersey during the 1760s was £175. Among the rioters were a miller, a minister, a sawmill owner, several slaveholders, and a farmer who set aside £230 for his son's college education.[52] Although the New Jersey insurgents represented a wide range of society, most were probably similar in status to participants in New York's manor rioting, whom Sung Bok Kim has described as "petty landed bourgeois."[53]

It is questionable whether agrarian unrest in New Jersey can be accurately characterized as the product of internal social discord pitting rich against poor, for economic interests forced disputants to cross class lines.[54] United in common concern with the proprietors were their many grantees in contested areas, mostly men of average means who feared losing their hard-earned property if the proprietors' claims were invalidated. Arrayed against them were not only numerous small farmers but also local elites. Among the leaders of the Elizabeth-Town Associates were Cornelius Hetfield, perhaps the town's wealthiest citizen, assemblyman John Crane, Joseph Bonnell, second justice of the supreme court, and Robert Ogden and Stephen Crane, both lawyers who later became Speakers of the assembly.[55] Resistance on the Harrison tract centered on Dollens Hegeman, Sr., a justice of the quorum, and Thomas Clawson, a wealthy planter.[56] John Bainbridge, Jr., who led opposition in Maidenhead to John Coxe's ejectment suits, was the son of a West Jersey Proprietor once nominated to the Royal Council.[57] Newark spokesman John Low was a merchant, an assemblyman, and a brother-in-law of the daughter of proprietor James Hude.[58] Most land claimants were men of middling status, and their arguments were articulated by local gentry; this finding, however, explains little about why some turned to violence and others did not.

The extent to which land claimants became implicated in forcible crowd actions varied considerably. Disturbances occurred from Ramapo to Trenton, but their geographic center was the Passaic Valley. No instances of violence were reported in Elizabeth Township proper, even near Turkey where land was highly vulnerable to recovery, and few broke out anywhere within the Elizabeth-Town tract. The most volatile areas were western Newark Township and the strip of land lying south of the disputed border of the Elizabeth-Town tract, between Bound Creek and the Passaic River. It is striking that the legal merits of nonproprietary titles were weakest in these same regions.

Witnesses named 137 participants in crowd actions, of whom 120 have been identified by residence. Two-thirds of the 120 were from Newark. Eighteen percent came from other localities outside the Elizabeth-Town tract. Fifteen percent lived within the tract (including most from Hunterdon County), but only one-third of this group was from Elizabeth Township, largely from Turkey.

One fact regarding involvement in crowd actions stands out: participation varied according to the legal circumstances affecting particular claims. In a letter to the colony's London agent, assembly leader Richard Smith noted a strong relationship between deficient legal standing and recourse to violence: "I observe thou had taken some pains to collect [th]e Case of a Tryal that had been appealed home on, & wch thou took to be the Case of those People Ryoting, But it was [th]e Case of the Elizabeth Town People wch is very different, from many of these Ryoters for they have only Indian Deeds & don't pretend any other Grant or at least are not like to be able to make out any other."[59] In associating rioting with Indian deeds, Smith was alluding to claims in western Newark Township. Titles there were not sanctioned by Carteret's patent of 1666, they contravened laws regulating Indian purchases, and some could not be produced for verification. "[T]he Generality of the Inhabitants of these Parts, who are Rioters," said one report of settlers beyond First Mountain, "are but lately come into *New Jersey*." Older Newark residents sold worthless quitclaims to such migrants, who accepted them out of ignorance or avarice. By the 1740s the grantees and their heirs were discovering that they faced eviction because the titles were certain to be vacated in court. It is not surprising that Newark claimants were reluctant to come to court.

Town leaders defended their lack of compliance with judicial proceedings by arguing that the provincial bench was biased and that only outside arbitrators could render a fair decision; but even when arbitration was employed, as in the test case of Horseneck, their Indian deeds fared as poorly as in regular judicial hearings.[60] It is not hard to imagine what emotions must have been aroused by the realization that no legal way remained to prevent one's family from being turned out of its home. Whether justifiable or not, here was tinder for an explosion.

No other community experienced more disturbances or counted more rioters among its population than Newark Township. At least 80 residents were named as participants in public disorders, and many more escaped identification. Approximately 300 townsmen participated in a jailbreak on January 16, 1745/6, although only 43 were indicted.[61] Since Newark had only 422 freeholders in 1755, the great majority of adult men must have rioted at one time or another.[62] Crowds elsewhere seldom numbered three dozen and rarely exceeded 5 percent of any township's adult males. Newark's name became linked with collective violence as early as 1746, when the dispossessors of several families were described as "a number of Persons, part of those who are commonly called the *Newark Rioters*."[63] Though Newark had no monopoly on coercion or intimidation, rioting was most closely associated with it.

The tensions and fears underlying forcible resistance in Newark were largely absent from Elizabeth Town, whose residents viewed adjudication as an opportunity to vindicate their claims. This willingness to seek redress within the legal system acted as a check on violence. East Jersey juries invariably gave possession to Elizabeth-Town litigants, and in *Fullerton v. Jones* the Privy Council had upheld title derived from the 1664 patent. As the proprietors observed, Elizabeth Townsmen were "bouyed up with the hopes of having their title established by the King."[64]

The township's residents did not have to face repeated barrages of proprietary lawsuits after 1735. It was rather the Elizabeth-Town Associates who aggressively expanded their claims into Morris, Somerset, and Hunterdon counties at the proprietors' expense. The associates' sales and leases outside Essex County minimized the chances that individual holdings in Elizabeth Township would be sued for recovery, and they provided an external source of money to defray legal expenses. Elizabeth Townsmen were thus spared the immediate threats, anxieties, and financial hardships occasioned by proprietary lawsuits elsewhere. This situation largely explains their reliance on the law, rather than force, to protect their property. The proprietors themselves offered evidence in this regard. Although James Alexander complained that Elizabeth-Town's claims were a cause of violence, even he had to admit that there was no information indicating that the associates had actually instigated riots.[65] Describing an incident in which he faced down an Elizabeth-Town crowd that gathered to resist the eviction of a widowed tenant in Peapack, Andrew Johnston stated that despite the group's efforts to appear menacing, its leaders "did not come with a design to oppose us by force."[66]

Other inhabitants of the Elizabeth-Town tract could not afford to be so confident. The burden of legal action by proprietors fell on Morris, Somerset, and Hunterdon counties. Trespass suits threatened farmers in those localities with onerous expenses and possible loss of their land. Unrest in Peapack and on the Great Tract, the much-publicized dispossession of Joseph Dalrymple, and the two jailbreaks of James Hampton in Morristown all attested to the doubts of freeholders and tenants on the tract's periphery that the 1664 patent protected their titles. Even within Elizabeth Township itself, unease was reported at Turkey, which lay within the Elizabeth-Town tract only if the tract's northern boundary was the Passaic River rather than Bound Creek.[67] Elizabeth Township remained quiet and confident from 1735 to 1754, while the anxiety projected into neighboring communities by its provocative land transactions smoldered and periodically flared up in outbursts of violence.

Sporadic disturbances occurred beyond the Elizabeth-Town and Newark purchases wherever defective proprietary deeds failed to protect land tenure. These claimants' cases had much legal merit, and juries seem to have generally upheld their titles. Few probably would have become implicated in public disorders had they not been victimized by abuses in the legal system.

Indications that the judiciary's integrity was compromised outraged defendants. They objected strongly that judges presiding over their trials were proprietors or their appointees, who sometimes used technical pretexts as excuses to set aside jury verdicts. Claimants on the Harrison tract gathered convincing testimony that Chief Justice Robert Hunter Morris used perjured information to vacate a verdict against his fellow proprietor Samuel Nevill.[68] Several Hunterdon County defendants likewise complained that a judge partial to John Coxe took the unprecedented action of ordering them to pay £525 in fees to Coxe's lawyer, despite the fact that they had just succeeded in having Coxe's ejectment suit against them dismissed.[69]

A more important catalyst of violence was the staggering cost of battling proprietary lawsuits. Only the Elizabeth-Town Associates could fund court expenses by selling reserves of land; in addition, they remained optimistic that an appeal to England would confirm their title again, as it had in 1697. Less fortunate claimants, though remarkably patient in adversity, found that litigation could be ruinous, whether or not their titles were ultimately vindicated. Court cases could drag on for years and seemed intended less to resolve the question of possession than to destroy the defendants' economic ability to resist. Victimized landowners considered this tactic legal blackmail and strongly condemned the proprietors' unwillingness to choose a few test cases for trial and then abide by the results. Costs as high as the £430 spent by one planter on the Harrison tract under suit by Samuel Nevill and John Coxe, or the attorney's fees of £525 mentioned in the preceding paragraph, taxed the resources even of wealthy defendants.[70] Success under such circumstances would be as disastrous as defeat. Groaning under heavy costs, facing judges they believed biased, and frustrated by the failure of favorable jury verdicts to protect their property, many desperate individuals concluded that the law offered little protection and that only force could end their ordeal of legal harassment.

Agrarian unrest never produced widespread, effective resistance to the eastern or western proprietors. The origins and legal merits of claims varied so widely that it proved exceptionally difficult to sustain an antiproprietary coalition for more than a short period. The Elizabeth-Town Associates refused to join with other land claimants, while cooperation among the latter groups was fragile and short-lived.

Conflicting boundaries and a history of mutual recrimination poisoned relations between Elizabeth Town and Newark.[71] The proprietors exploited friction between the towns by persuading Newark residents to sign affidavits supporting their contention that the Elizabeth-Town tract's northern boundary extended only to Bound Creek. The associates objected strongly to the use of such evidence, charging that its real intention was "to support the Claims of *Newark*, against that of *Elizabeth-Town*, as Purchasers of *Newark*."[72] The associates also held aloof from Newark lest any connection with known rioters prejudice their standing in court. When a coalition of claimants representing areas implicated in violence formed an antiproprietary committee in 1747, it is significant that no Elizabeth Townsmen joined.[73] On one occasion, Elizabeth-Town leaders went out of their way to frustrate the intended dispossession of a proprietary titleholder by a Newark crowd, by sending a timely warning to the intended victim.[74]

There is some evidence of joint action between Newark and other townships: disturbances uniting claimants from Newark and Maidenhead occurred in 1746 and 1747,[75] and in the latter year delegates from Newark, Maidenhead, and the Harrison tract managed to form a Committee of the Disaffected.[76] But such cooperative undertakings were uncommon. Leaders in Hunterdon, Middlesex, and Somerset counties, such as John and Edmund Bainbridge, David Brearly, and Dollens Hegeman, Jr., were more moderate than their Newark colleagues; they took bonds for good behavior and renounced violence in 1748 when a conditional pardon was offered. Indicted rioters in Newark, by contrast, refused to accept amnesty, and the town increasingly went its separate way.[77] Despite a common enemy, claimants were unable to overcome their differences, unite on strategy, and coordinate their efforts long enough to exert decisive influence on the government.

The colony's land disputes had little potential for widespread involvement beyond the areas immediately concerned in them. The proprietors enjoyed slight public support, but men whose property was not directly threatened showed no inclination to oppose them actively. A Newark crowd headed by Amos Roberts discovered this fact in early 1749 while attempting to gain support in Woodbridge. Woodbridge had already settled its differences with the proprietors, and Roberts's belligerent argument with a prominent townsman produced nothing but hard feelings on both sides. Tempers cooled short of fighting, but as the frustrated Newark townsmen left, one of them "Damn'd all the Township of Woodbridge, and Said there was not a Man in it."[78]

Despite the complexity of property disputes in New Jersey, there can be no doubt about the underlying issue. Neither land monopolization, landlord domination, nor quitrent obligations lay at the root of the troubles. The basis for conflict was not the conditions for holding land but title to vast tracts. It was precisely because possession, rather than rent payments, was at stake that tensions could escalate into violence. Quitrents were a nominal charge, low in relation to real estate values and little more than an irritating nuisance. On the other hand, widespread challenges to land tenure confronted men with grim prospects, not only the potentially ruinous cost of litigation but the still greater danger of loss of title, with the consequent agonizing alternatives of repurchasing one's former home at market value or being evicted. By the 1740s thousands of Jersey farmers had to reckon with this terrifying possibility, and some turned to force, whether justified or not.

The stark consequences of proprietary victories in the courts make it easier to understand why violence ensued than to explain why its use was so limited. Collective action in New Jersey shared basic similarities with the behavior of other eighteenth-century crowds (described by E. P. Thompson, George Rudé, and Pauline Maier) that aimed at rectifying threats to community welfare and exercised restraint by limiting the frequency and extent of public disorders.[79] Force was used sparingly in New Jersey's disturbances and virtually never endangered life. Only once did members of a crowd carry guns, and then reports circulated that "this Riot seems to Shock the more thinking part of the Rioters."[80] Dispossessions near Turkey almost ceased when spring arrived in 1747, because "it looked barbarous to turn out People so late in the Year, as it was planting Time, and hard to get New Places."[81] The jailbreaks of three men incarcerated for long periods without bail, while their trials were purposefully delayed, represented attempts to redress a denial of basic legal rights.[82] The generally defensive character of the incidents is striking; most were prompted by an arrest, an eviction order, or the occupation of a disputed lot by a proprietary titleholder. Crowd actions in New Jersey were well disciplined, limited in scope, reactive, and conducted with a minimum of violence.

The term *clubman* became synonymous with *rioter* in the decade following 1745, and its implications have great significance for understanding how self-imposed limits on collective action operated. Land claimants refused to carry guns or swords, even when they knew that their opponents were armed. They contrasted their own restraint with the support given by the eastern proprietors to their tenants along the disputed New York border, who allegedly released prisoners from sheriffs by force and once shot a New York constable's horse from under him.[83] Agrarian insurgents adopted the epithet clubman proudly, for it expressed their conception of how force should be used as a last resort. Blunt wooden weapons represented the minimal threat necessary to ensure the success of collective action, but they greatly lessened the chance of dangerous wounds. Furthermore, clubs sometimes served as a deterrent to violence by providing opponents with the excuse they needed not to resist overwhelming numbers of menacing men. The clubmen's goal was to intimidate rather than to inflict harm. Anyone choosing to fight under such circumstances accepted part of the responsibility for the consequences, yet stood little risk of serious injury.

The release of Robert Young and Thomas Sergeant from jail exemplifies the tactics that New Jersey crowds used to avoid bloodshed. Approximately three hundred individuals gathered in Newark on the afternoon of January 16, 1745/6. Their only weapons were cudgels or staves, although it was well known that an armed guard of thirty militia had been posted by the sheriff. The group's leaders tried to avoid a confrontation by negotiating for the prisoners' unconditional release. The sheriff, however, insisted that the men sign bonds to appear before the supreme court, which was heavily influenced by the proprietors. The crowd peacefully discussed the sheriff's terms for some time before concluding that they were unacceptable. As dusk approached, it was clear that action would have to be taken or the gathering would break up in failure. The "riot" began only then.

The crowd advanced on the prison, cursing neighbors who had been forced to stand guard and swearing to kill them if fired on. The militia officers directed the militiamen to cock their loaded muskets when the crowd was ten feet away. Tension rose as the clubmen pressed warily forward and the soldiers waited nervously for the command to aim and fire. The order never came. There was a small scuffle when clubmen broke through the militia tanks, but no one was badly hurt. The sheriff attempted to defend the jail and his honor by drawing his sword at the entrance but was driven off. The milling throng then unhinged the door and escorted Young and Sergeant home. A delegation later returned to complete the last item of unfinished business, repairing the breached jail door.[84]

Every step in this incident was calculated to avoid bloodshed. The assemblage initially remained orderly while leaders tried to gain their friends' release by negotiations. Lacking guns or swords, the crowd placed the militia in the impossible position of giving way or firing a volley at men who carried only staves. The officers and soldiers offered only token resistance. After parrying several cudgel thrusts with his sword, the sheriff also bowed to overwhelming numbers. The episode left no wounds more serious than cuts and abrasions. It is striking how well each side seems to have understood its opponents' intentions and the necessity of avoiding bloodshed. Such restraint should not be taken for granted. Serious violence was a very real possibility wherever emotions ran high. Land claimants were heard to promise that they would "pull [John] Coxe's Home down abot his Ears," that they would imprison their enemies in a backcountry pen, and that they would kill Samuel Nevill.[85] These threats were never carried out, but they should not be dismissed as idle bluster. There was always danger that public disturbances might crack through the restraints of moderation.

A critical factor in preventing excessive violence was the influence of those whom Samuel Nevill described as "Men of Fortune and great Estates," local gentry whose property was also jeopardized by the proprietors' lawsuits.[86] Their leadership was critical in keeping impetuous hotheads under control and directing unrest into conservative channels.

The gentry's collusion in acts of intimidation or even violence was consistent with contemporary attitudes toward civil disturbances. Americans familiar with English writings on political authority understood that a subject's right to oppose dangers to the community's welfare occasionally extended to challenging by force public officials who acted improperly. Educated men nevertheless realized that such expressions of dissatisfaction had definite limits, for citizens had a responsibility to prevent mayhem.[87] The social standing of gentlemen precluded personal participation in crowd actions, but their direction contributed greatly toward establishing strategies that minimized the possibility of violence and prevented assaults against the established social order.

Gentry influence helped ensure that civil disturbances in New Jersey would resemble local uprisings elsewhere in Anglo-America, which were "*extra-institutional* in character more often than they were anti-institutional."[88] Collective resistance was aimed at preventing the judicial system from being manipulated by the proprietors and at drawing the attention of responsible officials to the proprietors' alleged misdeeds. Participants in crowd actions intended not to place themselves beyond the law, but to force the government to guarantee their legal rights as British subjects.

A firm commitment to the rights of property also led men to moderate their actions while confronting authority. Land claimants saw property rights not as legalistic abstractions, but in almost moral terms, as the due reward for purchasing, clearing, and occupying the land in good faith. Secure property titles nevertheless required the protection of sheriffs, judges, and the court system. Even men in arms against biased judges and unscrupulous speculators realized that a distinction had to be made between the legal system *per se* and those individuals who would pervert it for selfish ends. This perspective was certainly more responsible for the infrequency of violence and the crowds' self-control than any ingrained sense of restraint inhibiting challenges to the wealthy and powerful.

New Jersey colonists exercised impressive self-control during the 1740s, as contrasted with episodes in the province's tumultuous past. East Jersey Puritans had been so anxious to escape quitrent obligations in 1673 that they eagerly, almost precipitously, renounced English allegiance during the Second Anglo-Dutch War. At the Middleton melee of March 25, 1701, rioters armed with guns assaulted a court where the governor presided, swore they would hang him if one of their wounded companions died, and refused to release him and several judges until the man recovered.[89] Nothing remotely comparable to those incidents happened between 1735 and 1754, despite the ominous peril to thousands of landholders. Although explosive, the disputes neither seriously endangered life nor menaced the government's legitimacy. Once an unstable outpost of Great Britain, New Jersey had become a settled society capable of minimizing recourse to violence while withstanding a high degree of stress. This important development occurred in little more than a generation. Crowd actions had ceased to be equivalent to anarchy; rather, they exhibited significant evidence of self-restraint and moral purpose.

On June 23, 1755, the last drama in the province's land disturbances was enacted at Newark. Fifty-six sullen men stood before Samuel Nevill, East Jersey proprietor and presiding judge of the court of oyer and terminer. Some may have been present earlier when emboldened insurgents promised to demolish the judge's home, and perhaps some had cheered the enraged farmer who described Nevill as a "son of a bitch" and threatened his life.[90] Now these men, almost all from Newark, listened quietly while they were reindicted for rioting by a grand jury that had been carefully chosen to include twice as many freeholders from Elizabeth as from their own township.[91] All but five threw themselves on the mercy of the court and received token fines of 5s.

The court's proceedings provided an appropriate ending for the inconclusive period of conflict. Most of the fifty-six men had been under indictment for nine years; they certainly submitted only on assurance of leniency. Nevill's imposition of minimal sentences contrasted sharply with the East Jersey proprietors' past insistence on draconian punishments for rioters. By mid-1755, it was evident that the passage of three years without serious violence had made such a harsh position inappropriate and that a continuation of the indicted men's defiant refusal to come to justice could lead others to conclude that the proprietors were unable to protect their property.

The land controversies had in effect become stalemated. The proprietors ceased pressing most of the trespass actions that had precipitated the initial disturbances and concentrated instead on ensuring that their own grantees and tenants would be neither dispossessed by legal actions nor intimidated into abandoning their titles. Most land claimants threatened by eviction proceedings had staved off the proprietors' efforts to evict them, but in reality they had gained little more than time in their struggle to vindicate their claims. All parties locked in the tangled web of land controversies seemed ready to consider a negotiated settlement. After 1755 most efforts to establish a mutually acceptable format for arbitration nevertheless failed, and by the Revolution the only title that had been definitively established was the proprietors' claim to 13,500 acres near Horseneck in Newark Township. An uneasy peace, broken only in 1770, meanwhile returned to the province.[92]

The agrarian upheaval in New Jersey ultimately stemmed from the failure of successive groups of proprietors to impose order on a highly disorganized process of frontier settlement. Unless prevented by outside interference, all colonial governments managed to solve this practical problem by establishing efficient, centralized systems of land registration. The only other similar conflicts occurred when unscrupulous speculators exploited ambiguous boundaries along New York's borders and in Pennsylvania's Wyoming Valley.[93] These disputes arose from localized controversies, rooted in circumstances untypical of colonial society in general. Even in New Jersey, where the problem of insecure land tenure was most pervasive, recourse to force was infrequent, restrained, defensive, and closely related to the legal standing of the property titles at issue.

Ordinary farmers and men of substance whose landholdings were under assault clearly believed that established legal procedures provided the best defense of their lives' work. With the exception of residents of Newark Township, violence was resorted to only after the judicial system had been discredited. Land claimants took pains to ensure that confrontations with public authority were structured as indictments of privilege rather than as attacks on the legitimate governmental institutions through which privilege operated. It is easy to view popular unrest in negative terms, as an expression of what individuals disliked about colonial society, but the positive insights that such episodes afford are far more valuable. Above all, patterns of agrarian discontent in New Jersey indicate that colonial Americans had a sophisticated understanding of how to apply selective, extralegal pressure in a conservative defense of property rights and that they could offer resistance with precision and determination even under conditions of extreme duress.

Notes

I wish to thank Jack P. Greene, James H. Merrell, Marc Harris, Rhys Isaac, and Arnd Bohm for their comments on earlier drafts. A version was presented to the Seminar for New Jersey Historians, sponsored by the New Jersey Historical Commission and the Department of History of Princeton University. Maps were drawn by Linda Yamane Merrell.

1. *American Weekly Mercury* (Philadelphia), Aug. 21–28, 1735.

2. Gary S. Horowitz, "New Jersey Land Riots, 1745–1755" (Ph.D. diss., Ohio State University, 1966), 67–97; John E. Pomfret, *The New Jersey Proprietors and Their Lands, 1664–1776* (Princeton, N.J., 1964), chap. 10; Edward Countryman, "'Out of the Bounds of the Law': Northern Land Rioters in the Eighteenth Century," in Alfred F. Young, ed., *The American Revolution: Explorations in the History of American Radicalism* (DeKalb, Ill., 1976), 41–42,49; Rowland Berthoff and John M. Murrin, "Feudalism, Communalism, and the Yeoman Freeholder: The American Revolution Considered as a Social Accident," in Stephen G. Kurtz and James H. Hutson, eds., *Essays on the American Revolution* (Chapel Hill, N.C., 1973), 271–274; Richard Maxwell Brown, "Back Country Rebellions and the Homestead Ethic in America, 1740–1799," in Richard Maxwell Brown and Don E. Fehrenbacher, eds., *Tradition, Conflict, and Modernization: Perspectives on the American Revolution* (New York, 1977), 79–86. See esp. Countryman, Brown, and Murrin.

3. The town's version is *An Answer to a Bill in the Chancery of New-Jersey at the Suit of John Earl of Stair, and Others, Proprietors of the Eastern-Division of New-Jersey, Against Benjamin Bond, and Others, Claiming under the Original Proprietors and Associates of Elizabeth-Town* (New York, 1752), 1–12. The proprietors' version is *A Bill in the Chancery of New-Jersey at the Suit of John Earl of Stair, and Others, Proprietors of the Eastern-Division of New-Jersey; Against*

Benjamin Bond, and Some Persons of Elizabeth-Town, Distinguished by the Name of Clinker Lot Right Men (New York, 1747), 22–41.

4. *Answer to the Elizabeth-Town Bill in Chancery*, 31.

5. *Elizabeth-Town Bill in Chancery*, 44.

6. The tract's northern boundary almost certainly was Bound Creek rather than the Passaic (William J. Magie, "New Light on Famous Controversy in the History of Elizabethtown," New Jersey Historical Society, *Proceedings*, N.S., II [1917], 147–150).

7. Mar. 30, 1743, *Minutes of the Board of Proprietors of the Eastern Division of New Jersey* (Perth Amboy, N.J., 1949–1960), II, 236. By 1675, 17,804 acres had been surveyed near Elizabeth Town (Edwin F. Hatfield, *History of Elizabeth, New Jersey; Including the Early History of Union County* [New York, 1868], 182–184).

8. Jan. 10, 1725/6, *East Jersey Proprietors' Minutes*, II, 13.

9. Dec. 3, 1735, *ibid.*, II, 42.

10. Aug. 19, 1741, *ibid.*, II, 127.

11. Aug. 23, 1743, *ibid.*, II, 285. Turkey lay north of the tract boundary as run from Bound Creek. See affidavit of Jeremiah Osborne, Nov. 20, 1740, *ibid.*, II, 133.

12. Dec. 4, 1735, *ibid.*, II, 43. See the Elizabeth-Town deed in Tewksbury Township, Hunterdon Co., described in the will of indicted rioter Jacob Shipman, Sept. 9, 1761, in William A. Whitehead *et al.*, eds., *Documents Relating to the Colonial, Revolutionary and Post-Revolutionary History of the State of New Jersey (Archives of the State of New Jersey*, 1st Ser., I–XLII [Newark, Trenton, Paterson, N.J., 1880–1949]), XXXIII, 383, hereafter cited as *N.J. Col. Docs.* On the town's activities in Somerset see "Journals of Andrew Johnston, 1743–1763," *Somerset County Historical Quarterly*, I (1912), 192, II (1913), 279, and III (1914), 196.

13. John P. Snyder, "The Bounds of Newark: Tract, Township, and City," *New Jersey History*, LXXXVI (1968), 96–98. Newark claimants evidently used the 1666 patent to buy lands outside the township. The will of John Dod, an indicted rioter from Newark, written June 25, 1768, mentions his purchase right, "over the mountain, at a place called the Great Swamp," which is in Morris County (*N.J. Col. Docs.*, XXXIII, 118).

14. David Ogden, *To the Several Persons Claiming under the Indian Purchases, Called the Mountain, Horseneck, and Van Giesen Purchases* (Woodbridge, N.J., 1767), 1–3; "The joint and several answers of Andrew Johnston, Lewis Johnston, John Burnet [*et al.*] . . . to the bill of Complaint of John Humphries, John Condict [*et al.*]," Stevens Family Papers, n.d., document #7867, N.J. Hist. Soc., Newark.

15. Horowitz, "N.J. Land Riots," 80–82.

16. The text is in *An Answer to the Council of Proprietor's Two Publications; Sett Forth at Perth-Amboy the 25th of March 1746, and the 25th of March 1747 . . .* (New York, 1747), 2.

17. Philip Carteret to Captains Post and Cornelius, May 26, 1666, *N.J. Col. Docs.*, I, 56.

18. *Answer to Council of Proprietor's Two Publications*, 3, 5.

19. When disinterested arbitrators decided the Horseneck tract, the Newark title lost (*New-York Gazette: or, the Weekly Post-Boy*, Jan. 22, 1770).

20. *Answer to Council of Proprietor's Two Publications*, 7.

21. Edward S. Rankin, "The Ramapo Tract," N.J. Hist. Soc., *Procs.*, L (1932), 375–382.

22. Commissions, Liber AAA, 38, 80, New Jersey State Library, Trenton.

23. *Ibid.*, 91; *New-York Gazette, revived in the Weekly Post-Boy*, Dec. 5, 1748, Jan. 2, 1748/9.

24. *First Publication of the Council of Proprietors of the Eastern Division of New Jersey, March 25, 1746* (New York, 1747), 5; *New-York Weekly Journal*, May 19, 1740.

25. Deeds critical to Coxe's tide are West Jersey Deeds, Liber A, 114, Liber B–I, 150, 179, N.J. State Lib. Coxe's title to the 30,000-acre tract was recognized in 1711 (Council of West Jersey Proprietors, Nov. 6, 1711, Meeting, Treasurer-Solicitor Group 12/7, p. 8, Public Record Office, London). See also affidavit of Joseph Stout, Dec. 10, 1754, in Ralph Ege, *Pioneers of Old Hopewell: With Sketches of Her Revolutionary Heroes* (Hopewell, N.J., 1908), 50–51, and will of Daniel Coxe, Mar. 21, 1737, *N.J. Col. Docs.*, XXX, 119.

26. Dollens Hegeman, "The Petition of the Subscribers being a Committee chosen and appointed by many Purchasers and Possessors of Lands in the Countys of Middlesex and Somerset" (1750), Robert Hunter Morris Papers, Box II, 3–6, N.J. Hist. Soc.; will of Daniel Coxe, Jan. 25, 1757, *N.J. Col. Docs.*, XXXII, 75–76; Henry Race, "The West Jersey Society's Great Tract in Hunterdon County," *The Jerseyman*, III (1895), 2–3; "Journals of Andrew Johnston," Apr. 24, 26, 1753, *Somerset Co. Hist. Qtly.*, I (1912), 187, 277.

27. Race, "W.J. Society s Great Tract," *Jerseyman*, III (1895), 1–5.

28. Robert Hunter to Lords of Trade, Aug. 27, 1714, *N.J. Col. Docs.*, IV, 197.

29. Richard Smith to Richard Partridge, Oct. 20, 1749, *N.J. Col. Docs.*, VII, 366–367.

30. Older-settled regions were already patented because East Jersey residents were intimidated into taking proprietary patents in the 1670s. Many later refused to pay the required quitrents, arguing that contracts signed under duress were unenforceable at law (Horowitz, "N.J. Land Riots," 29–31). Most land was patented as undeveloped at a halfpenny per acre, while meadows were charged twopence (*East Jersey Proprietors' Minutes*, I, 19).

31. Peter Sonmans Quitrent Book, 1707–26, N.J. Hist. Soc. Equivalent values for sterling and proclamation are calculated at the rate of £165 Jersey to £100 sterling (John J. McCusker, *Money and Exchange in Europe and America, 1600–1775: A Handbook* [Chapel Hill, N.C., 1978], 171–173).

32. Mar. 25, 1743, *East Jersey Proprietors' Minutes*, II, 227.

33. *Ibid.*, 11, xxii, xxviii.

34. Instructions to Thomas Gordon, Nov. 11, 1695, *N.J. Col. Docs.*, II, 112. See also Instructions to George Willocks, Dec. 9, 1697, *ibid.*, 192.

35. George Ryerse Record Book, 1752–1771, entries for 1752–1760, Special Collections Department, Rutgers University Library, New Brunswick, N.J.; May 7, 1740, Aug. 8, 1741, *East Jersey Proprietors' Minutes*, II, 112, 124. Rents did begin to rise in the 1760s, however.

36. Deeds listed 42,686 acres, but many did not specify the acreage in the survey, making the actual total larger (East Jersey Deeds, N.J. State Lib.).

37. Deeds listed 11,196 acres (*ibid.*).

38. "Journals of Andrew Johnston, 1743–1763," *Somerset Co Hist. Qtly.*, I (1912), 192 to IV (1915), 204.

39. *Ibid.*, Apr. 23, 1753, II, 187, and Feb. 25, 1761, IV, 115.

40. *Ibid.*, Apr. 22, 24, 1761, IV, 117–118, 199.

41. *Ibid.*, Oct. 9–10, 1753, II, 279, and Apr. 11, 1754, III, 21.

42. Such conditions were also common in West Jersey deeds, where fee simple titles were routinely sold (Pomfret, *N.J. Proprietors*, 117).

43. Woodbridge Freeholders Book, Mar. 26, 1737, N.J. State Lib.

44. *Elizabeth-Town Bill in Chancery*, 80.

45. *Ibid.*

46. *Ibid.*

47. Hegeman, "Petition of Subscribers," Morris Papers, Box II 3–5; *First Publication of the Council of Proprietors*, 5; Rankin, "Ramapo Tract," N.J. Hist. Soc., *Procs.*, L (1932), 375–382.

48. David Ogden to William Alexander, Dec. 13, 1769, William Alexander Papers, New York Public Library. Identical terms were offered earlier (David Ogden to Francis Spier, Dec. 22, 1744, *First Publication of the Council of Proprietors*, 7n).

49. Hegeman, "Petition of Subscribers," Morris Papers, Box 11, 3.

50. Race, "W.J. Society's Great Tract," *Jerseyman*, 111 (1895), 3–4; James T. Lemon, *The Best Poor Man's Country: A Geographical Study of Early Southeastern Pennsylvania* (Baltimore, 1972), 167.

51. Thomas Millidge, Map of West New Jersey Patent and Divisions at Horseneck, Mar. 3, 1774 (original at N.J. Hist. Soc., copy in *Genealogical Magazine of New Jersey*, XXVI [1951], 2–3); Dennis P. Ryan, "Landholding, Opportunity, and Mobility in Revolutionary New Jersey," *William and Mary Quarterly*, 3d Ser., XXXVI (1979), 575.

52. Abstracts of wills are in the *N.J. Col. Docs.*, XXX–XXXVIII. No wills probated after 1799 were used. Twenty-four inventories and 15 bequests were found, 20 from Newark and 19 others. Including bequests made the findings more inclusive but lowered median wealth since they averaged £39 less than inventories. The median of 20 Newark estates was £150 (mean £174), compared to a median of £350 (trimmed mean of L319, after excluding 2 inventories over £1,000) for the other 19. The median Newark inventory ranked among the highest 55% of N.J. inventory values for the 1760s, while the others' median ranked among the highest 20%. The median of 1,400 inventories (not including bequests) probated between 1761 and 1770 was £175 (*N.J. Col. Docs.*, XXXIII).

53. Sung Bok Kim, *Landlord and Tenant in Colonial New York: Manorial Society, 1664–1775* (Chapel Hill, N.C., 1978), 415.

54. While no work of progressive historiography comparable to Irving Mark's *Agrarian Conflicts in Colonial New York, 1711–1775* (New York, 1940) has analyzed N.J.'s land disputes, a progressive perspective emphasizing class antagonisms has been implicit in much of the literature. Donald L. Kemmerer, for example, posited a clash between feudal inclinations and democratic instincts in *Path to Freedom: The Struggle for Self-Government in Colonial New Jersey, 1703–1776* (Princeton, N.J., 1940), 190. A strong neo-progressive interpretation has appeared in the recent literature mentioning N.J.'s land conflicts (see above, n. 2).

55. Hetfield's personal property at death (1795) was £5,681 (*N.J. Col. Docs.*, XXXVII, 174–175). J. Crane sat in the assembly from 1744 to 1751. Ogden was Speaker from 1763–1765, and S. Crane from 1770 to 1771. Bonnell was second justice on the supreme court, 1739–1749.

56. Hegeman's commission is in Council Journal, Dec. 1, 1739, *N.J. Col. Docs.*, XV, 99. Clawson's personal property at death (1761) was L2,247 (*ibid.*, XXXIII, 81).

57. Robert Hunter to Lords of Trade, Aug. 13, 1715, *ibid.*, IV, 217.

58. Low sat in the assembly between 1744 and 1754. East Jersey Deeds name him as a merchant (Liber C-2, 269). His father was a New York merchant and his brother Cornelius attended the Inns of Court and married proprietor James Hude's daughter.

59. Richard Smith to Richard Partridge, Oct. 20, 1749, *N.J. Col. Docs.*, VII, 366.

60. *New-York Gazette: or, the Weekly Post-Boy*, Jan. 22, 1770.

61. *The [Third] Publication of the Council of Proprietors of East-New-Jersey* (New York, 1747), 31.

62. Rioters indicted May Term, 1746, *N.J. Col. Docs.*, VII, 457–458; Newark Freeholders List, 1755, N.J. Hist. Soc., *Procs.*, 2d Ser., XIII (1894–1895), 31–33.

63. *Second Publication of the Council of Proprietors of the Eastern Division of New Jersey . . .* (New York, 1747), 15.

64. *East Jersey Proprietors' Minutes*, II, 327.

65. James Alexander to Robert H. Morris, Feb. 1, 1750/1, Stevens Family Papers, document #8087.

66. "Journals of Andrew Johnston," Oct. 10, 1753, *Somerset Co. Hist. Qtly.*, II (1913), 280.

67. Affidavit of Jeremiah Osborne, Nov. 20, 1740, *East Jersey Proprietors' Minutes*, II, 133.

68. Hegeman, "Petition of Subscribers," Morris Papers, Box 11, 4. Gov. Belcher wrote that only an impartial commission of inquiry appointed to decide titles could end the disturbances and recommended the chief justices of New York, Connecticut, and Massachusetts. This sensible solution was never employed (Jonathan Belcher to Lord Hardwicke, Dec. 3,1751, Additional MSS, Vol. 35,909, p.152, British Museum [copy in Library of Congress]).

69. *Votes and Proceedings of the General Assembly of the Province of New-Jersey . . .* (Philadelphia, 1746), 36, 45, 56. Coxe disputed their charges.

70. Hegeman, "Petition of Subscribers," Morris Papers, Box II, 6.

71. Edward S. Rankin, "The Newark-Elizabethtown-Barbadoes Neck Controversy," N.J. Hist. Soc., *Procs.*, N.S., XI (1926), 353–364.

72. *Answer to the Elizabeth-Town Bill in Chancery*, 31, 36.

73. Petition of the Committee of the Disaffected, 1747, *N.J. Col. Docs.*, VII, 63–64.

74. Affidavit of Solomon Boyle, May 13, 1747, *ibid.*, 420.

75. State of the Facts, Concerning the Late Riots at Newark in the County of Essex, & in other parts of New Jersey, Dec. 24, 1746, *ibid.*, VI, 417. Another effort to unite titleholders on the disputed 4,500-acre tract near Cohansey in Salem Co. with claimants in Hunterdon Co. fighting Coxe's heirs was made in 1746 but evidently failed (A Brief State of Facts, Dec. 31, 1748, *ibid.*, VII,

213).

76. Petition of the Committee of the Disaffected, 1747, *ibid.*, VII, 63–64.

77. Council Journal, Nov. 29–30, 1748, *ibid.*, XVI, 11–15. It is likely that meetings held shortly before their capitulation by Amos Roberts of Newark were aimed at dissuading them (A Brief State of Facts, Dec. 31, 1748, *ibid.*, VII, 224).

78. Affidavit of William Gilman, Feb. 15, 1748/9, *ibid.*, VII, 232.

79. E. P. Thompson, "The Moral Economy of the English Crowd in the Eighteenth Century," *Past and Present*, No. 50 (1971), 76–136; George Rudé, *The Crowd in History: A Study of Popular Uprisings in France and England, 1730–1848* (New York, 1964); Pauline Maier, *From Resistance to Revolution: Colonial Radicals and the Development of American Opposition to Britain, 1765–1776* (New York, 1972), 3–26.

80. David Ogden to James Alexander, Dec. 1, 1749, *N.J. Col. Docs.*, VII, 369; affidavits of Abraham A. Phillips and Thomas Gould, Dec. 9, 1749, *ibid.*, 370–376.

81. Affidavit of Solomon Boyle, May 13, 1747, *ibid.*, 423.

82. See the affidavits on the release of Theophilus Burwell and Aaron Ball, both imprisoned for three months in 1749 without trial during the planting season (*ibid.*, 434–444). Simon Wyckoff's release in 1752 seems similar (*Votes and Proceedings of the General Assembly of the Province of New Jersey* . . . [Philadelphia, 1753], 9).

83. Hegeman, "Petition of Subscribers," Morris Papers, Box II, 8.

84. *New-York Weekly Post-Boy*, Jan. 20, Feb. 17, 1745/6; State of the Facts, Concerning the Late Riot at Newark, Dec. 24, 1746, *N.J. Col. Docs.*, VI, 401–403.

85. Affidavits of William Deare and Jarrit Wall, Sarah Martin, and Andrew Kelly, all dated July 20, 1747, *N.J. Col. Docs.*, VI, 467–470.

86. Charge to the Middlesex Grand Jury. Session of June 1747, *ibid.*, 457.

87. Maier, *Resistance to Revolution*, 41–42.

88. *Ibid.*, 5.

89. John E. Pomfret, *The Province of East New Jersey, 1609–1702: The Rebellious Proprietary* (Princeton, N.J., 1962), 74–75; Kemmerer, *Path to Freedom*, 3–4.

90. Affidavit of Andrew Kelly, July 20, 1747, *N.J. Col. Docs.*, VI, 468; A Brief State of Facts, Dec. 31, 1748, *ibid.*, VII, 215.

91. Essex Co., Court of Oyer and Terminer Minutes, June Term, 1755, Judiciary Records, Courts of Oyer and Terminer and Nisi Prius, N.J. State Lib. Twelve grand jurors were from Elizabeth, six from Newark, and three had names of freeholders in both; four grand jurors were former magistrates, certainly chosen on purpose.

92. A proprietary victory in arbitration over Horseneck led to protests by crowds in Newark, minor violence, and arson in Jan. 1770. The weak resistance dissipated after three men received heavy punishments, perhaps unjustly (*New York Gazette: or, the Weekly Post-Boy*, Feb. 20, Mar. 5, 1770).

93. Kim, *Landlord and Tenant*, 281–415; Philip J. Schwarz, *The Jarring Interests: New York's Boundary Markers, 1664–1776* (Albany, N.Y., 1979). On the Pennamite Wars see Wayland F. Dunning, *A History of Pennsylvania* (New York, 1948), 131–137.

Eight hard Dollars Reward.

RUN AWAY, a negro boy about 15 years of age, named JACK, has a down look, and is a very great liar. He was in Trenton laft Saturday night, and left it on Sunday morning. His intention is to efcape to the enemy. Whoever will fecure and deliver the faid negro boy to the printer hereof, fhall have the above reward, and reafonable charges paid. Trenton. July 10, 1781. I w

Fugitive slave advertisements, such as this one in the July 18, 1781, New-Jersey Gazette, reflected widespread fear that the colony's African Americans would react to the discrepancy between reality and Revolutionary rhetoric by joining Loyalist troops. Photograph courtesy New Jersey Historical Society.

3

The division of American historians into those emphasizing either consensus or conflict is particularly evident in the literature on the American Revolution. In *The History of Political Parties in the Province of New York, 1760–1776* (1909), Carl Becker postulated that in fact two simultaneous revolutions occurred in America, the first against England and the second, based on economic interests, over who should rule at home—conservatives or radicals, wealthy property owners and merchants or poorer farmers and craftsmen. Becker's ideas were later applied to an examination of the war's effects by J. Franklin Jameson in *The American Revolution Considered as a Social Movement* (1926). Jameson argued that the Revolution brought greater democracy and significant changes in four areas—the "status" of people, land ownership, commerce, and thought. He argued, for example, that many loyalists who left during and after the Revolution were large landholders whose property was confiscated, broken up, and sold, a process that created a measure of economic equalization in some areas. According to this view the Revolutionary conflict produced considerable change.

For those historians who have instead seen continuity as the more important thread in American history, the Revolution was one stitch in an ongoing seam. Change occurred gradually in colonial America. Considerable "democracy" as well as agreement on basic political premises existed both before and after the Revolution. The conflict was primarily with England, and American aims were "conservative," not revolutionary, because the colonists' main objective was to protect their existing "rights as Englishmen." In *The Ideological Origins of the American Revolution* (1967) and other works, Bernard Bailyn has argued that the Revolution became a "transforming" event that changed the "rights of Englishmen" to the "natural rights of all men." The political ideas that Americans agreed upon during this process were more significant than their disagreements.

Frederick Tolles, in his 1954 article "The American Revolution as a Social Movement Reconsidered," looked specifically at the results of the Revolution and concluded that Jameson had exaggerated the degree of change. When loyalist estates were confiscated, Tolles argued, they usually went to wealthy speculators who had the cash available to purchase them. Only gradually were these landholdings broken up and sold in smaller parcels. The Revolution had certainly brought changes, but only over the long haul.

The disagreement over how much and what kind of change the Revolution brought was heightened from the 1960s on by the increasing interest of scholars in studying history from "the bottom up." American history had long been the story of upper-class white males, while the society itself was heterogeneous from the start. Social historians were concerned that the actions of "inarticulate" people, those who left no written record, had been ignored while those of "great men," the wealthy upper classes who left a trail of manuscript letters, pamphlets, newspaper articles, and other documents, were excessively studied. The imbalance thus distorted the account of what had actually happened in the past.

To determine whether the American Revolution conserved what already existed or brought radical changes, social historians argued the necessity of examining the lives of everyday people as well as of the nation's political leaders, of studying common practices and popular ideas. They thus began to explore the lives of poor farmers, laborers, mariners, African Americans, women, and native Americans. The true consequences of the Revolution cannot be assessed accurately without taking into account the experiences of such minorities, as Gregory Dowd has argued with respect to New Jersey. Dowd not only addressed questions historians have been asking about American society as a whole in this period, but he also considered how these groups were *looked at* by others during and after the Revolution.

To study the "inarticulate," Dowd and other historians have had to use new sources—including the probate records, tax lists, and estate inventories mined by Purvis. Historians have also used court records from civil and criminal cases, merchants' and farmers' account books, archaeological evidence, material remains such as paintings, houses, furniture, and clothing, newspaper advertisements (including those for runaway slaves), and whatever diaries and letters these people produced. What sources could be used today to document the lives of those who have left few or no written records?

The Declaration of Independence contained two concepts of great significance—republicanism and equality. In *The Creation of the American Republic, 1776–1787* (1969), Gordon Wood argued that what Americans meant by "republic" grew during the course of the Revolution itself. To survive, a republic needed independent, virtuous citizens. How, then, did dependent and disenfranchised groups fit in the new nation? The concept of equality also changed. What started out as an idea that equated colonists to Englishmen in England soon came to mean far more. The Declaration of Independence claimed that all individuals were "created equal." How did (and do) Americans justify the contradiction between this ideal and their treatment of African Americans, women, native Americans, and other minorities? Did the American Revolution change the roles these groups were able to play in society? Did it change what they could do? Did it change how they were perceived?

Another issue relates to how historians date the Revolution. Did it start with the Stamp Act, the battles of Lexington and Concord, or the decision of Congress to assert independence? Did it end with the battle of Yorktown or the peace treaty? In *The Radicalism of the American Revolution* (1992), Wood has argued that while the Revolution was different from others in history, given "the amount of social change that actually took place" it was a "momentous upheaval . . . as radical and revolutionary as any in history." Wood ends the Revolutionary period at about 1830. Does extending the era to this date make a difference in how it is understood? How much had the United States changed in 1776, 1783, 1830? When does Dowd end the period? Finally, was the Revolution conservative or radical?

Suggested Readings

Bailyn, Bernard. *The Ideological Origins of the American Revolution.* Cambridge, Mass., 1967.

Davis, David Brion. *The Problem of Slavery in the Age of Revolution, 1770–1823.* Ithaca, N.Y., 1975.

Gerlach, Larry R. *Prologue to Independence: New Jersey in the Coming of the American Revolution.* New Brunswick, N.J., 1976.

Jameson, J. Franklin. *The American Revolution Considered as a Social Movement.* 1926. Reprint. Princeton, N.J., 1940.

Kerber, Linda K. *Women of the Republic: Intellect and Ideology in Revolutionary America.* Chapel Hill, N.C., 1980.

McCormick, Richard P. *Experiment in Independence: New Jersey in the Critical Period, 1781–1789.* New Brunswick, N.J., 1950.

Norton, Mary Beth. *Liberty's Daughters: The Revolutionary Experience of American Women, 1750–1800.* Boston, 1980.

Pingeon, Frances D. "Slavery in New Jersey on the Eve of Revolution." In *New Jersey in the American Revolution: Political and Social Conflict.* Trenton, N.J., 1970. 41–53.

Pole, J. R. "Suffrage Reform and the American Revolution in New

Jersey." *Proc. NJHS* 74 (1956): 173–94.

Riccards, Michael P. "Patriots and Plunderers: Confiscation of Loyalists Lands in New Jersey, 1776–1786." *NJH* 86 (1968): 14–20.

Tolles, Frederick B. "The American Revolution as a Social Movement Reconsidered." *American Historical Review* 60 (1954): 1–12.

Wood, Gordon S. *The Creation of the American Republic, 1776–1787.* Chapel Hill, N.C., 1969.

_____ . *The Radicalism of the American Revolution.* New York, 1992.

Young, Alfred F., ed. *The American Revolution: Explorations in the History of American Radicalism.* Dekalb, Ill., 1976.

◆ ◆ ◆ ◆ ◆ ◆

Declarations of Dependence: War and Inequality in Revolutionary New Jersey, 1776–1815

Gregory Evans Dowd

Shortly after British troops withdrew from the United States, New Jersey's "poet of the American Revolution," Philip Freneau, revised "The Rising Glory of America" to condemn Great Britain for employing foreign mercenaries, rebel slaves, and Indian warriors in a war against American women and children:

> Vengeance must cut the threat,—and Britain, sure
> Will curse her fatal obstinacy for it!
> Bent on the ruin of this injured country,
> She will not listen to our humble prayers,
> Though offered with submission:
> Like vagabonds and objects of destruction,
> Like those who all mankind are sworn to hate,
> She casts us off from her protection,
> And will invite the nations round about,
> Russians and Germans, slaves and savages,

New Jersey History 103 (1985): 47–67. Reprinted by permission of the author.

To come and have a share in our perdition—
O cruel race, O unrelenting Britain,
Who bloody beasts will hire to cut our throats,
Who war will wage with prattling innocence,
And basely murder unoffending women![1]

Embedded within this and other examples of early American rhetoric are clues toward the solution of a problem that has long fascinated American historians: How did white, male, republican writers and activists reconcile their revolutionary ideals with their customary disregard of the "equal rights" of blacks, women, and Indians? Why did the advocates of republican liberty fail, with apparent paradox, to confront the gulf between their revolutionary enthusiasm for the equality of men, and their acceptance of legal discrimination based on gender and race?

This essay will attempt to provide answers to these questions by examining the interplay of republican ideas with the reality of a revolutionary war. It will examine the manner in which the Patriots of New Jersey construed their changing world while they were constructing their government. It will argue that as these Patriots applied their republican "science of politics" to the social landscape about them, they interpreted the appalling violence of that world in ways that justified, for them, the persistence of American inequality. As they saw the forces of counterrevolution threaten their young state, they came to suspect the groups that they had always excluded from political equality of disaffection, corruption, and treason. When the republican ideals of propertied white men shined down on the deeply fissured terrain of New Jersey's fratricidal revolution, blacks, women, and Indians remained in the shadows.

The "Republican Synthesis"

Within the past twenty years a "republican synthesis" has come to dominate the study of early American political thought. As this synthesis has drawn the attention of scholars on both sides of the Atlantic, historians have paid particular attention to the republican conceptions of power, liberty, virtue, and corruption. The colonists, according to the republican school, drew upon an English tradition of political opposition that discovered in all politics a dramatic tension between the forces of power and liberty. Aggressive, thrusting power, they believed, naturally attempted to subvert delicate, passive liberty. Power, assisted by its ingratiating clients, could be checked only by virtue.[2]

The republican vision was of a triangular struggle: Power and virtue, both masculine personifications, struggled over feminine liberty, with power seeking to corrupt her and virtue rushing to her defense. Republicans of the eighteenth century, attempting to define the proper balance between power and liberty, invested their hopes in the virtue of the citizenry. Without such virtue, as William Paterson believed, "An artful Prince . . . abetted by a set of obsequious dependents, generally prepossesses the people in his favor, and does everything in his power to beguile them into a belief in their security and indeed fairly to lay them to sleep."[3]

Historians of the republican school have concentrated on the efforts of the founders to establish a polity and a political economy in which virtue would flourish and the republic prosper. In designing this polity, republicans held before their countrymen the image of an ideal citizen; he was a freeholding citizen-soldier, possessed of an unwavering concern for the public good, shunning luxury and self-indulgence. This ideal became the measure against which revolutionary thinkers placed would-be participants in the political nation.[4]

But ideological heritage did not alone influence the thinking of rebellious New Jerseyans. The ideology had its earthly context; each ideal type possessed its social or political counterpart. New Jersey's republicans did not need to ruminate in order to summon the vision of a powerful Britain struggling with virtuous, freeholding rebels over the issue of American liberty; rather, the vision lay clearly before them, in the social, political, and military struggles of a revolutionary war. The state saw some of the bloodiest fighting of the war; the British crossed it three times, raided it repeatedly from their base in New York City, and supported the counterrevolutionary activities of a large Loyalist population. As the crisis of the revolution deepened—as the safety of the new state was increasingly threatened both from within and without—white, male, republican thinkers confronted what they believed to be moral shortcomings and antirepublican machinations among those groups traditionally excluded from the political nation: blacks, women, and Indians.

Blacks

During the revolutionary era many of New Jersey's outspoken

republicans declared their opposition to slavery. Gov. William Livingston, who freed his slaves in 1778,[5] was typical in his recognition of the inconsistencies between republican liberty and Anglo-American slaveholding. Livingston, writing to the anti-slavery Quaker Samuel Allinson, called the institution "utterly inconsistent, both with the principles of Christianity & Humanity; & in Americans who have almost idolized liberty, peculiarly odious & disgraceful."[6] Others who opposed the institution exploited it for its propaganda value: in black slavery, they reasoned, was an illustration of Britain's miserable design for the colonies. At the College of New Jersey's 1780 commencement, for example, one student said of the slaves: "we have in them a picture of what cruel ravages oppression can make upon the human mind.—How much better should we have been, trampled on, insulted, and oppressed by foreigners?"[7]

The expression of such sentiments did not, however, release New Jersey's approximately eleven thousand slaves, about 8 percent of the population. New Jersey's republican thinkers may have agreed that black slavery and republican liberty were incompatible, but they questioned the legality and the expediency of abolition. Primarily they felt compelled to respect the property rights of slaveholders, for property was the principal source of that liberty that they believed bred virtue. For the government to single out one type of property for confiscation, they reasoned, would be tantamount to that very arbitrary exercise of power against which they struggled.[8]

But the sanctity of property was not their only concern. Racist thought, deeply embedded in New Jersey as well as in the South, also inhibited the abolition of slavery.[9] Like republican thought, racist thought was divorced neither from New Jersey society nor from the events of the revolution. As New Jersey's internal war dragged on, republicanism and racism became wedded in a manner that reinforced the traditional exclusion of blacks from political equality and may have prolonged their enslavement.

Shortly after the fighting broke out, and well before the adoption of the Declaration of Independence, Virginia's Loyalist Governor John Murray, Earl of Dunmore, unwittingly scored a propaganda coup for his rebel enemies when he declared, "all indented servants, Negroes, or others, (appertaining to Rebels) free, that are able and willing to bear arms, they going to His Majesty's Troops, as soon as may be, for a more speedily reducing the colony to a proper sense of their duty, to His Majesty's crown and dignity."[10] Dunmore's proclamation clearly articulated a position that had already achieved some currency among black and white Americans; fugitive slaves, if armed, paid, and directed by British authorities, would not only furnish His Majesty's troops with valuable information, but could disrupt the rebellious activities of slaveholding colonists.[11]

Even free blacks came under Patriot suspicion. In 1776 the Shrewsbury Committee of Observation required local blacks to turn in their firearms "until the present troubles are settled."[12] After it was reported that blacks had actually participated in Loyalist raids in Virginia, Philip Freneau, once a critic of West Indian slavery, now cried for deliverance, "not only from British dependence," but also "From the valiant Dunmore, with his crew of banditti, Who plundered Virginians at Williamsburg city."[13]

Freneau's easy identification of blacks with "banditti" became more widespread in New Jersey following two raids by "negroes and refugees" into Monmouth County. The first occurred at Shrewsbury in July 1779. Shortly afterwards, the *New-Jersey Journal* ran a poetic satire of the King's employment of escaped slaves:

> A Proclamation of late he sends
> To thieves and rogues, who are his only friends
> those he invites; all others he attacks
> but deference pays to Ethiopian blacks.[14]

There was another alarm the following June, when a "negro, who bears the title of Colonel, and commands a motly crew at Sandy-Hook," led another Loyalist raid into Monmouth County, attacking Capt. Joshua Huddy's home.[15] Seen through republican eyes, the raids clearly demonstrated the dangerous potential of the British to manipulate slaves.

In the final stages of the war, as Freneau's confidence in an American victory swelled and as the threat of black insurrection receded, the poet lampooned Dunmore, portraying the earl as wishing that "six years ago I had joined with your votes; Not aided the negroes in cutting your throats."[16]

For Freneau and for others, the British attempts to inspire slave insurrections confirmed certain aspects of revolutionary political thought. Because landowning was seen as a prerequisite to independence, and independence a prerequisite to virtue, the colonists would not accept the notion that the black allies of Britain fought as freedom fighters in their own interest. Rather, the Whigs saw the black soldiers as the hungry, outcast mercenaries of the British. They perceived the blacks as the deceived tools of monarchical oppression.

These attitudes had an immediate impact on New Jersey's blacks, both slave and free. During the revolution, New Jersey's Councils of Safety arrested blacks on the "Suspicion of intending to join the Enemy."[17] Denied equal protection before the law, the burden of proof of innocence rested upon white acquaintances, if any could be found. If none could be found, the blacks, presumed to be guilty of escaping to the British, were "sold to pay charges."[18] The *New-Jersey Gazette*, despite the antislavery opinions of its printer, Isaac Collins, carried advertisements for fugitive slaves that convey the same fear of black treachery: "Run away, a negro boy about 15 years of age, named JACK, has a down look, and is a very great liar. He was in Trenton last Saturday night, and left it on Sunday morning. His intention is to escape to the enemy."[19]

Fears generated by the war not only reinforced customary assumptions of black treachery, but also the republican distrust of propertyless persons. The widely held idea that power subverts fair liberty through the agency of desperate, servile dependents intertwined with the image of the treacherous black slave to quicken the republicans' conviction that blacks were the logical abettors of British tyranny. Once they defined blacks as the potential tools of despotism, the advocates of American liberty could more comfortably countenance the persistence of black slavery.

A comparison of New Jersey's patterns of both slaveholding and revolutionary violence with contrasting patterns in Rhode Island and New York lends support to the thesis that republican fears of British-inspired slave conspiracies delayed New Jersey's abolition. A purely economic interpretation of this delay cannot explain why Rhode Island and New York, two other northern states with substantial slave populations at independence, were quicker than New Jersey to abolish slavery. While economic concerns were critical, also important was an intense fear of free blacks, a fear that clearly worked to the slaveholders' advantage, but that was both expressed in republican terms and exaggerated by the peculiarities of New Jersey's revolution.

Of all northern states, only in New Jersey did fierce partisan warfare occur in counties with large slave populations. Rhode Island, with the third largest northern slave-to-free-person ratio, saw virtually no fratricidal warfare. The lines between British-occupied Newport and the rest of the state were clearly drawn; the fear of British agency among the slaves in rebel-held regions was consequently less pronounced. Rhode Island passed an abolition bill in 1784, twenty years before New Jersey. In New York, on the other hand, partisan warfare reached what may have been its northern apex but was concentrated in counties where slaveholding was uncommon: along the east bank of the Hudson River and on both banks of the Mohawk River. Where slaves were numerous, as in Queens, Kings, and Richmond counties, there was a comparative calm. Upstate New York's partisan warfare did aggravate the dread of counterrevolutionary conspiracies, which probably helped to delay New York's abolition until 1799. But in New Jersey slavery and civil war overlapped, and conspiratorial fears were far more powerful.

Partisan warfare in New Jersey was concentrated in the northeastern portions of the state. Bergen and Monmouth counties, where blacks comprised 20 and 12 percent of the populations, respectively, were racked by internal war, alarmed by real and imagined slave rebellions, and plagued with reports that slaves familiar with the disputed ground had crossed from British lines.[20] Such rumors and events fed the republicans' worst fears about both the treachery of slaves and their susceptibility to manipulation by the enemy. Defenders of slavery later seized upon such fears, which may in some measure explain New Jersey's tardy abolition.[21] Such fears may also shed light on the state's denial, at first customary and then legal, of civil equality to the state's free black men and women.

In what most scholars agree was an accident, and what many contemporaries saw as a sin of omission, the drafters of New Jersey's Constitution in 1776 extended the franchise to all free inhabitants worth £50. According to the letter of the law, free blacks should have been admitted to the polls. There is little evidence that blacks actually exercised this right before the early 1790s. In that and the following decade, however, as strife between Federalists and Republicans came to a head, the Federalists violated custom by soliciting the blacks' votes.[22] The staunchly Republican *Centinel of Freedom* reported one such instance in 1800: "Federal corruption displayed itself some time since, in its blackest colours, at Elizabethtown, when they brought forward many free blacks . . . , and persuaded them to vote for the Federal ticket."[23] Here again, though in a different context, republican rhetoric portrays blacks as the malleable tools of corruption, without the virtue required for citizenship in the republic. The press in New Jersey continued to exhibit concern about black voting until it was prohibited by law in 1807. That restriction, a bipartisan measure which passed the legislature by a margin of thirty-one to five, limited the franchise to free, white, adult men worth £50.[24] Republicans refused blacks equality largely because their theory of politics and their predisposition to racist thought led them to interpret revolutionary events in a manner that denied to blacks the capacity for virtuous manhood.

Women

The ideology of the American Revolution and the experience of the war itself also enabled white, male radicals to deny women a place in the political system. Republican rhetoric, in fact, implicitly libelled the character of women. Whig political language was full of masculine and feminine imagery. The major symbols— power, liberty, virtue, and luxury—each readily evoked a specific gender. Aggressive, thrusting, and intensely masculine power, as we have seen, hotly pursued and plotted against feminine, delicate liberty. Virtue, which derives from the Latin word for man (vir), carried the connotations of masculine strength and virility.[25] Selfless civic virtue not only defended fair liberty, it shunned effeminating luxury. "Let us guard," warned John Witherspoon, "against using our liberty as a cloke for licentiousness. . . . Let us endeavour to bring into, and keep in credit and reputation, everything that may serve to give vigour to an equal republican constitution . . . Let us check every disposition to luxury, effeminacy, and the pleasures of a dissipated life. Let us in public measures put honour upon modesty and self denial, which is the index of real merit."[26] Although such rhetoric placed action almost entirely within the masculine sphere—with power and virtue struggling over passive liberty—effeminate luxury might seduce virtue into a deceptive comfort, thus paving the way for the triumph of oppression. As New Jersey's Patriots struggled with their enemies, these republican images resonated remarkably well with the rebels' perception of events.

In mid-November 1776 the British made their first major incursion into New Jersey, seizing Forts Washington and Lee before crossing the state from New York to the Delaware River in pursuit of the rebels. Though repulsed from Trenton by the Continentals in December, the British remained in control of portions of the state until July 1777. During this thrust into the already divided colony, Gov. William Livingston collected the first of many reports that rapes and other atrocities had been committed against women by British and Hessian troops. In February,

Livingston wrote to Caesar Rodney, "Among other Points that I have in charge from the Congress to procure Affidavits of, concerning the Conduct of the Enemy upon their Irruption into this State, is their ravishing of Women."[27] Livingston's language suggests that these were eruptions within eruptions; that there were two types of rape occurring; the one metaphorical, the other, real.

Affidavits soon came in, though the government had the usual difficulties securing them. In March, Isaac Smith wrote to Livingston, "There are undoubtedly many more Instances of the like Kind happening to young Women but from a mistaken Modesty they conceal it. Widow Phillips's abuse was attended with this very singular & very shocking aggravation that it was committed in the Presence of her aged Father & Mother."[28] The crowning incident occurred in June 1780, when Hannah Caldwell was shot dead while home nursing her child. Reports quickly circulated that the culprit was a Hessian mercenary.[29] The Caldwell murder story survived well into the nineteenth century and gained a currency within New Jersey to rival that of the more nationally famous murder of Jane M'Crea. Shortly after the Caldwell incident, a College of New Jersey (now Princeton University) student deplored the "sufferings of virgin and matron innocence" at the hands of the British. "Let us remember," declared a classmate, "in order to add vigour to our genius, and force to our descending swords, that we are avenging the cause of virgin innocence."[30] Twenty years later, the *Centinel of Freedom* invoked the same language, asking its readers to resist Federalist power: "Say ye patriots of '76, have you so soon forgot when your aged matrons experienced the insults of a military host, when your virtuous daughters were marked out as the victims of the soldiers' most insatiable lust . . . can it be possible that you are so blind to your own interests as to have them taken without a struggle?"[31] Republican-minded citizens thus remembered the days when the pattern of events prophesied by their ideology vividly materialized in the heat of the struggle in New Jersey. Corrupt British power violated not merely abstract liberty but the very women of New Jersey. As if following the ideological model, the reporting of such incidents portrayed opposing males as actively fighting over New Jersey's defenseless daughters. To the republicans, moreover, women's defenselessness meant dependence upon men; as dependents women could not exercise true civic virtue.

The republican ideology, however, did not define feminine

characteristics as unwaveringly passive; an active, albeit corrupt, potential was also assigned to women. Whigs believed that, like effeminate luxury, women could be used by the crown as the seductive solvents of virtue. Revolutionary leaders like William Livingston strove both to defend the passive, virtuous, patriotic women of New Jersey, and to discover and punish the female agents of British power.

In September 1777, New Jersey's legislature approved an "Act for constituting a Council of Safety," which imposed a fine or imprisonment on any woman caught crossing enemy lines without the necessary authority. Second offenders faced the death sentence.[32] Livingston, who approved of the act, believed women to be more subject than men to the temptations of luxury. "Of all those who have applied to me," he wrote, "for recommendations to the commanding officer at Elizabeth Town to go to Staten Island or New York not above one in twenty appeared intitled to that indulgence; and many of them were as venemous Tories as any in the country. It is either from a vain curiosity (extremely predominant in women) cloaked with the pretence of securing their debts . . .; or for the sake of buying tea & trinkets (for which they would as soon forfeit a second paradise, as Eve did the first, for the forbidden fruit) that they are perpetually prompted to those idle rambles." Republicans believed that women lacked the necessary strength of physique and character to preserve their own virtue without the protection and guidance of men who were Patriots. Once seduced in the interest of the enemy they became especially dangerous. As luxury was the solvent of virtue, so could virtuous men, "from a mistaken complaisan[ce]," fall prey to the temptress.[33]

Livingston described his image of the Tory seductress as he rebuked the Continental Congress for releasing a woman charged with violating the law against crossing enemy lines. "I make not the least doubt," he said, "but that you & every other Member of Congress who have interested themselves in behalf of Mrs. Yard entertain a favourable Opinion of her; and that they really believe 'her late visit to New York was not only innocent but laudable.' But I also believe that Adam was deceived by Eve; and that Delilah got the better of Sampson."[34] In a state in which an estimated one third of the adult population retained its allegiance to the crown, it should not be surprising that women were suspected of working actively for the British. What is fascinating is the way the Patriots perceived this activity, the manner in which they brought to the events they witnessed a set of symbols that stood as guide posts for their interpretations. Power, liberty, virtue, and luxury—with all their masculine and feminine connotations, with all their potential for agency, action, and corruption—were ideological chords which strongly resonated to the dissonant strains of New Jersey's revolution.

The framers of the New Jersey Constitution of 1776 extended the franchise to women in the same way they granted the suffrage to blacks; that is, by accident. And as with blacks, though the constitution enfranchised all inhabitants worth £50, women were not admitted to the polls in significant numbers until the 1790s, when innovative thinking among Quakers and Federalists apparently led to the brief inclusion of women in New Jersey politics.

In a little understood move in 1790, the New Jersey Assembly revised the election law for several counties. Tradition has it that Joseph Cooper, a West Jersey Quaker, strongly advocated the enfranchisement of women, and that "to please him the committee reported a bill in which the franchise was confered upon voters referred to as 'he or she.' " Whatever Joseph Cooper's role was, it is remarkable that the bill passed with only three dissenting votes. When the provisions of the act were later extended to the rest of the state's counties, New Jersey had legally and explicitly enfranchised women. The wording may, however, have been tongue-in-cheek, for women still did not vote until the Federalist innovations of 1796 and 1797.[35] In the latter year, the Federalists, seeking electoral power, encouraged women to vote their ticket. This partisan move raised an uproar in the Republican press. Republican critics aired their anger in the *Centinel of Freedom*. One writer mixed sexual innuendo with anti-aristocratic language:

> Oh, what parade those widows made!
> some marching cheek by jowel sir,
> In stage or chair, some beat the air,
> and press'd onto the Pole, sir;
> While men of rank who played this prank
> beat up the widows quarters;
> Their hands they laid on every maid
> and scarce spared wives or daughters! . . .
> Now one and all proclaim the fall
> of Tyrants!—Open wide your throats,
> And welcome in the peaceful scene
> of government in petticoats!!![36]

Some Republicans chose to fight fire with fire, as did William Sanford Pennington, who boldly marched to the polls with a black woman in 1800. Ultimately, the Federalists recoiled from their innovations and accompanied the Republicans in voting for the explicit exclusion of blacks and women from the franchise in 1807.[37] That bill actually extended the white, male franchise to all taxpayers, which essentially meant white manhood suffrage. In practice this aspect of the bill meant little, for white manhood suffrage had been the norm since the politicization of poor white men in the early years of the revolution.[38] The two parties agreed, it seems, that while even those white men who were not truly "independent" could vote, women and blacks could not exercise the strength and independence of will necessary for virtuous participation in the polity. Republicans could argue that the propertyless whites had proved themselves in the struggles against Britain and aristocracy; republicans could not so perceive the contributions of blacks and women. Women could play the critical role of raising good Christian, republican children, and they could give comfort to their virtuous male protectors and defenders of liberty, but they could not act entirely of their own free will. These attitudes, latent in Whig political thought and reinforced by the republican interpretation of the war's events, would face challenges in the nineteenth century as women appropriated the language of virtue and identified the man's sphere as the source of corruption. Such changes would eventually signal the death of revolutionary republicanism.

Indians

By the time of the American Revolution, there were few Indians left in the state. Gov. William Franklin had reported in 1774 that some fifty or sixty of them lived on the Brotherton Indian Reservation in Burlington County. These, he noted, were a "quiet inoffensive People."[39] Although Franklin believed that all of the colony's Indians lived on the reservation, others lived in the neighborhoods of Vincentown, Crosswicks, Cranbury, and scattered throughout South Jersey. New Jersey's Indians, many of whom sought to conform to Anglo-American standards of behavior, posed no threat to the colony as it entered the revolution.[40] Following the revolution, John Witherspoon, whose fellow Presbyterians had actively supported the Brotherton reservation, wrote that their numbers had "dwindled away, so that there are few of them now left."[41]

Without a true Indian frontier, New Jersey suffered no serious Indian raids during the war. Yet Indians, like women and blacks, figured frequently in the writings and orations of New Jersey's republicans. And much as the revolutionaries denied the civic virtue of women and blacks, they denied the capacity of the so-called savages to act virtuously in their own tribal or national interest. When Indians took up arms against white frontier people, republicans in New Jersey interpreted the struggles as yet another manifestation of British corruption.

In the summer of 1777, British General Sir John Burgoyne issued a proclamation threatening the Patriots with Indian raids. William Livingston, quick to see the propaganda value in Burgoyne's broadside, published a gruesome parody of it in August. Livingston drew on the old, Puritan image of the Indians as Satan's hellhounds, but in this version, Burgoyne replaces the devil:

> I will let loose the dogs of Hell,
> Ten thousand Indians, who shall yell,
> And foam and tear, and grin and roar,
> And drench their maukesins in gore;
> To these I'll give full scope and play
> From *Ticondroge* to *Florida*;
> They'll scalp your heads, and kick your shins,
> And rip your guts, and flay your skins,
> And of your ears be nimble croppers,
> And make your thumbs, tobacco-stoppers . . .[42]

Anglo-Americans and black slaves on the frontier would probably have found little to laugh about in Livingston's parody. For them, the Indian war, with all its attendant horrors, was very real. From Ticonderoga to Florida, from the Gulf Plains to the Great Lakes, Creeks, Cherokees, Shawnees, Delawares, Iroquois, and a host of Northwestern nations took up arms in an attempt to arrest the expansion of the settlements. The Indians were more than willing to get essential supplies—arms and ammunition—from the British, but they were by no means under British control. Nor were they fighting in the name of any interest but that of their own people. Republicans, however, were quite as unwilling to concede that Indians had the capacity to fight in their own national interest as they had been to view the rebellious slaves as freedom fighters.

The most compelling symbol to come out of the West of Britain's cruel manipulation of the Indians was the figure of "The Great Renegade," personified by Simon Girty, a Pittsburgh Tory who fled west in 1778, joined the British Indian Department, and came to be charged by the Patriots with fomenting the Indian wars. In one popular captivity narrative of the day, Col. William Crawford, a Patriot, while suffering a slow immolation at the hands of his Delaware Indian captors, "called out to Simon Girty and begged of him to shoot him," but instead the Great Renegade jeered the dying man, "laughed heartily, and by all his gestures, seemed delighted at the horrid scene."[43]

But the Delaware Indians did not need a Simon Girty to encourage their hatred of white settlers in general, or of Crawford in particular. When they executed Crawford, they both retaliated against the Pennsylvania militia for its recent, cold-blooded massacre of ninety-six of their neutral, Christian kinsmen at Gnadenhutten and paid the colonel a personal debt, for he led the 1774 expedition that destroyed the Mingo Indians' Salt Lick Town.[44]

Following Crawford's death, an exchange of letters concerning it appeared in the *New-Jersey Gazette* between Gen. George Washington and the British commander in New York, Sir Guy Carleton. Carleton pointed out that the Indians had been attacked by Crawford and were fighting in defense of their villages. Washington, however, declared that he could not "ascribe the inroads of the savages upon our northwestern frontiers to the causes from whence your Excellency supposes them to originate: neither can I allow they are committed without directors from Canada. . . ."[45] The frontier war, as viewed from distant and tumultuous New Jersey, reinforced, indeed encouraged, the notion that the Indians were the treacherous agents of British authority, hired for baubles and trinkets to extinguish the spirit of fair liberty.

This image of the Indian as the puppet of Britain had a long tenure. In 1809, as the War of 1812 drew near, Philip Freneau assigned to England the responsibility for Indian war:

> Then arouse from your slumbers, ye men of the west,
> Already the indian his hatchet displays;
> Ohio's frontier, and Kentucky distrest;
> The village, and cottage, are both in a blaze:
> Then indian and english

No longer distinguish,
They bribe, and are bribed, for a warfare accurst;
Of the two, we can hardly describe which is worst.[46]

The republican notion that the Indians were the dangerous
dependents of British power might seem to us bizarre, for we
can clearly see the Indian wars as primarily defensive actions.
Even during the revolution settlers pushed westward; it was
indeed in these years that Anglo-Americans gained secure foot-
ings in Kentucky and Tennessee. What notions reinforced the
idea of the Indians' dependence on Britain, an idea that, significantly, permitted the Americans to ignore the Indians' claims to
territorial sovereignty and national self-determination? Foremost
among these, from a republican perspective, was that of Indian
savagery. The republicans placed the Indian savage, whether
noble or ignoble, outside of civil society. Without civilization,
they could hardly be expected to display civic virtue. Far from
exhibiting the qualities of the sturdy yeoman and the citizen-
soldier, Indian men—so the argument ran—did not even cultivate the soil. In the words of Elias Boudinot, "The objects which
engage their attention, and indeed their whole souls, are war
and hunting. Their haughty tempers will not condescend to
labour—this they leave to their women."[47] Republicans repeatedly accused Indian men of sloth—as their wives raised the
crops—and so they were also incapable of virtuous independence.

Although the radicals of the revolution universally decried
what they saw as British manipulation of the Indians, they disagreed with one another about the capacity of the Indians for
civilization. This was particularly true in the eighteenth century.
Some, notably Henry Knox, Thomas Jefferson, and, in New Jersey, Elias Boudinot,[48] strongly supported the efforts of missionaries and of government officials to bring "the arts" to the Indians.
If the Indians were taught civilization, they might be taught virtue. But even proponents of the civilizing mission disagreed with
one another. While Jefferson once claimed to hope for a mingling of Indians and whites, and indicated at another time that
Indians differed from whites only in culture,[49] Boudinot clearly
thought that Indians were innately inferior. "The enormities of
the Indians," he wrote, "form no excuse for the enormities of
white men. It has pleased heaven to give them but limited powers
of mind, and feeble lights to guide their judgments; it becomes
us who are blessed with higher intellects to think for them, and
to set them an example of humanity."[50]

Many other revolutionaries not only proclaimed the innate inferiority of the Indians, but also scorned any serious consideration of Indian education. According to the College of New Jersey President John Witherspoon, "The chief thing that a philosopher can learn from the Indians in New Jersey is, that perhaps the most complete experiment has been made here how they agree with cultivated life . . . On the whole it does not appear, that either by our young people going among them, or by their being brought among us, that it is possible to give them a relish of civilized life. There have been some educated at this college, as well as in New England; but seldom or never did they prove either good or useful."[51] Philip Freneau, portrayed by biographers as a friend of the Indian, also believed them to be uneducable. In his poem, "The Indian Student, or, Force of Nature," an Indian at college asks why

> . . . did I forsake
> My native wood for gloomy walls;
> The silver stream the limpid lake
> For musty books and college halls . . . [?]

> Where Nature's ancient forests grow,
> And mingled laurel never fades
> My heart is fixed;—and I must go
> To die among my native shades.[52]

Freneau, influenced by the noble savage theme then ascendant in Europe, meant the poem not so much to show the student's ineptitude, as to point up the shortcomings of civilization when compared with a sylvan existence.[53] But the theme of the Indians' incapacity for "cultivated life" is there, and—as with many examples of the noble savage theme—the Indians' alternative to civility is death. Other Freneau poems betray the same conviction, as is evident in such titles as "The Dying Indian" and "The Indian Burying Ground." It may not be too much to say that for Freneau, the much-acclaimed admirer of the children of nature, the only good Indian was a dying one.

Freneau hoisted his true colors in 1815, when, in "The Suttler and the Soldier," he said of the Indians

> They scarce are men—mere flesh and blood—
> Mere ouran-outangs of the wood,

Forever on the scent of blood,
And deers at heart.

When men, like you, approach them nigh,
They make a yell, retreat, and fly:
On equal ground, they never try
The warrior's art.[54]

But it was Witherspoon's student and Freneau's friend Hugh Henry Brackenridge of the Pennsylvania frontier who carried the critique of the Indians to its ultimate conclusion, arguing in 1802 "That the nature of an Indian is fierce and cruel, and that the extirpation of them would be useful to the world, and honorable to those who can effect it."[55]

Republican ideology had not a little to do with these sentiments. That Indian men were not full men was demonstrated, when viewed through the republican prism, by their failure to cultivate the soil, their reliance on the labor of women, and their treacherous dependence on Britain in both the American Revolution and the War of 1812. It should come as no surprise that the Americans refused even to discuss the notion of Indian territorial sovereignty at the Treaty of Paris, which ended the revolutionary war.

Jefferson, in his *Notes on the State of Virginia*, summed up that aspect of eighteenth-century political thought which most concerns this paper. "Dependence," he wrote, "begets subservience and venality, suffocates the germ of virtue, and prepares fit tools for the designs of ambition."[56] The events of the revolution, when seen through the lens of republican rhetoric, demonstrated the need for an independent, masculine citizenry. The expedient British alliance with fugitive slaves and western Indians implicated blacks and Indians as the dependent tools of overweening power. The suffering of New Jersey's women at the hands of British and Hessian troops reinforced the notion that women were weaker vessels who required virtuous guardians. For the revolutionaries of 1776, and their republican heirs of the early nineteenth century, the polity could only consist of white men: women had no role in government, blacks had little room in society, and for "savage" Indians there was, rather simply, no place at all.

Notes

An earlier version of this paper was read before the New Jersey Historical Commission's Teachers' Workshop, October 1983. My thanks to Prof. John M. Murrin and to the members of Princeton University's Graduate History Colloquium for their helpful comments.

1. Fred Lewis Pattee, ed., *The Poems of Philip Freneau: Poet of the American Revolution* (Princeton, N.J., 1902), 1:78–79.

2. The "republican school" is itself quite divided. Bernard Bailyn, in *The Ideological Origins of the American Revolution* (Cambridge, Mass., 1967), describes republican concepts clearly, though he has been criticized both for reducing colonial fears of conspiracy to paranoia, and for neglecting to moor republican ideology in a social context. Gordon S. Wood, in *The Creation of the American Republic, 1776–1787* (New York, 1969), agrees with Bailyn that the colonists drew on the English opposition tradition, but pays more attention than does Bailyn to the influence of social tensions on politics. His work thoroughly describes the transition of republicanism from an ideology of opposition to one of constructive government; see 31–34 for the concepts outlined in the text. John M. Murrin, in "The Great Inversion, or Court versus Country: A Comparison of the Revolution Settlements in England (1688–1721), and America (1776–1816)," in J.G.A. Pocock, ed., *Three British Revolutions, 1641, 1688, 1776* (Princeton, N.J., 1980), more firmly and surprisingly welds the republican school to the progressive school, suggesting not only that political disputes within the Republic were grounded in fairly clear social and sectional differences, but that the disputes followed an ideological pattern established in England during its Glorious Revolution settlement.

3. Quoted in John E. O'Connor, "William Paterson and the Ideological Origins of the Revolution in New Jersey," *New Jersey History 94* (1976): 12. For a rich discussion of the concept of virtue, see J.G.A. Pocock's "Virtue and Commerce in the Eighteenth Century," *Journal of Interdisciplinary History 3* (1972): 123–26, and *The Machiavellian Moment: Florentine Political Thought and the Atlantic Republican Tradition* (Princeton, N.J., 1975), 37, 506–8.

4. Jack P. Greene, *All Men Are Created Equal: Some Reflections on the Character of the American Revolution* (Oxford, 1976). Greene convincingly argues that republican political theory permitted the exclusion of blacks and women from political equality so long as the two groups were seen to lack the independence and civic competence necessary for virtue.

5. Leonard B. Rosenberg, "William Paterson and Attitudes in New Jersey on Slavery," *New Jersey History 95* (1977): 197.

6. Carl E. Prince et al., eds., *The Papers of William Livingston* (Trenton, N.J., 1979), 1:111–12.

7. Trenton *New-Jersey Gazette*, October 11, 1780, cited in *Documents Relating to the Revolutionary History of the State of New Jersey: Newspaper Extracts*, 5 vols., Archives of the State of New Jersey, 2d ser. (Trenton, NJ., 1901–1917), 5:31–35 (hereafter, *Doc. Rel. N.J.*). See also David Brion Davis, *The Problem of Slavery in the Age of Revolution* (Ithaca, N.Y., 1975), 274; Arthur Zilversmit, "Liberty and Property: New Jersey and the Abolition of Slavery," *New Jersey History* 88 (1970): 215–26.

8. Zilversmit, "Liberty and Property," 5–6, 222; see also Davis, *Problem of Slavery*, 257.

9. Zilversmit, "Liberty and Property," 220–25; Rosenberg, "William Paterson." I concur with Davis's treatment of the blacks' capacity for freedom; see Davis, *Problem of Slavery*, 166, 302–3. See also Edmund Morgan. *American Slavery, American Freedom: The Ordeal of Colonial Virginia* (Chapel Hill, N.C., 1976); William W. Freehling, "The Founding Fathers and Slavery," *American Historical Review 77* (1972): 81–93; John C. Miller, *The Wolf by the Ears: Thomas Jefferson and Slavery* (New York, 1977); and Winthrop Jordan, *White Over Black: American Attitudes toward the Negro, 1550–1812* (Chapel Hill, N.C., 1968).

10. Quoted in Benjamin Quarles, *The Negro in the American Revolution* (Chapel Hill, N.C., 1961), 19. See also Sylvia R. Frey, "Between Slavery and Freedom; Virginia Blacks in the American Revolution," *Journal of Southern History* 49 (1983): 375–98.

11. Frey, "Between Slavery and Freedom," 375–78.

12. Quarles, *Negro in the American Revolution*, 17.

13. Pattee, *Poems of Philip Freneau*, 1:139–40.

14. *Doc. Rel. N.J.*, 2d ser., 3:504; Quarles, *Negro in the American Revolution*, 114.

15. *Doc. Rel. N.J.*, 2d ser., 4:434–35, Quarles, *Negro in the American Revolution*, 147–48.

16. Pattee, *Poems of Philip Freneau*, 2:115; see also William Livingston's satire of British mercenaries in Prince et al., *Livingston Papers*, 1:224–33.

17. Prince et al., *Livingston Papers*, 1:338, 2:22.

18. Trenton *New-Jersey Gazette*, November 21, 1781. See also Prince et al., *Livingston Papers*, 1:338.

19. Trenton *New-Jersey Gazette*, July 18, 1781, cited in *Doc. Rel. N.J.*, 2d ser., 5:271.

20. For demography, see Arthur Zilversmit, *The First Emancipation* (New York, 1967), 4–5; Peter O. Wacker, *The Cultural Geography of Eighteenth–Century New Jersey*, vol. I in New Jersey's Revolutionary Experience series (Trenton, N.J., 1975), 15; and Thomas J. Archdeacon, *New Jersey Society in the Revolutionary Era*, vol. 17 in New Jersey's Revolutionary Experience series (Trenton, N.J., 1975), 11. For patterns of violence, see Edward Countryman, "Consolidating Power in Revolutionary America: The Case of New York, 1775–1783," *Journal of Interdisciplinary History* 6 (1976): 648–55; Leonard Lundin, *Cockpit of the Revolution: The War for Independence in New Jersey* (Princeton, N.J., 1940), 163–64; and Lewis F. Owen, *The Revolutionary Struggle in New Jersey, 1777–1783*, vol. 16 in New Jersey's Revolutionary Experience series (Trenton, N.J., 1975), 12. For rumored and actual slave insurgency, see Frances D. Pigeon, *Blacks in the Revolutionary Era*, vol. 14 in New Jersey's Revolutionary Experience series (Trenton, N.J., 1975), 21–23.

21. See, for example, Zilversmit's discussion of the proslavery argument that Quakers conspired to dominate the state through the manipulation of free blacks, in *The First Emancipation*, 186.

22. Marion Thompson Wright, "Negro Suffrage in New Jersey, 1776–1875," *Journal of Negro History 33* (1948): 171–75; Edward R. Turner, "Women's Suffrage in New Jersey, 1790–1807," *Smith College Studies in History* 1 (1916): 167–68; and John C. Miller, *The Federalist Era, 1789–1801* (New York, 1960),

264. See also William A. Whitehead, "A Brief Statement Connected with the Origin, Practice and Prohibition of Female Suffrage in New Jersey," *Proceedings of the New Jersey Historical Society*, 1st ser., 8 (1856): 101–5; Mary Philbrook, "Woman's Suffrage in New Jersey prior to 1807," ibid., 57 (1939): 87–98; Sophie H. Drinker, "Votes for Women in Eighteenth-Century New Jersey," ibid., 80 (1962): 31–45.

23. Newark *Centinel of Freedom*, December 9, 1800, 3; see also Turner, "Women's Suffrage," 166–69, and Wright, "Negro Suffrage," 171–77.

24. Wright, "Negro Suffrage," 175–76. New Jersey thus barred its black citizens from the polls a mere three years after having finally adopted gradual abolition.

25. Linda Kerber, *Women of the Republic: Intellect and Ideology in Revolutionary America* (Chapel Hill, N.C., 1980), 15; see also Pocock, *The Machiavellian Moment*, 37–38.

26. Quoted in Richard P. McCormick, *Experiment in Independence: New Jersey in the Critical Period, 1781–1789* (New Brunswick, N.J., 1950), 18.

27. Prince et al., *Livingston Papers*, 1:251; see also Linda Grant De Pauw, *Fortunes of War: New Jersey Women and the American Revolution* (Trenton, N.J., 1975).

28. Prince et al., *Livingston Papers*, 1:286.

29. DePauw, *Fortunes of War*, 17.

30. Trenton *New-Jersey Gazette*, October 11, 1780, cited in *Doc. Rel. N.J.*, 2d ser., 5:31–35.

31. Newark *Centinel of Freedom*, June 6, 1800.

32. Prince et al., *Livingston Papers*, 2:104.

33. Ibid., 2:519.

34. Ibid., 2:471.

35. A bill to disfranchise blacks and women was turned down by the assembly two years later. But like the "he or she" clause, the bill was introduced before women and blacks voted in significant numbers. See Turner, "Women's Suffrage," 167–69. See also Wright, "Negro Suffrage," 172–73; and Mary Beth Norton, *Liberty's Daughters: The Revolutionary Experience of American Women, 1750–1800* (Boston, 1980), 191–94.

36. Quoted in Turner, "Women's Suffrage," 172.

37. Wright, "Negro Suffrage," 175.

38. J.R. Pole, "Suffrage Reform and the American Revolution in New Jersey," *Proceedings of the New Jersey Historical Society* 75 (1956): 189.

39. *Doc. Rel. N.J.*, 1st ser., 10:447.

40. C.A. Weslager, *The Delaware Indians: A History* (New Brunswick, N.J., 1972), chap. 12; Frank J. Esposito, "Indian-White Relations in New Jersey, 1609–1802" (Ph.D. diss., Rutgers University, 1976), chap. 8.

41. John Witherspoon, *The Miscellaneous Works of the Rev. John Witherspoon* (Philadelphia, 1803), 312. The most thorough student of the Brotherton Reservation, Edward M. Larrabee, writes nothing of its revolutionary war experience. There are no substantive references to Brotherton in the newspapers of the period; it seems to have been too small and remote to have drawn much attention. The inhabitants undoubtedly wanted it that way. See Edward M. Larrabee, "Recurrent Themes and Sequences in North American Indian-

European Culture Contact," *Transactions of the American Philosophical Society*, new series, 66 (1976): 5.

42. Prince et al., *Livingston Papers*, 2:45.

43. John Knight, *Narrative of a Late Expedition* (Philadelphia, 1773 [sic., 1783]), 11–12.

44. Howard H. Peckham, ed., *The Toll of Independence: Engagements and Battle Casualties of the American Revolution* (Chicago, 1974), 94; Draper Manuscripts, Wisconsin Historical Society, file 14 J 116 (microfilm at Princeton University Library, Princeton, N.J.).

45. Trenton *New-Jersey Gazette*, December 11, 1782.

46. Freneau, "On the Symptoms of Hostilities," in Pattee, *Poems of Philip Freneau*, 3:293.

47. Elias Boudinot, *A Star in the West* (Trenton, N.J., 1816), 152.

48. See Reginald Horsman, "American Indian Policy in the Old Northwest 1782–1812," *William and Mary Quarterly*, 3d ser., 18 (1961): 35–53, Francis Paul Prucha, *American Indian Policy in the Formative Years* (Lincoln, Neb., 1962), 213–20; Bernard Sheehan, *Seeds of Extinction: Jeffersonian Philanthropy and the American Indian* (Chapel Hill, N.C., 1973); and Miller, *Wolf by the Ears*, for the opinions of Knox and Jefferson. Richard K. Mathews, in *The Radical Politics of Thomas Jefferson: A Revisionist View* (Lawrence, Kan., 1984), 53–76, extends Jefferson's views of blacks and Indians into his larger view of human nature. For Boudinot, see George Adams Boyd, *Elias Boudinot: Patriot and Statesman, 1740–1821* (Princeton, N.J., 1952), 252. Boudinot, in his last will and testament, left much money and land to missionaries for the conversion and Christianization of the Indians. He also endowed the Institute for Instructing and Educating the Heathen in Cornwall, Connecticut. Here, a student named Galagina, "The Buck," took Boudinot's name as his own, Christian name in 1818. This Cherokee leader, as Elias Boudinot, signed the Cherokee removal bill. See ibid., 254.

49. Miller, *Wolf by the Ears*, 65.

50. Boudinot, *A Star in the West*, xx.

51. Witherspoon, *Miscellaneous Works*, 312.

52. Pattee, *Poems of Philip Freneau*, 2:371–74.

53. For more on Freneau's allegorical criticism of civilization through the use of Indian characters, see the discussion of primitivism in Roy Harvey Pearce, *Savagism and Civilization: A Study of the Indian and the American Mind* (Baltimore, rev. ed., 1965), 143–46.

54. Pattee, *Poems of Philip Freneau*, 3:306.

55. Brackenridge, 5.

56. Thomas Jefferson, *Notes on the State of Virginia* (New York, 1964), 157.

A fervent republican and a signer of the Declaration of Independence, Abraham Clark (1726–1794) felt the Constitution should be ratified despite his concern about the rights of such small states as New Jersey and the kind of national government the document created. Photograph courtesy New Jersey Historical Society.

4

Historical debate over the Confederation period of the 1780s and the adoption of the United States Constitution continues the disagreement about whether the American Revolution was evolutionary or revolutionary. Here, too, historians tend to see either conflict or consensus and continuity to reflect the actions Americans took to establish fundamental laws for their new nation.

The debate centers around two issues. The first deals with the nature and severity of the problems experienced by the national and state governments under the Articles of Confederation. Was this truly, as the late nineteenth-century historian John Fiske described it, a "critical period" in American history? Or were the problems exaggerated by conservatives then, and by historians since? The second and related question is whether the Constitution was really necessary.

These issues were first clearly presented in Charles Beard's *An Economic Interpretation of the Constitution of the United States* (1913). Written at the height of the Progressive period, it reflected the concerns of that era with class and economic conflict. Beard thus argued, in a deliberately provocative manner, that the spirit of the Revolution was embodied in the Declaration of Independence and the Articles of Confederation. The Constitution represented a successful counterrevolution by conservatives who shared an interest in preserving particular forms of property (money, securities, manufacturing, trade, and shipping). Furthermore, because few could, or did, vote for the Constitution, America's sacred document was the result of an undemocratic conspiracy; the revered Founding Fathers were actually pursing their own self-interest. Merrill Jensen supported Beard's argument in *The Articles of Confederation* (1940) and *The New Nation* (1950) by maintaining that, with some alterations, the Articles would have sufficed for the new nation.

The consensus view of this period is quite different. Such historians as Edmund Morgan, in *The Birth of the Republic, 1763–89* (1956), maintained that the logic of both events and developing political theory led directly from the Declaration of Independence to the Articles of Confederation and then on to the Constitution. The later document was the fulfillment, not the denial, of the spirit of the Revolution. The faults of the Articles and disorders of the 1780s were indeed real. The Founding Fathers were public-spirited men, concerned with finding solutions to political and economic problems and not with lining their own pockets.

Some historians were specifically critical of Beard. Robert E. Brown and Katherine B. Brown, in *Virginia, 1705–1786: Democracy or Aristocracy?* (1964) and other works, saw the widespread political participation of the colonial period continuing after the Revolution. Forrest McDonald, in *We the People* (1958), presented a complex picture of various economic groups, with different interests in each state, relating in various ways to the Constitution and its provisions. He concluded that states that functioned independently of the national government and had done well under the weak Articles opposed the Constitution, while others that were dependent or had experienced problems during the Confederation period favored it. In a later work, *Novus Ordo Seclorum* (1985), McDonald turned to the philosophical ideas behind the Constitution, to the connection between ideology and action. For him the Constitution represented the culmination of the Revolution. It was the creative work of practical men who, from the ideas of their times as well as their own experiences, produced a new form of government to solve the problems of their country.

New Jersey presents some interesting problems in the context of this historiographical debate. As the following article shows, conflict and disagreement was pronounced in New Jersey during the 1780s over the payment of Revolutionary war debts and the use of paper money. How and why did residents of the state divide over these issues? Was their disagreement based on class or economic interests, or were other factors involved, such as sectionalism?

New Jersey residents disliked the Articles of Confederation from the outset, long before proposals arose at the Constitutional Convention to replace them with a totally new document. And despite the disagreements over economic issues New Jersey voted for the Constitution quickly and unanimously; on this mattter there was clear agreement. How can the apparent shift from conflict to consensus within the state be explained? How did the problems of the 1780s enhance discontent? Were New Jersey's founding fathers, such as William Paterson and William Livingston, protecting their own private interests in supporting the Constitution or the public interest of their constituents? Is the Constitution the fulfillment or overthrow of the Revolution? If the Constitution undid the Declaration, why did John Witherspoon, the firebrand Whig president of the College of New Jersey, sign the Declaration, serve in Congress under the Articles, and support the Constitution in the state ratifying convention?

New Jersey was after all a small state that lacked the historical independence of North Carolina or Rhode Island. Do Forrest McDonald's categories (independent or dependent) help in understanding New Jersey's response to the Constitution? What other reasons were there for the state's support of the Constitution?

Suggested Readings

Beard, Charles. *An Economic Interpretation of the Constitution of the United States.* 1913. Reprint. New York, 1941.

Beeman, Richard, Stephen Botein, and Edward C. Carter II, eds. *Beyond Confederation: Origins of the Constitution and American National Identity.* Chapel Hill, N.C., 1987.

Brown, Robert E. *Charles Beard and the Constitution: A Critical Analysis of "An Economic Interpretation of the Constitution."* Princeton, N.J., 1956.

Jensen, Merrill. *The Articles of Confederation: An Interpretation of the Social-Constitutional History of the American Revolution, 1774–1781.* Madison, Wisc., 1940.

_____ . *The New Nation: A History of the United States, 1781–1789.* New York, 1950.

Lurie, Maxine N. "The New Jersey Intellectuals and the United States Constitution." *Journal of Rutgers University Libraries* 69 (1987): 65–87.

McCormick, Richard P. *Experiment in Independence: New Jersey in the Critical Period, 1781–1789.* New Brunswick, N.J., 1950.

_____ . "The Unanimous State." *Journal of Rutgers University Libraries* 23 (1958): 4–8.

McDonald, Forrest. *We the People: The Economic Origins of the Constitution.* Chicago, 1958.

_____ . *Novus Ordo Seclorum: The Intellectual Origins of the Constitution.* Lawrence, Kans., 1985.

Murrin, Mary R. *To Save This State from Ruin: New Jersey and the Creation of the United States Constitution, 1776–1789.* Trenton, N.J., 1987.

O'Connor, John E. *William Paterson: Lawyer and Statesman, 1745–1806.* New Brunswick, N.J., 1979.

◆ ◆ ◆ ◆ ◆ ◆

New Jersey and the Two Constitutions

Mary R. Murrin

The English settled New Jersey in the mid-1660s, shortly after wresting the area from its original colonizers and their main commercial rivals, the Dutch. After the restoration of Charles II in 1660, his brother James, Duke of York, mounted a successful expedition against New Netherland. In 1664 James conveyed what is now New Jersey to two supporters of the royal court, John Lord Berkeley and Sir George Carteret. They had full title to the soil; they assumed they had governmental powers as well. The duke's chosen governor, Richard Nicolls, unaware of the duke's grant to Berkeley and Carteret, parceled out considerable acreage to various settlers.

Despite the uncertainty as to their legal right to rule, Berkeley and Carteret immediately drew up a frame of government for the new colony. Their "Concessions and Agreements" of 1665 offered liberal political and religious rights to prospective settlers. Yet initial harmony quickly yielded to conflict largely over the payment of quit rents and the competing land claims caused by the duke's grants of power to both a governor and the two proprietors. A brief Dutch reconquest in 1673–74 was largely uneventful; but the retrocession to England brought with it significant change.

In 1674 Berkeley sold his share to Edward Byllynge and John Fenwick, and in 1676 Carteret agreed to a partition of the province into East and West Jersey. For the next quarter century West Jersey developed under Quaker influence, while Carteret's East Jersey became more heterogeneous, attracting not only English Quakers but Dutch immigrants from New York, Puritans from New England, Anglicans from England, and both Presbyterians and Quakers from Scotland. The West Jersey proprietors issued a liberal frame of government, the West Jersey Concessions, in

In *The Constitution and the States: The Role of the Original Thirteen in the Framing and Adoption of the Federal Constitution*, edited by Patrick T. Conley and John P. Kaminski. Madison, Wisc.: Madison House Publishers, 1988. 55–75. Reprinted by permission of Madison House Publishers, Inc.

1677. Like its East Jersey counterpart, the Concessions were designed to attract settlers. Both guaranteed the basic rights of Englishmen, freedom of conscience, access to land, and participation in government. Both established general assemblies with elected lower houses. However, the West Jersey Concessions spelled out the powers of the assembly in greater detail and specified individual liberties, such as trial by jury, protection from arbitrary arrest, the secret ballot and a liberal code of laws. The East Jersey assemblies adopted a stringent criminal code modeled on the Duke's Laws of 1665.

During the period of division both Jerseys were beset by complicated questions of land ownership and by repeated challenges from New York to their independent status. In 1702 the proprietors, unable to rule effectively, surrendered all governing rights to the Crown. East and West Jersey became a single royal colony. Edward Hyde, Lord Cornbury, a cousin of Queen Anne, was New Jersey's first royal governor. Until 1738 the governor of New York also served, under separate commission, as governor of New Jersey, but beginning with Lewis Morris, New Jersey was permitted its own royal governor.

The proprietors retained their property interests, and New Jersey continued to be plagued with land disputes well after the Revolution. A Board of Proprietors of East Jersey (established in 1684 and headquartered in Perth Amboy) and a similar organization for West Jersey (established in 1688 and headquartered in Burlington) have continued in existence to the present day.

Problems under the Articles of Confederation

At the close of the Revolutionary War, New Jersey faced many of the same difficulties besetting other states. However, internal differences complicated the state's response to problems of debtor-creditor relations, currency, and the Continental debt. Distinctive patterns of ethnicity, land use, trade, and religion established during the proprietary period, when New Jersey was two colonies, were still evident. But although the two regions, East and West Jersey, were at loggerheads on possible solutions to these postwar problems, a decade of experience trying to resolve them made the state as a whole receptive to the Constitution. New Jerseyans believed the Articles of Confederation to be seriously flawed and were united on two major issues troubling the new nation—the disposition of western lands and Congress' need for a secure income.

The New Jersey legislature made its position on the Confederation quite clear in 1778. On June 16 it sent a remonstrance to the Continental Congress listing a number of objections to the proposed Articles of Confederation and urging their revision. The memorial New Jersey submitted devoted much space to issues of revenue, trade regulation, and western lands—topics of great importance during the next decade.

The legislature called for fixed state boundaries within five years, argued that Congress should have sole authority to regulate trade and impose customs duties, and observed that Congress should have authority over western lands so that all states might benefit rather than a few. On this last point the legislature observed plaintively,

> Shall such States as are shut out by Situation from availing themselves of the least Advantage from this Quarter, be left to sink under an enormous Debt, whilst others are enabled, in a short Period, to replace all their Expenditures from the hard Earnings of the whole Confederacy?

Congress listened, but it rejected the proposed revisions. In July, New Jersey delegate Nathaniel Scudder wrote to John Hart, the speaker of the New Jersey Assembly, urging the legislature to direct its delegates to ratify the Articles despite any disadvantages to the state. He pointed out that small states could be at a severe disadvantage if Congress began amending the Articles. Warning of the "fatal Consequences" should the Articles not be ratified and America be discovered to be "a Rope of Sand," Scudder asserted that "every State must expect to be subjected to considerable local Disadvantages in a general Confederation." In November, still convinced the Articles needed substantial revision, the legislature relented. New Jersey was the eleventh state to ratify, followed by Delaware and Maryland, two other small states that objected to the absence of any provision for the western lands.

New Jersey's objections were understandable. The Articles, which largely continued the constitutional relationship established under the Continental Congress, gave the Confederation Congress no power to tax, impose customs duties, or regulate trade (except by treaty). Under the Articles, and indeed after 1779, Congress no longer paid its bills simply by printing paper money. All governmental expenses, such as those required by the prosecution of the war and the servicing of the Continental debt, depended upon a system of requisition. Congress met its expenses by assessing each state a quota of the total amount. New Jersey had no source of income to satisfy these requisitions except by imposing direct taxes on its citizens. A small state with fixed boundaries, New Jersey had no western lands, no real port, and negligible foreign trade. Her merchants shipped through the ports of Philadelphia and New York City, and both New York and Pennsylvania exacted heavy import duties. As one historian has observed, New Jersey was like "a barrel tapped at both ends."

The Social Structure

New Jersey was an agricultural state: somewhere between 70 and 80 percent of the population of 150,000 owed its living in some way to the land. No town boasted more than 1,500 inhabitants. But despite the state's overall rural character, East and West Jersey exhibited important differences.

Dutch, English, Scots-Irish, Irish, and Germans made up the bulk of East Jersey's white population. Most of the state's black population of 10,000 (the majority slaves) lived in the northern part of the state, especially Bergen and Somerset counties. Economically, East Jersey was in New York City's orbit. It was a region of small family farms which produced little for sale. A few small manufactories and iron works and a number of artisans and shopkeepers completed the economic picture. Four of the state's largest towns—Newark, Elizabeth Town, Perth Amboy, and New Brunswick—were in East Jersey. English Calvinist and Dutch Reformed were the predominant religions; the Episcopal Church attracted fewer members.

West Jersey's population was more homogeneous, primarily English, with a few Germans, Finns, and Swedes. Politically it was dominated by Quakers who had not been enthusiastic supporters of either the war or measures to pay for the war. Economically the region looked to Philadelphia. Farms were larger, more prosperous than East Jersey's and produced some crops for sale. West Jersey escaped much of the devastation of the war, and few Continental creditors lived there.

Postwar Problems

The state, especially the northern part, was a major theater of battle between 1776 and 1780. One historian has called it "the cockpit of the Revolution." The clashing armies and the guerrilla warfare between patriots and the large loyalist population damaged and destroyed farms, houses, and towns. Farmers received payment for only a portion of the goods taken or destroyed. In 1779–80, when currency problems were at their height, federal officers left certificates or promises to pay. At war's end New Jersey was not only devastated; her citizens, particularly those in East Jersey, held a sizable portion of the notes and certificates which constituted the Continental debt.

The economic depression of the mid-1780s had a profound effect on relations between New Jersey's creditors and debtors. People who had speculated in land and goods on the easy credit of the inflationary wartime economy found themselves in debt as the economy contracted. The depression affected the entire American economy. British closure of the West Indies to American shipping cut off a major trade outlet. American merchants, who had restocked their wares on credit as the war ended, found few customers for their goods. A series of crop failures brought severe hardship to New Jersey's farmers, already in difficulty from wartime devastation, debt, and high taxes. The number of lawsuits for recovery of debt mushroomed.

East Jersey legislators tended to support any measures, such as paper-money bills, that helped the many debtors among their constituents and to vote against measures which required the spending of money. West Jersey legislators, often wealthier than their East Jersey counterparts and representing fewer debtors, opposed measures favoring debtors, including paper-money bills. A postwar dispute over the location of the dividing line between East and West Jersey significantly weakened the creditor influence within the legislature. The two boards of proprietors had surrendered political power when the Jerseys became a single royal colony in 1702, but they retained title to considerable amounts of land. The dispute over an improperly located dividing line occupied the attention of both groups of proprietors for several years as they argued the case before the legislature. Loath to offend potentially friendly legislators, the East Jersey proprietors mounted no opposition to prodebtor legislation. They won their case, but the two groups of proprietors, which might otherwise have combined to form a united procreditor front, exerted little or no influence on politics.

Paper Money

The Assembly passed a number of prodebtor measures in the early 1780s, including bills forcing creditors to accept paper money rather than specie, delaying court proceedings, releasing jailed debtors from confinement, and preventing the forced sale of debtor estates at reduced value. Creditors found the latter measure particularly reprehensible and believed that debtor-relief bills violated the sanctity of contracts and damaged public and private credit.

The 1785 session was marked by a fierce debate over a paper-money or loan office bill. The proposed loan office would issue paper money and lend it, at interest, to borrowers with sufficient landed security. Borrowers would repay the money in regular installments. As the loans were repaid, the principal would be withdrawn from circulation and destroyed. The interest payments would go to the state treasury for government expenses. The loan office had proved a convenient fiscal expedient in the past, especially in the middle colonies, and New Jersey's colonial experience with the device had been reasonably successful. The loan office debate provoked sharp exchanges from three of New Jersey's most influential political figures—Abraham Clark, William Livingston, and William Paterson.

Abraham Clark (1726–1794) was a figure of signal importance in New Jersey during the 1770s and 1780s. A signer of the Declaration of Independence, he either sat in the New Jersey Assembly or represented New Jersey in Congress for most of the period from 1776 to 1794. A man of fervent republican sympathies, he was the acknowledged champion of New Jersey's many indebted farmers, a position he eloquently presented in a series of anonymous newspaper essays and in a pamphlet entitled *The True Policy of New-Jersey, Defined*. Clark loathed privilege, distrusted lawyers, and had few kind words for merchants. At home he was a major advocate of paper money and other debtor-relief measures. In the wider arena he feared the economic power of New York and Pennsylvania over New Jersey and favored some expansion of congressional power, including a grant to the national legislature of authority over western lands. He represented New Jersey in the Annapolis Convention in September 1786, but he refused to accept appointment to the federal convention.

William Livingston (1723–1790) was governor of New Jersey from 1776 to his death in 1790. He served as one of New Jersey's delegates to both the First and Second Continental congresses before his selection as governor. Livingston was an accomplished polemicist, and his "Primitive Whig" essays made a forceful case for the hard-money, procreditor position. He served as one of New Jersey's delegates to the Constitutional Convention, but age and ill-health limited his contribution.

William Paterson (1745–1806) was a strong nationalist and, like Livingston, a vigorous Whig and staunch defender of property rights. A lawyer, Paterson was involved in two of the most divisive issues in New Jersey politics during the 1780S—the dividing-line controversy and debtor-creditor disputes. Paterson served in New Jersey's first and second provincial congresses, as New Jersey's attorney general, as one of New Jersey's delegates to the Constitutional Convention, and later as governor and then associate justice of the United States Supreme Court.

Advocates of the loan office bill argued that it would provide a necessary circulating medium for specie-poor New Jersey. Money did not circulate widely in the state's weak economy. In consequence, citizens found it difficult to pay either their debts or their taxes. Clark scornfully described the loan office opponents as "artful, designing men" and pictured creditors as "money-men . . . wishing for greater power to grind the faces of the needy."

Opponents of the loan office bill argued that paper money was a direct attack on the sanctity of contracts because it inevitably depreciated. If debtors were allowed to pay creditors in depreciated currency, creditors would be cheated of the amounts rightfully owed them. According to their arguments, money was not scarce; debtors were simply lazy individuals attempting to evade the payment of lawful debts. Livingston described debtors as "idle spendthrifts" and looked forward to the day "when laws [would] be made in favor of creditors instead of debtors; and when no cozening, trickish fraudulent scoundrel [should] be able to plead legal protection for his cozenage, tricks, frauds and rascality." Paterson argued for a decrease in the amount of money available because such a measure would "introduce a Spirit of Industry & Frugality . . . [and] compel people to work for the Bread they eat, and not go about seeking whom they may devour."

The legislature finally passed the paper-money bill in May 1786. The measure may have done little to relieve the situation of those in the most dire straits, but the legislature's attention to the agrarian discontent may have spared New Jersey from the kind of trouble Massachusetts experienced with Shays' Rebellion.

The weight of private debt made the problem of public debt more urgent. With no revenue from ports or western lands, New Jersey could meet congressional requisitions only by taxing its hard-pressed citizens, many of whom were the same Continental creditors Congress was raising money to pay. Not surprisingly, New Jersey was a strong advocate of alternative means to finance the central government.

During the war Congress and the states created several varieties of financial paper—certificates issued to pay for military supplies, notes given soldiers and militiamen in payment for services, and legal-tender paper money. Wartime inflation reduced its value nearly as fast as it was printed. Most of this financial paper was issued by Congress and constituted the Continental debt. New Jersey's citizens held about one-eleventh of this debt, a large amount for such a small state. This high percentage was attributable to the state's situation as a major theater of war.

Congress made several attempts to deal with its currency and debt problems. In 1780 it called in the old currency at a proportion of 1 to 40 and asked the states to issue new paper money. New Jersey arranged to redeem the old currency, but the new issue depreciated rapidly despite the state's vigorous efforts to maintain its value.

Many New Jerseyans had little faith in the new currency and declined to accept it. The controversy over its value developed largely along sectional lines. West Jersey legislators, whose region had little to lose because it had little of the old currency, favored redemption of the new issue at current rather than face value. East Jerseyans favored redemption at the higher face value. This would benefit the region's creditors and satisfy its fiscal conservatives, who viewed redemption at current depreciated value as a faithless repudiation of honestly incurred debt. Sectional divisions within the legislature prevented any resolution of the issue until after the October 1784 elections, when the political makeup of the Council (the upper house) changed. The Council and Assembly finally agreed on redemption at the depreciated value.

Western Lands

New Jersey's problems with the Confederation extended well beyond the currency issue. Many states were disturbed by the absence of any provision in the Articles for the disposition of trans-Appalachian lands claimed by some of the states under their colonial charters. New Jersey and other landless states, wanting to limit the western claims of states like Virginia, argued that the former Crown lands belonged in common to the Union. New Jersey's position was prompted both by its precarious economic situation and by the presence in the legislature of men who had invested in speculative land companies.

The land companies' claims to western lands were based on Indian deeds they had purchased. However, Virginia and other states, citing their original charters, claimed the same territory. In 1780 the New Jersey Assembly appointed a committee to investigate its citizens' western land claims. The Indiana Company, which counted many prominent citizens of New Jersey among its investors, was represented on the committee. Not surprisingly, the committee's report concluded that the lands belonged to the states in common. In December 1780 the Assembly sent Congress a memorial based on this report.

In January 1781 Virginia offered to cede the northern part of its western claim if all prior Indian claims were voided and Virginia's rights to the remaining territory were confirmed. New Jersey, among other states, objected strenuously. In October 1781 the New Jersey Assembly instructed its delegates to the Confederation Congress to oppose the cession and demand a resolution of the Indiana Company claim. Congress rejected Virginia's proposal in November, and the issue remained unresolved until March 1784, when Congress finally accepted the partial cession in a compromise which incorporated an understanding that the Indian grants would not be upheld.

Dissatisfied with the proposed compromise, New Jersey attempted to bring the land dispute before the Confederation as a suit between the states of Virginia and New Jersey. When this failed, New Jersey voted against the Virginia land cession. As late as March 1786, long after the land question had been resolved, New Jersey's legislature continued to instruct the state's delegates to oppose any western lands bill if the legislation might benefit one state exclusively.

New Jersey considered the western lands to be important, both as a source of revenue for the central government and as a prime area where the state's many impoverished farmers might seek a new start. However, the opening of the West to settlement depended upon the free navigation of the Mississippi River, and New Jersey's position on this issue differed from that of other northern states.

Britain had conceded the right to free navigation of the Mississippi River in the Treaty of Paris of 1783, but Spain actually controlled the region. To protect their territory, the Spanish closed the river to American shipping in 1784. Further, they demanded the renunciation of any American claim to free navigation of the Mississippi as the price of a commercial treaty.

Most of the northern states were quite willing to give up free navigation for a commercial treaty with Spain. A treaty would provide commercial opportunities for eastern cities hard-pressed by the postwar economic depression and give the new nation some commercial standing. Continued closure of the Mississippi River would prevent expansion into the West, an area all regions expected the South to dominate, and thus keep southern power in check.

The South promoted the opening of the West not only because expansion would increase its own influence but because the South feared the West might opt for independence if it were not brought into the Confederation quickly.

John Jay of New York, the American Secretary for Foreign Affairs, concluded that to insist on free navigation was futile, and he requested a change in his instructions. In August 1786 Congress agreed to Jay's proposed revision. Initially, two of New Jersey's three delegates supported revision. Virginia, convinced New Jersey might be persuaded that the opening of the West coincided with her best interests, directed James Madison to buttonhole Abraham Clark at the Annapolis Convention. Madison convinced Clark, who in turn helped persuade the New Jersey legislature to instruct the state's congressional delegates to restore the original demand for free navigation of the Mississippi.

A Spanish commercial treaty attractive to northern states blessed with ports and shipping industries was of little interest to a state with neither. The value of the western lands depended on opening the area for settlement. Once Congress controlled the western lands, New Jersey favored any course increasing their value.

New Jersey's Fiscal Problems with Congress

Congress' efforts to put its financial house in order did not end with the currency plan of 1780. In February 1781, before ratification of the Articles was complete, Congress asked the states to amend the document and give it the authority to levy a 5 percent tariff on certain imports—a move New Jersey favored heartily. Twelve states approved the 1781 impost, but passage required the assent of all thirteen. Rhode Island's negative vote killed the plan.

In September 1782 Congress made an emergency requisition on the states to pay the interest on the national debt. New Jersey's legislature took no action, an oversight which irritated the state's many Continental creditors. Stung by the public response, the legislature passed the required legislation in June 1783. In December the legislature moved to protect these creditors and bypass the requisition system it considered inequitable. It directed the state treasurer to pay the money directly to the federal public creditors resident in New Jersey rather than forward it to the Confederation treasury.

Meanwhile, Congress was again at work on a scheme to secure a regular source of income. In April 1783 it asked the states for the authority to levy a 5 percent tariff on certain goods for a period of twenty-five years. The proceeds would be used for public debt payments. In addition, it requested a supplemental revenue, also for twenty-five years, and the cession of all Crown lands still held by the states.

The New Jersey legislature had little reason to believe all thirteen states would agree to this impost when they had not approved the previous one. Nevertheless the legislature approved the duty and the land cession, but it delayed action on the supplemental revenue. In December 1783 the legislature authorized the necessary tax. It made it payable in paper money and ordered the printing of an amount equal to New Jersey's quota of the supplemental revenue. But as it did with the emergency requisition, it ordered the state treasurer to pay New Jersey creditors of the United States directly rather than forwarding any monies to the Confederation treasury. In December 1784 the legislature reaffirmed its decision and ordered the state treasurer to make no further payments on congressional requisitions until the states approved the impost.

As expected, all thirteen states did not ratify the financial plan. The significance of New Jersey's refusal to meet the requisition escaped notice because Congress made no new call for funds until September 1785 when it issued a requisition couched in language that enraged New Jersey's legislators. Congress announced it would not be responsible for interest payment made by any state to its own Continental creditors after January 1786.

Further, it refused to issue interest certificates to public creditors of any state which failed to comply with the requisition.

The legislature fumed. New Jersey had expected to be reimbursed at some future point for the payments made to Continental creditors. In a December 9 letter to the state's congressional delegation, New Jersey assemblyman Abraham Clark noted that New Jersey had incurred considerable expense by shouldering the financial burdens of Congress and was now about to be penalized for doing so. He also observed that New Jersey's citizens had lent money to Congress as private citizens. No action of the legislature of the state where they resided should interfere with repayment. Supplying New Jersey's share of the requisition required oppressive taxes, said Clark; moreover, the state's hard-pressed citizens also paid tariffs to both New York and Pennsylvania, contributing handsomely to *their* state treasuries. Clark described the requisition as a scheme to subvert the impost, the only practicable means of raising a revenue. The requisition system of Congress was "a burden too unequal and grievous for this State to submit to." In February the legislature resolved to take no action on the requisition until the impost was passed. And until the impost was passed, the state's congressional delegation was to vote against any expense to New Jersey unless the measure benefited the state or the Union in general.

Congress was shocked by New Jersey's defiant posture and quickly dispatched Charles Pinckney of South Carolina, Nathaniel Gorham of Massachusetts, and William Grayson of Virginia to placate the legislators and plead with them to reconsider. Pinckney painted a gloomy picture of the dissolution of the Confederation should the New Jersey legislature remain recalcitrant, and he touched on the grim consequences of such a breakup for small states like New Jersey. He suggested that a proper remedy to the perceived difficulties with the Confederation might be a state call for a general convention to amend the Articles. The legislators discussed the matter for three days and agreed to rescind the vote, but they continued to insist that the requisition system was unreasonable.

New Jersey's change of heart was more cosmetic than real. The state took no steps to comply with the requisition. Indeed, few states made any attempt to supply the requisitioned funds. By June 1786 Congress was nearly out of money.

New Jersey's fiscal rebellion lent considerable weight to calls for some reform of the Articles. Congress had coped as best it could with the unwieldy requisition system. New Jersey's refusal to comply with that system, which it perceived as grossly unfair, made the fragility of the Union apparent.

New Jersey Delegates in the Constitutional Convention

Virginia's invitation to a September 1786 convention at Annapolis to discuss congressional power over trade followed closely upon New Jersey's refusal to honor the requisition. New Jersey sent three delegates—Abraham Clark, William Churchill Houston, and James Schureman—and equipped them with liberal instructions. The trio was authorized to examine the trade of the United States and the several states, to consider a uniform system of trade regulations, and to deal with other matters as well.

It was an interesting delegation. Clark advocated some expansion in the authority of Congress and was particularly concerned about the economic domination of New Jersey by New York and Pennsylvania. Houston (1746–1788) was a prominent lawyer whose specialties were tax and financial questions. Schureman (1756–1824) was a prominent New Brunswick merchant who had served in both the New Jersey Assembly and the Confederation Congress. He was a staunch nationalist and a determined opponent of all paper-money measures.

Delegations from New Jersey, Virginia, New York, Delaware, and Pennsylvania attended the convention. No delegation arrived with the same instructions. Delegates from New Hampshire, Rhode Island, Massachusetts, and North Carolina did not arrive in time; the other states ignored the call. Under these circumstances the convention could reach no conclusions. However, the delegates returned to their states with a report proposing that another convention be held in Philadelphia in May 1787 and noting that "the Idea of extending the powers of their Deputies, to other objects than those of Commerce which has been adopted by the State of New Jersey . . . will deserve to be incorporated into that of a future Convention." Congress approved the recommendation in February 1787.

New Jersey, Pennsylvania, Virginia, Delaware, and North Carolina named delegates to the Constitutional Convention before Congress even endorsed the idea. With the exception of Rhode Island, which ignored the convention entirely, the remaining states chose delegates between February and June, in part spurred by the specter of armed resistance raised by Shays' Rebellion in Massachusetts.

New Jersey finally settled on William Livingston, Jonathan Dayton, William Paterson, David Brearly, and William Churchill Houston as delegates. Houston did not attend, possibly because of illness.

David Brearly (1745–1790) was a prominent lawyer who had helped draft the New Jersey constitution in 1776. He was the chief justice of the New Jersey Supreme Court from 1779 to 1789 and a judge of the U.S. District Court from 1789 to his death. He was a strong opponent of paper money and became a Federalist.

Jonathan Dayton (1760–1826) was the youngest man at the convention. He was a captain during the Revolutionary War but early established a reputation for imprudence. A member of a wealthy family, he owned large amounts of public securities and was an enthusiastic land speculator. At the convention he was a vigorous exponent of the rights of small states. Though considered Clark's protégé, Dayton became a Federalist.

Paterson proved to be the most important member of the delegation, though all five men went on to hold important state or federal office under the new Constitution.

The delegates to the Philadelphia Convention faced no easy task. First, they had to reach agreement on how radically to reform the Articles. Further, they had to achieve consensus on the amount of authority to be given the central government and how the states might be protected both from each other and from the central government.

Governor Edmund Randolph, head of the Virginia delegation, presented a series of resolutions on May 29. This Virginia Plan, drafted by Madison, called for a bicameral Congress with proportional representation. The lower house would be elected by the people, the upper house by the lower from a slate of nominees proposed by the state legislatures. Congress would choose the executive and could veto all state laws contravening the federal constitution. At least one supreme court and a system of inferior courts would make up the judicial branch. A council of revision consisting of the executive and several members of the judiciary would have a veto over the legislature.

The small states, including New Jersey, objected because the Virginia Plan would place them at a disadvantage. The larger states would control both houses and the executive. On June 15 Paterson presented a plan based on a reform of the Articles rather than an entirely new frame of government. This proposal would retain the Confederation's principle of equal representation for each state. In addition, Congress would receive limited power to tax and to regulate interstate and foreign commerce. The states would be freed from the requisition method of finance. Congress would control the disposition of western lands and could negotiate freely with foreign powers. The Paterson scheme also contained a provision making federal law and treaties "the supreme law of the respective states." This suggestion became the basis for the "supreme law of the land" clause in Article VI of the final document.

New Jersey's delegation was actually responsible for two proposals in support of equal representation. Brearly suggested that all existing state boundaries be redrawn, providing for thirteen precisely equal states. The convention made approving noises about the desirability of equitable boundaries, but it took no action.

The convention debated Paterson's scheme (also called the New Jersey or Small State Plan) for three days before rejecting it and deciding to use the Virginia Plan as the basis for debate. The small states continued to oppose proportional representation because it embodied some of their worst fears about the domination of small by large states. In July the convention broke the stalemate when it accepted a compromise calling for a two-house legislature, one house with representation based on population and the other with each state receiving equal representation.

Once New Jersey was assured of some form of equal representation, its delegation found the new Constitution quite a suitable frame of government, since it provided useful solutions for many of the problems New Jersey had first cited in 1778 when responding initially to the Articles.

The provisions allotting the federal government the power to regulate commerce (foreign and interstate), issue currency, and govern western lands, and the language upholding the sanctity of contracts, addressed the concerns of both East and West Jerseyans.

Stripping the states of the power to exact their own tariffs removed an economic burden from New Jersey and dissipated considerable hostility towards New York and Pennsylvania. The opening of the West would not only provide the new government a source of income but secure new opportunities for New Jersey's many impoverished farmers.

Throughout the Confederation period the state had suffered from depreciated currency and debt problems. New Jersey held a substantial portion of the Continental debt and had shouldered the heavy burden of interest payments to the state's Continental creditors, a burden the legislature believed should be the concern of the central government. There was little reason for any area of New Jersey to object to a new government which proposed to assume this debt. And New Jerseyans, appalled at the multiple and depreciating currencies and periodic repudiations of the Confederation years, were pleased with the prospect of a more stable financial system.

The form of government the convention produced owed more to Virginia's contribution than New Jersey's. Paterson's scheme rearranged the elements of the Confederation; Randolph's restructured the government. Still, New Jersey's contribution to the constitutional process was significant. The legislature's exasperation with the Confederation's mode of finance finally led to the flat refusal to comply with the requisition. This stand certainly encouraged the pursuit of more sweeping change among those states which sent delegations to Annapolis. New Jersey's broad instructions to its delegates were cited as a model, and the New Jersey Plan provided a useful corrective to the Virginia Plan.

The Constitution Ratified

The Philadelphia Convention's handiwork became public knowledge quickly. The full text of the Constitution appeared in the *Trenton Mercury* and in a New Brunswick broadside on September 25. In the first three weeks of October the legislature received several petitions from citizens of Salem, Gloucester, Middlesex, and Burlington counties calling for a ratifying convention. All expressed approval of the new frame of government; the most fervent was one from Salem, which read in part, "Nothing but the most immediate adoption of it can save the United States in general, and this state in particular, from absolute ruin."

Congress authorized the states to call ratifying conventions in late September. A month later, on October 29, the New Jersey legislature unanimously passed resolutions calling for a state convention. The elections were without incident, and on December 11 the delegates convened in Trenton at the Blazing Star tavern. Information about the convention's deliberations is scanty. According to the account published in the *Trenton Mercury*, the delegates spent December 11–13 selecting officers, discussing rules, reading the legislature's authorizing resolution, and examining the Constitution. On December 14, 15, and 16 the Constitution was analyzed section by section. On December 18 the Constitution was again read, debated, and unanimously approved. A ceremonial procession to the courthouse for a public reading followed ratification. The celebration was punctuated by fifteen rounds of musket fire, thirteen for the new nation and one each for Delaware and Pennsylvania, which had ratified before New Jersey. The delegates then repaired to a nearby tavern, seeking a more convivial atmosphere for the expression of their satisfaction with the completed task. The newspaper account makes it plain that the joy of the occasion was fixed in every heart and expressed with liquid abandon. The convention adjourned on December 19, but not before passing a final resolution promoting a location in New Jersey for the nation's capital. Months later the New Jersey legislature offered a large site not far from Trenton, but to no avail.

New Jersey's hopes of luring the new federal capital (authorized by Article I, Section 8, of the Constitution) to a site on the Delaware may have added to the state's enthusiasm for the new Constitution. Congress had actually met in Princeton in 1783 after the delegates departed Philadelphia in some haste, fleeing an angry contingent of Continental soldiers demanding back pay.

New Jersey's attempt to capture the federal capital ran afoul of both sectional rivalries and the struggle between those favoring a strong national government and those who did not. Congress, in turn, voted first for a site on the falls of the Delaware, then for two sites (one on the Delaware, one on the Potomac), then again for the site on the Delaware. Victory seemed within New Jersey's grasp, but lack of money made state construction of the buildings impossible. Though the South eventually prevailed, a New Jersey site was still a possibility while the state was engaged in the ratification process.

New Jersey had every reason to view the Constitution favorably, and there is no evidence of any substantial opposition to it within the state. None of the commentaries from beyond the state's borders indicated any doubt that New Jersey would ratify and do so quickly. Indeed, most of the debate in the new nation over the Constitution took place after New Jersey ratified. Abraham Clark, who could have registered significant opposition when the document was laid before Congress, remained quiet during ratification. Virginia's Richard Henry Lee proposed that Congress append a series of amendments detailing basic rights before forwarding the document to the states for ratification. His proposal, which included the provision for a second convention, might well have consigned the Constitution to defeat. Clark did not support Lee, and ten months later he explained his position in a letter to Thomas Sinnickson, a prominent Salem, N.J., merchant. Clark conceded he had not liked the Constitution because he believed it erected a consolidated rather than a federal government, and one which was unnecessarily oppressive. However, he had believed the document should be forwarded to the states as written, without approval or disapproval by the Confederation Congress, and he had hoped that the states would amend it as necessary.

The brief period of unanimity in New Jersey was not to last. Sectional divisions within the state had long been an important feature of political life. The two regions were different economically, socially, religiously, and ethnically. New Jerseyans were deeply divided over problems facing the state in the 1780s—debtor-creditor issues and the controversy over the loan office. The two regions agreed on little else but the deficiencies of the Confederation. The Constitution appealed to both sides. But the hostilities which had been expressed so forcefully in the loan office controversy and during the legislature's efforts to deal with the intense debtor-creditor situation reappeared during the first federal election. New Jersey's moment of concord then gave way to the accustomed pattern of sectional antagonisms, but these abated once more as the state achieved the distinction on November 20, 1789, of becoming the first to ratify the congressionally proposed Bill of Rights.

Essay on Sources

The major study of New Jersey during the Confederation period and the state's position on the Constitution is Richard P. McCormick, *Experiment in Independence: New Jersey in the Critical Period, 1781-1789* (New Brunswick, 1950). The New Jersey chapter in the present volume as well as a longer study, Mary R. Murrin, *To Save This State From Ruin: New Jersey and the Creation of the United States Constitution, 1776–1789* (Trenton, 1987), is based on McCormick's work.

For information on population, ethnic, religious, and land-use patterns, see Peter O. Wacker, *Land and People: a Cultural Geography of Preindustrial New Jersey; Origins and Settlement Patterns* (New Brunswick, 1975), especially chaps. 3–5. On politics and social structure, see Jackson Turner Main, *Political Parties before the Constitution* (Chapel Hill, 1973), chaps. 1, 6, 12, 13, and, by the same author, *Social Structure of Revolutionary America* (Princeton, 1965), chaps.

1, 3, 6. Information on wartime devastation can be found in Howard Peckham, ed., *Toll of Independence: Engagements and Battle Casualties of the American Revolution, 1763-1783: A Documentary History* (Trenton, 1975), which is a fertile source for quotations on wartime damage. On matters economic, see E. James Ferguson, *The Power of the Purse: A History of American Public Finance, 1776–1790* (Chapel Hill, 1961), chaps. 1–4, and John J. McCusker and Russell R. Menard, *The Economy of British America, 1607–1789* (Chapel Hill, 1985), especially chap. 9. On state and sectional rivalries, see Joseph L. Davis, *Sectionalism in American Politics, 1774–1787* (Madison, Wis., 1977) and Peter Onuf, *Origins of the Federal Republic: Jurisdictional Controversies in the United States, 1775-1789* (Philadelphia, 1983), chaps. 1, 2, 4, 7.

For biographical information on the major figures, see Paul S. Stellhorn and Michael Birkner, eds., *The Governors of New Jersey, 1664–1974: Biographical Essays* (Trenton, 1982), pp. 77-81, for Livingston; John E. O'Connor, *William Paterson, Lawyer and Statesman, 1745-1806* (New Brunswick, 1979) and James McLachlan, *Princetonians, 1748–1768: A Biographical Dictionary* (Princeton, 1975), pp. 437–440, for Paterson; Ruth Bogin, *Abraham Clark and the Quest for Equality in the Revolutionary Era, 1774–1794* (Rutherford, 1982); Richard A. Harrison, *Princetonians, 1776–1783: A Biographical Dictionary* (Princeton, 1981), pp. 31–42, for material on Dayton; and the McLachlan volume of *Princetonians*, pp. 643-47, for Houston.

Important sources of documentary material include Edmund C. Burnett, ed., *Letters of Members of the Continental Congress* (Washington, D.C., 1934; reprinted 1963), vols.7, 8; Merrill Jensen, John P. Kaminski and Gaspare J. Saladino, eds., *The Documentary History of the Ratification of the Constitution* (Madison, Wis., 1976–), vols. 1, 3, 13; the "Primitive Whig" essays from the *New Jersey Gazette*, courtesy of the William Livingston Papers project at New York University; and the pamphlet now identified as the work of Abraham Clark, *The True Policy of New Jersey, Defined* (Elizabeth-Town, 1786), in the Special Collections Department at Alexander Library, Rutgers University.

A former Federalist, Garret D. Wall was selected governor of New Jersey by a Jacksonian Republican legislative caucus in 1829. Though he declined to serve, his election marked the revival of partisan politics in the state. Photograph courtesy New Jersey Historical Society.

5

The men who wrote the Constitution of the United States in 1787 shared the assumption that political parties were bad because they could not help but be divisive. They declared as a consequence that parties should not and would not develop, and the structure of government they devised was based on this assertion. James Madison in *The Federalist Papers* foresaw the development of conflicting "interest" groups that would represent the different needs of American citizens. But he did not envision the political parties that quickly appeared in the 1790s, nor the two-party system that has characterized United States politics throughout most of its history.

As a result Americans have tinkered with their political system to make it work under conditions for which it was not originally designed. Historians in turn have tried to explain when and why parties appeared and how they developed and operated. Historians have also examined which voters have been attracted to which parties and why there were usually two parties (not more, as in Italy, or fewer, as in the former Soviet Union). The first American party system arose between 1791 and 1795 on the foundation of real political, economic, and ideological differences among Americans. The resultant Federalist and Jeffersonian-Republican parties fought over policies and offices until after the War of 1812, when the Federalist party declined because of its opposition to the war and a surge in nationalist feeling at its end. The election of 1824 was marked by a revival of political contests and followed by the re-emergence of a two-party system that Richard P. McCormick referred to as "the Second Party System" (1966).

Historians have tried to address numerous questions about this system. The first is when parties actually emerged. The initial contest (on the national level, the presidential election of 1828) was between John Quincy Adams, representing the National Republicans, and Andrew Jackson of the Jacksonian Democrats. A division emerged between Whigs and Democrats, but when? Or, more precisely, when did this split emerge on the national level and in different states, specifically New Jersey? Did the second-party system develop because of national issues, state interests, or a combination of both?

The second question concerns ideology. Historians have suggested that philosophical differences stimulated the creation of political parties. Whigs favored an active government, one that assisted in the development of commerce and manufacturing. Democrats preferred a limited government and a laissez-faire economy. The first represented the elite and wealthy, the second small farmers and workers. But American political parties have seldom been diametrically opposed in their viewpoints; they more often comprise coalitions of different interest groups. Thus, for example, it is necessary to ask if all Whigs in New Jersey were wealthy, and if all of them agreed on policy matters. If not, other factors must have influenced the development of parties.

An alternative explanation revolves around personalities. John Quincy Adams and Andrew Jackson were very different. As John William Ward noted in *Andrew Jackson: Symbol for an Age* (1953), Adams represented the East and was more intellectual; Jackson, by contrast, was seen as the western man of action. Each appealed to some voters and politicians and alienated others. But do voters support parties based on subjective likes and dislikes alone? Is this a sufficient explanation for the emergence of parties?

Whether ideology or personality accounts better for the creation of political parties, historians have noted the tendency of parties to be self-perpetuating. They become "electoral machines," winning offices for candidates by gathering votes and rewarding supporters with patronage appointments once in power. Recipients of jobs and other prizes support the party in the next election by voting and otherwise using their influence. In *The Behavior of State Legislative Parties in the Jacksonian Era: New Jersey, 1829–1844* (1977), Peter Levine has argued that such structural factors help explain what held together a diverse coalition.

Other historians have claimed that cultural differences have had greater influence in sustaining the party system. Herbert Ershkowitz, in *The Origin of the Whig and Democratic Parties: New Jersey Politics 1820–1837* (1982), argued that the "Whigs drew their support from evangelical Protestants, the Democrats had a constituency which included the Irish, German, and nonevangelical Protestants." Political scientists today might observe that Mormons are Republicans. But is there a uniform or strong correlation between ethnic, religious, and social background and party affiliation? If so, why does a particular religious or ethnic group support one party over another?

A related issue concerns the connection between the "first" and "second" party systems. Progressive historians claimed that in the debate over the Constitution Federalists became members first of the Federalist and then the Whig parties. Anti-Federalists became Jeffersonian-Republicans and then Democrats. Thus they posited a continuity in American politics based on class and ideological differences. Revisionists (the name given historians who challenge traditional interpretations of the past) have seen discontinuity in membership. Some Federalists, such as Joseph Bloomfield in New Jersey, became Jeffersonian-Republicans. Others switched affiliation from the Jeffersonian-Republicans to the Whigs. Did issues, personalities, ideology, or cultural differences guide these changes?

Suggested Readings

Birkner, Michael J., and Herbert Ershkowitz. " 'Men and Measures': The Creation of the Second Party System in New Jersey." *NJH* 107 (1989): 41–59.

Bowers, Claude G. *The Party Battles of the Jacksonian Period.* Boston, 1922.

Chambers, William Nisbet, and Walter Dean Burnham, eds. *The American Party System: Stages of Development.* New York, 1967.

Ershkowitz, Herbert. *The Origin of the Whig and Democratic Parties: New Jersey Politics, 1820–1837.* Washington, D.C., 1982.

Levine, Peter D. "The Rise of Mass Parties and the Problem of Organization: New Jersey, 1829–1844." *NJH* 91 (1973): 91–107.

_____ . "State Legislative Parties in the Jacksonian Era: New Jersey, 1829–1844." *Journal of American History* 62 (1975): 591–607.

_____ . *The Behavior of State Legislative Parties in the Jacksonian Era: New Jersey, 1829–1844.* Rutherford, N.J., 1977.

McCormick, Richard P. *The Second American Party System: Party Formation in the Jacksonian Era.* Chapel Hill, N.C., 1966.

Pessen, Edward. *Jacksonian America: Society, Personality, and Politics.* 1969. Rev. ed. Homewood, Ill., 1978.

Schlesinger, Arthur Jr. *The Age of Jackson.* Boston, 1945.

◆ ◆ ◆ ◆ ◆ ◆

Party Formation in New Jersey in the Jackson Era

Richard P. McCormick

American political historians have long been intrigued with the Age of Jackson and especially with the political ferment occasioned by Jackson's entrance upon the national political scene. Although it has always been apparent that the Jacksonian era was marked, among other features, by the formation of a new two-party system, the circumstances that gave rise to the parties have remained shrouded in obscurity. Our difficulties may be attributed largely to the fact that we have looked to events in the national capital to provide an understanding of the course of politics, whereas the crucial arena for observing party formation was in the individual states. It is therefore of some interest to examine political developments in New Jersey in that exciting period.

In the decade following the Treaty of Ghent, political interest and activity in New Jersey was on the decline. Traditional political distinctions between Federalists and Democratic-Republicans were somehow nurtured and kept alive, but on a state-wide basis the party of Jefferson had such a preponderance of numbers that the Federalists ceased to enter any contest above the county level. They could not expect to win state offices, for all officials—including the governor—were chosen by the joint meeting of the legislature. Neither could they hope to elect one of their party to Congress, for Congressmen in New Jersey were elected on a general ticket. Nevertheless, the Federalists remained at least the equal of their opponents in five of the state's thirteen counties, and they were a threat in three or four others.[1]

The Democratic-Republican party by 1824 was a mature organization that had enjoyed almost uninterrupted control of the state since 1801. It gave the appearance of being a well constructed, smoothly functioning machine, its main parts being

Proceedings of the New Jersey Historical Society 83 (1965): 161–73. Reprinted by permission of the author.

the township committees, county conventions and state convention. The last body—made up of delegates from each county—met biennially to nominate a Congressional slate and quadrennially to name presidential electors. Because of the decentralized nature of New Jersey politics, control of the party was not vested in a small clique, but was instead dispersed among the county chieftains. This condition, together with the fact that the party had not for many years been challenged on the state level and was therefore not well unified by the spur of competition, was to explain in part the breaking up of the party in the mid-1820s.[2]

The character of the election machinery in New Jersey was also to be of significance in the impending upheaval, for it was well adapted to mass participation in politics. Elections were held on the second Tuesday and Wednesday in October, except in presidential years when electors and Congressmen were chosen in November. All elections were by ballot, which could be either written or printed. In practice they were almost always printed, thereby facilitating straight party voting. The township was the voting unit and contained either one or two polling places. There was a legal requirement that adult males must be taxpayers in order to vote, but even if there had been a serious disposition to enforce this qualification, the techniques for doing so were inadequate. Consequently there was virtually universal white manhood suffrage.[3] During the years of apathy that followed the decline of Federalism, however, only a minority of voters went to the polls. Indeed, the most striking change that was to mark the Jackson era was the extraordinary increase in the size of the electorate.

Although there had been occasional rumblings of interest in the presidential question earlier in the year, it was not until late in 1823 that New Jersey began to rouse itself from its political lethargy.[4] From the first there was a marked lack of unanimity among political leaders in their choice of presidential candidates; Calhoun, Crawford and Adams all had substantial support within the ranks of the Democratic-Republicans.[5] Jackson's star was the last to rise, and there was little in the way of an organized campaign in his behalf until June 1824, when a public meeting in Salem issued a call for the friends of the General to gather in Trenton in September.[6]

The Jackson state meeting, attended by delegates from only seven of the thirteen counties, named an eight-man electoral ticket, at least three members of which were Federalists.[7] The movement was now well launched, and it is pertinent to ask who launched it. The evidence points fairly conclusively to the ubiquitous and notorious Colonel Samuel Swartwout of New York City. This former participant in the Burr Conspiracy, who was also a close friend of Andrew Jackson, was actually the chairman of the Jackson state convention, even though his connection with New Jersey was a tenuous one.[8] He was probably linked to the Salem meeting through Aaron Ogden Dayton, the nephew of another of his conspiratorial associates, Jonathan Dayton, for Aaron Ogden Dayton—a former Federalist—was secretary of both the Salem meeting and the state meeting.[9]

When the official Democratic-Republican state convention met on October 19th, the Jacksonians entered into a combination with the Crawfordites and forced the adoption of an electoral ticket made up of five Jackson and three Crawford men. The supporters of Adams thereupon withdrew and named their own set of electors.[10] Not content with the five-eighths of a loaf that the convention had awarded them, the ardent friends of Jackson assembled again a week later, on October 25th, and formed an all-out Jackson ticket.[11]

Eight days later the election opened, and for two days the people of New Jersey experienced the unfamiliar excitement of participating in a genuine presidential contest. Only once before—in 1808—had they been presented with the opportunity of voting for opposing slates of electors, and on that occasion over 33,000 ballots had been cast.[12] Now—in 1824—only 18,400 men voted. This figure approximated one-third of the potential electorate. By a narrow margin of 1000 votes, Jackson triumphed over Adams and carried nine of the thirteen counties.[13]

Under the circumstances, Jackson's victory must be regarded more as a successful and surprising political coup than as the result of a popular crusade. With the regular organization of the Democratic-Republican Party badly divided, the Jackson forces seized the initiative, created their own organization, and carried on a skillful campaign. It is impossible to discern any clear-cut bases for the cleavage between Jacksonians and Adamsites. Considerations of personal political expediency rather than concern with fundamental principles determined the allegiance of political leaders.[14]

No small share of the credit for Jackson's victory must be given to the leadership provided by former Federalists. Long denied an opportunity to rise to positions of state and national prominence, they eagerly climbed aboard the Jackson bandwagon, which was driven by Samuel Swartwout, and many of them were subsequently to become prominent Jacksonian officeholders.[15]

Such excitement as had been engendered by the presidential contest quickly subsided. The state elections in 1825 went off quietly, voters returned to their traditional party allegiances, and there seemed to be no general awareness that a new political era was at hand. In 1826, however, when the biennial state convention of the Democratic-Republican Party met, the "presidential question" was once more a divisive factor, and the session broke up in disorder, never to meet again. Each faction then met separately and nominated its own Congressional ticket.[16] One newspaper editor gave a succinct explanation of what lay behind the conflict: "Why simply that one man shall go *out* of, and another *into* office."[17]

In the October elections, the contest was between the Jackson Party and the Adams—or Administration—Party. The Adamsites scored an easy victory, carrying the state by 5000 votes out of a total of 25,000.[18] Again, this election was not a decisive test, for the Jacksonians had decided to wait until 1828 to make an all-out campaign. Their organization was rudimentary, in contrast to that of the Adamsites, which was largely the organization of the old Democratic-Republican Party, revived and strengthened by administration support and patronage.[19]

Soon after the state elections in 1827, which aroused little interest and resulted in a slight gain by the Jacksonians, the political pot began to bubble vigorously.[20] The Jacksonians led off with a state convention held on the anniversary of the battle of New Orleans. With evident enthusiasm, they named their electoral ticket and appointed a central state committee headed by Garret D. Wall.[21] The Adamsites held their convention on Washington's Birthday with a host of new faces—many of them former Federalists—conspicuous among the leaders of the session.[22] Quite obviously, the period of proscription had ended, and the Federalists were now participating fully in both the Jacksonian and Adamsite camps.

As the critical fall elections approached, campaigning by both parties reached an unprecedented peak of intensity. Early in October the state election was held, and it gave the Adamsites a victory by the slight margin of a thousand votes.[23] Some two weeks later—on October 23rd—the "Jackson Republican Convention," as it was now called, assembled again in Trenton. With every evidence of harmony a Congressional ticket evenly divided between former Federalists and former Democratic-Republicans was nominated.[24]

On November 4th and 5th the voters of the state responded to the pressures exerted on them by the two well organized and vigorous party machines by turning out more than 45,000 strong. Weeks later, when the official returns were finally published, they learned that Adams had triumphed by a majority of nearly two thousand votes and had carried all but four counties.[25] The real triumph, however, lay with the political managers of both parties who, without appeals to issues or to economic interest, had succeeded in bringing to the polls almost three times as many men as had cast ballots in 1824.

Seventy-two per cent of the adult white males voted in 1828 as compared with thirty-one per cent four years earlier. Vigilance committees, poll committees, township committees, county conventions, party organs, pamphlets, broadsides and personal appeals had all combined to arouse the voters and make them feel the urgency of the contest. No discernible issues, either state or national, were involved, other than those that centered on personalities. But the common man—the man who had rarely been stimulated to vote in national elections—now went to the polls, and he cast his vote as enthusiastically against as for the glamorous figure of Andrew Jackson.[26]

With the removal of their personal figure head from the presidential office, the Adamsites were dispirited and ineffective in 1829, and the Jacksonians swept the state for the first time since 1824.[27] Garret D. Wall, former Federalist, and foremost leader of the Jackson Party, was elected to the governorship, but he declined and accepted instead the appointment of United States District Attorney. Thereupon his future son-in-law, Peter D. Vroom, also a former Federalist, was chosen governor.[28]

Conscious of the growing strength of their party organization at the local level, but aware of the fact that they had not been able to win a state-wide election since their surprise triumph in 1824, the Jacksonians decided to change the rules of the game to suit their own ends in 1830. In control of the legislature, they enacted a law postponing the Congressional election in 1830 until late December, thus separating the state from the national election.[29] They had reason to fear the strength of their opponents, now organized under the National Republican banner behind a new hero, Henry Clay. Their strategy was probably sound, for although they retained control of the legislature, they lost the Congressional contest by a margin of nearly 1,100 votes out of a total of about 29,000.[30] The defeat of the Jacksonians was in part attributable to internal dissension, which manifested itself in the state convention and resulted in the choice of a Congressional ticket that displeased many in the party.[31] Although the party regained control of the legislature in 1831, their margin was slight, and it was evident that the election of 1832 was going to be fiercely contested by two well matched foes.[32]

It was at this period—in the early 1830s—that a significant new influence made its appearance in New Jersey politics. During the years 1830–1832 the legislature chartered the Delaware and Raritan Canal Company and the Camden and Amboy Railroad Company, which, merged together as the Joint Companies, were granted a monopoly of the canal and railroad traffic across the state between New York and Philadelphia. For many years to come this extremely valuable monopoly privilege was to be the target of attack by hostile transportation interests and was to be a major issue in state politics. Because the monopoly had been created by a Jacksonian legislature, and because many of the Jackson leaders were closely identified with the Joint Companies, the destinies of the party and the monopoly were intertwined. Correspondingly, those interests opposed to the monopoly were generally to be found in the National Republican—or Whig—Party. The rival transportation groups were especially active in the years 1832 to 1837, and during this period party politics were to be in many ways a projection of transportation politics.[33]

The influence of the transportation factor was evident as the parties prepared for the election of 1832. The five-member Jackson central committee, appointed in mid-March, included three directors of the Joint Companies and the editor of the leading pro-monopoly newspaper.[34] When the National Republicans held a Young Men's Convention in April, the presiding officer was the president of the Joint Companies' leading antagonist, the New Jersey Railroad and Transportation Company, and the secretary was a director of the same railroad.[35]

In addition to the transportation issue, the campaign also revolved around the bank question, which both parties agitated vigorously for popular effect. Elaborate organizations were perfected, with "Young Men" committees for the first time supplementing the work of the regular party machinery. Shortly before the October state elections, the county conventions met as usual to nominate candidates for the legislature and to elect delegates to the state conventions.[36] Forty thousand men turned out to vote for members of the legislature, an unprecedented total for a state election, and the National Republicans won this first test of strength by a small majority.[37]

A month later, however, when the national election took place, the tables were turned and the Jacksonians eked out a victory by the narrow margin of 463 votes out of the record total of over 47,000.[38] Seventy per cent of the adult white males voted. This indecisive triumph was the signal for the exultant editor of the chief party organ to proclaim:

> Hereafter we know no other name but *Democracy*—and the support of the administration is the *only* test of Democracy. The name of Jackson was but the signal—the watchword at which we rallied to the old Democratic landmarks—let us now maintain our stand upon the *old party principles*, and the *old party name*.[39]

In 1833—as in 1829—the Jacksonians overwhelmed their opponents, who could arouse little popular enthusiasm now that the magic name of Clay no longer served as their symbol of unity.[40] The Democrats showed nearly the same strength they had in 1832, but the National Republican vote declined sharply, especially in South Jersey, where it fell off as much as fifty per cent in certain counties. Religious issues, growing out of the Hicksite-Orthodox split among the Quakers, contributed to the defeat of the National Republicans as did the deterioration of their party organization.[41]

Looking forward to the 1834 election, the anti-Jacksonians seized upon the removal of the deposits from the Bank of the United States as the issue upon which they hoped to rally support. When New Jersey's two Senators refused to heed the instructions of the Democratic legislature on this question, they became—with the Bank—centers of party controversy. Reports of the endless debates in Congress kept the issue alive, although the local Democratic leadership was inclined to view the whole matter as remote, artificial, and even somewhat annoying. "If you were to stop talking," wrote Governor Vroom to Democratic Congressman James Parker, "people would not know that anything was the matter."[42]

But the "Bankites" continued to fulminate against Jackson, and their activities came to a head early in April when delegates from all parts of the state met in Trenton, ostensibly to memorialize Congress on the subject of the deposits. In reality, however, the meeting organized what very soon became known as the Whig Party.[43] It was the state committee appointed by this Bank meeting that later issued the call for a Whig State Convention to meet in August.[44]

The Democrats, despite some minor defections over the Bank controversy, remained substantially the same party in leadership and organization that they had been since 1828.[45] They held a state meeting in May for the purpose of drafting a set of resolutions approving the policies of the Administration, at the same time appointing party committees. In September, 670 delegates gathered in Trenton for the regular Democratic State Convention and with machine-like precision went through the formalities of renominating the old Congressional ticket.[46]

With both parties once again highly organized for what was universally regarded as a major contest, the total vote rose to a new high of 53,862—indicating that seventy-eight per cent of the adult white males had gone to the polls. The Democrats elected their Congressmen by a majority of a thousand votes and also retained control of the legislature.[47] Political observers agreed that the deciding factor in producing the Democratic victory was the vote cast by the Hicksite Quakers against the Whig ticket.[48]

With the election of 1834, a decade of transition in the history of political parties in New Jersey came to an end. For the next two decades, the Democrats and the Whigs, both well organized and usually evenly matched, were to contest for supremacy. Although the principles that distinguished one from the other were far from clear, each was able to command the firm allegiance of multitudes of voters.

The Jackson-Democratic Party, as it emerged and developed during the decade under consideration, was a new political organization; it could not be considered as a lineal descendant of the Democratic-Republican Party. It owed its origins largely to Federalist leadership, and former Federalists continued to be its most conspicuous helmsmen after it had become the dominant party in the state. They were attracted to the Jacksonian cause because it offered them an opportunity to win political preferment, and they were able to gain high positions in the party at an early date because the Democratic-Republican stalwarts chose to regard Adams as the legitimate successor to the presidency. The party was not organized around a set of principles, nor did it adopt any body of doctrine during the decade. Made up of disparate elements, it found its unifying symbol in Jackson and its unifying drive in the desire to win office.

The decade witnessed a new type of competition between parties that were becoming increasingly institutionalized. Men of abilities were willing to devote considerable attention to party affairs because politics offered a respectable, exciting, and lucrative career. They mastered and applied techniques of mass organization, recently made possible by improvements in transportation, communication and publication as well as by an electoral process that encouraged mass participation. Using these techniques with skill and energy, they competed intensely for votes. So well did they practice their profession that they succeeded in bringing to the polls nearly three-fourths of the adult white males in the state.

It would not be possible to find in this decade any evidence that the party situation reflected basic economic or social cleavages in the population. Certainly the Jacksonians were not participating in a class revolt or engaging in a radical crusade. Their most evident distinguishing characteristic subsequent to 1830 was their close identification with the monopoly of the Joint Companies. Before that date they were known chiefly for their allegiance to Jackson and for their partiality toward former Federalists. Their greatest accomplishment was so to arouse popular interest as to give new depth and meaning to the term "American Democracy."

Notes

1. The period is ably surveyed in Walter R. Fee, *The Transition from Aristocracy to Democracy in New Jersey, 1789–1829* (Somerville, N.J., 1933). As late as 1823, nineteen of the fifty-six legislators bore the Federalist label. (New Brunswick) *Fredonian*, Oct. 23, 1923. Federalists survived in large part because the county was the major political unit. Moreover, as partisan tensions declined, the legislators agreed that members from each county should enjoy "Senatorial courtesy" in matters of local appointments; Federalist politicians then could win elections to the legislature in several counties and share in the spoils of office. L. Q. C. Elmer, *The Constitution and Government of the Province and State of New Jersey* . . . (Newark, 1872), p. 211.

2. Even on the county level, the lack of competition from the Federalists encouraged intra-party contests and the frequent launching of "Union" tickets made up of Democratic-Republicans and Federalists. *Fredonian*, Oct. 22, 1818; (Elizabeth) *New Jersey Journal*, Oct. 16, 1822, Sept. 30, 1823; *Bridgeton Observer*, Oct. 18, 1823.

3. *New Jersey Laws*, Acts of Nov. 16, 1807, and June 1, 1820. Under this taxpayer qualification as many as three-fourths of the adult males actually cast ballots.

4. Gov. I. H. Williamson to Sen. Mahlon Dickerson, Dec. 16, 1823, Mahlon Dickerson Papers, N.J.H.S.

5. *New Jersey Journal*, Nov. 18, 1823; *Fredonian*, Feb. 12, 19, 1824; Charles F. Adams, *Memoirs of John Quincy Adams* (12 vols., Philadelphia, 1874–1877), VI, pp. 173–74, 253–54, 282–83, 479–80.

6. *Bridgeton Observer*, June 26, 1824. This Salem meeting was generally regarded at the time as marking the real start of the Jackson movement in New Jersey. "Amicus Republicae," *Fredonian*, Sept. 8, 1824.

7. (New Brunswick) *Times*, Sept. 22, 1824. The Federalists were James Parker, Joseph W. Scott and John Beatty, Jr.

8. Swartwout owned land with his brother in Bergen County. For the Colonel's background and his relations with Jackson, see Henry F. Du Puy, "Some Letters of Andrew Jackson," *Proceedings of the American Antiquarian Society*, N.S. XXX (1921), pp. 70–88. In mid-April, Swartwout had played a leading role in promoting Jackson's interests in New York City. *Fredonian*, Apr. 15, 1824.

9. [Charles Robson], *The Biographical Encyclopaedia of New Jersey* (Philadelphia, 1877), pp. 374–76.

10. *Times*, Oct. 27, 1824, *Fredonian*, Oct. 27, 1824.

11. *Bridgeton Observer*, Oct. 30, 1824. This final ticket contained six of the eight names proposed by the September meeting; five of the eight named by the state convention.

12. Minutes of the Privy Council, II, Nov. 12, 1808. N.J.S.L. Down to 1804, and again in 1812, the electors were not properly chosen. In 1816 and 1820 there had been no contest.

13. *Times*, Nov. 10, 1824; *Fredonian*, Nov. 17, 1824.

14. *Fredonian*, Nov. 10, 1824; Elmer, *Constitution*. pp. 189, 220, 224–25.

15. Among the prominent Federalists who took the lead in supporting Jackson were Garret D. Wall, Peter D. Vroom, James Parker, Henry S. Green, Aaron Ogden Dayton, Joseph W. Scott and William Chetwood. James Parker to G. D. Wall, Nov. 10, 1824, James Papers, R.U.L.

16. (Newark) *Sentinel of Freedom*, Sept. 26, 1826; (Trenton) *Emporium*, Sept. 30, 1826; (Bridgeton) *West Jersey Observer*, Oct. 7, 1826; [S. J. Bayard], A *Sketch of the Life of Com. Robert F. Stockton* (New York, 1856), pp. 60–62.

17. *Fredonian*, Oct. 4, 1826. See also *West Jersey Observer*, Oct. 7, 1826; *Sentinel of Freedom*, Sept. 26, 1826.

18. *Sentinel of Freedom*, Oct. 17, 1826; *Fredonian*, Nov. 1, 8, 1826. The Adams Party won the legislature, 41–16, and carried all but three counties—Sussex, Warren, and Hunterdon.

19. *Emporium*, Oct. 21, 1826; *Fredonian*, Oct. 25, Dec. 13, 1826; *Sentinel of Freedom*, Nov. 14, 1826; Bayard, *Stockton*, p. 63; Adams, *Memoirs*, VI, pp. 313–14.

20. *Sentinel of Freedom*, Oct. 23, 1827. Even as late as 1827, the old party labels still retained meaning in some counties. S. G. Opdycke to G. D. Wall, Aug. 28, 1827, G. D. Wall Papers, R.U.L.; *Fredonian*, Sept.–Oct., 1827.

21. *Sentinel of Freedom*, Jan. 15, 1828; *West Jersey Observer*, Jan. 12, 1828. The electors were all former Democratic-Republicans, but the Federalists were

assured that their claims would be recognized when the Congressional ticket was named. J. D. Westcott, Jr., to G. D. Wall, Jan. 18, 1828, G. D. Wall Papers, R.U.L.

22. (Mt. Holly) *New Jersey Mirror*, Feb. 27, 1828. Two former Federalists, Theodore Frelinghuysen and Aaron Leaming, were placed on the electoral ticket, and others such as Joseph C. Hornblower, L. H. Stockton, C. C. Stratton, William Pearson and William B. Ewing were active delegates. *West Jersey Observer*, Mar. 15, 1828.

23. *West Jersey Observer*, Oct. 13, 1828. The new legislature was to have 34 Adamsites and 23 Jacksonians.

24. *West Jersey Observer*, Nov. 1, 1828; *Sentinel of Freedom*, Oct. 23, 1828. The three Federalists were Vroom, Parker and Fowler. The "Administration State Convention," meeting on October 17, had named a Congressional slate that contained only one known Federalist— T. H. Hughes of Cape May. *New Jersey Mirror*, Oct. 29, 1828.

25. *Sentinel of Freedom*, Nov. 25, 1828; *West Jersey Observer*, Dec. 6, 1828.

26. Elmer, *Constitution*, p. 226.

27. *Sentinel of Freedom*, Oct. 20, 1829. They carried nine counties and secured a 39–18 majority in the legislature.

28. Elmer, *Constitution*, pp. 428–29.

29. *New Jersey Laws*, Mar. 2, 1830. Normally the state and national elections would have been held together on the second Tuesday and Wednesday in October.

30. *New Jersey Mirror*, Aug. 25, Oct. 20, 1830; Jan. 13, 1831.

31. *Sentinel of Freedom*, Nov. 16, Dec. 7, 21, 1830.

32. *New Jersey Mirror*, Oct. 27, 1831.

33. Wheaton J. Lane, *From Indian Trail to Iron Horse* (Princeton, 1939), passim; Robert T. Thompson, "Transportation Combines and Pressure Politics," *Proceedings of the New Jersey Historical Society*, LVII (1939), pp. 1–15, 71–86.

34. *New Jersey Journal*, Mar. 20, 1832.

35. *New Jersey Journal*, Mar. 27, Apr. 17, 1832. The directors of the New Jersey Railroad and Transportation Company were almost all National Republicans.

36. In Essex County the county conventions were not held until October 5th and 6th, only ten days before the election. *New Jersey Journal*, Sept.–Oct., 1832.

37. Although they secured a two-to-one majority in the legislature, their state-wide popular majority was under 2,000. *New Jersey Journal*, Oct. 16, 1832; *Emporium*, Oct. 30, 1832.

38. *Emporium*, Nov. 24, 1832. The Anti-Masonic vote was 480, enough to have significantly affected the outcome. Jackson carried Sussex, Warren, Hunterdon, Monmouth, Bergen and Somerset. South Jersey, Essex, Middlesex and Morris went for Clay.

39. *Emporium*, Nov. 10, 1832. Four years earlier, the same editor, Stacy G. Potts, had suggested to Garret D. Wall that the time had come for "the friends of Jackson to hoist the Republican flag." Evidently this proposal was regarded as being premature, for the Jackson label remained in use until 1832. Potts to

Wall, Nov. 8, 1828, G. D. Wall Papers, R.U.L.

40. *New Jersey Journal*, Oct. 22, Nov. 5, 1833; *Emporium*, Oct. 12, 1833. The Democratic majority was nearly 7,000, and they won every county except Essex and Cape May.

41. The Hicksites voted Democratic, largely because of their animosity toward Theodore Frelinghuysen, who had been opposed to them in their law suit with the Orthodox.

42. Vroom to Parker, Jan. 14, 1834, James Parker Papers, R.U.L. Two months later Vroom observed impatiently to Parker, "Neither of us can as yet see the end of the noise and clamor which the parasites of the Bank are endeavoring to excite and prolong." Vroom to Parker, Mar. 15, 1834. Ibid.

43. *New Jersey Journal*, Apr. 8, 1834; Vroom to Parker, Apr. 4, 1834, James Parker Papers, R.U.L. The name "Whig" came into use in New Jersey late in April.

44. *New Jersey Journal*, July 15, 1834. The leading figures in the newly christened party were for the most part men who had heretofore not occupied conspicuous positions in politics. Many were young men; a few were seceding Jacksonians; others had earlier been identified with the hierarchy of the old Democratic-Republican Party. Senators Samuel L. Southard and Theodore Frelinghuysen were the chief ornaments of the party.

45. Joseph W. Scott, Gen. Abraham Godwin, William Chetwood and James Cook were some of the moderately prominent figures who deserted to the Whigs. See also Vroom to Parker, May 20, 30, 1834, James Parker Papers, R.U.L.

46. *New Jersey Journal*, May 27, Sept. 16, 1834.

47. *New Jersey Journal*, Oct. 21, Nov. 4, 1834. The Democrats carried Bergen, Morris, Sussex, Warren, Hunterdon, Somerset, Monmouth, and Gloucester.

48. *New Jersey Journal*, Oct. 21, 1834; Vroom to Parker, May 30, 1830, James Parker Papers, R.U.L.

During the Civil War, after both the Raritan Bay Union and the North American Phalanx had ceased to operate, Rebecca Buffum Spring posed for a formal portrait. Photograph courtesy the Daugherty and Formichella families and New Jersey Historical Society.

6

Historical works appear in a number of formats. The oldest probably is the narrative, a descriptive, story-telling mode that embraces the ancient epic as well as the modern chronicle. Although it concerns itself with establishing precisely what happened in the past, the narrative, like all history, is also selective—an author must choose what details to include and what to leave out in order to tell a story. In so doing, the author makes a judgment, evaluates the evidence, and offers an explanation.

Other books and articles are mainly analytical, seeking to explain why something happened, to get at the "essence" of a country, people, or epoch, to pinpoint the most important characteristic or features of an event or a person. Analysis can be done on the basis of descriptive writing or statistical comparisons.

A third form is biography, which recounts one person's life in great detail both to show how the times influenced an individual and how an individual affected the course of events. In addition to making history more personal and alive, biography can show the reciprocal impact of people and the times in which they live.

But biographies also present interpretive problems. How typical is the person of the age in which he or she lived? If a person is unique or atypical, what exactly does biography teach except the life story of an idiosyncratic individual? Can enough information be found about a person to develop a well-rounded picture of his or her life? Can the biographer help but be influenced by a feeling of like or dislike for the person whose life is chronicled? Should biographers use psychology, and can modern psychological theories be applied to a previous age? Can we psychoanalyze the dead? If authors do not try to get under their subjects' skin, are they missing something?

The article that follows combines biography and analysis in the examination of the life of Rebecca Buffum Spring. How typical was she of women in nineteenth-century America? What do her experiences tell about the period in which she lived?

If republican ideology excluded women from citizenship by ascribing to them weakness, dependency, and vulnerability, as Gregory Dowd has argued in his earlier essay, Marie Mullaney has pointed out that these same attributes and others formed the basis of an alternative vision, a "cult of domesticity," by the early 1800s. The premise was that women were different from men, resided in a separate "sphere," and possessed *positive* attributes important for the preservation of a republic. Women were more sentimental; therefore, they could be counted on to do the "right" thing. Women's place was with their families in their homes. It was their responsibility to maintain the peace, sanctity, and integrity of the home and family, the central institutions of society. To women fell the task of educating children, the future citizens of the republic. By the late twentieth century, this picture of women's role appeared limiting, but in the nineteenth century it was regarded as a significant, and expanded, function.

To help educate children women could, and did, become teachers. To protect their homes and families they joined religious groups and formed organizations. To counter the effects of urbanization and industrialization, women supported or joined utopian communities. Women became members of Bible societies to distribute religious publications; they helped create Sunday schools to teach poor children. They joined in the temperance movement to rescue others from the evils of drinking. Some women became abolitionists; many others supported the more moderate cause of antislavery. Harriet Beecher Stowe argued in *Uncle Tom's Cabin*, after all, that slavery's greatest sin was the destruction of families.

By the middle of the nineteenth century, some women rejected the so-called "separation of spheres" and began instead to argue for an equality of the sexes. As women were "created equal," they should have the same legal and political rights as men. The desire for justice that came out of this argument fueled the early women's rights movement and bolstered the demand for suffrage, stated most clearly at the first women's rights convention at Seneca Falls, New York, in 1848. Seventy years passed before women won the right to vote, and they ultimately succeeded by stressing the contradictory ideas that they were equal to men and yet different, the specially designated holders of republican virtue.

What guided Rebecca Buffum Spring's involvement with reform? What ideas lay behind her efforts? Was she an early "feminist" (a term not used until after 1900), or was she acting in the way she thought best suited her domestic role as protector of home and family?

Suggested Readings

Beltz, Herman. "The North American Phalanx: Experiment in Socialism." *Proc. NJHS* 81 (1963): 215–47.

Bestor, Arthur. *Backwoods Utopias*. Philadelphia, 1950.

Degler, Carl N. *At Odds: Women and the Family in America from the Revolution to the Present*. New York, 1980.

Evans, Sara. *Born for Liberty: A History of Women in America*. New York, 1989.

Kerr, Andrea Moore. *Lucy Stone: Speaking Out for Equality*. New Brunswick, N.J., 1992.

Kirchmann, George. "Why Did They Stay? Communal Life at the North American Phalanx." In *Planned and Utopian Experiments: Four New Jersey Towns*, edited by Paul A. Stellhorn. Trenton, N.J., 1980. 10–27.

_____ . "Unsettled Utopias: The North American Phalanx and the Raritan Bay Union." *NJH* 97 (1979): 25–36.

Lewis, Jan. "The Republican Wife: Virtue and Seduction in the Early Republic." *William and Mary Quarterly*, ser. 3, 44 (1987): 689–721.

Rorabaugh, W. J. *The Alcoholic Republic: An American Tradition*. New York, 1979.

Sokolow, Jayme A. "Culture and Utopia: The Raritan Bay Union." *NJH* 94 (1976): 89–100.

Tyler, Alice Felt. *Freedom's Ferment: Phases of American Social History from the Colonial Period to the Outbreak of the Civil War*. Minneapolis, Minn., 1944.

Walters, Ronald G. *American Reformers, 1815–1860*. New York, 1978.

◆ ◆ ◆ ◆ ◆ ◆

Feminism, Utopianism, and Domesticity: The Career of Rebecca Buffum Spring, 1811–1911

Marie Marmo Mullaney

For more than two decades, historians have been putting women into the history books, retrieving their achievements and contributions, and delineating the differences in the historical experi-

New Jersey History 104 (1986): 1–22. Reprinted by permission of the author.

ence of the sexes. In New Jersey, scholars have recently embarked on an ambitious project, aiming to catalogue within one volume the biographies of hundreds of women of significance and renown in the state's past.[1] Placing women's experiences into the historical record is important for more than purely compensatory reasons, however. Due to the efforts of historians of women, knowledge of women's collective experience has reached the stage where biography may be used to uncover and isolate larger questions about the relationship between women and the wider society: The manner in which women sought to effect social change, the sorts of changes they envisioned, and the relationship between their public activism and their feminist commitment.

Exemplar of Reform

A biographical analysis of one New Jersey woman is particularly useful in this regard. Rebecca Buffum Spring was centrally involved in two significant episodes of nineteenth-century state history, the North American Phalanx and the Raritan Bay Union, utopian communities that placed New Jersey in the forefront of antebellum America's fascination with communitarianism and social reform.[2] She was also an ardent abolitionist, who visited insurrectionist John Brown in prison, petitioned for his release, and saw to it that the bodies of two of his raiders were buried in free Northern soil. In addition, her Quakerism linked her to dozens of other achieving women whose religiously based belief in the spiritual equality of the sexes triggered their assumption of public roles. Spring's commitment to reform also stemmed from familial influence. Her father, merchant and inventor Arnold Buffum, was the first president of the New England Anti-Slavery Society, and her sister, Elizabeth Buffum Chace, a well known lecturer in Europe and America, was active in prison reform, pacifism, abolition, and suffrage. Thomas Earle, presidential aspirant William Birney's running-mate on the Liberty Party ticket of 1840, was her first cousin.

Spring was one of the most widely known women in nineteenth-century America. She was a kind of American *salonière*, whose New York City home was a favorite gathering spot for the cultural, political, and literary intelligentsia. Her circle of friends and associates reads like a contemporary *Who's Who* of illustrious personages on both sides of the Atlantic Ocean. She numbered among her personal friends Fredrika Bremer,

William Henry Channing, Lydia Maria Child, Bronson Alcott, Albert Brisbane, Julia Ward Howe, Horace and Mary Mann, William and Mary Howitt, Horace Greeley, and Caroline Severance. She was acquainted with Charles Dickens, Harriet Martineau, William Wordsworth, Thomas Carlyle, Giuseppe Mazzini, Ralph Waldo Emerson, and Henry David Thoreau. Her deep personal friendship with Margaret Fuller is most noteworthy, for it was as a traveling companion to Spring and her husband Marcus that Fuller made her celebrated European voyage in 1845. The Springs' role in bringing Fuller to Europe is rarely mentioned in the literature on the acclaimed feminist and transcendentalist.

Although Spring's name is mentioned in the histories of Quakerism, utopianism, and abolitionism, she has escaped the sustained attention of historians, remaining virtually unknown in the history of American social reform. Yet her career is a significant one. Active as she was during an especially critical period in the history of American women, her experiences and motivations cast light on the wellsprings of American feminism. The middle decades of the nineteenth century saw not only the birth of the first movement for women's rights, but the emergence of the genteel cult of the lady with its encumbering notions of domesticity. Spring reflected these divergent threads, for she was a curious blend of reformer and conservative, feminist and traditionalist. A study of her life helps to reassess and reinterpret not only the roots of nineteenth-century feminism, but the relationship between feminism and the larger currents of moral and social reform. On a secondary level, an analysis of Spring's career provides a good opportunity to reevaluate the ideological roots of nineteenth-century communitarianism in New Jersey, clarifying and highlighting as it does the surprisingly nonsocialistic aspirations of the communities' founders.

Early Years

Rebecca Buffum Spring was born in Providence, Rhode Island, on June 8, 1811, the fourth of seven children of Arnold Buffum and Rebecca Gould. She lived in Rhode Island as a child before the family moved to Fall River, Massachusetts, in 1823. The Buffums prized learning, and their daughters attended the Quaker-run Smithfield Academy. In common with other young women of the antebellum period, they organized the Smithfield Female Mutual Improvement Society, a literary club whose members met weekly to read useful books and exchange original compositions on religious and political themes.

Two concerns dominated Rebecca Buffum's girlhood: education and abolition. Her father's influence was paramount in both. To promote the use of several of his inventions, Arnold Buffum made three trips to Europe during her youth, activities that served to politicize his family. Impressed with the advances then being made in England toward the education of factory children, and learning of various educational theories being tested on the continent, he interested his daughters in opening a factory school for mill children. Following after her sisters Elizabeth and Lucy, Rebecca Buffum taught at such schools in Fall River and Uxbridge, Massachusetts. The integrated mill school at Uxbridge was one of the first of its kind in the area. In 1834, when her father moved to Philadelphia to open a hat shop, Rebecca Buffum taught at the Philadelphia Colored Infant School that was supported by many Quakers and abolitionists. A creative and unique institution, it was both integrated and coeducational.

While in Europe, Arnold Buffum had studied the slave trade with Thomas Clarkson, an advocate of the total abolition of slavery in the British colonies. He also met the English abolitionist William Wilberforce. Upon his return to America he and eleven abolitionist friends met in Boston to launch the New England Anti-Slavery Society. The result of his activities was to interest his daughters in abolition work. As their father organized societies across New England, the Buffum daughters went from house to house distributing antislavery pamphlets. While Rebecca Buffum taught in Philadelphia, all of her sisters joined the Fall River Female Anti-Slavery Society, whose members petitioned Congress and held fairs to raise money for food and clothing for runaway slaves. Although these activities met with local resistance—even from Quakers, with Arnold Buffum being asked to resign his membership in the Smithfield Monthly Meeting—persecution only heightened Rebecca Buffum's resolve. At age twenty-three, according to her sister, Rebecca Buffum's letters were "throbbing with tender sympathy" for the cause of the slave.[3] In 1838 she participated in a women's antislavery convention in Philadelphia, attended by such luminaries as William Lloyd Garrison, Theodore Weld, Angelina Grimké, and Maria Chapman. Here she gained firsthand knowledge of the dangerous passions enflamed by abolitionists, as she witnessed the mob burning of the newly dedicated Pennsylvania Hall of Liberty where the convention was being held.[4]

An Unconventional Marriage

Rebecca Buffum's passion for abolition and social reform was shared by the man who became her husband, dry-goods merchant Marcus Spring. Born in Uxbridge, Massachusetts, on October 21, 1810, Spring was a Unitarian and a cultured, highly literate, self-made man. An avid reader of economics, philosophy, and classical literature and a lover of art and music, he was interested in the improvement of the factory classes and had worked with Arnold Buffum in aiding runaway slaves. Married in Philadelphia on October 26, 1836, the Springs shared a romantic, companionate, and egalitarian union. Their collected letters reveal a relationship that belies the standard image of married life in antebellum America.[5]

According to historians, mid-nineteenth-century American society was characterized in large part by rigid gender-role differentiation both within the family and society as a whole, leading to the emotional segregation of women and men.[6] Etiquette books, advice manuals on child rearing, religious sermons, guides to young adults, medical texts, and school curricula all suggest that most nineteenth-century Americans inhabited a world composed of distinctly male and female spheres that were determined by the immutable laws of God and nature. According to antebellum advice givers, marriage subjugated woman to man, for Christianity indicated no "perfect equality of rights" between husband and wife.[7]

Women's problems in adjusting to marriage were compounded by the fact that men and women grew up in relatively homogeneous sexual groups. Letters and diaries from this period detail the existence of sexually segregated worlds inhabited by human beings with different values, expectations, and personalities. Much of the emotional stiffness and distance usually associated with Victorian marriage may be seen as a consequence of the homosociability of nineteenth-century American society. With marriage, both women and men had to adjust to life with a person who was, in essence, a member of an alien group.[8]

The Springs, however, deviated from common cultural standards considerably, for their collected correspondence readily reveals the uniqueness of their marital bond. Over and over again Rebecca Spring's letters speak of her passionate attachment to "my precious one, my husband and dearest friend." "I feel it is a blessed privilege to have such a dear friend to love as you are," she wrote, "one whom I can so entirely respect, one so near my idea of human perfection." "Thou are the dearest and best friend I have in this world. You strew my path of life with roses. You take away the thorns. God was good to me when He gave me such a friend. May He make me worthy to be so blessed."[9]

Marcus Spring echoed these sentiments. Equally passionate, his letters reveal his distress when business affairs all too frequently took him away from home. Sensitively he wrote how he longed to have his wife "here on my lap with your arm around my neck, and we talking over all that interests us and reading through each other's eyes the happiness that would fill both our hearts."[10] Rebecca Spring frequently conducted business affairs during her husband's absence. Their letters reveal the mutuality of their intellectual interests as they commonly exchanged details of reading or shared private opinions and thoughts. Marcus Spring encouraged both of them to learn all they could during their separations so that "we may have the more to talk about when we meet."[11]

One consequence of Rebecca Spring's deeply companionate and egalitarian marriage was that she never appeared to have developed the kind of all-encompassing, same-sex friendship that historians have identified as central to the lives of many women in the male-dominated nineteenth century.[12] Despite a myriad of relationships with important figures of antebellum America, Rebecca Spring never had one such attachment. Marcus Spring participated in her friendships with a host of achieving nineteenth-century women whose correspondence was just as frequently addressed to him as to his wife.

Communitarian Interests

Rebecca Spring's relationship with her husband was as unique and pioneering for its time as the communitarian ventures that resulted from their shared political ideals. The pair are best known in New Jersey history as the chief stockholders of the North American Phalanx and the founders of the Raritan Bay Union.[13] Their interest in communitarianism stemmed from various sources. Rebecca Spring's concern for the condition of factory workers had been awakened during her girlhood in industrial Fall River. During the early years of her marriage, she thought of establishing a cooperative colony for people living in the New York City slums to foster appreciation of art, music, and the classics. Marcus Spring shared her concern to improve living standards for the urban poor. An 1845 European tour rekindled his interest in the establishment of a community where people could live in cleanliness and plenty within a spiritual environment. As a small step in this direction, he solicited subscriptions from merchant friends to fund a bathhouse in New York City. The Springs were personal friends with poet and editor William Cullen Bryant, whose son-in-law Parke Godwin was one of America's foremost communitarians. Readers of the *Dial*, they bought stock in the Brook Farm community in Massachusetts and even encouraged Rebecca Spring's younger brother, Edward Buffum, to find a place there. Communitarianism also had familial roots for Rebecca Spring's sister, Lydia Buffum, was a member of Adin Ballou's Hopedale community.

It was the Springs' friendship with editor and publisher Horace Greeley that proved decisive in sparking an attempt at communal living. Greeley had become enamoured of French socialist ideas through the influence of Albert Brisbane, the son of a well-to-do land speculator from Batavia, New York, who had himself become acquainted with socialist thought during a European study tour. Upon returning to the United States, Brisbane became a leading propagandist for communitarianism, conducting a vigorous recruitment campaign through lectures, periodicals, pamphlets, articles, and correspondence. By 1842 Greeley had begun to donate space in his *New York Tribune* for columns expressing Brisbane's views, and it was there that the Springs read Brisbane's utopian tract, *The Social Destiny of Man*. When Greeley solicited support for the funding of a communal experiment, they decided to take a chance.

In 1843 a joint-stock company organized by Brisbane, Greeley, and Marcus Spring purchased a 673-acre farm near Red Bank, New Jersey, thereby inaugurating one of the most successful communitarian experiments of the period. The North American Phalanx lasted twelve years, averaging an annual population of 150. Its chief industry was farming, at which it was highly successful. The products of the Phalanx mills—wheat, rye, buckwheat flour, mustard, cornmeal, and hominy—became widely known, especially in New York. The Phalanx is also credited with marketing the first boxed cereal sold in the United States. The colony started the practice of sending choice fruits and vegetables in attractively marked containers to New York City markets. Peaches, apples, pears, plums, nectarines, grapes, strawberries, and tomatoes were grown in such abundance that to service the expanding market, the Phalanx purchased a part interest in steamboats that ran from Red Bank and Keyport.

Despite these successes, however, discord over a variety of issues troubled the community. By 1853 factionalism had become so acute that a group of thirty families, clustered around the Springs, withdrew from the Phalanx to form their own community in nearby Perth Amboy. The 268-acre Raritan Bay Union, as it was called, aimed to give as much emphasis to the manufacturing and mechanical trades as to agriculture. A wharf was built on the Raritan River, and private houses, workshops, artists' studios, a laundry, bakery, restaurant, and community building with rental apartments were constructed. Farms and workshops were rented to individuals, whose produce and products were sold in New York City by an agency of the community. Although the Raritan Bay Union attained a greater cultural and literary prominence than the North American Phalanx, it was never as successful economically. Its fate was much less spectacular, surviving as a communal organization only until 1857.

Progressive Education

Even during its own lifetime, the Raritan Bay Union as an experiment in communal living came to be overshadowed by the progressive school that the Springs established on its premises. In common with other nineteenth-century experiments where there was a close affinity between educational and communal ideals, the Union's "central focus," according to Rebecca Spring, was education.[14] Christening their creation Eagleswood, the Springs brought to it a fascinating collection of teachers and scholars. Headed by its principal, Theodore Weld, Eagleswood hosted some of the most renowned radicals of the day in a famous series of Sunday evening lectures. Henry David Thoreau, Bronson Alcott, William Cullen Bryant, Horace Greeley, and Ralph Waldo Emerson visited and spoke there, along with Unitarians, Quakers, abolitionists, spiritualists, phrenologists, and advocates of women's rights, temperance, dress reform, and Hungarian freedom. All found an atmosphere of free inquiry and benevolence at the colony.[15]

Feminism also had a place at Eagleswood. A remarkable collection of women taught at the coeducational school: Sarah and Angelina Grimké, Elizabeth Palmer Peabody, Catharine Inness Ireland, and Mary Mann. With such women as role models, Eagleswood provided a supportive environment highly conducive to feminine achievement, offering students the opportunity to break the bonds of contemporary female stereotypes. Girls were encouraged to speak up at public gatherings, to act in plays, and to excel in athletics.[16] Despite the novelty that surrounded her, however, Rebecca Spring persisted in relatively traditional roles. She served as hostess at the Sunday evening colloquia and taught in the school, but she does not appear to have exercised any leadership role.

Abolition, not feminism, remained her primary concern. An 1852 trip to Cuba and South Carolina left her revolted at the conditions under which slaves lived and worked. An avid supporter of the new Republican Party, she established a station of the "underground railroad" at Eagleswood. Her most celebrated activity was a missionary visit to insurrectionist John Brown after his attack on the federal arsenal at Harpers Ferry, Virginia, in 1859. Comforting Brown in his last hours, she promised to bury the bodies of two of his raiders, Absolom C. Haslett and Aaron Dwight Stevens, in free soil. Despite heated local resistance, the burial was conducted at Eagleswood as promised.

During the Civil War, the Springs supported a school for the children of slaves and financed a soup kitchen to aid the increasing number of fugitives and refugees traveling north in the wake of the Emancipation Proclamation. To meet the needs of the nation, Eagleswood was converted into a military academy. Although Rebecca Spring had to reconcile her pacifism to the idea of training young boys for military duty, she believed the move was necessary to serve the cause of freedom. She personally supervised the strict codes of religious and moral discipline that were enforced at the school and played hostess to the continual flow of visitors. Fulfilling her lifelong cultural interests, she was instrumental in creating an art colony on the premises, which hosted such celebrated practitioners as William Page, George Inness, Louis Tiffany, and James Steele MacKaye.

By the late 1860s the Springs wearied of caring for the large estate, and the academy officially closed at the end of 1868. Rebecca Spring busied herself in these years with family and cultural pursuits. After her husband's death in 1874, she moved to California, where she lived until her own death in 1911. The experiments in New Jersey were never far from her thoughts, however. "Poor, dear Eagleswood," she lamented frequently during her last years, "that sacred spot. How we planted and built and spent money there! A noble company gathered to develop a society that would create harmony, love, and usefulness. Now I sit on the grave of great hopes . . . I look back to see a light that went out from it—small, but bright and pure and true. I believe some holy work is yet to be done through our Eagleswood."[17]

The Mixed Motives of Reform

According to Spring, she and her husband had been willing "to give everything," even their lives, for the sake of their utopian ideals.[18] Yet they were not the sort of people one would typically associate with utopian communal schemes. Wealthy, Yankee, white, Republican, Protestant, and self-indulgent, theirs was a life of breeding, gentility, and comfort. Surrounded by servants, they mingled with the New York literatii, spent evenings at the opera or fashionable *soirées*, dined at Delmonico's restaurant, and took extended trips abroad. Although reading popular moralists of the time frequently inspired Marcus Spring to act "more brotherly toward that unfortunate class whom we call servants,"[19] he and his wife could be baldly condescending to those they employed, complaining of "lazy and insolent attitudes," and slovenly personal habits, or remarking that a particular girl was "remarkably neat for Irish."[20] Nor was Marcus Spring exactly an altruistic or progressive employer. In a revealing letter, he informed his wife of one particularly fortuitous business arrangement: Buying up 150,000 pounds of damaged cotton that had been salvaged from a fire-gutted warehouse, he promptly hired 250 men, women, and children to pick it over and dry it out, paying them from a nickel to fifty cents for their labors. Most were of the "loafer sort," he assured her, "that would be begging or perchance stealing, if not doing this. It is rather a pleasant thing to reflect that we may be keeping a good many from mischief and cultivating habits of industry."[21]

With such attitudes, the Springs clearly reflected the views of the rising commercial plutocracy of the day. While sincerely committed to moral reform and regeneration, they were determined to remake society in their own class and culture-bound vision of what was, according to Rebecca Spring, "the way people ought to live."[22] Her motives in supporting communitarianism were philanthropic, entrepreneurial, and religious, not specifically socialistic. Although she called herself a socialist "because the Bible teaches socialism,"[23] her inspiration might more accurately be termed Christian socialism. Perhaps the greatest influence on her utopianism was William Henry Channing, one of the leading theologians of liberal Protestantism in New England. A personal friend of the Springs, he had organized the Religious Union of Associationists in Boston in 1846. Also named the Church of Humanity, it aimed to reconcile "the Christian Church to Social Reform."[24]

Spring's communitarian vision was also deeply rooted in her Quaker background. A key feature of her creed, in the words of its founder George Fox, was the conviction that men and women "could live in accordance with the injunction of the Sermon on the Mount, not in a future Kingdom of Heaven but here and now in this world of flesh and blood."[25] With their belief in the latency of the inner light in every human being, the Quaker commitment to perfectionism involved helping others to be perfect— not only by exhortation and spiritual consolation, but in more tangible forms as well.[26] The depth of Rebecca Spring's religious sentiment is evident in her personal papers. According to her, the Springs wanted to gather around them a "truly Christian neighborhood . . . a term that expressed in one word all virtues of Peace, Kindness, Temperance, and Holy Lives."[27] They hoped for a nonsectarian "loving community," based on the "only law of life in God's kingdom, . . . a better home for people, where people would learn better to live and love."[28] Because of the primacy of their religious motives, it was precisely the absence of sufficient religious spirit that prompted the Springs' displeasure with the North American Phalanx. They mistook the community's climate of religious tolerance and pluralism for irreligion, and their efforts to establish a fixed liturgy there was one of the main causes for its undoing.[29]

The rival colony they established, the Raritan Bay Union, advertised itself as a place where "all ties—Conjugal, Parental, Filial, Fraternal, and Communal sanctioned by the Christian Religion, would be strengthened and purified."[30] The Springs hoped to attract to their model community people who wished "to combine efficient work with refined conditions . . . who are longing for self-supporting industry with a choice of congenial companions, and who wish to unite domestic comfort and quiet with culture and cheerful society."[31] The Raritan Bay Union was really more of a planned community than a socialistic one. Its prospectus was as attractive, appealing, and non-ideological as that of any suburban real-estate development, advertising its bountiful amenities and healthful blend of country air with urban sophistication. "Sufficiently distant from the city to secure the many enjoyments and the healthful influences, moral and physical, of refined country life," the Raritan Bay Union boasted "a good school, combining the most complete appointments and arrangements for thorough education, physical as well as literary, scientific, artistic, social, and spiritual."[32]

Both the North American Phalanx and the Raritan Bay Union were designed to solve individual and family problems, and to provide models for the reform of the less than perfect society around them. Yet, although social consciousness was at the heart of the Springs' communitarianism, both were patently capitalistic ventures, in which, according to Marcus Spring, "all capitalists, clerks and all, should be mutually interested," giving "great satisfaction to all the parties concerned—architects, masters, workmen, and journeymen."[33] Unlike other contemporary socialists, the Springs preached not class conflict, but class harmony and reconciliation. Sharing the transcendentalist faith in the infinite worth of the individual and his ability to work out his own destiny, they retained a capitalist conviction of the dignity of labor. On this the Raritan Bay Union prospectus was clear: "Every man will be paid for what he does and no man will be paid for nothing."[34] With such sentiments, the Springs clearly branded themselves as part of an emerging commercial class of property-minded and respectable individuals who linked business success with personal virtue. Significantly, they looked to private efforts—to individual capitalists like themselves—to effect much-needed social change.

This repeated emphasis on the virtues of individualism also made them strange communitarians. Although they were the largest single shareholders, the Springs never moved to the North American Phalanx; Rebecca Spring was adamantly determined to remain in her newly constructed Brooklyn home. At the Raritan Bay Union, the Springs also preferred to live apart from the communal dwelling, settling in the mansion house of the former owner. Because of the Springs' conviction that private property was fundamental to civilized society, property was never held in common in either community.[35] Traditional marital practices, with their attendant traditional sex roles, also remained intact.[36]

Feminism in Perspective

Just as it is wrong to assume that socialism was at the root of the Springs' communitarianism, so too is it difficult to place feminism, at least as it is usually defined, at the heart of Rebecca Spring's activism. Spring was never a public worker in reform, in contrast to her sisters Elizabeth and Lillie, who held office in suffrage organizations and published essays and articles on their work, or to other Quaker women like the Grimkés, Lucretia Mott, and Abby Kelley who took to public platforms to espouse the cause of the slave. While the feminists of this period expended much energy arguing for dress reform and attacking the unhealthful fashions donned by the women of their day, Rebecca Spring never challenged the tight stays, bustles, or voluminous petticoats then in vogue. Always "richly dressed and luxuriously deposed,"[37] she condemned the bloomer costume that enjoyed a short-lived fascination among New Jersey communitarians. Anxious to rebut the popular attitude that the communities were "composed of long-haired men and short-skirted women,"[38] she facetiously told a friend that she had to wear her dresses long enough "to make up for others wearing theirs too short."[39] She was even more displeased to learn that her sisters Sarah and Elizabeth had tried the bloomer outfit for a while.

Nor did she ever accept contemporary feminist rhetoric tracing women's bondage to restrictive family roles. With Rebecca Spring, children and family always came first: she even cut short a European tour because of her sadness at leaving her young daughter behind in the United States. Totally devoted to her three children, she spent her days with them, reading them stories, playing with them, hearing their lessons. Her diary was filled with prayers and entreaties that "their goodness and truth be reflected also from me, that I too may be a blessing."[40] Although a few remarks in Spring's diary attest to her fatigue and frustration due to the constraints of child care, and to her difficulty in writing "with the dear boy ever hanging to me, pulling me and talking,"[41] never did her remarks approach the anger of contemporaries like Elizabeth Cady Stanton, who lambasted the "sacrifice" of women in the "isolated household,"[42] or the vehemence of Elizabeth Palmer Peabody, who longed "to quit the old diseased carcass which now goes by the name of civilization."[43] Although Stanton looked longingly to communal life as a path to women's radical emancipation from the isolated household,[44] Rebecca Spring's hopes for utopian living never took on this dimension. She resisted moving to the North American Phalanx altogether, and continued to live in privacy and luxury at the Raritan Bay Union.

From her papers, it is clear that her conventional femininity caused a rift in her friendship with Margaret Fuller. In an especially revealing letter, Fuller strongly challenged Spring's conviction that "it is still better to give the world [a] living soul, than a part of [one's] life in a book."[45] Although Spring had read Fuller's *Woman in the Nineteenth Century* "with the deepest feeling,"[46] she reserved her highest praise for the fact that the author much loved the Springs' young son Edward. There was a vast difference in temperament and ideals between Spring and her friend. Her personal papers reveal the strains between the two: The fact that Spring never quite approved of Fuller's actions, particularly her love affair and subsequent marriage to Count Giovanni Ossoli, her out-of-wedlock pregnancy, and her passion for the Italian Risorgimento.[47] When during their European tour Fuller made a literary pilgrimage to the home of George Sand, Spring refused to accompany her. Sand was a woman of whom she also did not approve.[48] Familiarity seemed to breed contempt, at least during their trip. Confidentially Spring wrote home to a friend that she was glad to leave Fuller behind in Italy, to see her go her own way.[49] The differences between the unlikely friends were not lost on contemporaries. An English clergyman named Goodwyn Barnaby who once met Spring at a dinner party in London recalled being "enraptured by her charms"; this in stark contrast to an unfortunate friend "who had to listen to Miss Fuller . . . [and] was talked to death." The poor man, said Barnaby, "would have preferred a quiet hand at whist."[50]

Contemporaries themselves seemed to recognize the tensions and ambivalence that marked Spring's career, and moved to correct false assumptions drawn from her achieving life. In 1922 an old family friend wrote to the editor of the *Perth Amboy Evening News* to correct the impression left by a previous article that Rebecca Spring had come to Perth Amboy "to found a free love colony." Indignantly he insisted that the Springs were a "perfectly respectable, devoted married couple, highly cultivated people . . . who came here to make a home."[51] Yet others of a more nontraditional persuasion also went away puzzled when they first met Rebecca Spring. John Brown's brother Frederick had expected "a sensible woman, who isn't too fine to do her housework, and doesn't wear dresses dragging in the dirt." Spring's more publicly active sister Elizabeth was quick to correct him, however, warning that he would find instead "a woman who never gets up to breakfast, seldom goes into her kitchen, and wears skirts trailing on the ground."[52]

Retrospect on a Career

Spring's contrasting blend of activism and traditionalism may be one reason why she has escaped the attention of historians. The letters that remain among her papers are disappointing, seldom yielding insights into her ideology or politics and containing few if any blatantly feminist overtones. Though her religious sentiment and abolitionist credo are obvious, her political ideals are markedly undeveloped. Her utopian vision is spelled out in simple terms. "What we dreamed of . . . is the way people ought to live."[53]

Rebecca Spring wrote her autobiography, entitled "Auld Acquaintance," at the age of eighty-nine. If it is true, as students of the genre contend, that the value of an autobiography is in its revelation of an individual's basic conception of self and personality,[54] then hers is especially significant, for it tells about the meaning of her life as she understood it. Understandably rambling and at times incoherent considering her age at the time, the tone is decidedly nonpolitical. "'Rich in friends' is a happy saying of the Swedes," she begins, "and I have been urged to write about the friends who have enriched my life."[55] The autobiography is nothing more than that, an account of the friends and acquaintances she had—another telling indication of her conventional femininity. In keeping with the standard model of the female personality structure as identified by psychologists,[56] Spring was a woman who consciously defined herself in terms of her relationship with other people.

Spring's career holds a valuable lesson for historians. Despite seeming contradictions, Rebecca Spring was a feminist, as she was anxious to have women shape and influence American society. Although she disavowed feminist rhetoric and methods, she believed women should play important social roles and not be isolated from the forces affecting American life. The goals she worked for were feminist ones, even though she may have differed from contemporaries like Stanton and Anthony in her conception of how female influence should be exerted. The apparent tensions and ambivalence at the heart of Spring's career mirrored the larger dilemma at the core of emergent nineteenth-century feminism: Whether women should assert female influence as a function of their differences from men or on the basis of their human equality. These two strands of feminism, what may be called the domestic and the public, competed for the allegiance of American women, and Rebecca Buffum Spring, like thousands of others in the nineteenth century, clearly chose the former course.

Rebecca Spring was a "lady" in the nineteenth-century sense of the term; she exemplified the ideal of femininity in antebellum America. Gentle, refined, cultured, sensitive, religious, moral, and loving, she personified what historians have termed the cult of true womanhood—the notion that women are moral and domestic creatures whose task is to create a heavenly and wholesome environment for their families, "a bright, serene, restful, joyful nook of heaven in an unheavenly world."[57] A corollary of the cult of true womanhood—that women's special moral gifts, already manifest in the home, could be made applicable to all society—runs throughout her biography. With morality and domesticity the vehicles for her activism, she was a living embodiment of the faith expressed by her friend William Henry Channing, that as "more and more . . . opportunity will be offered to women to train and use their gifts, . . . the world [will] find out what womanhood is. . . . The regeneration of the future will come from the exalting influence of woman."[58]

As a young woman, Spring chose to teach at a school for black infants because she was convinced she could "do more good in that way than in any other."[59] Her utopianism stemmed from a similar conviction that women could expand their influence from their own domestic circle, making their communities and their cities joyous, safe, and moral extensions of their families. Such moral communities rooted in strong family lives could undo the "sad consequences of neglected households." If neglected households spawned evil, strong ones could be powerful engines of social reform. "I believe," Spring once said, "that the tired man on his way home from work who knows that a good well-cooked supper is waiting for him in his home is less likely to stop at the grog shop than one who expects no such comfort."[60] The sentiment may have been simplistic, but it was a conviction shared by thousands of other nineteenth-century women who devoted their lives to the temperance crusade.

For all her adventurism, Spring's humanitarianism was rooted in a very traditional view of woman's role, with nurturance and sustenance at its heart. "I think that we are put into this world to do all the good we can and to help make it more beautiful," she once told a news reporter in Los Angeles. "You know that when you can, you should make two blades of grass grow where one grew before."[61] Like her contemporary Catharine Beecher, she believed women were uniquely qualified to heal social divisions and work as meliorative rather than destructive agents of social change.[62] For Rebecca Spring, this was the larger significance of her rescue mission to John Brown. She had never met Brown personally, nor did she fully approve of his actions.[63] Yet, in the words of her husband, she hoped that her journey would convince Americans that "nothing but love for whites and blacks, and the spirit of peace and human brotherhood" would set the country right on the slavery question.[64]

Spring's visit illustrated another central tenet of the cult of true womanhood: The belief that one of women's most important functions was to be comforter and nurse, one of their greatest privileges to be a "ministering spirit at the couch of the sick."[65] A commitment to this credo prompted Spring's visit. Accompanied only by her twenty-two-year-old son Edward, her suitcases packed with bandages and medical supplies, Rebecca Spring made the journey at considerable risk, considering the passions Brown's raid had aroused. Greeted by hostility and icy stares, she entered the jailhouse surrounded by a menacing mob, "by a sea of angry eyes and clenched and threatening hands." Yet she persevered, convinced that "when men fight and hurt each other, women should go and take care of them."[66] She drew sustenance from the realization that "Brown's last days [had been] made bright and cheerful by the presence of loving women." It was a sentiment Brown shared. "I think more of women than ever before," he told her, "since you and my sister have come to me this long distance, alone and unprotected."[67]

Spring's conviction of women's proper function deepened as she aged. Living alone in California, her husband dead and her fortune gone, she suffered numerous personal sorrows and disappointments. Yet as she wrote to an old friend, "to cheer and help others" remained "the best solace in sorrow" she ever found. "And there are always those who need such help."[68] In California, Spring became a charter member of the Friday Morning Club founded by her old friend Caroline Severance, and was later chosen honorary first vice-president of the National Federation of Women's Clubs. Work in the women's club movement suited Spring's temperament, for it too was consistent with the doctrine of domesticity. While clubs had diversified programs, their main focus was literary and cultural. Clubs sponsored musical performances, dramatic productions, poetry readings, and discussions of current events. With a membership composed of affluent, white, native-born women like herself, she found this atmosphere congenial, for the study of art and literature was not as radical as suffrage work. The proponents of the cult of true womanhood had long insisted that women had an inherent interest in culture: The arts could potentially uplift everyone, much like women were supposed to do. Clubs kept women like Spring intellectually alive, promoting culture, the study of art and literature, and an interest in contemporary events, while affording women opportunities for self-expression and self-improvement. For these reasons, scholars have found a feminist core in the club movement, despite its otherwise genteel and conservative connotations.[69]

The problem of characterizing Spring ideologically is similarly difficult. Although more flamboyant reformers have captured the most scholarly attention, this hardly makes for a thorough understanding of how feminine self-consciousness effected social change in nineteenth-century America. Sarah Hale, the influential editor of *Godey's Lady's Book*, one of the primary literary expressions of the cult of true womanhood, always commanded more adherents than Elizabeth Cady Stanton.[70] Scholars agree that Stanton's vituperation, her railing against the sexism of the Bible, for example, slowed the pace of suffrage advance and separated her from the mainstream of American womanhood.[71]

Spring's social consciousness, on the other hand, seems to have been more typical of feminist activism than the radicalism of her more celebrated contemporary. Like Spring, thousands of women in this period effectively transformed the cult of true womanhood, using cultural stereotypes of feminine virtue to exert special influence in education, temperance, abolition, prison reform, community service, and social work. By invoking their supposed natural talents, women used the ideology of the home to escape its confines, winning status and recognition in the public sphere of men.

As a reformer deeply interested in the central ideas of the nineteenth century, Rebecca Spring's career illustrates the rich diversity of activities characteristic of nineteenth-century American feminism. Her feminism was of a subtle, not strident, variety, an outgrowth of her humane interests in education, religion, and culture. In this way, her experience parallels that of many other women of the period, for each of these concerns was key to the flowering of feminism in nineteenth-century America.

Notes

Research for this article was supported by a grant from the New Jersey Historical Commission, whose generous assistance I gratefully acknowledge. I would also like to thank Carl Lane, formerly of the New Jersey Historical Society, for his assistance with sources, and my former student Michele Barbetta, whose internship at the Society first alerted me to the Springs and their work.

1. The Women's Project of New Jersey, Inc., *Out of the Garden: Lives of New Jersey Women*, forthcoming [published as Joan Burstyn, ed., *Past and Promise: Lives of New Jersey Women* (Metuchen, N.J., 1990)].

2. See Arthur Bestor, "American Phalanxes" (Ph.D. diss., Harvard University, 1938), and *Backwoods Utopias* (Philadelphia, 1950); Mark Holloway, *Heavens On Earth* (New York, 1960); John Humphrey Noyes, *Strange Cults and Utopias of 19th Century America* (1870; reprint, New York, 1966); Alice Felt Tyler, *Freedom's Ferment* (Minneapolis, 1944), pt.2; and Michael Fellman, *The Unbounded Frame: Freedom and Community in Nineteenth-Century Utopianism* (New York, 1973).

3. Lillie Buffum Chace Wyman and Arthur Crawford Wyman, *Elizabeth Buffum Chace, 1806–1899: Her Life and Its Environment* (Boston, 1914), 1:47.

4. On the burning of the Pennsylvania Hall of Liberty, see Thomas E. Drake, *Quakers and Slavery in America* (Gloucester, Mass., 1965), 155–157.

5. This portrait of the Springs' relationship is drawn from their papers in the Raritan Bay Union Collection, MG 285, New Jersey Historical Society (hereafter, RBU-NJHS).

6. See Carroll Smith-Rosenberg, "The Female World of Love and Ritual," in *A Heritage of Her Own: Toward a New Social History of American Women*, ed. Nancy F. Cott and Elizabeth H. Pleck (New York, 1979), 311–42.

7. Lee Virginia Chambers-Schiller, *Liberty, A Better Husband: Single Women in America: The Generations of 1780–1840* (New Haven, 1984), 47–66.

8. Smith-Rosenberg, "Female World of Love and Ritual," 316–318; Lillian Faderman, *Surpassing the Love of Men: Romantic Friendship and Love between Women from the Renaissance to the Present* (New York, 1981), 180.

9. Rebecca Spring (hereafter, RS) to Marcus Spring (hereafter, MS), October 22, 1838, May 3, 1840, July 6, 1844, and June 24, 1846; and RS to J.L. Kearney (hereafter, JLK), November 12, 1902, RBU-NJHS.

10. MS to RS, May 17, 1840, RBU-NJHS.

11. Ibid.

12. See Faderman, *Surpassing the Love of Men*; Smith-Rosenberg, "Female World of Love and Ritual"; William Taylor and Christopher Lasch, "Two Kindred Spirits: Sorority and Family in New England, 1839–1846," *New England Quarterly* 36 (March 1963): 23–41; and Martha Vicinus, *Independent Women: Work and Community for Single Women, 1850–1920* (Chicago, 1985).

13. Unless otherwise noted, this discussion of the North American Phalanx and the Raritan Bay Union, is based on: Herman J. Belz, "The North American Phalanx: Experiment in Socialism," *Proceedings of the New Jersey Historical*

Society 81 (October 1963): 215–46; Julia Bucklin Giles, "The North American Phalanx," paper delivered to the Monmouth County Historical Association, November 18, 1922, North American Phalanx file, Monmouth County Historical Association Library, Freehold, New Jersey; Maud Honeyman Greene, "Raritan Bay Union, Eagleswood, New Jersey," *Proceedings of the New Jersey Historical Society* 68 (January 1950): 1–20; George Kirchmann, "Why Did They Stay? Communal Life at the North American Phalanx," in *Planned and Utopian Experiments: Four New Jersey Towns*, ed. Paul A. Stellhorn (Trenton, N.J., 1980), 10–27, and "Unsettled Utopias: The North American Phalanx and the Raritan Bay Union," *New Jersey History* 97 (Spring 1979): 25–36; Eric R. Schirber, "The North American Phalanx" (M.A. thesis, Trinity College, 1972); Charles Sears, *The North American Phalanx, an Historical and Descriptive Sketch* (Prescott, Wis., 1886); Jayme A. Sokolow, "Culture and Utopia: The Raritan Bay Union," *New Jersey History* 94 (Summer–Autumn 1976): 89–100; Norma Lippincott Swan, "The North American Phalanx," Monmouth County Historical Association *Bulletin* 1(May 1935): 35–65; Harold F. Wilson, "The North American Phalanx: An Experiment in Communal Living," *Proceedings of the New Jersey Historical Society* 70 (July 1952): 188–209; and Kalikst Wolski, "A Visit to the North American Phalanx," ibid. 83 (July 1965): 149–60.

14. RS, "Auld Acquaintance," unpublished autobiography, 1900, 106, in Rebecca Spring Papers, Henry E. Huntington Library, San Marino, California (hereafter, RBS-HHL); RS to JLK, August 9, 1885, RBU-NJHS.

15. Robert H. Abzug, *Passionate Liberator: Theodore Dwight Weld and the Dilemma of Reform* (New York, 1980), 259–74; Gerda Lerner, *The Grimké Sisters from South Carolina* (Boston, 1967), 329–38; and Benjamin P. Thomas, *Theodore Weld: Crusader for Freedom* (New Brunswick, N.J., 1950), 225–35.

16. On the feminist atmosphere of Eagleswood, see Joan Burstyn, "Education and the Changing Perception of Women's Roles," unpublished paper delivered at the First Symposium Celebrating Women's Spheres: Three Centuries of Women in Middlesex County and New Jersey, October 1983; Moncure Daniel Conway, *Autobiography: Memories and Experiences* (Boston, 1904), 1:332; and Sara (Read) Lovell, "Recollections of My Youth," manuscript, RBU-NJHS.

17. RS to JLK, August 9, 1885, and October 25, 1897, RBU-NJHS.

18. RS to JLK, August 1907, RBU-NJHS.

19. MS to RS, May 20, 22, 1838, RBU-NJHS.

20. See, for example, RS to MS, May 3, 1840, and RS, Diary Fragments, February 26, 1844, RBU-NJHS.

21. MS to RS, July 11, 1840, RBU-NJHS.

22. RS quoted in Lillie Buffum Chace Wyman, *American Chivalry* (Boston, 1913), 58.

23. RS in *Los Angeles Record*, 1905, newspaper clippings, RBU-NJHS.

24. For Channing's influence on Spring, see RS to JLK, August 9, 1885, RBU-NJHS.

25. William L. Hedges, "John Woolman and the Quaker Utopian Vision," in *Utopias: The American Experience*, ed. Gairdner B. Moment and Otto F. Kraushaar (Metuchen, N.J., 1980), 97.

26. Ibid.

27. RS to JLK, August 9, 1885, RBU-NJHS.

28. RS to MS, December 13, 1852, RBU-NJHS.

29. Noyes, *Strange Cults*, 487, 491; Sears, *North American Phalanx*, 12–14.

30. Provisional Prospectus of the Raritan Bay Union," RBU-NJHS.

31. Ibid.

32. Ibid.

33. MS to Margaret Fuller (hereafter, MF), April 17, 1850, RBU-NJHS.

34. Noyes, *Strange Cults*, 488–89.

35. RS to JLK, August 9, 1885, RBU-NJHS.

36. Dorothy W. Hartman, "Women in Utopia: Ideology and Reality at the North American Phalanx," *Women's Spheres Symposia: Selected Papers* (New Brunswick, N.J., 1985), 33–40.

37. Wyman, *American Chivalry*, 51.

38. Swan, "North American Phalanx," 35.

39. RS to JLK, August 1907, RBU-NJHS.

40. RS, Diary Fragments, March 13, 1844, RBU-NJHS.

41. RS to MS, May 3, 1840; RS, Diary Fragments, February 23, 1865, RBU-NJHS.

42. Elizabeth Cady Stanton to Paulina Davis, December 6, 1852, RBU-NJHS.

43. Swan, "North American Phalanx," 46. A standard biography of Stanton is Lois Banner, *Elizabeth Cady Stanton: A Radical for Woman's Rights* (New York, 1980).

44. Elizabeth Cady Stanton to Paulina Davis, December 6, 1852, RBU-NJHS.

45. RS, "Auld Acquaintance," 87.

46. RS, Diary Fragments, February 26, 1844, RBU-NJHS.

47. See MF to RS and MS, December 12, 1849, and February 5, 1850; RS to MF, April 14, 1850; MS to MF, April 17, 1850; and MS to Ralph Waldo Emerson, March 1850, RBU-NJHS.

48. RS, Random Notes to "Auld Acquaintance," RBU-HHL.

49. RS to "Meggie," May 7, 1847, RBU-NJHS.

50. Wyman, *American Chivalry*, 55.

51. Emily King Paterson, *Perth Amboy Evening News*, April 28, 1922.

52. Elizabeth Buffum quoted in Wyman, *Elizabeth Buffum Chace*, 1:207.

53. RS quoted in Wyman, *American Chivalry*, 58.

54. Katharine T. Corbett, "Louisa Catherine Adams: The Anguished 'Adventures of a Nobody,'" in *Woman's Being, Woman's Place: Female Identity and Vocation in American History*, ed. Mary Kelley (Boston, 1979), 69.

55. RS, "Auld Acquaintance," 2.

56. Judith M. Bardwick, *Psychology of Women* (New York, 1971), 157–58.

57. On the cult of true womanhood, see Gerda Lerner, "The Lady and the Mill Girl," in Cott and Pleck, *A Heritage of Her Own*, 182–96; Barbara Welter, "The Cult of True Womanhood," in *The American Family in Social-Historical*

Perspective, ed. Michael Gordon (New York, 1973), 224–50, and "The Feminization of American Religion: 1800–1860," in *Clio's Consciousness Raised: New Perspectives on the History of Women*, ed. Mary Hartman and Lois W. Banner (New York, 1974), 137–57.

58. Channing quoted in Welter, "Feminization," 146.

59. RS quoted in Wyman, *Elizabeth Buffum Chace*, 1:46.

60. RS to JLK, August 31, 1903, RBU-NJHS. For the temperance movement, see Ian R. Tyrrell, *Sobering Up: From Temperance to Prohibition in Antebellum America* (New York, 1979).

61. "Literary Productions and Research Notes of Beatrice Borchardt," RBU-NJHS.

62. On Beecher, see Kathryn Kish Sklar, *Catharine Beecher: A Study in American Domesticity* (New York, 1973).

63. RS, Autobiographical Fragments, RBU-NJHS.

64. MS to RS, November 7, 1858, RBU-NJHS.

65. Welter, "Cult of True Womanhood," 203.

66. See RS, "In An Angry City to Visit Brown," *New York Post*, October 30, 1909; also RS to Elizabeth Palmer Peabody, July 5, 1860, RBU-NJHS.

67. RS, Random Notes on Brown Visit, RBU-NJHS.

68. RS to JLK, November 14, 1906, RBU-NJHS.

69. See Karen J. Blair, *The Clubwoman As Feminist: True Womanhood Redefined, 1868–1914* (New York, 1980).

70. Ann Douglas, *The Feminization of American Culture* (New York, 1977), 45.

71. See, for example, Aileen S. Kraditor, *The Ideas of the Woman Suffrage Movement, 1890–1920* (Garden City, N.Y., 1965), 64–75.

An Act

For the Gradual Abolition of Slavery.

—

Sec. 1. **B**E *it enacted by the Council and General Assembly of this State, and it is hereby enacted by the authority of the same,* That every child born of a slave within this state, after the fourth day of July next, shall be free ; but shall remain the servant of the owner of his or her mother, and the executors, administrators or assigns of such owner, in the same manner as if such child had been bound to service by the trustees or overseers of the poor, and shall continue in such service, if a male, until the age of twenty-five years, and if a female until the age of twenty-one years.

2. *And be it enacted,* That every person being an inhabitant of this state, who shall be entitled to the service of a child born as aforesaid, after the said fourth day of July next, shall within nine months after the birth of such child, cause to be delivered to the clerk of the county whereof such person shall be an inhabitant, a certificate in writing, containing the name and addition of such person, and the name, age, and sex of the child so born ; which certificate, whether the same be delivered before or after the said nine months, shall be by the said clerk recorded in a book to be by him provided for that purpose ; and such record thereof shall be good evidence of the age of such child ; and the clerk of such county shall receive from said person twelve cents for every child so registered : and if any person shall neglect to deliver such certificate to the said clerk within said nine months, such person shall forfeit and pay for every such offence, five dollars, and the further sum of one dollar for every month such person shall neglect to deliver the same, to be sued for and recovered by any person who will sue for the same, the one half to the use of such prosecutor, and the residue to the use of the poor of the township in which such delinquent shall reside.

3. *And be it enacted,* That the person entitled to the service of any child born as aforesaid, may, nevertheless within one year after the birth of such child, elect to abandon such right ; in which case a notification of such abandonment, under the hand of such person, shall be filed with the clerk of the township, or where there may be a county poor-house established, then with the clerk of the board of trustees of said poor-house of the county in which such person shall reside ; but every child so abandoned shall be maintained by such person until such child arrives to the age of one year, and thereafter shall be considered as a pauper of such township or county, and liable to be bound out by the trustees or overseers of the poor in the same manner as other poor children are directed to be bound out, until, if a male, the age of twenty-five, and if a female, the age of twenty-one ; and such child, while such pauper, until it shall be bound out, shall be maintained by the trustees or overseers of the poor of such county or township, as the case may be, at the expence of this state ; and for that purpose the director of the board of chosen freeholders of the county is hereby required, from time to time, to draw his warrant on the treasurer in favor of such trustees or overseers for the amount of such expence, not exceeding the rate of three dollars per month ; provided the accounts for the same be first certified and approved by such board of trustees, or the town committee of such township ; and every person who shall omit to notify such abandonment as aforesaid, shall be considered as having elected to retain the service of such child, and be liable for its maintenance until the period to which its servitude is limited as aforesaid.

A. Passed at Trenton, Feb. 15, 1804.

———◆———

Many New Jerseyans objected to gradual manumission on the grounds that it would impede farming in areas where white labor was then scarce. The bill, which nonetheless became law in 1804, was worded in such a way that slavery continued to exist in the state until the passage of the Thirteenth Amendment. In Acts of the Twenty-Eighth General Assembly of the State of New Jersey *(Trenton, 1804). Photograph courtesy New Jersey Historical Society.*

7

One of the central contradictions in American history has been between the statement in the Declaration of Independence that "all men are created equal" and the existence of slavery. The British were quick to point this inconsistency out, and the Revolutionary generation itself wrestled with the problem. One result was an expansion of what equality meant, at least in part through the abolition movement, which supported the emancipation of and equal rights for African-American people. Because there were fewer slaves in the North (where farms were smaller and crops more diversified) and because particular religious groups (the Quakers in West Jersey, for example) supported abolition from theological arguments, the institution was abolished above the Mason-Dixon Line by 1804. Or was it? The following article proves that slavery actually persisted in New Jersey until 1866.

This surprising fact raises a number of questions. Historians have traced the development of two separate societies in America after 1800. The North increasingly became capitalistic and thus turned to commerce and manufacturing; the South remained largely agrarian, moving from the cultivation of tobacco and wheat to an obsession with cotton. At the same time slavery became the South's "peculiar institution"—and another element that distinguished the two sections. What happens to this traditional view once the existence of northern slavery is acknowledged? Are the two sections of the country all that different?

The same question can be asked when we look at what happened to those slaves who were freed in the North. How were they treated? What did it mean to be a freedman? How far was the idea of equality taken in practice in nineteenth-century America, North and South? If Americans have not been color-blind in either section, can northerners condemn southerners for their actions? Because some northern industries—for example, cotton textiles—were dependent on staples slaves cultivated and harvested, did the North not also profit from slavery? Does this place the later Reconstruction efforts and the civil rights movement in a different perspective?

Why was New Jersey the last northern state to move toward abolition? What made New Jersey different? Were there more slaves in New Jersey than elsewhere, and, if so, did economic interest play a role? If not, the essay by Gregory Dowd suggested another possible explanation—the state's experiences in the American Revolution. In much of New Jersey that conflict was a bitter civil war, particularly in areas where slavery was prominent. The British appealed to slaves to run away and fight with the loyalists. Did these two facts, working together, leave a legacy of fear of African Americans greater than that in other northern states?

Proponents of ending slavery argued that there were several ways that the institution could be ended in the United States and elsewhere in the world. One was to compensate owners, to lessen their resistance and the financial impact of losing their property; after all, they had paid for their slaves in the first place, and one of the fundamental principles of American law is that private property cannot be taken without compensation. Yet it was argued that compensation would deplete the national pocketbook.

A second proposal was immediate confiscation. To many Americans, slavery was wrong not only because it contradicted the idea of equality upon which their country was founded, not only because it destroyed families (the foundation of civilized society), but also because it was *sinful*. It violated fundamental religious teachings about how people should treat one another. It was based on the use of force rather than on "brotherly love." The two approaches, compensation and immediate abolition, appealed to two conflicting components of American ideology, protection of property and support of equality.

New Jersey ultimately opted to abolish slavery but to do so gradually. The children of slaves would be freed after they came of age, after they had compensated their owners for the expense of having purchased them through their own work and when they were old enough to support themselves and not be a public burden. This solution was a compromise, an effort to get around the American dilemma: it reflected New Jersey's conservatism and its traditional respect for property. This latter fact helps explain why a gradual method was used to abolish slavery in New Jersey, rather than the more direct measures used in some other states. However, some African Americans argued that the *slaves* should have been compensated for being treated as property to begin with and that gradual manumission unnecessarily prolonged the institution of slavery.

There is another broad issue raised by this article, a reflection of the time in which it was written. The author used the term "Negro" and published his article in the *Journal of Negro History*. Like other words, the meanings and connotations of the term have changed over time; in the seventeenth century "democratic" was sometimes a pejorative term, the equivalent of calling someone a "communist" during the Cold War. Forty years ago "Negro" was acceptable; earlier, the term "colored" had been, as the title of the National Association for the Advancement of Colored People, founded in 1910, makes clear. But terms suggested today in place of "Negro"—"Black," "black," or "African American"—are also problematic. Many argue that to use "black" instead of African American focuses inappropriately on race rather than ethnicity; European immigrants are called Irish American, Italian American, or German American according to their country of origin. But not all persons of African descent have come directly from Africa, such as Jamaicans, and not all Africans are black. Different generations of African Americans disagree on the use of these terms. Which term do you think is most appropriate, and why?

Suggested Readings

Gardner, D. H. "The Emancipation of Slaves in New Jersey." *Proc. NJHS* 9 (1924): 1–24.

Litwack, Leon F. *North of Slavery: The Negro in the Free States, 1790–1860.* Chicago, 1961.

McManus, Edgar J. *Black Bondage in the North.* Syracuse, N.Y., 1973.

Price, Clement A. *Freedom Not Far Distant: A Documentary History of Afro-Americans in New Jersey.* Newark, N.J., 1980.

Williams, Robert J. "Blacks, Colonization, and Antislavery: The Views of Methodists in New Jersey, 1816–60." *NJH* 104 (1984): 51–67.

Wright, Giles R. *Afro-Americans in New Jersey: A Short History.* Trenton, N.J., 1989.

Wright, Marion M. Thompson. "New Jersey Laws and the Negro." *Journal of Negro History* 28 (1943): 156–99.

Zilversmit, Arthur. *The First Emancipation: The Abolition of Slavery in the North.* Chicago, 1967.

_____ . "Liberty and Property: New Jersey and the Abolition of Slavery." *NJH* 88 (1970): 215–26.

◆ ◆ ◆ ◆ ◆ ◆

The Persistence of Slavery and Involuntary Servitude in a Free State (1685–1866)

Simeon F. Moss

It is a common assumption that slavery was abolished at an early period in the northern states. Few persons realize how long slavery persisted in New Jersey. In fact, slavery in New Jersey was not completely abolished until the adoption of the Thirteenth Amendment in 1866. It is the purpose of this paper to show the persistence of slavery and other forms of involuntary servitude in New Jersey down to the Civil War. Emphasis has been placed on population statistics throughout, giving the relationship of slave population to total population.[1] The free Negro is considered as a product of manumission, and the rise of equalitarian sentiments in the revolutionary generation. How the growth of a large free population affected the general attitudes toward the free Negro, is another major consideration of this study.

Negro Slavery in the Proprietary Period

Negro slavery early took root in the Proprietary Colony of New Jersey. Slaves were probably brought in by the first English settlers, although the earliest allusion to slavery is made in the Concessions and Agreements of the Proprietor, in which slaves are mentioned as a basis for the allotment of land to settlers.[2] Negro slaves are not mentioned specifically as such, but there is sufficient evidence to substantiate the fact that, prior to 1675, slavery was an accepted institution in the Colony. An act was passed during this year forbidding individuals from harboring, transporting, or entertaining apprentices, servants, or slaves.[3] By 1680, Colonel Lewis Morris of Shrewsbury had over sixty Negro slaves employed in his iron works and about his plantation. This was one-half of the total number of slaves in the Colony.[4] Within

The Journal of Negro History 35 (1950): 289-310. Reprinted by permission of *The Journal of Negro History*.

ten years the diffusion of slave ownership must have been rapid in northern New Jersey, for by 1690 nearly all of the inhabitants of this area owned slaves.[5]

Laws concerning the Negro slave also attest to the fact that the slave population of the Colony was rapidly increasing. After the act of 1682, which required owners of Negro slaves in East Jersey to give their chattel sufficient victuals and clothing, bills were passed with increasing regularity. Most of the bills were intended to strengthen the power of the master over his slave. Since during this period, the Colony was separated into two provinces, East and West Jersey, it is significant to note that a majority of the laws with reference to slavery were enacted in East Jersey where the slave population was most numerous.[6] The rise of anti-slavery sentiment in the areas of Quaker predominance, explains the comparative sparsity of slaves in West Jersey.

Throughout the Proprietary and Royal period, Perth Amboy served as the chief port of entry for slaves into East Jersey.[7] Coopers Ferry (now Camden), opposite Philadelphia, was the entrepôt for slaves into West Jersey. Negroes were brought from Africa to the West Indies where they were seasoned, that is, acclimated to the more temperate regions, instructed in the rudiments of the English language, and shipped to the American Colonies.[8] On their arrival at the port the slaves, usually chained in groups of two, were led into a large barracks where they were kept until auctioned. Slaves were usually imported in small numbers, consequently they created no problem at the ports of entry.[9] Here they were sold soon after their arrival.

The chief reason for the importation of slaves under the Proprietors was to increase the working force of the Colony.[10] Most of the slaves were used as agricultural workers and domestic servants. This was especially true in the Raritan and Minisink Valleys.[11] These areas were populated by persons of German and Dutch extraction, who had no objection to the use of slave labor. In fact, the large plantations possessed by the Dutch and German tenants made them particularly receptive to slave labor.[12] While the settlers of the eastern portion of the Colony were interested in slavery, as early as 1680 those of the Western part had come under the influence of the Quakers of Pennsylvania, and they remained rather indifferent to the institution.[13] In 1696 the Quakers of New Jersey united with their brethren from Pennsylvania to recommend to the members of their own sect to refrain from the importation of slaves, or the employment of them.[14]

Negro Slavery under Royal Control

By 1702, when the Proprietary Colony of New Jersey reverted to Royal control, the slave population was rapidly increasing, although some expressions of anti-slavery attitudes were to be found. Pre-revolutionary agitation set the stage for manumission and gradual emancipation. Forecasts of what were to come after the Revolution are frequently signaled throughout the Colonial Period.

From its beginning, slavery in New Jersey had been actively encouraged by the crown. Queen Anne in her instructions to Lord Cornbury in 1702, urged him to take all measures to encourage the importation of slaves, "so that the colony might have a constant and sufficient supply of merchantable Negroes at moderate rates," supplied by the Royal Africa Company.[15] The earliest record of Negroes imported into New Jersey are those of the Customs House of Perth Amboy in 1726. There were no Negroes imported from 1698 to 1717 inclusive. From 1718 until 1726, a total of 115 slaves arrived at the port of Perth Amboy. All of the slaves came from the West Indies. The largest cargo of fifty came from Barbados and St. Martins on the *Sloop George* in 1721. The collector of the port certified that no Negroes had been imported from Africa or Madagascar during this period.[16]

Four census records of Colonial New Jersey are available for comparison. Allowing for their inaccuracies, for which Greene and Harrington have compensated, they give an excellent index of the relationship of the slave population to the total population, throughout the period. The censuses are those of 1726, 1738, 1745, and 1772.[17] The percentage of the total population which the slave constituted remained fairly constant throughout the period. In 1726 the percentage of slave population to total population was 8%. In 1738 it still stood at 8%. By 1745 it had decreased slightly to 7.7%. The percentage of slave population then began to rise, and it had again reached 8% by the first official census. Certain counties consistently led in high percentage of slave population to total population. Bergen County's slave population not only exceeded that of any other county in actual numbers throughout the Colonial Period, but also in the percentage of slave population to total population. Somerset, Middlesex, and Monmouth Counties were also leaders in the number of slave inhabitants, as well as in the percentage of slaves to total population. The analysis shows that those Counties which comprised East Jersey under the Proprietors, exceeded those of

West Jersey in slave population and in percentage of slave population to total population. Probably the most interesting conclusion to be drawn from this analysis is the fact that the percentage of slave population to total population remained fairly stable throughout the Colonial Period.[18]

To control the slave trade, the legislature of New Jersey early took measures to place prohibitive duties on slaves. Later acts of the legislature veered toward total prohibition of the slave trade. Legislative attempts to regulate the importation of slaves began with the Act of 1714. This bill, introduced into the Assembly in the session of 1713–1714, laid a duty of £10 on Negro, Indian, and Mulatto slaves.[19] The Royal Governor of the Colony in a letter to the Board of Trade justified the Act as one, "calculated to encourage the importation of white servants for the better peopling of the country." He referred to a law of Pennsylvania, which had had a similar effect.[20] This act expired in 1721. Attempts to renew it precipitated a conflict between the Assembly and the Council which was to go on for almost half a century. The British Government through its spokesmen in the colonies, consistently encouraged the slave trade because it was a Royal Monopoly and lucrative source of revenue to the crown. On the other hand, the members of the Colonial legislature, realizing that the further importation of slaves would be economically detrimental to the Colony, staunchly opposed any action that would force an unwelcome and unwanted source of population on them.

The bills passed in 1739 and 1744 looked toward the entire prohibition of the importation of slaves from abroad.[21] In 1739, the Assembly rejected such a bill, while in 1744 another was vetoed by the Governor. Commenting on the bill of 1744, the Governor wrote the following letter to the Board of Trade.

> This bill the Council considered abstractedly [*sic*] from any instructions your majesty has in relation to the African Company, which many of the gentlemen of the Assembly we suppose are not acquainted with, and only weighed the advantages and disadvantages that would arise to the people of the colonies upon that bill's passing into law. By that bill was plainly intended an entire prohibition of all slaves being imported from foreign parts, no less than a duty of £10 being imposed on all grown slaves imported from the West Indies, and £5 on all those imported directly from Africa.

At this time the Royal Governor believed that even the mere

discouraging of importation was undesirable. He further maintained that the Colony had a great need for laborers, because many of the former inhabitants of New Jersey had left for the West Indies, and farmers and trading men found it difficult to carry on their occupations.[22]

Once more the question of a duty on slaves came up for legislative discussion. This time in 1761.[23] Because slaves could be imported into New Jersey duty free, great numbers had been landed there to escape the duties imposed in New York and Pennsylvania. To prohibit the use of New Jersey as a dumping place for slaves which were to be eventually smuggled into one of the Colonies on either side of it, the inhabitants of New Jersey petitioned for a law to place a duty on slaves high enough to discourage this procedure. Governor Hardy disapproved of the bill, and sent this message to the General Assembly.

> By the twenty-sixth article of his majesty's instructions I am forbid to give my assent to any act imposing duties on Negroes imported into this province payable by the importer or upon any slaves exported that have not been sold in this province and continue there for the space of twelve months. I have sent you this notice to avoid giving unnecessary trouble to the house.[24]

Later, Hardy wrote a letter to the Lords of Trade informing them of his action in suspending the bill of 1761 until he could get the king's assent. He explained that the reason for laying a higher duty in the Western division of the state than in the eastern part, was because the Province of Pennsylvania had a higher duty, £10, on slaves than did New York, where the duty was only £2.[25]

Governor Hardy's appeal to the Lords of Trade had its desired effect, and the Assembly secured permission for the levying of a different scale of duties in the two sections of New Jersey. An Act of 1769, primarily intended as a revenue act, was the last passed previous to the Revolution which had a direct effect on the numerical growth of the slave population of the state. One of its clauses did much to retard manumissions. It repealed that section of the Act of 1713 which gave liberal terms of manumission, and placed the burden of the support of the indigent freedman directly on the slaveholder who had manumitted him.[26] Some slaveholders, unable to shoulder this monetary burden, had to forego manumitting their slaves.

Reviewing these attempts of the Colonial legislature to curtail the slave trade, one sees that the Colonists after 1714, wanted to restrict slave importation, but that the crown, through its royal governors, did everything it could to maintain the slave trade unimpeded.

Two lines of anti-slavery agitation developed soon after the first legislative act was passed to regulate the importation of slaves. One approach was economic, which will be discussed in a later section, the other was humanitarian. Most of the early attacks made on slavery were launched by the Friends, who had objected to slavery from a humanitarian standpoint for many years prior to 1702. This sect continued its anti-slavery agitation until the middle of the nineteenth century. In 1729 the Friends became the first group to censure the importation of slaves. Thirteen years previous to this, in 1716, they had gone on record with a left-handed disavowal of slavery. The minutes of the meeting clearly express their views. "It is desired that Friends generally do as much as may be to avoid buying such Negroes as shall hereafter be brought in, rather than offend any Friends who are against it . . . yet this is only caution, not censure."[27]

Outstanding among the anti-slavery crusaders during the quarter century before the Revolution was John Woolman of Mount Holly. In his extensive travels throughout the Colonies, he gained first hand knowledge of the plight of the slave. In 1743, he began his long and persistent opposition to slavery. Through his efforts, anti-slavery feeling in the Colony was brought to the attention of the legislature, where it resulted in Acts restricting the slave trade. Believing that human bondage was incompatible with the Christian religion, Woolman urged the members of the Society of Friends to work against the purchasing and keeping of slaves. Although Woolman desired that all slaves should be manumitted at the earliest possible moment, he realized that the mode of living and the annual expenses of some of the slaveholding Friends made it impractical for them to set their slaves free without changing their whole way of life. To these, he recommended more humane treatment of their slaves.[28]

The American Revolution and Slavery in New Jersey

The spirit of independence contributed no inconsiderable part of the decline of slavery in New Jersey. While the gradual abolition of slavery was not effected until the Post-Revolutionary period, immediately prior to the Revolution anti-slavery sentiment seems to have swept the state. Petitions to the legislature from the citizens of Burlington, Cumberland, Middlesex, Monmouth, and Hunterdon Counties were presented to the legislature in 1773, "setting forth the evils arising from human slavery."[29] In October, 1774, the Colonists, then united in opposition to British Colonial policy, turned their thoughts to the unfortunate slaves among them. They signed an agreement that they would purchase no slaves imported after the first of December, "after which we will neither be concerned in it ourselves nor sell our commodities or manufactures to those who are concerned with it."[30] On the eve of the Revolution six Counties—Salem, Cumberland, Burlington, Monmouth, Middlesex, and Essex—petitioned the legislature to restrict slavery.[31]

During the period of the Revolution, the struggle for self-preservation overshadowed all attempts to abolish or restrict slavery. Many feared that a loosening of curbs on the slave population while the war was in progress, might encourage them to desert their masters and espouse the Loyalist cause. But others felt differently. They asserted that ameliorating the lot of the slave might make him a steadfast friend of freedom. In 1778 Governor Livingston urged the General Assembly to make provision for the manumission of slaves, but was persuaded to withdraw his proposal on the grounds that times were too critical to permit a consideration of the question. Livingston personally abhorred slavery, and he set his slaves free during the war. He was convinced that the practice of holding slaves was utterly inconsistent with the principles of Christianity and humanity. Slave-holding by those, "who almost idolized liberty," he believed to be particularly odious and disgraceful.[32]

The Manumission Movement

Manumissions began early in the eighteenth century. The first recorded act of manumission is to be found in the will of Rabakah Stacy of Burlington County, who gave her "nager woman" Jane, her freedom and twenty shillings yearly for life. This will was recorded in 1711.[33] An analysis of the Abstracts of Wills for the entire Colonial period reveal that numerous manumissions were effected despite the fact that the master was required by law to give security for slaves set at liberty. It was also a frequent practice to defer manumission through the process of indentured servitude. Where this was done, the will usually stipulated the number of years a slave would have to serve under the indenture, after which he was to be set free. In addition to deferred manumissions, masters also resorted to conditional manumissions of various kinds. Thomas Standford of Salem stated in his will in 1722 that Cornelius Niew Kierke, his Negro man, was to have his freedom at the decease of the testator's wife, if it is decided that he had behaved well.[34] Marion Gilchrist of Middlesex County, in her will of 1744, decreed that her Negroes Solomon, Mary, and Cornelius were to have their freedom as specified in the indenture for, "civil behavior and obedience to me in my old age."[35]

The areas in which early manumissions and indentures predominated were those in which Quaker influence was prevalent. Shrewsbury, in Monmouth County, was a large Quaker settlement, and led in manumissions throughout the Colonial Period.[36] By the middle of the eighteenth century, many had become convinced that parts of New Jersey were not fitted for the employment of slaves, particularly the newly settled regions of the northern and southern parts of the state where the winters were too severe for the unacclimated Africans. In addition to this, by 1750, the large plantations of the Raritan and Minisink Valleys had become overstocked with slaves. Seeing that no other alternative presented itself, many slaveholders freed their slaves because of economic necessity.[37] A slave was set free in Shrewsbury in 1756, on the condition that he pay the testator's daughter 40 shillings a year.[38] This arrangement reveals that the manumitted slave must have been able to earn his own keep and maintain his property as though he were a free man. This form of self redemption was similar to the practice of hiring out slaves.

The Revolutionary spirit created a climate favorable to manumission. Increasing numbers of petitions were sent to the legislature, anti-slavery societies pressed their agitation, and the inhabitants of the Colony became more and more favorably disposed toward manumission. While the war was in progress, manumissions decreased, but this was the case chiefly because slave labor was necessary for the maintenance of a sufficient supply of goods and agricultural products for the Continental Army. Before there could be freedom for the Negro, slave owners felt that there had to be freedom from England, and an analysis of the wills for the Revolutionary period shows that only one slave was manumitted in the ten year period between 1774 and 1783.[39]

War service was a basis for the liberation of male slaves immediately after the conflict. Slaves who had served honorably in the military forces were usually given their freedom by act of the legislature. Such an act of manumission would recite the war record of the slave, and set him free for life. An excellently preserved manuscript of the Act Setting Free Peter Williams Late The Property of John Heard, is available for study in the office of the State Archivist in Trenton. Heard had entered Loyalist lines with his slave Peter, who returned in 1780 to serve with the Revolutionary troops until the end of the war. When Heard's estate was confiscated, his slave Peter became the property of the State. The State in consideration of Peter's services stipulated that, "said Peter Williams is hereby declared to be manumitted and set free from slavery and servitude as fully to all intents and purposes as though he had been free born and continued in such a state of freedom; any law or usages to the contrary not withstanding." This act was passed on September 1, 1784.[40] A similar act was passed in 1789 with respect to another Negro, Cato, who had rendered essential services to his state and to the United States as a member of its armed forces.[41] The Revolutionary annals of Newark cite among its heroes Cudjo, a black man. He was a slave owned by Benjamin Coe, and served as a substitute for his master as a member of the Continental Army. Here he fought side by side with the white Patriots. For his services in the field, Cudjo was given his freedom by his master, and nearly an acre of ground on High Street in Newark.[42]

Immediately after the war, and previous to any legislative action, the impulse to freedom was translated into action in the wills of a large number of the slave-holding populace. These wills are usually specific in giving the conditions under which manumission was to take place. Slaves were given their freedom at a specified age or on the death of the slaveholder. As a rule the slave was given a small amount of money or goods with which to begin his free life.[43]

The Act of 1786 set the pattern for future gradual emancipation laws.[44] This Act prohibited the importation of slaves for sale in New Jersey, and provided for manumission by the certificate of two Justices of the Peace of the County in which the master resided, or two overseers of the poor of the Township.[45] The simplicity of the process of manumission by deed, provided for by the Act of 1786 is shown by a deed recorded in Burlington County.

> We the subscribers, two of the justices of the peace for said county do certify that the bearer Pomjuy Stewart is manumitted and set free by his master Richard Potts of the Township of

Hanover and County aforesaid in conformity, to an act of the Assembly of this state in that case made and provided in witness of which we have herein set our hand.

20th. January 1794

[signed]

Isaiah Cogwille

Joel Cook[46]

Manumission accounted for the rapid shift in negro population from predominantly slave to predominantly free between 1790 and 1820. The free Negro population began to rise rapidly after the enactment of laws of manumission. In 1790 the free Negro population was a little greater than one-fifth of the total Negro population. By 1800 the free population had risen to one third of the total Negro population. In 1810 there were two freedmen for every slave. The period of most rapid numerical growth of free population corresponds with the period of most rapid decline of the slave population. From 1800 to 1830, free Negroes increased from 4 thousand to 18 thousand, while the slave population declined from 12 thousand to 2 thousand. In comparison with other states New Jersey's relative rank with reference to free negro population rose from ninth to sixth, while her relative rank with reference to total Negro population showed a decline from eighth to thirteenth position. In comparison with the two adjoining states, New York and Pennsylvania, New Jersey's rate of decrease in slave population is less rapid than either. It is gratifying however, to see that the slave population showed a more uniform decline throughout the fifty year period from 1790 to 1840, in spite of the fact that the manumission laws of New Jersey were less advanced than those of either New York or Pennsylvania.[47]

The next important manumission act to follow the act of 1786 was the Gradual Abolition Act of 1804, which provided that every child born of a slave within the state of New Jersey should be nominally free after July fourth, 1804, but should remain the servant of the owner of the mother until the age of twenty-five, if a male, or twenty-one if a female.[48] The effects of this law on master-slave relationships were so sweeping that soon many slaveholders banded together to petition for its repeal. A group of petitioners from Bergen County expressed alarm at the serious and dangerous consequences of the law, which they considered as unconstitutional, impolitic, and unjust. They considered it an infringement on the rights of slaveholders whom they believed had an unlimited right to the services of the offspring of their slaves because they had clothed, protected, and supported them in their youth. Moreover, they argued that supporting the children of slaves who were to be eventually free, constituted an excessive tax on the slaveholder.[49] The citizens of Salem County submitted a petition containing 36 signatures, in which they stated their grievances against a proposed supplement to the Act of 1804.

> Your memorialists reside in the midst of a population which contains within it a large number of that unfortunate race who are to be affected by the provision of that bill, and we believe that the most serious evils will result to this community from its passage. In this County, as well as in all western Counties of New Jersey there is no white laboring population sufficient for the farming interest, and we do seriously believe that the passage of the law will cause so much difficulty that the farmers will not be able to procure workmen for their farms. Your memorialists need only remind your honorable body that the black population is exceedingly ignorant and prejudiced and cannot be expected to yield that regard to the law which is evoked from the white citizens of the state.[50]

Morris County also submitted a petition in which the signers stated why they deemed such a law to be inexpedient at the time. The petitioners charged that it took from the individual a considerable portion of his property without his consent, taxed the individual slaveholder for the support of children born of slave parents, a tax not felt by the community at large. This Act did not free the slave, they declared, but merely demanded his services for a number of years. Rather than place an unequal burden on any segment of the populace, they advocated a system of manumission which would make the burden equal.[51]

Because of the persistence of the illegal slave trade after 1807, Congress passed a law in 1820 imposing the death penalty on those found guilty of engaging in it. This illicit trade was carried on in New Jersey throughout the second decade of the nineteenth century. Slaves could be easily smuggled from New Jersey into Delaware or Maryland in rowboats or small sailing ships. Evidence of the illegal trade in New Jersey was brought to the attention of the legislature by petitioners from Middlesex County.[52] This petition reviewed the previous Acts designed to bring about the abolition of slavery in the state, then went on to discuss the conditions which had brought about a revival of the illegal slave trade in New Jersey. The high price for which prime field hands could be sold in the deep south seems to have been the chief reason. The trade, they said, was carried on openly between Perth Amboy and New Orleans. A vehement condemnation of this practice ended the petition.

The Act of 1820 was the third in a series of Laws which led to the gradual abolition of slavery in New Jersey. It strengthened the previously mentioned Acts, and made manumission an even simpler process than it had been hitherto. It did not, however, complete emancipation, for slavery was not wholly abolished in New Jersey until the ratification of the Thirteenth Amendment. So beneficial was the operation of gradual emancipation that by 1830 the free Negro population had increased almost fifty percent over that of 1820. One of the larger slaveholding Counties, Somerset, possessed only seventy-eight full slaves by 1830.[53]

The movement for gradual abolition culminated in the Law of 1846. This Act abolished the slave in name as such, and declared him an apprentice for life. It made all children born of apprentices after 1816 free persons.[54] The Act of 1846 is also significant for the educational requirement that it set for apprentices. When this law was passed, there were less than six hundred slaves in the state, and by 1850 this number had decreased to approximately two hundred. Whether these were apprentices under the terms of the Act of 1846 or Negroes illegally held in slavery is something impossible now to determine as this distinction was not made by the census takers.

There is no evidence as to the degree the educational requirement of the Act of 1846 was enforced, or to what degree substitutes in money payment to the state could be made in lieu of the educational requirement. Educational provisions for the slave were first made in 1788, in anticipation of further gradual emancipation legislation. This Act made the teaching of slaves to read, compulsory under a penalty of £5.[55] Judging from the number of runaway slaves who could both read and write in the period before the Revolutionary war, it is logical to assume that many slave holders had followed the practice of giving their bondsmen the rudiments of an education long before the Act of 1788.[56]

The Free Negro in New Jersey

The free Negro in the three decades before the Civil War, lived in a society that was alien to him, for it was intended for two classes only—free whites and Negro slaves. There were at times certain objections to slavery. Slaves were too numerous, work for them was insufficient, or the slave economy did not fit into the economy of a particular County. If, however, there were some who were occasionally critical of slavery, there were a large number consistently hostile to the free Negro. By 1830, the free Negro constituted 88% of the state's total Negro population. By 1840 it stood at 99%.[57] Individual instances of free Negroes may be found during the Colonial period, but their increase did not become great until legislative acts encouraging manumission were passed. The members of the Provincial Assembly seem to have held the free Negro in low esteem. In an Act which they passed in 1714, the legislators speak of the free Negro population as, "idle and slothful people, and prove often a charge to the place where they are." Masters who set slaves free were required to post "sureties" so that the freedman would not become a public charge.[58]

The freedman usually got a start in his new life through the beneficence of his former master, who on setting him free gave him a small sum of money, or perhaps the tools with which he had worked. Margaret Valentine of Somerset County freed her man, Charles, and gave him all of his shoemaking tools.[59] Another thoughtful master provided a milk cow and a bed for his slave couple.[60] Others were given land, wearing apparel, and articles of household furniture.

Before manumission became an accepted procedure, the free Negro in New Jersey seems to have enjoyed the same rights and privileges under the law as free white persons.[61] Negro freedmen were allowed to vote until 1807, when his suffrage rights were revoked.[62] As early as 1793, by implication, a free Negro, who could show that he had a legal residence and clear proof of his freedom was entitled to vote.[63] Shortly after this, Governor Pennington is said to have escorted a strapping "negress" to the polls in Essex County, where he joined her in the ballot.[64] Some free Negroes possessed a goodly amount of property. Robert Aaron, a free black of Somerset County, left $250 to the Dutch Reformed Church of Bedminster. An inventory of his estate showed that his possessions were fairly extensive, when his will was filed in 1802.[65]

Most free Negroes carried on the occupation which they had learned as slaves. Many continued to serve their former masters. Very few free Negroes moved from the immediate area in which they had lived as slaves. An analysis of the percentage of Negro population to total population from 1800 to 1840, shows no pronounced increase or decrease of Negro population in any of the Counties.[66] Free Negroes who moved into the urban areas, usually became domestic servants. Only spotty data is available concerning competition between the free Negro worker and the white worker. It is an established fact, that as the free Negro population increased, the drive to exclude him as a legitimate member of society became intense.[67] The years from 1830 until the enactment of the Thirteenth Amendment constituted a period of extreme restriction, both socially and economically, for the free Negro. He was denied many civil rights, considered a social misfit, and feared by white workers as a threat to their occupational security.

The historical records of Princeton give the occupational status of three of the outstanding free Negroes in that community, for the era after 1820. Betsey Stockton was a domestic servant for the household of Dr. Ashbel Green, president of the College of New Jersey. Peter Scudder was a bootblack at the College, and he sold apples and ice cream to the students of the College and Seminary. He accumulated some property and owned and operated an ice cream shop and confectionery on Nassau Street. Anthony Simmons kept an oyster cellar, ice cream parlor, and confectionery on Nassau Street. He also was a caterer for large family dinners and association banquets. When he died in 1868, he left a will in which he disposed of about half a dozen houses in Princeton. He also left a house to his church for a manse.[68]

All indications point up the fact that as long as the free Negro population of the state remained small, these persons enjoyed much the same rights and privileges as did the white population. However, after gradual emancipation had begun, and the free Negro population increased as a result of it, restrictions and discriminations made against him, soon relegated the free Negro to the status of a second class citizen.

Conclusion

The large plantations of the Proprietary and early Colonial Period offered a stimulus to the growth of the slave population of New Jersey, and as long as the plantation economy remained dominant, slavery was essential to its existence. The circumscribed areas available for plantation monoculture soon placed a limitation on the slave population of New Jersey. When farms became overstocked with slaves, their importation was no longer encouraged or desired by the Colonists. Acts limiting the importation of slaves by placing duties on them, attest to the fact that, by the middle of the 18th century, slavery was a dying institution in New Jersey. The uniformity of the ratio of slave to total population also shows that the slave population did not increase relatively to any great extent. After manumission began the percentage of Negro to total population shows a gradual decline.

The coup de grace to slavery was given by the Revolutionary war. Ideas engendered in the struggle for freedom from Great Britain carried over to the slave, and led to the laws of gradual emancipation. By 1810 the slave population of New Jersey was less than one percent of the total population. An enigma was also created by emancipation. The economic threat of a free Negro population soon led to a reaction against them.

Despite the fact that New Jersey was early classified as a free state, the movement for abolition of slavery was a long and tedious one. In the period previous to the Civil War the free Negro in New Jersey enjoyed a status which was hardly better than that enjoyed by the freedmen under the Black Codes of the South.

Notes

Standard Abbreviations
1 NJA-New Jersey Archives, 1st and 2nd Series.
2 NJHSP-New Jersey Historical Society Proceedings.

1. Greene and Harrington, *American Population before the Federal Census of 1790* (Columbia University Press, 1932), pp. 106–109.

2. Lee, Francis B., *New Jersey As A Colony and As A State* (New York, 1903), Vol. VI, p. 25.

3. Ibid., p. 43.

4. Sypher, J. R. and Apgar, E. A., *History of New Jersey* (Philadelphia, 1870), p. 47.

5. Snell, James P., *A History of Sussex and Warren Counties* (Philadelphia, 1881), p. 77.

6. Franklin, John H., *From Slavery To Freedom* (New York, 1947), p. 93.

7. Mellick, A. D., *The Story of an Old Farm* (Somerville, 1889), p. 220.

8. See Table V appended [not included].

9. Ibid.

10. Leaming, A. and Spicer, J., *The Grants Concessions and Original Constitutions of the Province of New Jersey* (Philadelphia, 1778), p. 21.

11. Lee, pp. 30–31.

12. Mellick, p. 227.

13. Franklin, p. 93.

14. Sypher and Apgar, p. 47.

15. Lee, p. 27.

16. See Table V [not included].

17. See Table I [not included].

18. See Table I [not included].

19. Gordon, T. F., *History of New Jersey* (Trenton. 1834), p.47.

20. Keasbey, A. Q., Slavery In New Jersey, *NJHSP* III Series Vol. IV, p.42.

21. Lee, p.29.

22. *NJA*, I Series Vol. XV, pp. 384–385.

23. Heston, Alfred M., *Slavery and Servitude In New Jersey* (Camden, 1903), p. 9.

24. *NJA*, I Series Vol. IX, p. 345.

25. Ibid., p. 383.

26. Keasbey, *NJHSP*, p. 92 et seq.

27. Heston, p. 16.

28. Gardner, D. H., The Emancipation of Slaves in New Jersey. *NJHSP* III Series Vol. IX, pp. 1–21.

29. Lee, p. 33.

30. Heston, p. 15.

31. Connelley, Slavery In Colonial New Jersey. *NJHSP* III Series Vol. XIV, p. 119 et seq.

32. Gardner, *NJHSP*, p. 225.

33. *NJA*, Abstracts of Wills, Vol. I, p. 437.

34. Ibid., p. 438.

35. *NJA*, Abstracts of Wills, Vol. II, p. 201.

36. This conclusion has been reached from a study of the abstracts of wills for the entire Colonial Period. Further detailed statistical data is available in my notes on this subject.

37. Heston, p. 9. Also see Mackey, *Land and Labor in Colonial New Jersey* (Seminar paper to be found in the Princeton University Library), pp. 39–40.

38. *NJA*, Abstracts of Wills, Vol. IV, p. 125.

39. A study of the Abstracts of Wills, *NJA*, for this period has led to this conclusion.

40. File of Original Petitions, State Archivists Office, Trenton, New Jersey.

41. Allinson, S., *Acts of The General Assembly of The State of New Jersey*, p. 538.

42. Atkinson, Joseph, *History of Newark* (Newark, 1878), p. 117.

43. This data is taken from the Abstracts of Wills, *NJA*.

44. See Table III [not included].

45. Allinson, pp. 1783–1788.

46. State Archivist's Manuscript File, Trenton, N.J.

47. See Table III [not included].

48. Mellick, p. 228.

49. Bergen County Petitions to the Legislature requesting the repeal of the New Jersey Abolition Act of 1804, State Archivists Office, Trenton, N.J.

50. Petition to the members of the Legislative Council of New Jersey, State Archivists Office, Trenton, N.J.

51. Morris County Petitions to the Legislature, 1806, State Archivists Office, Trenton, N.J.

52. Petition from the inhabitants of the County of Middlesex to the General Assembly, State Archivists Office, Trenton, N.J.

53. Mellick, p. 228.

54. Cooley, Henry S., *A Study of Slavery in New Jersey*, Johns Hopkins University Studies, Vol. XIV, pp. 28–29.

55. Woodson, Carter G., *The Education of the Negro Prior to 1861* (New York, 1915), p. 74.

56. See Table III [not included].

57. Ibid.

58. Connelley, *NJHSP*, p. 199.

59. *NJA*, Abstracts of Wills, Vol. VII, p. 366.

60. Ibid., p. 413.

61. Washington, Booker T., The Free Negro in Slavery Days. *Outlook*, Vol. XCIII, pp. 107–114.

62. Ibid., p. 112.

63. Heston, p. 10 (note).

64. Atkinson, p. 142.

65. *NJA*, Abstracts of Wills, Vol. X p. 7.

66. See Table III [not included].

67. Jackson, Luther P., *Free Negro Labor and Property Holding in Virginia* (New York. 1942, p. 3.

68. Hageman, J. F., *Princeton and Its Institutions* (Philadelphia, 1879), Vol. II, p. 210–211.

MARCUS L. WARD,

The Soldier's Friend,

FOR

Governor of New Jersey

---o---

(AIR--TRAMP, TRAMP, TRAMP.)

---o---

Written by R. B. Nicoi, author and publisher of a choice
collection of Popular Songs—printed on fine note paper,
and sent to any part of the United States, postage free,
on receipt of price.

Terms—14 copies, 50 cts.; 30 copies $1; or $25 per 1,000,

Address—R. B. Nicoi, care of Gibson Brothers, printers,
271 Penna. Avenue, Washington, D. C.

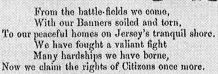

From the battle-fields we come,
With our Banners soiled and torn,
To our peaceful homes on Jersey's tranquil shore.
We have fought a valiant fight
Many hardships we have borne,
Now we claim the rights of Citizens once more.

CHORUS.

Tramp, tramp, tramp, the boys are marching,
Cheer up, Marcus, we will come,
And a helping hand shall lend
To elect "The Soldier's Friend,"
And defeat the trait'rous Copperheads at home.

In the battle front we fought
During all the great campaign,
Till the Rebels and Rebellion met their doom;
So we'll rally to the Polls,
And a victory will gain
O'er the Copperheads, our *enemies*, at home.
Chorus.

How those trait'rous hounds rejoiced,
When our cause looked dark and drear,
Is well known to every son of Liberty;
During all the tug of war
They were fighting in our rear—
But we soon shall gain a final victory.
Chorus.

We are marshalled for the strife,
And we come with all our might,
To maintain the cause which traitors would subdue;
Then three cheers for Mr. Ward,
For the Union and our Rights,
For New Jersey and her Bonny Boys in Blue.

*During the war, New Jersey Democrats turned a deaf ear to Union
soldiers' pleas for the right to vote in the field; Marcus L. Ward of the
fledgling Union-Republican party was thus "the soldier's friend." Defeated
by the "out and out Douglas man" Joel Parker in his bid for the New
Jersey governor's seat in 1862, Ward won handily in 1864. Photograph
courtesy New Jersey Historical Society.*

8

For some historians, the Civil War was a consequence of cultural differences stemming from the growth of two distinctive civilizations with divergent styles of life and outlooks. For others, it was the result of an economic clash between capitalism in the North and agrarianism in the South that led to variant views on such public policies as the tariff, western land sales, and banking. A third interpretation places the blame on political disagreements over how to interpret the Constitution, what form of union it created, and what role it provided for state and national governments. Finally there is the question of slavery, condemned by abolitionists as the ultimate evil and defended by southerners as a positive good.

Whatever the explanation, all emphasize the differences between North and South. Only in the border states such as Tennessee, Maryland, and what became West Virginia did cultures, economic interests, political ideas, and views on slavery overlap. New Jersey, although in the North, has been seen as a "border state" because its situation resembled theirs more than it did most northern states.

The following selection describes some surprising aspects of homefront politics in New Jersey during the Civil War. Given the persistence of slavery in New Jersey, the presence of such unique features should not be all that striking. Maurice Tandler has pointed out that New Jersey voted against Lincoln in both 1860 and 1864 and that Democrats maintained their hold on state politics throughout the war. That party divided into different factions; some Democrats were openly sympathetic to the South and thought that the Confederacy should be permitted to leave the Union unopposed. There was also a vocal contingent of "Copperhead" politicians and newspaper editors who made their opposition to the Illinois "railsplitter," Republicans, the war, and the draft well known. There are indications that support for abolition even among New Jersey's Republicans was lukewarm at best; some expressed an open racism.

What in New Jersey's past makes its divided attitudes during the Civil War comprehensible? First, abolition came late and gradually to the state because both economic interest in slavery and racism remained strong; that racist attitudes continued during and after the war should not be unexpected. Second, New Jersey had a history of close elections; its behavior in the 1864 Lincoln-McClellan race continued a pattern and did not necessarily indicate a shared sentiment about slavery specifically. Third, residents had divided in previous wars. There were large numbers of loyalists in New Jersey during the American Revolution; the antiwar Federalists regained power during the War of 1812. Fourth, New Jersey, like other northern states, had economic and social ties to the South. The leather industry in Newark produced numerous pairs of cheap shoes purchased by plantation owners for their slaves. Many southerners attended Princeton, while others vacationed at Cape May and other early resorts. Fifth, New Jersey showed some support for state's rights ideas as well as for federal sales of western lands to create revenue. It was William Paterson and the New Jersey delegation that had pushed for the protection of the states at the Constitutional Convention. Finally, New Jersey was traditionally conservative. Going to war was a drastic step, and the implications of the conflict became more radical after the Emancipation Proclamation. What additional factors might explain why New Jersey appeared to be a "border state" during the Civil War?

Was New Jersey in fact all that different in this period? Comparative analysis shows that there were Copperheads in other mid-Atlantic states during the Civil War, particularly New York and Pennsylvania. Neither of these neighboring states met all their manpower obligations willingly, on time, or completely; New Jersey in fact compares favorably on these measures. For much of the war northern armies scored few victories while the toll of killed and wounded mounted, and with it objections to government policies. Opposition to the draft led to vicious riots in New York City. Racism was present throughout the North; the Emancipation Proclamation did not receive unanimous approval. The Democratic party did not disappear during the war. Can New Jersey in truth be considered unique at this time?

Other questions might be asked about New Jersey and its residents during the Civil War. Tandler has noted that James W. Wall, a leading Democrat, was arrested and imprisoned because of his antiwar "diatribes." How much dissent and criticism of the government is permissible in a free country during wartime? When does the individual overstep the bounds of his rights and cross the line into treason? How should the government react? Are its powers rightly different in war than in peace? What constitutes a misuse of power? Clearly Wall and his Republican opponents had different answers to these questions, and historians have criticized Lincoln's actions during the war in these respects. Yet the same problems appeared during World War I, World War II, and the Vietnam conflict. Can Americans yet claim to possess a clear understanding of the distinction between individual rights and government powers during wartime?

Suggested Readings

Foner, Eric. "The Causes of the American Civil War: Recent Interpretations and New Directions." *Civil War History* 20 (1974): 197–214.

Knapp, Charles M. *New Jersey Politics during the Period of Civil War and Reconstruction.* New York, 1924.

McPherson, James M. *Battle Cry of Freedom: The Civil War.* New York, 1988.

Neely, Mark E., Jr. *The Fate of Liberty: Abraham Lincoln and Civil Liberties.* New York, 1991.

Pressly, Thomas J. *Americans Interpret Their Civil War.* Princeton, N.J., 1954.

Randall, J. G. *Constitutional Problems under Lincoln.* 1926. Rev. ed. Urbana, Ill., 1951.

Siegel, Alan A. *For the Glory of the Union: Myth, Reality, and the Media in Civil War New Jersey.* Rutherford, N.J., 1984.

Stampp, Kenneth M. "The Irrepressible Conflict." In *The Imperiled Union: Essays on the Background of the Civil War.* New York, 1980.

Wright, William C. "New Jersey's Military Role in the Civil War Reconsidered." *NJH* 92 (1974): 197–210.

◆ ◆ ◆ ◆ ◆ ◆

The Political Front in Civil War New Jersey

Maurice Tandler

At an early Union party rally for Lincoln and Johnson in 1864, John F. Farnsworth of Illinois told his Newark audience that he

Proceedings of the New Jersey Historical Society 83 (1965): 223-33. Reprinted by permission of the author.

had been advised against speaking in New Jersey because "there were no Lincoln men there and it was a God-forsaken place."[1] Although this remark evoked great laughter from the assembled party faithful, New Jersey's Union-Republicans usually found it less than funny to be reminded of the State's political apostasy. The only Northern state with both a Democratic governor and an annually-chosen Democratic legislature, New Jersey was an object of unconcealed scorn to Union men outside the State. "In no other Free State," declared the New York *Tribune*, "are disloyal utterances so frequent and so bold as in New Jersey."[2]

Such criticism caused much anguish. This lament of a Jersey expatriate in Illinois was typical: "As a native born Jerseyman, I love her reputation, and when I am so often compelled to hear the anathemas hurled against her, which I do hear; and when I think how all this has come to pass, and by whose acts, I get to be fighting mad at those who have brought this shame upon us."[3] Alexander G. Cattell need scarcely have reminded his fellow Lincoln elector, Marcus Ward, as he did shortly before Election Day in 1864 that "The moral effect of a victory in New Jersey would be worth more than the vote of even a larger State."[4] As it turned out, New Jersey's redemption had to be postponed; the Lincoln men were beaten by eight thousand votes and "favorite son" George B. McClellan was the beneficiary of the State's seven electoral votes.

If to Unionists New Jersey was blighted with Copperheadism, to the Opposition it stood as "a city on a hill to the Democratic party in other States."[5] On the eve of the election of 1860 the New Jersey Democracy had been hopelessly divided despite an eleventh-hour fusion attempt. Yet within two years the party breach was healed sufficiently to inflict severe damage on the Republican cause.

The key to Democratic success in the political battles of the war years was the remarkable unanimity displayed by the party in its opposition to the Lincoln Administration. To be sure, a fair number of War Democrats—usually, but not always, of anti-Lecompton antecedents—had augmented Union ranks; James M. Scovel of Camden and Martin Ryerson of Sussex County typified this group. But these men were branded as renegades, indistinguishable from the "Black Republicans." Nevertheless, despite the amalgam of anti-Republicanism, which sufficed to insure electoral success, party unity was strained by a diversity of opinion concerning the war effort itself. Democratic leadership was divided into two factions, whose boundaries were not at all clearly delineated.

On the one hand, there was the radical wing of the party. This faction, whose power base lay in Bergen County (a playground for New York Copperheads), held extreme anti-war views. Among the leading lights of the so-called Peace Democracy were such stalwarts as Thomas Dunn English, Daniel Holsman, Rodman M. Price, C. Chauncey Burr and James W. Wall. From the beginning of hostilities this noisy and militant group was obsessed with Northern responsibility for the war, and some were at all times ready to acquiesce in Southern independence as a *sine qua non* of peace. Such a statement as the following by Rodman Price is a good example of the stridency of radical rhetoric: "I charge that the Republican party have all the disunionists and traitors, they have broken the Constitution and dissolved the Union . . . I regret that New Jersey ever permitted her troops to invade the soil of any State, in hostile array, without consent of the authority of the State, being first heard. . ."[6] On the other hand, there was a larger and more moderate group in the party, which stood ready to support what it deemed the legitimate war effort and to condemn any and all "unconstitutional" acts of the government at Washington. The views expressed by Garrit S. Cannon of Bordentown were shared by many party members:

> Whilst I am a Democrat as warmly attached to its time honored principles, whilst I am as much opposed as ever to Republicanism in every shape, I feel it is my duty to oppose Secession and all its aiders, abettors, sympathizers and apologists with as much energy and sincerity as I ever have and ever will oppose Abolitionism and its kindred heresies . . .

> I desire to remain perfectly free to support the Democratic candidate for Governor if he is in my judgment a patriotic and loyal man, and in favor of suppressing this infamous and unjustifiable Rebellion. If he is not I do not wish by word or deed to commit myself in any way to his support.[7]

When the Democrats wisely nominated Joel Parker for the governorship in 1862, party factionalism was temporarily submerged. Rodman Price, for one, offered his congratulations, and Parker replied, "I am glad the nomination appears to give satisfaction and I hope it will unite the party."[8] It is most doubtful whether the Democrats could have amassed their fifteen thousand vote majority in that election with an extreme anti-war man at the head of the ticket. As H. N. Congar pointed out in an election post-mortem to the defeated candidate, Marcus Ward: "Against you the Democrats nominated a strong candidate for Governor. He was an out and out Douglas man, and yet the traiterous Breckinridge men supported him in their hatred of Republicanism. We had nothing against him and a dominant party for him."[9] As New Jersey's second war governor, Parker pursued a middle of the road policy exemplified in the slogan "The Union as it was, the Constitution as it is." Despite the cabal of Peace Democrats in the State Legislature, the bulk of the party generally followed the more prudent course of supporting the war while criticizing specific acts of the Federal government.

As the party of the "outs" on the national level, New Jersey Democrats could indulge freely in attacks on the Lincoln Administration, while complete control of the State's political machinery after 1863 gave them a powerful advantage in local contests. Without question, their most effective vote-getting issue was slavery. Suspension of *habeas corpus* and suppression of anti-war journals, no mean issues themselves, paled in comparison with the specter of Negro emancipation by the Federal government. In 1862 the Emancipation Proclamation was certainly a potent factor in causing the Union party's defeat in New Jersey, and elsewhere, for that matter.

The Democrats saw in emancipation vindication of their long-held views as to the abolitionist character of Republicanism. Their opposition to it rested on the twin pillars of constitutionality and racism. In a speech to the House of Representatives in the spring of 1862, Nehemiah Perry of Newark rang the changes on the constitutionality theme:

> The American Union can exist no longer than the Constitution remains safe from the insidious attacks of these abolition doctrines . . . If I understand, sir, anything of the object of the war, it is designed for the preservation of the country, and not for its destruction; yet you propose to annihilate the great institution of the South . . . Sir, if you love your country better than the negro, the Union better than party, drop these diverting, ruinous measures . . . Millions for the Union, not one cent for abolition.[10]

The Democrats gained considerable political capital by exploiting the deep-set fears of their white constituents. In a deliberate attempt to cultivate this "backlash" vote, they painted lurid pictures of the economic consequences of cheap labor and of racial amalgamation which they claimed would follow a mass migration of Negroes into the state. Their newspaper organs printed harrowing stories of "Black Republican" farmers in the agricultural counties hiring contrabands at ten cents a day and turning away needy white laborers.[11] The Honorable Andrew Jackson Rogers, Representative from the Fourth Congressional District— and one of the more unsavory Democratic politicos—told his constituents in 1864 that "They must vote for McClellan to prevent the long-heeled and thick-lipped Ethiopian from competing with the white population in wages, and also to save our sons and daughters from marrying and mixing with the negroes."[12] At Democratic rallies all over the state during that campaign, McClellan was hailed as "the White Man's President." This issue was used by the party with telling effect.

Generally, civil rights questions involving freedom of speech and of the press arouse slight popular concern. But during the war, New Jersey's Democrats were opportunely presented with several cases of political martyrdom, the most notable being the arrest of the irrepressible Col. James W. Wall of Burlington and his incarceration in Fort Lafayette.

Wall was a popular figure in the state. His father, Garret D. Wall, had been a United States Senator during the heyday of Jacksonian Democracy. A former Mayor of Burlington, Colonel Wall was much sought after on the lecture circuit, but he was best known as a leader of the Democratic party. One of the most vocal of the radical Democrats, he resembled his arch-enemy, Commodore Robert F. Stockton, in both his lack of personal modesty and his stormy temper. Wall was a man capable of violent dislikes. He never forgave James Buchanan, or the Stocktons, for the appointment of John P. Stockton, and not himself, as Minister to Rome in 1858, and he wrote several abusive letters to Buchanan. Senator John R. Thomson, the Commodore's brother-in-law, had to explain to the retired President that "we do not consider any thing he says or does, as worthy of any attention, whenever his feelings or prejudices are at all concerned."[13] Imagine then how Wall's feelings were aroused when on September 11, 1861, a United States Marshal and four deputies, accompanied by the Mayor of Burlington and three of his police, showed up at Wall's house with an arrest warrant.

Wall's exertions in behalf of the peace movement in the first months of the war had led him into an early collision course with the Federal government. As a frequent contributor to Ben Wood's New York *Daily News*, a sheet not especially noted for its devotion to the Union cause, Wall specialized in anti-Administration diatribes. He later recalled: "During the Reign of Terror, I was the only man in the State who had the nerve to stand forth in defense of the liberty of thought, of speech and of the press, and the true principles of the Democratic faith."[14]

At the time of his arrest Wall was dining with his family. When the U.S. Marshal announced the purpose of his visit, the outraged Wall voiced his displeasure by grabbing the unfortunate agent's neck and flinging him across the room. After a wild free-for-all, in which one of the arresting officers was knocked out, the prisoner was subdued and dragged into the street, hatless, with his clothes torn, and hustled off to a waiting train and Fort Lafayette. No charges were preferred against him, and within two weeks of his arrest he was released upon taking an oath of allegiance. Needless to say, he received a hero's welcome on his return to Burlington.

As a hapless victim of Black Republican tyranny, Wall's arrest inspirited the ranks of the peace men and served to attract many new recruits to the anti-Administration cause. Encouraged by the widespread sympathy for his ordeal, Wall wasted few opportunities of subjecting the Washington authorities to his special brand of lurid invective. In a speech at Burlington in 1862 he likened them to "human vampires sucking blood from the country's veins, while with the gently fanning wings of honied words, and patriotic profesions, they lulled their victims into unconsciousness of their designs."[15] His great moment came early in 1863 when the New Jersey Legislature, of Peace Resolutions notoriety, elected him to fill the Senate seat vacated by the death of John Thomson. It is perhaps fortunate that the Colonel's subsequent peace-mongering activities were discreetly overlooked. In a January 1863 letter to Buchanan, Wall intimated that he had received hints of a return trip to Lafayette. He wrote: "How I longed that they would put the threat in execution. The effort would have cost the Administration the life of one marshall: as after my release I went armed to the teeth. The protest of a dead marshall on my doorstep would have been full of eloquent meaning for the scoundrels at the head of affairs."[16]

To the Democrats, of course, the nation's number one scoundrel was the man in the White House. These old Jacksonians, taking a page out of the Whig book, blasted the President as "Abraham the First," and in place of "honest old Abe" inscribed their placards "Abraham Lincoln: First in War and First in the Pockets of his Countrymen." Such publications as E. N. Fuller's Newark *Evening Journal* and C. Chauncey Burr's *Old Guard* directed a steady stream of personal abuse at the President; "ignoramus," "obscene, joking old railsplitter," "nation's buffoon," and "deluded and almost delirious fanatic" were among the choicer of their epithets. And when Union war aims had broadened to include abolition of slavery, Rodman Price raved: "Lincoln means to divide this Country. Every abolitionist is a disunionist—and a traitor—& he is an abolitionist. He has been false to his oath and to his Country. He is impeachable before God & man. He stands reeking in the blood of his countrymen."[17]

In the face of such militant Democratic opposition, support of the President by New Jersey's young Union party was ineffectual, as the election results demonstrate. One must bear in mind that a formal Republican organization, as such, had not existed in the State prior to the Civil War. It is true that the Federal patronage was at the disposal of the state organization, and this did prove a stimulus to party development. But the party's close identification with the National Administration was a two-edged sword, especially in the early years of the war, as every reversal on the field of battle inured to the benefit of the Democratic party.

In comparison with such states as Indiana, Ohio and Pennsylvania, New Jersey Republicans operated at a further disadvantage. The implied constitutional provision against soldier voting in the field removed a potentially valuable weapon from the Union arsenal. That the Democrats were cognizant of this was made clear when in 1864 the State Legislature ignored the nearly 140 petitions signed by over 37,000 Jerseymen asking for passage of an authorization bill.[18]

Democratic ascendancy in New Jersey had long before the Civil War pushed politics to the right, as it were, and the State's Republicans were an eminently conservative lot. In the pre-convention maneuvering for the party's Presidential nomination in 1860, the "Opposition" leadership had rallied around favorite son William L. Dayton, because it was widely felt that William H. Seward could never carry New Jersey, or the other doubtful states. And when it became obvious to the Jersey delegation at Chicago that Dayton had no following outside his native state, they threw their support to Abraham Lincoln as the most available candidate. During the campaign the issue of protectionism received equal stress with that of the territorial question.

With few exceptions the leaders of the State's Union-Republican party gave unqualified support to the policies of the Lincoln Administration and eschewed the early Radical demands for a more vigorous anti-slavery policy. The small Radical faction in

New Jersey consisted principally of a few German leaders—Dr. Louis Greiner and attorney Charles Bocherling, to name but two—, but they moved outside the inner party circles. And H. N. Congar, long-time editor of the Newark *Daily Mercury*, who might have been expected to gravitate towards the Radical position, was out of the way in Hong Kong, where he was serving as United States Consul.

If the party was in substantial agreement on the necessity of sustaining the national government, the same could not be said of its attitude towards the single most powerful corporation in the state: the Camden and Amboy Railroad Company. Leaving aside the economic issues involved, formidable as they were, the chief difference of opinion revolved around the extent to which the interests of the Democratic party and the monopoly were tied together. According to some Union party leaders the State could never be redeemed until the Company was shorn of the monopoly privileges which allowed it to exercise its pernicious influence in state politics. Thomas H. Dudley, our consul in Liverpool, was of this opinion, and after Lincoln's defeat in New Jersey in 1864 he wrote home:

> I am not in the least disappointed though deeply mortified at the result in my own state poor New Jersey. It was the same old tale that the monopoly would graciously permit us on this occasion to carry the state. I have heard this at least for twelve times during the last twenty years. It proved to be a lie each time, and was from the beginning intended as a cheat to delude us . . . You might just as well attempt to go to Heaven through a place that I will not name as to expect a Republican triumph through the Camden & Amboy R R Co. Why they own the Copperhead party. They in fact are a mere appendage to the Company. You owe it to yourselves as a people, to the state you love, and to the people of the Union, *to get rid of this monopoly and set the state free.*[19]

Despite the abortive anti-monopoly crusade undertaken by that supreme opportunist, James Scovel, and by Joseph C. Potts—both former Democrats, incidentally—, the party leadership resisted all attempts to put their state organization on record against the Camden and Amboy. The fact is that too many good Republicans were enthusiastic devotees of the monopoly, as was Joseph P. Bradley, its chief counsel and a member of the Board of Directors.

As far as the rank and file of the Union party of the state was concerned, the overarching consideration was successful prosecution of the war. They were well aware that victory in the field would lead to victory at the polls. The unrestrained joy and relief with which the people of New Jersey received the news of Appomattox is nowhere better illustrated than in this letter written the following day by the Chairman of the Union State Executive Committee, Charles Perrin Smith:

> I was sick all day and all last night, but hearing cheers about midnight, I repaired to the telegraph office—rightly supposing that the *end* had arrived. Lee has surrendered with all his army! Four years ago I was as certain of this ultimate result, and I have not for a moment wavered in the opinion. I hastened home, lit the gas from top to bottom of the house,—threw open all the windows, ran out the Stars and Stripes over my front door, *fired a musket twice in the street*, woke every body up, and and went to bed sick again in body, but elated beyond description in spirits.[20]

With the war triumphantly concluded, the prospects of the Union party never seemed brighter and New Jersey Republicans looked forward with unreserved optimism to the fall gubernatorial election. Their confidence was buttressed by what they regarded as a sure-fire issue—the opposition of the State's Democrats to the Thirteenth Amendment. Marcus L. Ward—"the Soldiers' Friend," *par excellence*—was renominated, and all the indications were that he would not be forgotten by the Boys in Blue come November:

> We have hung the Rifle up, we will keep our powder dry
> While we use the Ballot thus we sheath the Sword;
> Then remember each of you, that a loyal Jersey Blue
> Will not vote for any but for Marcus Ward.[21]

As the party of the Union and of the martyred Lincoln, the Republicans entered the canvass with that religious zeal which only sight of the promised land can inspire. "I would almost give my right arm to carry the State against the Copperheads," said the editor of the Trenton *State Gazette*.[22] Given a climate of opinion where it was an insult to accuse a man of having voted for McClellan, he was able to keep his arm. On Election Day, 1865, the Republicans were finally victorious, carrying the governorship and gaining control of the State Legislature. The election results were hailed throughout the country, but nowhere more enthusiastically than in the redeemed state. One can imagine the surging emotions of the correspondent who addressed these lines of congratulation to the Governor-elect: "'God be praised': not so much, that Marcus L. Ward is elected Governor, as that the people of New Jersey, have at 'the eleventh hour', returned from all manner of wickedness, and declared themselves Loyal and true to the *Union*."[23]

Notes

Mr. Tandler's article, with minor revisions, was presented originally as a seminar paper at the Fourth Annual American History Workshop of the New Jersey Civil War Centennial Commission, held at Rutgers University on December 19, 1964.

1. *Newark Daily Advertiser*, September 15, 1864.

2. As quoted in *Sussex Register* (Newton), June 6, 1862.

3. James D. Cleaver to Marcus L. Ward, July 28, 1865, Marcus L. Ward Papers, New Jersey Historical Society (NJHS).

4. Cattell to Ward, October 25, 1864, ibid.

5. Thomas B. Pierson to Peter D. Vroom, November 16, 1863, Peter D. Vroom Papers, NJHS.

6. Undated memorandum [probably October 1863] in Rodman M. Price Papers, Rutgers University Library (RUL).

7. Cannon to Price, June 26, 1862, ibid.

8. Parker to Price, September 8, 1862, ibid.

9. Congar to Ward, December 31, 1862, Ward Papers.

10. *Congressional Globe*, 37th Congress, 2nd session (March 6, 1862), pp. 1103–1106.

11. *Newark Daily Advertiser*, August 8, 1862.

12. Ibid., October 8, 1864.

13. Thomson to James Buchanan, April 28, 1861, James Buchanan Papers, Historical Society of Pennsylvania.

14. Wall to Buchanan, June 29, 1865, ibid.

15. *The Constitution: Originating in Compromise, It Can Only Be Preserved by Adhering to its Spirit, and Observing Its Every Obligation. An Address Delivered by James W. Wall, Esq., at the City Hall, Burlington, February 20, 1862* (Philadelphia, 1862), p. 57.

16. January 4, 1863, Buchanan Papers.

17. Undated memorandum, *op. cit.*, Price Papers.

18. Josiah H. Benton, *Voting in the Field: A Forgotten Chapter of the Civil War* (Boston, 1915), p. 270.

19. Dudley to Ward, November 27, 1864, Ward Papers.

20. Smith to Thomas H. Dudley, April 10, 1865, Thomas H. Dudley Collection, Huntington Library, San Marino, Calif. Quoted with permission.

21. *Song of the Loyal Band* (Newark, n.d.). Photocopy in Marcus L. Ward Papers, RUL.

22. Jacob R. Freese to Ward, September 8, 1865, Ward Papers, NJHS.

23. Charles E. Elmer to Ward, November 13, 1865, ibid.

"A Merry Bunch, Atlantic City," stereoview, about 1890. Though touted in its own promotional literature as a high-toned resort for "representatives of the best society," Atlantic City actually catered to a middle- and working-class crowd, many of them day excursionists. Photograph courtesy New Jersey Historical Society.

9

As historians have studied different aspects of the past, their main interest has shifted since the 1960s from politics to economics, from laws to society. Political historians have focused on ideas and institutions, the formation of political parties, and voting requirements and patterns. Economic historians have considered industrialization, monetary policies and institutions, and the changing ways people have earned a living. Legal historians have analyzed constitutions and laws, judges' lives, and methods of handling crime. More recently, social historians have sought to recreate the lives of everyday people, to examine class and class differences. The following selection is from a social history of one resort town that deals with forms of entertainment and attitudes toward both class and recreation during the Victorian era in the United States.

In 1852 Absecon Island had only marshes and sand dunes to offer visitors. Less than thirty years later, Atlantic City had achieved national status. Who was attracted to this new resort? According to the publicity releases of its boosters it drew the rich and well-born from all over the East. In fact, the city's pull was far more limited in terms of both class and distance. Charles Funnell has raised questions about the relationship between class and entertainment. Did rich and poor enjoy the same forms of recreation and go to the same vacation places? Do they today? Are golf, tennis, and skiing, for example, sports for all classes? Who goes to baseball games and such places as Great Adventure? What role do financial status, class, and taste play in how Americans choose to use their leisure time? Why has Funnell characterized Atlantic City as both "crude" and "magnificent"?

Atlantic City's entertainment created problems for many Victorian Americans because it made apparent some of the conflicts and contradictions in their society. Vacations were meant to be enjoyable, but pleasure and morality sometimes clashed. Most laborers worked six days a week, but on the seventh day, meant to be a day of rest, Sunday "blue laws" closed stores and prohibited the sale of liquor—and thus defined the limits of acceptable relaxation. Sunday was also the only day most tourists could make trips to the shore, but that the town's facilities stayed open so that visitors would make the most of their limited leisure time violated both laws and sensibilities. If amusements closed visitors stayed away, and the resort's businesses made no profit.

Atlantic City was also advertised as a family resort at the same time publications heralded the opportunites for singles to meet there. However, some of the forms of entertainment that drew single people, including saloons, gambling, and prostitution, offended families. Yet even those Victorians who established laws regulating entertainment did not always agree on or enforce "correct" standards. Does New Jersey still have "blue laws"? Where do law and society draw the line between pleasure and morality today?

Another interesting aspect of entertainment in the Victorian era is the impact of technological advance. Just as railroads opened areas of the country for settlement in the 1800s, made the transportation of goods easier and cheaper, and fueled industrialization by creating the need for large-scale production of iron and steel, they made Atlantic City possible. The resort was on a direct line from Philadelphia. Railroads enabled large crowds to travel inexpensively to Atlantic City, not for the summer or week as vacationers had done earlier, but for the day. Most Atlantic City tourists still spend only a day there.

Technology also provided new machines to entertain visitors once they came. The ferris wheel, merry-go-round, and roller coaster were mechanical wonders that drew crowds as strongly as the ocean and the boardwalk. Today technological developments continue to provide both updated versions of older machines and new forms of entertainment. What kinds of rides are available at Great Adventure and DisneyWorld, and how do they compare with those at Atlantic City a century ago?

Atlantic City drew workers as well as tourists. Many of those who labored to keep the city running were African American. How were these workers regarded and treated? Did segregation exist in Atlantic City, and, if so, what form did it take? Here, too, Victorians compromised moral and ethical standards with the desire for profits. How does the treatment of African Americans in the city compare with their treatment in other places during this time?

Atlantic City in the Victorian era was not unique; though it was larger and more famous, it resembled other shore towns in many fundamental ways. Its story reveals much about general attitudes towards class, recreation, and race in the North.

Suggested Readings

Cunningham, John T. *The Jersey Shore*. New Brunswick, N.J., 1958.

Dulles, Foster Rhea. *America Learns to Play*. New York, 1940.

Foster, Herbert J. "Institutional Development in the Black Community of Atlantic City, New Jersey: 1850–1930." In *The Black Experience in Southern New Jersey*, edited by David C. Munn. Camden, N.J., 1985. 32–48.

Mrozek, Donald J. *Sport and American Mentality, 1880–1910*. Knoxville, Tenn., 1983.

Uminowicz, Glenn. "Recreation in a Christian America: Ocean Grove and Asbury Park, New Jersey, 1869–1914." In *Hard at Play: Leisure in America, 1840–1940*, edited by Kathryn Grover. Amherst, Mass., 1992. 8–38.

Wilson, Harold F. *The Story of the Jersey Shore: A Social and Economic History of the Counties of Atlantic, Cape May, Monmouth and Ocean.* 2 vols. New York, 1953.

_____ . "Victorian Vacations at the Jersey Shore." *Proc. NJHS* 77 (1959): 267–71.

◆ ◆ ◆ ◆ ◆ ◆

Newport of the Nouveaux Bourgeois

Charles E. Funnell

Many different kinds of people patronized Atlantic City in the turn-of-the-century period, but the ambiance of the resort was lower middle class. From this class came the greatest number of visitors and the largest part of the city's revenue, and accordingly the atmosphere of Atlantic City was a product of lower-middle-class preferences and aspirations. Many people today believe, and some at the time asserted, that the city was then an upper-class resort. Articles appearing recently in popular magazines have offered a casual sketch of the gentility and elegance of the Victorian resort, its swell tone and distinguished patronage. We will speculate on the causes of this attitude in the last chapter, but here we must consider why it is basically erroneous.

Bedizened, gauche, extravagant, conniving, ingenuous—Atlantic City from the start depended on the lower middle class for its success, and was the charming preposterous artifact of its customers' tastes.

Before beginning, it is necessary to consider the class structure applied here. The most useful divisions for the town's history are upper class, upper middle class, lower middle class, lower class, blacks, and bums. The upper class is divided into "society," defined strictly as individuals listed in the *Social Register* for Philadelphia, and the nouveaux riches, those enjoying wealth but not yet accepted by the traditional upper class. The upper middle class consists mainly of professional people, substantial businessmen, executives, and the like. Also, and importantly, newspaper editors. To the lower middle class belong lesser white-collar workers of all varieties, including the many different kinds of clerks staffing the commerce and retail trade of Philadelphia. Many of these are women, employed in growing numbers as salesgirls. The lower class consists of factory workers, male and female, and other laborers engaged in heavy, tedious, and generally unremunerative work. Blacks include residents of Atlantic City and visitors from Philadelphia, and are properly considered apart from all classes of whites, in a period which witnessed the acme of racial sentiment in American society. Economically trivial but socially interesting, bums are the *Lumpenproletariat* of unemployed drifters and down-and-outs.

Many observers of Atlantic City believed, or liked to believe, that it was an expression of high society. A Pennsylvania Railroad pamphlet of 1889 spoke of the "representatives of the best society" which frequented the resort. In 1897 a member of the Atlantic City Hotel Men's Association, expansively describing the future of the town in the twentieth century to a Philadelphia businessmen's group, predicted that a bicycle path recently built between the city and its resort would be improved to a broad highway for the wealthy: "A modern Appian way, upon which the rich and pleasure-loving people, blessed with fine horses, can drive down from Philadelphia in their carriages." John F. Hall, editor of the *Daily Union*, boasted that "there is hardly a family of any prominence residing within a thousand miles of this favored region that has not at one time or another occupied, as host or guest, one of the beautiful homes which form the crowning glory of the town." The resort's Easter Parade, one of the annual highlights, drew great crowds to promenade the Boardwalk. *Harper's Weekly* said of it in 1908: "Practically all of the Easter guests here are people of wealth and fashion. . . . Seventy-five per cent of their names figure in the social registers of their home cities."

Such claims, of course, are immediately suspect. If they are to be believed, Atlantic City was hot on the trail of Newport for the patronage of the Four Hundred. Was the resort in fact laying hold of the fashionable clientele of the Quaker City?

An examination of the "hotel personals" which the *Daily Union* regularly printed in the 1890's is illuminating. While not captioned "social column," these lists clearly were the cream of the visiting crop in the newspaper's eyes. They were compiled from the registers of the principal (and most expensive) hotels that lined the Boardwalk, a selection device which simplified the editor's task, since these great structures embodied the town's most forceful claim to elegance and sophistication. An examination of twenty-six weekly lists—chiefly in 1890, 1893, and 1894, when they were prominently and extensively featured in the newspaper—yields 467 names of distinguished visitors. These were all from Philadelphia (if a visitor came from a different city, the *Daily Union* noted that fact). A comparison of these names with the appropriate *Social Registers* yields 10 definite listings and 5 possible listings. Lest it be thought that the resort press was too yokel an affair to recognize society when they saw it, similar data from the *Philadelphia Inquirer* may be added. Of 327 distinguished visitors to Atlantic City (1892, 1894, 1901), 14 are found in the *Social Register*. In addition, of 142 arrivals on a single day at a dozen hotels (including the prestigious Traymore, Windsor, and Chalfonte), 4 are listed.

But perhaps Philadelphia society, while not thronging the hotels, maintained a sizable cottage community at the seaside. The Social Register Association published a summer edition in 1900 which gave 763 addresses of individuals or families, listed in the winter register at Philadelphia residences, who had summer homes elsewhere. Only 31 of them gave a summer address for Atlantic City, and 7 of these are not private homes but hotels. Though this edition of the register gave the same information for society members from Baltimore, Washington, New York, Chicago, and Boston, only one individual from these cities had a summer residence at the resort. Taking the summer addresses of the first two hundred Philadelphians in the register, we find fully half of them choosing the fashionable Philadelphia suburbs (such as Chestnut Hill and the Main Line), with most of the rest scattered among various northeastern resorts and foreign countries. Seven preferred Atlantic City. In sum, if high society was not utterly absent at the City by the Sea, there was something less than a surfeit of tweed on the Boardwalk.

Who were these "distinguished visitors" then? The brief descriptions attached to some of the names in the *Daily Union* give an idea. They are offered as given, with no attempt to harmonize the syntax: "Pennsylvanic Cycle Co.," "the well known brick manufacturer," "a prominent official in the passenger department of the Pennsylvania Railroad," "candidate for District Attorney of Philadelphia," "a prominent businessman," "a prominent merchant," "a well known carpet manufacturer," "a prominent Philadelphia Civil Engineer," "a prominent member of the Quaker City bar," "manager . . . of the Philadelphia Press," "a well known Philadelphia letter carrier," "publisher and printer," "one of Philadelphia's most prominent physicians," "a well known Philadelphia shoe manufacturer," "a well known Philadelphia fruit dealer," "a prominent iron merchant," "Select Councilman of the Tenth Ward," "President of the Penn Mutual Life Insurance Co.," "President of the Fire Association of Philadelphia," "real estate agent," "publisher of The First Ward News," "of Common Council's," "the well known Philadelphia politician," "a prominent Philadelphia lumber merchant," "well known wholesale grocer of Philadelphia," "the 8th street shoe merchant," "Recorder of Deeds of Philadelphia." Also, twenty-one physicians.

These were the elite of business, manufacturing, government, publishing, and the professions. They were not high society. How a "well known Philadelphia letter carrier" made the list is anyone's guess; the inclusion seems ironic, but it was probably meant seriously. In six instances, ladies at the great hotels are specifically described as high society: "a pretty society lady of Germantown," "a popular acquisition to the large number of society representatives stopping at the Waverly," "a leader of society of Philadelphia," "a handsome blonde and prominent in Philadelphia social circles," and others. Yet none of these ladies is listed in the *Social Register*. It cannot be said that a blueblood never trod the strand, but society stayed away from the town with marked assiduity. Most of the rich who did come were the men who gave the Gilded Age its name, the nouveaux riches who were forging industrial America and growing fat on the proceeds. With them came the upper middle class, who could afford some of the same luxuries in more modest degree. The pseudo-snobbery of resort literature was partly aimed at both groups. If they couldn't be invited to Newport, they could buy their way into Atlantic City, but they would have to share the city with the classes they were escaping from. One article put it in just these terms:

> The ultra-swell and almost no one else go to Lenox, Bar Harbor, Newport. Swell and near-swell and folks "just comfortable" go to places like Asbury Park. Into Atlantic City ever day in the season are dumped ultra-, almost-, and near-swell, folks comfortable and uncomfortable, and absolutely every other kind by the thousands; for that's Atlantic City.

There are numerous indications that those not having a vested interest in the promotion of the resort regarded it as lowbrow in atmosphere. The year 1894 was a black one for the national economy, but the *Philadelphia Inquirer* claimed that the resort had acquired new visitors from "influential society" and the "wealthy classes, ranging from the tens to the hundreds of thousands valuation." The author of the article, while seemingly sympathetic to the resort's interests, gave it a backhanded slap: "Some of these people came because they were tired of other resorts and wanted novelty, which they certainly get here, and others visited here because they could not afford to go to the more ultra and consequently much more expensive resorts." In 1909 a visiting journalist sardonically portrayed the nouveaux riches in the town. These are not the "Financiers" or the "Titans" whom Theodore Dreiser portrayed; these are bush-league robber barons:

> These men are mainly railroad men and manufacturers—not the heads of railways, but assistants and deputies and lieutenants. They have money in abundance without being vastly rich, and they come to Atlantic City because it so exactly suits their barbarous ideal of what is fine.
>
> They never think of anything outside the subject of iron or coal or pork or wheat or railway rates. They incarnate crass materialism in its most hopeless form.

The *Daily Union* complained in 1892 that the resort was failing to attract "the patronage of millionaires" because it lacked a really posh hotel of the "first class Ponce de Leon" variety. Indeed, by 1887 Atlantic City was already developing a suburb named Chelsea, to which its upper-middle-class natives were retreating. The locals had begun to sniff at their customers.

Although the resort's nouveaux riches might be crass materialists, they were not always humorless. The *Inquirer*, observing that powerful Philadelphia politicians are often seen at the shore, mentions an anecdote of "George W. Ledlie, the generous and big-hearted Port Warden of the Thirty-second ward, and the gentleman who has 4300 men working for him on his electrical traction work in Philadelphia and other cities." The tale is not without relevance to Atlantic City's moneyed customers and to Gilded Age ethics:

> Mr. Ledlie tells a story, which is worth repeating, of an old firm of coal dealers who had as an employe an individual who was about as dumb and thick-headed as they come. This failing on the man's part became so apparent, finally, that the firm decided to discharge him. To bring this about, one of the members, with his visage full of foreboding portent, said: "Say, Bill, what do you know anyhow?"
>
> The employe said: "Well, not much, boss. But I know that 1800 pounds makes a ton." That the man was kept on the firm's pay-roll, it is needless to say.

Quite apart from transient patrons, many of the resort's upper-middle-class users were resident throughout the summer in the city, renting the great number of cottages which the locals vacated for the season to pull in some extra money. Editor Hall estimated that there were over four thousand cottages on Absecon Island and that fully half of them were rented each summer. Such seasonal residents were often professionals and executives who commuted from Philadelphia, apparently each day, leaving their families by the seaside. A Camden and Atlantic Railroad brochure of 1883 encouraged this trade, while in 1893 the Reading Railroad sold twenty-trip commutation tickets for $17.50. This portion of the resort's clientele was reliable and dull, the least colorful part of the visiting population. It was certainly welcome, yet the garish, intense pleasure industries of the Boardwalk were aimed at the more transient customers. The cottagers spent their money peacefully and left comparatively little historical record.

At the other end of the social spectrum were the blacks, both resident and visiting. Evidence of their activities is hard to come by, for while the resort was highly dependent on black labor, it was anxious not to advertise the presence of blacks to potential white customers. Since most blacks were poor, they could hardly constitute a large tourist population. On the other hand, merely by working in Atlantic City they were able to avail themselves of some of the pleasures of the resort. The New Jersey state census of 1905 shows that, of 426 resident blacks, only 38 had been born in New Jersey. Of the vast majority not native to the state, 130 had been born in Virginia, 86 in Maryland, 43 in Washington, D.C., 34 in Pennsylvania, and 27 in North Carolina. A total of 47 were from fifteen other states, and individuals had come from Cuba, England, and Australia. A great many no doubt lived in Philadelphia before seeking work in the resort. Nevertheless, directly or indirectly they found themselves in a very special community, some of whose pleasures could not be denied them.

It was a situation not entirely agreeable to the local establishment. In 1893 the *Inquirer* complained:

> What are we going to do with our colored people? That is the question. Atlantic City has never before seemed so overrun with the dark skinned race as this season, probably because the smaller proportion of visitors makes their number more prominent. At any rate, both the boardwalk and Atlantic avenue fairly swarm with them during bathing hours, like the fruit in a huckleberry pudding. This has gone so far that it is offending the sensitive feelings of many visitors, especially those from the South. . . . Of the hundreds of hotels and boarding houses which stud the island from one end to the other, it is probable that not a dozen could be found in which white help is employed. And when to the thousands of waiters and cooks and porters are added the nurse girls, the chambermaids, the barbers and bootblacks and hack drivers and other colored gentry in every walk and occupation of life, it will easily be realized what an evil it is that hangs over Atlantic City.

Although this complaint is a good expression of the contradictory mentality of a white culture which employed blacks for every personal service and yet was distressed by the thought of mingling with them in the surf, it is nevertheless an admission that the city made no real attempt to exclude blacks from the beachfront. The article went on to say that in Asbury Park the problem had been solved by the founder and "original proprietor" of the resort, who restricted blacks to certain defined areas. But in Atlantic City, with ownership diffused in hundreds of hands, no such unified suppression was possible. The author conceded that only the collaboration of all the beachfront proprietors could keep the blacks in their place, a collaboration which (one suspects) was unlikely. Seven years later the *Washington Post* complained of the way local blacks by the hundreds were invading the bathing districts "heretofore patronized by the best visitors." Conditions were similarly lax off the beach: "After the colored waiter serves his master's supper he can go out and elbow him on the Boardwalk, crowd him in the cars, or drink at the very next table to him in almost any cafe." But it would be wrong to imagine that blacks at the resort were always coldly viewed. In July 1900 the *Inquirer* good-naturedly (if condescendingly) mentioned "a beautiful young colored lady becomingly garbed in broad, longitudinal stripes of black and orange alternating and carrying an indescribable, unmentionable parasol into the surf with her to shield her complexion from tan and freckles while in water up to her neck."

Of course, Atlantic City was not in fact completely integrated. Various kinds of informal segregation were practiced everywhere. The *Daily Union* records the criticism of a black Pennsylvania newspaper concerning the "color line" in the resort. Although black servants could sit in the pavilions along the Boardwalk, wealthy black tourists were denied admission. Such inverted discrimination in favor of poor over wealthy blacks was perfectly logical, given the racial convictions of the whites. After all, the servants had to be in Atlantic City: the black tourists did not.

The amount of black excursionism to Atlantic City is, as has been suggested, harder to determine than the use of facilities by local blacks. Nevertheless, it is clear that during the 1890's there was an annual outing to the resort for blacks from Philadelphia and the surrounding area. The *Daily Union* reported the visit of five thousand blacks to the Seaview Hotel and excursion district on September 3, 1891. They used public conveyances, swam, and enjoyed themselves at the Seaview's dance hall and carrousel. The date, September 3, is interesting. At that time Labor Day had not yet been made a national holiday and September 1 marked the end of summer at the shore, after which resort trade quickly dried up. It may be that the blacks who organized the excursion chose a date just after the close of the season to avoid offending the whites. Moreover, the money would be welcome as a post-season windfall.

The *Inquirer* observed in September 1896 that "one of the harbingers of fall is . . . the annual excursion of colored citizens from Pennsylvania, Delaware and New Jersey to the seashore." The visitors that year remained in the lower Boardwalk area, and "the beach below Texas avenue was devoted exclusively to the dusky bathers." The newspaper approvingly commented on their orderliness, for there were very few arrests and "the race weapon, the 'razor,' was conspicuously absent." In September 1897 the annual black excursion drew eleven carloads over the Pennsylvania Railroad and twenty-five over the Reading. Some travelers report-edly came from as far away as Maryland for the event. The 1898 convocation prompted the *Inquirer* to remark that there was "no more disorder than there would be were the gathering composed of an equal number of whites."

Whether Atlantic City's hospitality to blacks warmed as the decade advanced is not clear from the limited evidence, but in 1897 there was a holiday during the regular season in mid-August for "the belles and beaux of the colored quarter" of Philadel-phia. They chartered two gaily decorated streetcars with musi-cians aboard for a round-trip party over the length of Absecon Island. Another August excursion took place the following year, and on August 22, 1899, the Baptist National Colored Congress met at Atlantic City, where "Miss G. H. Hoggers, of Philadelphia, caused a sensation when she said that God knew his business when he made the negro black, and that he should not seek to get white by using cosmetics." Black excursionism continued into the twentieth century, as evidenced by a postcard dated from Atlantic City in August 1909: "Never saw so many of the Col-ored race on any train. 11 cars of them. 27 whites *only.*"

Thus it appears that while blacks suffered under the traditional exploitations and disadvantages of racial prejudice at the resort, they nevertheless enjoyed certain opportunities to outflank white society. Racial barriers more rigidly enforced elsewhere were hard to preserve at the seaside, and sometimes they were largely relaxed. Moreover, blacks were able to achieve some political power, as we shall see later.

At the very bottom of the heap of the resort's users was a group which contributed neither money nor labor, and therefore was not welcome. Atlantic City wanted a smiling face, for important reasons shortly to be discussed, and the presence of tramps dis-turbed the smile. There was a good deal of pathos in their situa-tion: "Ten tramps, like a flock of sheep, being chased down the railroad track by officer Piner was an amusing sight witnessed by many this morning. As the summer season progresses these undesirable visitors make their appearance, stealing rides in freight cars." The city's policy was to hustle tramps as quickly as apprehended over the drawbridge back to the mainland. Bums who applied to the city jail, however, were given overnight lodg-ing. Perhaps this service was granted on the condition of their leaving town, though this is only conjecture. At any rate, in 1897 a total of 471 persons were admitted as "Lodgers," "Tramps," and "Bums" to the city jail. The authorities had a habit of categorizing them: 229 were classified as "Americans," 129 as Irish, 38 as black, 36 as German, 4 as Jews, and 2 as English. The *Daily Union* complimented the Jews on their "excellent showing," "considering the large numbers in this city and the fact that many are constantly traveling . . . in their effort to earn their livelihood." The resort had particular trouble with tramps during the severe depression beginning in 1893 (the worst to hit America until the Great Depression of the 1930's); in that year a detachment of Coxey's Army passed through town, to the great amusement of the employed. This was a novel incident, but hoboes were a recurrent problem. In 1908 it was observed: "There are no beggars around to bother [the visitor]; they and the tramps are run out of town as soon as discovered." By 1912 the Salvation Army had an "industrial home" in the resort, and the Volunteers of America had a lodging house for transients of both sexes. Such was seaside life for those who tarnished the Gilded Age.

Between the extremes of the rich and the déclassé stood the lower middle and lower classes. Certainly these two groups were distinct from each other, but together they comprised the great mass of visitors to the resort. Evidence points to the numerical preponderance of the lower middle class, with the lower class coming in its wake and enjoying whatever its modest means would allow. In terms of numbers, the greater part of the accommodation industry was directed toward the lower middle class, while the values expressed in the resort's entertainment were those of citizens vigorously striving for the good life which they believed they could attain and which they imagined the upper middle class and rich to enjoy. It seems likely that upper-middle-class observers tended to lump the lower middle and lower classes together. A laborer in clean shirt with wife and family would be as acceptable and as "respectable" as a petty clerk and his family. So long as the lower-class visitor had money to spend, he might "pass" as lower middle class. From the visitor's viewpoint, the clerk in an insurance office certainly would not consider himself on a par with the hod carrier. Nevertheless, both belonged to the less-moneyed group of tourists, instead of the blue-ribbon trade which some promoters fancied Atlantic City should attract. The local upper middle class who ran the large businesses, edited the newspapers, and cranked out the publicity for the town viewed this great mass of visitors with mixed feelings. Though the hosts wanted their money and recognized that the resort depended on their patronage, they often wished their guests were someone else.

It is necessary to consider how the hotel industry fit into the needs of the lower middle class. It is obvious that the great hotels were beyond their range. The Traymore charged $3.00 to $5.00 a day, as did the Brighton. The United States Hotel and the Dennis demanded $3.00 to $3.50, while Haddon Hall had accommodations from $3.00 to $4.00. No shopgirl from Wanamaker's or ticket agent for the Pennsylvania Railroad was going to pay that much unless he was on a mad spree. On the other hand, a study of 225 of the principal hotels in 1887 shows that most of them charged far less. The most common daily charge (73 hotels) was only $1.50 to $2.00 for room and board. On a weekly basis, the cost was lower. A total of 91 hotels offered weekly room and board for $8.00 to $12.00, this being the most common price range of the many schedules available. In 1890 clerical workers in steam railroads and manufacturing averaged $848 a year; thus $8.00 for a week's lodging and food would represent about half a week's salary. It seems reasonable to suppose that such hotels would be well within their range. Annual real wages for other kinds of workers included: $1,096 for government employees in the executive branch, $878 for postal employees, $794 for ministers, $687 for workers in gas and electricity, $439 for workers in manufacturing (nonclerical), and $256 for teachers. Here the economic blurring of the classes emerges, however different their aspirations and working conditions might be. Schoolteachers simply could not afford hotel rates; a trolley-car driver might. But in the main, the lower middle class could meet the prices of the majority of hotels in Atlantic City, assuming that their stay represented a holiday for which they had saved. Qualifications are in order. The larger the hotel, the more expensive it tended to be: with one exception, the eleven largest were above the $1.50–$2.50 range. They comprised 5 percent of the total number of hotels, yet had 23 percent of the total number of rooms. The 91 hotels which offered room and board for $8.00–$12.00 weekly comprised 40 percent of the total number of hotels, yet had only 25 percent of the total number of rooms. In other words, only about one fourth of the hotel space could be had at the cheapest rates. Yet these smaller houses were probably more consistently full. A newspaper clipping in a scrapbook compiled in 1885 indicates that at peak season only the big hotels had room available, whereas second-rate hotels and boardinghouses were crammed full. Moreover, when demand exceeded supply, hotel men practiced "doubling up" in the rooms, a maneuver which could hardly have been used in the most expensive and prestigious houses. Thus the smaller, cheaper hotels, though lacking in space, utilized their space more fully.

The principal bailiwick of the lower middle class was the boardinghouse, not the hotel. Unfortunately, their rates are not recorded, though they must have ranged from the price of the cheapest hotels down to a good deal lower. In return for lower rates, the boardinghouse offered relatively humdrum accommodations and food. One fastidious reporter for *The New York Times* was reduced to desperation in his search for a hotel room on a summer evening in 1883:

> I passed a large boarding-house with a crowd on the front porch and somebody banging a piano in the parlor. I was almost far enough gone to seek for shelter in a boarding-house, but not quite. Even in my desolate condition I pitied the dwellers in an Atlantic City boarding-house and passed on.

Still, boardinghouses, though lacking the glamour of even a small hotel, made available to the lower middle class a means of extended vacationing; without them they could have afforded only daily excursions. Estimating the number of boardinghouses is difficult, since there was no legal obligation for a proprietor to call his hostel by the name of "boardinghouse" or "hotel." In addition, the nebulous term "cottage" was often favored, no doubt for its implication of class as well as its lack of clarity. *Gopsill's Directory*, the standard Atlantic City guide in this period, lists the "hotels, cottages, and boardinghouses" for each year. A fair estimate would place boardinghouses, in name or in fact, at about three fifths the annual total:

1882–83	311	1896	610
1884	349	1897	582
1885	362	1898	590
1886	382	1899	621
1887	443	1900	649
1888	506	1901	715
1889	506	1902	739
1890	522	1903	665
1891	570	1904	689
1892	541	1905	696
1893	512	1906	683
1894	552	1907	682
1895	600	1908	716

The above figures show that, measured by the number of establishments, the accommodation industry developed steadily in the 1880's, wobbled but developed in the 1890's, and leveled off after 1902. Apparently the hard times of the 1890's did not drive many boardinghouses and hotels out of business. Nevertheless, prosperity was not identical with being open for business. The impact of depression on a mass resort is apparent in an *Inquirer* article of 1893:

> Nearly every branch of business has felt the depression. The small hotel-keepers, who run their houses largely on speculation from season to season, have the most to fear, and several of them are tottering in the balance. A few weeks of good business would put them on their feet again, and this is what all are praying for. The big houses, like the Windsor, Brighton and Dennis, which draw their patronage almost exclusively from the fashionable and moneyed elements of society, are doing well, because these elements of society will always flock to seaside resorts as long as the resorts last.

When the economic fortunes of average Americans faltered, those of Atlantic City faltered as well. Widespread hard times inevitably touched the majority of resort businessmen, and if the town's few most prestigious services had a clientele with a reserve to fall back on, it could only make the general drought more irksome.

Atlantic City could not have existed without the railroads, and the railroads could not have existed without the lower middle and lower classes. During summer weekdays, lower-middle-class families and young single people poured into town on their annual vacations, and their fares sustained the railroads, which waited for weekends to make the big killing. Just like the resort, the railroads needed successful weekends for a profitable season. On twelve or thirteen weekends hinged the prosperity of the entire year, and in fact Sundays were most critical of all. The six-day workweek was the general practice in the nineteenth century; thus employees not on vacation had one day a week into which to cram their summer pleasure. The excellent rail service between Atlantic City and Philadelphia made a round trip in one day feasible, and the railroads recognized that they must encourage this mass patronage with low rates. The narrow-gauge Philadelphia and Atlantic City Railway was built for this purpose in 1877, offering fares that Hall claims went as low as fifty cents for a round trip. Travel to the resort increased swiftly: "The crowds in the city were so large at times, especially over Sunday, as to nearly exhaust the supply of meat, milk, bread and provisions in stock." Generally, round-trip excursions cost $1.00 or $1.50, and in 1880 the fare was increased to $1.75. A protest meeting was organized in the resort, probably as a response to the threat the raise posed to the excursion trade. The West Jersey and Atlantic Railroad, controlled by the Pennsylvania, was organized in 1880 specifically to attract "the medium and poorer classes." The fare was "the astonishing sum of fifty cents each— less than hackfare from Market street Philadelphia, to the Park." The expense of travel could be reduced still further from prevailing excursion rates by organizing charters, a popular practice. In 1880 Hillman and Mackey advertised themselves as sole agents soliciting group excursions on the Camden and Atlantic Railroad, and invited churches, fraternal organizations, and other interested assemblies to make early reservations for choice summer dates. On the mass patronage of the ordinary tourists the railroads were able to maintain service which provided for upper-middle-class and upper-class visitors as well.

There are many random indications of the essentially lower-middle-class appeal of the resort, in addition to the evidence of lodgings and transportation. Excursion houses had a long history at the seaside. Built at the terminals of railroads entering the city, they provided a reception point, an entertainment pavilion, a dining hall, and an amusement park for the weekend crowds. The Seaview Excursion House aimed at the popular market, with "its broad piazzas, its numberless facilities for amusement, and its enormous dining-hall, which can be changed on occasion into a Jardin Mabille, with flowers and fountains." The West Jersey Excursion House featured solid excursion-oriented food, like "fish, chicken, roast meats, vegetables, pies, pudding, ice cream, tea and coffee." It provided free music and dancing in the ballroom, a bar, a bowling alley, and a pool room, and bathing suits and lockers could be rented for twenty-five cents. The Seaview announced that "the large and spacious Ball Room will be used for Roller Skating every evening except Wednesday," while the Ocean House had a "Billiard Room Attached." Later, in 1911, the Hygeia Hotel promised the "Free use of shower bath," whence, apparently, its name. Its price range went as low as fifty cents, because it was on the "European plan," which meant that the visitor of modest means could bring his own food. Most amusements admitted customers at five cents or ten cents apiece, aiming at high-turnover, low-cost entertainment. Applegate's Pier let in baby carriages for free, with an eye to thrifty mothers. Heinz Pier, which charged nothing for admission, featured an "art exhibit" of fine rugs, ceramics, figurines, and paintings. But the company sought to develop a mass market for its "57 Varieties" through samples and demonstrations. A souvenir postcard introduced the housewife to the mysteries of canned goods. "Four Ways of Serving Heinz's Baked Beans With Tomato Sauce" included "The Usual Way" ("Place the can in boiling water for ten to fifteen minutes, then open and serve. *Especially desirable for luncheons*") and a fearsome recipe for "Bean Salad" ("Place portions of the contents of a can of Heinz's Baked Beans in individual salad dishes. Pour over each portion a tablespoonful of Heinz's Mustard Salad Dressing"). Endless details reveal the mass orientation of Atlantic City.

If Atlantic City was primarily a lower-middle-class resort, then the next question concerns the basic function it performed for its clientele. In simplest terms, the answer is: it was there to dispense pleasure. The thousands of different people who flocked to the city shared an extraordinary community of feeling which could not exist under normal urban conditions, because, unlike the conventional city, Atlantic City had a single purpose. The Boardwalk was a stage, upon which there was a temporary suspension of disbelief; behavior that was exaggerated, even ridiculous, in everyday life was expected at the resort. The rigidities of Victorian life relaxed, permitting contact between strangers and the pursuit of fantasies. The imprimatur of the absurd was upon Atlantic City. In later years it would be the scene of fantastic stunts which came to be expected in the merrily bizarre atmosphere of the place—aviation feats, a gigantic operating typewriter, a colossal marathon dance derby, the gaudy and grotesque Miss America Pageant. Examples from the 1890's include a balloon ascension and parachute drop, Pain Pyrotechnic Company's Battle of Manila at Inlet Park (together with the explosion of the *Maine* and a mammoth portrait of Admiral Dewey in fireworks), a female baseball club, and a challenge supper of "oysters and sugar, pure soap, watermelon and molasses" undertaken by three visitors who wagered that "the one who first became ill after eating certain dishes agreed upon by the trio should 'set up' a wine supper for the less distressed members of the party." The town was a gargantuan masquerade, as visitor deceived visitor, and entrepreneurs fooled them all. And people wanted to be deceived, to see life as other than it was, to pretend that they were more than they were. America was starved, as today, for festivals. The culture was groping toward common bonds in an industrial world, bonds that could humanize and integrate urban life without reimposing the restrictions of the old village form of society. Atlantic City provided a location of common understanding, together with a diminution of customary restrictions. The fluidity it offered was the countervailing force to a culture too rigid, with expectations in excess of possibility.

Pleasure at the resort meant not only fluidity but also the illusion of social mobility. Whether such an illusion is a good thing depends on the philosophical inclination of the observer, whose attitude will be affected by the degree to which the actual mobility of the society approximates the illusion. No attempt will be made here to improve upon Stephan Thernstrom's analysis in *Poverty and Progress*, which maintains that America did provide its citizens with real mobility, but not in the rags-to-riches manner of the Horatio Alger novel. For present purposes, let it be noted that the crowds at Atlantic City very much liked the fantasy world which surrounded them, and that it was skillfully and ingeniously presented by men who shared their hopes for the realization of the fantasy.

One form of fluidity found at Atlantic City was increased contact between the sexes. It is not possible here strictly to separate actuality from illusion, but only to make some observations. Common sense suggests that meetings between males and females of like class, socially and economically, were far easier in a resort than in the outside world. Young men with prospects, money to spend, and the desire to meet girls would take their annual vacations there. Single girls could visit the resort in the company of girl friends, or with relatives or parents who might well be understanding, or even alone. The excursions seem to have been gay parties from beginning to end. With the anonymity provided by a great transient city went a kind of prior legitimation of contact. No one went to Atlantic City for solitude, at least not in summer. So anyone who went there could expect to meet strangers, and could feel relatively assured in seeking introductions. This process was similar to today's computer dating, in which selection of mutually compatible couples is not the point. Rather, the computer, with its prestige in a science-worshipping society, provides a technological and therefore social ratification of the meeting of strangers with like motivation. Single people who went to Atlantic City could expect that other single people would have motives similar to theirs. This was a great breaker of barriers, and was of real benefit to the people involved.

Of course, not all mingling at the resort was of the approved sort, nor did the easygoing informality of seaside life always yield wholesome fruit. In July 1896, a local constable invaded a Kentucky Avenue hotel at one in the morning to arrest a couple who had registered as "Mr. and Mrs. C. R. Duff." "Sensational developments are expected at the hearing," the *Inquirer* duly informed its readers, for the adulterous pair were allegedly well known in Philadelphia. A detective, hired by an outraged husband, had shadowed them to discover who was plumbing "Mrs. Duff." Sometimes the temptation to exceed social proprieties proved compelling, as in the case of a young man who "implanted four osculatory bits upon the ruby lips of a woman whose acquaintance he did not enjoy." The judge before whom this scapegrace appeared rejected his defense that he was unable to restrain himself, and "decided that there was not sufficient provocation, though he admitted that the victim of the kisser was fair to gaze upon." He nailed the culprit for five dollars a kiss, and "would not consent to a discount on a lot of four, but insisted that the trespasser upon the dignity of woman should pay $20." "Dan and Mary," a couple from Chicago, found Atlantic City a bit too casual for the prosperity of their relationship:

> She accused Dan of having boldly flirted with others of her sex, to which the lover mildly protested. With the cunning that is proverbial in the feminine world, Mary pretended that she believed Dan, and matters went along smoothly again. But the storm broke in all its fury yesterday, when Daniel, after having enjoyed a surf bath, during which he cast sheep's eyes at a fair female bather, returned to his bath house. Mary had seen his doings, and she was mad clear through, so she decided that in order to prevent a reoccurrence of such scenes she would treat her derelict lover to another bath. Straightway she procured a box of lye, which she poured into a bucket of water. Then, as Daniel hove in sight she prepared for the act of her life. When within a few feet . . . Mary took good aim and fired.

Dan was obliged to seek a quick rinse before repairing to a magistrate to have his sweetheart arrested. But at length he gallantly declined to press charges, and was reunited with his fiery mistress. Incidents such as these doubtless were exceptions to the happier rule of pleasant boy-girl encounters.

As an aid to the mixing of the sexes, Applegate's Pier had a

"Lover's Pavilion." The *Daily Union* snickered at a Baltimore ordinance forbidding public kissing, imagining what a riot such a law would cause if enacted at the seaside. Guvernator's Mammoth Pavilion had an inner sanctum, curtained off, which sold liquor to young people and was accordingly a popular place among them.

> A noteworthy feature was that many of these young people who were entertaining each other did not seem to be very well acquainted. Their speech and actions did not indicate such, any how [sic]. As an example may be cited the determined efforts of a rosy-cheeked lad of not more than eighteen years, surely, to discover the "real name" of the maiden who accompanied him.

Beyond this, increased sexual contact existed on the level of illusion. This in itself could have concrete results, because expectations encouraged fulfillment. It is undeniable that the public believed Atlantic City to be a great mingler of the sexes. A postcard from the turn of the century shows two ladies in a rolling chair who have just run down a well-dressed young man. Flat on his back, he gallantly salutes them. "Just ran across an old friend on the Boardwalk," says the caption, but behind the weak humor is substance, the fantasy of women assuming the role of sexual aggressors. A flowery bit of prose in John F. Hall's history extols the romantic milieu of the resort: "It must be borne in mind that the Goddess of Love is the divinity that presides at the seashore and the matches that are made within sight of the sea, while not as numerous as the sands on the beach, are of frequent occurrence." Such attitudes were congruent with the official sanction given the family, and in a city that prided itself on being the Family Resort, it is not surprising that faith in the availability of marriage is frequently proclaimed. This did not deny the element of chance, which made the game more exciting and poignant. Heston's handbook for 1888 shows a male hand clasping a female hand, and the legend: "The Autumn Break-Up—They May Never Meet Again." But at least they had met the first time, and getting contacts for the long winter was probably the strategic objective of many Philadelphians.

In spite of the make-believe atmosphere along the Boardwalk, however, it was necessary to bear in mind the prudent considerations of the real world which resumed after vacation's end. An 1873 article mentioned "whole rows of unmatched girls" who waited by the shore for partners "equal to them in social position." There was much latitude for deception here, the making of alliances that would end in bitter disillusionment. But when the Cinderella romance did come true, and in an honorable way, it was cause for celebration, a vindication of the capitalistic faith that the individual could transcend class. A story from the *Inquirer* in 1893 is straight out of Horatio Alger:

> A wedding will take place quietly at this resort tomorrow, which if all the details were known, would disclose one of the most romantic stories of the season. The bride is a young Philadelphia girl who is well-known among the employes of Wanamaker's, where she has held a position as saleswoman for several years past. She came down last week to spend her vacation at the shore, and during the gay round of pleasure she encountered a young Western man.
>
> The pair were strangely attracted to one another, and the upshot of the acquaintanceship will be tomorrow's ceremony. The bridegroom comes from Colorado, and is reputed to be the sion [*sic*] of one of the wealthiest families of the Centennial State.

But even without romance, the feeling of being part of a great crowd with a common purpose was intrinsically pleasurable. A promotional pamphlet exalted "the crowd itself," in which each participant figures as does another wave in the sea. A visitor mentioned how he liked to "bathe in people" at the resort. It was a huge party, with everyone putting on his best face as befitted the situation. The sores of industrial living and working were hidden from view, just as the resort took care to railroad its bums out of town.

Since there was a heightened awareness of forms of behavior appropriate to a pleasure city, fads arose which the masses seized upon. They conferred a feeling of belonging, a "society" of those outside society. Fads also testified to the loneliness that was a part of city living, for a fad is an artificial attempt, inherently frantic, to create or to heighten identity where insufficient identity is felt. Fads in Atlantic City took such diverse forms as the use of certain words, the wearing of particular objects and items of clothing, interest in what is *au courant*, and even the adoption of certain roles.

> Talking of love and pretty girls, we do not have any more flirtations, they are called "mashes"—"don't you forget it." This is the day of slang phrases; at cards you are told that "you can't some-

times most always generally tell how things will turn out"; as for the bathing "it is just too awfully nice for anything."

The *Inquirer* warned its readers in July 1896 to avoid being judged "not in it" by laying in a supply of comic lapel buttons. Messages in use on the Boardwalk included: "If you love me, grin"; "I am somewhat of a liar myself, and there are others"; "I am mamma's darling, whose darling are you?"; and the succinct "Yes, darling." The young man could wear one proclaiming, "Give me your hand," to which the "summer girl" could respond with another which said, "I will be a sister to you."

In 1897, someone discovered that a burning incense taper carried in the coiffure would discourage Jersey's saber-toothed mosquitoes, and this practical innovation quickly became an item of fashion. As crowds of women strolled the Boardwalk by night, the effect was "quite startling, resembling somewhat the firefly." Vacationers also liked to have friends autograph their cigarettes as keepsakes, and white duck sailor hats were similarly used, the object being the hieroglyphic effect attained by great numbers of signatures. For a brief time, daring young men wore a single silk garter made of flashy ribbon with a silver buckle as they paraded the beach. Young women were fond of attracting attention by performing athletic exercises on the sand, such enthusiasts being generally of generous endowments and often of economical inclinations in the use of yard goods for bathing costumes.

At the century's end, "Hello, My Baby" was so popular that this "mongrel ballad" could scarcely be escaped along the waterfront, while the "latest dude dress" was reported to be a white jersey shirt worn "Chinaman style outside of the pantaloons." Men were advised to turn up the cuffs of their white flannel trousers if they wished to be in style. Palmistry was in favor, especially among the ladies, who queued up to consult various "professors," "gypsy queens," and other savants "just arrived from Paris." The palmists had "all sorts of queer-sounding cognomens, some of which are regular jaw-breakers," and were attired in "some fantastic costume" to impress "the fair patron with the weight of their marvelous powers." Previously, phrenology had been the "summer girl's" pet interest, and her aspiring gallant might be cruelly diverted from "a conversation of particular personal interest" with "How's the development of your bump of amativeness?"

Ladies' bathing suits became more abbreviated and more

colorful as the end of the century approached. Part of the reason was the increasing number of women learning to swim (who appreciated not having to drag pounds of spare cloth through the water) and part the growing hedonism of American society. "Time was," said the *Inquirer*, "when women went into the water with long, baggy trousers down to their heels, while over these hideous garments hung flannel skirts. But that was in the old days before the world began moving at the pace it seems to be going at now." Women were eager to keep up with bathing-suit fashions, and the typical costume of 1898 "would scarcely fill the much talked of collar box." The more daring abandoned stockings and began to abbreviate their skirts. Bicycle clothing influenced bathing-suit design toward trimness, much to the delight of male "kodak fiends." A new female type emerged, "the bicycle girl, mayhap astride a man's wheel, scorching up and down the strand, with her golden hair hanging down her back and robed in a natty bathing suit, the colors of which outrival the noise of the bell, with her jaws going at a rapid pace because of the wad of tutti-frutti she has hidden within." Novelty was possible in street wear, too. For the Fourth of July 1896, one enterprising young lady "combined patriotism and style" by wearing a shirtwaist fashioned from a silken American flag, with a body of blue studded with stars and sleeves of red and white stripes.

A more esoteric fad, the "widow craze," struck Atlantic City in 1893. The widow possessed a mystique of "experience" which the maiden never enjoyed, an earthly wisdom made respectable by the hand of God. The black clothing, drab in color but not necessarily in design, was an immediate attention getter, and widows were allegedly in demand. Their avowed bereavement recommended itself to the solicitations of gallant strangers. An attractive blond widow was to be seen every afternoon at a certain time on the merry-go-round, dressed in the "most exquisite style."

The "summer girl" has joined the great auk in extinction, but she was once a prevalent shorebird. She deserves to be considered more as a role than a fad, perhaps, for she reappeared with each *fin de siècle* summer to bewitch male vacationists. "At a distance you would take this creature for an angel and no mistake, for she seems the personification of modesty and grace. Nudge up a little closer—if you can—and alas, you will observe that she has that naughty little twinkle in her eye." With her "coquettish commingling of sea shore freedom, natural feminine vanity and womanly longing for admiration," she was a sentimental favorite of journalists. But the efforts of young ladies to act the summer girl could make for amusement, too.

> A sensation . . . was furnished on Tuesday by three very pretty, stylish and modest young ladies who went into the water wearing, for the first time, suits that had been made especially for them, cut from thin white flannel. They didn't know, poor things, the terrible shrinking power of salt water, or they would not have gone in . . . They had not been in the water five minutes till a group of horrid men had assembled directly in front of where they were bathing. One of the girls, wonderingly, made a survey, and the result horrified her. The three of them were living pictures of "Venus Rising from the Sea." The white flannel was clinging with a tenacity worthy of a far better cause, and the black stockings showed through the material as though it was tissue paper, and indeed it was not much better. Being nice, modest girls they made a break at once for the bath house, but on their way thither ran a gauntlet far more awful than any ever encountered by Fenimore Cooper's Indian fighters.

Fashionable yet unspoiled, alluring yet virginal, surrounded by imploring suitors whom she coyly evaded, the summer girl was the archetype of female desirability. She was altogether too delicate a flower for the twentieth century.

New York City might have its Four Hundred, but Atlantic City had its Forty Thousand. Anyone could join who had an aptitude for vogue and a fancy to belong to an "elite." In the confined area of the resort—and along its nerve track, the Boardwalk—fads could spread quickly. They occupied the evanescent middle range of repetitive behavior, halfway between the gesture too private to be stylish and the cliche too well known to be distinctive. In a normal city, fads applied to sections of the population, whereas Atlantic City was one great show on a city scale, and everyone was potentially in on the act.

Imitation of the upper class was a primary component of the symbolic mobility which the resort afforded its lower-middle-class users. The many pseudo-sophisticated portraits of the city offered in promotional materials were designed to impart a patrician glamour to a plebeian spa, and far from substantiating the prestige of the place, they prove just the opposite. Atlantic City was low-flung, but it palmed itself off in high-toned terms. The promoters had a good ear for what appealed to their audience, and they were not wanting in boldness. Dr. Boardman Reed, a vigorous booster, composed a brochure for the Pennsylvania Railroad which touted the advantages of his home town as a health resort relative to Florida, the western states, and Europe, but these places were noncompetitive with Atlantic City for 95 percent of its customers. The object could only have been to gild the Jersey coast with glamour rubbed off more remote utopias. Similarly, the imposingly titled "Academy of Music" presented lowbrow fare like comic opera and "Professor Bartholomew's Trained Horses." Overstuffed names like these were usual throughout the town. Many called the fifth boardwalk, completed in 1896, the "Esplanade." But the events of 1898 generated a rumor that this elegant title had a Spanish origin, obliging the embarrassed Esplanadists to retreat hurriedly to the more humble "Boardwalk" to avoid "anything that savors of the Dons."

Probably the most baroque and certainly the most long-lived ersatz phenomenon was the Boardwalk rolling chair. It began as an aid for invalids, but one entrepreneur realized its wider potential. He started renting a fleet of them with attendants, and they rapidly caught on. They were floridly designed along the lines of Brown Decades' aesthetics, with swan-necked prows and heart-shaped dips in the backrests. Thickly padded with comfortable cushions and equipped with robes, they offered to the most proletarian customer willing to spend some change an American version of the sedan chair, the classic attribute of effete aristocracy. The chair pusher was probably the only servant most visitors ever had. Rolling chairs were popular subjects on postcards—just the thing to impress people back home. They were the epitome of nouveau bourgeois.

> Afterward, well wrapped up, a ride in a rolling chair is within the range of possibility, and when one has been wheeled for a stretch along the Boardwalk, dined at the celebrated tables for which our hotels are noted and afterward listened to a high-class concert, he or she is ready to smile a welcome to the sandman.

One of the most important devices by which the lower-middle-class visitor created the illusion of having a higher-class status was clothing, for when nobody knew anybody else, clothes assumed an exaggerated importance in attributing status. Victorian styles allowed rather more yardage for creating effect than today's taste recommends.

The Piers at Atlantic City are the happy hunting grounds for those of the fair sex who love to see beautiful gowns or to display stunning ones in their own wardrobe. Saturday and Sunday nights the crowd is thickest . . .

[One] simple but vastly pretty gown [recently seen] was white organdy made over grape-colored silk. The yoke, which extended over the sleeve top, was of pleats and grape velvet ribbon . . . alternately arranged in groups, edged with a quilling of organdy, velvet bordered. The sleeves were mousquetaire, with a ruche at the wrist, and the waist itself repeated the perpendicular lines of the yoke, but at greater intervals.

The belt and stock were very deep violet satin ribbon and a big bow nestled at the left corner of the yoke. The skirt had a ruching laid in points, which was edged top and bottom with velvet, and above it following the same outline were three rows of the same ribbon. Ruche and ribbon rows were repeated at the foot of the circular flounce. Stunning little gown it was even if not specially original.

Dress standards were high at Atlantic City, both in contemporary terms and even more so from the perspective of the melancholic informality of the present Age of Denim. Gowns, bonnets, and parasols for the ladies and suits, cravats, and skimmer hats for the men were in order for beach strolls. Victorian decorum prevailed right up to mean high-water mark.

While fancy clothing was usual throughout the season, on one particular occasion there was an immense resort-wide competition to be the best-dressed. This was Atlantic City's Easter Parade, copied from the older event on New York's Fifth Avenue. Like the Miss America Pageant at a later date, the Easter Parade was a ploy of local businessmen to pull in shekels outside the normal holiday season. The mild weather of springtime allowed promenading, even if the ocean was too brisk for swimming, and the event was highly popular. One weekend near the turn of the century, for example, allegedly drew nearly forty thousand passengers over the railroads. The Boardwalk each year was jammed rail to rail by a crowd dressed in springtime finery. An army of the nouveaux bourgeois, like the fevered vision of a megalomaniac haberdasher, marched in review past equally well-dressed spectators. This was the white society which found cakewalks so amusing. Yet in its turn it performed a ceremony that to the unanthropological eye was every bit as ridiculous. It was a mass imitation of the upper class, an awkward assumption of the externals of elegance, and as such a parody of itself and its model.

Atlantic City was for sale. High society might be for sale too, in the long run, but it erected barriers against the too easy assault of wealth upon its ranks. A mellowing process was employed, to give time for the aura of the stockyard or the dime store or the roundhouse to dim a bit. New families seeking admission on the basis of wealth and power passed through a generational apprenticeship which allowed sons or grandsons into the ranks of the patriciate, but excluded the patriarch who had done the dirty work. Edward D. Baltzell in *Philadelphia Gentlemen* describes how this worked. But Atlantic City sold its wares cash-on-delivery, and the pocketbook was its only coat of arms. There was a limit to illusion, which the town never forgot: at the end of every fantasy was a hand poised over a cash register. An emphasis on buying and selling pervaded the resort and typified it throughout its history, producing an unabashedly vigorous commercial atmosphere. Every inch of the Boardwalk was engineered to tickle silver out of the jingling pockets of the throng. When the city of Chicago investigated the resort's water-recreation facilities in 1913 and compared them with its own, it was pleased to see that the difference was favorable to the boys in Cook County. It was noted that maximum profit, not convenience and service to the public, was the overriding purpose of the Jersey resort. Searching for upper-class trappings, Atlantic City inaugurated an annual horse show in 1899, prompting editor Hall to express equal enthusiasm for the horseflesh and the profits of the display. A visitor was disgusted when St. Nicholas' Church charged admission to its dedication, "in common with everything else" at the resort, and an *Inquirer* article remarked how the city's businessmen "pile it on" in their systematic extortions. That was a secret of Atlantic City. Though particular charges tended to be small, the methodical way in which everything had its fee led to cumulative effects unhappy for the visitor. The steady trickle of nickels and dimes was the making of fortunes and the undoing of personal budgets as well.

The principal shearing of sheep took place in the scores upon scores of small stores which abutted the Boardwalk on the land side. So long as the stroller was not looking at the ocean, he was looking at something for sale. These petty shops contrasted curiously with the pompous hotels, for they were lower in tone, a kind of lower-middle-class commercial foothills to the great structures behind them. They also moved huge quantities of goods to lower-middle-class customers who could not afford the swank hostelries. But, like the hotels, they encouraged a parallel impulse to consume, to revel in the first full flush of prosperity which urbanization and industrialization were bringing to the common people. The great hotels beyond the foothills would be conquered someday; today the masses could buy from the shops for a taste of high life. It was good stage setting. It encouraged the lower middle class to continue to struggle for utopia by way of materialism, in which it had unshakable faith. It peddled rhinestones by the curb, and held the diamonds a bit further off.

And the things that were sold! Racy postcards, "Genuine Japanese corylopsis talcum," tinsel brooches, agate ornaments, "lurid Naples landscapes on pearl shells," coral, Japanese fern seeds, "Indian" moccasins, Kewpie dolls, Swiss woodcarving, photographs bedizened with gold lacquer, and a heroic device to cut apples open in the shape of a water lily. The visitor could buy an improving tintype to grace his mantel back home ("A stalwart maiden . . . in a boat which stood on end, pulling through the surf with an oar, and dragging a drowning man . . . into the boat with her free hand. The legend was 'Saved'"). Or he could have a glass of "pure orange juice" from a big machine which consumed huge piles of ripe fruit before his eyes ("These machines in several instances are mere dummies, and the great stock of oranges that appear to be passing through the fake crusher is the same old pile that was doing business early in July"). Then there were deviled crabs, lemonade, soda pop, tutti-frutti, Gilt Edge Beer, Fralinger's Salt Water Taffy, Gage's Ice Cream, Zeno Chewing Gum, George Smith's Cream Java Coffee, and innumerable other syrups, jellies, doughs, liquids, and solids to lick, chew, munch, gulp, and swill.

Confronted with so much wonderful junk so relentlessly proffered, visitors engaged happily in recreational buying, as dozens of desires not previously known to exist suddenly sprang into being and demanded fulfillment. All of life seemed to be for sale. Buying itself as a sort of pleasure was institutionalized for good and all in American culture. So far from being simply a convenience for the crowds, selling became a chief entertainment, engaging the passions more deeply and consistently than the ocean ever could. Recreational buying was a new phenomenon at the time. Whereas today it is an obvious element in the success of the suburban shopping center, through which it has become a principal locus of community, in Victorian America it was a novelty that the beneficiaries—the merchants—discovered slowly. The Boardwalk stores at first sold souvenirs and refreshments, and only later extended their wares as they discovered what the crowds wanted. But the entrepreneurs of the resort rose to the occasion handsomely, learning to speak a materialistic language the masses understood. Washington & Arlington's New Unlimited Monster Shows shrewdly tacked on its bill of fare a note pointing out its "steam organ, costing [$]10,000." "Munkacsy's Christ Before Pilate" ("The young woman who recites a little piece and tells all about the picture, explains what is not on the bills, that the picture is 'after' Munkacsy") was touted as "the $100,000 painting." Roving Frank's Gypsies promised that the traditional service of palm reading would be done by "All New Gypsies," a message which belied the spirit of clairvoyance as completely as it fingered the pulse of the times.

The merchants, promoters, and hotelkeepers themselves could only be impressed by the success which had descended on the town. Like their customers, they were a bit overwhelmed by the place, and, as though rubbing their eyes to make sure it was all real, they liked to reassure themselves with endless recounting of the growth in profits and numbers of visitors. They had many anxieties, for their welfare depended on factors that were either partially or totally out of their control: the press of Philadelphia, the laws of New Jersey, public taste, weather, the character of the resort, competition among themselves, and so forth. They had always predicted success for Atlantic City, and yet, now that it was here, was not a certain alchemy involved? Hence they searched for unique factors that would explain their city's fortune, that would imply permanence and eliminate the alchemy of success. The world of things for sale which so appealed to their customers appealed also to themselves. One could sell the goodness of life, and one could buy it—or so it seemed. And if this was true, then the goodness of life had descended upon both merchant and customer along the Boardwalk. Since happiness could be approached by measurable units, the businessmen of Atlantic City were measurers by nature. The Victorians were no Puritans. It was not for them to hasten through this vale of sorrow; they had made it a valley of opportunity. It was necessary now only to remind oneself that opportunity had no sorrows.

Until he settled in Atlantic City, Joseph Fralinger was a loser. Born in 1848 and orphaned at the age of six, he terminated a sporadic education at an early age to work as a glass blower. When strikes drove him from his job, he tried his hand at the fish-and-produce business in Philadelphia. Next he managed the Quaker City Base Ball Club and organized his own team at Philadelphia's Jumbo Park, but the illness of his wife forced him to move to Atlantic City. Here he started the unsuccessful "August Flower" baseball club, then moved to Wilmington, Delaware, where he again failed to turn a profit on yet another team. Back he came to Atlantic City. "Foreseeing the possibilities in catering to the tastes of visitors who were beginning to flock to the local beaches," he dispensed cider, apples, and lemonade to the Boardwalk crowds, juggling lemons to attract attention. He also began to manufacture saltwater taffy, at that time sold in trifling quantities for five cents a bag, but he hit on the idea of putting up larger quantities in boxes to take home. One weekend he ventured a purchase of two hundred boxes, sold out before Sunday noon, and frantically turned to oyster boxes from a sea-food shop to satisfy the demand. Fralinger's fortune was made. He became so prosperous that he was able to buy an interest in amusement rides, acquire beachfront real estate, and build the Academy of Music on the Boardwalk. He rebuilt the Academy after fires in 1892, 1898, and 1902, and remodeled it in 1908 for lease. It became the celebrated Nixon's Apollo Theatre. Before he died, Fralinger owned homes in Atlantic City, Miami Beach, and Schwenksville, Pennsylvania, and was a pillar of the resort community.

John Lake Young (1853–1938) was the kind of businessman who had the eye of the times. Born in the village of Absecon to an oysterman and his wife, he was left fatherless at the age of three. As the official story goes, he sacrificed education as a youth to labor for his living, and by the age of thirty was working as a carpenter doing patchwork on the Boardwalk and pavilions. One day he met Stewart McShea, a Pennsylvania baker who had come to the resort for his health. The baker had capital to invest, the carpenter had ideas. Together they bought a pavilion, converted it to a roller-skating rink, and "made loads of money." When the popularity of skating flagged, they turned to the carrousel. "If they made money before they made ten times as much in this new enterprise." In 1891 they bought Applegate's Pier opposite the carrousel, rented out its stores and booths for increasingly stiff fees, and "money just simply rolled their way." McShea retired to enjoy his wealth in 1897, but Young persevered, attracting hordes of customers to the pier's auditorium, theater, ballroom, aquarium, and net hauls of fish (Young could identify forty-eight species for the crowd). In 1906 he triumphantly opened the new Million Dollar Pier, "one of the big engineering achievements of the present day," on which he located his personal concrete "Italian-style villa," with three stories, twelve rooms, and a conservatory and garden. Eventually he owned ten miles of beachfront property ("a goodly part of which is marketable at the tidy price of $1500 a front foot"), more land in Florida, two steam yachts, a fleet of sailing craft, hotels and cottages, and the proud memory of having entertained President William Howard Taft in his home. For John Lake Young, "eminently noteworthy as an example of that product of American achievement known as the self-made man," the good life had been reached literally by way of nickels and dimes.

The popularity of vaudeville in Atlantic City is an excellent illustration of the kind of patronage the resort attracted and the aspirations these people had. Many vaudeville shows were performed at the lower end of the Boardwalk, the plebeian end, which contrasted with the relatively sedate section toward the inlet to Absecon Bay. An elemental atmosphere prevailed in the "pavilion theatre" district, packed with excursionists.

> There we find the fakir who shouts over his counter of hot sausages, mustard and rolls, "Take a bit of courage and eat something, gents. You've got to eat, and here's the place to do it." We find the "Three baseballs for five. Everytime you knock a baby down you get a good cigar" man, and hosts of others.

Here, too, were beer gardens, saloons, open drinking bars, "The Haunted Forest" exhibition, shooting galleries, toboggan rides, "flying horses," carrousels, dinner-ticket and rental-bathing-suit hawkers, a champion weight guesser, "fake" shows, dancing pavilions, and a number of cheap boardinghouses and hotels. Into this section flocked a large fraction of the resort's trade, the less affluent part. These people were the lower middle class which Albert F. McLean, in his book *American Vaudeville as Ritual,* describes as the "New Folk," but which in the present study are called the nouveaux bourgeois.

McLean believes that the bulk of vaudeville audiences consisted of rising white-collar workers and their families, who were in transit toward upper-middle-class status. This group increased eightfold between 1870 and 1910, to over five million members. They were only one or two generations away from rural life in America or in European peasant villages, but they were thoroughly acculturated and had left their old ways behind. Vaudeville managers designed their shows to appeal to the aspirations of the lower middle class while remaining comprehensible to the lower class. Immigrants just off the boat would need some familiarization with American life before they could appreciate vaudeville, a fact which is borne out by the kinds of shows performed at Atlantic City. In 1903 Lew Dockstader and His Great Minstrel Company staged a tableau entitled "The Sunny South," featuring a scene described as "The Colored Heaven": "Showing a Southern colored man in one of his happiest moments. 'The Watermellon [*sic*] Song'. . . sung by Manuel Romain." This same singer also offered "Sadie, the Princess of Tenement Row." These were themes that the immigrant could not really appreciate, while the slum dweller would find it hard to share a romantic feeling about "Tenement Row." They were lower-middle-class themes, suiting the taste of those familiar with American life and above the dirt sill of urban existence.

Vaudeville managers came to emphasize the "moral" quality of their shows, for two reasons: vaudeville was suspect to Protestant Christianity, and its basic appeal did not reside in sexual themes anyway. Rural, evangelical Protestantism traditionally had been hostile to public amusement, but in the late nineteenth century church leaders were divided on the question. Progressive Protestant clergymen, eager to relate their faith to the increasingly urban American population, began to discriminate between the use and abuse of amusement, a concession that vaudeville managers were quick to exploit. They were quite willing to keep their shows "respectable," since fundamentally their success was due to the glorification of materialistic success in industrial society, a theme which the clergy did not construe as objectionable. Vaudeville began to separate into two paths, "high-class" vaudeville and variety. Variety, which was not aimed at a family audience, was more bawdy and vigorous. It eventually turned into straightforward burlesque. Its respectable relative advertised itself as "refined vaudeville," "polite vaudeville," or "family vaudeville" to make its purpose clear, while managers labored to eliminate any taint of vice from their theaters and to prevent obscenities from being uttered in stage speeches. As such, high-class vaudeville was widely regarded as safe fare for such vulnerable listeners as young children and pregnant mothers. But the emphasis on "refinement," while it pacified the churches, had a coincidental effect much more powerful with its New Folk customers. It had snob appeal, playing on their desire to share in the life of the upper middle class by surrounding vaudeville with the trappings of upper-middle-class taste. The managers' claim that they wanted the "carriage trade" was actually addressed not to the gentry but to the plebeians, just like the high-flown promotional literature of the resort.

There is a good deal of documentation to demonstrate that most of the vaudeville in Atlantic City chose to take the "high-class" route as the more profitable alternative to variety. Doyle's Pavilion on the Boardwalk presented "Highclass Vaudeville" in 1900, as did the highly important Young's Ocean Pier Theatre a year later. The Amphitheatre on the Boardwalk announced that "Ladies and Children Can Attend Unaccompanied," while the Iron Pier Music Pavilion at its grand opening in 1894 promised to be "Devoted Strictly to High-Class Vaudevilles." The Empire was most explicit of all. Besides presenting "Continuous Highclass Vaudeville," it was "Patronized By The Elite," who enjoyed its "Elegantly Appointed Buffet." In fact, it was "The Only Music Hall in the City Conducted on a Strictly European Plan." This meant that the Empire served food but one did not have to buy it. The nifty rhetoric made it seem a club for the patriciate, but it hastened to assure its customers that the gilt of glamour entailed no financial consequences that were not entirely voluntary. In such manner did morality and materialism, two themes constantly on the mind of the nouveaux bourgeois, go hand in hand in Atlantic City.

Nothing more vividly illustrates the lower-middle-class soul of Atlantic City than the class sensitivity in the promotional output of the town's boosters, within and without. These men were generally of the upper middle class or were in the pay of upper-middle-class interests. They included people like the reporters for the Philadelphia newspapers and pamphleteers for the railroads. Among them were John Hall, editor of the *Daily Union* and local historian, and A. L. English, founder of the *Atlantic City Review*, who sold out to Alfred Heston in 1884 to write a promotional history of the resort. Heston in turn issued his series of handbooks, the single most important publicity device besides the Philadelphia press. Such men found themselves in an awkward and contradictory position. Local promoters belonged to the city's upper middle class. They recognized the importance of lower-middle-class patronage to the resort, wished to encourage it, and at the same time felt superior to it. Ideally, Atlantic City should be an upper-class resort, even though they knew full well its real character. At the same time, they resented the upper class, because it enjoyed elegance and privilege they would never attain. A similar enmity was felt toward the upper middle class of Philadelphia, supposedly their equals, because they were estimable frogs in a much bigger puddle: the editor of the *Bulletin* was not in the same league as the editor of the *Daily Union*. In Philadelphia, writers for the great newspapers could hardly refrain from snickering at the lowbrows of the seaside resort and their plebeian trade. They knew they had great power to affect Atlantic City's prosperity in the articles they wrote, each one bound to impress thousands of readers with the desirability or undesirability of the resort. Moreover, journalists outside Philadelphia were not boosting the resort the way the locals were. They were attracted by an easy source for a colorful article, but they did not feel the necessity for strict loyalty which resort journalists did. They could afford to express some negative feelings about the people there. Still, their articles were a vital element in boosting Atlantic City, and hence may be considered a part of the promotional literature.

The concern with class in resort advertising and journalism is consonant with the history of the period. Turn-of-the-century America witnessed such disturbing upheavals as Haymarket and Pullman, and the depression of 1893, a plunge of unprecedented severity for the masses. Americans could see plenty of evidence of class structure about them and the poverty and hardship that were the lot of the unfortunate. Though it was widely believed that thrift, hard work, and exploitation of readily available opportunities would enable deserving citizens to transcend the barriers of class, and allow the society to assimilate the hordes of ragged aliens that swarmed into America in search of a livelihood, the specter of revolution could not be ignored. The promotional literature of Atlantic City contained many touching examples of class mixing by the seaside, reassuring declarations of harmony to quiet the fears of readers and visitors and to reaffirm their belief that America successfully accommodated its different classes. Sometimes, however, these accounts were tinged with class antagonism which belied their benign intent.

Rand, McNally's *Handy Guide to Philadelphia and Environs of 1895* identified Atlantic City as "a thoroughly democratic place" devoid of "caste prejudice." It was "no uncommon sight to see the children of millionaires and the little ones of laboring men riding happily on the merry-go-round at the same time, and perhaps to find the parents fraternizing on the Switchback Railway." Applegate's Pier fathered a jingle in the same mode:

> Four spacious decks high in the air,
>   The old, the young, the millionaire,
> The worthy poor as well,
>   Seek health and rest, all find the same,

Shielded from sun as well as rain,
A paradise to dwell.

Faith in the benevolence of American society is rather lugubriously embodied in a tableau presented at Young's Pier during the 1908 season:

> When the curtain rises on the first scene the snow is falling on a busy street, where Christmas purchasers, moving rapidly past each other, present life in its different phases of wealth and poverty. A drunkard is about to be "run in" by a policeman, when the wife and child of the former make an eloquent pantomimic appeal and the good-natured officer releases his prisoner. A colored waif, with newspapers beside him, has fallen to sleep in the snow and the man in blue, passing along, sees him and covers his face with a newspaper.

An *Inquirer* vignette of democracy in the shallows depicted "the most haughty and conservative of Walnut street beauties in boldly neglige [*sic*] attire laughingly receiving the splashings of a denizen of 'de Fourt' ward." The "pretty shop girls from the big Market street stores" were taught to swim by "big, athletic clubmen who would scarcely deign to notice them in the scurrying throngs along Chestnut street after 6 o'clock." Another reporter claimed that "the four-dollars-a-week young man spending his year's savings in a vacation trip jostle[s] the pompous millionaire freely, and very likely flirts with the millionaire's daughter right before the old man's eyes."

The *Inquirer* covered the Hebrew Charity Ball of 1894, an affair of "Jewish society of the highest class," at which "we are elbowing men who hold in their hands the business of many communities" and who "can transfer millions by the stroke of their pens." These are "men who are respected more and more, admired, by their fellow men and their colleagues." The author of a Pennsylvania Railroad pamphlet of 1889 attempted to dazzle his readers with the high-class atmosphere of Atlantic City, but achieved a portrait both sardonic and curiously naive: "When Lent comes and the fashionable world takes its well-earned rest, there is no more fitting refuge in which it can undergo its self-denial in pleasurable quiet, while it recuperates its wasted energies in penitential rest, than this haven by the sea." A somewhat different tone pervaded *The Casino Girl*, a two-act musical staged at the Academy of Music in 1901. Its characters included such gentry as "pilsener Pasha, a brewer, whose introduction of beer into Egypt won for him his title," and "Mrs. H. Malaprop Rocks, a leader of St. Louis Society, better half of 'Rocks and Company,' pork packers of the western town."

In contrast to these views of the wealthy at the shore, it was reported that "slumming" was among the amusements of the resort. "The smaller concert gardens further down the island, which put up a complete variety show in connection with their concerts, attract the lower elements of society, although it not infrequently happens that parties of fashionables who delight in breaking loose and doing unconventional things when away from home are seen in these places." A writer for *The New York Times* suggested a trip to Atlantic City to see "Tom, Dick, and Harry and their girls." "It is almost worth a visit to see how the average Philadelphian amuses himself at the seashore." There is "no ruffianism" and the resort is "well-policed." "On the whole" the place is "quite as attractive as Coney Island," surely a back-handed compliment.

Atlantic City's role in presenting the illusion of social mobility must be seen in light of the class sensitivity evident in resort literature. The attention to class among resort commentators emphasizes the fundamentally lower-middle-class character of the town, and not only expresses satisfaction at the harmonizing potential of American society but also displays class antagonisms at variance with the supposed harmony. The history of the great plebeian resort demonstrates why it is possible to see turn-of-the-century America as either the Gilded Age or the Brown Decades, depending on the surface from which the light is reflected.

Notes

226 "representatives of the best society" *Atlantic City By the Sea*, p. 7.

226 "A modern Appian way" Dale, *Twentieth Century*.

226 "there is hardly a family" Hall, *Daily Union History*, p. 231.

226 "Practically all," John Steevens [sic], "The Charm of Eastertide at Atlantic City," *Harper's Weekly*, April 18, 1908, p. 20. Hereafter referred to as "Eastertide."

227 "467 names" ACDU, July 16, 21, 26, 28, December 1, 8, 15, 22, 29, 1890; February 22, 1892; June 3, July 24, 1893; July 2, 16, 23, December 3, 10, 17, 31, 1894; July 23, 1895; July 20, 23–25, August 6, 7, 1900. Hereafter referred to as ACDU Society Listings.

227 "appropriate Social Registers" *Social Register, Philadelphia,* 1893, VII, 3 (New York: Social Register Association, November 1893); *ibid.,* 1894, VIII, 2 (New York, Social Register Association, November 1893); *ibid.,* 1900, XIV, 3 (New York: Social Register Association, November 1899). The *Social Registers* for 1890–92 were not available to me, but the use of the 1893 volume (published in November 1892) probably makes little or no difference. It seems unlikely that the number of individuals listed in the *Social Register* in 1890, but not listed three years later, would be very large. Moreover, the *Social Register* had the habit of listing recently deceased members of society, so the loss of names by death would be further reduced.

227 "327 distinguished visitors" "Society by the Seaside," *PI,* July 17, 1892, p. 12; "Society at the Seaside," *PI,* July 24, 1892, p. 12; "Society," *PI,* July 31, 1892, p. 12; "Summer Resorts," *PI,* July 22, 1894, p. 9; "Beside the Bounding Billows," *PI,* July 14, 1901, Summer Resort Section, p. 4; "Beach Costumes of Fair Bathers" and "The Social Whirl," *PI,* July 21, 1901, sec.2, p. 11.

227 "14 are found" *Social Register, Philadelphia, 1893; Social Register, Philadelphia, 1894; Social Register, Philadelphia, 1901,* XV (New York: Social Register Association, November 1900).

227 "142 arrivals" "Beside the Bounding Billows," *PI,* July 14, 1901, Summer Resort Section, p. 4.

227 "763 addresses" *Social Register, Summer 1900,* XIV, 19 (New York: Social Register Association, 1900).

228 "brief descriptions. . . in the *Daily Union*" ACDU Society Listings.

228 (Descriptions of ladies) *Ibid.*

229 "The ultra-swell" O'Malley, "Board-Walkers," p. 233.

229 "Some of these people came" "Atlantic City," *PI,* August 5, 1894, p. 9.

229 "These men are mainly" "Baedeker," p. 46.

229 "failing to attract" Editorial, ACDU, January 28, 1892, p. 4.

229 "Chelsea" Heston, 1887, pp. 73–74.

230 (Ledlie story) "Summer Resorts," *PI,* July 22, 1894, p. 9.

230 (Hall estimate of cottagers) Hall, *Daily Union History,* pp. 227–31.

230 (C & A brochure) *Summer Sketches,* pp. 15–19.

230 "commutation tickets" "A Rush to the Seashore," ACDU, June 26, 1893, p. 1.

230 "little historical record" They did form a Cottagers' Association in 1889, primarily to protest the routing of train tracks through the city and to seek lower commutation rates to Philadelphia. The organization seems to have withered away after two years.

231 (Geographical origins of blacks) Trenton, New Jersey State Library, Archives and History Bureau, "New Jersey State Census, 1905. Atlantic City."

231 "What are we going to do. . .?" "Down by the Sea Shore—Atlantic City," *PI,* July 23, 1893, p. 10.

231 "could keep the blacks in their place" *Ibid.*

231 "*Washington Post* complained" ACDU, July 23, 1900, p. 1.

232 "a. . .young colored lady" "Some Curious Scenes Depicted on Beach at

Gay Atlantic City," *PI*, July 28, 1900, p. 3.

232 "criticism of a black . . . newspaper" ACDU, August 8, 1891, p. 1.

232 "black tourists" Little evidence has emerged of how such restrictions were enforced. It seems most probable that the white community had a fair consensus on how the blacks should be treated, and that a reproving word from a hostler, waiter, or passing citizen sufficed to enlighten black offenders of the code. Moreover, a black who sought his pleasures where he was not wanted had to calculate that appeal might be made to his employer by an angry white. Atlantic City must have had certain aspects of a "company town," since the single-purpose economy precluded most alternative kinds of employment. On the other hand, there were many employers, preventing the monopoly which made the disciplinary potential of the company town so oppressive.

232 "five thousand blacks" ACDU, September 3, 1891, p. 1.

232 "post-season windfall" In one of Alfred Heston's scrapbooks is an undated clipping from a Bucks County (Pennsylvania) newspaper which from internal evidence, must have appeared about 1904. It records: "Yesterday over 6,000 negroes were here to enjoy the annual colored excursion of the first Thursday in September." Heston, "Reminiscences of Absecon."

232 (*Inquirer* descriptions of black excursions) "The City by the Sea, *PI*, September 6, 1896, p. 21; "Colored People Invade Atlantic," *PI*, September 2, 1897, p. 12; "Atlantic City," *PI*, September 4, 1898, p. 15.

233 (August excursions of blacks) "In the Merry Throng Down by the Sea," *PI*, August 18, 1897, p. 12; "Discussed Race Problem," *PI*, August 23, 1899, p. 5; New Brunswick, New Jersey, Rutgers University Library, New Jersey Collection, postcard file.

233 "Ten tramps" "Itinerant Visitors Warned," ACDU, June 21, 1893, p. 1.

233 (Tramps in jail) "City Jail Records," ACDU, January 29, 1897, p. 1.

234 (Depression of 1893) ACDU, June 23, 1893, p. 4.

234 (Coxey's Army) "At the Seaside—Atlantic City," *PI*, August 12, 1894, p. 9.

234 "There are no beggars" O'Malley, "Board-Walkers," p. 238.

234 (Salvation Army, Volunteers of America) Brett, "Black and White," pp. 725–26.

235 "study of 225. . .hotels" Heston, 1887, pp. 131–34.

235 (Annual wages) Paul L. Douglas, *Real Wages in the United States, 1890–1926* (Boston: Houghton Mifflin Company, 1930), table following p. 392.

235 "the lower middle class could meet the prices" Comments one newspaper: "The grand hotels serve the wealthy, but the moderate ones give entertainment to thousands." Newspaper clipping from unidentified Bucks County (Pennsylvania) newspaper, ca. 1904, in Heston, "Reminiscences of Absecon."

235 "newspaper clipping" "Atlantic City Sketches."

235 "doubling up" "Greatest and Best—Our Island City," ACDU, July 4, 1891, p. 1.

236 (*Times* reporter) "A Sunday Sea-Side Resort," *NYT*, August 14, 1883, p. 3.

236 "three fifths the annual total" In 1887, for example, Heston's handbook lists 212 "hotels," while *Gopsill's Directory* lists 443 "hotels, cottages, and boardinghouses." It is a safe bet that Heston did not omit anything worthy of the name "hotel." In fact he included many establishments with a dozen rooms or less. Thus, 47 percent (212/443) should certainly be reduced to obtain a rough estimate of the proportion of hotels to the total number of lodging places.

236 (Table) All figures in this table except that for 1884 were compiled from *Gopsill's Atlantic City Directory for 1882–1883* (Philadelphia: James Gopsill, 1882) and *Gopsill's Atlantic City Directory* (Philadelphia: James Gopsill's Sons), volumes for 1885–1908. The figure for 1884 was compiled from *Holdzkom and Company's Atlantic City Cottage and Business Directory for 1884* (Atlantic City: Holdzkom and Company, 1884).

237 "hard times of the 1890's" It is possible that some might be induced to open a boardinghouse when depression struck. If, for example, an Atlantic Avenue merchant saw his trade dry up, his wife might decide to start a boardinghouse in their home, since even marginal profit was better than none.

237 "Nearly every branch" "At the Summer Resorts—Atlantic City," *PI*, July 16, 1893 p. 10.

238 "The crowds in the city" Hall, *Daily Union History*, p. 197.

238 "protest meeting" Obviously, the excursion trade did not appeal equally to all business interests in the resort. Broadly speaking, there were two major economic camps in Atlantic City who were potential rivals. The first consisted of the proprietors of the large and prestigious hotels, other businessmen catering to upper-middle-class patronage, local professional and religious leaders, and citizens not directly dependent on a mass-resort economy. The second included small hotel and boardinghouse keepers, and amusement operators. On the fringes of the second group were businessmen of varying respectability and legality, such as Boardwalk hawkers, small-time entertainers like sand "sculptors," operators of unlicensed saloons and Sunday-closing violators, gamblers, brothel proprietors, and so forth. Conflict between the economic camps figures prominently in Chapter 5, "Babylonian Days," over the issue of Sunday liquor selling. Naturally, the excursion crowd was of nil (or even negative) interest to the high-class resort businessmen, even if it was the lifeblood of the others.

238 "astonishing sum" English, *History*, p. 154.

238 (Hillman and Mackey) "Atlantic City Sketches."

238 (Seaview Excursion House) "A New Atlantis," p. 620.

238 (West Jersey Excursion House) "Atlantic City Sketches."

238 "Ball Room . . . Billiard Room" English, *History*, p. 223.

239 (Applegate's Pier) Heston, 1887, p. 15.

239 (Heinz Pier) Postcard, author's collection; trade card, author's collection.

239 (Stunts of the 1890's) "Visitors of a Day at Atlantic City," *PI*, August 12, 1898, p. 2; "Atlantic City," *PI*, August 21, 1898, p. 15; "Rain Swept the Long Boardwalk," *PI*, August 24, 1897, p. 5; "With the Merry Throng at the Seaside Resorts," *PI*, August 10, 1899, p. 5.

240 "Single girls" Dreiser superbly describes the pleasures of newly found

social opportunity in *Sister Carrie*, when Carrie meets Drouet on the train to Chicago.

241 "Mrs. Duff," "four osculatory bits," "Dan and Mary" "A Sunday Stroll at Atlantic," *PI*, July 13, 1896, p. 7; "Review of the Passing Show at Atlantic City and Cape May," *PI*, August 2, 1899, p. 6; "Atlantic City's Merry Throng of Seekers After Pleasure," *PI*, August 1, 1899, p. 14.

242 "Lover's Pavilion" Heston, 1887, p. 54.

242 "Baltimore ordinance" ACDU, June 28, 1893, p. 4.

242 "A noteworthy feature" "At Atlantic City: The Evening Bulletin's' Exposure Bears Good Fruit," *PB*, August 12, 1890, p. 1.

242 "Just ran across" Atlantic City, Public Library, Local History Collection, scrapbook of postcards. Hereafter referred to as "Atlantic City Postcards."

242 "It must be borne in mind" Hall, *Daily Union History*, p. 252.

242 "Such attitudes were congruent" Yet Atlantic City, by providing the opportunity for illicit sex, could be a threat to family values. The shopgirl's dream lover might turn out to be a rake, the shopgirl might discover a bit of the tart in her own soul, or the upstanding young man might avail himself of a lady of easy virtue. But it is possible that, on a higher level, illicit sex helped the family to survive.

242 "The Autumn Break-Up" Heston, 1888, p. 68.

242 "unmatched girls" "A New Atlantis," p. 615.

243 "a wedding will take place" "Atlantic City Romance," *PI*, August 23, 1893, p. 5.

243 "the crowd itself" *Cape May to Atlantic City: A Summer Note Book* (N.p.: Passenger Department, Pennsylvania Railroad Company, 1883), p. 39. Hereafter referred to a *Cape May to Atlantic City*.

243 "bathe in people" "The Spectator," *Outlook*, CIV (July 26, 1913), 719.

243 "Talking of love" lapel buttons "Atlantic City Sketches"; "Atlantic City," *PI*, July 19, 1896, p. 18.

244 (Incense tapers, other fads) "Gay Atlantic," *PI*, August 8, 1897, p. 20; "The City by the Sea," *PI*, August 23, 1896, p. 18.

244 "Hello, My Baby," clothing styles, palmistry, phrenology "Atlantic City," *PI*, August 6, 1899, sec. III, p. 1; Atlantic City, Public Library, Local History Collection, loose newspapers in folders, *Atlantic Journal*, July 30, 1890, p. 1; "Atlantic City," *PI*, July 22, 1900, sec. II, p. 8; "Atlantic City," *PI*, July 12, 1896, p. 18.

245 (Bathing suits, "bicycle girl," Fourth of July) "Atlantic City," *PI*, August 14, 1898, p. 15; "Atlantic City Sands," *PI*, August 15, 1897, p. 20; "The City by the Sea," *PI*, July 5, 1896, p. 18.

245 "widow craze" "At the Summer Resorts—Atlantic City," *PI*, July 2, 1893, p. 10.

245 "the summer girl" "Belles of the Beach at Gay Atlantic," *PI*, July 22, 1900, Half-Tone Supplement, p. 1; "Atlantic City," *PI*, July 28, 1895, p. 14.

246 "everyone was potentially in on the act" Fads not only are an attempt to create community, they are also (as a corollary) the expression of a felt lack

of community. The feverish pleasures of Atlantic City bespeak not only what the culture could deliver—for a price—to its members, but also what it withheld from them.

247 (Reed brochure) Reprinted in English, *History*, pp. 183–94.

247 "Academy of Music" "Don't Be Slow: A Great Rush for the Academy's Opening Bill," ACDU, June 22, 1893, p. 1; McMahon, *So Young*, pp. 43–44.

247 "Esplanade" "Atlantic City," *PI*, July 10, 1898, p. 13.

247 (Rolling-chair design) Somers Point, New Jersey, Atlantic County Historical Society, Silas R. Morse Scrapbook, 1840–1928. Hereafter referred to as "Morse Scrapbook."

247 "Afterward, well wrapped up" Hall, *Daily Union History*, p. 237.

247 "The Piers at Atlantic City" "Some Gowns Seen at Atlantic City," *PI*, September 3, 1899, Half-Tone Supplement, p. 7.

248 "Easter Parade, copied" Steevens, "Eastertide," p. 22.

248 "forty thousand passengers" Hall, *Daily Union History*, pp. 247–49.

249 (Baltzell) Edward D. Baltzell, *Philadelphia Gentlemen: The Making of a National Upper Class* (Glencoe, Ill.: Free Press, 1958).

249 "pocketbook. . .coat of arms" In 1922, a visiting New Zealand woman exclaimed: "Dollars is the password here. You can have what you want if you are prepared to pay for it. Not so at Newport, where the amazing mansions of New York's Four Hundred are like a battlement along the cliff, warning off intruders." Nellie M. Scalon, "American Cities As Seen by a New Zealand Woman," *NYT*, October 29, 1922, sec. VIII, p. 2.

249 "Chicago investigated" Special Park Commission, *Report of Investigation of Bathing Beaches* (N.p.: Chicago City Council, 1913).

249 "horse show" Hall, *Daily Union History*, p. 243.

249 "St. Nicholas' Church" "Atlantic City Sketches."

249 "pile it on" "Down by the Sea Shore—Atlantic City," *PI*, July 30, 1893, p. 9.

250 "And the things that were sold!" "The Spectator," pp. 718–19; Warner, "Their Pilgrimage," p. 682; "Acid in the Juice," *PI*, September 2, 1899, p. 3.

251 (Entrepreneurs' new language) Helen C. Bennett, "Come On In—The Water's Fine!" *American Magazine*, August 1926, pp. 45, 144; ACDU, August 21, 1890, p. 4; "Atlantic City's Foul Blots," *PI*, August 4, 1895, Sunday Supplement, pp. 21–22; ACDU, August 29, 1900, p. 4.

251 (Fralinger's career) Heston, *South Jersey*, IV, 211.

252 (Young's career) *Ibid.*, IV, 415–16; "Atlantic City," *PI*, September 3, 1899, sec. III, p. 4; "Atlantic City," *PI*, July 22, 1900, sec. II, p. 8.

253 "There we find the fakir" "At the Seaside—Atlantic City," *PI*, August 26, 1894, p. 9.

253 (McLean) Albert F. McLean, *American Vaudeville as Ritual* (Lexington: University of Kentucky Press, 1965). Hereafter referred to as *American Vaudeville*.

253 "Immigrants just off the boat" *Ibid.*, pp. 40–41.

254 (Dockstader shows) Atlantic City, Public Library, Local History Collection, Alfred M. Heston scrapbook, "Good Times Book, vol. I, Trips 1894–1895."

Hereafter referred to as "Good Times Book."

254 (Analysis of vaudeville) McLean, *American Vaudeville*, pp. 35–36, 66–83.

255 (Doyle's Pavilion) ACDU, August 17, 1900, p. 4.

255 (Young's Ocean Pier Theater) Atlantic City, Public Library, Local History Collection, untitled scrapbook of theater programs. Hereafter referred to as "Scrapbook of Theater Programs."

255 (Iron Pier) ACDU, July 23, 1894, p. 1.

255 (The Empire) ACDU, July 30, 1900, p. 4.

256 "snickering at the lowbrows" Recall the *Times* reporter who was appalled by an Atlantic City boardinghouse.

256 (Rand,McNally) William E. Meehan, *Rand, McNally and Company's Handy Guide to Philadelphia and Environs, Including Atlantic City and Cape May* (Chicago: Rand,McNally and Company, 1895), pp. 163, 168–69.

256 "Four spacious decks" ACDU, July 5, 1890, p. 1.

257 "When the curtain rises" Gaston Lichtenstein, *A Visit to Young's Pier at Atlantic City, N.J.*, reprinted from the *Tarborough Southerner*, Tarborough, N.C. (Richmond, Va.: William Ellis Jones, 1908), pp. 3–5.

257 (Inquirer vignette) "Down by the Sea Shore—Atlantic City," *PI*, July 9, 1893, p. 10.

257 "Another reporter" "At Atlantic City: A Record of Unique Characteristics," undated clipping (from *The Tribune* [?]) in "Atlantic City Sketches."

257 (Hebrew Charity Ball) "Down by the Sea—Atlantic City," *PI*. July 29, 1894, p. 9.

257 "When Lent comes" *"Atlantic City By the Sea*, p. 6.

257 (The Casino Girl) "Good Times Book"

258 "slumming" "Down by the Sea Shore—Atlantic City," *PI*, July 9, 1893, p. 10.

258 "It is almost worth a visit" "A Sunday Sea-Side Resort," *NYT*, August 14, 1883, p. 3.

A champion of workmen's compensation laws but unfriendly to unions, Mahlon Pitney stood firmly in the mainstream of the Progressive movement. Photograph courtesy New Jersey Historical Society.

10

Progressivism is a generic term American historians apply to the efforts of social reformers around the turn of this century, but they differ on how precisely to define and use the word. Frustrated by the issue, Peter Filene concluded in 1970 that the term should be discarded. Progressives were a diverse group with different goals and values. Together, Filene observed, they displayed "a puzzling and irreducible incoherence." In contrast, Richard L. McCormick and Arthur S. Link in *Progressivism* (1983) willingly incorporated numerous reformers with varying philosophies and agendas under the term. In the article that follows, Michal Belknap has argued that United States Supreme Court Justice Mahlon Pitney from New Jersey, whom previous authors had cast as a reactionary "capitalist tool," was in fact a Progressive.

Who were the Progressives? How did they differ from other reformers and from those whose practices they sought to reform? Was there a definable Progressive program or set of objectives? What did these reformers expect to accomplish, and how successful were they? What does Pitney's career show about Progressivism in the nation as a whole and in New Jersey specifically?

In *The Age of Reform* (1955), Richard Hofstadter argued that the Progressives were middle-class "victims of an upheaval in status" whose "deference and power" were challenged by the rise of big business and organized labor. Progressive reforms, he argued, in effect lashed out at opponents on both ends of the economic spectrum, at least in part to maintain the group's position in society. Numerous historians have attacked Hofstatder's premise. Based on profiles of Progressives and of their opponents, David Thelen concluded that there was no appreciable difference in class, occupation, or the tension each experienced from social change. Instead of being a movement restricted to urban middle-class professionals, historians have discovered rural, working-class, and immigrant support for Progressivism. As a middle-class lawyer from an old-stock New Jersey family, Pitney may have fit the old profile of a Progressive, but others with identical credentials were not reformers while some from very different backgrounds were.

Why did Pitney and others become Progressives? A number of developments at the end of the nineteenth century seem to have triggered their reaction. First, the social gospel theology of various religious groups heightened interest in social justice. This "new theology" included a concern for the general welfare and emphasized an active involvement in the community. Second, the depression that began in 1893 led many to conclude that new programs were necessary. Third, "muckraking" journalists had revealed widespread economic and political corruption. Progressives may have felt that preventive medicine was necessary; the way to avoid the spread of socialism and other radical movements was to temper the capitalist system. How did Pitney's support for Progressive measures emerge? What was there about New Jersey politics at the end of the nineteenth century that led men like him to conclude that reforms were necessary? What power did corporations and the trusts in the state possess?

Reflecting their diverse backgrounds, Progressive reformers had a wide variety of objectives. They advocated two methods for dealing with the trusts, either breaking them up or regulating them. They also proposed a series of political reforms, including the direct election of senators, the direct primary, the secret ballot, and laws to eradicate such corrupt practices as buying votes at the polls and in the legislature. Finally, they sought social measures such as minimum wages for women, restrictions on child labor, workmen's compensation, and pure food and drug laws. Which of these reforms did Pitney support and which did he oppose? Which succeeded and which did not? Based on his attitudes toward labor and corporations, including the railroads, was he a "conservative" or "liberal" Progressive? What, if anything, does Pitney's position suggest about the nature of the Progressive movement in New Jersey?

Belknap's essay on Pitney provokes two other questions about Progressives. The first considers their tolerance, or lack thereof, for differences and dissent. Some historians have described the Progressives as middle-class moralists who wanted to impose their standards on society as a whole and who, in the process, displayed a certain condescension toward the working classes, hostility towards immigrants, fear of radicals, and refusal to accept dissent, particularly during wartime. To what extent did Pitney exhibit these attitudes? What standards did Pitney and other judges in his time use to decide what was acceptable wartime dissent, and how do those standards compare to what prevailed in the Civil War years?

Second, how does one assess the historical role of such figures as Supreme Court judges? Legal historians ask whether or not a judge was "great"; political historians rank presidents. What standards are and should be used in this evaluative process? Should judges be compared only to others of their period or to those of later times?

To compare historical figures to those who have succeeded them runs the risk of "presentism," evaluating the past by modern standards. Not to do so, on the other hand, may make their lives and history irrelevant to present-day readers.

Suggested Readings

Buenker, John D. "Urban, New-Stock Liberalism and Progressive Reform in New Jersey." *NJH* 87 (1969): 79–104.

Chambers, John Whiteclay II. *The Tyranny of Change: America in the Progressive Era, 1890–1920.* 2d ed. New York, 1992.

Filene, Peter. "Obituary for Progressivism." *American Quarterly* 22 (1970): 20–34.

Hofstadter, Richard. *The Age of Reform.* New York, 1955.

Link, Arthur S. *Wilson: The Road to the White House.* Princeton, N.J., 1947.

McCormick, Richard L., and Arthur S. Link. *Progressivism.* Arlington Heights, Ill., 1983.

Noble, Ransom E. *New Jersey Progressivism before Wilson.* Princeton, N.J., 1946.

Thelen, David P. "Social Tensions and the Origins of Progressivism." *Journal of American History* 56 (1969): 323–41.

Tobin, Eugene M. "The Progressive as Humanitarian: Jersey City's Search for Social Justice, 1890–1917." *NJH* 93 (1975): 77–98.

Wiebe, Robert H. *The Search for Order: 1877–1920.* New York, 1967.

◆ ◆ ◆ ◆ ◆ ◆ ◆

Mr. Justice Pitney and Progressivism

Michal R. Belknap

I. Introduction

In a book published in 1912, Marxist historian Gustavus Myers branded the United States Supreme Court a tool of the domi-

Seton Hall Law Review 16 (1986): 381-423. Reprinted by permission of *Seton Hall Law Review.*

nant capitalist class.[1] Part of the evidence he offered to support his characterization was the appointment that year of Associate Justice Mahlon Pitney, a native of what Myers called "that essentially plutocratic town," Morristown, New Jersey.[2] This was, he claimed, an event that gratified the great capitalist interests and "was inimical to the workers."[3] Summarizing Justice Pitney's career in 1969, historian Fred Israel also pictured him as a conservative bulwark against innovation,[4] notable mainly for his persistent hostility to labor.[5]

Such characterizations of Pitney are inaccurate. He did hand down a number of antiunion decisions, and he did interpret the income tax amendment in a manner arguably favorable to the wealthy, but this judge was no tool of the capitalists. Indeed, Pitney opposed monopoly in both the political and judicial arenas. Although hostile to trade unions, he wrote opinions that advanced the interests of unorganized workers, especially those victimized by industrial accidents. Far from being a die-hard reactionary, Mahlon Pitney was a judge whose career reflected the Progressivism that dominated American politics during the early years of the twentieth century. Some of Pitney's ideas seem illiberal today, but many of the reformers of his own time shared his views. Consequently, they gave him their political support. As a state judge, and later as a United States Supreme Court Justice, he took positions on issues similar to those of contemporaries whom historians have labeled "Progressives." That appellation fits Pitney too, for his judicial opinions mirror concerns, values, and biases characteristic of Progressivism.

II. Progressivism

Pitney's judicial opinions link him to the "[c]onvulsive reform movements [that] swept across the American landscape from the 1890s to 1917."[6] These movements promoted a variety of economic, political, and social changes, which their proponents believed would "improve the conditions of life and labor" and stabilize American society.[7] Progressive reform crusades were extremely diverse. As several historians have pointed out, Progressivism was not a unified movement. Progressives pursued a variety of goals; indeed, they often disagreed among themselves, even about how to achieve commonly held objectives.[8]

On no issue were the disagreements among reformers sharper than on the question of what to do about the giant combinations of capital that Americans referred to inaccurately and pejoratively as "the trusts."[9] One group of Progressives, for whom Theodore Roosevelt was the most prominent spokesman, considered bigness in business inevitable and desirable. Rather than smashing the trusts, they argued, the Federal Government should subject them to continuous administrative supervision.[10] It should distinguish between those that behaved themselves and those that did not, and it should use intermittent law suits to discipline the miscreants.[11] Woodrow Wilson and his advisor in the 1912 presidential campaign, Louis Brandeis (later a colleague of Pitney on the Supreme Court), favored a vastly different approach. They idealized small economic units, and rather than regulating monopolies, they wanted to break them up by enacting legislation that would effectively outlaw giant combinations of capital.[12]

Progressives of this type held views deeply rooted in the American past, views that had been widely accepted since before the Civil War. Both Jacksonian Democrats and the leaders of the infant Republican party of the late 1850's were deeply suspicious of corporations and economic concentration. They feared that these might restrict the options open to wage earners and small entrepreneurs and interfere with the efforts of these groups to attain economic independence and upward social mobility. The Democratic version of this antebellum ideology emphasized conflict between labor and capital, but most Republicans believed there was a harmony of interests between different social classes. For this reason, the Republicans opposed self-conscious, working-class actions such as strikes, which they saw as interfering with the rights of others. They believed that an individual might quit any job he chose, but that it was wrong for him to join with others to shut down his employer or to keep those who wanted to work from doing so.[13] Unions, like corporations, were aggregations of power that threatened the opportunities of enterprising members of the middle class.[14] Hostility toward combinations of both labor and capital was central to the thinking of the advocates of laissez faire,[15] who gained intellectual pre-eminence in the United States during the decades after the Civil War.

Turn-of-the-century Supreme Court Justice John Marshall Harlan, known as a rigorous enforcer of the antitrust laws, also exhibited a distinct lack of sympathy for workers' organizations.[16] Even Brandeis, although a friend of the trade union movement, "was absolutely opposed to the closed shop as a form of labor despotism."[17] As late as 1909, Woodrow Wilson declared, " 'I am a fierce partizan [sic] of the Open Shop and of everything that makes for individual liberty.'"[18] To many small employers and middle-class professionals, unions seemed like just another type of monopoly—originated for the same reasons as the industrial monopoly and likely to produce similar results.[19] During the late 1890's and the early years of the twentieth century, the average middle-class citizen viewed himself as a member of an unorganized, and therefore helpless, consuming public, threatened from above by mushrooming trusts and from below by workers combining to protect themselves.[20]

Historian Richard Hofstadter once characterized Progressivism as "the complaint of the unorganized against the consequences of organization."[21] His thesis that it was caused by the status anxieties of the middle class[22] has by now been largely refuted by other scholars.[23] There were, however, other reasons for members of the unorganized middle class to feel threatened by the growing power of big business above and trade unions below. One was inflation. During the period from 1897 to 1913, the cost of living rose thirty-five per cent. Although the increase was modest by today's standards, the Country was then emerging from a period of deflation, and the public tended to blame rising prices on "the sudden development of a vigorous, if small, labor movement, and an extraordinary acceleration in the trustification of American industry."[24] The second important reason for the development of reform sentiments within the unorganized middle class was a sudden increase in public awareness of the extent to which big corporations were corrupting the political process in order to advance their own interests at the expense of other segments of American society.[25] The fears and resentments of the middle class were certainly not the only reasons for the development of Progressivism,[26] but they do explain the career of Mahlon Pitney and its relationship to that reform movement.[27]

III. *The New Jersey Years*

A. Background and Early Life

Progressives were mostly old-stock Americans with British ethnic backgrounds who came from economically secure middle-class families.[28] Religiously, they were most often Calvinists, affiliated with denominations such as the Congregationalists and the Presbyterians.[29] In a day when few Americans went to college, most Progressives were college graduates.[30] A majority of those active in politics were lawyers.[31]

In other words, the typical Progressive reformer was someone very much like Mahlon Pitney. Pitney's ancestors had come to New Jersey from England in the early 1700's, and the great grandfather for whom he was named served in George Washington's army during the Revolutionary War.[32] The future Justice was born the second son of attorney Henry C. Pitney on the family farm near Morristown on February 5, 1858.[33] He attended private schools in Morristown, and as befits a New Jersey Presbyterian, he enrolled at Princeton in 1875.[34]

Pitney studied hard at Princeton, and during his senior year, he played first base on and managed the baseball team.[35] Among his classmates were Robert McCarter, who would later serve as attorney general of New Jersey,[36] and Thomas Woodrow Wilson, who was destined to become President of the United States.[37] On November 30, 1915, the class of 1879 held a reunion at the White House hosted by President Wilson and attended by, among others, Justice Pitney.[38]

After graduating from Princeton, young Mahlon followed his father into what was rapidly becoming the family profession— law. H. C. Pitney, a country lawyer who had served as prosecutor of the pleas for Morris County in the 1860's, capped a successful career by becoming a vice chancellor in 1889, a position he held until 1907.[39] His sons, Henry C., Jr. and John O. H. (founding partner of Pitney, Hardin, Kipp & Szuch) also took up the practice of law.[40] " 'I could hardly have escaped it,' " Mahlon once remarked.[41] After discussing career options with his father, he decided that following graduation, he would read law in the elder Pitney's office.[42] That form of preparation for the bar proved to be less than thrilling. " 'I found the work very dull at first, and Blackstone very dry reading,'" the future Supreme Court Justice admitted later.[43] On the other hand, he learned an immense amount, " 'most of it from [his] father who was a walking encyclopedia of law.'"[44]

B. Law Practice

After a period of intense cramming with his close friend Francis J. Swayze (who would be his colleague on the New Jersey bench and rival for a seat on the United States Supreme Court),[45] Pitney took and passed the bar examinations. He was admitted as an attorney at law and solicitor in chancery in 1882, and three years later he became a counselor.[46] For the first seven years after his admission to the bar, Pitney practiced alone in Dover, New Jersey.[47] There he acted as counsel to the Cranbury Iron Company, which he also served as a director and an officer.[48] In addition, Pitney found time to manage a Dover department store.[49]

When his father was appointed vice chancellor in 1889, Mahlon returned to Morristown to take over H. C.'s firm, Pitney & Youngblood.[50] He achieved a reputation as both a skillful appellate advocate and a clever trial lawyer.[51] By 1894, Pitney was "justly regarded as one of the leading legal lights in New Jersey."[52]

C. Political Career

1. Congress

In the fall of 1894, Pitney entered politics, running for the House seat from the Fourth Congressional District.[53] Like his father, Mahlon was a Republican, and the Fourth was normally a Democratic stronghold.[54] In 1894, the Country was in the depths of a depression, however, and voters troubled by hard times were turning against the party of Democratic President Grover Cleveland.[55] Although a newspaper supporting his opponent, Johnston Cornish, stated that "no Democrat [could] be expected to vote for Mr. Pitney, because he represents in the most radical degree every principal [sic] of Republicanism that is distasteful to a Democrat,"[56] many obviously did. Pitney carried the district by 1407 votes.[57]

During his first term in the House, Speaker Thomas B. Reed named him to both the Committee on Reform in the Civil Service and the powerful Appropriations Committee.[58] Although Pitney seldom opened his mouth on the floor,[59] the performance of the quiet freshman from New Jersey obviously pleased "Czar" Reed. When Pitney stood for re-election in 1896, the Speaker traveled to Morristown to give a major address and to endorse his candidacy.[60] Pitney again prevailed at the polls, defeating Democrat Augustus W. Cutler by 2977 votes.[61]

During his second term in the House, he assumed a somewhat higher profile, frequently participating in debate.[62] Pitney spoke out against what he regarded as the excessively large appropriations proposed for various departments of the Government.[63] He also served on the committee to which the Alaska boundary dispute was assigned. All of its members were asked to prepare briefs on the controversy, and Pitney's was so "exhaustive that he was assigned to manage the passage of the . . . report" that the committee presented to the full House.[64]

2. State Senate

Although successful, Pitney's second term ended prematurely. He resigned on January 5, 1899 to take a seat in the New Jersey Senate.[65] Both he and his wife, the former Florence Shelton, "longed to return to Morristown and their friends" there.[66] In addition, Pitney wanted to be governor.[67] Early in 1898, he made the obligatory pilgrimage to the Camden railroad office that served as the headquarters of New Jersey's Republican "boss," William J. Sewall, seeking Sewall's endorsement.[68] He did not get it. The "boss," who favored another candidate, told Pitney that he had to broaden his base in state politics before seeking the governorship.[69] Assured by Sewall that if elected to the New Jersey senate he could have the minority leadership, Pitney ran for the Morris County seat in November of 1898,[70] winning by a plurality of 831 votes.[71]

When the Republicans gained control of the upper chamber in 1900, he became president of the senate.[72] During his three years in Trenton, Pitney won acclaim for a thorough "study of the proposed Morris Canal abandonment scheme," which he revealed was almost exclusively for the benefit of the lessee of the canal, the Lehigh Valley Railroad.[73] His efforts prevented consummation of this dubious project[74] and even won him praise from a newspaper otherwise highly critical of the state senate.[75]

Pitney's success in Trenton made him a leading contender for the Republican gubernatorial nomination and a likely winner of the state's highest office.[76] Before the 1901 election, however, the Chief Justice of the New Jersey Supreme Court, David A. Depew, resigned.[77] Governor Foster M. Voorhees elevated Associate Justice William S. Gummere to the chief justiceship, and on February 5, 1901, he nominated Pitney to fill the resulting vacancy.[78] On that day, Pitney also celebrated his forty-third birthday.[79] His fellow senators quickly confirmed their colleague from Morristown,[80] bringing an end to his career in elective politics.

3. Progressive Politician

His career suggests that Pitney was part of the emergent Progressive movement that was just beginning to gather momentum around the Country when he abandoned the political arena for the bench. To be sure, Pitney took traditional Republican positions on the issues in his two races for Congress.[81] As historian George Mowry has pointed out, however, most of those who would later be identified as Progressives were conservatives in the middle 1890's.[82] In the landmark Presidential election of 1896, these nascent Progressives opposed William Jennings Bryan, who, as the candidate of the Democratic and Populist parties, advocated the free and unlimited coinage of silver as a panacea for the economic woes of American farmers and workers.[83] Certainly, Pitney was part of this opposition. " 'What we need,' " he thundered, " 'is . . . not more money, but more confidence and more business.' "[84] Pitney's Princeton classmate Woodrow Wilson, now remembered as a Progressive governor and President, took a similar position. He denounced Bryan and cast his ballot for a breakaway faction of the Democratic party that favored retention of the gold standard.[85]

What made reformers of men such as Wilson and Pitney were the economic and political abuses of the great corporations.[86] Such abuses were particularly serious in New Jersey, where during the 1880's and 1890's, the legislature adopted a series of laws designed to facilitate the formation of holding companies and monopolies.[87] Between 1896 and 1913, the state did a bargain-counter business in corporate charters, enriching its treasury with filing fees while giving a legal home to all of the largest holding companies in the Nation and a majority of the lesser trusts as well.[88] Their rush to incorporate in New Jersey earned her the nickname "the mother of trusts."[89] Particularly offensive to New Jerseyans themselves were the utility companies, which controlled gas, electric, trolley, and street railway service in the northern part of the state.[90] Backed by the major banks and insurance firms, these corporations enjoyed intimate relations with the leaders of both the Democratic and Republican parties, many of whom had financial interests in the companies.[91] It is hardly surprising that utilities benefited from extremely favorable franchise arrangements and quite low taxes.[92]

During the period from 1905 to 1912, these firms came under attack by reformers in both political parties. The first to take the offensive were the so-called "New Idea" Republicans, led by Jersey City Mayor Mark Fagan, his corporation's counsel, George Record, and Essex County Senator Everett Colby.[93] By 1906, the "New Idea" men had become such a potent force in the northern part of the state that the Republican majority in the legislature hastened to endorse their demands for increased taxation of railroad property and for legislation imposing limitations on the franchises that local governments routinely granted to utility corporations.[94] In 1911, Democratic Governor Woodrow Wilson joined the assault. His administration secured passage of legislation creating a board of public utility commissioners and investing it with the power to set rates and regulate service.[95]

Fourteen years before that measure became law, Mahlon Pitney had spoken out against abuse of the public by a utility corporation. In particular, he focused on the United States Electric Lighting Company, a firm that for years had enjoyed a monopoly franchise for lighting the streets of the Nation's Capital. In an 1897 debate on the floor of the House of Representatives, Pitney vigorously attacked the lighting company and endorsed the efforts of the District of Columbia Commissioners to give some of its business to a competing firm.[96] No company "that has the full control in a matter of this sort can be trusted to care for the public interests," Pitney told his colleagues.[97] What would best serve the interests of consumers was competition.[98] The following year, in probably his most famous House speech, Pitney defended his home state against charges by Populist Congressman "Sockless" Jerry Simpson of Kansas that New Jersey was guilty of coddling the trusts. Although denouncing Simpson for preaching a doctrine that would "lead us directly to socialism," Pitney endorsed "reasonable measures of regulation for the government of corporations" and the use of the equity powers of the judiciary to prevent corporate abuses.[99] As he left the New Jersey Senate for the bench in 1901, he denounced "bills . . . contrived for the purpose of establishing or bolstering up a partial or total monopoly."[100]

D. State Judge

Like his political rhetoric, Pitney's performance as a state judge reflected attitudes commonly associated with Progressivism. He served as an associate judge of the New Jersey Supreme Court from February 19, 1901 to January 22, 1908.[101] During this tenure, he wrote a total of 167 opinions, dealing with a wide variety of civil and criminal legal problems.[102] Only four times did the court of errors and appeals reverse one of his decisions.[103]

Pitney's performance earned him a promotion. When Chancellor William J. Magie retired in January of 1908, Governor J. Franklin Fort nominated him to a full seven-year term as Magie's

successor.[104] The senate, not even bothering with the usual reference to committee, quickly confirmed the choice.[105] During
Pitney's four years and two months as chancellor, he headed
both the law and equity branches of the court of errors and
appeals.[106] He handed down forty-seven decisions on the law
side and approximately eleven on the equity side.[107] His responsibilities as chancellor also included coordinating the work of
the vice chancellors, who presided over the various districts into
which the state was then divided.[108] This made him briefly the
superior of his father, who had already submitted his resignation before Mahlon's appointment, but remained on the job for
a few months after his son took office.[109] As chancellor, Pitney
inaugurated the practice of having all the vice chancellors meet
two or three times a year to discuss any problems they were
experiencing in their districts.[110] What attracted the attention of
the press, however, was his "scoring [of] the Camden law firm of
French & Richards for oppressive conduct in attempting to charge
the Amparo Mining Company $75,000 for legal fees" by reduc-
ing the firm's fee to only $12,500.[111]

The Amparo Company had more reason to applaud Pitney's
performance on the state bench than did most corporations. His
decisions in cases challenging efforts to subject railroads to
increased taxation revealed the continuing development of the
incipient Progressivism that he had displayed as a politician. The
constant in these rulings was the identity of the losing party; it
was always the railroad. For example, Pitney spurned[112] the Bergen
and Dundee Railroad's challenge to the constitutionality of the
1905 Duffield Act,[113] a measure subjecting all property of railroads and canals except their "main stem" to taxation by local
governments. He also upheld the validity, under both the state
constitution and the fourteenth amendment,[114] of 1906 legislation that removed the main stem classification from property
formerly so denominated[115] and equalized the tax rates on that
part of railroad and canal property subject solely to state taxation with the rates on other New Jersey real property.[116]

Pitney again rebuffed railroads when they complained about
the amount of their tax assessments[117] and when they objected
to the inclusion of particular pieces of real estate in the "second
class" category subject to local taxation.[118] He ruled in favor of
the mayor and aldermen of Jersey City in a suit against both the
State Board of Equalization and the Central Railroad Company
of New Jersey.[119] The suit arose after the board, at the instigation
of the railroad, ordered a reassessment of all real property in the

community without giving notice to other taxpayers.[120]

Pitney also supported Jersey City's Progressive Republican administration in two disputes with local street railway companies. In 1905, he ruled that the municipality could collect a license fee from the North Jersey Street Railway Company.[121] Two years later, Pitney upheld as reasonable a municipal regulatory ordinance requiring North Jersey and another company to provide sufficient cars during rush hour so that all passengers could have a seat and no one would have to wait more than five minutes for a ride.[122]

This latter decision reflected Pitney's desire to see corporations regulated and controlled. Although he could wax eloquent about "the marvelous progress of the past half century in every line of human effort, carried on . . . more and more through the instrumentality of corporations,"[123] he deeply distrusted the increasing separation of ownership from control and the concentration of economic power into fewer and fewer hands,[124] two factors that distinguished corporate evolution at the turn of the century. His ideal corporation was a little democracy in which directors were elected annually for limited terms, real power rested with the shareholders, and minority rights were respected.[125] An equity judge, Pitney thought, should use his powers to preserve this ideal and at the same time to protect the public from corporate abuses such as restraint of trade.[126]

The nineteenth-century attitudes that permeated his corporation decisions also governed his approach to labor law. In the case of *Brennan v. United Hatters, Local 17*,[127] Pitney expressed his distaste for a union's claim that the value of belonging to it "consist[ed] in participation in a more or less complete monopoly of the labor market in the particular trade in question."[128] He subsequently cited *Brennan* as holding that the state constitution guaranteed a painter the "right to seek and gain employment in his lawful occupation,"[129] and added that, consequently, a union "had no right to interfere with him in his employment merely because he was not a member."[130] Finally, in *George Jonas Glass Co. v. Glass Bottle Blowers' Association*,[131] Chancellor Pitney upheld a sweeping injunction[132] issued by Vice Chancellor Bergen[133] against a labor organization that had attempted to pressure an employer into unionizing his factory. Besides instigating a strike and a boycott and picketing the plant, the union apparently had resorted to threats, intimidation, and even bribery to deprive Jonas Glass of a work force until the firm agreed to its demands.[134] Pitney characterized the union's actions as "a war of subjugation against the complainant corporation."[135] In issuing the injunction, Vice Chancellor Bergen was careful to emphasize that he was not disputing the right of workers to form a union or to state peacefully to others their position in a labor dispute.[136] Pitney, on the other hand, expressed distaste for a state statute that appeared to legalize both unions and strikes. He declared that if this law really permitted the use of peaceable measures to induce workmen to quit their jobs or refuse to enter someone's employment, it would have to be unconstitutional.[137]

Because Pitney's hostility toward unions was inspired by their tendency to monopolize in the labor market,[138] it did not extend to unorganized workers. In tort cases decided while he was on the New Jersey bench, he ruled in favor of injured workmen about as often as he ruled against them.[139] He did once make rather heartless use of the doctrine of contributory negligence, employing it to reverse a jury verdict in favor of a fourteen-year-old boy whose hand had been crushed in his employer's machine.[140] In another case, Pitney declined to adopt the so-called vice-principal exception to the fellow-servant rule, thus precluding a telephone lineman from recovering against his employer for injuries caused by the negligence of his foreman.[141] On the other hand, he consistently took the position that employers must furnish their employees with safe tools and a safe place in which to work, and he would not allow those who failed to do so to avoid liability by hiding behind the fellow-servant doctrine.[142] In viewing workers favorably while loathing their organizations, Pitney was not unique.[143] "[F]or many a progressive the rise of the labor union was as frightening as the rise of trusts."[144]

Pitney's hostility to unions placed him squarely within the mainstream of the Progressive movement, as did his support of governmental efforts to regulate saloons[145] and to combat other forms of vice.[146] In addition, Pitney impressed Progressives by prodding a Hudson County grand jury into indicting for election fraud some opponents of Jersey City's New Idea mayor, Mark Fagan, men who, according to the *Newark Evening News*, had concocted a "conspiracy to override the will of the people."[147] A charge to a Passaic County grand jury also attracted favorable attention. In it, Pitney lashed out at local officials for failing to enforce the liquor laws and called for action against election officers in Paterson, who were alleged to have submitted false returns.[148]

His judicial support for causes dear to their hearts made him politically appealing to Progressives.[149] In 1906, some Morris

County friends launched a campaign to elect Pitney to the United States Senate.[150] Their bandwagon never really got rolling, however, and even his hometown backers finally abandoned it in the legislature. Nevertheless, Essex County's New Idea senator, Everett Colby, stuck with Pitney all the way by both nominating and voting for him.[151]

In the summer of 1907, President Theodore Roosevelt, then emerging as an outspoken champion of Progressivism,[152] encouraged New Jersey Republicans to nominate Pitney for governor.[153] That idea appealed to a Jersey City "Colbyite," who was impressed by the fact that the justice had made the railroads pay an additional $4,000,000 in taxes.[154] Pitney, however, did not get the gubernatorial nomination, despite being regarded as an acceptable candidate by a great majority of those who identified themselves with the New Idea movement.[155] He continued to be mentioned as a prospect for the governorship, though, and when Democrat Woodrow Wilson ran for that office in 1910, he thought his classmate might well be his opponent.[156]

IV. Supreme Court Justice

A. Appointment

Pitney was headed not for the governor's office in Trenton, but for the Supreme Court in Washington. Although President William Howard Taft considered him for one of three open seats on the Court in 1910,[157] he ultimately gave those positions to other men.[158] Taft returned to Pitney after Associate Justice John Marshall Harlan died in October of 1911, but the chancellor was not his first choice for that appointment.[159] Scholars have never satisfactorily explained why the President finally chose Pitney for the Harlan seat.[160]

Perhaps the most important reason was his broad political appeal. During the early months of 1912, Taft was locked in a fight for control of the Republican party with his predecessor, Theodore Roosevelt, who was seeking to deny him renomination and to capture the top spot on the GOP ticket for himself.[161] The President and his political strategists believed that New Jersey could become a crucial battleground in this contest.[162] Ultimately, this belief proved decisive in Taft's choice of a replacement for Harlan.

The President first offered the appointment to his Secretary of

State, Frank Knox, who declined the honor.[163] For several months after that, the leading contenders appeared to be Secretary of Commerce and Labor Charles Nagel and Judge William C. Hook of the Court of Appeals for the Eighth Circuit. Nagel lost out because he was too old, lacked prior judicial experience,[164] and had made himself unpopular with labor by supporting immigration.[165] Some people objected to Hook because of his concurrence in a decision upholding an Oklahoma statute that allowed railroads to provide sleeping, dining, and chair cars for whites without making comparable facilities available to blacks.[166] Others disliked his issuance of an injunction prohibiting the city of Denver from constructing a new water plant and "requir[ing] it instead to buy [out] a private water company whose franchise had expired."[167] In addition, state railroad commissioners and Progressive governors from western states complained that Hook's approach to rate making was prorailroad.[168] That was not the sort of nominee Taft needed at a time when he was laboring to keep Progressives from deserting to the Roosevelt camp.[169]

Pitney was. Franklin Murphy, a former governor of New Jersey and then the state's Republican National Committeeman, pushed him for the job. Murphy was a strong Taft supporter,[170] and because he hoped to be selected as his running mate, he was anxious to ingratiate himself with the President. Taft was scheduled to give a speech in New York City in February of 1912. With the objective of promoting his political fortunes in New Jersey, Murphy arranged for Taft to stop over in Newark on the way there to attend a luncheon at the ex-governor's home and a Republican reception at the Essex County Country Club.[171] At Murphy's house, the President sat next to Chancellor Pitney.[172] They had a pleasant conversation,[173] and a week later, on February 19th, Taft offered the chancellor a seat on the Supreme Court.[174]

Pitney was in many ways just what the President had been looking for. He was an experienced judge, but at fifty-four, he still had many years of judicial work before him.[175] In addition, he was from the Third Circuit, which had been unrepresented on the Supreme Court for a number of years.[176] A desire to correct that situation was one of the reasons Taft had approached Knox, and only reluctantly had he turned his attention to candidates from further west.[177] After dining with Pitney, the President, a former judge himself,[178] spent several hours reading a number of his opinions.[179] These apparently confirmed a favorable assessment of Pitney's abilities that Taft had received from New Jersey Vice Chancellor James E. Howell in 1910.[180] Finally,

Pitney was from New Jersey. Taft had become convinced that he had to name someone from that state.[181]

Although the chancellor satisfied many of the President's other criteria, political considerations eventually earned him a seat on the Supreme court. Taft considered at least three other New Jersey judges,[182] among them Pitney's friend Justice Swayze.[183] Swayze, who was Governor Murphy's initial choice for the job, had the support of United States Senator Frank O. Briggs [184] and even the chancellor himself.[185] Howell had advised the President, however, that Pitney was preferable because of his more extensive involvement in politics.[186] Eventually, Pitney became Murphy's choice.[187] The ex-governor was a conservative who considered the Progressive movement dangerous, but he recognized the value of appeasing those Republicans who were attracted to it because they needed their vote.[188] Thus, he invited two or three Progressives, among them Senator Colby, to his luncheon, an event arranged to generate enthusiasm for the Taft movement.[189] The appointment of Pitney was almost certainly another move of the same kind, intended to curry favor with the New Idea men and thus help Taft retain control of the New Jersey Republican party.[190]

Reaction to the nomination from within the state was extremely positive,[191] and Governor Wilson commended Taft's choice.[192] To the rest of the Country, however, Pitney "was 'an unknown quantity.' "[193] The *New York Times* nevertheless predicted that the Senate would quickly and easily confirm him.[194]

The *Times* was wrong. First, the president of the Iowa Federation of Labor protested the Pitney appointment to Senators from his state.[195] He failed to substantiate his objections, however, because his argument was based on *Frank & Dugan v. Herold*.[196] As the nominee swiftly pointed out, the Pitney who had granted a sweeping injunction against picketing and other union activity in that case was his father.[197] Mahlon Pitney claimed not to be an enemy of labor,[198] and the president of the New Jersey Federation of Labor, who was also a Hudson County assemblyman, supported him, claiming to be unable to recall any decision by the chancellor that had borne heavily against union interests.[199] He apparently had forgotten *Jonas Glass*. When the Senate took up the nomination on March 8th, Charles A. Culberson, a Texas Democrat, raised objections to the *Jonas Glass* decision.[200] It aroused enough controversy that the Senate had the opinion printed.[201] For three days, Senators read and debate raged.[202] At one point during the executive sessions on the nomination, Pitney's supporters reportedly lacked sufficient votes for confirmation.[203] Governor Wilson, Senator James E. Martine, and other leading New Jersey Democrats sprang to the defense of their state's native son,[204] and on March 13th, the Senate approved Taft's choice by a vote of fifty to twenty-six.[205] The division was basically along partisan lines, although four Insurgent Republicans did join twenty-two Democrats in voting "no."[206]

B. Supreme Court Decisions

Five days later, Pitney took the oath of office,[207] beginning a tenure on the Supreme Court that would last for just under eleven years.[208] A durable Justice, he was seldom absent from the Bench, participating in all but nineteen of the 2412 decisions that the Court rendered during his tenure.[209] Pitney authored a total of 268 opinions, speaking for the majority on 244 occasions, dissenting 19 times, and writing 5 concurrences.[210]

1. Taxation

For lawyers practicing today, Pitney's most important opinion is *Eisner v. Macomber*.[211] In that case, he defined income for purposes of the sixteenth amendment, drawing the line between those additions to wealth that were subject to the Federal income tax and those that were not.[212] The specific question in *Eisner* was whether stock dividends constituted taxable income.[213] Congress had passed a law in 1916 treating them as if they did,[214] but the financial community expected the Court to hold that measure unconstitutional. Early in his opinion, Pitney explained the intent of the disputed act.[215] Apparently, he mumbled as he did so.[216] An agent for Dow Jones misunderstood him as saying not that Congress had sought to tax stock dividends as income, but that the Court was holding it had the power to do this.[217] The Dow Jones man rushed out to wire the news to Wall Street.[218] The result was a brief plunge in stock prices.[219] When the false report was corrected, however, the market recovered what it had lost and more.[220]

The stock market's favorable reaction to Pitney's actual opinion probably did not surprise Justice Louis Brandeis. In a strong dissent, he charged, "If stock dividends representing profits are held exempt from taxation under the Sixteenth Amendment, the owners of the most successful businesses in America will . . . be able to escape taxation on a large part of what is actually their income."[221] Brandeis's Populist rhetoric was nearly as unjustified a reaction to Pitney's opinion as the collapse of stock prices. Informed observers recognized that *Eisner* had not created much of an opportunity for the distribution of tax-free profits, and virtually all of the voluminous scholarly literature that the case generated supported Pitney's position.[222]

That is hardly surprising, for the Justice from New Jersey had become something of a tax specialist. *Eisner* was only one of six majority opinions that he wrote explicating the concept of income as it related to the sixteenth amendment.[223] Pitney also spoke for the Court in cases involving Federal taxation of corporations,[224] inheritances,[225] and imports.[226] In addition, he wrote a total of twenty majority opinions[227] and one dissent[228] dealing with various constitutional issues raised by state tax measures.

2. Labor Unions

Although Pitney devoted more attention to taxation than to any other subject, as one of his biographers has pointed out, "It is in the area of labor decisions . . . that the Justice made his most significant contribution."[229] These were also the opinions that earned him his reactionary reputation.[230] As a member of the Supreme Court, Pitney continued to exhibit the hostility toward unions that he had displayed on the New Jersey bench.[231] In a 1915 case known as *Coppage v. Kansas*,[232] he held unconstitutional a state statute that made it unlawful for employers to require their workers, as a condition of employment, to agree not to join a labor organization.[233] Pitney insisted that he was not questioning "the legitimacy of such organizations," but added, "Conceding the full right of the individual to join [a] union, he has no inherent right to do this and still remain in the employ of one who is unwilling to employ a union man."[234] Pitney viewed the Kansas statute as one designed for "leveling inequalities of fortune" through "an interference with the normal exercise of personal liberty and property rights . . . and not an incident to the advancement of the general welfare."[235] Not even a national emergency, he argued in a later case, could justify legislative interference with management's freedom to negotiate with its workers for the employment terms it wanted.[236]

Pitney's antistatist attitudes did not cut both ways. Although hostile to governmental interference with employers' freedom of action, he generally gave enthusiastic support to governmental interference with the liberty of unions. Pitney remained a champion of the labor injunction. In *Paine Lumber Co. v. Neal*,[237] he argued unsuccessfully that open-shop sash and door manufacturers were entitled under the Sherman Antitrust Act[238] to have a Federal court enjoin a boycott of their products by the Brotherhood of Carpenters and Joiners and certain unionized firms. Later, as a spokesman for the majority in *Hitchman Coal & Coke Co. v. Mitchell*,[239] Pitney held that a coal-mining company that had required its employees to agree to work on a nonunion basis might have a Federal district court restrain the United Mine Workers from trying to organize its labor force.[240] In a revealing passage, he declared: "Defendants' acts cannot be justified by any analogy to competition in trade. They are not competitors of plaintiff; and if they were their conduct exceeds the bounds of fair trade."[241] Pitney believed that a union had no right to reduce an employer's freedom of choice through economic coercion, although he regarded it as perfectly acceptable for management to limit the independence of workers by making them agree not to join a union in order to obtain a desperately needed job.[242] *Hitchman Coal* and *Eagle Glass & Manufacturing Co. v. Rowe*,[243] which was decided the same day on *Hitchman Coal's* authority, exhibit what one commentator had characterized as a "zeal bordering on vindictiveness in an effort to strike at labor."[244]

Despite his deep and long-standing hostility toward unions, Pitney wound up supporting their position in his last labor law decision. The New Jersey Justice gave no preliminary indication that he would soon support a judicial inroad on the formidable restrictions on organized labor and union activity that he had helped to erect. Speaking for the Court in a January 1921 case called *Duplex Printing Press Co. v. Deering*,[245] he upheld the action of a Federal district court, which had enjoined a secondary boycott organized by the International Association of Machinists in an effort to force a manufacturer to unionize.[246] Pitney ruled this way despite the fact that the district court had based its injunction on the antitrust laws.[247] He refused to acknowledge that by enacting section 20 of the Clayton Act[248] in 1914, Congress had made conduct of the type in which the machinists had engaged lawful and nonenjoinable under those statutes. Justice Brandeis responded with a powerful dissent in which he argued that rights were subordinate to the interests of the community and that how far "industrial combatants" might push their struggle was some thing for the community's representatives in the legislature to decide and "not for judges to determine."[249] Certainly that had never been Pitney's view, but he was not a man who clung to his own conclusions out of vanity, and he could be persuaded by study to change his mind.[250]

Twelve months later, in *Truax v. Corrigan*,[251] the New Jersey Justice adopted Brandeis's position. Taft, who was then Chief Justice, assigned Pitney to write an opinion invalidating an Arizona statute that forbade the issuance of injunctions in labor disputes. Pitney soon received a memorandum from Brandeis opposing the decision, which he "read with interest."[252] The New Jersey Justice then changed his vote, joining his critic in dissent.[253] Pitney's opinion suggested his sympathies still lay with businessmen seeking assistance from the courts rather than with unions,[254] and he declined to endorse "the wisdom, or policy, or propriety" of the Arizona law.[255] It now seemed clear to him that the labor injunction could be abolished "in the normal exercise of the legislative power of the State."[256]

3. Industrial Accidents

Pitney's dissent in *Truax* "demonstrates that it would be an error to dismiss him simply as an antilabor judge."[257] Although too oriented toward the individualistic world of the nineteenth century to appreciate that unions might be necessary counterweights to rapidly expanding aggregates of capital (whose legitimacy he also could not accept), the Justice from New Jersey did have some understanding of America's emergent industrial society. Like a number of his colleagues on the Supreme Court, he was willing, where union activity was not involved, to give a wide berth to state labor regulations.[258] Thus, for example, Pitney wrote opinions upholding the constitutionality of Missouri[259] and Oklahoma[260] statutes that required employers to give workers who either quit or were fired letters setting forth the nature and duration of their service and the reasons for its termination.

Like his *Truax* dissent, both of these decisions came near the end of his service on the Supreme Court. Much earlier, however, in cases arising under the Federal Employers' Liability Act (FELA) and state workers' compensation statutes, Pitney had displayed the sympathy for unorganized workers already apparent during his years as a New Jersey judge. Compensating laborers injured in the course of their employment, which was the purpose of these laws, was a long-standing Progressive objective, which he supported every bit as vigorously as did such outspoken champions of reform as Theodore Roosevelt.[261]

Four years before Pitney's appointment to the Supreme Court,

Congress had enacted the FELA,[262] a statute that abolished the fellow-servant rule in cases where interstate railroad workers sued their employers for on-the-job injuries.[263] The FELA also greatly modified for purposes of such litigation two other common employers' defenses—contributory negligence[264] and assumption of the risk.[265] During his tenure on the Court, Pitney decided a total of sixteen cases arising under the FELA. Twelve times he ruled in favor of the injured worker or his estate.[266] In two of the cases that the railroad won, the issue before the Court was not whether the railroad was liable, but only whether the damages that the plaintiff had recovered were excessive.[267] In a third case, Pitney disposed of all of the substantive issues in a manner favorable to the worker, but reversed a jury verdict in his favor because some local practice rules in the jurisdiction where the case arose had not been followed.[268] Similarly, in litigation arising under the common law of torts[269] and the Safety Appliance Act,[270] he ruled for railroad employees injured on the job.

It was in cases involving workers' compensation statutes, however, that Pitney aligned himself most dramatically with Progressivism. At the time of his appointment to the Supreme Court, states had begun to enact laws that made employers liable without fault for injuries that their workers suffered on the job; usually these statutes also limited the amount that the victim could recover.[271] New Jersey was a part of this national trend. In 1911, Woodrow Wilson secured enactment of a workers' compensation statute for the state.[272] By then, it had become apparent that traditional tort litigation served the interests of employers no better than it served those of employees; even the National Association of Manufacturers had concluded that compensation systems were inevitable and probably desirable.[273]

Nevertheless, in the 1911 case of *Ives v. South Buffalo Railway*,[274] the New York Court of Appeals unanimously struck down the first state law creating one, holding that it violated both the New York Constitution and the fourteenth amendment.[275] Constitutional law experts, led by Dean Roscoe Pound of Harvard, denounced the *Ives* decision in the press,[276] and Theodore Roosevelt expressed a desire to see every judge who had participated in the case removed from the bench.[277] In a February 1912 speech, Roosevelt, who was then mounting his challenge to Taft, urged giving the people the right to recall judicial decisions holding statutes unconstitutional.[278] Although denounced by the American Bar Association, Roosevelt's proposal and his concomitant attack on judicial power in general elicited a surprising amount of support, even within the legal community.[279]

If the judiciary were to avoid a successful assault on its authority, it had to adjust constitutional law to accommodate legislation ensuring compensation for the victims of industrial accidents. Mahlon Pitney did that. In the wake of the *Ives* decision, New York amended its constitution and then enacted a new workers' compensation law limited to employees in supposedly hazardous industries.[280] In 1916, that statute came before the Supreme Court in *New York Central Railroad v. White.*[281] The employer argued that this law struck "at the fundamentals of constitutional freedom of contract."[282] Speaking for the Court, Pitney disagreed, holding that it was "a reasonable exercise of the police power of the State."[283] Pitney reasoned that the pecuniary loss caused by an employee's death or injury had to fall somewhere and that these damages were, after all, the result of an operation out of which the employer expected to derive a profit.[284] Pitney concluded that it was not "arbitrary and unreasonable for the State to impose upon the employer the absolute duty of making a moderate and definite compensation in money to every disabled employee."[285]

In a companion case, in which the Court upheld an Iowa statute, Pitney declared "that the employer has no vested right to have these so-called common-law defenses perpetuated for his benefit, and that the Fourteenth Amendment does not prevent a State from establishing a system of workmen's compensation without the consent of the employer, incidentally abolishing [these] defenses."[286] The New Jersey Justice also spoke for the Court in *Mountain Timber Co. v. Washington.*[287] The statute at issue in that case, unlike the New York law upheld in *White*, required employers in hazardous industries to contribute to a state fund for the compensation of injured workmen, whether or not any injuries had ever befallen their own employees.[288] Thus, a careful firm had to help pay for the harm caused by its negligent competitors. Nevertheless, stated Pitney, because "accidental injuries are inevitable," it could not "be deemed arbitrary or unreasonable for the State, instead of imposing upon the particular employer entire responsibility for losses occurring in his own plant or work, to impose the burden upon the industry."[289]

Four Justices dissented in *Mountain Timber.*[290] This suggests that the Court had not been nearly as unified in support of the other two decisions as their reported unanimity indicates. Years later, Brandeis said of Pitney, "But for [him] we would have had no workmen's compensation laws."[291] Originally, the New Jersey

Justice "had been the other way," but "Pitney came around upon study,"[292] grasping the economic and sociological arguments for workers' compensation. He then voted to sustain those laws and wrote admirable opinions explicating the rationale for doing so.[293]

For the rest of his tenure on the Court, Pitney remained a champion of workers' compensation. He upheld as consistent with the fourteenth amendment the extension of New York's scheme to embrace all employers of four or more workers (even those in industries that were not hazardous)[294] and to provide payments for disfiguring injuries that did not deprive their victims of income-earning capacity.[295] Furthermore, when the Court held that a New York court's application of New York law to the case of a stevedore fatally injured while working upon the navigable waters of New York amounted to an impermissible invasion of the exclusive maritime jurisdiction of the Federal judiciary, Pitney entered a vigorous dissent.[296] Although usually ruling in favor of the employee, he would go the other way when this was necessary to protect the integrity of a comprehensive workers' compensation system. This was also demonstrated in the case of an injured Texan who sought a higher recovery than his state's compensation act allowed by bringing a common law tort action against his employer.[297]

On the other hand, Pitney held that if a legislature gave laborers the option of either settling for the amounts authorized by a compensation statute or bringing tort actions against their employers (whose common law defenses it severely restricted), this violated neither the equal protection clause nor the due process clause.[298] The states, he wrote in the *Arizona Employers' Liability Cases*,[299] "are left with a wide range of legislative discretion, notwithstanding the provisions of the Fourteenth Amendment; and their conclusions respecting the wisdom of their legislative acts are not reviewable by the courts."[300] Novelty was not a constitutional objection.[301] The statute that the Arizona Legislature had enacted imposed no new financial burden on hazardous industries; the very nature of these industries made damages from accidental injuries inevitable.[302] All this law did was require the party who organized and took the profits from an enterprise to treat these damages like other costs of doing business, such as paying wages.[303] He could consider them in setting prices and thus pass through the cost of accidents to the consumer, rather than leaving injured workers, their dependents, and public welfare agencies to bear the burden.[304] Acceptance of such modern notions about spreading the costs of accidents, so incompatible with the fundamental assumptions of turn-of-the-century tort law,[305] apparently did not come easily to Pitney.[306]

That it came at all is indicative of the extent to which one of the reform movements associated with Progressivism molded his thinking. Pitney did not always take a Progressive position in labor cases. For example, he voted against both a Federal child labor statute[307] and a state minimum-wage-for-women law.[308] Nevertheless, his positions in cases involving both unions and unorganized workers reflected the attitudes of Progressive reformers to a surprising extent.

4. Antitrust and Economic Regulation

The stands Pitney took in litigation arising under the anti-trust laws and various state and Federal regulatory statutes also mirrored the attitudes of Progressive reformers. The lack of sympathy for railroads, which was such a notable feature of his career on the New Jersey bench, persisted after his appointment to the Supreme Court. In disputes between carriers and shippers, Pitney exhibited a consistent preference for the latter.[309] He rejected railroads' challenges to orders of the Interstate Commerce Commission,[310] and was almost equally unreceptive to their constitutional complaints about the rules and rates imposed upon them by state regulatory agencies.[311] Pitney also continued for the most part to support the efforts of municipal governments to regulate the corporations that provided their citizens with utility services.[312]

The antimonopoly bias that had animated him during his days as a New Jersey congressman and judge manifested itself in cases arising under the Sherman Antitrust Act. "As a rule, he joined with the majority where it upheld and gave vitality to the Act, and could be counted among the dissenters where the Court resorted to 'strained and unusual' interpretations of the facts to uphold the legality of challenged practices."[313] When a Supreme Court that was growing noticeably more conservative[314] ruled in 1917 that the exclusive leasing agreements that the United Shoe Machinery Company had used to dominate the entire shoe manufacturing business did not violate the Sherman Act, Pitney joined Justices Day[315] and Clarke[316] in protesting its decision. When the Court employed the "rule of reason" to justify rejecting the Government's efforts to dissolve the United States Steel Corporation, he again stood with these two colleagues in dissent.[317] Pitney was, according to one scholar, the Supreme Court's "most consistent supporter of congressional policy as detailed . . . in the antitrust law."[318]

5. Civil Liberties

Although Theodore Roosevelt might not have applauded them, Pitney's votes in support of governmental efforts to control monopoly, like his rulings upholding Federal attacks on liquor[319] and prostitution,[320] were very much in the Progressive tradition.[321] So too was Pitney's endorsement of the National Government's attack upon dissent during World War I. For Progressives, among them President Wilson, American participation in "the war to end all wars" was a great crusade, in which the Nation fought to eradicate militarism, to protect liberalism, and to spread democracy.[322] Believing shared convictions were the cement of society, the Government resorted to publicity and appeals to conscience to unite the Nation behind this greatest of all reform efforts.[323] The results were intolerance, vigilantism, and persecution.[324] Congress passed the repressive Espionage[325] and Sedition[326] Acts, and despite the apparent inconsistency between those measures and the first amendment, the Supreme Court affirmed their constitutionality and regularly sustained convictions obtained under them.[327] Even the great Justice Oliver Wendell Holmes, Jr., before penning the first of his famous "clear and present danger" dissents, handed down three decisions in this vein.[328]

Pitney was in good Progressive company when, in *Pierce v. United States*,[329] he upheld the convictions of four Socialists under section 3 of the Espionage Act[330] based primarily on their distribution of a pamphlet called *The Price We Pay*.[331] This leaflet characterized the war as fought for the benefit of capitalists like J.P. Morgan, wailed about recruiting officers hauling young men away to awful deaths, predicted a rise in food prices, and accused the Attorney General of being so busy jailing those who failed to stand for the playing of "The Star-Spangled Banner" that he had no time for prosecuting speculators.[332] "Common knowledge," Pitney believed, "would have sufficed to show at least that the statements as to the causes that led to the entry of the United States into the war against Germany were grossly false; and such common knowledge went to prove also that [the] defendants knew they were untrue."[333] In his opinion, a jury might have found that *The Price We Pay* could tend to cause insubordination in the armed forces and to obstruct recruiting.[334]

Brandeis, on the other hand, considered it inconceivable that the lurid exaggerations with which this pamphlet was filled could induce any serviceman of normal intelligence to risk the severe penalties prescribed for refusal of duty.[335] In dissent, he pointed out the harm that could be done to the democratic political process if arguments were treated as criminal incitements merely because they seemed unfair, mistaken, unsound, or intemperate "to those exercising judiciary power."[336] His was a message lost on Pitney, who joined the majority that upheld numerous other convictions under the Espionage and Sedition Acts and related state statutes.[337]

In voting to jail opponents of the war, Pitney reflected the temper of his times. His greatest weakness was an inability to question the accepted wisdom of his own day. Thus, he affirmed a district court decision that had denied a writ of habeas corpus to Leo Frank, who was convicted of murder in an Atlanta trial so dominated by a mob that the defendant had to be absent from the courtroom when the jury returned its verdict.[338] Because Frank had failed to raise the matter of his exclusion from the courtroom promptly and because the Georgia courts had considered and had rejected his contention that the jury had been influenced by the threatening atmosphere that surrounded the trial, Pitney ruled that the defendant had not been denied his fourteenth amendment right to due process of law.[339]

Such exaggerated deference to state authority and such callous insistence that violations of fundamental rights by state institutions lay beyond Federal control were not peculiar to Pitney. They remained typical of the Court as a whole until well into the 1920's.[340] Furthermore, in refusing to impose national conceptions of due process on Georgia, Pitney was taking a position consistent with the one he adopted in other cases far less controversial than Leo Frank's.[341] Still, Holmes could see what Pitney could not: "Whatever disagreement there may be as to the scope of the phrase 'due process of law,' there can be no doubt that it embraces the fundamental conception of a fair trial . . . Mob law [cannot be] due process."[342] Within less than a decade, the Court would inform the states, through a Holmes opinion, that the fourteenth amendment limited their discretion at least that much.[343]

C. Resignation and Death

By the time it did this, Mahlon Pitney was no longer on the

Bench. The Justice who reflected so well the attitudes of the Progressive era departed from the Supreme Court soon after Progressivism came to an end in the sour aftermath of World War I.[344] In early 1922, while attending a rededication of the Philadelphia room where the Court had held its first session, Pitney suffered what doctors diagnosed as "a blood clot on the brain."[345] Chief Justice Taft urged him to take some time off,[346] and he did.[347] Upon his return to Washington, Pitney still could not resume a full workload. Taft regarded him as a "weak" member of the Court, and after his "breakdown," he assigned him no further cases.[348] Pitney wrote only three more opinions before the end of the Term.[349]

Then, in August 1922, he suffered a massive stroke.[350] Pitney now recognized that he would have to leave the Court.[351] Unfortunately, if he did so, he would not be eligible for a pension; he had completed the required ten years of service, but was still six years short of the mandatory seventy years of age.[352] Congress enacted special legislation enabling Pitney to retire,[353] however, and he did so on December 31, 1922.[354] A little less than two years later, on December 9, 1924, New Jersey's third Supreme Court Justice died at his house in Washington.[355] Then, for the last time, he came home to Morristown.[356]

III. Conclusion

Neither contemporaries nor historians have ranked Pitney with the greats of the Supreme Court. Even among the four New Jersey Justices, he tends to be the forgotten figure. Nonetheless, Pitney deserves more credit than he has received. At the time he sat, a previously rural and agrarian America was struggling, often without really knowing quite how to go about it, to adjust to life as an urban and industrial society. That, at bottom, was what Progressivism was all about.[357] The Country needed judges who would support, rather than use their judicial power to thwart, the sometimes unwise but mostly necessary initiatives of a great reform movement. The Nation found one in Mahlon Pitney. Of all the Justices who sat on the Supreme Court during his tenure, "Pitney was the most consistent supporter of national reform legislation."[358] His opinions are as murky as one critic has charged,[359] but he was not the reactionary some have made him out to be.[360] Thrust onto the national scene by New Jersey Progressivism, and a mirror of its values and biases, Justice Pitney was a contributor to whatever success the Progressive movement achieved, both in his native state and in the Nation as a whole.

Notes

The author wishes to thank Ms. Loni Freeman for her invaluable help with the research for this article.

1. *See* G. Myers, *History of the Supreme Court of the United States* 783–85 (1912, reprint 1925).

2. *Id.* at 783.

3. *Id.* at 784.

4. Israel,"Mahlon Pitney," in 3 *The Justices of the United States Supreme Court 1789–1978: Their Lives and Major Opinions* 2001 (L. Friedman & F. Israel eds. 1980).

5. *See id.* at 2005.

6. A. Link & R. McCormick, *Progressivism* 1 (1983). This book is the best short survey of Progressivism. It also provides a good introduction to the scholarly literature on the subject.

7. *Id.* at 2.

8. *See id.*

9. Most of these big businesses were not true trusts. John D. Rockefeller did accomplish a horizontal combination of competing firms in the oil industry in 1882 by creating a trust. G. Porter, *The Rise of Big Business, 1860–1910,* at 56 (1973). After 1889, however, such a horizontal combination was normally achieved by creating a holding company incorporated under the laws of New Jersey. *See id.*

10. *See* J. Garraty, *A Short History of the American Nation* 368–69 (2d ed. 1974).

11. *See id.* at 369.

12. *See* T. McCraw, *Prophets of Regulation* 111 (1984).

13. *See generally* E. Foner, *Free Soil, Free Labor, Free Men: The Ideology of the Republican Party Before the Civil War* 16–17 (1970) (discussing the free-labor outlook).

14. *See id.* at 20, 22, 25.

15. *See* Benedict, "Laissez-Faire and Liberty: A Re-evaluation of the Meaning and Origins of Laissez-Faire Constitutionalism," 3 *Law & Hist. Rev.* 293, 308 (1985).

16. For Harlan's views on concentrations of capital and the enforcement of the Sherman Antitrust Act against them, *see* G.E. White, *The American Judicial Tradition: Profiles of Leading American Judges* 136–38 (1976). For his attitudes toward unions and his views on liberty of Contract in the labor market, *see* his opinion in Adair v. United States, 208 U.S. 161 (1908).

17. P. Strum, *Louis D. Brandeis* 343 (1984).

18. A. Link, *Wilson: The Road to the White House* 127 (1947) (footnote omitted). During his 1910 campaign for governor, Wilson repudiated what he had said earlier about unions, claiming he had not really meant it. *Id.* at 159, 184.

19. G. Mowry, *The Era of Theodore Roosevelt: 1900–1912*, at 100 (1958).

20. R. Hofstadter, *The Age of Reform* 170 (1955).

21. *Id.* at 216. *Contra* R. Wiebe, *The Search for Order: 1877–1920 passim* (1967) (arguing Progressivism was part of effort to impose order upon chaotic, new society created by rapid industrialization).

22. *See* R. Hofstadter, *supra* note 20, at 135. Hofstadter states:

It is my thesis that men of this sort [Progressive reformers], who might be designated broadly as the Mugwump type, were Progressives not because of economic deprivations but primarily because they were victims of an upheaval in status that took place in the United States during the closing decades of the nineteenth and the early years of the twentieth century. Progressivism, in short, was to a very considerable extent led by men who suffered from the events of their time not through a shrinkage in their means but through the changed pattern in the distribution of deference and power. *Id.*

23. *See* A. Link & R. McCormick, *supra* note 6, at 7 ("No interpretation has been more sharply criticized than Hofstadter's status-revolution theory.").

24. R. Hofstadter, *supra* note 20, at 168–69.

25. *See id.* at 172–73.

26. Arthur Link and Richard McCormick contend that "middle-class interpretations of Progressivism" are meaningless because at the turn of the century, most Americans were part of the middle class. A. Link & R. McCormick, *supra* note 6, at 7–8. While it is true that only a minority of Americans were not members of the middle class, it does not follow that the concerns of the middle class did n(ot inspire some of those who belonged to it to become reformers.

27. It may be that an interpretation of Progressivism that emphasizes the reaction of the middle class to what its members perceived as threats from above and below is more useful for explaining the development and nature of that phenomenon in the region from which Pitney hailed—the urban Northeast—than in the South and Middle West, where the organization of the working class into labor unions had not progressed nearly as far as it had in states such as New Jersey.

28. *See* G. Mowry, *supra* note 19, at 86.

29. *See id.* at 86–87.

30. *See id.* at 86.

31. *See id.*; *see also* Thelen, "Social Tensions and The Origins of Progressivism," 56 *J. Am. Hist.* 323, 330–34 (1969) (arguing that Progressives came from backgrounds similar to those of their conservative opponents).

32. *See* Israel, *supra* note 4, at 2001.

33. *Id.*

34. *Id. See generally Obituaries*, 48 *N.J.L.J.* 29, 29 (1925) (summary of Pitney's life).

35. *Obituaries*, *supra* note 34, at 29.

36. *Id.; see also Princeton College, The Class Of 1879: Quindecennial Record 1879–1894*, at 85 (1894) (stating Pitney was "in frequent conflict with" McCarter) [hereinafter cited as *Class of 1879*].

37. Israel, *supra* note 4, at 2001.

38. *Newark Evening News*, Dec. 1, 1915, in Mahlon Pitney Papers (in the personal possession of James C. Pitney, Morristown, New Jersey) [hereinafter cited as Pitney Papers]; *see* Letter from Woodrow Wilson to Mahlon Pitney (Nov. 22, 1915), in Pitney Papers, *supra*.

39. *See Bench and Bar of New Jersey* 209 (1942).

40. *See Obituaries, supra* note 34, at 29.

41. A. Breed, "Mahlon Pitney: His Life and Career—Political and Judicial" 8 (undated, unpublished thesis, Princeton University).

42. *See id.* at 8–9.

43. *Id.* at 9.

44. *Id.* at 10.

45. *See id.* at 9.

46. *See id.* at 9–10; Letter from Wilbur F. Sadler, Jr. to Mahlon Pitney (May 5, 1914), in Pitney Papers, *supra* note 38.

47. A. Breed, *supra* note 41, at 10.

48. *Id.*

49. *See id.*

50. *Id.*

51. *See id.* at 11.

52. *Class of 1879, supra* note 36, at 85. Robert McCarter, Pitney's classmate at Princeton and frequent rival at the bar, once wrote, "The aggravating fact about Pitney was that whatever he did, he did well." R. McCarter, *Memories of a Half Century at the New Jersey Bar* 89 (1937). This included chess, dancing, and golf, as well as the practice of law. *Id.* at 88–89.

53. *See Obituaries, supra* note 34, at 29–30; A. Breed, *supra* note 41, at 12.

54. *See supra* note 53.

55. *See* Gould, "The Republican Search For a National Majority," in *The Gilded Age* 171, 183 (H. Morgan ed. 1970).

56. *True Democratic Banner*, Sept. 27, 1894, in Pitney Papers, *supra* note 38.

57. A. Breed, *supra* note 41, at 12.

58. *See id.*

59. It is interesting to note that the *New York Daily Tribune* later claimed, "Pitney surprised some of the old-timers by making a number of excellent speeches during his first term in Congress." *N.Y. Daily Tribune*, May 10, 1897, in Pitney Papers, *supra* note 38. *The Congressional Record*, however, lends no support to this bit of Republican puffery.

60. *See Morris County Chronicle*, Oct. 16, 1896, in Pitney Papers, *supra* note 38.

61. A. Breed, *supra* note 41, at 13.

62. *Id.*

63. *See id.*

64. *Obituaries, supra* note 34, at 30.

65. *See* A. Breed, *supra* note 41, at 14.

66. *Id.*

67. *See id.* at 16.

68. *Id.* at 15; Israel, *supra* note 4, at 2002.

69. *See* Israel, *supra* note 4, at 2002.

70. *Id.*

71. *Obituaries, supra* note 34, at 30.

72. *See id.*

73. *Id.*

74. *Id.*

75. *See* Letter from Mahlon Pitney to the Editor of the Sunday *Call* (Mar. 28, 1901), in Pitney Papers, *supra* note 38. In his letter, Pitney complained, "You give me full credit for the defeat of the Morris Canal bill." *Id.* He also defended the integrity of the New Jersey Legislature: "And I want to say, Mr. Editor, that your wholesale denunciation of the Senate as debauched, corrupt, incapable of good action and subservient to the bosses is as cruel and unjust an accusation as I have ever read." *Id.*

76. Israel, *supra* note 4, at 2002; Obituaries, *supra* note 34, at 30; A. Breed, *supra* note 41, at 16.

77. A. Breed, *supra* note 41, at 17.

78. *Id.*

79. *Id.*

80. *Id.*

81. Besides defending the gold standard, Pitney also supported that traditional Republican bromide, the protective tariff. *See infra* notes 83–84 and accompanying text. In 1894, a Democratic newspaper characterized him as "a Protectionist of the rankest and most radical sort." *True Democratic Banner*, Sept. 27, 1894, in Pitney Papers, *supra* note 38.

82. G. Mowry, *supra* note 19, at 87.

83. *See* Fite, "Election of 1896," in 2 *History of American Presidential Elections* 1787, 1822 (A. Schlesinger ed. 1971) . Many American farmers were deeply in debt. Bryan's proposal for the free and unlimited coinage of silver into money would have produced inflation, thus lightening the burden of their debts. *See* J. Hicks, *The Populist Revolt* 315–16 (1931). The idea was not very appealing to urban workers, however, for it would have meant a shrinkage in their real wages. *See* Fite, *supra*, at 18, 22–23. As Pitney pointed out in a speech on the House floor on February 3, 1898, the free-silver issue caused New Jersey Democrats to desert their party by the thousands in 1896. *See* 31 *Cong. Rec.* 165 app., 167 app. (1898).

84. *Morris County Chronicle*, Oct. 16, 1896, in Pitney Papers, *supra* note 38.

85. *See* A. Link, *supra* note 18, at 25.

86. *See id.* at 134–35.

87. *Id.* at 134; R. Noble, Jr., *New Jersey Progressivism before Wilson* 4–6, 9–11 (1946); see McCurdy, "The Knight Sugar Decision of 1895 and the Modernization of American Corporation Law, 1869–1903," 53 *Bus. Hist. Rev.* 304, 322–23 (1979). As McCurdy notes, "Between 1891 and 1894 the rise of the New Jersey corporation overshadowed all other aspects of the trust problem in the public mind." *Id.* at 328. Particularly useful to the great industrial combinations of the era were two Acts of the New Jersey Legislature. One authorized New Jersey corporations to do business outside the state and to issue their own stock in order to purchase stock in other corporations. *See* Act of May 9, 1889, ch. 265, §§ 1, 4, 1889 NJ. Laws 412, 412, 415. The other allowed corporations organized for any lawful purpose to carry on business anywhere, to hold securities in other concerns, and to issue their own stock in payment for property. *See* Act of Apr. 21, 1896, ch. 185, §§ 7, 49, 50, 1896 N.J. Laws 277, 280, 293–94, 294. The latter law also gave corporations organized under it wide power to alter their charters. *See id.* §28, 1896 N.J. Laws at 286.

88. *See* A. Link, *supra* note 18, at 134.

89. *Id.*

90. R. Noble, Jr., *supra* note 87, at 10–11.

91. *Id.* at 9–10.

92. *Id.* at 10–11.

93. *Id.* at 24, 51.

94. *Id.* at 65 n.3, 66–71.

95. A. Link, *supra* note 18, at 262–63; *see also* Act of Apr. 21 1911, ch. 195, 1911 N.J. Laws 374 (creating the Board of Public Utility Commissioners).

96. *See* 29 *Cong. Rec.* 1448–55 (1897). When Representative Baker of New Hampshire argued that the new firm, the Potomac Company, would have to tear up the streets in order to lay a conduit for its lines, Pitney replied, "[S]o far as my personal feeling is concerned, if the Commissioners had any discretion they might better authorize the tearing up of a few blocks more of the sacred pavements of Washington, in order to break up this controlling monopoly that has been here for so many years." *Id.* at 1453.

97. *Id.* at 1454.

98. *Id.* at 1455.

99. 31 *Cong. Rec.* 167 app. (1898).

100. Letter from Mahlon Pitney to the Editor of the Sunday *Call* (Mar. 28, 1901), in Pitney Papers, *supra* note 38.

101. Israel, *supra* note 4, at 2003; A. Breed, *supra* note 41, at 17–18.

102. Israel, *supra* note 4, at 2003.

103. *Id.*

104. *See* Obituaries, *supra* note 34, at 30.

105. *Id.* When his friend Francis Swayze expressed regret about his leaving the supreme court, Pitney told him "that [he] would like to be *both* a Supreme Court Justice and Chancellor." Letter from Mahlon Pitney to John R. Hardin (Jan. 25, 1908), in Pitney Papers, *supra* note 38.

106. Israel, *supra* note 4, at 2003, A. Breed, *supra* note 41, at 20.

107. A. Breed, *supra* note 41, at 20.

108. *See id.*

109. Family legend has it that Chancellor Pitney was once seen by a friend at a railroad station with a dour look on his face. Asked what was bothering him, he replied that he was on his way to reverse a decision of his father. Interview with James C. Pitney, Grandson of Justice Pitney, in Morristown, New Jersey (Apr. 15, 1985). At a banquet held to honor Pitney shortly after his appointment to the United States Supreme Court, his Princeton classmate, then-Attorney General Robert H. McCarter, recalled "those scenes at [Pitney's] father's home at Morristown, when [he] would return from Trenton and announce that the Court of Errors and Appeals had reversed the decision of Vice Chancellor Pitney, the judgment being rendered by Pitney, J." "Jersey's Honor to Justice Pitney," 35 *N.J.L.J.* 139, 140 (1912) [hereinafter cited as "Jersey's Honor"].

110. A. Breed, *supra* note 41, at 20.

111. *Newark Evening News*, June 8, 1910, in Pitney Papers, *supra* note 38. Both French and Richards were friends of the chancellor; in reducing their fee, he rejected arguments made on their behalf by his Princeton classmate, Robert McCarter. *See id.*

112. *See* Bergen & Dundee R.R. v. State Bd. of Assessors, 74 *N.J.L.* 742, 67 A. 668 (1907).

113. Ch. 91, 1905 N.J. Laws 189.

114. *See* Central R.R. v. State Bd. of Assessors, 75 *N.J.L.* 120, 67 A. 672 (Sup. Ct. 1907), aff'd, 75 *N.J.L.* 771, 69 A. 239 (1908).

115. *See* Average Rate Law, ch. 82, 1906 N.J. Laws 121.

116. *See* Perkins Act, ch. 280, 1906 N.J. Laws 571; *see also* Act of Apr. 18, 1906, ch. 122, 1906 N.J. Laws 220 (defining "main stem").

117. *See* Tuckerton R.R. v. State Bd. of Assessors, 75 *N.J.L.* 157, 67 A. 69 (Sup. Ct. 1907).

118. *See In re* New York Bay R.R., 75 *N.J.L.* 389, 67 A. 1049 (Sup. Ct. 1907); *In re* United N.J.R.R. & Canal, 75 *N.J.L.* 385, 67 A. 1075 (Sup. Ct. 1907), *rev'd*, 76 *N.J.L* 830, 71 A. 275 (1908).

119. *See* Mayor of Jersey City v. Board of Equalization of Taxes, 74 *N.J.L.* 753, 67 A. 38 (1907).

120. *See id.* at 754, 67 A. at 39.

121. *See* Mayor of Jersey City v. North Jersey St. Ry., 72 *N.J.L.* 383, 61 A. 95 (Sup. Ct. 1905). The Company, a successor in interest to the Jersey City & Bergen Railroad Company, claimed that a supplement to the charter of the Jersey City & Bergen, passed by the legislature in 1867, exempted it from license fees imposed by a local government. *Id.* at 387–88, 61 A. at 96. *But cf.* Fielders v. North Jersey St. Ry., 68 *N.J.L.* 343, 363, 53 A.404, 411 (1902) (stating that an ordinance requiring street railway companies to pave the portion of the street over which their tracks passed was an illegal tax not justifiable as an exercise of the police power).

122. *See* North Jersey St. Ry. v. Mayor of Jersey City, 75 *N.J.L.* 349, 67 A. 1072

(Sup. Ct. 1907). At the end of his opinion in the *North Jersey* case, Pitney announced that a like result had been reached previously in a similar case. *Id.* at 354, 67 A. at 1074; *see also* State v. Atlantic City & S. R.R., 77 *N.J.L.* 465, 72 A. 111 (1909) (sustaining effort of the attorney general to forbid a railroad from owning stocks and bonds of a street railway company).

123. *See* Warren v. Pim, 66 NJ. Eq. 353, 399, 59 A. 773, 790 (1904) (Pitney, J., concurring). In this case, Pitney was part of a seven-to-six majority that affirmed a decision handed down by his father. *See id.* at 428, 59 A. at 802.

124. *See id.* at 364, 373, 378, 386–87, 59 A. at 777, 780, 782, 785 (Pitney, J., concurring).

125. *See id.* at 395–97, 59 A. at 789 (Pitney, J., concurring).

126. *See* 31 *Cong. Rec.* 167 app. (1898).

127. 73 *N.J.L.* 729, 65 A. 165 (1906).

128. *Id.* at 739, 65 A. at 169.

129. Levin v. Cosgrove, 75 *N.J.L.* 344, 347, 67 A. 1070, 1071 (Sup. Ct. 1907).

130. *Id.* at 347–48, 67 A. at 1071. It is not at all clear that this is really a holding of Brennan; the reasoning in the opinion is extremely murky. *See* Brennan, 73 *N.J.L.* at 742–43, 65 A. at 170–71.

131. 77 *N.J. Eq.* 219, 79 A. 262 (1908).

132. The injunction restrained the defendants as follows:

First. From knowingly and intentionally causing or attempting to cause, by threats, offers of money, payments of money, offering to pay expenses, or by inducement or persuasion, any employe of the complainant under contract to render service to it to break such contract by quitting such service.

Second. From personal molestation of persons willing to be employed by complainant with intent to coerce such persons to refrain from entering such employment.

Third. From addressing persons willing to be employed by complainant, against their will, and thereby causing them personal annoyance, with a view to persuade them to refrain from such employment.

Fourth. From loitering or picketing in the streets or on the highways or public places near the premises of complainant with intent to procure the personal molestation and annoyance of persons employed or willing to be employed by complainant, and with a view to cause persons so employed to refrain from such employment.

Fifth. From entering the premises of the complainant against its will with intent to interfere with its business.

Sixth. From violence, threats of violence, insults, indecent talk, abusive epithets, annoying language, acts or conduct, practiced upon any persons without their consent, with intent to coerce them to refrain from entering the employment of complainant or to leave its employment.

Seventh. From attempting to cause any persons employed by complainant to leave such employment by intimidating or annoying such employes by annoying language, acts or conduct.

Eighth. From causing persons willing to be employed by complainant to refrain from so doing by annoying language, acts or conduct.

Ninth. From inducing, persuading or causing, or attempting to induce, persuade or cause, the employes of complainant to break their contracts of service with complainant or quit their employment.

Tenth. From threatening to injure the business of any corporation, customer or person dealing or transacting business and willing to deal and transact business with the complainant, by making threats in writing or by words for the purpose of coercing such corporation, customer or person against his or its will so as not to deal with or transact business with the complainant. *Id.* at 221–22, 79 A. at 263.

133. *See* George Jonas Glass Co. v. Glass Bottle Blowers Assoc., 72 *N.J. Eq.* 653, 66 A. 953 (Ch. 1907), aff'd, 77 *N.J. Eq.* 219, 79 A. 262 (1908).

134. *See id.* at 655, 66 A. at 954.

135. *Jonas Glass*, 77 *N.J. Eq.* at 221, 79 A. at 263.

136. George Jonas Glass Co. v. Glass Bottle Blowers Assoc., 72 *N.J. Eq.* 653, 662, 66 A. 953, 957 (Ch. 1907), *aff'd*, 77 *N.J. Eq.* 219, 79 A. 262 (1908).

137. *See Jonas Glass*, 77 *N.J. Eq.* at 224, 79 A. at 264. The statute read as follows:

That it shall not be unlawful for any two or more persons to unite, combine or bind themselves by oath, covenant, agreement, alliance or otherwise, to persuade, advise, or encourage, by peaceable means, any person or persons to enter into any combination for or against leaving or entering into the employment of any person, persons or corporation.

Act of Feb. 14, 1883, ch. 28, §1, 1883 N.J. Laws 36, 36. In a mildly critical editorial, the *Newark Evening News* argued that Pitney had not overlooked this statute, but had ignored the strikers' "constitutional rights of personal liberty and free speech." *Newark Evening News*, Feb. 15, 1911, in Pitney Papers, *supra* note 38.

138. *See Jonas Glass*, 77 *N.J. Eq.* at 224, 79 A. at 264.

139. *See infra* notes 140–142 and accompanying text. He ruled for workers three times and against them four times. *See id.* If one discounts Delaney v. Public Serv. Ry., 82 *N.J.L.* 551, 552, 82 A. 852, 852 (1912), in which he affirmed a nonsuit because the plaintiff had presented no evidence of the defendant's negligence beyond the fact that its pneumatic jack had injured him, there is an even split.

140. *See* Diehl v. Standard Oil Co., 70 *N.J.L.* 424, 57 A. 131 (Sup. Ct. 1904). The decision in Gill v. National Storage Co., 70 *N.J.L.* 53, 56 A. 146 (Sup. Ct. 1903) seems also to be based on the doctrine of contributory negligence but it may rest on the principle of assumption of the risk; the opinion is extremely unclear.

141. *See* Knutter v. New York & N.J. Tel. Co., 67 *N.J.L.* 646, 52 A. 565 (1902).

142. *See* Burns v. Delaware & Atl. Tel. Co., 70 *N.J.L.* 745, 59 A. 220 (1904); Hopwood v. Benjamin Atha & Illingsworth Co., 68 *N.J.L.* 707, 54 A. 435 (1903); Smith v. Erie R.R., 67 *N.J.L.* 636, 52 A. 634 (1902).

143. *See generally* R. Hofstadter, *supra* note 20, at 238 (Progressives "[o]n one side . . . feared the power of the plutocracy [and] on the other the poverty and restlessness of the masses").

144. G. Mowry, *supra* note 19, at 99–100.

145. *See, e.g.*, Meehan v. Board of Excise Comm'rs, 75 *N.J.L.* 557, 70 A. 363 (1908) (upholding constitutionality of "Bishops' Law," which required inte-

riors of taverns to be in full view from public street during hours when sale of liquor was forbidden by law); Croker v. Board of Excise Comm'rs, 73 *N.J.L.* 460, 63 A. 901 (Sup. Ct. 1906) (upholding municipal ordinances designed to keep saloons closed on Sunday); Bachman v. Inhabitants of Phillipsburg, 68 *N.J.L.* 552, 53 A. 620 (Sup. Ct. 1902) (holding license issued to proprietor of beer saloon should be set aside because it had been obtained through fraud). The hostility of Progressives toward saloons arose from a belief that immigrants drank too much. *See* A. Link & R. McCormick, *supra* note 6, at 102–03.

146. *See, e.g.*, Ames v. Kirby, 71 *N.J.L.* 442, 59 A. 558 (Sup. Ct. 1904) (upholding jailing of Atlantic county man for bookmaking). *See generally* A. Link & R. McCormick, *supra* note 6, at 68–69 (discussing society's weakness of character).

147. *Newark Evening News*, Nov. 2, 1907, in Pitney Papers, *supra* note 38.

148. *See* clipping from unidentified newspaper, Jan. 10, 1907, in Pitney Papers, *supra* note 38.

149. Although his judicial rulings clearly served to enhance his political appeal, Pitney insisted in 1912 that he had never allowed politics to influence his decisions. "[H]e had simply considered what he believed to be the justice of the case and acted accordingly." "Jersey's Honor," *supra* note 109, at 143.

150. *See* Letter from Frederick Gordon to the Editor of the *Newark Evening News* (Jan. 11, 1907), in Pitney Papers, *supra* note 38. The *Evening News* commented favorably on Pitney as a possible Senatorial candidate. *Newark Evening News*, Sept. 4, 1906, in Pitney Papers, *supra* note 38.

151. R. Noble, Jr., *supra* note 87, at 83 n. 59; see *The Jerseyman*, Jan. 25, 1907, in Pitney Papers, *supra* note 38.

152. *See* G. Mowry, *supra* note 19, at 210–12, 218–20 (discussing Roosevelt's "Progressive" steps).

153. *See Newark Public Ledger*, Aug. 10 (year unidentified), in Pitney Papers, *supra* note 38.

154. *See* Letter to the Editor of the *New York Times*, Aug. 9, 1907, in Pitney Papers, *supra* note 38.

155. *See Newark Evening News*, July 27, 1907, in Pitney Papers, *supra* note 38.

156. *See* undated clipping from unidentified 1910 newspaper in Pitney Papers, *supra* note 38. In 1915, Morris County Republicans sought to promote the idea of a Pitney Presidential candidacy. *See Newark Evening News*, Nov. 24, 1915, in Pitney Papers, *supra* note 38. The Justice, however, then serving on the United States Supreme Court, released a letter to them saying he could not see his way clear to permit the use of his name as a candidate. *See Newark Evening News*, Nov. 30, 1915, in Pitney Papers, *supra* note 38.

157. *See* Letter from William H. Taft to James E. Howell (Sept. 15, 1910), in Pitney Papers, *supra* note 38. On September 15, 1910, President Taft wrote to Vice Chancellor James E. Howell of the court of chancery in Newark, whom he had contacted earlier about the qualifications of Justice Francis Swayze. *See id.* He had put Swayze on the eligible list and now wanted "to get [Howell's] judgment as to the comparative ability of Justice Swayze and Chancellor Pitney; also a statement as to . . . their ages." *Id.*

158. Willis Van Devanter was named to the Associate Justiceship vacated by Edward D. White when the latter was elevated to Chief Justice. Joseph R. Lamar replaced William Moody, and Charles Evans Hughes was named to the seat formerly held by David J. Brewer. *See generally* 9 A. Bickel & B. Schmidt, Jr., *History of the Supreme Court of the United States: The Judiciary and Responsible Government 1910–21*, at 3–85 (1984) (chapter entitled "Mr. Taft Rehabilitates the Court").

159. *See infra* notes 163–169 and accompanying text.

160. Fred Israel attributes the appointment to the impression that Pitney made on Taft when they met at a dinner in Newark the week before the appointment was made. *See* Israel, *supra* note 4, at 2003. Henry J. Abraham attributes it to political strategy related to the struggle between Taft and Theodore Roosevelt for the 1912 Republican nomination, but he fails to explain the relationship between the two satisfactorily. *See* H. Abraham, *Justices and Presidents: A Political History of the Appointments to the Supreme Court* 162–63 (1974). After extensive research, the late Professor Alexander Bickel concluded, "The origins and the method of the Pitney selection are not discoverable." A. Bickel & B. Schmidt, Jr., *supra* note 158, at 326.

161. *See* A. Link, *supra* note 18, at 468–69. Although Roosevelt had hand-picked Taft to succeed him, he became dissatisfied with his choice when Taft drifted in a conservative direction, coming into increasing conflict with the Progressive insurgents in Congress. *See* W. Harbauch, *Life and Times of Theodore Roosevelt* 402 (new rev. ed. 1963).

162. *See* H. Abraham, *supra* note 160, at 163.

163. A. Bickel & B. Schmidt, Jr., *supra* note 158, at 318–19. Knox had also declined an appointment to the Supreme Court offered to him by Roosevelt, and Taft did not really expect the Secretary to accept at this time. *See id.*

164. *Id.* at 326.

165. H. Abraham, *supra* note 160, at 163. Nagel's first wife was Louis Brandeis's sister. A. Bickel & B. Schmidt, Jr., *supra* note 158, at 326 n.26.

166. A. Bickel & B. Schmidt, Jr., *supra* note 158, at 322–24. The case was McCabe v. Atchison, T. & S.F. Ry., 186 F. 966 (8th Cir. 1911), aff'd, 235 *U.S.* 151 (1914). Hook's association with that decision made it likely that his nomination would add to the race-related political problems the administration was already experiencing in Oklahoma. *See* A. Bickel & B. Schmidt, Jr., *supra* note 158, at 323–24. The administration had previously refused to challenge the disfranchisement of black voters by a grandfather clause in Oklahoma, and it later acquiesced in an unauthorized prosecution attacking that device brought by an insubordinate Republican United States Attorney. *Id.* at 323.

167. A. Bickel & B. Schmidt, Jr., *supra* note 158, at 321. The case was City of Denver v. New York Trust Co., 187 F. 890 (8th Cir. 1911), rev'd, 229 *U.S.* 123 (1913).

168. A. Bickel & B. Schmidt, Jr., *supra* note 158, at 320–21. The decision to which the governors and railroad commissioners particularly objected was Missouri, Kan. & Tex. Ry. v. Love, 177 F. 493 (W.D. Okla. 1910), aff'd, 185 F. 321 (8th Cir. 1911).

169. *See generally* W. Harbaugh, *supra* note 161, at 401–06.

170. *See N.J.Journal*, Feb. 21, 1912, in Pitney Papers, *supra* note 38 (stating Murphy was a Taft delegate at the Republican National Convention).

171. *See N.J.Journal*, Jan. 22, 1912, in Pitney Papers, *supra* note 38; *N.J.Journal*, Feb. 12, 1912, in Pitney papers, *supra* note 38.

172. A. Breed, *supra* note 41, at 22.

173. *Id.* at 23. Pitney and Taft had met earlier, once having played golf together at Chevy Chase, Maryland. *Id.* at 22. The game of golf would continue to provide something of a bond between them after Pitney's appointment. *See* Letter from Mahlon Pitney to the President (June 18, 1912), in Pitney Papers, *supra* note 38 ("I wrote last week from Washington to Messrs Von Lengerke & Detmold, Fifth Ave. Bldg., New York City, from whom I buy my golfing supplies, asking them to send you a dozen small size Zome Zodiacs.").

174. *See* Letter from William H. Taft to Mahlon Pitney (Feb. 19, 1912), in Pitney Papers, *supra* note 38. While the two of them were driving from Newark to New York on February 12th, Taft told Murphy that he would likely appoint Pitney. A Breed, *supra* note 41, at 23.

175. *See* H. Abraham, *supra* note 160, at 163; J. Semonche, *Charting the Future* 267 (1978).

176. *See* H. Abraham, *supra* note 160, at 163.

177. *See* A. Bickel & B. Schmidt, Jr., *supra* note 158, at 318–19.

178. Taft had been a judge on the Ohio Superior Court from 1887 to 1890 and a judge on the United States Court of Appeals for the Sixth Circuit from 1892 to 1900. A. Mason, *William Howard Taft: Chief Justice* 12 (1964).

179. A. Breed, *supra* note 41, at 23.

180. *See* Letter from James E. Howell to William H. Taft (Sept. 15, 1910), in Pitney Papers, *supra* note 38.

181. *See* "Jersey's Honor," *supra* note 109, at 143–44.

182. *See id.* at 140.

183. J. Semonche, *supra* note 175, at 266. Semonche claims that Swayze was the leading contender from New Jersey. *Id.* Certainly, that is what Pitney thought. *See* A. Breed, *supra* note 41, at 22.

184. *See* A. Breed, *supra* note 41, at 26–27.

185. *Id.* at 22. Briggs was also a Taft supporter. *See id.* at 26–27. According to Robert McCarter, Murphy at first urged Taft to appoint Swayze. Taft responded by offering to appoint Swayze to the United States Court of Appeals for the Third Circuit. R. McCarter, *supra* note 52, at 85.

186. Letter from James E. Howell to William H. Taft, *supra* note 180. After Pitney's selection was announced, the *New York Times* reported, "The appointment of the Chancellor, who has long been a prominent figure in New Jersey politics, will tend, it is thought, to throw the influence of New Jersey leaders to the President." *N.Y. Times*, Feb. 19, 1912, in Pitney Papers, *supra* note 38.

187. *See N.Y. Times*, Feb. 25, 1912, in Pitney Papers, *supra* note 38; *see also* A. Breed, *supra* note 41, at 22 (Murphy and Pitney were close friends).

188. R. Noble, Jr., *supra* note 87, at 23.

189. *See* A. Breed, *supra* note 41, at 22.

190. Bickel asserts that Taft "decided to nominate Pitney in the teeth of the progressives." A. Bickel & B. Schmidt, Jr., *supra* note 158, at 328. Bickel is guilty of reading history backward, however, assuming that Taft knew at the time he made the appointment the sort of controversy that it would ignite. *See infra* notes 195–206 and accompanying text. He also views the opposition to Pitney's confirmation as more Progressive than it was. *See infra* note 206 and accompanying text. Pitney was a close friend of the conservative Franklin Murphy. A. Breed, *supra* note 41, at 22. Murphy probably regarded him as a true conservative, like himself and the President, but someone appealing enough to Progressives to attract support for Taft from the New Idea wing of the party. That is probably what he told the President during the latter's Newark visit, and it is likely what Taft had in mind when he made the appointment. *See supra* notes 170–174 and accompanying text.

In Washington, political observers commented that the Pitney appointment would have a sharp bearing on the political contest for control of New Jersey, which would be developing within the next few weeks, and that it would help Taft hold the state against the Roosevelt supporters who were "set[ting] things in line" to give New Jersey's delegates to their man. *See N.Y. Times*, Feb. 19, 1912, in Pitney Papers, *supra* note 38.

191. *See* A. Breed, *supra* note 41, at 30–31.

192. *Id.* at 32.

193. A. Bickel & B. Schmidt, Jr., *supra* note 158, at 329.

194. *N.Y. Times*, Feb. 19, 1912, in Pitney Papers, *supra* note 38.

195. A. Bickel & B. Schmidt, Jr., *supra* note 158, at 329.

196. 63 *N.J. Eq.* 443, 52 A. 152 (Ch. 1901).

197. A. Bickel & B. Schmidt, Jr., *supra* note 158, at 330.

198. *Id.* at 330 n.41.

199. A. Breed, *supra* note 41, at 31–32.

200. A. Bickel & B. Schmidt, Jr., *supra* note 158, at 331; *N.Y. Times*, Mar. 9, 1912, in Pitney Papers, *supra* note 38; *see also supra* notes 131–137 and accompanying text (discussing Pitney's opinion in *Jonas Glass*).

201. 48 *Cong. Rec.* 3011 (1912).

202. A. Bickel & B. Schmidt, Jr., *supra* note 158, at 331.

203. *See Newark News*, Mar. 13, 1912, in Pitney Papers, *supra* note 38.

204. *See id.*; A. Breed, *supra* note 41, at 33.

205. *Newark News*, Mar. 13, 1912, in Pitney Papers, *supra* note 38.

206. A. Bickel & B. Schmidt, Jr., *supra* note 158, at 332. Although four Insurgent (Progressive) Republicans voted against Pitney, one of his leading supporters in the Senate confirmation debates was William E. Borah of Idaho, also an Insurgent. Professor Bickel somewhat grudgingly acknowledges that "[the] Insurgents did not unite against him." *Id.* Earlier, Bickel implies that they should have done so because Pitney was supported by the president of the National Association of Manufacturers. *See id.* at 329. What he fails to point out is that this endorsement came only after "labor agitation" had nearly defeated Pitney in the Senate. *See generally* A. Breed, *supra* note 41, at 33–36 (discussing Senate debates on Pitney's labor positions).

207. *See* A. Breed, *supra* note 41, at 36.

208. *See* Israel, *supra* note 4, at 2004. Pitney served for 10 years, 9 months, and 12 days. *Id.*

209. *Id.*

210. *Id.*

211. 252 *U.S.* 189 (1920).

212. Pitney wrote that income was "*not* a gain *accruing* to capital, not a *growth* or *increment* of value *in* the investment; but a gain, a profit, something of exchangeable value *proceeding from* the property, *severed from* the capital however invested or employed, and *coming in*, being '*derived*', that is, *received* or *drawn by* the recipient (the taxpayer) for his *separate* use, benefit and disposal." *Id.* at 207.

213. *Id.* at 199.

214. *See* Revenue Act of 1916, ch. 463, §2(a), 39 Stat. 756, 757 (current version at 26 *U.S.C.* §61 (Supp. II 1984)).

215. *See* Eisner, 252 *U.S.* at 201–05.

216. *See* A. Bickel & b. Schmidt, Jr., *supra* note 158, at 508.

217. *See id.*

218. *Id.*

219. *See id.*

220. *Id.* at 509.

221. Eisner, 252 *U.S.* at 237 (Brandeis, J., dissenting).

222. A. Bickel & B. Schmidt, Jr., *supra* note 158, at 509. On the other hand, the Supreme Court was "unquestionably ready in the next generation to overrule *Eisner v. Macomber*, [but] could not find the occasion to do so." *Id.*
It is not surprising that Pitney defined income restrictively and thus limited what the National Government could tax under the sixteenth amendment. New Jersey had refused to ratify that amendment. *See* A. Link, *supra* note 18, at 267–68. Governor Wilson had supported it, and the assembly had passed it without a dissenting vote in 1911. *Id.* The Senate, which was controlled by Pitney's Republican party, had refused to go along, however. *Id.*

223. *See, e.g.*, Miles v. Safe Deposit & Trust Co., 259 *U.S.* 247 (1922); Rockefeller v. United States, 257 *U.S.* 176 (1921); United States v. Phellis, 257 *U.S.* 156 (1921); Peabody v. Eisner, 247 *U.S.* 347 (1918); Lynch v. Hornby, 247 *U.S.* 339 (1918); Southern Pac. Co. v. Lowe, 247 *U.S.* 330 (1918).

224. *See, e.g.*, LaBelle Iron Works v. United States, 256 *U.S.* 377 (1921); United States v. Cleveland, C.C. & St. L. Ry., 247 *U.S.* 195 (1918); Hays v. Gauley Mountain Coal Co., 247 *U.S.* 189 (1918); Anderson v. Forty–Two Broadway Co., 239 *U.S.* 69 (1915); Stratton's Independence, Ltd. v. Howbert, 231 *U.S.* 399 (1913); McCoach v. Minehill & S.H.R.R., 228 *U.S.* 295 (1913).

225. *See, e.g.*, United States v. Field, 255 *U.S.* 257 (1921).

226. *See, e.g.*, St. Louis, J.M. & S. Ry. v. J.F. Hasty & Sons, 255 *U.S.* 252 (1921).

227. *See, e.g.*, Texas Co. v. Brown, 258 *U.S.* 466 (1922); Citizens Nat'l Bank v. Durr, 257 *U.S.* 99 (1921); Bowman v. Continental Oil Co., 256 *U.S.* 642 (1921); F.S. Royster Guano Co. v. Virginia, 253 *U.S.* 412 (1920); Travis v. Yale & Towne

Mfg. Co., 252 *U.S.* 60 (1920); Shaffer v. Carter, 252 *U.S.* 37 (1920); Wagner v. City of Covington, 251 *U.S.* 95 (1919); American Mfg. Co. v. St. Louis, 250 *U.S.* 459 (1919); Mackay Tel. & Cable Co. v. City of Little Rock, 250 *U.S.* 94 (1919); Leary v. Mayor of Jersey City, 248 *U.S.* 328 (1918); Postal Tel. Cable Co. v. City of Newport, 247 *U.S.* 464 (1918); United States Glue Co. v. Town of Oak Creek, 247 *U.S.* 321 (1918); Crew Levick Co. v. Pennsylvania, 245 *U.S.* 292 (1917); Illinois Cent. R.R. v. Greene, 244 *U.S.* 555 (1917); Louisville & N.R.R. v. Greene, 244 *U.S.* 22 (1917); Greene v. Louisville & Interurban R.R., 244 *U.S.* 499 (1917); St. Louis S.W. Ry. v. Arkansas, 235 *U.S.* 350 (1914); Singer Sewing Mach. Co. v. Brickell, 233 *U.S.* 304 (1914); Ohio Tax Cases, 232 *U.S.* 576 (1914); United States Fidelity Co. v. Kentucky, 231 *U.S.* 394 (1913).

228. *See* Union Tank Line v. Wright, 249 *U.S.* 275, 287 (1919) (Pitney, J., dissenting).

229. Israel, *supra* note 4, at 2004.

230. *See* J. Semonche, *supra* note 175, at 298.

231. *See* Levitan, "Mahlon Pitney—Labor Judge," 40 *VA. L. Rev.* 733, 748 (1954).

232. 236 *U.S.* 1 (1915).

233. *Id.* at 26. Such agreements were commonly referred to as "yellow-dog contracts." In striking down this statute, Pitney relied on an earlier case in which the Court had invalidated a Federal statute outlawing yellow-dog contracts for railroad workers. *See id.* at 9–18 (citing Adair v. United States, 208 *U.S.* 161 (1908)). For a criticism of both Coppage and Adair, *see* Powell, "Collective Bargaining Before the Supreme Court," 33 *Pol. Sci. Q.* 396 (1918).

234. Coppage, 236 *U.S.* at 19.

235. *Id.* at 18.

236. *See* Wilson v. New, 243 *U.S.* 332, 377 (1917) (Pitney, J., dissenting). In order to prevent a nationwide strike by several railway unions during a period of increasing military preparedness prior to American entry into World War I, Congress had reduced the workday for the railroad industry to eight hours, but had provided that railroad workers should continue to receive the same pay they had gotten for working longer hours. *See generally* Belknap, "The New Deal and the Emergency Powers Doctrine," 62 *Tex. L. Rev.* 67, 79–81 (1983) (discussing the Wilson case and the national emergency powers doctrine).

237. 244 *U.S.* 459, 472 (1917) (Pitney, J., dissenting).

238. Ch. 647, 26 Stat. 209 (1890) (codified as amended at 15 *U.S.C.* §§1–7 (1982)).

239. 245 *U.S.* 229 (1917).

240. *Id.* at 261–62.

241. *Id.* at 259.

242. *See* Powell, *supra* note 233, at 421–22.

243. 245 *U.S.* 275 (1917).

244. Levitan, *supra* note 231, at 744.

245. 254 *U.S.* 443 (1921).

246. *Id.* at 478–79.

247. *See id.* at 461.

248. Ch. 323, §20, 38 Stat. 730, 738 (1914) (current version at 29 *U.S.C.* §52 (1982)).

249. "Duplex Printing," 254 *U.S.* at 488 (Brandeis, J., dissenting).

250. *See* A. Bickel & B. Schmidt, Jr., *supra* note 158, at 585.

251. 257 *U.S.* 312 (1921).

252. Letter from Mahlon Pitney to Mr. Justice Brandeis (Nov. 3, 1920), in Louis D. Brandeis Papers, folder 14, manuscript box 114 (available at Harvard Law School Library) [hereinafter cited as Brandeis Papers]. In a note on the back of a memorandum on Truax v. Corrigan, which he wrote sometime during the 1920 Term, Pitney stated: "At the last Term the conference voted to reverse, and opinion was allotted to me. Being unable, on further examination, to write in accordance with the vote, I circulated this Memorandum as a report." Memorandum by Justice Pitney in No. 72, Oct. Term 1920, in Brandeis Papers, *supra*, folder 9, manuscript box 7.

253. Conversations between L.D.B. and F.F., in Brandeis Papers, *supra* note 252 folder 14, manuscript box 114; see *Truax*, 257 *U.S.* at 344 (Pitney, J., dissenting).

254. *See Truax*, 257 *U.S.* at 346–47 (Pitney, J., dissenting).

255. *Id.* at 349 (Pitney, J., dissenting).

256. *Id.* at 348 (Pitney, J., dissenting). Somewhat earlier, Theodore Roosevelt had evolved from a defender to an opponent of the labor injunction. *See* J. Lurie, *Law and the Nation, 1865–1912*, at 59 (1983). During the period from 1894 to 1896, he denounced those who opposed this device, but by 1901 through 1902, he endorsed the right of labor as well as the right of capital to combine. *See id.* at 59–61. By 1907, Roosevelt admitted that there were good reasons for some of the attacks that had been leveled at the labor injunction, and in 1908, he sent a special message to Congress denouncing the way some judges used their power to issue injunctions. *Id.* at 62–63.

257. Levitan, *supra* note 231, at 748.

258. *See id.* at 752.

259. *See* Prudential Ins. Co. v. Cheek, 259 *U.S.* 530 (1922).

260. *See* Chicago, R.I. & Pac. Ry. v. Perry, 259 *U.S.* 548 (1922).

261. On the attitudes of Roosevelt, Congress, and the Progressive movement concerning compensation for the victims of industrial accidents, see A. Bickel & B. Schmidt, Jr., *supra* note 158, at 205–13. *See generally* Friedman & Ladinsky, "Social Change and the Law of Industrial Accidents," 67 *Colum. L. Rev.* 50 (1967).

262. Ch. 149, 35 Stat. 65 (1908) (codified as amended at 45 *U.S.C.* §§51–60 (1982)).

263. *Id.* §1, 35 Stat. at 65 (current version at 45 *U.S.C.* §51 (1982)).

264. *Id.* §3, 35 Stat. at 66 (current version at 45 *U.S.C.* §53 (1982)).

265. *Id.* §4, 35 Stat. at 66 (current version at 45 *U.S.C.* §54 (1982)).

266. *See, e.g.*, Philadelphia, B. & W.R.R. v. Smith, 250 *U.S.* 101 (1919); South-

ern Ry. v. Puckett, 244 *U.S.* 571 (1917); Erie R.R. v. Welsh, 242 *U.S.* 303 (1916); Spokane & I.E.R.R. v. Campbell, 241 *U.S.* 497 (1916); San Antonio & A.P. Ry. v. Wagner, 241 *U.S.* 476 (1916); Chicago & N.W. Ry. v. Bower, 241 *U.S.* 470 (1916); Chesapeake & O. Ry. v. Proffitt, 241 *U.S.* 462 (1916); Great Northern Ry. v. Knapp, 240 *U.S.* 464 (1916); Seaboard Air Line Ry. v. Horton, 239 *U.S.* 595 (1916); Kanahwha & Mich. Ry. v. Kerse, 239 *U.S.* 576 (1916); North Carolina R.R. v. Zachary, 232 *U.S.* 248 (1914); Missouri, Kan. & Tex. Ry. v. Wulf, 226 *U.S.* 570 (1913).

267. *See* Chesapeake & O. Ry. v. Gainey, 241 *U.S.* 494 (1916); Chesapeake & O. Ry. v. Kelly, 241 *U.S.* 485 (1916).

268. *See* Chesapeake & O. Ry. v. De Atley, 241 *U.S.* 310 (1916).

269. *See* Gila Valley, G. & N. Ry. v. Hall, 232 *U.S.* 94 (1914).

270. *See* Texas & Pac. Ry. v. Rigsby, 241 *U.S.* 33 (1916); Southern Ry. v. Crockett, 234 *U.S.* 725 (1914).

271. *See* A. Bickel & B. Schmidt, Jr., *supra* note 158, at 581; Friedman & Ladinsky, *supra* note 261, at 69–72.

272. A. Link, *supra* note 18, at 263 (footnote omitted). In 1910, an alliance of New Idea Republicans and Democrats had tried to secure the enactment of legislation abolishing the fellow-servant doctrine and other antiworker tort defenses, but Old Guard Republican strength in the senate had forced them to settle for a measure that only partially fulfilled their objectives. *See generally* Tynan, "Workmen 's Compensation for Injuries," 34 *N.J.L.J.* 164 (1911) (discussing New Jersey's workmen's compensation statute).

273. *See* Friedman & Ladinsky, *supra* note 261, at 65–69. Although the assumption of the risk, contributory negligence, and fellow-servant doctrines all favored the employer, judges had riddled these rules with so many exceptions that often an injured worker could win despite them. *See id.* at 65. In addition, they were a source of labor unrest and thus interfered with management efforts to "rationalize and bureaucratize" enterprises. *Id.* Legal fees were a burden on employers as well as employees because they tended to eat up much of whatever judgments workers did manage to recover. *Id.* at 66.

In 1910, President Taft, set up a commission "to investigate employers' liability and workmen's compensation." A. Bickel & B. Schmidt, Jr., *supra* note 158, at 210. Although headed by conservative Republican Senator George Sutherland of Utah, it submitted a report in 1912 recommending that the FELA be replaced with a compulsory workmen's compensation statute. *Id.* Ironically, organized labor opposed workers compensation legislation. J. Weinstein, *The Corporate Ideal in the Liberal State: 1900–1918*, at 43 (1968). This was mainly because of the limitations on recovery that such laws usually contained. *See id.* Union leaders tended to see legislative abolition of the tort defenses traditionally relied upon by employers as a preferable alternative. *See id.*

274. 201 N.Y. 271, 94 N.E. 431 (1911).

275. *See id.* at 317, 94 N.E. at 448.

276. Friedman & Ladinsky, *supra* note 261, at 68.

277. J. Lurie, *supra* note 256, at 71; *see also* Friedman & Ladinsky, *supra* note 261, at 68 n.69 (President Theodore Roosevelt expressed revulsion at notion of employees bearing financial burdens occasioned by their work-related ac-

cidents).

278. Stagner, "The Recall of Judicial Decisions and the Due Process Debate," 24 *Am. J. of Legal Hist.* 257, 257–58 (1980).

279. *See id.* at 259–64.

280. *See* New York Cent. R.R. v. White, 243 *U.S.* 188, 192–97 (1917).

281. 243 *U.S.* 188 (1917).

282. *Id.* at 206.

283. *Id.*

284. *Id.* at 205.

285. *Id.*

286. Hawkins v. Bleakly, 243 *U.S.* 210, 213 (1917).

287. 243 *U.S.* 219 (1917).

288. *Id.* at 219–20.

289. *Id.* at 244.

290. *See id.* at 246.

291. A. Bickel & B. Schmidt, Jr., *supra* note 158, at 585 (footnote omitted).

292. *Id.* (footnote omitted).

293. *See generally* Powell, "The Workmen's Compensation Cases," 32 *Pol. Sci. Q.* 542, 553–69 (1917) (discussing Pitney's workers' compensation decisions). According to Bickel, "[W]hat Pitney came around to was a narrow and particular ground of decision." A. Bickel & B. Schmidt, Jr., *supra* note 158, at 585. The Court accepted the reasonableness of the statute before it, but reserved the right to strike down others later if it did not like them. *Id.* Although offensive to proponents of judicial restraint such as Bickel, Pitney's reliance on this approach, rather than on deference to legislative judgments, serves to demonstrate his commitment to Progressive policies. In an article written shortly after these decisions, Thomas Reed Powell of the Columbia Law School commended the reasoning of Pitney's opinions precisely because of his acceptance of " 'economic and sociological arguments' " of the type that the New York Court of Appeals had dismissed in Ives "as not pertinent to the constitutional issue." Powell, *supra*, at 560. Powell stated, "Mr. Justice Pitney's opinion on the constitutionality of workmen's compensation legislation sets an example of judicial reasoning for judges everywhere to emulate." *Id.* at 569.

294. *See* Ward & Cow v. Krisky, 259 *U.S.* 503 (1922).

295. *See* New York Cent. R.R. v. Bianc, 250 *U.S.* 596 (1919).

296. *See* Southern Pac. Co. v. Jensen, 244 *U.S.* 205, 223 (1917) (Pitney, J., dissenting).

297. *See* Middleton v. Texas Power & Light Co., 249 *U.S.* 152 (1919). The employee had argued that the Texas workers' compensation statute violated the equal protection clause of the fourteenth amendment because it discriminated between those persons working for employers who had chosen to bring themselves under the system and those working for employers who had not. *See id.* at 156.

298. *See* Arizona Employers' Liability Cases, 250 *U.S.* 400 (1919).

299. 250 *U.S.* 400 (1919).

300. *Id.* at 419.

301. *Id.*

302. *Id.* at 424.

303. *Id.*

304. *See id.* at 427.

305. *See generally* G. White, *Tort Law in America* 61–62 (1980) (explaining early twentieth century views on tort law).

306. Originally, the "Arizona Employers' Liability Cases" were assigned to Justice Holmes. *See* A. Bickel & B. Schmidt, Jr., *supra* note 158, at 586. He wrote an opinion that took the tack that all risk of damages should be imposed on the employer because he could pass them through to the public. *See id.* at 587. Holmes's majority fell apart when the other members of it saw what he had written. *See id.* at 587–88. At this point, there were four dissenters—including the Chief Justice, who had at first been with Holmes. *Id.* at 586–88. The opinion was also too strong for some of those who continued to favor upholding the Arizona statute. *Id.* at 586–87. One of those was Pitney, to whom the case was reassigned. *See id.* at 589. Yet, the opinion that he produced talked about the ability of employers to spread the cost of accidents and also stressed judicial restraint, the other theme Holmes had planned to emphasize. *See id.*

307. *See, e.g.,* Hammer v. Dagenhart, 247 *U.S.* 251 (1918). *See generally* S. Wood, *Constitutional Politics in the Progressive Era: Child Labor and the Law* (1968) (discussing child labor reform). On this issue, Pitney was also out of line with New Jersey, which had passed legislation in 1903 and 1904 forbidding the employment of children under age 14 in mines, workshops, and factories, and limiting the number of hours per day and per week that youths aged 14 through 16 could be employed in such enterprises. *See* R. Noble, Jr., *supra* note 87, at 122–25. It strengthened these measures in 1907 and 1910 with laws that limited the hours of children under age 16 working in mercantile establishments and banned night work in factories by all persons under age 16. *Id.*

308. *See, e.g.,* Stettler v. O'Hara, 243 *U.S.* 629 (1917) (per curiam); *But see* A. Bickel & B. Schmidt, Jr., *supra* note 158, at 593–603 (discussing Stettler). Immediately after Stettler was argued, Pitney voted with a five-member majority that favored holding the Oregon minimum-wage-for-women statute unconstitutional. *Id.* at 595. The decision had not yet been handed down for some unknown reason when one member of the majority, Justice Lamar, died. *See id.* at 598. The case was restored to the docket and reargued, but Lamar's replacement, Louis Brandeis, had to disqualify himself because he had participated as counsel in the first argument. *Id.* at 598–99. No other Justice changed his position, and thus an equally-divided Court affirmed an Oregon Supreme Court decision upholding the law. *See id.* at 602.

Although voting twice against a minimum-wage law for women, Pitney was part of the majority that upheld an Oregon statute setting maximum hours for both men and women and requiring time-and-one-half pay for overtime work. *See* Bunting v. Oregon, 243 *U.S.* 426 (1917). According to one scholar, the reason why he voted for this law, but against the one at issue in

Stettler, was a strong hostility to wage setting. *See* J. Semonche, *supra* note 175, at 342 n.46.

309. J. Semonche, *supra* note 175, at 279; see, e.g., Spiller v. Atchison, T. & S.F. Ry., 253 *U.S.* 117 (1920); Arkadelphia Milling Co. v. St. Louis S.W. Ry., 249 *U.S.* 134 (1919); Morrisdale Coal Co. v. Pennsylvania R.R., 230 *U.S.* 304, 315 (1913) (Pitney, J., dissenting); Mitchell Coal & Coke Co. v. Pennsylvania R.R., 230 *U.S.* 247, 267 (1913) (Pitney, J., dissenting); Pennsylvania R.R. v. International Coal Mining Co., 230 *U.S.* 184, 208 (1913) (Pitney,J., dissenting).

310. *See, e.g.,* O'Keefe v. United States, 240 *U.S.* 294 (1916); Kansas City S. Ry. v. United States, 231 *U.S.* 423 (1913).

311. *See, e.g.,* Darnell v. Edwards, 244 *U.S.* 564 (1917); Phoenix Ry. v. Ceary, 239 *U.S.* 277 (1915); Michigan Cent. R.R. v. Michigan R.R. Comm'n, 236 *U.S.* 615 (1915); Louisville & N.R.R. v. Finn, 235 *U.S.* 601 (1915).

312. *See, e.g.,* Lincoln Gas & Elec. Light Co. v. City of Lincoln, 250 *U.S.* 256 (1919); Puget Sound Traction, Light & Power Co. v. Reynolds, 244 *U.S.* 574 (1917). *But see* City of Denver v. Denver Union Water Co., 246 *U.S.* 178 (1918).

313. Levitan, *supra* note 231, at 761.

314. *See* A. Bickel & B. Schmidt, Jr., *supra* note 158, at 415; J. Semonche, *supra* note 175, at 422–23.

315. *See* United States v. United Shoe Mach. Co., 247 *U.S.* 32, 75 (1918) (Day, J., dissenting).

316. *See id.* at 75 (Clarke, J., dissenting).

317. United States v. United States Steel Corp., 251 *U.S.* 417, 466 (1920) (Day, J., dissenting).

318. J. Semonche, *supra* note 175, at 423.

319. *See, e.g., Ex parte* Webb, 225 *U.S.* 663 (1912).

320. *See, e.g.,* Zakonaite v. Wolf, 226 *U.S.* 272 (1912).

321. On Progressive attitudes concerning the control of liquor and prostitution, see A. Link & R. McCormick, *supra* note 6, at 69, 79, 102–03.

322. *See* D. Kennedy, *Over Here: The First World War and American Society* 51 (1980).

323. *See id.* at 74–75.

324. *See id.* at 75–88.

325. Ch. 30, 40 Stat. 217 (1917).

326. Ch. 75, 40 Stat. 553 (1918).

327. *See generally* Levitan, *supra* note 231, at 763–67 (discussing Supreme Court's treatment of cases under Espionage and Sedition Acts).

328. *See* Debs v. United States, 249 *U.S.* 211 (1919); Frohwerk v. United States, 249 *U.S.* 204 (1919); Schenck v. United States, 249 *U.S.* 47 (1919).

329. 252 *U.S.* 239 (1920).

330. Section 3 provided:
Whoever, when the United States is at war, shall willfully make or convey false reports or false statements with intent to interfere with the operation or success of the military or naval forces of the United States or to promote the success of its enemies and whoever, when the United States is at war, shall

willfully cause or attempt to cause insubordination, disloyalty, mutiny, or refusal of duty, in the military or naval forces of the United States, or shall willfully obstruct the recruiting or enlistment service of the United States, to the injury of the service or of the United States, shall be punished by a fine of not more than $10,000 or imprisonment for not more than twenty years, or both.

Espionage Act, ch. 30, §3, 40 Stat. 217, 219 (1917).

331. *Pierce*, 252 *U.S.* at 253.

332. *See id.* at 245–47.

333. *Id.* at 251. Brandeis attributed Pitney's certitude that he knew the real causes of World War I to his Presbyterianism. Conversations between L.D.B. and F.F., in Brandeis Papers, *supra* note 252, folder 14, manuscript box 114. Brandeis stated, "Pitney . . . personally is very kindly, though in many ways naive and wholly without knowledge but still can't shake his Presbyterianism or doesn't realize he is in its grip." *Id.*

334. *Pierce*, 252 *U.S.* at 249.

335. *Id.* at 272 (Brandeis, J., dissenting).

336. *Id.* at 273 (Brandeis, J., dissenting).

337. *See* Israel, *supra* note 4, at 2008.

338. *See* Frank v. Mangum, 237 *U.S.* 309 (1915). *See generally* L. Dinnerstein, *The Leo Frank Case* (1968).

339. Frank v. Mangum, 237 *U.S.* 309, 338–40 (1915). Brandeis remarked, "Pitney had a great sense of justice affected by Presbyterianism but no imagination whatever." Conversations between L.D.B. and F.F., in Brandeis Papers, *supra* note 252, folder 14, manuscript box 114.

340. *See* P. Murphy, *The Constitution in Crisis Times: 1918–1969*, at 82–83 (1972).

341. *See, e.g.,* Collins v. Johnston, 237 *U.S.* 502 (1915); Lem Woon v. Oregon, 229 *U.S.* 586 (1913); Ensign v. Pennsylvania, 227 *U.S.* 592 (1913); cf. Prudential Ins. Co. v. Cheek, 259 *U.S.* 530 (1922) (applying Federal due process principles to a state law).

342. Frank v. Mangum, 237 *U.S.* 309, 347 (1915) (Holmes, J., dissenting).

343. *See* Moore v. Dempsey, 261 *U.S.* 86 (1923).

344. *See generally* B. Noggle, *Into the Twenties* (1974).

345. A. Breed, *supra* note 41, at 164. Breed actually says Pitney suffered this illness in early 1921, but this appears to be a typographical error. *See* Israel, *supra* note 4, at 2009.

346. *See* Letter from Chief Justice Taft to Justice Pitney (Jan. 20, 1922), in Pitney Papers, *supra* note 38.

347. Letter from Pitney to Chief Justice Taft (Jan. 21, 1922), in Pitney Papers, *supra* note 38.

348. A. Mason, *supra* note 178, at 213.

349. A. Breed, *supra* note 41, at 164.

350. *Id.* at 165.

351. *Id.* According to certificates submitted to the Senate Judiciary Commit-

tee from four physicians, by November, Pitney was also suffering from hardening of the arteries and Bright's disease. S. 4025, 67th Cong., 3d Sess., 63 *Cong. Rec.* 272 (1922).

352. *See* A. Breed, *supra* note 41, at 165–66.

353. *Id.* at 166.

354. *Id.* at 165.

355. *Id.* at 167.

356. *See id.*

357. *See generally* S. Hays, *The Response to Industrialism: 1885–1914* (1957).

358. J. Semonche, *supra* note 175, at 308 n.7.

359. *See* H. Abraham, *supra* note 160, at 179.

360. *See id.* at 163–64; cf. Israel, *supra* note 4, at 2001 (Pitney adequately fulfilled the role of a Supreme Court Justice).

Historically aligned with workers, Paterson police sided with management in the 1913 strike. The force, including its six-year-old mounted division, worked to quell the labor action on the premise that outsiders were its leaders. But police efforts only strengthened the numbers and resolve of striking textile workers. Photograph courtesy the Botto House, American Labor Museum, Haledon, New Jersey.

11

Since the late nineteenth century, economists and historians have both described and analyzed the American labor movement, an area of inquiry in which considerations of American "exceptionalism" have been critical. Compared to many other western industrialized countries, the labor movement in the United States has been distinguished by its lack of class consciousness, its conservative emphasis on "bread and butter issues" (wages, hours, conditions of work), and its failure to develop separate political parties.

In Europe and elsewhere, industrial workers have tended to respond to their situations much as Marxist theory suggested they might, uniting against capitalists to demand a greater ownership of the goods they helped to create and establishing separate "labor" parties. The "failure" of American labor to organize in its own class interest has been attributed to the existence in the United States of universal suffrage, the two-party system, and the persistent, widespread belief in the possibility of mobility (social, economic, and geographic). Moreover, the religious and ethnic diversity of workers, the divisions between skilled and unskilled labor, and long-held distinctions between craft and industry have been credited with inhibiting the organization of laborers. American workers were more conservative than their European counterparts; labor's support of radical ideas or actions was widely viewed as the result of foreign (immigrant) or outside influences. In addition, partly because labor historians have often sympathized with workers, they have sometimes suggested that manufacturers and police colluded to repress labor.

Early labor historians concentrated primarily on institutions—the growth of specific unions, for example—and on events such as strikes. The emergence of social history led to a "new" labor history that has emphasized the importance of culture in the structure of labor-management relations. Labor historians have examined the influence of ethnic background, religion, community, and gender on workers and their attitudes and on the workplace. In addition, they have tried to assess the role of mill and factory workers themselves in organizing unions and calling strikes. Finally, historians have added new questions to their traditional concerns. What were the consequences for labor of changes in management techniques and factory organization? What effect did new technology have on the way work was performed?

Paterson, an early site of industrialization, is a good place to try and answer some of these questions. The city's laboring population represented diverse ethnic and religious backgrounds and occupied both skilled and unskilled jobs. There were skilled weavers from England as well as unskilled dyers from Italy. A few were anarchists, some were socialists, and others supported the nonpolitical craft unions of the American Federation of Labor. Labor unrest was endemic in Paterson and was capped by a dramatic strike in 1913 that attracted a great deal of national attention and comment. Paterson's long industrial history and tense labor climate have attracted many historians, including Steve Golin.

Does Paterson's example confirm or refute the idea of American exceptionalism? Was there a radical class consciousness among the workers, or were they conservative? To answer this question, it is necessary to ask what workers sought through the 1913 strike. Did they wish, as Marxist theory would suggest, to control the "means of production," or did they seek only to improve working conditions, to curtail hours, and to increase wages? How did workers conduct the strike? How did workers' diverse backgrounds affect their ability to mount joint efforts against the mill owners?

Many labor historians have analyzed the role of the Industrial Workers of the World, the "Wobblies," in the 1913 strike. At the height of its power just before World War I, the I.W.W advocated one large union of all workers. Big Bill Haywood, John Reed, and other I.W.W activists came to Paterson to support the strike effort. What specific roles did they play? Did the strike emerge because of outside agitation or indigenous discontent? Just as Purvis's article asked a similar question about who led colonial mobs in the land riots, who were the real leaders of the Paterson strike? What was the relationship between the intellectuals who gave support to the strikers and the workers themselves? What role did the police, particularly chief John Bimson, play in the strike? Did they always support the manufacturers?

One of the reasons weavers in Paterson struck was because of an alteration in the rules of work. What was the significance of the shift from two to four looms? To ask a broader question, who benefits from technological advances? If new machines are built, who profits from their increased efficiency? Are workers justified in fearing change? What might the consequences be of failure to take advantage of new technology for a company, and for society as a whole?

Suggested Readings

Brody, David. "The Old Labor History and the New: In Search of an American Working Class." *Labor History* 20 (1979): 111–26.

Fogelson, Nancy. "They Paved the Streets with Silk: Paterson, New Jersey Silk Workers, 1913–1924." *NJH* 97 (1979): 133–48.

Foner, Philip. *History of the Labor Movement in the United States*. 7 vols. New York, 1947–1986.

Gish, Clay. "The Children's Strikes: Socialization and Class Formation in Paterson, 1824–1836." *NJH* 110 (1992): 21–38.

Golin, Steve. "The Paterson Pageant: Success or Failure?" *Socialist Review* 69 (1983): 45–78.

_____ . *The Fragile Bridge: Paterson Silk Strike, 1913*. Philadelphia, 1988.

Gutman, Herbert G. *Work, Culture, and Society in Industrializing America: Essays in American Working-Class and Social History*. New York, 1978.

_____ . "The Reality of the Rags-to-Riches 'Myth': The Case of the Paterson, New Jersey, Locomotive, Iron, and Machinery Manufactures, 1830–1880." In *Nineteenth-Century Cities: Essays in the New Urban History*, edited by Stephan Thernstrom and Richard Sennett. New Haven, Conn., 1969. 98–124.

Kazin, Michael. "Struggling with Class Struggle: Marxism and the Search for a Synthesis of U.S. Labor History." *Labor History* 28 (1987): 497–514.

Lipset, Seymour Martin. "Trade Unionism and the American Social Order." In *The American Labor Movement*, edited by David Brody. Lanham, Md., 1971. 7–29.

Osborne, James D. "Italian Immigrants and the Working Class in Paterson: The Strike of 1913 in Ethnic Perspective." In *New Jersey's Ethnic Heritage*, edited by Paul A. Stellhorn. Trenton, N.J., 1978. 10–34.

Schatz, Ronald W. "Labor Historians, Labor Economics, and the Question of Synthesis." *Journal of American History* 71 (1984): 93–100.

Scranton, Philip B., ed. *Silk City: Studies on the Paterson Silk Industry, 1860–1940*. Newark, N.J., 1985.

Tripp, Anne Huber. *The I.W.W. and the Paterson Silk Strike of 1913*. Urbana, Ill., 1987.

Zieger, Robert H. "Robin Hood in the Silk City: The I.W.W. and the Paterson Silk Strike of 1913." *Proc. NJHS* 84 (1966): 182–95.

◆ ◆ ◆ ◆ ◆ ◆ ◆

Bimson's Mistake: Or, How the Paterson Police Helped to Spread the 1913 Strike

Steve Golin

On the first day of the great 1913 Paterson silk strike, Police Chief John Bimson arrested three out-of-town speakers at Turn Hall. Patrick Quinlan, Carlo Tresca, and Elizabeth Gurley Flynn had come to Paterson at the request of the strike committee, which had asked the national I.W.W. (Industrial Workers of the World) to send speakers. On the morning of February 25, Tresca and Flynn had just finished speaking to two thousand striking broad-silk weavers when Quinlan arrived at Turn Hall, exchanged words with Bimson, and was taken directly to the police station. Having arrested Quinlan, Bimson gave the others a choice—leave town for good or join Quinlan in jail. Samuel Kaplan, a fourth outside speaker, agreed to leave town, but Flynn and Tresca chose jail. Bimson admitted that in a strictly legal sense he was exceeding his authority, but, in a larger sense, he regarded the arrest of the outside agitators as "preventative medicine." With them out of action, he and the mayor explained to reporters, he would be able to keep the strike within manageable bounds.[1]

Bimson's assumption, almost as common among historians today as it was among policemen and editorial writers in 1913, was that the famous out-of-town speakers were the brains behind the strike; by themselves the silk workers were incapable of effectively challenging the power of the mill owners. It followed that the way to control the strike was to cut off its head. But Bimson's assumption was false, and from the very beginning his strategy backfired. As his captives were led out of Turn Hall, "fifteen hundred strikers waiting outside nearly went wild at seeing Miss Flynn

New Jersey History 100 (1982): 58-86. Reprinted by permission of the author.

in the clutches of Bimson." On the way to the police station, "all the efforts of four mounted policemen, and the frightful clubbing meted out to the marchers, failed to disperse Miss Flynn's escort.[2] For Bimson this was but a taste of what was to come. Partly because of his efforts, the strike spread uncontrollably. To grasp why the silk workers reacted as they did to Bimson's use of force, we need to understand their history much better than he did.

This essay will examine the collective experience of the Paterson silk workers as a way of explaining their actions and reactions during the first two weeks of the strike. It was their strike. Their needs drove it; their hard-won unity made it possible; their accumulated wisdom guided it. Through the democratic organization of the strike they participated in all major decisions and retained final authority.[3] The I.W.W. speakers themselves recognized and welcomed (at least in the beginning) the fact that the real leaders of the strike were the silk workers themselves.

Toward the end of the second week of the strike, Big Bill Haywood (who had just arrived in Paterson) tried to persuade Paterson's Rabbi Leo Mannheimer that the workers themselves were in control of the strike. The two men were talking in Turn Hall, and their dialogue went like this:

> MANNHEIMER: Oh, Mr. Haywood, I'm so glad to meet you. I've been wanting to meet the leader of the strike for some time.
> HAYWOOD: You've made a mistake, I'm not the leader.
> MANNHEIMER: What! You're not? Well, who is he?
> HAYWOOD: There ain't any "he."
> MANNHEIMER: Perhaps I should have said "they." Who are they?
> HAYWOOD: This strike has no leaders.
> MANNHEIMER: It hasn't! Well, who is in charge of it?
> HAYWOOD: The strikers.
> MANNHEIMER: But can't I meet some responsible parties somewhere? You know I represent the other churches of the city, the Catholic fathers and the Methodist ministers are awaiting my report. I would like to find out all I can and then maybe we could come to some agreement with the millowners.
> HAYWOOD: The millowners already know what the strikers want.
> MANNHEIMER: They do! Why some of our leading citizens don't even know yet.
> HAYWOOD: That's funny. I just got off a train from Akron a

couple of hours ago and I know.

MANNHEIMER: Will you please tell me?

HAYWOOD: It's very simple. They want the eight-hour day, abolition of the three- and four-loom system in broad silks, abolition of the two-loom system in ribbons, and the dyers want a minimum wage of twelve dollars per week.

MANNHEIMER: Well, well! I must say it's strange we haven't heard this!

HAYWOOD: There's an awful lot of things you never heard of, Parson.

MANNHEIMER: Do they have a strike committee, and where do they meet?

HAYWOOD: Right in this hall, every morning at eight o'clock.

MANNHEIMER: Who are they?

HAYWOOD: I don't know; and if I did I wouldn't tell.

MANNHEIMER: How many are there?

HAYWOOD: One hundred and twenty-seven.

MANNHEIMER: One hundred and twenty-seven! My God! What can we do with a strike committee of one hundred and twenty-seven that meets in a public hall before all the rest of the strikers?

HAYWOOD:: I don't reckon you can do much 'cept the heavy looking on, Parson.[4]

Rabbi Mannheimer persisted in trying to mediate. For his efforts he was forced by the manufacturers to give up his position in Paterson, but he never gave up his assumptions. Throughout the strike he regarded Haywood and the other I.W.W. speakers as the parties responsible for the disciplined behavior of the strikers. "I cannot refrain from paying tribute to the leadership of William Haywood, Elizabeth Gurley Flynn, Patrick Quinlan, Adolph Lessig, and Carlo Tresca," Mannheimer wrote in the *The Independent* in May. "For 13 weeks they have held in check and directed an army of 25,000 men and women."[5] Despite his good intentions Mannheimer failed to understand either the strike or the silk workers who created and controlled it. Unlike Mannheimer, most leading Patersonians did not want to mediate the strike, but to crush it. But they too misread the evidence (indeed misread their own experience) in the same way that Mannheimer did, and for the same reason: they assumed that working people would not do what they were doing unless someone was directing them from outside.

Bimson's second in command, Police Captain Andrew J. McBride, maintained with apparent sincerity that the majority of strikers did not want to strike. Testifying in 1914 before the Federal Commission on Industrial Relations, Captain McBride insisted that the I.W.W. had used violence and threats of violence to force the workers to leave the mills. "The leaders came here and declared a strike and adopted tactics to get them out." But if I.W.W. employed force, why did not the police simply use greater force to protect the workers who wanted to stay in the mills? Captain McBride's answer to this question drew on his experience, and undermined the rest of his testimony. "We have been warned by people working in the mills if we stayed around there they would leave work; that they did not want to work in a mill which was considered a scab mill by the police being around it."[6] Not the fear of violence but the shame of being perceived as a scab was uppermost in the minds of even the few who worked during the strike. The rabbi, from his perspective, had emphasized the orderliness and peacefulness of the strike, whereas the police captain stressed the extent of violence and disorder. But these perspectives converged: neither the captain nor the rabbi could accept what his own evidence suggested, namely that praise or blame for the strike belonged to the silk workers themselves.

Bimson's superior, Mayor Andrew F. McBride, was also questioned closely by the federal commission. Mayor McBride (no relation to the captain) testified that the silk workers originally had walked out for a lark, that they had stayed out almost five months, and that during this time they had suffered, many of them greatly. Then why, he was asked by William O. Thompson, lawyer for the commission, had they not simply gone back to work when the strike stopped being a lark?

> McBride: The agitators (i.e., the I.W.W. speakers) preached if there was any break in the line . . . the bosses would become more arrogant and conditions would become more intolerable and finally they would be treated just like slaves. . . .
> Thompson: And these people had been working in the mills for some time before they went out on strike?
> McBride:: Yes.
> Thompson: They were acquainted with their employers?
> McBride: Largely, I believe.
> Thompson: But in your opinion they preferred to take the word and say-so of outside agitators who came in at that time, and so they stayed out?
> McBride: Why, many of them were absolutely influenced by the preaching of the outside agitators. They believed every-

thing that was told them, and you could not talk with them.[7]

What Captain McBride attributed to the use of violence, Mayor McBride attributed to the seductive force of words. In either event the cause of the actions of the silk workers was located outside them and their history in the tactics and propaganda of the I.W.W. The strikers were controlled from out-of-town. This was the common assumption of the mayor, the police captain, and the rabbi. Ironically, each had been told the workers' version of the strike. The rabbi had been told by Haywood that the silk workers democratically controlled the strike through their strike committee. The captain had been told even by nonstrikers that they did not want police protection, because they would not be scabs. And the mayor had been told by the silk workers that they regarded this strike as the decisive one, which they had to win to prevent the manufacturers from making conditions intolerable. Especially in his capacity as a physician, the mayor had heard this version, over and over again: "I have been in practice for 25 years and have treated many of them for years and years and was very intimate with them, but I could not talk with them. It got so I would not discuss it with any of my patients."[8]

But the mayor, the captain, and the rabbi were unable to grasp what they were told. Paterson's leading citizens (the mayor and other politicians, the police chief and captain, the clergy and the mill owners) all had had personal experience of dealing with the silk workers. But few, in the nature of the case, had experienced the workers as equals. And when for five months in 1913 they were compelled to deal with the silk workers as equals, they could not grasp the meaning of their experience. They attributed the strength and solidarity and staying power of the workers to the national I.W.W. leaders.

Historians, while correcting contemporary biases toward the strikers on many particular points, have perpetuated the general tendency to devaluate their achievements. The discipline, unity, and intelligence of the strikers have been acknowledged by scholars but attributed to the influence of the I.W.W. The fullest account of the strike is by Melvyn Dubofsky, in *We Shall Be All*, his history of the I.W.W. Dubofsky notes that "when inquiring journalists asked the strikers who their leaders were, the workers shot back: 'We are all leaders.'" Yet Dubofsky also quotes (approvingly) a contemporary account praising the I.W.W. outside organizers for having "put into the 25,000 strikers a spirit that has made them stand together." Despite what he knows Dubofsky apparently cannot believe that working people, as a result of their own thinking about their experience, could create their own unity or come to consciousness of themselves as a class. In his version of the strike, as in the versions of contemporaries, the I.W.W. was the actor, the silk workers were acted upon. Following the lead of Rabbi Mannheimer, Dubofsky asserts that the national I.W.W. or organizers "held in check an army of 25,000." It follows from Dubofsky's assumption of passive workers, who were made into effective strikers by outside agitators, that class consciousness was injected into Paterson's workers from outside and above. Though he cites Flynn's view that class consciousness grew out of the silk workers' experience in trying to change their conditions ("sounding almost like John Dewey, she noted that education is not a conversion, it is a process"), Dubofsky concludes one sentence later that, "the Wobblies attempted to convert the immigrants from their diverse Old World religions to a new single-minded faith in the class struggle." The actual struggles of the Paterson silk workers, stretching well back into the nineteenth century, are entirely absent from Dubofsky's account.[9] Where agency is attributed to outside agitators, there is no need to waste time on the history of the local workers.

Similarly, Philip Foner, in the other major account of the 1913 strike, dismisses the prior history of the silk workers in one sentence. Like Dubofsky, Foner recognizes that the strike was unusual in the degree of rank-and-file control. "The I.W.W. theory that leadership must spring from the mass was put into practice in Paterson." The general strike committee of local people, including nonmembers of the I.W.W., "was in charge of conducting the struggle." But Foner, like Dubofsky, seems imprisoned in a set of assumptions that prevent him from making use of what he knows about the democratic control of the strike. The silk weavers, Foner wrote, "entrusted control of the strike to the I.W.W." In his account, too, the I.W.W. organizers appear to possess the active controlling will, whereas the mass of silk workers provide the raw material which they act upon. "The ready response to the I.W.W. strike call can be easily understood," wrote Foner. "The silk workers were tired of A.F. of L. indifference to their needs, and it only required a militant appeal for action to crystallize the latent discontent."[10] There was, however, nothing "latent" about discontent in Paterson, as we will see. The only thing latent is the assumption that discontented workers passively wait for some national organization to galvanize them into action.

The myth that the silk workers were a divided and disorganized mass, incapable of taking effective action on their own behalf, has prevailed from 1913 to the present. Most historians continue to share Bimson's predilection for focusing on the articulate outside agitators.[11] Forgetting what they know about the democratic control of the strike, often dismissing as irrelevant the previous history of the strikers, historians (with one exception) have located primary responsibility for the strike outside the ranks of the strikers, in the national I.W.W.

The important, though partial, exception is James Osborne. In a 1976 paper on the 1913 strike, and more recently in a dissertation on Paterson's immigrant workers up to and including 1913, Osborne has studied the workers themselves. He succeeds in placing the strike in the context of Paterson's history: the history of the silk industry, of immigration, and of class conflict. Seen in this context, the 1913 strike ceases to appear as the product of I.W.W. activity. Osborne rightly concludes that historians, like contemporaries, have "glossed over the role of the millhands in the strike" and exaggerated the role of the I.W.W. In reality, "the I.W.W. exercised very little authority over the day-to-day functioning of the strike, partly because the I.W.W. ideology held that the workers were quite capable of managing their own affairs, and partly because the city's workers had their own deeply entrenched strike traditions." Osborne's valuable and permanent contribution is to take the history of the strikers seriously. He has retrieved much valuable information about the work habits and communal traditions of both the old (e.g., British) and the new (e.g., Italian) immigrants. But Osborne misses the chance to show the development of the Paterson working class from the older to the newer immigration. Embracing a historical perspective that stresses the "primitive" characteristics of first-generation industrial workers, Osborne exaggerates the importance of immigrant strike violence. This violence he then reads into the 1913 strike as an explanation for its failure. Because over the years silk workers had developed no bureaucratic union organization for carrying out orderly collective bargaining, Osborne concludes that they were "helpless" in the face of the determination of the police chief and mayor to crush their disorderly strike.[12] Anything but helpless, as we shall see, the silk workers were even able to turn the police offensive to their advantage. Osborne finally fails to break with the dominant tradition of seeing the silk workers as incapable of acting effectively for themselves. Locked into his model of primitive characteristics, he misses the growing unity and sophistication of the Paterson labor movement.

The general silk strike of 1913 represented the climax of this growth. It was the culmination of years of struggle by the ribbon weavers, the dye workers, and the broad-silk weavers. The ribbon weavers gave the strike a leaven of skilled, militant workers with a long history of struggle in Paterson and a strong sense of their rights as Americans. The dye workers provided the solid core of disciplined proletarians willing to picket and to go to jail, and able to rally support for the strike from a strong immigrant community. The broad-silk weavers first achieved unity among English-speaking and immigrant, skilled and semiskilled weavers, thereby creating the basis for unity among all silk workers. This essay connects the history of each of the three main groups of strikers with the outbreak of the 1913 strike and the silk workers' response to Bimson's use of force.

Paterson Weavers

The first ribbon weavers in Paterson were hand-loom weavers, who owned their own looms and supplied the power with their hands and feet. These ribbon weavers were highly skilled mechanics who made their warps themselves, while their wives and children did less skilled work, like quill winding, and helped them turn the loom when they were tired. They owned their homes in Paterson and expected to be treated with the respect due artisans. In Europe they had been independent artisans working out of their homes or in the small workshops of master weavers. From the silk centers of France, Germany, Switzerland and especially England, they had come to Paterson in the 1860s and 1870s, bringing their traditional work habits and a sense of their traditional rights. In Paterson most of the work was done in old cotton mills that had been empty since cotton had failed in the 1830s (Given a chance by a high U.S. tariff placed on imported silk in 1861, the developing silk industry utilized both the abandoned cotton mills and the skilled machinists who had originally come to build them.). But despite the factorylike atmosphere of the workplace, the work itself was still done on hand looms, and the old artisan traditions of the skilled hand-loom weavers took firm root in Paterson.[13]

In the 1870s the power loom came to silk. Equipped with an automatic device that stopped the loom when the silk thread broke, the new loom could be attended by women and girls, who were both less expensive and more manageable. In broad silk the male weavers fought a delaying battle against the power loom, which nevertheless gradually replaced the hand loom during the 1880s. But in ribbon weaving power lagged behind. Not until 1889, when a high-speed automatic ribbon loom was introduced, could embroidered designs on ribbon goods be produced efficiently by power looms. For the very reason that power came to silk so much later than to cotton and other textiles (because, that is, of the fineness of the thread and the resistance of the artisan-weaver) power came to ribbon weaving last. Throughout the 1890s some hand-loom ribbon weavers were still working in the old way in Paterson. It is true that the use of technology, including all the improvements made on the power loom, enabled Paterson's manufacturers both to capture markets from the less mechanized European silk industry and to attract capital away from Paterson's older types of industry so that by 1900 they had succeeded in making Paterson "Silk City," the "Lyons of America." But the new technology did not solve their labor problems or transform their work force as much as they had hoped. In 1880 one manufacturer had singled out the English as especially troublesome: "They are generally a bad set, a very bad set. They are so tainted with a communistic spirit that we prefer to have nothing to do with them." The troublesome habits and attitudes of the hand-loom weaver outlived the hand loom.[14]

Weavers continued to be difficult from management's point of view, because they continued to be skilled. Silk looms, even when driven by power, were more delicate and specialized than looms used for weaving other textiles, requiring experienced eyes to watch them and skilled hands to start up and adjust them. Consequently, not only did the industrial revolution in the weaving of silk start later than in the weaving of other textiles, but the efforts of the silk weavers to protect themselves against its effects were more successful. In Paterson, through the last two decades of the nineteenth century and the first two decades of the twentieth, weavers contested manufacturers for control over both the rate of technological change and the distribution of its benefits. Especially in ribbon weaving their fight was not hopeless, because their skills remained an important part of the productive process. The high-speed looms were run by women and girls, as the manufacturers had intended. But in 1913, experienced skilled weavers were still necessary to weave the heavier grades of ribbon on German looms. These skilled weavers no longer owned their own looms, of course, but they did own their tools. In the ribbon trade, and to a lesser extent in broad silk, the male striker of 1913 was a skilled workman, heir to a long tradition of independent artisans.

It was a militant tradition. In weaving as in broad silk, strikes were endemic in Paterson. Shop strikes were everyday occurrences. Strikes of entire trades (which became split into increasing numbers of small and medium size broad-silk and ribbon shops as the industry grew) were less common and harder to organize. The 1913 strike was only the third time the ribbon weavers struck en masse (the first had been in 1877). Protesting against a wage cut, ribbon weavers from one mill went to the seven other ribbon mills and persuaded the weavers to join them. Despite the depressed economic conditions of 1877, the ribbon weavers held firm, and their wages were restored. Afterward the silk manufacturers complained that the mayor and the aldermen of Paterson had failed to provide potential strikebreakers with sufficient police protection. Convinced that the community was more sympathetic to the weavers than to them, the manufacturers threatened to raise a private militia.[15]

The second general strike of ribbon weavers was in 1894, and again they achieved at least a partial victory. In Paterson (and in New York City) ribbon weavers won a uniform piece-work scale. The 1894 strike shared many of the features of the great 1913 strike. There was mass picketing when needed, and strikebreakers were mocked as "scabs" and followed even to their homes. Out-of-town speakers, including socialists and anarchists, addressed the strikers, placing their struggles in a broader framework, and the speeches were translated into five languages. A crowd of strikers sang the "Marseillaise." At the climax of the strike, 550 ribbon weavers marched from New York to Paterson and held a demonstration. Several days later 800 strikers from Paterson marched to New York, taking along several wagons of provisions, and musical bands. The mass picketing and verbal intimidation of scabs, the mixing of nationalities, the outside speakers, the international songs, even the climactic trip to New York, all entered into the main tradition of Paterson silk strikes, and reappeared on a larger scale in 1913.[16]

As an old-timer recalled during the strike of 1913, the great difference between the two strikes was that in 1894 Paterson's authorities did not take the side of the manufacturers.[17] The neutrality of the mayor and police in the 1894 battle helped shape the future strategy of both sides. For the weavers, peaceful mass picketing of the mills and humiliation of anyone still working in them became the central strike strategy. The battle strategy of the mill owners in the years from 1894 to 1913 focused on two main thrusts: to try to gain political control over the Paterson police, and simultaneously and wherever possible, to move their mills out of Paterson.

The first objective continued for a time to elude the manufacturers. As the twentieth century began they were still unable to wield the city's police force as a weapon against pickets. Paterson in 1900 belonged as much to the workers as to the manufacturers. As if in recognition of that fact, the manufacturers began to flee Paterson. Between 1890 and 1910 there was a great rush to build annexes in Pennsylvania. Although the absolute decline of Paterson's silk industry did not begin until the textile slump of the 1920s—in 1910 there was a record number of silk mills (276) in Paterson, employing over 20,000 people—the silk industry was nevertheless growing faster in Pennsylvania than in Paterson. The same improvements in technology that enabled the Paterson manufacturers to hire unskilled workers, usually women and children, enabled them to move a large part of their business to the coal mining towns of Pennsylvania. In Pennsylvania coal towns the local authorities did not have divided loyalties, and were able as a rule to intimidate the miners' wives and children who constituted the work force in the new silk mills and plants. More than simply the opportunity to pay lower wages was involved in the move to Pennsylvania, a leading manufacturer acknowledged in 1901. Labor in Pennsylvania was more reliable, "and it was less liable to labor troubles, which are incident to Paterson."[18]

The new ribbon-weaving mills that sprang up in Pennsylvania were equipped with the high-speed automatic looms and employed women and children exclusively. But in Paterson in 1913, skilled male ribbon weavers still constituted about half of the city's ribbon weavers. And the total number of ribbon weavers employed in Paterson at the time of the great strike, including the less-skilled women and girls, still exceeded the number of either dye-workers or broad-silk weavers. By 1913, it is true, all the gains won in 1894 had been wiped out by the employers' counteroffensive. Even the skilled weavers on the heavy looms had suffered improvements: the looms had been lengthened and a second deck added. Wages had continually declined. Restoration of the uniform price scale for piece work (which the manufacturers had reluctantly accepted in 1894 as a way of ending the strike) appeared in the 1913 strike as an almost utopian demand of the ribbon weavers.[19]

"The wages have decreased in proportion as the loom improved," insisted a striking ribbon weaver in 1913. To him, the relationship between improved technology and falling wages seemed neither natural nor inevitable. Ribbon weavers believed that the value of their labor increased as their productivity increased; therefore improvements in the loom should have meant higher wages. As another striking weaver put it,

> We don't object to improved machinery. We welcome improved machinery, if we can get some benefit from it outside of making the work easier or making it possible to produce more goods; but as a rule we never receive any benefit from any improved machinery they put into the mills. On the contrary, we get a cut in wages whenever there is a new method made on a loom. Instead of giving us a benefit from it the benefit is really taken away from us and the manufacturer gets the benefit instead of the worker. So that improved machinery does not help us. It only antagonizes the workers the more, because they can see themselves that they can produce more under the improved machinery; still they get less wages.[20]

The ribbon weavers refused to believe that the tendency of modern machinery to render their labor cheaper was irreversible. By contrast, the ribbon-mill owners bowed before the process of historical change, which they interpreted as progress. Their attitude was reflected by a manager of two Paterson mills, one employing male ribbon weavers on German looms and the other female weavers on high-speed looms. To him the skilled male weavers simply had no future; all their protests and strikes could not change that fact:

> A good deal of trouble comes from the fact that the silk business is passing through a change, that it is gradually becoming a business for females; that in the next 15 to 20 years the males employed in the silk industry will be nil. The change is coming very fast. For instance, as far as ribbons are concerned, the high-speed looms are mostly being run by females. The German looms are gradually changing from male to female and, as I say, in 15 to 20 years, or possibly less time, the mills will mostly be run by female labor.[21]

The long struggle between the skilled ribbon weavers and the mill owners, which reached its climax in the strike of 1913, was never merely a dispute about wages. Rooted from the beginning in a conflict between two ways of life and two experiences of history, it came to reflect two fundamentally different views of social change. To the owners and managers, capitalism appeared given; within it social change occurred more or less automatically as the result of the search for profit. To the ribbon weavers, social change could result from the conscious actions of people with similar interests, and there was nothing inevitable about capitalism. By 1913 socialism had in fact become the dominant ideology of the ribbon weavers. Their spokesman, Louis Magnet, was an active member of the Socialist party, and the bulk of their strike leadership were socialists.[22] By 1913 many skilled ribbon weavers had concluded from their long history of struggle that their problems could not be solved within the framework of capitalism.

As the success of the ribbon weavers in earlier strikes had driven the manufacturers to discover new strategies, so the success of the manufacturers' counteroffensive after 1894 drove the ribbon weavers to seek new solutions. On the shop level in the years before 1913, the ribbon weavers had experienced their new impotence:

> We asked the boss what are you paying for the job; if we did it would amount to an offense to the boss, and if you were to ask, "Can you not pay a little more for this job?" it was almost equivalent to a discharge, so domineering did some of the employers— had they become—that the workers were afraid to go before the boss, almost afraid to state their grievances to one another, for fear that the employer would use [the] weapon that his economic position gives him in discharging them.

Within the shop the balance of power had shifted sharply toward the employer. Able to employ increasing numbers of semi-skilled female weavers, with an overabundance of skilled male weavers consequently competing for jobs, the ribbon manufacturer appeared, for the first time in Paterson's history, as the dictator of the shop. If a weaver "individually went to the office and made complaints in regard to the price he was told that if he didn't like it he could quit; that there were lots of workers only too glad to come and take his place. And that was generally the answer of the manufacturers to the men who would individually complain." Some employers continued to negotiate piece rates with individual ribbon weavers or with their representatives, as they had been accustomed to doing in the past. But, explained Magnet, speaking precisely, "if it should have reached the ears of some employers that a committee was going to be formed or there was even talk of a committee being sent to the employers, they would be singled out and systematically discharged." Militant ribbon weavers, unaccustomed to such treatment, reconsidered their tactics and strategy in the years before 1913. On a tactical level they realized that they had to walk out as a group first, and present demands afterward, when it was too late for the employer to intervene.[23] Strategically, they increasingly thought in terms of political power, on a larger and larger scale.

"The militancy of the factory workers is hard to imagine without the legacy of artisan protest against the encroachments of capital into the spheres of production," wrote Alan Dawley in his study of the shoe workers of Lynn, Massachusetts. Dawley persuasively contrasts the labor movement in Lynn, possessing a rich craft heritage, with the labor movement in the textile industry. "The textile industry in New England began at the factory stage, having gone through no prior development under a domestic system. Consequently, labor had no opportunity to establish its household independence, to create pre-factory customs in the work process, or to develop the means to resist industrial capitalism as an encroachment on established patterns of work and life. The presence of all these conditions in the shoe industry appears to make the difference between an aggressive and a defensive labor movement."[24] Paterson's silk industry, which superficially contradicts Dawley's hypothesis about the textile industry, actually tends to confirm it. In silk, the American textile industry did not begin as a modern industrial system. Among the silk weavers of Paterson, especially the ribbon weavers, there was an old tradition of craft pride and independence, and a sense of their rights as artisans and as citizens, which they brought with them to the modern mill. As late as 1913, a significant minority of the silk workers in Paterson owned their own tools and possessed skills needed, and not easily replaced, by their employers. In keeping with Dawley's hypothesis, much of the aggressiveness of Paterson's labor movement and its growing orientation on power in the shop and the nation was a result of the influence of these skilled weavers.[25]

A Tradition of Militance

There was, however, a separate tradition of militance in Paterson's labor movement, which shaped the 1913 strike as much as did the craft tradition of the skilled weavers. Dyers' helpers were the proletarians of the silk industry. If the skilled ribbon and broad-silk weavers gave the strike its upright posture and its aggressively forward look, the dyers' helpers constituted the backbone of the strike and its central nervous system.

Dyeing was a modern chemical industry. In contrast to silk weaving, in which many small shops flourished alongside larger ones, silk dyeing had been housed in sizable concerns ever since it first split off from the mills as a separate branch of the industry in the 1870s. In the summer the steam was suffocating; in the winter the steam condensed and froze. Working in teams of seven or eight, under the supervision of a master dyer, the dyers' helpers added chemicals to the silk. They routinely touched boiling chemicals and, in order to determine whether the acid content was right, they even had to taste the chemicals.[26]

As unskilled workers, dyers' helpers were paid at rates comparable to those of other unskilled laborers, or about $11 or $12 per week in 1913. In practice, however, dyers' helpers were unemployed roughly half the year, and only averaged about $6 per week. Skilled ribbon weavers were still making $3 to $3.50 per day in Paterson in 1913, and averaging over $14 per week.[27] Within the silk industry, the ribbon weavers and dyers' helpers stood at nearly opposite poles. As craftsmen and English-speaking Americans, the skilled ribbon weavers were struggling in 1913 to protect a whole way of life. As Italian-speaking proletarians, the dyers' helpers were fighting for a chance to live.

The militant tradition of the dyers' helpers was rooted not in a common craft but in community—namely, the Italian community of Paterson. (During the great migrations from southern and eastern Europe, many textile towns became fragmented into a myriad of ethnic communities. In Paterson, however, the Italians dominated the new immigration.) Many of the Italians who came to Paterson in the 1880s were northerners, who had worked as skilled silk weavers or dyers in Piedmont or Lombardy. But in Paterson they became dyers' helpers. After 1890 southern Italians began to arrive in great numbers. They worked alongside northerners in the dye houses, while some more fortunate northerners became broad-silk weavers or even ribbon weavers. The dye houses, however, remained the focal point of Paterson's

Italian community, and the northerners continued to set the cultural and political tone of that community.[28]

Conflicts with management in the dye houses and mills, and with the police in the street, shaped the Italian experience and unified it. Northern or southern, skilled or unskilled, radical or religious, they were given the worst jobs, for the least money, and treated most brutally when they tried to fight back. Exploited and oppressed together, they created together a fighting community. Among the major groups of strikers in Paterson in 1913, the dyers' helpers were closest to the stereotyped picture of near-starving workers who strike in the desperate hope of somehow increasing their wages. But even in the case of the dyers' helpers what needs to be emphasized is the extent to which their strike behavior in 1913 was not merely the reflex of their economic condition, but rather was shaped by a sophisticated tradition of revolt. Through violent struggle with Paterson's dye manufacturers and police, the dye workers tempered their northern Italian inheritance, and made themselves into the effective strike force that they were in 1913.

Italian immigrants, especially from the north, had brought their own theories and agitators with them. During the 1890s Paterson became the international center of Italian anarchism. The Italian anarchist group in Paterson published an Italian language newspaper and a journal, and encouraged fellow immigrants to think in terms of class rather than in terms of their region of origin. It also encouraged them to think in terms of violence. In 1900 the king of Italy was assassinated by an anarchist from Paterson; anarchists in Paterson continued for some years to celebrate the assassination date.[29] In 1902 a dyers' strike, with the help of the anarchists, became the bloodiest strike in Paterson's history.

The Italian dyers' helpers took the lead in the 1902 strike. Twenty workers from two dye houses began the strike on their own initiative, and it spread rapidly. At one dyeing plant three Italian workers and one policeman were shot. The manufacturers pressed the mayor to request the militia from the governor, but in keeping with Paterson tradition the mayor refused. The dye workers were successful in shutting down their branch of the industry, but were unable to force their employers to give in to their wage-and-hour demands. The strike was stalemated, foreshadowing the long stalemate in the strike of 1913. The only way for the striking dye workers to augment their forces was by precipitating a general strike of all branches of Paterson's silk industry. Calling a mass meeting, they invited leading anarchists to speak. The anarchists urged the use of whatever force was necessary. Marching to the weaving mills, the dyers' helpers forcefully emptied them. This time eight workers and one policeman were shot, and now the mayor asked the governor to send the militia. The use of violence boomeranged. The Italian dyers' helpers became isolated, as both the weavers and the English-speaking dye-workers drew back from them. The militia stayed in Paterson while the defeated dye workers drifted back to work.[30]

The 1902 strike proved a setback for Paterson's labor movement as a whole. Sensing that for the first time public opinion had swung in their favor, the dye and silk manufacturers used the violence of the 1902 strike as an excuse for renewing their counteroffensive against the political influence of Paterson's workers. And this time they were successful. Aided by public hysteria over anarchists and prejudice against Italians, and armed with the threat of moving even more of their business to Pennsylvania, Paterson's manufacturers won victory after victory. The old police chief, who for more than thirty years had guided the department along its moderate course in strikes, was suspended. His captain, previously known as a hard-liner and publicly denounced as such by the workers, was promoted to chief. This new chief had never respected the traditional right of Paterson's silk workers to picket peacefully. As far back as 1877, as a young policeman, he had contested the customary control of the streets by workers. In 1894 he had drawn his gun to threaten angry pickets. In 1901, when silk workers had praised the old chief for refusing to prohibit their public meetings, they had denounced his captain for "abuse of his authority."[31] In 1902 Captain John Bimson became chief of police.

Five years later, in 1907, a business-sponsored reform of the city's government freed Chief Bimson from popular control. In place of the aldermen and mayor, an elected board of commissioners became responsible for overseeing the police. The new commissioners immediately made their intentions plain by increasing the size of Bimson's force by over fifty percent. The reaction time of the police was shortened by installation of a telegraph system that connected the patrolmen with headquarters. The police were also given a mounted division to accompany police patrols, and a new "Italian Division." Bimson hired two Italian detectives for the new department and established a precinct station in the predominantly Italian Riverside section. The following year those leaders of the Italian anarchist group who had not fled Paterson in 1902 were arrested, and their journal was permanently closed down.[32] Bimson came to power in the backlash from the dyers' helpers strike in 1902. His specific mandate as police chief was to keep the Italians in line.

The defeat of the 1902 strikers changed the approach of the Italians as well. Treated like the enemy, the whole Italian community came together behind the dyers' helpers. In 1913 the entire community, including tradesmen, would organize its considerable resources through the Sons of Italy and put them at the disposal of the strikers. The dyers' helpers themselves learned from 1902. The Italian labor movement emerged from defeat with a new sense of the limitations of violence; the influence of the anarchists within the movement declined, even before they were closed down by Bimson. During the 1913 strike Haywood noticed the difference: "These Italians have showed a spirit seldom credited to their class in this city and they should be congratulated."[33] The self-discipline of the Italian dyers' helpers in 1913, in contrast to their wholesale violence of 1902, has typically been attributed to the restraining influence of the I.W.W., in accordance with the widespread assumption that the I.W.W. speakers were the brains behind the strike.[34] But the dyers' helpers listened to the advice of the I.W.W. speakers only because it dovetailed with their experience. The calling of the militia in 1902, the promotion of Bimson, the expansion and modernization of the police force, and the administrative reform designed to give Bimson a free hand had visibly altered the balance of power in Paterson. After 1902 the dye workers could no longer hope to hold Paterson by force (as they had for a while in 1894). Straightforward violence could hurt the manufacturers and the police, who now directly served under them, but it could no longer win a strike. The disciplined militance of the Italian dyers' helpers in 1913, which Tresca and other speakers reinforced, was their response to defeat in 1902 and its aftermath.

Broad-Silk Weavers

Paterson's silk workers in 1913 were no raw mass, waiting to be molded by the I.W.W. Both the skilled ribbon weavers and the Italian dyers' helpers had traditions of their own, which shaped their responses to the manufacturers and police, and to the I.W.W. Despite their great contribution to the strike of 1913, however, the dyers' helpers and ribbon weavers did not begin it. The broad-silk weavers triggered the events of 1913; prior to their call for a general strike on February 25, the strike belonged to them. Consequently, unlike the ribbon weavers or dyers' helpers, the broad-silk weavers have received considerable attention in the literature on the strike. Their immediate history has been examined in detail and their ethnic origins have received considerable comment.[35] But what has not been sufficiently emphasized even in the case of the broad-silk weavers is the extent to which they were seasoned veterans of the labor movement.

The broad-silk weavers were, in fact, the inheritors of not one but two converging lines of struggle. Like the ribbon weavers, the broad-silk weavers were heirs to a craft tradition that in Paterson went back to the hand-loom weavers. Like the dyers' helpers, the broad-silk weavers were heirs to traditions—from southern and eastern Europe—of collective protest and radical ideas. In this sense the broad-silk weavers contained within their own history the militant traditions of both the ribbon weavers and the dyers' helpers. Uniting the craftsmen's experience in shop struggles with the communal rebelliousness of Paterson's new immigrants, the broad-silk weavers were ideally situated within the silk industry to inaugurate its first general strike.

Many of the broad-silk weavers of 1913 had been skilled textile workers in Europe. Some northern Italians, having worked with silk or wool in Italy itself, or in France or Switzerland, became broad-silk weavers in Paterson. Jews began coming to Paterson in large numbers after the turn of the century. "Like the northern Italians," writes a historian of New Jersey's ethnic communities, "this Jewish proletariat was experienced in strikes, labor organizations, and radical movements."[36] From the textile centers of Warsaw, Bialystok, and especially Lodz, they came to the broad-silk mills, where, as the latest comers, they were generally given the least-skilled and lowest-paid jobs. In Paterson the Jews and the northern Italians found themselves, for the first time, working in a technologically advanced industry, tending automatic looms, and vulnerable, as semiskilled workers, to further "improvements" in the work process. This experience provided a basis for unity not only with each other but also with Paterson's English-speaking broad-silk weavers. In 1913 skilled English-speaking weavers were still making fine broad-silks on Jacquard looms in Paterson. But they were no longer protected, as prior generations of Paterson's artisan-weavers had been, by an apprenticeship system that controlled entry to the trade. English-speaking broad-silk weavers, northern Italians, and Jews saw their trade becoming progressively deskilled. In 1913 they would join together in defending their skills and their older ways of working.[37]

Class struggle, which brought the Italians together as a community, split the Jews in Paterson apart. In 1913 there were actually not one but two Jewish communities. Jews from Germany, who came to Paterson in the late nineteenth century, were often owners or managers of silk mills and formed a Jewish upper class; to the newcomers from Poland, the German Jews seemed more German than Jewish. As relatively recent entrants into the business, the Jewish broad-silk manufacturers were resented by their workers and accused of particularly sharp practices. With the Polish Jews moving into Paterson's Jewish neighborhood, in the heart of the city—"Jewtown," as it came to be called—the German Jews moved out, to the fashionable East Side. Jewishness no more unified these older and newer immigrants than Catholicism united the Irish and Italians. In each case, the decisive experience for the newcomers, shaping their sense of community, was the experience of becoming industrial proletarians. The "Wops and Jews," as Bimson's police called them, were harassed by the authorities and shunned by American Federation of Labor unions. Their militant backgrounds and their similar experiences in Paterson encouraged them to draw together across ethnic lines and become allies.[38]

The alliance between the Italians and Jews represented one of the great strengths of the 1913 strike; the alliance between skilled and unskilled (or semiskilled) workers constituted the other. Each alliance was initially forged in the crucible of the broad-silk industry, before reaching out in 1913 to encompass the movement as a whole. It was in the broad-silk mills that Italians and Jews, that skilled and semiskilled weavers came together in opposition to the stretch-out.

The increase, or stretch-out in loom assignments had first become an issue for the broad-silk weavers in the early 1880s, simultaneously with the change over from the hand loom to power. The labor movement in the broad-silk industry had begun before the coming of the Italians or the Jews, as a protest of the skilled weavers against the increase from one to two looms. This tradition of protest, and the system of values on which it rested, continued to inform the struggle of the broad-silk weavers. Their objection was not to improved machinery but to the fundamental inequality that enabled manufacturers to secure the benefits of improvements for themselves. In 1881 a skilled weaver had noticed that "every month the bosses increase the . . . improvements in machinery and thus the workers can tend to more machines and produce more. But the general complaint in all mills is, that for producing two thirds more the workers only get one third more pay." The insistence of this right to be paid in proportion to his productivity was a trade mark of the artisan-weaver. In 1913, speaking in the still recognizable tones of the skilled weaver, the general strike committee made the same point: "The manufacturers must realize that the improvement of machinery means something besides increasing the already swollen fortunes of a few unscrupulous and money-mad barons. That the toiler who feeds and clothes the world must have a fairer and more just share of the wealth he creates. This they demand as a right, not as a favor."[39] From the 1880s through 1913, there was a continuous thread of protest by the skilled broad-silk weavers against the manufacturers' attempts to monopolize the benefits of increasing productivity.

Beyond protest, the intellectual triumph of the broad-silk weavers was to grasp the logic of what had been done to them, in order to prevent it from being done again. In the 1880s their resistance to the doubling of loom assignments had been ineffective, for two reasons. Striking in isolated shops, they were easily defeated; the remedy for this was to strike together. But also they were defeated because they were tempted by the higher wages that, at first, resulted from working two looms. Even though wages fell behind productivity, they still rose; the broad-silk weaver who worked two looms made more than the weaver who worked one. But the increase was only temporary, lasting only so long as the manufacturers were winning acceptance for the heavier loom assignments. Afterward, profiting from the higher productivity and the resulting surplus of labor, the manufacturers gradually reduced wages until weavers who were fortunate enough to work steadily were running two looms for virtually the price of one. This problem was harder to solve. Its solution depended on the ability of the broad-silk weavers to analyze the long-term tendencies of further increased loom assignments and to reject as a group the short-term advantages offered by the manufacturers. If some weavers agreed to work a larger loom assignment in return for higher pay, it would soon stampede the others to submit, since everyone's price per loom would soon fall. A chance for successful opposition to a new increase in loom assignments depended on a near-impossible unity between the more and less skilled, between the English-speaking, the Italian, and the Jewish weavers. Between 1911 and 1913 the broad-silk weavers of Paterson achieved this nearly impossible unity.

In 1911 one Paterson broad-silk manufacturer doubled the loom assignment of some of his weavers to four looms. Henry Doherty rearranged his looms so that one weaver could tend to four of them, and equipped them with the automatic stop motion. Doherty received prior approval for his plan from the A.F. of L.'s United Textile Workers, which had recently organized most of his weavers. He would use four looms only on the cruder forms of silk, and four-loom weavers would make more money than two-loom weavers (though not twice as much more). But when Doherty began to implement his plan, his weavers struck. Ordered back by the union officials, they turned to another union, Local 25 of the Socialist Labor party. Striking again in 1912, they reached out to other broad-silk weavers and other issues. When the settlement of the 1912 strike left the original issue of four looms unresolved, the three-and-four-loom system spread in Doherty's mill to less crude forms of silk and to other broad-silk mills in Paterson. In January 1913 Doherty's broad-silk weavers went on strike yet again. This time they turned to Local 152 of I.W.W. And this time they would take out all the broad-silk weavers with them.

But why did Doherty's weavers repeatedly strike, against the dictates of their first union, and despite the mistakes of their second? And why did the other weavers increasingly support them in resisting the four-loom system? It was not primarily a question of the difficulty of the work itself. Weaving was not heavy work; rather it was "tedious work," as one weaver put it, "and a man's nerves must be on the tense all day, and he has to be right there on the job with the work he does." Tending four broad looms, in place of two, made a weaver more tense and was harder on his eyes—even with the automatic stop, a weaver antici-pated breaks, catching the early signs and making adjustments—but it was not impossible to do.[40] Nor was it simply a question of wages: four looms did indeed pay better than two. Doherty's weavers repeatedly struck, and the other broad-silk weavers joined them because they understood the long-term effect of the larger loom assignment.

With each weaver producing twice as much, fewer weavers would be needed. Adolph Lessig, a broad-silk weaver, explained the process to the Commission on Industrial Relations in 1914: "All the weavers realized that if the thing became general throughout the trade, the three and four looms, it meant the filling of the street with unemployed, which would mean a general reduction in wages, and that is what all the weavers realized." When asked by a commission member how the employers originally got weavers to run two looms instead of one, Lessig answered, "By the same methods and process Mr. Doherty is using today, by appealing to the hungriest of the workers and making him believe that he is always going to continue on making that amount of money." Drawing on their history in Paterson, the broad-silk weavers were able, as a group, to resist the lure of temporarily higher wages:

> THOMPSON: If the rates of pay offered to the workers who would remain had been sufficient, would there still have been a complaint that the weavers would have refused to use the new system?
> LESSIG: Well, the workers all realized that it was only a matter of time: that the wages must come down if they were going to have that army of unemployed. They were wise enough to see that.[41]

Newspaper accounts of the outbreak of the 1913 strike denied that the broad-silk weavers showed wisdom. The strike was "a protest against new and improved machinery," wrote a *New York Times* reporter from Paterson on February 25. In fact no new machinery was involved in the speed-up, except for the automatic stop-motion, which was not really new. But the reporter was eloquent in defense of the manufacturers' point of view. The new machinery "permits fifty silk weavers to do the work; that formally [*sic*] required 100." The weavers were blind opponents of progress, the Luddites of the twentieth century, according to the *New York Times*.

> To show how futile the strike is and how hopeless it is to expect that modern machinery can be eliminated because weavers don't like to lose their old positions, members of the Board of Trade called attention to this paragraph in the call of the I.W.W. for a general strike:
> "The new four-loom system must be stopped. If we allow this new system to exist hundreds of workers will not be able to find jobs as loom-fixers, twisters, and warpers, and will crowd into the dye houses at any price they can get. The wages of all silk workers will therefore be cut down to the lowest possible level of starvation. Your mill may be the next one to adopt the four-loom sys-

tem. Show your disapproval by striking all together. Don't scab on your future by remaining at work. . . ."

It also pointed out that the introduction of the newest machine was being opposed by the same protests which marked the introduction of the weaving machines in England in the last years of the eighteenth century.[42]

With this wisdom the *New York Times* closed its account. But the strike had just begun.

The broad-silk weavers fought, not against progress, but for a progress that would not be against them. To have a chance of success, they needed more than unity among themselves. They needed unity among all the silk workers. In 1902 broad-silk workers had remained at work, albeit somewhat reluctantly, during the big dye-workers' strike; during the broad-silk weavers' strike of 1912, the dye workers had returned the compliment. Amidst rumors that they were going to support the broad-silk weavers in 1912, the dyers' helpers had been offered "an increase of wages of one dollar a week. In this way the talk of going on strike was abolished," explained a dye worker. "Many of the workers appreciated the generosity of the employers, but there were amongst the wiser ones dissatisfaction and they considered it a great insult. They did not fail to see that the advance in wages was thrown at them as a robber would throw a bone to a barking dog."[43] In 1913, having seen their gains of the previous year whittled away, the dyers' helpers went out as a body in support of the broad-silk weavers. They would not scab on their future. They had learned what the Jews and Italians within the broad-silk industry had learned, and what the I.W.W. speakers (who had themselves tested it in other struggles) would never tire of repeating: that each trade or branch within the industry as a whole could only advance if they all joined together, as a class.

The I.W.W. did not create unity among the strikers; the strikers created their own unity. Unity grew out of their prior experiences, as a reasoned response. It is this that Bimson did not understand. Like his captain and his mayor, he apparently did not think of the silk workers as people who learned from experience. When most of the broad-silk weavers and some dyers' helpers went out on strike on February 25, Bimson did not take their demands seriously. To him, as to the *New York Times*, their strike was merely a disturbance. They could not stop progress. (Their job was to make silk, not history.) Believing that silk workers were objects of others' activities, never subjects of their own,

Bimson looked for the power behind the strike, and found it in the I.W.W. leaders. To limit the disturbance he had only to separate the strikers forcefully from their out-of-town shepherds, and then herd them back to work.

In fact, the reaction of the strikers to Bimson's police offensive immeasurably strengthened the strike. This reaction troubled the *New York Times* reporter on the very first day of the strike. The strikers allowed the out-of-town speakers to be arrested without actually rioting. "But for many hours after the arrests the strikers moved in disorganized masses about the town, threatening the police and the Mayor, and denouncing the treatment accorded them." The agitation continued at night. "Detectives on duty tonight in the distinct where the silk weavers live brought in word that secret meetings were going on in many of the houses and that the strikers seemed much agitated and alarmed. About 2,000 more had joined the strike tonight." Throughout the first week Bimson's tactics continued to help the strike. Speaking at a large Friday night meeting, Wilson P. Killingberg, secretary of the Socialist Party of New Jersey, asked for a vote of thanks for Bimson, "the man who won our strike." Killingberg later explained that "when the constitution was abrogated by the authorities, in closing down the halls, arresting speakers and clubbing citizens, such a feeling of disgust arose among the workers that it became a very simple matter to call out shop after shop." Flynn agreed with this analysis. The attempts at police repression, she told the strikers in March, had solidified their ranks; shops that originally had not wanted "agitators" to address them now called on the strike committee for speakers. By the beginning of the second week of the general strike about five hundred silk workers a day were joining Local 152, the dye houses and broad-silk mills were shut down, and Flynn, Tresca, and Quinlan were again addressing daily meetings of the strikers at Turn Hall and Helvetia Hall. Asked why he was not carrying through his threats about preventing the outside agitators from speaking in Paterson, Bimson looked "somewhat crestfallen," according to the *New York Call*. "What's the use," he said, "I did the best I could."[44]

Bimson's attempt to use force to prevent Flynn, Tresca, and Quinlan from speaking brought the ribbon weavers, particularly, into the strike. During the first week, while the dyers' helpers joined the strike, delegates from the various ribbon shops were in contact with the strike committee. On Monday evening, March 3, and again on Tuesday evening, March 4, the ribbon weavers gathered by themselves in Helvetia Hall, to debate the question of joining the general strike. The Tuesday meeting lasted late into the night and resulted in the decision to strike. What pushed the ribbon weavers over the edge was their outrage at Bimson's violation of their rights. Historically, Turn Hall and Helvetia Hall had been the meeting places of Paterson's workers. How could the police dictate who could speak in them, or under what condition they might remain open? Veterans of Paterson's labor movement, skilled ribbon weavers expected that their customary and constitutional rights would be respected during strikes. When Bimson violated these rights in the opening days of the strike, he served notice that everything Paterson's silk workers had won over the years was under attack. Trying to explain "the rapid spread of the strike," Louis Magnet, the spokesman of Paterson's ribbon weavers, thought that "the action of the city authorities in trying to suppress the constitutional right of free speech had a great deal to do with inciting . . . those law-abiding, liberty-loving Americans who believe that the constitutional rights of each and every citizen would be preserved under any circumstances." "The ribbon weavers, the aristocrats of the industry, decided to come out in support of the general strike," exulted the I.W.W. weekly, *Solidarity*. "This almost unprecedented situation is largely the result of the resentment of the working class against the high handed and outrageous action of the police."[45]

During the second week, celebrating the remarkable spread of the strike, the *New York Call* gave credit where credit was due. Chief Bimson and Mayor McBride, it said,

> have seen the work of their hands in the tying up of the entire trade of the city, the idle silk mills and dyehouses, the impossibility of procuring scabs—there are heroes enough of the breed, but they haven't the necessary skill. . . .
>
> When the first move was made by a small number of strikers, [Bimson and McBride] persuaded themselves that it was more a foolish childish prank than anything else; that the workers had no grievance and that under the circumstances they should be caned like naughty children and sent back to the looms. . . . The outside agitators were rounded up. . . . Bimson was hailed by the local press as the savior of Paterson society. Leave it to old Bimson. Who said he was too old for the job? Had he been in command years ago, at the time of the previous trouble, there would have been no trouble. He knows how to handle these malcontents who give Paterson a bad name. He doesn't talk—he acts. . . .
>
> And Bimson did all that was expected of him—and a little more

for good measure—and he succeeded—in tying up the silk industry of Paterson.[46]

Bimson indeed miscalculated: the strikers were not children
but grown men and women with memories of their own. His
reliance on force and his focus on the outside agitators were based
on the assumption—shared by the managers, ministers, and
mayor—that the silk workers could not act on their own behalf.
This assumption would prove costly. The unprecedented unity
forged by the broad-silk weavers, dyers' helpers and ribbon weavers in the first two weeks of the strike would last for almost five
months despite the pressure of hunger and the increasing temptation of individual shop settlements, and would deprive the
city of enormous funds and the manufacturers of their summer
and fall seasons. From the beginning the strike belonged to the
silk workers themselves. Before Flynn or Tresca said a word to
the strikers, the basic direction of the strike had been laid down.
The calling of the strike, the aggressiveness of the workers, their
intelligence, and tactical flexibility—all preceded the coming of
the national I.W.W. leaders to Paterson.

Conclusion

It is true that the national I.W.W. had helped indirectly to bring
the ribbon weavers into the strike, by sending the out-of-town
speakers to Paterson. And the national organization helped bring
the dye workers into the strike by reintroducing the demand for
the eight-hour-day. But in each case local people controlled the
process. Militant silk workers in Local 152 had taken up the
demand for the eight-hour day, and the dye workers responded
to it out of their own needs and their own history.[47] The outrage
of the ribbon weavers at Bimson's denial of free speech to the
outside speakers, who had been invited to town by local workers,
was shaped by their historic sense of their rights in that town;
like Bimson himself, the ribbon weavers acted in terms of their
understanding of previous battles in the class war in Paterson.
In a sense, the greatest contribution of the I.W.W. to the strikers
was that, unlike Bimson or other unions or most historians, it
respected them and their history.

When Haywood arrived in Paterson on Friday, March 7, he
found the weaving mills and dye houses already shut down and
the strike well-organized. He could see that there was little for

him to do, and soon decided to return for a while to Akron, to resume the more difficult task of organizing striking rubber workers there. While in Paterson he stressed familiar I.W.W. themes. "I have come to Paterson not as a leader," he told the strikers in Turn Hall on Saturday. "There are no leaders in the I.W.W.; this is not necessary. You are the members of the union and you need no leaders. I come here to give you the benefit of my experience throughout the country." And by way of emphasis he added: "The union belongs to you." From the gallery, a voice cried out in English: "And we're going to keep it, too."[48]

Notes

1. *New York Times*, February 26, 1913, 22; *New York Call*, February 26, 1913, 1; Appeal to Reason, August 16, 1913, 2.

2. *New York Call*, February 16, 1913, 1.

3. As they proved during the last phase of the strike, when a majority of the strike committee rejected the advice of the I.W.W. speakers. See Elizabeth Gurley Flynn, "The Truth about the Paterson Strike," in *Rebel Voices: An I.W.W. Anthology*, ed. Joyce L. Kornbluh (Ann Arbor, Mich., 1964), 222–23.

4. *Solidarity*, April 19, 1913, 2. I have eliminated Frank Pease's editorial comments from the dialogue.

5. Leo Mannheimer, "Darkest New Jersey," *Independent* (May 29, 1913) 74:1190.

6. U.S. Commission on Industrial Relations, *Industrial Relations, Final Report*, Senate Executive Doc. no. 415, 64th Cong., 1st, 1916, 3:2565. (Hereafter cited as *Report of C.I.R.*) For a summary of local testimony blaming the strike on the I.W.W. see Morris William Garber, "The Silk Industry of Paterson, New Jersey, 1840–1913; Technology and the Origins, Development, and Changes in an Industry" (Ph.D. diss., Rutgers University, 1968), 254–56.

7. *Report of C.I.R.*, 2554–55.

8. Ibid., 2555.

9. Melvyn Dubofsky, *We Shall Be All: A History of the Industrial Workers of the World* (Chicago, 1969), 271, 272, 274. The only other silk strike Dubofsky mentions is the 1912 strike. In place of the history of the silk workers, he gives the history of the I.W.W. attempts at organizing Paterson.

10. Philip S. Foner, *The Industrial Workers of the World, 1905–1917* (New York, 1965), 365–67.

11. Perhaps because so many silk workers were recent immigrants, historians have generally taken it for granted that the national I.W.W. organizers supplied unity and direction. "Divided immigrant workers could call a strike and stone scabs," writes Joseph R. Conlin about Lawrence and Paterson, "But

it took the I.W.W. to impress on the disorganized mass a powerful union which won strikes on specific issues." *Big Bill Haywood and the Radical Union Movement* (Syracuse, N.Y., 1969), 147. For a similar emphasis, see Kornbluh, *Rebel Voices*, 199, and Nancy Fogelson, "They Paved the Streets with Silk: Paterson, New Jersey, Silk Workers, 1913–1924," *New Jersey History* (Autumn, 1979): 137.

12. James D. Osborne, "Italian Immigrants and the Working Class in Paterson: The Strike of 1913 in Ethnic Perspective," in *New Jersey's Ethnic Heritage*, ed. Paul A. Stellhorn (Trenton, N.J., 1978), 20, 30; Osborne, "Industrialization and the Politics of Disorder: Paterson Silk Workers, 1880–1913" (Ph.D. diss., University of Warwick, 1979), 323 and *passim*. The older work of James E. Wood is similarly useful on the continuities in the Paterson labor movement: "History of Labor in the Broad-Silk Industry of Paterson, New Jersey, 1879–1940" (Ph.D. diss., University of California, 1941), 73–315.

13. Evald Koettgen, "Making Silk," *International Socialist Review*, 14 (March 1914): 552–53; Schichiro Matsui, *The History of the Silk Industry in the United States* (New York, 1930), 154; Garber, "The Silk Industry of Paterson," 166, 172; Osborne, "Industrialization and the Politics of Disorder," 43–44.

14. Garber, "The Silk Industry of Paterson," 166, 185, 228; Matsui, *The History of the Silk Industry*, 138.

15. Matsui, *The History of the Silk Industry*, 148, 188, 206; *Report of C.I.R.*, 2604, 2589; *Solidarity*, April 1, 1913, 1; Wood, "History of Labor in the Broad-Silk Industry," 137; Herbert Gutman, "Class, Status and Community Power in Nineteenth-Century American Industrial Cities; Paterson, New Jersey: A Case Study," *Work Culture and Society in Industrializing America* (New York, 1976), 242–46.

16. Wood, "History of Labor in the Broad-Silk Industry," 156–59; *New York Call*, March 3, 1913, 2.

17. Frederick Mott, in *New York Call*. March 3, 1913, 9.

18. Ruth Tierney, "The Decline of the Silk Industry in Paterson, New Jersey" (M.A. thesis, Cornell University, 1938), 16–18; Garber, "The Silk Industry of Paterson," 228.

19. *Solidarity*, April 19, 1913, 1; *Report of C.I.R.*, 2427; Koettgen, "Making Silk", 553.

20. *Solidarity*, April 19, 1913, 1; *Report of C.I.R.*, 2596.

21. *Report of C.I.R.*, 2492.

22. Flynn, "The Truth about the Paterson Strike," 216.

23. *Report of C.I.R.*, 2573, 2595.

24. Alan Dawley, *Class and Community: The Industrial Revolution in Lynn* (Cambridge, Mass., 1976), 228–29.

25. The independence of the skilled ribbon weavers eventually proved troublesome even to Flynn, and after the strike she blamed their socialism and supposed conservatism for the defeat. (Flynn, "The Truth About the Paterson Strike," 223–24) Because historians have been too impressed with Flynn's later version, and because they have tended to lump together the English-speaking male ribbon weavers with other English-speaking silk workers (espe-

cially with the small number of highly skilled, highly paid loom-fixers and twisters and warpers, who had belonged to A.F. of L. craft unions for years and who opposed the strike) historians have missed the key role played by the skilled ribbon weavers. See, for example, Osborne, "Industrialization and the Politics of Disorder," 300–302; Dubofsky, *We Shall Be All*, 271, 281; and Graham Adams, Jr., *Age of Industrial Violence, 1910–1915: The Activities and Findings of the United States Commission on Industrial Relations* (New York, 1966), 246.

Actually the least skilled workers in Paterson's silk industry, known as hard-silk workers, were the most difficult of all large groups of workers to involve in the strike. See, for example, *Paterson Evening News*, April 18, 1913, 1.

26. *Report of C.I.R.*, 2444–45; *Solidarity*, May 3, 1913, 2; Koettgen, "Making Silk," 554.

27. *Report of C.I.R.*, 2427, 2595; Matsui. *The History of the Silk Industry*, 201–2; *Outlook* 104 (June 7, 1913): 285–86. Note that the average for ribbon weaver included unpaid hours and even unpaid days when the weaver was fixing a loom or making a holdfast with a new set of warps. *Report of C.I.R.*, 2604.

28. Rudolph J. Vecoli, *The People of New Jersey* (Princeton, N.J., 1965), 191; Osborne, "Italian Immigrants and the Working Class in Paterson," 23; James D. Osborne, "The Paterson Strike of 1913; Immigrant Silk Workers and the I.W.W. Response to the Problem of Stable Unionism" (M.A. thesis, University of Warwick, 1973), 26; Matsui, *The History of the Silk Industry*, 187.

29. Vecoli, *The People of New Jersey*, 191.

30. Wood, "History of Labor in the Broad-Silk Industry," 181, 189; Osborne, "Industrialization and the Politics of Disorder," 230.

31. Osborne, "Industrialization and the Politics of Disorder," 115, 129–30, 135, 251–53, 276. The old chief's suspension was only temporary, and he returned to his post for a few years. But his suspension signalled a new era in police-community relations.

32. Osborne, "Italian Immigrants and the Working Class in Paterson," 19, 28–29.

33. *Paterson Evening News*, May 19, 1913, 1.

34. See, for example, *The United States of America vs. William D. Haywood, et al.*; Indictment on sections 6, 19, and 37 of the Criminal Code of the United States and section 4 of the Espionage Act of June 15, 1917 (Chicago, n.d.) 11751–52.

35. See especially Garber, "The Silk Industry of Paterson," 246–50; and Martin Mooney, "The Industrial Workers of the World and the Immigrants of Paterson and Passaic, New Jersey: 1907–1913" (M.A. thesis, Seton Hall University, 1969), 63–71.

36. Vecoli, *The People of New Jersey*, 193. On the northern Italians, Osborne, "The Paterson Strike of 1913," 26, 28, and "Industrialization and the Politics of Disorder," 177, 178.

37. Wood, "History of Labor in the Broad-Silk Industry," 176; William D. Haywood, "The Rip in the Silk Industry," *International Socialist Review*, 13, no. 11 (May, 1913): 785; Osborne, "Industrialization and the Politics of Disorder," 61. Osborne unaccountably plays down the importance of Jews in

the 1913 strike, claiming that "it was, in fact, an Italian strike" (Osborne, "Italian Immigrants and the Working Class in Paterson," 21). Though evidence of Jewish activities keeps slipping into his account of the strike ("Industrialization and the Politics of Disorder," 287, 288, 293, 303, 319, 321), he misses the importance of Italian-Jewish unity in 1913.

38. Mooney, "The Industrial Workers of the World", 37, 38; *Report of C.I.R.*, 2573, 2586; Wood, "History of Labor in the Broad-Silk Industry," 76; Edward S. Shapiro, "The Jews of New Jersey," in *The New Jersey Ethnic Experience*, ed. Barbara Cunningham (Union City, N.J., 1977), 306; *Report of C.I.R.*, 2594. For similar examples from other cities of Italian-Jewish alliances during this period, see David Montgomery, *Workers' Control in America: Studies in the History of Work, Technology and Labor Struggles* (Cambridge, Mass., 1979), 100; and John H. M. Laslett, *Labor and the Left: A Study of Socialist and Radical Influences in the American Labor Movement, 1881–1924* (New York, 1970), 109–12.

39. Garber, "The Silk Industry of Paterson," 238; Wood, "History of Labor in the Broad-Silk Industry," 141; "Statement of the General Strike Committee," *Paterson Evening News*, May 29, 1913, 1, 9.

40. *Report of C.I.R.*, 2429, 2468.

41. Ibid., 2454, 2471. Lessig was a local I.W.W. leader. But Thomas Morgan, the local A.F. of L. leader who had negotiated the introduction of four looms with Doherty, explained the process and the strike in almost identical terms. See ibid, 2416–17. On the weaver's grasp of the process, see also Mary Brown Sumner, "Strike of New Jersey Silk Workers," *The Survey* 30 (April 19, 1913): 81.

42. *New York Times*, February 26, 1913, 22. The *New York Times* version of the general strike call is accurate but highly condensed. For the unedited version, see *Solidarity*, March 1, 1913, 4.

43. *Solidarity*, May 3, 1913, 1. On 1902, see Wood, "History of Labor in the Broad-Silk Industry," 187, 188.

44. *New York Times*, February 26, 1913, 22; *New York Call*, March 1, 1913, 1; March 4, 1913, 1; March 6, 1913, 2; and March 19, 1913, 3; *Paterson Evening News*, March 12, 1913, 1, 9. On Bimson's contribution and surrender, see also *Solidarity*, March 15, 1913, 1. Haywood too acknowledged Bimson's help: "It was in the very beginning that we received our first assistance from the police force." *Solidarity*, April 19, 1913, 1. See also *Report of C.I.R.*, 2524.

45. *Report of C.I.R.*, 2573, *Solidarity*, March 15, 4; *Paterson Evening News*, March 3, 1913, 1, 7 and March 5, 1913, 9; *New York Call*, March 5, 1913, 1. Bimson was similarly helpful with some of the English-speaking broad-silk weavers. Most of these skilled weavers joined the Jewish and Italian broad-silk weavers on the first day of the general strike, but some remained at work. By the second week, angered at the attempts of the police to violate the strikers' rights, they were all out.

46. *New York Call*, March 5, 1913, 6.

47. But this is part of another, longer story. The present essay is part of an ongoing book-length study of the 1913 strike. I deal elsewhere with issues only touched on here, such as the demand for the eight-hour day, and the

role of women, of the Socialist Party, of violence, of the A.F. of L., and of Local 152 in the strike.

48. *Paterson Evening News*, March 8, 1913, 1, 9. Haywood was gone by Wednesday, March 12, though of course he later returned to Paterson. See ibid., March 11, 1913, 1, 9 and March 12, 1913, 1.

Prohibition Is a Live Issue in This Campaign

Supported by Republican party bosses David Baird, Edward C. Stokes, and Edmund Wakelee, Newton A. K. Bugbee ran for governor in 1919 with equivocating positions on both Prohibition and the zone-based trolley fare increase proposed by the Republican-controlled Public Service Railroad Corporation. State Democrats parodied Bugbee's fence-straddling, and in the end his argument that opposing Prohibition was tantamount to nullifying the Constitution fell on deaf ears in New Jersey. Democratic Party campaign advertisement in the Newark Evening News, October 27, 1919. Photograph courtesy New Jersey Historical Society.

12

Warren Stickle's article on the election of 1919 in New Jersey raises a broad spectrum of issues, the most obvious being how people vote, why they make their selections, and what the consequences have been. But the 1919 election also reveals much about attitudes toward law and liquor, the fear of dissent, and even the words people use to express dislike.

Government structure, issues, personalities, and culture influence voting trends, just as they help account for the origins and development of political parties. The decision to go to the polls in the first place can be affected by laws making it easy or difficult to exercise the franchise. Suffrage restrictions, the secret ballot, primary elections, and registration requirements have also affected turnout. Once in the polling booth, voters respond variably to issues and personalities based partly on cultural background—the ethnic, religious, and family ties that bind them to certain identities and associations.

In the election of 1919, as they often had before, New Jersey voters bucked the trend in the country at large, and in the Northeast in particular, by voting for the Democratic candidate for governor. To determine what lay behind their choice, political scientists and historians have analyzed voting returns by district, examined party platforms, and surveyed local newspapers and contemporary correspondence. Based on his research, Stickle determined that some factors were unimportant compared to the issues in the campaign, particularly trolley fares, prohibition, and law and order. Prohibition, Stickle has argued, was the one question that clearly divided voters.

But what determined a voter's choice for or against Prohibition? In the country as a whole, advocates of Prohibition generally were rural, old-stock, evangelical Protestants. Prohibition's opponents tended to be urban, often Catholic immigrants. Does this cultural division define New Jersey's experience adequately?

New Jersey in 1919 is an interesting case study of the consequences when issues clash with culture-related political ties. The election was especially significant because it led to a political realignment. Many voters shifted their customary support from one party to another. Historians have commonly identified 1928 or 1932 as the year when the "New Deal Coalition" was formed in a nation as a whole: immigrants, Catholics, laborers, and urban residents increasingly voted for Democratic candidates. The election of 1919 caused the shift to occur earlier in New Jersey than elsewhere and, Stickle has argued, opposition to Prohibition was behind it.

Unpopular and widely ignored, Prohibition not only changed the way people voted; it also affected their attitude toward law. What are the consequences for the legal system when government passes laws large numbers of citizens do not respect? What happened in New Jersey, and elsewhere, after the election of 1919? Can and should a government impose one standard of behavior on everyone?

The position of liquor in American society illustrates well how cultural attitudes change constantly. In the Jacksonian era many Americans saw liquor as the source of all social evils, the cause of poverty, insanity, and crime in weak individuals. By the early twentieth century Americans tended to blame society, or a person's environment, rather than individuals for such problems. Society's imperfections caused poverty, and poverty led to drinking; people drank to escape from the sorrow and inequity of the real world. Today many view such problems as a failure of both society and individuals working in tandem. And solutions also are perceived differently: Prohibition, once called the "noble experiment" and a governmental intervention of unprecedented scale, after all did not work.

Because Prohibition did not end drinking and led to widespread disrespect for the law, scholars have been critical of the movement. Yet the health-conscious 1980s, with its increased awareness of the connection between drinking, illness, and car accidents, made it harder to dismiss the AntiSaloon League as just an illiberal aberration in American history. Like Progressive reformers, Prohibition advocates have been criticized for their intolerance of immigrants and workers, who tended to drink more than other members of society (or at least to do so in such public places as saloons).

The rhetoric of the election of 1919 shows other prejudices as well. The Russian Revolution occurred in 1917, the Red Scare in the United States in 1919. The resultant wave of fear led to the deportation of radical immigrants. In New Jersey charges of Bolshevism, anarchism, treason, and sedition were leveled first against shipyard workers in Camden who rioted against trolley fare increases, and then against the "wet" candidate for governor. These allegations were as much a carryover from the wartime emphasis on 100 percent Americanism, patriotism, and conformity as they were a reflection of widespread interest in Prohibition. What do the terms politicians use to define and denigrate their opponents reveal about the prejudices and fears of their times?

Suggested Readings

Clark, Norman H. *Deliver Us from Evil: An Interpretation of American Prohibition.* New York, 1976.

Furnas, J. C. *The Life and Times of the Late Demon Rum.* New York, 1965.

Lender, Mark E., and James K. Martin. *Drinking in America: A History.* New York, 1982.

Murray, Robert K. *The Red Scare: A Study in National Hysteria, 1919–1920.* Minneapolis, Minn., 1955.

Sinclair, Andrew. *The Era of Excess: A Social History of the Prohibition Movement.* New York, 1964.

Timberlake, James H. *Prohibition and the Progressive Movement, 1900–1920.* Cambridge, Mass., 1963.

◆ ◆ ◆ ◆ ◆ ◆

The Applejack Campaign of 1919: "As 'Wet' as the Atlantic Ocean"

Warren E. Stickle III

Prohibition had a pervasive social, religious, moral, economic and political effect on New Jersey and the nation for more than a decade. Emerging as the dominant national issue of the Twenties, it changed American life in many ways—its social attitudes, its morals, its drinking habits, its religious fervor, its economic institutions, its concept of reform, its attempt at Americanization and its politics. Not least among its effects, Prohibition upset historic Republican roots and fostered the rejuvenation of the New Jersey Democracy. The ability of the Democratic Party to make its anti-Prohibition stance the central and winning issue of the gubernatorial campaign of 1919 constituted the beginning of a political realignment that would continue throughout the Twenties, making the Democratic Party the party of urban America. This critical decade for New Jersey Democracy began

New Jersey History 89 (1971): 5–22. Reprinted by permission of the author.

with what one local newspaper appropriately labelled "The Apple-jack Campaign."[1]

After 1916 the Wilsonian coalition was in decline throughout New Jersey and the nation, marking a period of transition and defeat for the Democratic Party. In the Garden State, Republicans swept the presidential, gubernatorial, and senatorial campaigns of 1916, won both the long and short term senatorial posts in 1918, and controlled the congressional and legislative delegations throughout this period. With the armistice of 1918, a new era arrived—an era of adjustment and change, of conflict and tragedy for New Jersey and the nation. Racial disturbances rocked twenty-five municipalities throughout the nation. Labor unrest reached its peak with the Seattle general strike, the Boston police strike, and major strikes in the steel and coal industries. A series of bombings in the spring of 1919, creating fear of terrorism and Bolshevism, ignited the Red Scare. The League of Nations' crisis and the battle for ratification fragmented much of the national spirit and divided the nation. The continuation of war-time Prohibition and the implementation of the Volstead Act frustrated America's thirst, alienating thousands of immigrants and Newer Americans. A spiraling inflation gripped New Jersey and the nation as prices rose as much as 105 per cent above 1914 levels.[2] "The mythical goose that lays golden eggs," quipped the *Paterson Evening News* on October 28, 1919, "has nothing on the hen which lays ordinary ones, at present prices." The events of 1919 led to a growing disenchantment with Wilsonian Democracy at home and abroad, and a national resurgence of Republicanism, a prelude to "normalcy." The Republican Party won almost all elections north of the Mason-Dixon line and west of the Mississippi, making a shambles of the Wilsonian coalition of 1916.[3] Only in the Garden State was the Democratic Party successful, and there only because the local party had put together a multi-factional, urban, "wet" coalition of Newer Americans on the issue of opposition to prohibition.

As each political party, reflecting the unrest and turbulence of the times, struggled for self-definition, the party primaries took on added significance. The Republican Party witnessed a four-way battle for the gubernatorial nomination. William N. Runyon, President of the Senate, became acting Governor with the election of Governor Walter Edge to the United States Senate in 1918. A lawyer, municipal judge and State Senator from Union county, he was essentially a conservative, "dry" politician who had supported Taft in 1912. Tracing his ancestry back to the French-

Huguenot settlements in 1668, he represented Protestant old-stock America. His ultra-dry position garnered the support of the Anti-Saloon League in the primary of 1919.[4]

At the time of Runyon's elevation to the governorship, Newton A. K. Bugbee of Trenton was already campaigning for the nomination. A businessman, banker, and political moderate, Bugbee was well known to New Jersey Republicans because of his service as Chairman of the powerful Republican State Committee from 1913 to 1919 and State Comptroller from 1917 to 1919. He received the support of such local GOP bosses and organizations as David Baird of Camden county, the Edge machine of Atlantic county and former Governor Edward C. Stokes, who had replaced Bugbee as GOP State Chairman in 1919.[5] The support of the local party machinery was Bugbee's greatest asset in the primary battle.

The continuation of war-time Prohibition and the comparative "dryness" of Bugbee and Runyon brought a "wet" candidate into the primary struggle. A lawyer, district court judge, and prosecutor for the Pleas Court of Essex county, Thomas L. Raymond enjoyed much support in Newark and throughout Essex county because of his service as mayor and later city commissioner in charge of streets and public improvements in Newark. Although he was relatively unknown outside of northeastern New Jersey, his frank "wet" appeal attracted much support during the primary race.[6]

The fourth Republican candidate for governor, Warren C. King of Middlesex, was relatively unknown throughout the state and received no support from the state organization even in his own county. Although he had successfully organized the Manufacturers' Council of New Jersey, King's political appeal was severely limited. Despite large expenditures and a vigorous campaign, he polled less than five per cent of the GOP primary vote and had no impact on its outcome.[7]

While Runyon, Bugbee, Raymond, and King fought for the Republican nomination, a struggle for the leadership of the Democratic Party was also taking place in the Garden State. A businessman, bank president, State Comptroller from 1911 to 1917, and State Senator from Hudson county, Edward I. Edwards received the support of Frank Hague's Hudson county machine, and of fourteen other county leaders. Although personally "dry," Edwards opposed Prohibition. One of his original supporters was Essex county's Democratic boss James Nugent. It appeared at first that Hague and Nugent had agreed upon the distribution of patronage if Edwards was victorious. But as Nugent's influence in the Edwards campaign declined, the Essex leader repudiated his former support of Edwards and declared his own candidacy, claiming that he was going to give the people a choice on Prohibition because Edwards was only "moist." The candidacy of James Nugent, an Irish-Catholic lawyer, who had served as Chairman of the Democratic State Committee (1907–1912), and boss of Essex county, resulted in a confrontation with Frank Hague for control of the Democratic Party in the Garden State, a struggle that would determine party leadership for the next thirty years.

The third Democratic candidate for governor was a hardy perennial, Frank M. McDermit. An Irish-Catholic lawyer from Newark, he had lost an Assembly race in 1886, a State Senate race in 1908, and three campaigns for United States Senator in 1910, 1912, and 1918. A supporter of Henry George's single tax and an advocate of federal ownership of public utilities, McDermit posed no threat to the Edwards-Nugent power struggle.[8]

Although Prohibition was the dominant issue in 1919, a conflict over trolley fares helped shape the campaign and set its tone. On August 1, 1919, the Republican-controlled Public Utility Board of Commissioners approved the nation's first trolley zoning fare system, which had been devised by the Public Service Railroad Corporation. Instead of paying a seven-cent flat fare and one cent for a transfer, riders under the new system would pay three cents for the first mile, two cents for each additional mile, and would have no transfer privileges. The purpose of zoning was to achieve a more equitable fare—the farther one traveled, the higher the cost.[9] However, the zoning fare plan quickly became a political football.

Before the new system went into effect on Sunday, September 14, the GOP gubernatorial candidates had voiced their disenchantment with Public Service and the new fares. Arguing for a "just fare," Bugbee suggested that the people "are not getting a square deal," but he offered no immediate solution. Raymond denounced the new system as "an unreasonable charge" and advocated postponement of its adoption. Governor Runyon, however, refused to act without a full investigation; consequently no action was taken before the zoning fare system was implemented.[10]

Edwards vigorously attacked the Utility Board for its "little regard for the interests of the people." Since Essex and Hudson counties, with one-half New Jersey's population, had no representation on the Board, he called for a Board elected according to districts. On the eve of the system's implementation, he vigorously attacked the Public Service Company and the zoning system, calling the latter "outrageous and nothing short of a gigantic swindle." In a full-page advertisement in sixty newspapers, Edwards asserted that the attitude of Public Service was: "The Public be Damned—We want the money." The President of Public Service labelled Edwards "mendacious, vicious, and debasing," a "vulgar demagogue," an "incendiary anarchist," and "Bolshevist agitator." Many began to respect Edwards for the enemies he was making.[11]

Of all the major candidates for governor, James Nugent contributed least to the zoning fare debate. The *Jersey Journal* noted on September 5, that Nugent was reluctant "to adopt the prevailing fashion and jump on the Public Utility Commission." As Nugent continued sidestepping the fare issue, Edwards' supporters pointed out that the Essex Democrat had previously acted as a counselor for Public Service and held shares of stock in the company. "I'll hang Jim Nugent with the Public Service before we get through this campaign," shouted Mayor Charles Gillen of Newark, an Edwards supporter.[12] Only on primary day did Nugent finally speak out against the zoning fare system.

The Garden State was rudely shocked by civil disorders that accompanied the implementation of the zoning fare system, especially in Camden. On the first working day of the new system, shipyard workers in Camden smashed doors and windows and refused to pay their fares. The next day, several trolleys were wrecked, and attempts were made to burn bridges and grease rails. Obstacles blocked the tracks and shots were fired at trolleys. When motormen and conductors refused to take their trolleys out, service was dispensed. The zoning fare system "has resolved itself into a question of law and order," declared Mayor Charles Ellis of Camden. "Anarchy in a mild form has raised its head in Camden and must be crushed . . . Bolshevism will not be tolerated." Finally, militia reserves were called to the scene on September 19 to preserve order and protect property. The shipyard workers responded with a trolley boycott, adopting a slogan of "Five cent fare or walk." And walk they did. The boycott was partially successful as trolleys carried few or no passengers, and daily receipts dropped from an average of $50 to $100 per car, to only $2 or $3.[13]

The Republican candidates reacted strongly to the uproar in this traditionally Republican bailiwick. Bugbee supported the demands of Mayor Ellis and other Camden citizens for a flat rate of five cents within Camden and one cent per mile beyond the city limits. Raymond charged that Adjutant-General Gilkyson, Bugbee's campaign manager, had "called out the militia to protect the Public Service in Camden." Governor Runyon ordered the Utility Board to show cause why it should not be removed from office for neglect of duty and misconduct of office. He claimed, furthermore, that the Adjutant-General had dispatched the militia without requesting the governor's permission, and tried to link Bugbee with Public Service.

It is exceedingly difficult to draw any measurable conclusions as to who benefited from the zoning fare crisis. Although Bugbee polled 62.4 per cent of the vote in Camden, the support of the Baird machine appears to have been more significant than the trolley issue. Since Edwards' margin of victory in Camden was less than 400 votes, the trolley issue seems not to have been decisive. The reaction to the zoning fare system was considerably less outside of Camden and elsewhere played only a relatively minor role in the election.[14] Clearly other issues such as Prohibition and control of local party machinery determined the outcome of both primaries.

Prohibition ultimately became the most significant issue in 1919. While all the Democratic candidates were "wet," the Republican party found itself divided over Prohibition. Contending that "Prohibition is not a state issue," Governor Runyon declared that "the problem is one not of prohibition or non-prohibition, but rather respect for the fundamental law of the land." As the "dry" champion, he received the political and financial support of the Anti-Saloon League. Not only did the League support the Governor, but it threatened to run a separate candidate, Filmore Condit, should either Bugbee or Raymond win the primary.[15]

While Runyon sought to collect the "dry" vote, Raymond made a conscientious effort to cultivate the "wet" vote. Devoting his campaign to upholding "the personal liberty of the American people," he stressed New Jersey's equal and concurrent power with Congress and pledged himself to nullify a search law within the Garden State and to start proceedings to repeal the Eighteenth Amendment. Although he denounced "lawlessness in any form," the former Newark mayor was the only Republican candidate to oppose Prohibition.[16]

In contrast to the extremes of Raymond and Runyon, Bugbee tried to take a middle position. Since he was not known as a Prohibitionist and was believed to be personally "wet," his candidacy drew the support of known "wets" such as State Senator Charles O. Pilgrim of Essex and former Senator Emerson Richards of Atlantic county. By repudiating the platform of the State League of Republican Clubs which had called for a referendum on Prohibition, the Trentonian bypassed the fears of both "wet" and "dry" groups. Announcing that the "liquor question is already settled," he admonished the people to "stop chasing rainbows" and "get down to the realities of life" by cooperating "in the enforcement of the law." "I would as soon dishonor the flag or demolish the public school system," declared Bugbee, "as I would violate the Constitution of the United States." Accepting the enforcement of Prohibition as inevitable, Bugbee sought to neutralize it as a political issue. "Among Bugbee's supporters," declared the *Jersey Journal* on September 12, "are a lot of Republicans who prefer to pussyfoot on the liquor question." Bugbee's assumption of a middle position made him the candidate best able to unite the various factions of the Republican Party.[17]

"All of the Democratic candidates for the gubernatorial nomination are 'wet,'" declared the *Trenton Evening Times*. "Each is endeavoring to have it appear that he is the 'wettest' of the crowd." But James Nugent's vigorous, outspoken attack on Prohibition clearly identified him as the "wettest" candidate in either party: the *raison d'etre* of his candidacy was opposition to Prohibition. He carried this message to all sections of the state, bitterly attacking the Anti-Saloon League as "pseudo-reformers" who by "chicanery and deceit, by coercion and intimidation" wanted "to rule or ruin" America. "This election will decide," declared Nugent at a Sea Girt rally, "whether we shall lower the Stars and Stripes and replace 'Old Glory' with the banner of the arrogant Anti-Saloon League." Adopting a position similar to that of Raymond, Nugent claimed that the Eighteenth Amendment infringed on constitutional rights and denounced it as "a monstrosity of fanaticism and fundamental lawlessness." He promised to utilize "all the resources of our sovereign State to defeat Prohibition," and personally to take the Eighteenth Amendment to the Supreme Court and act as counselor for the people of New Jersey. "Prohibition will not come in this State," Nugent declared, "if we have the men in office to stand up against it." "The paramount issue of this campaign is the question of Prohibition," Nugent reminded the voters. "Everyone knows this. I made Prohibition the issue in this state. . . ." And, indeed, he had.[18]

Although every Nugent speech was devoted solely to his opposition to Prohibition, Edward I. Edwards was not to be outdone. He frequently reminded voters that he had cast one of the nine votes against ratification of the Eighteenth Amendment in the

State Senate. He stressed the concurrent powers of the sovereign state and promised to veto any legislation enforcing Prohibition within the Garden State. "If you do not believe that I will go farther than James R. Nugent in the matter of Prohibition," declared Edwards repeatedly, "and do it in an intelligent, legal way, do not vote for me—vote for Nugent." By the end of the primary campaign, Edwards' position had become so "wet" that the *Jersey Journal* suggested he was trying "to 'out-Nugent Nugent' in promises" on Prohibition.[19]

On primary day the voters clarified "the most puzzling race since the establishment of the primary system." The returns showed that Bugbee had won a narrow victory, polling 64,245 votes to 57,876 for Runyon, a slim margin of only 6,369. Raymond finished third with 39,373 votes and King received but 7,276 votes. In this four-way race, Bugbee polled only 38.07 per cent of the GOP vote compared to 34.23 for Runyon, 23.39 for Raymond and only 4.31 for King.[20]

Bugbee's moderate policies and his ability to straddle the Prohibition issue attracted many voters. He drew support from both "wets" and "drys" and ran especially well in his native South Jersey. Most significantly, he ran best where he had the support of the local organization, essentially in Camden, Atlantic and Mercer counties. With the backing of Pierre P. Garven's organization, Bugbee was also able to carry Hudson county. In his native Trenton, he received a spectacular 71.8 per cent of the vote and polled more than 62.0 per cent in Camden. But in other areas of the Garden State, Bugbee fared poorly. He ran a poor third in Newark, and other cities like Elizabeth and Paterson revealed a disappointing vote. He polled less than 14 per cent of the vote in populous Essex county. Clearly, the northeastern, urban, polyglot areas did not fall to the Trenton Republican.

Governor Runyon piled up a huge vote in his native Union county, especially in Elizabeth, and won ten of twenty-one counties. He ran well in the central and northwestern "dry" rural counties, where the endorsement of the Anti-Saloon League drew great support to his candidacy. A steady rain which fell throughout election day perhaps curtailed an even larger rural vote for Runyon, particularly in southern New Jersey.

Thomas Raymond swept his native city of Newark and polled 51 per cent of the vote in Essex county. Significantly, his Essex county vote represented 40 per cent of his state-wide total, thus exhibiting the limited appeal of his candidacy in other areas of the state. However, he did carry the city of Passaic and ran well in Paterson; he also garnered scattered "wet" support in Camden, Trenton and other cities.

No patterns emerged from the various sectors of the urban community. In the cities of 50,000 population or more, Newer Americans comprised at least 60 per cent of the population in sixty-five wards.[21] Of these, Bugbee carried 31, Runyon and Raymond 17 each. Each candidate carried the Newer American wards where he was well known and where he had organizational support. The Republican primary returns thus revealed the importance of Prohibition and the local party machinery.

The fundamental problem confronting the Republican party thus was the task of uniting all factions behind the Bugbee candidacy. How would the nominee run in the northeastern cities and the Newer American wards? Could the local organizations marshal the "wet" voters behind the "dry" candidate? Or would the Raymond vote defect to the Democrats? These questions confronted the Trenton Republican as he turned to face the Democratic primary victor in the general election.

The decisive factor in the Democratic primary was Edwards' ability to garner support from the local Democratic Party machinery throughout the Garden State. In early July most of New Jersey's twenty-one Democratic county chairmen pledged their support to the Hudson Democrat. But Edwards' greatest asset was Frank Hague's political machine in Hudson county. "We know how to get majorities," shouted Hague. "We've got the organization to do it."[22] On primary day, Hague made good his boast.

The primary returns revealed that Edwards had won a clear victory, polling 56,261 votes to 43,612 for Nugent, a margin of 12,649; McDermit gathered only 5,095 votes. Edwards' percentage of the vote reached 53.6, compared to 41.6 for Nugent and 4.8 for McDermit. Edwards piled up a huge majority in Hudson and carried fifteen counties. In Jersey City, the vote ran 9 to 1 for Edwards and individual districts showed spectacular results. The sixth district of Ward 2 (Hague's Horseshoe district) cast 300 votes for Edwards, 1 for Nugent; the seventh district was 178–0, the eighth ran 225–2, and the ninth was 190–1. Districts in wards one, three, four, five, ten and eleven showed similar results. Hague's majority in Hudson neutralized Nugent's gains in Essex, Union, Passaic and Mercer counties and carried Edwards to victory. Clearly, Hague emerged "from the Democratic primaries as the new Democratic State leader."[23] Proclaiming Hague "a genius in his field," the *Newark Evening News* on September 24, called him "a gentleman who promises to claim a larger share of public attention in the future than heretofore." Within six weeks, Hague provided new evidence to support these predictions.

Nugent's defeat has clouded the source and significance of his vote in the Democratic primary. Campaigning vigorously on the sole issue of Prohibition, the Essex boss ran well in the urban "wet" areas of the state, sweeping Newark, Trenton, Paterson and Elizabeth, and consequently carrying Essex, Mercer, Passaic and Union counties. He clobbered Edwards by a 6–1 margin in his native Newark and polled 79.9 per cent of the vote in Essex county. But where in the cities did Nugent garner his support? He swept all eight Newer American wards in Trenton, all eleven in Newark, both in Irvington, seven of nine in Elizabeth and nine of ten in Paterson. Only in Passaic did Edwards carry all three Newer American wards. He won only six of forty-three Newer American Wards outside of Hudson. Obviously, Nugent had put together an urban coalition of Newer Americans outside of Hudson county on his anti-Prohibition issue. But the urban, "wet" Newer American coalition was not numerous enough to overcome the efficiency of the Hague machine. With Nugent's defeat, his supporters were left with no alternatives except to support Edwards or sit out the election. They chose the former because of his Nugent-like opposition to Prohibition.

After the primaries, each party held its state convention and drafted a platform amenable to the nominee.[24] On the utility problem, the Democratic Party denounced the "inequity and unfairness . . . [of the] miserable and botched zone system." It demanded the ousting of the existing Utility Board, the election of a new Board, and the restoration of a five-cent flat rate. The Republicans proposed a fair, flat rate, based on an impartial valuation of the properties of the utility company, so that rates could be based on the actual money invested in such properties. Before the platform differences could have much impact on the campaign, however, the trolley crisis subsided. After two weeks of consultations between the Public Service Company and the Utility Board, a compromise solution was found. Instead of the original zone fare system of 3 cents for the first mile, 2 cents for each additional mile, and no transfer, the substitute plan called for 5 cents for the first two miles, 1 cent for each additional mile and 1 cent for a transfer. Although the zoning plan was only modified and the Utility Board remained in office, the compromise diluted the issue; its impact on the campaign was negligible.

On the fundamental issue of Prohibition, the GOP platform

declared that the Eighteenth Amendment had been ratified by more than the necessary two-thirds of the states and would become the law of the land on January 16, 1920. The party declared that "ratification can no longer be considered as necessary or as a political issue in this or any state," and pledged itself to uphold the Constitution and enforce the laws of the land. The Anti-Saloon League came out for Bugbee, and Filmore Condit of Essex Fells, as he withdrew from the race, announced that "We Anti-Saloon men can get more from the Republicans than we can from the Democrats." Quickly the Republican Party became associated with the "dry" issue and defense of law and order. Conversely, the Democratic Party proclaimed its decisive opposition to Prohibition. Announcing that "Prohibition has no proper place in the fundamental law of the nation," the party pledged itself "to oppose by all lawful means the ratification or enforcement" of Prohibition, and "to lead the movement which will eventually result in its repeal." Stressing "the concurrent powers granted to the states by that amendment," Democrats pledged that the "liberty of the individual citizen in New Jersey will be protected by legislation."[25] On the leading issues of the day, party lines had been drawn, and the five-week battle for "applejack" had begun.

While Edwards adopted a Nugent-like stand on Prohibition, Bugbee struggled to find a winning issue. Attacking "Frank Hague and his raiders from Hudson county," the Trentonian raised the issue of bossism, but Edwards' defeat of Boss Nugent and the conspicuous GOP bosses in southern New Jersey undermined Bugbee's charges.[26] Still groping for an issue, Bugbee desperately turned to national problems, contending that the election of Edwards would be viewed as an endorsement of Wilson's foreign and domestic policies. The attempt to stress national issues fell flat, as Prohibition dominated the campaign. "The last thing that the voters were thinking of," declared the *Newark Sunday Call* on November 9, "was the League of Nations or the effect of the election on next year's campaign."

As the deck of issues was shuffled and reshuffled, one card turned up continually—Prohibition. Although Bugbee contended that Prohibition was not an issue and pledged himself to support and defend the Constitution, he drank a glass of beer in Clifton to prove that he was personally "wet," although politically "dry."[27] Conversely, Edwards was personally "dry," but politically "wet." In mid-October he told one audience that "I am from Hudson County and I am as 'wet' as the Atlantic Ocean."

On October 18, in Perth Amboy, Edwards allegedly stated that if he was elected governor, he would make New Jersey "as 'wet' as the Atlantic Ocean."[28] He defended state's rights and called for nullification of the Constitution.

Bugbee saw in this the issue he had sought; he quickly seized the banner of law and order and carried it throughout the remainder of the campaign. Edwards was not just "wet"; now he was a Bolshevik, an anarchist, guilty of treason and sedition. "The overshadowing, overwhelming question we Jerseymen are now called upon to decide," declared Bugbee in Camden on October 20, "is whether we are to be loyalists or nullificationists." Republican spokesmen compared Edwards to John C. Calhoun and "the South Carolina nullifiers of old." The next day the Trentonian suggested that "if it had not been for the fact that the Democrats have injected an issue into the campaign that has no place there, there would be no campaign."[29] While Bugbee attacked Edwards for "preaching treason and sedition" at a Singer plant rally in Elizabeth, one worker shouted: "To hell with him! He is the man who would take away our beer." Frequently, Bugbee and GOP speakers linked anarchy, treason, sedition, secession, nullification, and Bolshevism to Edwards' opposition to Prohibition.

The issue of Prohibition reached a climax when the Volstead Act was passed by a Republican-controlled Congress over Wilson's veto one week before Garden Staters went to the polls. New Jersey as well as the nation was officially "dry." Ballantine and Schlitz shifted their advertisements from beer to ginger ale. One saloon-keeper who remained open observed: "It needed but a few flowers to make it a first class funeral."[30] The immediacy of Prohibition became acutely apparent to all.

In the last week of the campaign Edwards intensified his battle for "the preservation of personal liberty by all lawful means at our disposal." The Association Opposed to National Prohibition told Garden State voters: "Don't be fooled!! . . . New Jersey Need Not Concur." Bugbee, too, vigorously stepped up the tempo of his campaign. Discussing the "one overwhelming, overshadowing issue in this campaign," the Trentonian shouted that "the Democratic platform is a lie. The pledge of the Democratic candidate for governor is a lie." "Tomorrow New Jersey will vote on one question and one only. My opponent has raised only one issue in this campaign," declared Bugbee on election eve. "If he [Edwards] should be elected, . . . it will mean that the majority of the people of New Jersey desire the nullification of the Constitution." Later that same evening in Morristown, he concluded his campaign by declaring: "This is the issue: Loyalty as against nullification. Law and order against lawlessness. Patriotism as against sedition. You are at the crossroads tonight. Tomorrow you must take one of the two roads." The campaign had ended.[31] At the crossroads there was but one sign—"Applejack"—and without hesitation, Garden Staters took that path.

Seldom in the history of this or any state has a political campaign narrowed down to one issue. But in the "Applejack campaign," the issue had been clearly drawn by both parties and their spellbinders. As far as the man in the street was concerned, "liquor," declared the *Camden Post-Telegram* on November 4, "is the really big question." If ever a referendum was held on Prohibition (prior to 1932), it was the New Jersey gubernatorial campaign of 1919.

The "Applejack campaign" polarized Garden State politics as never before. Edwards swept the large cities, carrying Jersey City, Newark, Trenton, and Elizabeth. Republican Gibraltars were shocked as the "wet" vote went solidly to the Hudson Democrat. The Raymond vote in the primary shifted to Edwards, especially in Newark and Trenton. In Newark Bugbee ran behind the combined Republican primary vote in five wards largely dominated by Italians and German-Americans; in some wards, the dropoff was nearly 30 per cent. In Trenton, Bugbee ran behind the combined GOP primary vote in 39 of 71 districts, mostly Newer American areas. Without doubt a silent protest had occurred in 1919, and Newer Americans in the large urban centers began a shift to the Democratic Party.

The candidates and the press agreed that Prohibition had dealt the Republican Party a severe setback. "If the election of Edwards . . . means anything," declared the *Paterson Evening News*, "it indicates that the sentiment in this state is decidedly wet." In Newark, it was the same story. "The consensus of opinion is that Edwards' strong anti-Prohibition stand was unconquerable," noted the *Newark Star Eagle*. The voters had "but one purpose," declared the *Newark Sunday Call* on November 9, "to register their emphatic disapproval of Prohibition." The press throughout the state echoed the sentiment that the issue was the question of "wet" or "dry."[32]

The candidates agreed with the press. "I feel this election indicated that New Jersey is very 'wet,'" declared Newton A. K. Bugbee. "The ballots were not cast along the line of political partisanship. It was a matter of 'wet' and 'dry.'" "I construe my election," Edwards observed, "as an indication of the people of this state concerning national Prohibition."[33]

To the political parties, the candidates, the press, and the man in the street, the battle for "applejack" was real. Immediately after Edwards' victory, several hundred immigrants and Newer Americans started out on a tour of Paterson, looking for "applejack," but found that they could not buy a drink. Returning home they charged that things would be different after Edwards was inaugurated.[34] It would be a long wait for a legal drink but in 1919, "New Jersey," declared a national magazine, "is decidedly wet."[35]

Notes

1. *Elizabeth Daily Journal*, Nov. 4, 1919.

2. William E. Leuchtenburg, *The Perils of Prosperity, 1914–1982* (Chicago, 1958), 66–77; Frederick Lewis Allen, *Only Yesterday* (New York, 1981), 1–72; David A. Shannon, *Between the Wars: America 1919–1941* (Boston, 1965), 1–30; Robert K. Murray, *Red Scare: A Study of National Hysteria, 1919–1920* (New York, 1955); Andrew Sinclair, *Era of Excess: A Social History of the Prohibition Movement* (New York, 1962).

3. David Burner, *The Politics of Provincialism: The Democratic Party in Transition, 1918–1932* (New York, 1968), 28–74.

4. *Newark Star Eagle*, Sept. 20, 1919.

5. *Newark Star Eagle*, Sept. 18, 1919.

6. *Elizabeth Daily Journal*, Sept. 20, 1919.

7. *Elizabeth Daily Journal*, Sept. 20, 1919.

8. *Jersey Journal*, Sept. 12–20, 1919; *Elizabeth Daily Journal*, Sept. 12–20, 1919; *Newark Star Eagle*, Sept. 12–20, 1919.

9. *Paterson Evening News*, Aug. 1, 1919.

10. *Trenton Evening Times*, Sept. 11, 1919; *Newark Star Eagle*, Aug. 29, 1919.

11. *Trenton Evening Times*, July 25, 1919; *Jersey Journal*, Sept. 13–20, 1919.

12. *Newark Star Eagle*, Aug. 26, 1919.

13. *Camden Post-Telegram*, Sept. 15–30, 1919.

14. *Camden Post-Telegram*, Nov. 1–10, 1919.

15. *Newark Sunday Call*, Aug. 10, 1919.

16. *Newark Star Eagle*, Aug. 8, 1919.

17. *Trenton Evening Times*, July 7, 14, 17, 1919; *Newark Sunday Call*, Aug. 17, 31, 1919.

18. *Trenton Evening Times*, July 7, 18, 28, Aug. 15, 1919; *Newark Star Eagle*, Sept. 13, 19, 1919; *Newark Sunday Call*, Aug. 10, 1919.

19. *Jersey Journal*, Sept. 19, 1919; *Elizabeth Daily Journal*, Sept. 20, 1919.

20. All general election returns and final county primary returns were found in the *Legislative Manual of the State of New Jersey, 1920* (Trenton, 1920). City and ward returns for the primary were found in the local newspapers since no state records exist. The quotation is from the *Newark Star Eagle*, Sept. 22, 1919.

21. Newer Americans are defined as the foreign born and those of foreign-born or mixed parentage. Statistics are from the fourteenth and fifteenth censuses of the United States.

22. *Newark Star Eagle*, Aug. 26, 1919.

23. *Jersey Journal*, Sept. 24, 1919. "It was at bottom a factional fight [between Hague and Nugent] by which the public profited slightly." *Nation*, CIX (Oct. 4, 1919), 451. See also Dayton D. McKean, *The Boss: The Hague Machine in Action* (Boston, 1940), 46–51.

24. The platforms may be found in the *Legislative Manual of the State of New Jersey, 1920* (Trenton, 1920), 244–256.

25. *Trenton Evening Times*, Sept. 30, Oct. 1, 1919.

26. *Camden Post-Telegram*, Oct. 16, 1919.

27. The *Newark Sunday Call* correctly suggested that "the voters are not interested in the private habit of candidates, but only in what may be expected of them if elected." Oct. 19, 1919.

28. *Paterson Morning Call*, Oct. 27, 1919. After the election Edwards confessed: "I did not say I would use legal means to make New Jersey as 'wet' as the Atlantic Ocean. I was misquoted. What I said was I would use legal power to prevent the enforcement of the Prohibition amendment. That I have always said." *Trenton Evening Times*, Nov. 7, 1919. But during the last three weeks of the campaign Edwards made no effort to repudiate the statement. As far as the populace was concerned, Edwards was going to make the state "as 'wet' as the Atlantic Ocean."

29. *Newark Star Eagle*, Oct. 21, 1919.

30. *Newark Evening News*, Oct. 31, 1919.

31. The campaign dialogue can be found in all large city newspapers.

32. *Paterson Evening News*, Nov. 5, 1919; *Newark Star Eagle*, Nov. 5, 1919. Among other newspapers which saw Prohibition as the decisive factor were the *Trenton State Gazette*, Nov. 5, 1919, the *Trenton Evening Times*, Nov. 5, 1919, and the *Camden Post-Telegram*, Nov. 13, 1919.

33. *Paterson Evening News*, Nov. 5, 1919; *Literary Digest*, LXIII (Nov. 22, 1919), 18.

34. *Paterson Evening News*, Nov. 6, 1919.

35. *Review of Reviews*, LX (Nov., 1919), 472.

The first woman to be elected to the United States Congress from east of the Mississippi, Mary Norton (center) was joined by (from left) Jeannett Rankin (R.-Montana), Frances P. Bolton (R.-Ohio), Margaret Chase Smith (R.-Maine), and Edith Nourse Rogers (R.-Massachusetts) during her twenty-five years there. Photograph courtesy Special Collections, Rutgers University Libraries, New Brunswick, New Jersey.

13

Marie Mullaney's article on Rebecca Buffum Spring dealt, in part, with the origins of the women's movement in nineteenth-century America. The suffragettes who pushed for the vote developed two parallel lines of argument. Some justified voting as a right, a recognition of women's equality; others maintained that it would raise politics to a higher level because women were more moral than men. Gary Mitchell's analysis of the career of politician Mary Norton raises questions about what happened to women in the United States after the Nineteenth Amendment, which granted women the right to vote, was ratified in 1920. First, to what extent did women vote and hold office? Second, did women's political participation change the character of politics? Third, how did the women's suffrage movement position itself in the conflict between women's assertions of equality and the view that women had special character, roles, and needs?

Certainly women had great expectations once the right to vote was won. Suffrage proponents believed that women would no longer just "stay at home," that they would participate in politics as "free and equal citizens." They anticipated the creation of female political organizations, the nomination of women candidates for office, the passage of legislation to benefit members of their sex, all supported by the turnout of a large group of new voters acting as a block. In fact, none of these things came to pass. By the mid-1920s women's political power had actually declined, not to be revived until the mid-1960s. Even then equal political participation was still an ideal, not a reality.

Several factors help to explain this outcome. First, the fight for suffrage gave women a false sense of their shared concerns. Women, like men, were divided by race, religion, ethnic background, and class. When they voted, these attributes were as important as gender. In addition, women frequently acquiesced to long-standing cultural notions that their role was in the home—and sometimes to their husbands' beliefs that women should not vote. Women showed an inclination to follow the advice of the men in their families. In other words, the idea that women would vote as a bloc along gender lines was a myth, and as a result male politicians soon showed less willingness to defer to women, to nominate them for office, or to support their causes.

Women were also initially hesitant to run for office, in part because they lacked experience and in part because men deliberately discouraged them. Practically, women found it hard to break into politics; cultural constraints made it harder still. As a result, the first women who held office were widows who took over their husbands' terms. Seldom did they run for re-election on their own merits. Women who achieved prominence during the New Deal usually owed their positions to personal ties with either Roosevelt or his wife Eleanor. Not until the mid-1970s did women begin to run for political office on their own in significant numbers. Not until 1992 did they win election in noticeable numbers, and even then New Jersey had only one congresswoman; the state stood forty-first in the nation in the number of women state legislators. Not until 1993 did New Jersey elect its first woman governor.

Once women achieved office, they were not particularly successful in obtaining either equal rights or special programs for members of their sex. In part, they lacked the numerical strength necessary to pass such legislation. Old divisions also inhibited them: women policymakers could not agree on what course of action to follow (whether, for example, to form their own political party or work through the existing ones) or on their objectives (an equal rights amendment or shorter working hours). The old contradictions were perpetuated in a division between so-called "social feminists" and "hard-core feminists."

How does Mary Norton, the first woman elected to the House of Representatives from the Democratic party, fit into this picture of the role of women in American politics after suffrage? She successfully ran under her own steam and was re-elected many times. Yet, as William H. Chafe pointed out in *The American Woman* (1972), Norton ran with the support of Frank Hague, who wanted the "honor" of sending the first woman Democrat to the House. Hague picked a woman as well because he believed he would be able to control her; she would never, he thought, be his rival. Did Mary Norton, for all of her success, escape the limits that American politics had historically placed on women?

What were some of the reactions and comments that Norton's presence in Congress provoked from other congressmen, and what do these reactions indicate about cultural ideas and expectations?

Consider another question. How did Norton see herself? What role did she think she should play? Mitchell quoted her to have stated, "It's up to women to stand for each other." What did she mean by this? During her early career in Congress Norton supported three specific issues—the vote for women who lived in the District of

Columbia, their right to serve on juries under equal terms with men, and the right of all women to equal treatment under the immigration laws. What do these reforms reveal about Norton's outlook?

One final broader question arises. When Americans elect politicians, who do they expect them to represent? Should a woman represent all of her constituents, or does she have a special obligation to members of her gender? And should politicians vote according to their consciences or their constituents' demands?

Suggested Readings

Burstyn, Joan N., ed. *Past and Promise: Lives of New Jersey Women.* Metuchen, N.J., 1990.

Carroll, Susan J. *Women as Candidates in American Politics.* Bloomington, Ind., 1985.

Chafe, William H. *The American Woman: Her Changing Social, Economic and Political Roles, 1920-1970.* New York, 1972.

Degler, Carl N. *At Odds: Women and the Family in America from the Revolution to the Present.* New York, 1980.

Evans, Sara. *Born to Liberty: A History of Women in America.* New York, 1989.

Gordon, Felice. "After Winning: The New Jersey Suffragists in the Political Parties, 1920-30." *NJH* 101 (1983): 13-25.

_____ . *After Winning: The Legacy of the New Jersey Suffragists, 1920-1947.* New Brunswick, N.J., 1986.

Hartmann, Susan M. *From Margin to Mainstream: American Women and Politics since 1960.* Philadelphia, 1989.

Mandel, Ruth B. *In the Running: The New Woman Candidate.* New Haven, Conn., 1981.

O'Neill, William. *Everyone Was Brave: A History of Feminism in America.* Chicago, 1969.

Werner, Emmy W. "Women in Congress: 1917-1964." *Western Political Quarterly* 19 (1966): 16-30.

◆ ◆ ◆ ◆ ◆ ◆

Women Standing for Women: The Early Political Career of Mary T. Norton

Gary Mitchell

We have had Congresswomen for nearly two decades, and as Congresswomen they have been pretty good Congressmen, but the time has come for them to remember that they do represent women in a rather special way. Women are interested in them, read what they say and try to keep posted on what they do, and do have a sense of personal regard for them unshared by their brothers save in individual instances. .

—Ellis Meredith[1]

I think that women should first of all be interested in other women, interested in other women's projects, their dreams, and their ambitions. It's up to women to stand for each other.
—Mary T. Norton[2]

Throughout her life, in social welfare work and in politics, Mary Norton sought to secure victories for women. From her entry into Congress in 1925, until she left in 1950, Norton represented women—intending to do so from the start—in that special way that Ellis Meredith cited. This she did in addition to representing her Jersey City constituency. Norton's many careers and achievements would require voluminous consideration. It has been said that she is probably "the most important woman politician this country has ever known." Her career, to some, "reads like a feminine Horatio Alger success yarn," a description accurate in its dramatic impulse but which misses the politics of sisterhood which guided her rising movement.[3] This article is necessarily confined to an examination of a single dimension of her political work and covers but one segment of her middle life. The article focuses on her entry into politics and her early

New Jersey History 96 (1978): 27-42. Reprinted by permission of the author.

Congressional career as they each in turn affected, and were affected by, women and the legacy of sisterhood left in the wake of the suffragist's victory in 1920.

When Mary Norton was elected to Congress in 1924 she became the first woman Representative of the Democratic Party, and the first woman to be elected to the House from east of the Mississippi. She served continuously till 1950 when she retired from Congress, but not yet from political life, at the age of 75. Norton represented the Democratic stronghold of Jersey City in Hudson County, New Jersey. But coming from Boss Hague's baili-wick does not fully explain Norton's rise in politics. Neither does a summary reference to Hague correctly place the context in which Norton developed as a politician and leader of her party. Though this article deals with Norton's early political career, it sets forth what Norton did for women, or with women in mind, and what she meant, both personally and politically, to the women of her time. Questions concerning Frank Hague must be answered elsewhere.

The ratification of the woman suffrage amendment in 1920 resulted in a new focus for the energies that Norton had previously devoted to social welfare work. Up to that time, her attention had been consumed in work directed at ameliorating the plight of working-class women in industrial Jersey City. As a middle-class woman who had led an independent, working life for over ten years, she had turned her attention to the cause of her working-class sisters and their children, for whom a patriarchal and androcentric society did not provide.

With ratification a certainty, Hague's political instincts had him begin preparing for the effect that newly-enfranchised women would have. He called on Mary Norton, knowing of her successes in welfare work, and asked her to begin organizing women for the Democratic Party. Norton herself thought Hague would get greater help and be proceeding with greater fairness if he sought out those who had worked actively for suffrage to do organizational work. But at his behest, and fueled by her own desires and ambitions, Norton agreed to begin organizing women into Jersey "Democracy." She was made the Democratic State Committee's first woman member, representing Hudson County.[4]

As a member of the State Committee, Norton plunged into a public career. Although widely experienced in dealing with public officials and business people, Norton had little experience speaking before the mass audiences with which she would now come in contact. Her confidence was shaky, but the outpouring of support she received from women with whom she had worked gave her needed encouragement. Of her first political rally she wrote: "I looked up into the gallery, and there, filling the place, smiling and waving, I saw my four hundred faithful members of the day nursery. My 'gang' was there!"[5]

At the end of that same meeting, Norton's new endeavors got another boost as she listened to another speaker, Carrie Chapman Catt, discuss suffrage. Catt's eloquence moved Norton to think of "the long struggle, . . . the hardships endured by women of great vision . . . [who] had not fought . . . battles for themselves, but for women in the years to come. . . ." As Catt finished, Norton's thoughts (as remembered in her memoirs) echoed Emma Goldman's declaration that true emancipation begins "in woman's soul" and that women's freedom would reach as far as woman's power to achieve that freedom reaches. The enlivening speech gave Norton a vision of a new world in the making in which women's battles were to be initiated at the interface of "that intangible something we call Soul" and the hard reality of politics. This was where she now knew her energies would go, sure that at the night's end "Mary Norton was launched on a political career."[6]

That was 1920. The next three years Mary Norton spent organizing women into the Democratic Party so women could obtain the power to achieve real freedom. She also campaigned around the state for local, state and national tickets. In 1921 she was elected vice-chairperson of the Democratic State Committee. In her autobiography she writes of the obstacles with which she was confronted in organizing women and of her motivations for the work of those years.

She would go to meetings around the state expecting to speak to audiences of women; instead, she would often be greeted by groups of hostile men, opposed to her organizing "their" women. Invariably, Norton would side with the women. Through such experiences she realized the practical dimensions of such opposition: the men were "fearful that [organized women] might interfere with them in running . . . the election district." At one meeting, with women in attendance but outnumbered by men, she asked for discussion. She recalled, "We had it—plenty of discussion. The women won. We elected the officers of the club. . . ." This outcome was "much to the disgust of the men, who evidently wanted to control" any and all organization.[7]

At another meeting, Norton "found the place filled with men, but not one woman present." Boldly she confronted the group, asking "Where are your women? This was supposed to be a meeting for women." This challenge was greeted with her being told "Our women are home . . . where you ought to be." Now she "really saw red," but still wanting to be effective and somehow get to the women she "managed to control myself and spoke quietly." Trying to defuse the explosive hostility and get off the defensive, Norton began her speech gently, telling the men of "a new responsibility . . . given to women"—and then, as she recalls, she "really let them have it!" As she concluded, the leader of the men's group stood up and publicly apologized. A new date was set for the women's meeting, which then led to one of the best women's organizations of the state.[8]

Norton believed that such resistance did not go without having an adverse effect and suggested that many women did not continue in politics because of "difficulty with the men in control of the counties or districts." Her county of Hudson was not typical she found, for "many county leaders did not co-operate and they did dominate." Women then would become "discouraged by [this] lack of cooperation on the part of the men," although she would try to instill in her sisters her belief that "wherever women persevered they usually won, even against great odds."[9]

Norton's motivation for such work as she did in those years immediately following the enfranchisement of women came from the legacy left by the suffragists. Before ratification in 1920 she had never been an active suffragist, although "she never was an anti"; she had "realized all the time that the vote would help women immeasurably. . . ." Politics just had not seemed accessible or immediately relevant to her concerns. Rather, "welfare work consumed her vigor and verve." Thus, it was not that Norton did not believe in women's suffrage, but that, as she later wrote, at the time it did not "mean to me what it meant to so many women who had [been] ardently work[ing] for suffrage."[10]

However, with ratification of the suffrage amendment, Norton was soon to grasp its meaning. She told the first convention of New Jersey Democratic Women, organized through her leadership in 1923, that "we should well feel proud . . . when we consider the full importance of this right of franchise." Speaking from her own vantage she acknowledged that it

came to many of us not because of anything we did to merit it, but rather through the grinding work and heartaches of those splendid women of this and a past generation whose ideals and vision ever prompted them to go on in the face of the most disheartening rebuffs.

Stating the issue and championing her earlier suffragist sisters, Norton told the women she had brought together:

> Surely we owe them a great obligation. . . . Their task was difficult but they never faltered—always looking away and beyond, and the picture they visioned was that of the greatest good to womenkind—to place in our hand a weapon which, if properly used, would bring to the women of our generation and countless generations to follow, the great advantages which must accrue as a result of . . . our work in this new field.[11]

Indeed, Norton adopted the position of a most militant and hopeful suffragist: "Our Country has progressed to an extraordinary degree during our lifetime," she told an audience of women at the 1927 Women's World Fair in Chicago, "but the greatest single achievement of that period has been wrought through the enfranchisement of women." She called the suffragists "farseeing women" with "their indomitable will and never ending faith in the cause of women," asserting "to those pioneers should we bend our knee in grateful homage . . . that through their labors a new day has dawned for the women of America." Promising to "hold the torch high and keep the faith," Norton cautioned her sisters to remember "that our service is a transient thing but that our standards may be followed by generations to come." She had come to think of suffrage "as though she had sponsored it in its infancy."[12]

Though she experienced dramatic changes in her own consciousness, some attitudes she encountered in working to organize women were relics of past conditions and carry-overs of reaction. Such attitudes ranged from regarding women in politics as "more or less of a curiosity" to those of some, particularly some men, who still opposed suffrage for women. Before the women of her district were strongly organized, she sometimes found "they used to vote on the sly . . . to escape the wrath of an old-fashioned, domineering, husband." Once she was personally stung by a candidate on behalf of whom she had been speaking. The candidate had not liked her remarks; she thought her speech was a good one. As she finished and left the platform, he came up to her, "shook his head in a disgusted manner and muttered: 'And they gave women the vote!'" In characteristic Norton understatement, she called this episode her "first lesson in practical politics," one which—to make the point—made her "even more anxious than ever before to continue."[13]

In 1923 Norton was asked to run for Freeholder in Hudson County, accepted and was elected. She credited the women who had worked for suffrage with preparing the opportunity that presented itself. Upon her victory she "wanted to pay part of my debt to my fellow women to whom I owe much." So she conceived the idea for a County Maternity Hospital. "Counties have always cared for their aged paupers," she declared to a reporter, "but it had never occurred to any county to care for its young mothers. To me, it seemed the most important need." Given her past experience with the medical care available to the working-class women of Jersey City, Norton's evaluation of the need for comprehensive and inexpensive obstetric and gynecological care for her constituents was consistent and to be expected.[14]

Her concern, though, was baffling to her fellow-freeholders. Moreover, Norton told them she wanted to be "considered as a worker and a person rather than as a woman." That she did not want her sex to be an obstacle in her path seemed beyond their understanding. Norton was not surprised, for she had known from the beginning that the other freeholders, all men, had not "looked upon a woman on the board too happily." When she brought up the idea of a county maternity hospital, the suggestion "almost broke up the meeting." Some members of the board, she believed, "thought I was just a little bit crazy." She then went directly to Hague, whom she interested in the idea. Hague told her the men on the board could be persuaded, but they "will have to come to it gradually." With Hague on her side, Norton was relieved for she had learned that he had been asked to discourage her interest in the project. With Norton continuing her efforts at persuasion and investigating the means to obtain state authorization to so expend county funds, and Hague backing her, the Board capitulated. Norton sought out Catherine Finn, a state legislator from Hudson County, to introduce a measure in the legislature to authorize the financing of her project. With Finn's help, Norton's wish to do something for Hudson County women was on its way to realization.[15]

A year after her election as Freeholder, opportunity again came knocking for Norton when Hague backed her as a candidate for Congress. It threatened to be a Republican year, even in Democratic Hudson, but Norton credits women with continually urging her to move ahead. Women recalled to her the campaigns of 1922 and how she had travelled throughout the county and state in support of many candidates. Now her "'gang' insisted that I ought to do a bit of stumping for myself . . ." Though she hesitated to leave her hospital after only seeing it through a year in the planning stage, Norton resigned from the Board of Freeholders to accept the organization's nomination as a Congressional candidate. That fall of 1924 she campaigned for her own election to the House of Representatives and, as Vice-chairperson of the Democratic State Committee, stumped the state for the entire ticket. Having organized women in most counties, she knew the state well.[16]

The result of the election surprised her, for it turned out that "in 1924 there were only two Democrats elected in Hudson County and I was one of them." Traditionally Democratic Hudson had indeed had a Republican year, as had the country. Democrats were overwhelmingly defeated, yet Norton polled a plurality of 17,000. Some years later Hague confided to her that he had been just as surprised by the outcome and honestly could not "take much credit for my election." As one might expect, Norton gives credit to the support of women who elsewhere deserted the men on the Democratic ticket. Hague's foresight in putting Norton up as a candidate had evidently paid off, for as Norton remembered, he had been "worried about what [women] would do to upset the leadership of men." Fearing he could not beat them, he tendered to Norton a Congressional run (albeit in a difficult year) as if to ask women to join with him. Thus Hague could point to one more piece of evidence that his organization was responsive to women's demands. Responsive he needed to be, for in his ambitions he needed their help.[17]

When Mary T. Norton became Congresswoman Norton she met the same attempts to dismiss her as ornamental, and was treated with the same lack of seriousness, that greeted earlier women upon their arrival in Congress. But she was not about to be made a joke or a curiosity. One newspaper account had her declaring "Emphatically that she had no desire to receive concessions because of her sex," and adding that "she did not anticipate giving any concessions" either. Similarly, she refused to "have her photograph taken while she stood in front of a stove and while she hung clothes on the line." Scoffing at these contrived ideas, she told the photographer who asked her to adopt such poses that as a Representative her business would be with legislation, adding "I do not expect to cook, and I do not expect to wash any clothes in Congress. . . . Why tell the world about those things?" Logic, she stated, had guided her life and it was there to stay. She based her success on such principles as having "always treated everyone as if he or she had brains," and it was her opinion that "for that reason people like me."[18]

In her early congressional career, Norton's activity gained for her a reputation of firmness and effectiveness. On one occasion she so assiduously lined up support for a bill she had offered that one member "facetiously inquired, 'Is Mrs. Norton now the leader of the New York Delegation?'" Even as a minority member of some minor committees she "kept the committees actively engaged." Significantly, the usually inactive and unconcerned District of Columbia committee was stirred into considerable activity by its first woman member. The Congresswoman would "find something continually that the committee should pass upon," although most members cared little about and were reluctant to invest energy in matters concerning the voteless citizens of the Nation's capital. Largely due to Norton's pressure, the Committee became "a very, very active one." She was to profit by the spotlight, too.[19]

As she did throughout her career, the Congresswoman turned her energies to women's causes and raised issues with a mind to securing justice for her sisters. During her first term she got the District Committee to report out two bills she wanted for the women of Washington. They could not vote for her, but she would still champion their right to equality with Washington's similarly voteless, though male, persons.

One of the bills dealt with the authorization by which policewomen might be hired in the District. The bill precipitated a clash between Representative Norton and Mina Van Winkle, a former New Jersey suffrage leader and then head of the Women's Bureau of the Washington, D.C. Police. Van Winkle objected to changes Norton wanted the Committee to make in the bill Van Winkle herself had drafted. The bill needed to be amended, Norton thought, "so that men and women on the force would be on a basis of absolute equality."

Norton's concerns were that policewomen, like policemen, be required to wear uniforms while on duty, that they be required to have "substantially the same" "prerequisite mental training and experience" before being appointed to the force, and that the guides to their duties not allow one more latitude than the other. Van Winkle's provisions would have required "additional educational requirements . . . for policewomen" beyond those set for policemen, so as not to have "an undesirable type . . . placed on the police force by political appointment." Additionally, she opposed mandatory uniforming of women officers and wanted women to be allowed "more latitude in the performance of the duties of their offices than [as allowed] policemen." Norton's objections were to any provisions, such as those regarding uniforms and latitude, which would differentiate a policewoman's work from that of a policeman. She feared that such provisions would enable the Police Department to keep policewomen confined to a narrow set of duties and in a separate sphere of activities from those handled by policemen. In Norton's mind, "Women fought for suffrage in order to be on an equal basis with men." Hence, "there should be no more sex lineups in public office, . . . women should have equal opportunity to participate in public life and should . . . accept equal responsibility . . ."

As the only woman member of the Committee and because of her leadership work in Jersey City, Norton's opinion carried great weight with her colleagues. She explained that "as an advocate of the Woman's Bureau . . . I should like to see these changes made in the bill to safeguard policewomen from the criticisms which are made against them." The charges that "young policewomen attract attention of men on the streets with a view to arresting them" ought not be leveled at the women themselves, Norton informed the Committee; for it seemed that the Metropolitan Police Department was primarily interested in the women on its force to the extent that they could pose as prostitutes. Norton's opposition to the distinctions made on account of sex in the Van Winkle provisions was intended to prevent the law from circumscribing policework for women and, with duplicitous regard for the female officers, specifying a "special class of work performed by them." Furthermore, she added that "enemies of the Woman's Bureau" and of policework for women use such provisions to attack women officers regardless of the reality of their role.

Her points of opposition were intended to speed passage of the bill, not skuttle it, she wanted her colleagues to know. She believed the Policewoman's Bill would not pass "as long as the present inequalities remain in the measure. . . ." Moreover, she wanted it understood that she believed "a great amount of good" can be done by women, as well as men, in police work, adding that she personally favored "an increase in the number of policewomen" and "the raising of the status of the Woman's Bureau so that it will be on the same basis as other bureaus of the Metropolitan Police Department."[20]

The same term saw Norton introduce a bill to grant the women of Washington, D.C., the right to serve on juries. This bill met with resistance and was carried over to the 70th Congress. Consequently, on being re-elected to a second term Norton re-introduced the measure. All during hearings on the bill she worked indefatigably for its passage. She rounded up large numbers of Democratic votes, even while Southern Democrats opposed the measure. But on the floor some of her support deserted her, Democrats teaming with New England Republicans to force an amendment providing that women could be excused from jury service by a simple request to be excused. Norton stood staunchly for exact equality in this duty of citizenship. She rose to oppose the amendment even as several Democrats tried futilely to motion her down. Firmly she declared her convictions that "women, as well as men, should present their excuses to the judgement of the court when they are unable to serve on juries." Five Congresses and ten years later she would, as Chairperson of the District Committee, obtain the support of the District Commissioners and officials of the local courts for the measure she had pressed for, and see the day when women were put "on an equal footing with men" by striking all sex discrimination from the jury service law in the District of Columbia.[21]

In the 70th Congress, Norton sponsored a proposal suggested by a twenty-one-year-old Brooklyn woman urging that "the nation's young womanhood . . . be allowed to participate in summer training activities similar to the citizens training camps conducted by the Army" for young men. With the other two women in Congress at her side, Norton sought the same opportunity for girls as had been offered to boys under the auspices of the Federal Government. With characteristic directness, her statement announced: "I think it is high time the government took the lead in building up the health of its young women."[22]

She campaigned for women in more personal, if still legislative, ways too. Having introduced in the 69th Congress a general pension bill calling for an increase in the monthly pensions of all Civil War widows, only to see her measure reduced in committee, Norton returned to the 70th Congress ready with a new tactic. Carrying on the fight for what she thought due to the women the bill would affect, Norton proceeded to introduce special pension bills for every woman whose case was called to her attention. Through strenuous efforts she accomplished her end by taking the arguments to the Pensions Committee in each individual case and having the special bills collectively contained in a single House resolution.[23]

On still another front, Norton spoke out in strong support of immigration equalization for women. Congressional action of September 22, 1922 had provided that in marriages of Americans to foreigners, neither person would forfeit the citizenship of their own country. However, if a marriage was effected prior to that date, the woman and the man would each be affected differently, a man retaining his citizenship but a woman losing her citizenship by virtue of marriage to a foreigner. Norton sponsored a bill to provide a means by which women who were residing in the United States as of that date could regain their citizenship.[24]

The current law discriminated against women in the reverse circumstances, too. A male citizen could go abroad and marry and bring his wife back with him as a non-quota immigrant. Through legislative remedy Norton sought to promote sex equality by conferring upon women the rights possessed by their brothers who married foreigners—that women would be provided the same entry rights in bringing a foreign-born husband to this country as a non-quota immigrant. Discussing the case of an Italian woman of Newark, by birth a citizen of the United States, who married abroad and fell victim to the sex discrimination of the immigration statutes, Norton asked "Why shouldn't she be allowed the privilege of bringing in her husband, she being a citizen, as a man is privileged in entering the country with his bride?" She reminded her male colleagues who had written the androcentric law and who had let the equalization measure languish that the situation "is most unfair and yet the wheels of Congress grind so slowly that this measure has been pending for the past two years."[25]

While busily advocating women's interests in legislative matters, Norton continued to speak around the state and country urging women's participation in politics. Norton saw a sense of discouragement growing among women with regard to political activity midway through the decade that began so formidably with the passage of woman's suffrage. Her response to these women reflected her practical knowledge of politics and organizational work, tinged with a feminist appeal to boost failing spirits. As she told a group of college women in 1925, "we must remember that women have had only four years with the power of the vote while men have had it for a long, long time and they have not accomplished so much that we need to be discouraged with our part so far." Through such talks as this Norton sought "to transfer my experiences to other women who are groping and unsure of themselves." She found that "many of those women, who like myself were inexperienced and feeling their way, told me that I did give them courage. . . ." By putting her sisters at ease, letting them know what to expect, and sharing with them her own dreams and ambitions, Norton hoped to stimulate their interests, enlarge their options and raise their expectations of themselves.[26]

So it should not have been surprising when, at the start of her second term in Congress, she attacked the patriarchal cast of her male colleagues' attitudes. However, the shock shook her Congressional brethren. Candidly, she charged: "Men don't want women in Congress—and don't you think they do." Although she herself was beginning to be accepted through the sheer force of the determination she exuded, she threatened to "break out" of her token status and treat her male colleagues accordingly—a prospect over which she would chuckle. Letting it be known that she did not believe "in any discrimination because of sex" she demanded that women be accepted with regularity when they came to Congress.[27]

A home-town paper, knowing its Congresswoman's attitudes, editorially supported her and suggested it was to Norton's credit that, in contrast to her male colleagues' attitudes toward women, she had "no objection to men sitting in Congress." Praising Norton's idea that "Congress is a place for citizens to render public service, not a place for one sex or the other to render that service," the editorial looked ahead to a day when, through the efforts of Congresswoman Norton and like-minded others, Congress would be elected upon such principles, and expected then that "the work of Congress will be more intelligently done than it has been in the past." Such was the backing she received (and came to expect) from her constituency.[28]

In 1928 Norton warned of a "social leader 'complex' in the political development of American womanhood." In politics, too many women were letting "someone else do their thinking for them." As a caveat to her own alarm she allowed that "we are only eight years old in the world of politics" and "in this period we have advanced far, but there is much more to learn." However, to continue their successes, she was convinced "women must learn to stand on their own feet. . . ." Sisterly advice and criticism such as this was always offered without malice and was intended in a constructive vein to move women to act.[29]

Norton would hold herself to the same standards, too. Discussing the confusion of the times, she spoke of "one who is a pioneer in her particular line" in a talk to the Baltimore Press Club admitting "it has often been puzzling to decide which is the better course in many questions affecting not only her district but the cause of women in general." This uncertainty existed even though early in her political career she had determined that what mattered the most "to me personally" was what "I did or left undone . . . as it affected the status of women . . . in the years to follow." She thought the real heroines were "the women who fought for suffrage" and knew what her career owed to "the great courage, broad vision and tremendous energy of those women," and wanted to follow their example. But with characteristic modesty and a respectful solemnity she wondered how she would be able to do so: her aid to the cause could "be but secondary to their splendid contribution." Her hope was "to live long enough to see many women in the Congress"; she predicted that "when this comes to pass . . . a better understanding shall be reached between men and women in politics." About this she had no second thoughts for she considered a career in government and politics a worthy endeavor, telling women "not [to] be content to leave the task to men."[30]

Speaking as a member of Congress, her message to women was to "take an interest in politics and aspire quite freely to become members of Congress." With an almost contemporary feminist acuity for the confluence between the personal and the political, Norton tried to demonstrate to women who would not let themselves imagine a plunge into politics "the close relation between politics and details of everyday home life." Attempting to bridge the strangeness, distance and almost unwholesomeness that things political might bring to mind, she would have it known that "any woman interested her own family and her own community is interested in politics." She wanted women to see that politics and government "have a real meaning," that such work was something "women, as well as men, should have part in." "Men," she would announce, "have been lords of creation politically too long." Therefore women should "have no hesitancy in coming to Congress."[31]

So strong was the Congresswoman's desire to have her sisters join her in Washington that she hoped for women's success regardless of party. Medill McCormick of Illinois, a woman whom Norton had met in Chicago at the Women's World Fair, received support and an endorsement from Norton as a result of the political sisterhood that Norton urged transcend party lines. Of McCormick, a Republican, Democrat Norton volunteered to reporters, "I don't know of any woman who should have better equipment to run. . . . She should make a very worthwhile contribution to Congress if she wins a seat. . . ." Norton welcomed the possibility of McCormick's election, explaining "[w]hile Mrs. McCormick and I are of opposite political faiths, I should be very glad to see her in Congress"—"I shall be very glad to have a woman sit in the Illinois delegation." Not only in Illinois, but even in her own New Jersey, this Democratic Congresswoman would put sisterhood ahead of party when it came to electing women. Speaking before 300 women in Bloomfield, she called for recognition of Republican women by their party. She told the gathering that the Republican Party "should have sent a woman from New Jersey to keep me company in the House," exclaiming that, irrespective of party "she would have met with a cordial welcome from me, for I don't think there are nearly enough women in public office as there should be."[32]

Even in these early years, Norton allowed no limit to women's horizons in politics. In 1926, she "saw no reason why a woman should not be a governor in the east as well as in the west," and well expected women to covet the Presidency—and obtain it when their strength mounted. Indeed, to increase women's political strength is what Mary Norton had set out to do. Whenever an opportunity occurred—and if it didn't she would set out to make one—Norton would aid and speak on behalf of women candidates, anxious as she was to have them elected.[33]

Her own Congressional career continued to grow. With a Democratic Congress elected in 1930, Congresswoman Norton, who by that time had become the ranking Democrat on the House District Committee, became Chairwoman Norton—the first woman to chair a Congressional committee. Later, she would chair two other Congressional Committees and become the first member of Congress to chair three committees. Upon her appointment to chair the District Committee, she noted that she was "conscious of the fact that a woman in a new position is always open to more criticism than a man would be in the same position, that her mistakes are magnified." The double standard that she had ardently attacked for a decade would now make a target of her.[34]

Chairing the Committee, Norton met with both humorous and indignant rebuffs from her male colleagues. A Republican of

West Virginia, Representative Bowman let her know that it was the first time in his life that he had been controlled by a woman. Chairwoman Norton replied that her position was a first for her too and she "rather like[d] the prospect" of presiding "over a body of men." A Democrat's comment was not as amusing when he suggested a man would be much more efficient at the head of the House District Committee. Admitting that his chairwoman was a "fine conscientious, hardworking woman," Representative Quinn of Pennsylvania attributed her disability to the fact of her sex. Norton was stung by such blatant sex prejudice. A Washington newspaper wrote at the time that Quinn's comments were "enough to arouse any woman's ire, especially a feminist like Mrs. Norton."[35]

Defending her record and willing to have it compared with any other member who chaired a committee, Norton denounced her Democratic detractor as a bigot and a "freshman" who ought to know his place. "A few men," she angrily told reporters, "will always consider women inferior, but, of course, that simply means the superiority complex is overworked. . . . Of course, there are always men who want to start a 'back-to-the-kitchen' movement." She added that Quinn had only been a member of the District Committee for six months and was "merely a freshman." Quinn became defensive at Norton's attack, asserting that he had had a long career in Pennsylvania politics and was no "freshman" when it came to politics. He felt he had not said anything at which Norton should have taken such offense. Obviously, the Congresswoman thought otherwise.[36]

As Chairperson, the Congresswoman knew—more than anyone—"the reaction my service will have on women in public life." With both boldness and a now characteristic confidence, Norton could see that new responsibilities would be beginning in her life "because we pioneers in political office must always keep in mind the effect of our work upon the public mind in its reaction to granting power to women through public office." Another opportunity to chair a committee later in the second decade of her political career would leave her with a similar feeling of "great responsibility." Were she a success, "others will reap the benefit." If she should fail, "other women will suffer." For Mary Norton, being "the first woman in a position" meant a responsibility that "troubled me more than the honor."[37]

The end of the decade that began with the suffrage victory saw Mary Norton continue her stout defense of women's entry into the give-and-take of practical politics, indeed, into every field of endeavor. Her early political career and her first few terms in Congress evidence the two, almost dialectical, feminist principles that would follow her all through her life—her demand that women be seen as persons, that her record and career be viewed without regard to sex and her continuous espousal of and activity to benefit women's forays and full participation in politics and the public world. At the time, a Washington newspaper described the City's new "mayor" (i.e. the chairperson of the District Committee) as "essentially a feminist." With surprise, the reporter noted that her entire office force was composed of women, from the choice and coveted Committee clerkships to her chauffeur, executive secretary, administrative assistant, and other secretaries and assistant clerks. "Women make her office a Mecca," the reporter wrote, "troop[ing] up there on all sorts of missions." Another writer noted the same circumstances, quoting Norton as being "strong for women" and describing her belief that women were qualified to pursue positions throughout the fields of business and government. Citing the Congresswoman's "absolute faith" in women's "ability, sincerity, loyalty and integrity," the reporter waxed ecstatic that Norton "carries out her convictions and has an office that is 'manned' entirely by women!" The article then "venture[d] to say that she is about the only woman as 100% consistent as this." Such was not news to New Jerseyans, as *The Hudson Dispatch* commented, for "[i]n New Jersey it has been known for long that Mrs. Norton is distinctly a feminist. . . ."[38]

In 1926, first-term Congresswoman Norton was called "a modern woman, . . . a shrewd politician, a great vote-getter and an extremely dangerous adversary on the platform." In the 1930's, a Washington journalist suggested "one could write a book on her other claims to fame." But in 1975, the centennial anniversary of her birth, she is a little-known, almost forgotten figure in New Jersey history. In her time—for a period of over thirty years—she was considered the most prominent woman in American politics. She was commonly described as "one of the most dynamic and powerful personalities on the political scene."[39]

But even as a half-forgotten predecessor of women's endeavors in American politics, Mary T. Norton, has affected our reality. She is one whose struggle has made American politics a bit more progressive and democratic. Her story remains to be written. But her life helped pave the way for the activity of the resurgent feminism of the recent past.

Notes

1. Ellis Meredith, "What Six Congresswomen Could Do," *Democratic Digest* (June, 1935), 7.

2. "Have You Heard?" *Erie Daily Times* (Erie, Pa.), May 13, 1935, Scrap Books, Mary Norton Papers, Rutgers University Library. Hereafter cited as MNP.

3. James Nevin Miller, "Congresswomen, and How They Grew," *Washington Post*, Feb. 29, 1936, Scrap Books, MNP.

4. "A Woman Legislator Who Had the Courage of Her Convictions," *Wardman Park Vista*, Jan. 17, 1926, Scrap Books, MNP; Mary T. Norton, "Madam Congressman," unpublished autobiography, 35-39, MNP.

5. *Hudson Observer* (Hoboken), Oct. 11, 1922; Norton, 39, 50.

6. Norton, 39.

7. Norton, 45.

8. Norton, 46.

9. Norton, 47; untitled, handwritten manuscript notes to "Madam Congressman," Box 6, MNP.

10. *Jersey Journal* (Jersey City), Oct. 5, 1925; press release, Democratic National Committee, Aug. 31, 1928, Box 4, MNP; "A Congresswoman from New Jersey," *The Charm* (March, 1926), 27, Box 7, MNP; Esther Van Wagoner Tufty, "Profile of a Great Lady," *Jersey Journal*, c. 1946, Box 7, MNP; manuscript notes, Box 6, MNP; Helen F. Meagher, "Through the Door of Welfare," *Woman's Voice* (April, 1931), Box 7, MNP; Helen F. Meagher to Mary T. Norton, Mar. 26, 1931, Box 1, MNP.

11. Address delivered to Convention of Democratic Women, Newark, N.J., Sept. 5, 1923, Box 5, MNP.

12. Address at Women's World Fair, Chicago, May 24, 1927, Box 1, MNP; *The Lowell Sun* (Lowell, Mass.), Jan. 16, 1926, Scrap Books, MNP.

13. *Hartford Courant*, July 14, 1957, Box 7, MNP; Norton, 43.

14. *Atlantic City Sun*, Dec. 15, 1929, Scrap Books, MNP.

15. *Sunday Star-Ledger* (Newark, N.J.), June 23, 1946; Norton, 52-54; Helen F. Meagher to Mary T. Norton, Mar. 26, 1931, Box 1, MNP.

16. *Knickerbocker Press* (Albany, N.Y.), Nov. 6, 1924, Scrap Books, MNP; Norton, 55-56.

17. Manuscript notes, Box 6, MNP.

18. *Knickerbocker Press*, Nov. 6, 1924; *Washington Post*, c.1940, Scrap Books, MNP; Norton, 57-58.

19. *Jersey Journal*, Apr. 29, 1926; *Newark Sunday Call*, July 18, 1926, Box 7, MNP.

20. *Jersey Journal*, June 8, 1926, Scrap Books, MNP.

21. *Jersey Journal*, Apr. 29, 1926; unidentified newspaper clipping, c. March, 1937, Scrap Books, MNP.

22. *Jersey Observer*, May 5, 1926, Scrap Books, MNP.

23. *The Hudson Dispatch*, Dec. 30, 1928; *Jersey Journal*, Feb. 24, 1928; *Jersey Journal*, c. 1928, Scrap Books, MNP.

24. "Mrs. Norton Discusses Bills in Which She is Interested," *Jersey Journal*, c. 1928, Scrap Books, MNP.

25. "Mrs. Norton Discusses Bills in Which She is Interested," *Jersey Journal*, c. 1928, Scrap Books, MNP.

26. *Jersey Journal*, Oct. 5, 1925, Scrap Books, MNP; Norton, 43-44.

27. *Evening World* (New York), Dec. 13, 1927, Scrap Books, MNP.

28. *The Hudson Dispatch*, Dec. 19, 1927, Scrap Books, MNP.

29. *Jersey Journal*, Mar. 22, 1928, Scrap Books, MNP.

30. Address to Baltimore Press Club, Mar. 1, 1927, Box 5, MNP.

31. "A Congresswoman from New Jersey," Tufty, Box 7, MNP; *New York World*, Jan. 17, 1930, Scrap Books, MNP; *World-Telegram* (New York), c. July, 1934, Scrap Books, MNP; *Newark Sunday Call*, July 18, 1926, Box 7, MNP.

32. *Jersey Observer*, July 28, 1928; *Jersey Journal*, c. Sept., 1927, Scrap Books, MNP; *Independent Press* (Bloomfield, N.J.), Nov. 3, 1933, Scrap Books, MNP.

33. *Newark Sunday Call*, July 18, 1926; *Jersey Journal*, c. Sept., 1927, Scrap Books. MNP.

34. M.E. Hennessy, "A Woman is The Real Mayor of Washington," unidentified clipping, c. 1930, Scrap Books, MNP.

35. *Jersey Observer*, Dec. 26, 1931, Scrap Books. MNP; "Chairman Norton . . . Angered by 'Efficiency' Story," unidentified clipping, c. June 11, 1935, Scrap Books, MNP.

36. "Chairman Norton . . . ," Scrap Books, MNP; "Quinn's Remark on Women Draws Rep. Norton's Ire," unidentified clipping, c. June 11, 1935, Scrap Books, MNP; *Jersey Observer*, June 11, 1935.

37. *Washington Daily News*, July 24, 1934, Scrap Books, MNP.

38. *Washington Post*, Feb. 7, 1932, Box 7, MNP; *Pelham Sun* (Pelham, N.Y.), Aug. 26, 1932, Scrap Books, MNP; *The Hudson Dispatch*, Feb. 18, 1932, Scrap Books, MNP.

39. Miller, Scrap Books, MNP; *Newark Star-Eagle*, Apr. 26, 1932; *Jersey Journal*, Nov. 3, 1938.

*Originally adamantly opposed to Roosevelt's candidacy but a firm sup-
porter after the 1932 Democratic convention, Jersey City Mayor Frank
Hague could deliver so many votes that FDR put aside his dislike of the
mayor and accepted his invitation to open the campaign in New Jersey.
Hague greeted FDR at Sea Girt on August 27, 1932, before about 100,000
people, perhaps the largest political rally ever held in the United States to
that date. Photograph courtesy UPI/Bettmann.*

14

The career of Jersey City mayor Frank Hague raises two questions with which American historians have wrestled for some time. The first is how to look at and evaluate the role of "bosses" in politics. The second is whether political machines controlled by bosses are a thing of the past or also of the present. If they are as extinct as the dinosaurs, when and why did they die?

Historical opinion about bosses and their political role has changed over time. During the Progressive Era bosses were blamed for the corruption that was rampant in cities, criticized for their ties to the immigrant community (which seemed to trade its votes for favors), and faulted for their relationship to the business community, which paid bribes for preferential treatment. At the outbreak of the Second World War party bosses were condemned for an excessive use of power compared at the time to that of the rising fascists in Europe. Historians and critics charged that boss control of government embraced an undemocratic and intolerable suppression of individual rights, as well as inefficiency and unwarranted expense.

In more recent years historians have been less inclined simply to condemn boss rule than to describe and explain how it operated and the services it provided. Machine politics reached significant proportions at the end of the nineteenth century when cities grew at a rapid pace and immigrants arrived in enormous numbers. The boss bridged the gap between inadequate services and human needs. He provided job counseling when there were no unemployment offices, food baskets before food stamps and other welfare programs, assistance to businessmen before economic development bureaus, and a personal touch in an increasingly impersonal world.

Whether evaluating boss rule or trying to determine its balance of costs and services, historians have generally agreed that its days as a widespread American institution were numbered by the 1930s. The New Deal provided an assortment of social welfare services previously offered by the machine, such as social security, aid for families with dependent children, and subsidies for public works projects. The rise of big labor unions meant that they also took on some of the functions of the political machine, furnishing assistance in the event of arbitrary treatment, providing greater job security, and working for higher wages. At the same time the end of large-scale immigration, a consequence of both the restrictive laws passed after

World War I and of the Depression (which made the United States a less attractive destination), shrunk the pool of traditional boss support. Bosses who survived the 1930s were an exception to the rule.

Hudson County's Frank Hague, like other bosses, has been roundly condemned for his dictatorial qualities. Dayton D. McKean in *The Boss* (1940) specifically charged that the Hague organization "systematically and successfully utilized the methods of terrorism . . . that have characterized the fascist régimes in Europe." The rights to freedom of speech and assembly were trampled in Jersey City. Government was inefficient and expensive; the school system was inadequate and plagued with cronyism. In contrast to this clear condemnation, Lyle Dorsett attempted a more detached appraisal. How does he evaluate Hague? What services did the Hague machine provide for residents, as well as for churches and businessmen, in return for their support? What, for example, did citizens receive in return for their investment in the large, expensive Jersey City Medical Center? Why did Jersey City voters keep Hague in office for so long?

Frank Hague first rose to power as a reform candidate in 1913. By 1932 criticism of his personal wealth and lifestyle, as well as his political methods and activities, was widespread. There were predictions that he could not remain in power much longer. But Hague outlasted even the New Deal, the reputed dragon slayer of boss rule. Dorsett has argued that the New Deal actually rescued Hague. Why did this happen? What did Hague have that Roosevelt needed, and what did Hague receive in return?

The relationship between the boss and the president was a pragmatic one, based on the needs of each. Roosevelt could be devious as well as practical. In 1940 he decided to try to oust Hague by quietly encouraging Charles Edison to act as a counterweight by running for governor of New Jersey. Although Edison was elected, the plan did not succeed, and Hague remained in office until 1947. Why did the reform effort fail? What does its failure suggest about the staying power not only of Hague but of political machines in general?

The Hague machine in Jersey City was replaced in 1949 by the Kenny machine. Does machine politics still exist today? If it does, what functions does it perform, and where? To survive, boss-driven political machines need to provide something no one else offers in return for the votes and support they receive. Historians have come to agree that this process is reciprocal, not just the rule of bosses over voters.

Suggested Readings

Brownell, Blaine A., and Warren E. Stickle, eds. *Bosses and Reformers: Urban Politics in America, 1880–1920*. Boston, 1973.

Callow, Alexander B., Jr., ed. *The City Boss in America: An Interpretive Reader*. New York, 1976.

Colburn, David R., and George E. Pozzetta. "Bosses and Machines: Changing Interpretations in American History." *History Teacher* 9 (1976): 445–63.

Connors, Richard J. *The Cycle of Power: The Career of Jersey City Mayor Frank Hague*. Metuchen, N.J., 1971.

Foster, Mark S. "Frank Hague of Jersey City: The Boss as Reformer." *NJH* 86 (1968): 106–17.

Greene, Lee S., ed."City Bosses and Political Machines." *Annals of the American Academy of Political and Social Science* 353 (1964): 15–121.

Lemmey, William. "The Last Hurrah Reconsidered: The Kenny Era in Jersey City, 1949–1972." In *Cities of the Garden State: Essays in the Urban and Suburban History of New Jersey*, edited by Joel Schwartz and Daniel Prosser. Dubuque, Iowa, 1977. 127–43.

———. "Boss Kenny of Jersey City, 1949–1972." *NJH* 98 (1980): 6–28.

McKean, Dayton D. *The Boss: The Hague Machine in Action*. Boston, 1940.

Murray, Joseph M. "Bosses and Reformers: The Jersey City Liberty Movement of 1957." *NJH* 103 (1985): 33–67.

O'Connor, Edwin. *The Last Hurrah*. Boston, 1956.

Rapport, George C. *The Statesman and the Boss: A Study of American Political Leadership Exemplified by Woodrow Wilson and Frank Hague*. New York, 1961.

Stave, Bruce M., ed. *Urban Bosses, Machines, and Progressive Reformers*. Lexington, Mass., 1972.

✦ ✦ ✦ ✦ ✦ ✦

Frank Hague, Franklin Roosevelt and the Politics of the New Deal

Lyle W. Dorsett

William Dean Howells once said that "the kindlier view of any man is apt to be the truer view." This is probably true, but few journalists have applied it to Frank Hague. Aside from a 1937 feature article in the already disreputable *Literary Digest* (the *Digest's* days were numbered after it predicted Landon would defeat Roosevelt in 1936), most writers portrayed the boss of Jersey City as a "Dictator—American Style" or "King Hanky-Panky." Hague's city, it was argued, was an "occupied area" under the rule of New Jersey's "Hitler."[1]

There is some truth in the image journalists created of Hague. As with most images, though, the distance between reality and the impressions expressed by opponents is great. Hague was no angel but he always had a large popular following. One of the reasons people in Jersey City liked Frank Hague was that they could identify with him and his humble beginnings. He was born in the Horseshoe in downtown Jersey City. The Horseshoe got its name in 1871 after the Republicans gerrymandered most of the city's Democrats into one assembly district, bordered by Hoboken in the north and the Hudson River on the east, and rounded off to the west and south in a horseshoe shape.

In 1876, the year Hague was born, Jersey City's population was approximately 120,000. About one-fifth of this number was foreign-born, and many of those came from Ireland. Most of the immigrants and native-born laborers were forced to raise their families in the Horseshoe, close to their places of employment, where rent was the lowest. It was down among the railroad yards, noisy wharves, and soot-blackened factories that Frank Hague was born. Although most of the neighbors lived in crowded tenements, Frank's Irish-born father managed to move his Irish bride and eight children into a dilapidated frame house when he graduated from a blacksmith's job to become a guard at a local bank.[2]

New Jersey History 94 (1975-76): 21–35. Reprinted by permission of the author.

Frank nearly died as an infant, a fate which would not have been unusual in a late nineteenth century city, especially among slum children. But he had a strong constitution and grew into a tall, lean, strong boy with sandy-colored hair and striking blue eyes. A typical rowdy of the Horseshoe, Hague ran in a gang, swam in the river, and fought in the streets. His mother saw to it that he regularly attended Mass, but no one succeeded in getting him to school very often. Indeed, in the sixth grade at the age of fourteen, he was expelled for habitual truancy, thus ending his formal schooling. From P.S. 21 he went to work as a blacksmith's helper, and then took an unskilled job with the Erie Railroad. In his spare time he worked out in a gymnasium and became a rather good boxer. While fighting in the gym he met a professional lightweight named Joe Craig. Looking for an opportunity to get out of the railroad yards and into a suit and tie, Hague made a deal with Craig, became his manager, and was able to turn his back on work clothes and common labor forever.[3]

During his years as Craig's manager, Hague became well-known in the Horseshoe. He spent many hours around the Cable Athletic Club and the Greenwood Social Club where he distinguished himself as the local fashion plate in impeccably clean shirts and four-buttoned, double-breasted plaid suits. Those who knew him believed his ambitions to be modest. He wanted to avoid the toil of manual labor, dress smartly, and eventually get a job on the police force. As a matter of fact, he demonstrated no particular interest in politics, and initially entered it unexpectedly on the initiative of others. Hague's political career began when a well-known saloonkeeper in the Horseshoe, Nat Kenny, decided to challenge the Democratic boss of the neighborhood, Denny McLaughlin. Kenny had no interest in holding public office himself, but he wanted to become the behind-the-scenes power in the Horseshoe Democracy. McLaughlin held no public office either, but he had many friends in the area and could deliver a large block of votes for candidates of his own choice at election time. Just prior to a special election in 1896 to elect constables and members of the Street and Water Board, Kenny was searching for some men who were popular in the Horseshoe. It was suggested that young Frank Hague, who was well known in the clubs and as a fight manager, would be a good choice to run for constable. Hague was asked to run; he accepted, and went on to win.[4]

This victory was all Hague needed to realize that his calling was politics. The man of modest ambitions quickly developed a monumental appetite for power and prestige. He worked faithfully for the regular Democratic organization until Jersey City heard the nation-wide clamor for reform. Then in 1913, Hague became a reformer. He called for cleaning the "bosses" out of city hall and bringing honesty and efficiency to city government. The boy from the Horseshoe won the election and became a city commissioner and later Mayor of Jersey City. And in the mayor's office he stayed until his voluntary retirement in 1947.[5]

During those early years in the mayor's office, Hague carefully tended to the business of building a political machine. His following was enlarged by keeping his promises of modernizing the city's fire and police departments. Eventually he had lieutenants in every ward of the city. Their job was to care for the needy and then get the vote out on election day. In middle-class neighborhoods the boss established social clubs where people could relax, play, and socialize. For the business community, both small and large, there were tax breaks and other favors. Hague also had the patent support of the Roman Catholic Church in Jersey City. The boss contributed large sums of money and some magnificent gifts to the church, and in return, he had its endorsement at election time. Furthermore, deliberate efforts were made to do favors for Jews and Protestants. Several well-known and influential Rabbis and Protestant ministers were on the city payroll as "utility men" or "special inspectors."[6]

By the time Franklin Roosevelt launched the New Deal, Hague was a powerful and popular mayor with an efficient and loyal organization at his command. The seamier side of his character and the most ruthless tactics of his machine had not yet come to light. Consequently, Hague was the undisputed leader of the New Jersey Democratic Party by 1932, and he went to the national convention at Chicago militantly anti-Roosevelt. Hague's idol was Al Smith, and the New Jersey boss used every ounce of influence at his disposal to see him nominated. If Roosevelt had been inclined to hold a grudge against anyone in Al Smith's camp it would have been toward Hague. The arrogant, wise-cracking boss of Jersey City was Smith's floor manager at the convention, and it was he who told reporters in Chicago that if nominated, Roosevelt would not carry even one state east of the Mississippi.

This was a big crow to swallow, but Hague was an audacious man with enough appetite for the task. Immediately after the convention Jim Farley went to Atlantic City to rest and recuperate from the strain and pressure of the battle for the nomination. He was not there long before he received a phone call from

Hague. "He said," Farley remembered, "there was no soreness on his part over what had happened, that he was whipped in a fair fight, and that if Governor Roosevelt would come to New Jersey to open his campaign, he would provide the largest political rally ever held in the United States."[7]

Regardless of how much bitterness Roosevelt felt toward Hague, one thing was certain; he was not about to seek revenge. New Jersey, after all, was a populous state with a sizeable block of electoral votes, which traditionally went to the Republican candidate. For Roosevelt to refuse the aid of the state's most powerful Democrat would be suicidal. There was no hope of carrying New Jersey without Frank Hague's endorsement.

Always the realist, Roosevelt extended the olive branch, accepted Hague's invitation, and opened his presidential campaign with a speech delivered in front of Governor A. Harry Moore's home at Sea Girt. Jim Farley estimated that between 100,000 and 115,000 people were present to hear Roosevelt at what was probably the largest political rally ever to take place in the United States. Roosevelt was markedly impressed by the demonstration. If Hague could do this, he probably could put the state in the Democratic column in November. The boss of Jersey City was speaking the nominee's language, and it appeared that the hatchet was buried forever. Indeed, some months after the general election when Hague had delivered the vote for Roosevelt, he wrote a note to the President. "Your recognition of our State Organization had been substantially manifested and in return I feel we owe you this pledge of loyalty. Should the occasion ever arise when New Jersey need be counted, I am yours to command."[8]

This letter reveals the heart of the Roosevelt-Hague relationship. Hague delivered the vote as promised in 1932. In return, the President showered the New Jersey boss with favors. As long as the favors poured in, Hague would use his machine to support Roosevelt, and as long as Roosevelt needed Hague, the favors would be forthcoming.

The evidence shows that from the outset of the New Deal, Frank Hague was in complete control of all federal patronage in the state. Federal appointments were not filtered through the Governor or New Jersey's Senators. On the contrary, the Mayor of Jersey City made all the decisions. Governor A. Harry Moore was inundated with appeals for help in finding various kinds of federal jobs. Almost invariably he answered the applicants in the way he wrote to a Newark, New Jersey man in August, 1933.

"I do not have the power," exclaimed the Governor "to appoint to these Federal positions. They are made upon recommendation of the local organizations to Mayor Hague, who, in turn, sends them in . . . I would suggest that you also get in direct touch with the mayor."[9]

When Hague wrote to Roosevelt that "your recognition of our State Organization had been substantially manifested," he implied that everyone in the Roosevelt Administration was being generous. No one wanted to offend Frank Hague and his organization. Jim Farley did his best to help if the cause was legitimate. The Postmaster General believed in party regularity. The Hague machine had put Roosevelt over in New Jersey, so it deserved New Jersey's share of the spoils. Typical of Farley's willingness to assist the Hague machine was an incident in 1934. Governor A. Harry Moore, a loyal Hague man, called upon Farley to use his influence to restore a friend to a post with the Civil Works Administration as an aeronautical inspector. It seems that the man was competent, but that his services were already covered by others in the state. Farley took the case to the Secretary of Commerce, who controlled this particular level of appointment. Although the man did not get his old job back, he was given another post of equal caliber.[10]

It is true that Farley always worked well with the big-city bosses. He talked their language, believed in party organization, and held with the philosophy that the winners should take the spoils. It is also true that Farley hoped to become president some day, and he believed his friendship with bosses like Hague would enhance his chances. However, there were limits to which Farley would go to win political support, for he was a man of unimpeachable integrity. An issue surrounding Farley and Hague which sheds light on this point came in the late 1930's after Hague had faithfully delivered the delegates and the votes in two presidential contests. As Postmaster General, Farley received evidence which proved that Frank Hague had one of his henchmen opening every piece of mail that went to or came from one of his political enemies. In a fit of anger, the usually jovial Farley stormed in to see the President for orders on how to proceed with arrest and prosecution. To Farley's disappointment, Roosevelt said: "Forget prosecution. You go tell Frank to knock it off. We can't have this kind of thing going on. But keep this quiet because we need Hague's support if we want New Jersey."[11]

Harry Hopkins was another who did his best to curry favors

with Frank Hague. An ex-social worker, Hopkins learned the game of politics fairly well, and he too had ambitions that went beyond the cabinet and ministership of relief. Striving to please Jersey City's boss, Hopkins gave Hague charge of over 18,000 CWA jobs in 1934. Then Hopkins appointed Hague's man, William Ely, as the first director of the Works Progress Administration in the state. During the thirties New Jersey employed between 76,000 and 97,000 annually through WPA.[12]

That Hopkins lacked the courage or the will to clamp down on Boss Hague is abundantly clear. New Jersey was one of the worst states in the nation when it came to political abuses in FERA and WPA. Hopkins was inundated with evidence from his own investigators and from injured citizens. Stacks of testimony and sworn affidavits testify to widespread political coercion. Men and women who held federal positions in New Jersey were forced to vote for the machine's candidates. Furthermore, it usually took connections to find employment in the first place. All jobholders were expected to "tithe" three per cent of their salaries to the machine at election time. Politics became so flagrantly interwoven in WPA that one director always answered his office phone, "Democratic headquarters!" Even where it was argued that Republicans controlled relief programs it was well known that Hague actually had his guiding hand in the system because he always rewarded a group of "machine Republicans" who worked faithfully for him by voting in Democratic primaries or becoming "Republicans for Hague."[13]

Hopkins not only ignored the overwhelming evidence of politics in relief programs, but he was up to his neck in it himself. New Jersey's state Director of Relief, William Ely, probably had some notion of ultimately building his own machine through the relief program. Consequently, he occasionally circumvented Hague's wishes on patronage if he thought he could do it and not get caught. Hopkins, however, used his personal influence to see that Hague's friends found jobs. In 1936, for example, Hopkins phoned Ely about a gentleman and said "Frank is very anxious to give him a job." Ely assured the Federal Minister of Relief that "I think maybe we can work it out." Then on another occasion, after a plea from Hague, Harry Hopkins decided to stretch the letter of the law and take WPA funds which were earmarked for labor costs and use them to buy seats and plumbing for Jersey City's new baseball stadium. Hague knew he was asking Hopkins to violate the law but assured him it was for a good cause inasmuch as the facility was to be named Roosevelt

Stadium and the president was going to be there for the grand opening. Once again Hopkins bowed to the throne in Jersey City and pressured Ely to look for a way to engineer the boondoggle for Hague.[14]

Besides these special favors from Hopkins, Frank Hague derived many other benefits from the New Deal. He estimated that his organization gave away approximately $500,000 a month through FERA to hungry families of the unemployed. WPA spent over $17,000,000 in Jersey City and Hudson County between 1933 and 1938, and by 1939, WPA had poured nearly $50,000,000 into the community. The machine took political advantage of every dollar and every job which the federal government provided.[15]

All of the federal support was helpful but some of the projects could be used more advantageously than others. The monumental Jersey City Medical Center, for instance, was built largely with grants and loans from the Public Works Administration. This gigantic complex was composed of seven buildings—the highest of which has twenty-three floors. All in all, the facility encompassed ninety-nine floors with 2000 beds. At the time of construction it was the third largest hospital in the world. The Medical Center was Hague's pride and joy. To focus attention on his pet project, he got President Roosevelt to come and lay the cornerstone in October, 1936. The Hudson County boss humbly thanked Roosevelt for the federal funds which were making the project possible. Once the center was finished, though, Hague unabashedly took full credit for extending medical care to everyone who could not afford to pay. He likewise took great delight in attention-getting extravaganzas at the hospital. Without fail, Mayor Hague appeared at the children's ward each Christmas with a lieutenant who was dressed as Santa Claus and bearing gifts for all. With great resourcefulness Frank Hague squeezed every ounce of political advantage out of the Medical Center. When election time drew near, the boss saw to it that families who had received hospital services were sent bills with enclosed notes informing them that if they went to see their district leader they could get their bills reduced or completely written off.[16]

In the final analysis, the combined efforts of Roosevelt, Farley, Hopkins, and countless other administrators insured New Deal benefits for the Hague machine. As a careful student of Hague's career concluded, "the fact that the New Deal worked through, rather than in competition with, Frank Hague heightened the dependence of Jersey City families on his organization during the depression decade. The CWA, PWA, WPA, etc., provided resource strength for the Hague machine as it became a vast employment and relief agency."[17]

If it was not for the fact that Roosevelt needed the large majorities Hague turned out for him in Hudson County—indeed Roosevelt could not have carried New Jersey in 1932, 1936, 1940 and again in 1944 without those margins—it is difficult to imagine the President aligning himself with Frank Hague. Roosevelt probably would have allowed due process to take its course in 1938 when Farley exposed the mail-opening incident, except for reasons of political expediency. If Jersey City's Mayor had not been a tried and true political asset, he would have gone the route of Kansas City's Tom Pendergast, upon whom Roosevelt unleashed the T-men in 1939. At least he would have met the fate of James Michael Curley, who never received New Deal favors because Roosevelt considered him a liability. This is so because unlike Fiorella LaGuardia, Edward Kelly, and Edward Flynn—three urban bosses Roosevelt genuinely liked and enjoyed being with—Frank Hague disgusted him. A key to Roosevelt's personal feelings toward politicians was the frequency of their social visits to Hyde Park. While numerous people met the president at his birth place for brief political meetings, only those Roosevelt thoroughly enjoyed picnicked there or socialized with their families overnight. It is significant that Hague attended only one luncheon at Hyde Park. The only time Mrs. Hague and the boss socialized with Roosevelt was on board a ship, *U.S.S. Indianapolis*, in 1934 to review the fleet. And this outing was a perfunctory political gathering which included a number of dignitaries and their wives from New Jersey and New York.[18]

Roosevelt, like many New Dealers, found Hague repulsive. A pushy, arrogant, domineering man, Hague once dictatorially boasted "I am the law" to a man who questioned the legality of one of his decisions. The New Jersey chieftain had the physique of an athlete, sharp features, and piercing ice blue eyes. He prided himself on his superb physical condition and enjoyed walking the feet and legs off his associates. His aggressive style complemented his obsessive personality. While he could be flexible when necessary for political advantage, he was a true believer when it came to several issues of the time.

Hague was militantly anti-Communist. Typical of many of the Americans he represented, he ignorantly equated Communism, socialism, and organized labor. In the name of preserving democracy, he pitched civil liberties to the wind. He said that civil liberties were bunk for anyone "working for the overthrow of the government"; and he advocated the establishment of concentration camps in Alaska for American radicals.[19]

Intellectually Frank Hague never grew beyond the elementary grade education he received in Jersey City's Horseshoe district. The capitalistic system was good in his eyes, and 100 per cent American. To the "Hudson County Hitler," as civil libertarians dubbed him, the Socialist Party and its leader Norman Thomas was subversive. Consequently, when Norman Thomas tried to speak in Jersey City, the Hague-controlled police force stood idly by while angry Hagueites pelted him with rocks and rotten vegetables. Thomas was detained by police without cause, and the Mayor followed this up by banning the socialist from speaking in Jersey City.[20]

Inasmuch as the local industrialists whom he admired and from whom he received so much support were adamantly opposed to the CIO, Hague did all in his power to oppose organized labor's entrenchment in New Jersey. However, this anti-labor stand was not merely a facade to garner the continued support of the Chamber of Commerce and industrial magnates. That Hague, the true believer, really viewed it as a Communist conspiracy against the American system is evident in his dogged attempt to find evidence of Communist connections by scanning the mail of New Jersey's CIO organizers. While Hague viewed all organized labor as a threat, his most poisonous venom was saved for the CIO. Of co-founder John L. Lewis, the demagogue from Jersey said he was merely "window dressing"—he was "a puppet of the Communist Party."[21]

By the late 1930's Hague unflinchingly resorted to police-state tactics of framing political opponents through the machine-controlled courts. Some apparently innocent persons were jailed for committing no crime other than challenging the "law" of Frank Hague. By 1937 and 1938, President Roosevelt drew increasing criticism from irate citizens, as well as from journalists who spoke for the liberal press. Given all of the adverse publicity and growing pressure, it is not at all surprising that Roosevelt allowed a situation to develop which could have worked to his advantage.[22]

It should be recalled that Roosevelt encouraged Joseph V. McKee to enter the mayoralty race in New York City in 1933 to insure Tammany's defeat—and hopefully to elect Fiorello LaGuardia. Regardless of who won, either McKee or LaGuardia, Roosevelt came out the winner. He had his hand in the contest but remained aloof enough to capitalize either way the race went. Then in 1938 in Missouri, Roosevelt played the game of subtly encouraging Lloyd Stark in his battle with Tom Pendergast. The President refused, however, to take sides openly until it was clear Stark had the Democratic Party fairly well in hand in Missouri. By 1940 a similar situation had developed in New Jersey. Hague was under constant attack for his fascist-style control of Hudson County, but to attack him openly as Farley suggested was dangerous. The danger lay in the fact that Hague did control the Democratic machinery and without his allegiance Roosevelt could not carry New Jersey.

Roosevelt's plan was to use his Secretary of the Navy, Charles Edison, son of Thomas A. Edison, to test the anti-Hague sentiment in New Jersey. If Edison could wrest control of the pro-Roosevelt forces in the state away from Hague, then Roosevelt could count New Jersey in the Democratic column in elections, yet be rid of the embarrassment of the notorious boss of Jersey City. Roosevelt's New Jersey scheme was delicate. The President had to encourage Edison to launch a reform crusade against the boss, but he had to appear above the battle himself. If Hague thought Roosevelt was in on the coup, then it could be "goodbye New Jersey" in 1940.

The plan seemed especially plausible in light of the Republican victories in Jersey's off-year elections in 1938. The word which reached the White House was that Republicans won for two reasons. First, citizens were embittered by Roosevelt's attempt to pack the Supreme Court. Secondly, laborers who ordinarily voted Democratic deserted the party because of Hague's bitter fight against the CIO. This was the first time Hague had not delivered for the New Deal. Was he losing his grip? The best way of finding out, given Roosevelt's way of thinking, was to send up a trial balloon and get a reading.[23]

Circumstances and events conspired to make Charles Edison the trial balloon. By 1940 Roosevelt knew war was imminent. In order to avoid making preparedness appear to be a Democratic Party monopoly, he wanted to appoint Republicans to key defense positions. How fortuitous it was that the Secretary of Navy was from New Jersey. If Edison resigned and ran for governor of New Jersey, he could open a cabinet post for a Republican, and at the same time, test the wind for breaking Hague's hold on the state. Like McKee and LaGuardia, Charles Edison was taken in by Roosevelt's facade of sincerity. Like so many others, he went out to do battle for Roosevelt only to find that it was his own fight—

the President's aid would never be forthcoming.

The plan was quickly implemented. Edison entered the Democratic primary and to the surprise of many received Hague's endorsement. He resigned from the cabinet and Republican Frank Knox was appointed. When Roosevelt accepted Edison's resignation he told him "I hope you will be elected—and I say this because you have a deep-seated feeling of responsibility to good government and efficient government, which I hope will be recognized by the people of your State." Edison was elected, and Roosevelt sent him a leather notebook as a gift of congratulations.[24] On the same day in 1940 that Edison was elected governor, Frank Hague delivered a whopping Hudson County vote for Franklin D. Roosevelt. Hague had worked hand-in-glove with Chicago's Edward Kelly at the national convention to railroad the President through for an unprecedented third term, and he followed up with a huge margin in Jersey City which Roosevelt needed to carry the state.

Soon after Edison entered the governor's mansion, he launched an all-out crusade against the Jersey City boss. For the three years of his term he battled the boss, and frequently went to Washington to consult with the President. Although Roosevelt could lend behind-the-scenes encouragement to Edison, the trial balloon, he never publicly or openly declared his opposition to Hague and his tactics of repression and demagoguery.[25]

Charles Edison was in almost every way the antithesis of Hague. He was well educated and reflective, where Hague was ignorant and impetuous. Edison had warm eyes, a sincere smile, and calm and somewhat rounded, soft features, whereas Hague had dashing cold eyes, chiseled features, and the lean, hungry look of a hawk. Edison was a calm, reasonable, and articulate speaker, and Hague was hard, flamboyant and impulsive. Edison was an idealist, and his rhetoric was reminiscent of early twentieth-century progressives. He had no organization and made no attempt to build one. Hague, on the other hand, was a calculating realist who understood that organization was essential to winning and keeping office, and that an organization was built on patronage and favors rather than party ideals.[26]

Edison also had the severe handicap of being unable to succeed himself as Governor after one three-year term because of the state constitution. During his three years in office he managed to embarrass Hague, pushed forward the movement for a new state constitution, and gave the citizens some relief from the extraordinarily high taxes they were paying under the Hague-controlled, highly wasteful government. In the final analysis, though, the trial balloon showed Hague to be indestructible without more drastic action. A journalist with the *New Republic* summed up Edison's impact and Hague's reaction quite well. "After three years in office," wrote Willard Wiener, "Edison has retired to private life. He has materially weakened Hague's stronghold on the people of New Jersey and has provided a favorable opportunity to launch, with federal help, a campaign of liberation. But Hague is still strongly entrenched, with his chief support found in Washington and the Catholic Church, which he has played for all it is worth."[27]

As time passed it was clear that Hague could be embarrassed but not destroyed. It would have taken action such as Farley suggested in the late 1930's but which Roosevelt would have no part of. In other words, Hague would have to be sent to prison if the Jersey City machine was to be toppled. But Frank Hague was destined to remain in power until he voluntarily retired from office in 1947 at the age of seventy-one. Roosevelt refused to destroy Hague—which he certainly could have done—because the man who ruled Jersey City politics for nearly half a century was more valuable to the President at the helm of New Jersey's Democracy than he was in prison.

Notes

The author thanks the American Philosophical Society for a grant which helped finance the research for this essay.

1. Marquis W. Childs, "Dictator—American Style," *Reader's Digest*, XXXII (Aug. 1938); Jack Alexander, "King Hanky-Panky of Jersey," *Saturday Evening Post*, 213 (Oct. 26 1940); Willard Wiener, "Hague is the Law," *New Republic*, 110 (Jan. 31, 1944); *Literary Digest*, 123 (May 22, 1937).

2. Mark S. Foster, "The Early Career of Mayor Frank Hague" (M.A. thesis, U. of Southern California, 1968), 5–7; Sutherland Denlinger, "Boss Hague," *Forum*, XCIX (Mar. 1938).

3. Dayton D. McKean, *The Boss: The Hague Machine in Action* (Boston, 1940), 20–27; Denlinger.

4. Foster, 7–8; McKean, 26–29.

5. Mark S. Foster, "Frank Hague of Jersey City: The Boss as Reformer," *New Jersey History*, LXXXVI (Summer, 1968), 106–117.

6. Richard J. Connors, "The Local Political Career of Mayor Frank Hague," (Ph. D. diss., Columbia U., 1966), ch. III; Wiener, 110; McKean, ch. 8, 9;

Foster, "Reformer," 107–8.

7. James A. Farley, *Behind the Ballots* (New York, 1938), 158.

8. Farley, 158; Hague to Roosevelt, Nov. 24, 1933, President's Personal File 1013, Roosevelt Mss., Hyde Park.

9. A. Harry Moore to Joseph Melici, Aug. 12, 1933, A. Harry Moore Mss., State Library, Trenton, file "Federal 1932–1934."

10. Correspondence in A. Harry Moore Mss., Trenton, file "Federal, 1932–1934."

11. Interview with James A. Farley, Dec. 18, 1966.

12. Connors, 130; Arthur Macmahon et al., *Administration of Federal Work Relief* (Chicago, 1941), 199.

13. Political Coercion, New Jersey 610 WPF, National Archives; Lorena Hickok to Harry Hopkins, Feb. 11, 1936, Box 89, Narrative Field Reports, FERA-WPA, Roosevelt Library, Hyde Park.

14. Hickok to Hopkins, Feb. 11, 1936, Box 89, Narrative Field Reports. FERA-WPA, Roosevelt Library; transcripts of telephone conversations between Hopkins and Ely, Jan. 6,16, 1937, and between Hopkins and Hague, Jan. 14, 1937, Harry Hopkins Mss., Box 93, Roosevelt Library.

15. McKean, 103–4.

16. McKean, ch. 10; Connors, 130.

17. Connors. 130.

18. President's Personal File 1013, Roosevelt Library; interview with James A. Farley, Dec. 28, 1966.

19. Bruce Blivens, Jr., "Will the Witness Step Down?" *New Republic*, 95 (June 29, 1938).

20. "Liberty in Journal Square," *New Republic*, 95 (May 18, 1938); "Mayor Hague's Long Shadow," *New Republic*, 95 (June 15, 1938); McAlister Coleman, "Hague's Army Falls Back," *Nation*, 147 (Nov. 26, 1938).

21. Heywood Broun, "Shoot the Works," *New Republic*, 95 (Jan. 19, 1938).

22. "Mayor Hague's Long Shadow," *New Republic*, 95 (June 15, 1938); *New York Times*, Feb. 18, 1938; McKean, 144. See also materials in Official File 300, New Jersey 1938 and File 134, Roosevelt Library, for correspondence relating to Hague and civil liberties. Among the periodicals which put Hague under fire and sometimes Roosevelt for tolerating him, see especially the *Nation* and *New Republic* in 1937 and in 1938.

23. Edward Whalen to Roosevelt, Dec. 29, 1933, Official File 300, Democratic National Committee, 1938, New Jersey, Roosevelt Library.

24. Charles Edison to Roosevelt, Dec. 30, 1940, President's Personal File 3159, Roosevelt Library; press release, June 24, 1940, President's Personal File 3159, Roosevelt Library.

25. President's Personal File 3159, Roosevelt Library.

26. Edison's speeches and letters were in Charles Edison Mss., State Library, Trenton.

27. Jack Alexander, "Ungovernable Governor," *Saturday Evening Post*, 215 (Jan. 23, 1943); Wiener, 110.

Promoted as a "town for the motor age," Radburn, New Jersey, combined the features of an English garden city with a street system that, though connected to major highways, was to insulate residential spaces from the automobile. But its limited area and the Depression kept it from achieving the full range of goals planners envisioned for it. Photograph dated September 19, 1929, from undated pamphlet, Radburn, The Town for the Motor Age; *courtesy New Jersey Historical Society.*

15

Historians deal not just with written documents but with assorted material and visual relics of the past as well. Influenced by art historians and anthropologists, recent historians have become concerned with "material culture," the objects (such as pottery, furniture, tools, and equipment) that people use in everyday life. Architectural historians have traced the changing styles and construction techniques of buildings. Urban historians have examined maps, street plans, architectural renderings, and photographs not only to understand the location of cities, their growth rates, and their institutional structure but also to determine how buildings are designed and how people use space. Their objective is to discover not just the layout of American urban areas but also how planners expected them to work, how people hoped to live.

Radburn in Fair Lawn, Bergen County, is a particularly interesting example of a planned community. This suburb started as an experiment meant to provide an alternative urban area for New Jerseyans and a model for the rest of the country. Cities planned and built from scratch have been created from time to time all over the world. However, the migration to America and the westward movement of many of its people offered a unique opportunity for such planned communities. Colonial proprietors, religious leaders, speculators and boosters, railroad companies and industrialists—all developed proposals for towns, many of which John W. Reps reproduced in *The Making of Urban America* (1965).

Urban planners found ideas for planned cities in both old and new sources. The earliest plans for American cities resemble the fortified towns of Europe, a natural result of the fact that they were viewed as outposts in an unsafe world. A few New England villages followed a linear pattern with houses strung out alongside a river or road, but the most common plan used in America was the grid with two sets of parallel streets at right angles to one another that formed square or rectangular blocks. Neat, orderly, and easy to survey, the grid also enabled speculators to reap quick profits.

Yet by the late eighteenth century, cities based on this plan were seen as monotonous and boring. The plans in the 1790s for the new capital, Washington, D.C., added diagonal streets for interest. By the 1830s another pattern came into vogue, although it was never as popular as the grid. Influenced by the Romantic movement in general and the design of English gardens in particular, planners in the United States began to map out curving streets and oddly shaped blocks, first for cemeteries and parks and then for suburban developments. Llewellyn Park in South Orange, New Jersey, built in 1853, incorporated elegant homes for the wealthy surrounded by winding streets and a parklike setting.

The plan for Radburn was also influenced by the design of English gardens, but it went further. Radburn was meant to be an experiment in both "physical and social planning." The objective was to create a self-contained community that embodied a solution to the traffic problems caused by the automobile. As originally conceived, houses, schools, stores, and industries were fitted into a rural landscape. Unlike Llewellyn Park, whose residents were wealthy, Radburn was intended to draw its inhabitants from the middle and working classes.

The rise of the automobile made suburban communities like Radburn both possible and necessary. As statistics make clear, by the 1920s the need to include provisions for motor vehicles was becoming urgent. In 1910 there were eight thousand automobiles registered in the United States; by 1920 there were more than eight million and by 1930 more than twenty-three million. The rate of increase slowed during the Depression and World War II but again expanded rapidly afterward: in 1950 there were more than forty million cars registered and by 1955 more than fifty-two million. It is no wonder that the post-1950 suburban population of New Jersey exploded.

In the proposed layout of Radburn, curving, wide streets replaced the grid pattern to permit the efficient flow of through traffic; narrower streets led to houses. Numerous streets ended in cul-de-sacs that provided privacy and traffic control. Houses were clustered together to leave space for open parklands, and detached single-family homes were mixed in with semi-attached and multi-unit buildings. From a modern perspective, the plan hardly seems innovative, but it was novel when it was designed. Radburn was planned to accommodate the automobile, but what happened when the plans were put in place? How much of the original design of houses and streets was implemented? What happened to the concept of constructing an entire community? What did Radburn become, and why?

A final aspect of the plan for Radburn is worth considering. The proposed community was designed to provide for all aspects of life—education, recreation, living, and working. It was originally expected to house "a wide range of income groups" so that there would be bankers and shopkeepers, teachers and laborers—every type of working person a community would need to take care of itself. However, building costs raised the expense of housing and thus restricted who could live there. Radburn became a middle-class "bedroom suburb." What have Americans done since to provide moderate- and low-income housing? What are the consequences for communities of the failure to design such housing? What does segregation of housing by income do to a community and to its relationship with communities around it?

Suggested Readings

Lapping, Mark B. "Radburn: Planning the American Community." *NJH* 95 (1977): 85–100.

McKelvey, Blake. "Planning the City Beautiful." Chap. 8 in *The Urbanization of America, 1860–1915*. New Brunswick, N.J., 1963.

_____ . "An Outburst of Metropolitan Initiative: 1920–1929." Chap. 2 in *The Emergence of Metropolitan America, 1915–1966*. New Brunswick, N.J., 1968.

Reps, John W. *The Making of Urban America: A History of City Planning in the United States*. Princeton, N.J., 1965.

Wright, Gwendolyn. *Building the Dream: A Social History of Housing in America*. Cambridge, Mass., and London, 1981.

✦ ✦ ✦ ✦ ✦ ✦

Lessons in Land Use: Radburn and the Regional Planning Association of America

Daniel Schaffer

A town built to live in—today and tomorrow. A town 'for the motor age.' A town turned outside-in—without any backdoors.

From *Planned and Utopian Experiments: Four New Jersey Towns*, edited by Paul A. Stellhorn. Trenton, N.J., 1978. Reprinted by permission of New Jersey Historical Commission.

A town where roads and parks fit together like fingers on your right and left hands. A town in which children never dodge motor-trucks on their way to school. A new town—newer than the garden cities, and the first major innovation in town-planning since they were built.

Geddes Smith on Radburn[1]

Sunnyside Gardens and Radburn and the Greenbelt towns were but finger exercises, preparing for symphonies that are yet to come.

Lewis Mumford[2]

Bergen County in northern New Jersey represents the archetypal affluent American suburb. Its landscape is characterized by detached single-family houses centered on spacious, well-kept lawns; busy state roads lined with a variety of malls and light industrial plants; an eight-lane interstate highway slicing through the county to facilitate access to other areas; and a sprinkling of colleges, parks, golf courses, and country clubs. Pursuit of private wealth and satisfaction defined by material success are the foundations of the county's ideal, and the privately owned home and automobile give both meaning and structure to its suburban way of life.

The values and lifestyles of the majority of families who reside in Bergen County are basically the same as those of other suburbanites throughout the country.[3] With a median family income exceeding thirteen thousand dollars a year, with 16 percent of its adult population college-educated, with every conceivable type of store and service available in three large shopping centers and along two state highways, Bergen County is what most people consider a suburban paradise—with the benefits and liabilities associated with such an environment.[4] Pockets of poverty exist, and the construction of high-rise apartments along the Hudson River in Fort Lee has changed the complexion of the County's southeastern section. But the private house, the highway, and the bustling shopping center have left an indelible mark upon both the landscape and the residents in this area of New Jersey.

Picture, if you will, an alternative environment for Bergen County. Instead of an endless clutter of individual lots and houses, with commercial establishments stretched along the length of major highways, imagine a constellation of relatively self-contained communities separated by green, open space. Each community would contain between twenty-five and fifty thousand people. Housing, commerce, and industry would all be integrated in the original site plan, so that most of the residents' daily needs could be met within the confines of the community. But the towns would not be entirely isolated entities. A sophisticated transportation network would bind them together to permit access to a diversity of cultural activities that only a large population of several hundred thousand people could support. A system of mass transit and "townless highways" or parkways would lace through open space permanently devoted to agriculture and recreation. This "undeveloped" area would not only provide food for the communities but also give them physical definition. Unplanned suburban growth—or what one student of urban America has called "land pollution"—would be replaced by a plan for orderly, systematic land use. Indeed the word "undeveloped" in its conventional sense would no longer apply, for each parcel of land would be developed to fill a specific purpose in a balanced urban-and-rural environment.[5]

Hidden within Bergen County's extensive suburban development lies Radburn, a small, almost inconspicuous manifestation of this larger vision of balanced regional growth. Radburn, originally conceived as a town for twenty-five thousand people, exists today as a community of three thousand residents forming a section of the Borough of Fair Lawn. Though Radburn's growth has been aborted, its site plan has served as an ideal model for urban planners since the existing elements of the community were introduced in 1928. But American planners have too often separated the technical achievements of Radburn—such as the use of cluster housing and cul-de-sacs (dead-end streets)—from the social and regional context in which these ideas were developed. The purpose of this paper is to discuss Radburn as an experiment in physical and social planning intended not to improve the suburban environment as it exists but rather to change the nature of land use and development throughout the United States.

Advertised as "the town for the motor age," Radburn was the first planned community to consider the automobile a vital part of the American way of life, but one that should not be permitted to dominate the landscape.[6] Twenty years after the construction of Radburn, Clarence Stein, one of the community's chief architects and site planners, stated that "the Radburn idea" sought to discover "how to live with the auto," or perhaps more precisely, "how to live in spite of it!"[7] To overcome the problems created by the automobile required a radical rethinking of the relationship of homes, streets, gardens, paths, parks, neighborhoods and highways. A functional relationship among these elements was attained through the creation of the "safety-hurst or superblock," Radburn's basic unit of construction. Instead of the predominant residential or commercial grid or checkerboard pattern of 200-by-600-foot rectangular blocks, the planners of Radburn introduced large interior spaces of 1200 feet by 1800 feet, uninterrupted by vehicular traffic. Each of these "superblocks," circumscribed by a roadway that directed automobiles around rather than through the community, had an interior area ten to fifteen times the size of a conventional American city block. Instead of the inefficient, unsightly maze of garages and alleys typical of American development at that time, Radburn contained open spaces averaging four to six acres in size set aside for common interior parkland. This design created a direct link between the parks and homes.[8]

In Radburn, the community was protected, but not entirely insulated, from vehicular traffic. The width and length of each roadway was predetermined by the role it would play in the transportation network of the community. Express or arterial highways would connect Radburn to other towns; secondary or connector roads would tie together the six superblock units originally planned; and finally service roads or cul-de-sacs would provide residents with direct access to their houses. This plan prevented the roadway from dominating the environment and thus becoming the most significant factor in the town's development. Since the roadways were planned to serve specific functions, they varied substantially in width. Indeed the cul-de-sacs were built as narrow as 20 feet, a more than adequate size for the limited use they would receive. This preplanned, functional street system enabled the designers of Radburn to confine roadways to 21 percent of the development instead of the approximately 35 percent in conventional American subdivisions.[9]

Slotted into the edges of the superblocks, the cul-de-sacs were lined with ten to eighteen houses apiece, creating a ratio of seven homes per acre—almost twice the density of conventional suburban developments. Clustering houses and laying out smaller, less numerous streets preserved a good deal of land within the superblock for common interior parkland. Of the 149 acres ultimately developed as a part of Radburn, twenty-three acres (about 15 percent of the total area) consisted of green open space to be shared by the entire community. The money saved through a

25-percent reduction of the space used for streets and utility lines even provided the capital to construct and landscape the common parks. This fact led Henry Wright, Sr., one of Radburn's chief site planners, to conclude that "these parks come to us for almost nothing—merely the price of the virgin land—" because they "do not have to be served by sewers, water, gas and all sorts of things, as they would have to be if the street ran along in front of them."[10]

Although almost half of the houses in Radburn were single-unit dwellings, they were not erected on typical quarter- or half-acre building lots. Indeed Radburn could never have been built if conventional zoning ordinances had been in effect in Fair Lawn during the 1920s. Such laws, which typically divided the land into a set of identical lots, would have precluded cluster housing. Instead of platting the land as an initial step, the planners of Radburn began by creating a pleasing relationship among the houses to be erected along each cul-de-sac. Once they had positioned the houses, they determined the size and shape of each lot. By reversing the conventional process of development, the Radburn site plan freed the architect from the restraint imposed by rigid geometric patterns and permitted him to experiment in innovative methods of land development. Various types of housing—single-unit, semiattached, row, and multiunit dwellings—could all be incorporated in the original design of a single superblock to avoid the one-dimensional quality of detached, one-family homes common in the conventional American suburb.

To create an attractive diversity of housing, as well as to save space and money, about 50 percent of the houses in Radburn were either attached or multiunit dwellings. By varying the roof lines, colors, external compositions, and textures of the houses, the designers of Radburn developed a diverse residential environment. This variety was created, not despite the construction of row houses, but because of it. Through the use of a number of simple but effective techniques the architects of Radburn's attached houses avoided the monotony associated with row houses in places like Philadelphia and Baltimore. Moreover, the construction of cluster housing provided the opportunity to overcome the conformity dictated by suburban development that carved the land into identical lots.[11]

A system of walkways connected the houses with the interior parkland. Underpasses and overpasses between the superblocks permitted a complete separation of vehicular and pedestrian traffic. The site plan protected the pedestrian from the dangers presented by the automobile and freed the driver from the inconveniences created by the pedestrian. This accomplishment led the *New York Times* to editorialize that Radburn represented "the first deliberate attempt to harmonize the rights of the pedestrian and of the motorist."[12] Since no home was more than 400 feet from either the parkland or a major roadway, Radburn provided accessibility to both the automobile and the natural environment. With the danger and congestion caused by gas-driven vehicles emerging as a fundamental problem in twentieth-century America, and with the nation's increasing emphasis upon leisurely and recreational activity, it was Radburn's apparent ability to address these two issues in a successful manner that elicited a positive response from the planning profession.

To reduce the impact of the automobile upon the residential areas even further, each home was given two entrances of equal importance—one on the cul-de-sac, designed for the delivery of goods and services, and the other on the pedestrian walkway or parkland, intended for leisure and recreational activities. "At Radburn we have abolished the backyard and made it the front yard," proclaimed Louis Brownlow, the municipal consultant to the firm financing the construction of Radburn. "We have tried to do away with the backdoor and we are building houses that have no backs, but have two fronts."[13] Perhaps nowhere was this idea more clearly expressed than in the floor plan of a Radburn house. Unlike the layout of the conventional American house, the interior design of a house in Radburn was turned "outside in." Rooms designed for family use and sleeping, which had traditionally fronted the street, faced the walkways or parkland. And the utility rooms, such as the kitchen, overlooked the noisier, less aesthetically pleasing cul-de-sacs instead of the landscaped backyards. In other words, the "integrated framework" created a house with "two faces" looking out on two views, of which "the one is paved, the other mainly green." Each entrance, like each specialized roadway, was developed as a part of the site-plan to serve a specific function.[14]

None of the elements in the "Radburn idea" was entirely new. First, in Central Park, built in the mid-nineteenth century, Frederick Law Olmsted, Sr., had completely separated pedestrian and vehicular traffic. Although those responsible for Radburn lived and worked in New York City, Olmstead apparently did not serve as the source of their inspiration. The use of common interior parkland and cul-de-sacs in the English garden cities of

Letchworth and Welwyn provided a more immediate example for Radburn's site planners. Indeed, Stein and Wright visited these English communities on a "special investigation trip" before planning Radburn. Second, in the 1920s, a specialized highway system was in its initial stages of development in the United States. Westchester County in New York State had constructed a small network of limited access parkways; and New Jersey had designed cross-county thoroughfares like railway lines to bypass towns and admit traffic only at particular locations similar to railroad terminals. Finally, even houses oriented toward the parkland had been experimented with in Sunnyside Gardens, Queens, the first community planned under the influence of those who were ultimately responsible for the "Radburn Idea."[15]

In Radburn, however, these concepts were synthesized and broadened into a new environmental design. The common interior space in an English garden city was the size of a small courtyard, and its primary purpose was to create a tranquil retreat for the residents; in Radburn it was expanded in both size and purpose to become the fundamental element of the residential environment protected from the automobile. In the United States, the specialized highway systems constructed during the 1920s were rarely sophisticated enough to do more than distinguish parkways and expressways from ordinary city streets. In Radburn, the planners applied Benton MacKaye's conception of a "highwayless town" and "townless highway." Instead of reinforcing the conventional methods of development, Radburn's intricate functional street system, designed in relation to residential areas and open space, contained the potential for the creation of a new pattern of land use.[16] Thus Radburn struck a responsive chord among urban planners because it synthesized the concerns and ideas which the profession had expressed for the past two decades. These factors led Thomas Adams, the general director of the Regional Plan of New York, who was perhaps the most noted planner in the United States during the 1920s, to call Radburn "the most forward step in town planning in America."[17]

The design techniques—including the superblock, the specialized highway system, the complete separation of pedestrian and vehicular traffic, and the turned-around houses—were devised to direct the residents' attention away from the street and toward the parkland. The institutions and facilities basic to any community would all be accessible via the walkways in the park. Although the designers of Radburn did not believe that the physical layout of a community determined social values, they were convinced that the site plan was not a neutral factor. Whereas the automobile frayed the social fabric of American communities, Radburn's planners maintained that the parkland (constructed in relationship to educational, civic and commercial centers) would generate an atmosphere conducive to neighborliness and cooperative effort.

"Small neighborhoods are essential for eye-to-eye democracy," Stein proclaimed in *Toward New Towns for America*, an autobiographical account of his professional career. "This is basic, not only for local contentment, but for national freedom and world-wide security."[18] The sentiment expressed in this statement characterizes the social values which shaped the principles of the "Radburn idea." The site plan at Radburn represented more than a series of technical solutions to the problems of housing and congestion facing twentieth-century America. For those who designed Radburn, it provided the potential for creating a face-to-face village atmosphere in a modern industrial society.

To construct such a social environment, the "neighborhood unit" concept was used in Radburn. Originally designed for twenty-five to thirty thousand residents, the town was divided into three neighborhoods ranging in size from five to ten thousand people. In the simplest terms, a "neighborhood unit" could be described as two superblocks with radii of no more than one-half mile. However, the size of each "neighborhood unit" was actually determined by the number of children (and therefore the number of households) needed to support an elementary school, which would serve not only as an educational facility for the children but also as a cultural center for adults. In addition to the elementary schools, a high school—symbolically located at Radburn's highest point of elevation—was envisaged as the institution that would bind the entire community together. Just as the church provided the nexus for community activities in a colonial New England town, so would the school in Radburn. As another tool used to shape an environment that would facilitate community interaction, the school provided the forum where residents could exchange their ideas and interests.[19]

The conception of community development embodied in the "Radburn idea" was borrowed largely from the principles of the English garden-city movement. This town-planning movement had developed from the writings of an obscure English court stenographer, Ebenezer Howard, who in 1898 had published *Tomorrow: A Peaceful Path to Real Reform* (now known under the title of the 1902 edition, *Garden Cities of To-Morrow*). Howard's emphasis on planned dispersion that would create a poly-nucleated pattern of development has served as the foundation of the garden-city movement throughout the twentieth century, and it provided the basis for the construction of Radburn.[20]

Howard's ideas were transplanted to the American landscape by a small, informal organization called the Regional Planning Association of America (RPAA). Throughout its ten-year existence (1923–1933) the association rarely had more than a dozen active members, and it never operated on a budget exceeding $2,500 annually.[21] In place of a strong institutional framework, the RPAA relied on a shared commitment to dealing with the problems of housing, urban reform, and regional development. Architects and planners Clarence Stein, Henry Wright, Sr., Frederick L. Ackerman, and Robert D. Kohn; conservationist Benton MacKaye; urban critic and author Lewis Mumford; economist Stuart Chase; and realtor Alexander Bing formed the nucleus of the group. "Never a formal organization with an office, a staff, a regular publication, and a schedule of meetings," historian Mel Scott has stated, "the association was really no more than a circle of friends held together by a broad conception of planning."[22]

From the outset, the RPAA was committed in principle to the construction of garden cities throughout America. But the association realized that the building of communities, not to mention the "comprehensive planning of regions," was an extraordinarily complex process requiring enormous experience and capital. As a first step toward its ultimate goal, the RPAA was instrumental in the planning of Sunnyside Gardens (1924–28) in Queens, New York, where Stein and Wright served as the chief site planners and architects. Built on a seventy-acre tract in the shadow of Manhattan's skyline, Stein described Sunnyside as "a dress rehearsal" on the "cramped stage" of New York City's grid pattern. Encouraged by the success of this preliminary investigation, in 1927 the RPAA began to discuss plans for the nation's first garden city. These discussions, held at the Hudson Guild Farm in Netcong, New Jersey, ultimately led to the "Radburn idea" and the construction of Radburn.[23]

But from the initial conversations, it was apparent that Radburn would compromise a number of Howard's basic principles. The protective greenbelt, an essential component of the garden city, was abandoned in Radburn because of the cost and difficulty of acquiring large tracts of land near the nation's large metropolitan centers. Members of the RPAA realized that Radburn's site plan, which included an expressway along the northern boundary and a strip of parkland on the eastern edge of the community, gave insufficient protection from the onslaught of suburbanization on the adjacent land. Built on one square mile of land without the five-mile greenbelt recommended by Howard, Radburn would lack the physical definition and the rural-urban balance integral to a complete garden city.

In Howard's model, the garden city was a relatively self-contained community incorporating agricultural, residential, commercial, and industrial facilities. The absence of a greenbelt around Radburn left the area open to development and therefore jeopardized the production of foodstuffs on it. The RPAA relinquished this garden city principle in the initial stages of discussion. The members also realized that it would be difficult to attract industry to a new community. They chose Fair Lawn in part because of its proximity to the markets in New York City and Paterson. The George Washington Bridge, then under construction, and a proposed state highway across Bergen County would eventually tie Radburn to the New York metropolitan area. The Erie Railroad, with a station servicing Radburn, would provide another means of transportation for the town. The planners set aside ample space for industrial development, but they overestimated the strength of Radburn's geographic location. "We found," Stein reminisced twenty years after the construction of Radburn, "that industry lives in the present." Proposals for a sophisticated transportation network in the future were not enough to attract industrial establishments into the community. When Radburn opened in May 1929, the Erie Railroad was "a secondary branch which went nowhere of importance," the George Washington Bridge was still under construction, and designs for Bergen County's state highway were first being drafted. Even if the Great Depression had not struck five months after the first residents arrived, it would have been difficult to establish a strong industrial base for the community. Conceived as a garden city, Radburn emerged as a "satellite town" that would depend upon the surrounding area for employment opportunities.[24] The economic collapse of the 1930s destroyed even that vision. With three thousand people, Radburn became a small section of Fair Lawn—part of a dormitory suburb contrary to the RPAA's ideal.

In his model, Howard included housing for a wide range of income groups so that each garden city would be a microcosm of the larger society. In the conferences leading to the construction of Radburn, it soon became evident that the community would not be able to accommodate a large spectrum of the population. As Stein lamented,

> if the poorly paid workers were admitted into the garden city, the industry that used them would have to subsidize these workers' houses or advance their wages; there was no other way of providing them with the barest minimum of good houses unless the garden city duplicated the very conditions that it existed to escape from.[25]

The standard of housing and the number of community facilities the RPAA proposed in America's first garden city would price the working class out of the housing market. In January 1928, when the City Housing Corporation announced that it would finance the construction of Radburn, some hoped that skilled laborers and craftsmen would be able to purchase the houses. But prices during the first year ranged from $7,900 to $18,200, more than twice the average price of an American house in the late 1920s.[26] The high cost of maintaining a home in Radburn meant the community would contain affluent business executives and educated professionals. The first survey of Radburn, conducted in 1933, showed that 87 percent of the men had some college education and almost all of them held white-collar or professional positions. The social composition of Radburn hardly resembled the portrait drawn by Howard in his depiction of the garden city.[27]

To maintain the integrity of the site plan and to prevent speculative development, Howard called for the municipal ownership of land and a system of leaseholding rather than renting. Through a program of long-term rentals, periodically adjusted to reflect rising land values, Howard believed that the "unearned increment" obtained through individual speculative investment could be translated into a "collectively earned increment" to benefit all the residents.[28]

But the sacred tradition of private homeownership in the United States prevented this scheme from being transferred to Radburn. Except for the apartment units, houses in Radburn were sold individually rather than leased by the construction company or a private realtor. The common interior parkland was held in trust for the community by The Radburn Association, an "extramunicipal" government organized to conduct the town's political affairs.* Thus the backbone of Radburn's neighborhoods—the park—was protected from private speculation and development and preserved for the benefit of the entire community. But the method of attaining that goal was rooted in the American experience more than in Howard's ideas of municipal land ownership. The restrictive deeds established in the wealthy, romantic nineteenth-century suburbs of Roland Park, Maryland, and Llewellyn Park, New Jersey, and in the more contemporary development of Forest Hills, New York, built before World War I, served as the precedents for Radburn's political structure.[29] To placate potential investors and homeowners, the planners used traditional methods of real-estate development (based on deed restrictions placed on private contracts and mortgages) instead of the potentially revolutionary concept of public ownership.

Thus the experiment at Radburn failed to conform to several of the basic tenets of Howard's garden city. Since Radburn lacked a greenbelt, it was vulnerable to suburban sprawl, and since it failed to attract industry, it could never achieve the economic and social balance that was at the heart of Howard's reform measures. But despite these serious compromises, Radburn adhered to enough garden city principles to differ substantially from other residential developments throughout the country. "We committed our share of mistakes," Charles Ascher, the author of Radburn's land-use covenants, recently admitted, "but everything was planned."[30] Howard's emphasis on rational, systematic development—in contrast to the haphazard, incremental growth in most cities and suburbs—remained at the center of the "Radburn idea." Just as Howard had advocated, the site plan at Radburn was set up to limit the population to between twenty-five and thirty thousand people. Even before Radburn was designed, the RPAA concluded that an American garden city should not have more than fifty thousand residents because, in the words of Stein, a larger number of people would "complicate and heighten the costs of any city life." Without a lid on population growth, the RPAA feared Radburn would suffer from the

---

*The residents of Radburn are also citizens of the Borough of Fair Lawn, and must pay taxes to the municipal government. The Radburn Association is a "government within a government" equivalent to the contemporary homeowners' associations found in planned-unit developments and condominiums. Residents are required to pay an assessment fee to the association based on a percentage of the property tax. In Radburn the money is used for administration, park maintenance and recreational and cultural programs.

same problems that plagued conventional suburban development. Like Howard, the association contended that a community's ability to function was directly related to the size of the population.[31]

Since Howard had concluded that each community should stop growing at a predetermined point, the success of the garden-city movement depended ultimately on a pattern of land use that extended beyond the design and construction of one town. Howard envisioned a network of "social cities"—six limited-size communities surrounded by and linked to a larger "central city." As each community reached its population limit, it would cease to grow, and a process of "domestic colonization," or planned internal migration, would take place, leading to the creation of another garden city. Although each community would be relatively self-sufficient, it would be bound to all the others by a modern rapid transit system to facilitate social intercourse and to provide the structure for wide-ranging cultural activities. Thus Howard imagined a matrix of garden cities separated from each other by permanent belts of green open space. He believed that in such a scheme "each inhabitant of the whole group" would "enjoy all the new advantages of a great and modern city; and yet all the fresh delights of the country."[32]

The RPAA agreed in the main with Howard, and his vision inspired the construction of Radburn. But a variety of sources contributed to the organization's broad concept of regionalism. The mid-nineteenth-century French provincial movement, the principle of "geotechnics" first presented by the Scottish academician and activist Patrick Geddes, and studies in "regional ecology" conducted by American scientists John Wesley Powell, Nathan Shaler, and Morris Davis all filtered into the program for regional development articulated by the RPAA.[33] Geddes exerted a strong influence on the entire group, especially Mumford, who in the words of one scholar provided the "connective tissue" which held the principles of the RPAA together.[34] Geddes's analysis of the devastating effects of "conurbations"—tentacle-like webs of factories, mills, slums, and dormitory suburbs extending over the landscape—corresponded to the RPAA's critique of American society, while Geddes's alternative pattern of land use based on the unity of "place, work and folk-environment, function and organism"—provided a framework on which the RPAA hoped to build a program for regional development.[35]

Although members of the RPAA shared many values, perhaps it is unfair to suggest that the organization's concept of regionalism consisted of a single vision. As Mumford has recently written,

> all of us thought of planning in terms of some larger corporate organization than the community. MacKaye thought in continental terms and even liked—to my horror—to speak fondly of the Appalachian Empire. . . . Stein thought originally in terms of the State or the Region, as the latter was very vaguely defined in his own mind.

The organization, however, agreed on one principle. Just as the house could no longer be treated in isolation from the streets, utility lines, and parks which contributed to the larger environment, the community could not satisfactorily serve as the basis of any comprehensive plan for land development. But only in the most abstract terms or in aborted experiments like Radburn could the organization represent the regional vision it offered as an alternative to piecemeal growth.[36]

The inability of the RPAA to present a distinct regional plan may be less a failing than it first appears. With the sensibilities of skilled craftsmen, the members appreciated not only the potential but also the limitations of their work—whether these influences were economic, social or technical. In contrast to academic and professional overspecialization, the RPAA was organized primarily as a study group or educational forum designed to broaden the expertise of its members. Trained as architects, conservationists, economists, and site planners, they all viewed their own disciplines as parts of the overall issue of land use and development. Indeed the association was convinced that a regional plan would unfold only through a comprehensive, interdisciplinary approach. As Mumford put it, "unlike city planning, regional planning is not merely the concern of a profession: it is a mode of thinking and a method of procedure." The sense of process suggested in this statement affected each activity conducted by the RPAA, including the construction of Radburn.[37]

If the meetings held by the RPAA were educational forums, then the two communities influenced by them—Sunnyside Gardens and Radburn—provided the practical experience or field work necessary to explore the association's theories in practice. "The main point to remember is the experimentation of our group," Mumford has emphasized, "our willingness to make small mistakes instead of plunging into bigger ones."[38] This spirit of experimentation enabled Stein to reflect upon Radburn as "a splendid adventure: a voyage of discovery in search of a new and practical form of an urban environment to meet the actual requirements of today. This exploration opened up and charted the way—no matter how limited the settlement remains."[39]

Both the RPAA's commitment to regional development and its self-conscious experimental approach were basic to the evolution of the "Radburn idea." Any study of the history of the community must consider these two aspects to understand the full dimensions of the experiment. The Radburn design, with its superblock structure and its strict attention to the problems created by the automobile, marked a significant departure in the history of American urban planning. But the parkland, forming the core of the superblock, constituted only a part of what architectural historian Walter Creese has referred to as the "internal green," which itself is only one element of a comprehensive program for balanced regional growth. The "Radburn idea," not only as a physical construct but also as a part of a larger social and regional program, can only be understood through a study of garden city principles, or what Creese calls the "external green."[40] Radburn, lacking a regional pattern of development, was destined to turn into a suburb with a distinctive site plan. Instead of providing an alternative to traditional suburban development, the community was consumed by the process of land use its planners sought to change.

In 1928, Radburn was regarded as a small "initial step" toward the construction of garden cities for America. Within a few months after opening, it emerged as a dormitory suburb. Studying its distinctive site plan and strong sense of community, planners have long praised Radburn's technical innovations as ends in themselves. But for those who devised the "Radburn idea," the site plan was a means toward an end, a set of tools designed to shape an alternative to conventional patterns of land use on a regional scale. Among those who belonged to the RPAA Radburn was "but a finger exercise preparing for symphonies that are yet to come."[41]

Notes

1. Geddes Smith, "A Town for the Motor Age," *Survey Graphic* 59 (March 1, 1928): 695.

2. Clarence Stein, *Toward New Towns for America*, with an introduction by Lewis Mumford (Cambridge: MIT Press, 1973), p. 17.

3. For an analysis of the suburb in history see Sam Bass Warner, Jr., *Streetcar Suburbs: The Process of Growth in Boston 1870–1900* (Cambridge: Harvard University Press, 1962); Warner, *The Private City: Philadelphia in Three Periods of Its Growth* (Philadelphia: University of Pennsylvania Press, 1974); Kenneth T. Jackson, "The Crabgrass Frontier: 150 Years of Suburban Growth in America," in *The Urban Experience: Themes in American History*, ed. Raymond A. Mohl and James F. Richardson (Belmont, Calif.: Wadsworth Publishing Co., 1973); Joel Schwartz, "The Evolution of the Suburbs," in *Suburbia: The American Dream and Dilemma*, ed. Philip C. Dolce (New York: Anchor Press, 1976). For a then-and-now sociological analysis of the suburb, see Harlan Paul Douglass, *The Suburban Trend* (New York: The Century Co., 1925); and Herbert J. Gans, *The Levittowners: Ways of Life and Politics in a New Suburban Community* (New York: Pantheon Books, 1967).

4. U.S., Bureau of the Census, *1970 Census of the Population: Characteristics of the Population*, vol. 1, pt. 32 (Washington, D.C.: U.S. Government Printing Office, 1973), pp. 559–61. According to the 1970 census, the median family income throughout the United States was $8,231, and 10.7 percent of the population had completed four years of college or more. U.S., Bureau of the Census, *1970 Census of the Population: Characteristics of the Population: Summary Section 1*, vol. 1, pt. I (Washington, D.C.: U.S. Government Printing Office, 1973), pp. 94, 386.

5. Carl Feiss, "New Towns for America," *Town and Country Planning* 28 (January 1960): 235.

6. See the promotional literature distributed by the City Housing Corporation, the company that financed the construction of Radburn. The material may be found in the Radburn Library in Fair Lawn, N.J. For example, "Radburn Garden Homes" (New York, September 1, 1930); "Announcing Radburn, A New Town" (c. 1930). Also Henry M. Propper, "A New Town Planned for the Motor Age," *American City* 38 (February 1928): 152–54; "Radburn's Unique Plan Shows Results," *American City* 41 (November 1929): 142–44; Geddes Smith, "The Radburn Way," *Outlook* 153 (October 16, 1929): 257; Henry Wright, Sr., "Planning a Town for Wholesome Living," *Playground* 22 (March 1929): 182–84.

7. Stein, *Toward New Towns*, p. 41.

8. For the innovative features of the "Radburn idea" and the fundamental challenge the concept presented to traditional urban planning techniques, see Stein, *Toward New Towns*, pp. 37–73; also Roy Lubove, *Community Planning in the 1920's: The Contribution of the Regional Planning Association of America* (Pittsburgh: University of Pittsburgh Press, 1962), pp. 23–27; Mark Lapping, "The Middle Landscape and American Urban Theory (Ph.D. diss., Emory University, 1972).

9. Henry Wright, Sr., " 'Cul-de-Sac' Streets Effect Marked Economies," *American City* 39 (December 1928): 148–49; "The Radburn Plan," *National Real Estate Journal* (September 30, 1929): 74–76; Stein, *Toward New Towns*, p. 48.

10. Wright, "Wholesome Living," p. 684.

11. These innovations were first used in government-sponsored housing conducted by the Emergency Fleet Corporation and the United States Housing Corporation. See *Report of the U.S. Housing Corporation: Houses, Site-Planning,*

Utilities (Washington, D.C.: U.S. Government Printing Office, 1919), pp. 71–74; also Roy Lubove, "Homes and a Few Well Placed Fruit Trees: An Object Lesson in Federal Housing," *Social Research* 27 (Winter 1960): 469–86.

12. *New York Times*, January 26, 1928.

13. Louis Brownlow, "Building for the Motor Age," *Housing Problems in America: Proceedings of the Tenth National Conference on Housing* (New York: National Housing Association, 1929), p 149.

14. Clarence Stein, "Cities to Come," ca. 1955, Clarence Stein Papers, Olin Library, Cornell University, Ithaca, N.Y.

15. For a discussion of the ideas and experiments which influenced the creation of the "Radburn idea" see Stein, "Cities to Come"; Henry Wright, Sr., "The Autobiography of Another Idea," *The Western Architect* 39 (September 1930): 137–41. For further information on Sunnyside, which along with Radburn stands forth as one of America's most innovative experiments in community planning, see Stein, *Toward New Towns*, chap. 2, also Alexander Bing, "Sunnyside Gardens: A Successful Experiment in Good Housing at Moderate Prices," *National Municipal Review* 15 (June 1926): 330–36; Lewis Mumford, "Houses—Sunnyside-Up," *The Nation* 120 (February 4, 1925): 115–16; Henry Wright, Sr., *Rehousing Urban America* (New York: Columbia University Press, 1935), pp. 37–41.

16. For a description of the "highwayless town" and "townless highway," see Benton MacKaye, "Roads vs. Shuttles," *American City* 44 (March 1931): 125–26, "Townless Highways—To Relieve Through-Traffic Congestion and Restore a Rural Wayside Environment," *American City* 42 (May 1930): 94–96; and MacKaye and Lewis Mumford, "Townless Highways for the Motorist," *Harper's* 163 (August 1931): 347–56.

17. Thomas Adams, Edward Bassett, and Robert Whitten, "Neighborhood and Community Planning: Problems of Planning Unbuilt Areas," in *Regional Survey of New York and its Environs*, Thomas Adams, Gen. Director (New York: Committee on the Regional Plan of N.Y. and its Environs, 1929), vol. 7; *Neighborhood and Community Planning*, p. 256.

18. Stein, *Toward New Towns*, p. 225.

19. The "neighborhood unit" concept was first devised by Clarence Perry and appeared in "The Neighborhood Unit, A Scheme of Arrangement for the Family-Life Community," in *Neighborhood and Community Planning*, pp. 22–140. The four basic elements embodied in Perry's analysis—the school, open space, commercial facilities, and the deflection of traffic around rather than through the community—were all incorporated into the "Radburn idea." See Mark B. Lapping, "Radburn: Planning the American Community," *New Jersey History* 95 (Summer 1977): 93–94.

20. Ebenezer Howard, *Garden Cities of To-Morrow*, F. J. Osborn, ed. (1946 ed. of 1898 ed. [*To-morrow: A Peaceful Path to Real Reform*], Cambridge: MIT Press, paper series, 1965).

21. Regional Planning Association of America, "Minutes," June 7, 1923, October 17–19, 1927, Clarence Stein Papers.

22. Mellier Goodin Scott, *American City Planning since 1890* (Berkeley: University of California Press, 1969), p. 223.

23. Stein, "Radburn and the Radburn Idea," Clarence Stein Papers.

24. Stein, *Toward New Towns*, p. 39.

25. Regional Planning Association of America, "Minutes," October 8–9, 1927, Clarence Stein Papers.

26. For the price of houses in Radburn see Louis Brownlow, "New Town Planned for the Motor Age," *International Housing and Town Planning Bulletin* (February 1930): 4–11.

27. For the demographic composition of Radburn during its early stages of development, see Robert Bowman Hudson, *Radburn: A Plan for Living* (New York: American Association for Adult Education, 1934).

28. Howard, *Garden Cities*, p. 59.

29. For a discussion of the Radburn Association see Charles Ascher, "How Can a Section of a Town Get What It Is Prepared to Pay For?" *American City* 40 (June 1929): 98–99; Ascher, "The Extra-Municipal Administration of Radburn: An Experiment in Government by Contract," *National Municipal Review* 18 (July 1929): 442–46; Ascher, "Community Life in Radburn," *Survey* 66 (April 15, 1931): 99–100; Ascher, "Private Covenants in Urban Redevelopment," in *Urban Redevelopment: Problems and Practices*, ed. Coleman Woodbury (Chicago: University of Chicago Press, 1953).

30. Interview with Charles Ascher, New York City, December 1977.

31. Regional Planning Association of America, "Minutes," October 8–9, 1927, Clarence Stein Papers.

32. Howard, *Garden Cities*, p. 142.

33. For a discussion of the individuals who exerted an influence upon the Regional Planning Association of America see Lewis Mumford, "Modest Man's Enduring Contributions to Urban and Regional Planning," *Journal of American Institute of Architects* 65 (December 1976): 19–29; also Lubove, *Community Planning*, pp. 83–105; Carl Sussman, ed., *Planning the Fourth Migration: The Neglected Vision of the Regional Planning Association of America* (Cambridge: MIT Press, 1976), pp. 1–45.

34. Ibid., p. 19.

35. Patrick Geddes, *Cities in Evolution: An Introduction to the Town Planning Movement and to the Study of Civics* (New York: Harper and Row, 1971), p. 198.

36. Sussman, *Migration*, p. 21.

37. Lewis Mumford, "Regions, To Live In," *Survey* 54 (May 1, 1925): 152.

38. Lewis Mumford, letter to author, November 16, 1977.

39. Stein, *Toward New Towns*, p. 67.

40. Walter Creese, *The Search for Environment: The Garden City, Before and After* (New Haven: Yale University Press, 1966), p. 303.

41. Lewis Mumford, Introduction to *Toward New Towns*, p. 17.

The corner of Somerset and Waverly streets in Newark's Third Ward, 1930. By the First World War, the Newark News *called the area "unrestricted, haphazard, muddled, ignorant and irresponsible," a jumble of commercial, industrial, and domestic structures. Already overcrowded by the time of the Great Migration from the South, the ward grew into one of the most densely populated and unhealthy areas in the nation by 1940. Photograph courtesy Newark Public Library.*

16

For the twenty years or more print and broadcast journalists have been calling Newark, New Jersey's largest city, a sick community. By the 1960s, its housing stock was severely deteriorated, its industry had fled, and its population had decreased. Those left behind were in need of greater governmental services but were least able to pay the taxes needed to supply them. Clement Price's article on Newark's African-American population analyzes the role segregation has played in making Newark a troubled place. When and where did segregation develop? What is behind the city's decay? How does Newark's decline compare to that of other major American cities since World War II? Finally, how does an understanding of the history of segregation and urban decay improve one's perspective on the unrest of the 1960s, as well as on the problems that cities continue to face?

Historically and practically, racism, discrimination, and segregation differ. Racism is a cultural attitude that has been present in America since its settlement. It ascribes an inferior status based on color. Discrimination uses this supposed inferiority to justify unequal treatment. Segregation, the insistence on separate facilities for blacks and whites, developed later, but historians disagree about precisely where and when "Jim Crow" practices and legislation first appeared. In *The Strange Career of Jim Crow* (1955), C. Vann Woodward argued that there was no segregation in the South during slavery or under Reconstruction. Segregation appeared in the 1890s as a consequence of the Populist movement's challenges to southern politics. In contrast Leon Litwack, in *North of Slavery* (1961), noted that segregation existed in the North before the Civil War. Other historians, disagreeing with Woodward, have argued that Jim Crow laws adopted in the South after 1890 merely expressed in legal form practices that long predated them; moreover, segregation was more prevalent in urban than rural areas. Newark's example shows the complexity of questions about segregation and discrimination. Public schools in the city were legally segregated from 1828 to 1909, but afterwards *de jure* segregation was replaced by *de facto* segregation as blacks became an increasing percentage of the population. Segregation in the use of such public and private facilities as swimming pools, restaurants, theaters, and stores had existed before World War I but grew much worse afterward. During the Depression even such social service agencies as the Salvation Army segregated their relief efforts. World War II brought increased black militancy for civil rights, a new state constitution in 1947, and the creation of a state Division against Discrimination.

Despite segregation in many areas of urban life, housing in Newark originally was largely integrated. During the Depression, one resident recalled, "Our block was integrated . . . We had everything— Italians, Jews, Negroes—every kind of people." But after 1940 blacks were increasingly restricted to the central part of the city. Their overall poverty and deliberate discrimination on the part of white real estate agents and property owners helped assure their segregation in the center city, as did "white flight" to the suburbs.

What explains the complex pattern that segregation took in both the North and the South? What connection do historians see between the growth of African-American population in the city and increasing residential and institutional segregation? Price has argued that the seeds of decay were planted in Newark between 1890 and 1920. The city's problems stemmed from lack of space, insufficient housing, and poorly designed and constructed buildings. Provisions for health care were inadequate. In addition, because of its location near New York City, Newark had long been a commuter community. Few people both lived and worked in Newark, which meant they paid little attention to the problems of the city and often paid no taxes. Discrimination against blacks in employment was also a long-standing problem resulting in chronic low income and widespread unemployment. How many of these problems were also characteristic of other cities in New Jersey, such as Trenton, Camden, and Plainfield, and of others in the country?

In the mid-1960s, in the heat of the summer, rioting broke out in cities all across the United States. Political commentators at the time, and historians since, have identified a variety of causes both long and short term, including the accumulated frustration of poverty and discrimination, the war on Vietnam, and the inescapable heat of the urban summer. The civil rights movement and growth of black nationalism led to greater expectations and a lessening interest in accommodation. The decades-old problems of massive unemployment and a dilapidated housing stock also contributed to the firestorm. Did these historic problems contribute to the riot in Newark? How have race relations in this and other cities changed since the riots? What, if anything, have urban renewal and gentrification done to cities affected by racial violence? How does the Los Angeles riot of 1992 affect our perspective on, and our understanding of, these issues?

Suggested Readings

Cunningham, John C. *Newark*. 1966. Rev. ed. Newark, N.J., 1988.

Jackson, Kenneth T., and Barbara B. Jackson. "The Black Experience in Newark: The Growth of the Ghetto, 1870–1970." In *New Jersey since 1860: New Findings and Interpretations*, edited by William C. Wright. Trenton, N.J., 1972. 36–59.

Litwack, Leon. *North of Slavery: The Negro in the Free States, 1790–1860*. Chicago, 1961.

"Perspectives: The Strange Career of Jim Crow." *Journal of American History* 75 (1988): 841–68.

Porambo, Ron. *No Cause for Indictment: An Autopsy of Newark*. New York, 1971.

Price, Clement A. "The Struggle to Desegregate Newark: Black Middle Class Militancy in New Jersey, 1932–1947." *NJH* 99 (1981): 215–28.

_____ . "The Strange Career of Race Relations in New Jersey History." In *The Black Experience in Southern New Jersey*, edited by David C. Munn. Camden, N.J., 1985. 10–17.

Woodward, C. Vann. *The Strange Career of Jim Crow*. 1955. Rev. ed. New York, 1974.

Wright, Giles R. *Afro-Americans in New Jersey: A Short History*. Trenton, N.J., 1989.

Wright, Marion M. *The Education of Negroes in New Jersey*. New York, 1941.

✦ ✦ ✦ ✦ ✦ ✦

The Beleaguered City as Promised Land: Blacks in Newark, 1917–1947

Clement A. Price

After the Civil War, Newark took on a distinctive image as an industrial, working-class city, and its industrial base enlarged and diversified during the remainder of the nineteenth century. Thousands of Irish, Germans, Italians, Russians and Poles settled in the city and enriched its life. But labor was their major contribution. With its ample supply of workers, its accommodating city government, and its proximity to a waterway and to New York City, Newark was the industrialists' ideal city, and at the turn of the century the business leadership labeled it the "City of Opportunity." It had grown into a major center of workshops and factories populated largely by foreign-stock working class.[1]

Within the next thirty years much of Newark's industrial promise emerged and the population continued to grow. A political reform movement in the early twentieth century replaced the boss-dominated aldermanic system with a commission government; too, the city established an agency to plan urban growth. Yet beneath the veneer of municipal progress and the promise of individual success, the years from 1890 to 1920 marked a period of transformation which slowly undermined the quality of life in some areas and ushered in a long process of urban decay. Many American cities experienced similar growth pains during these years, but in Newark the consequences were dramatic enough to imperil the city's future. Problems which at the turn of the century had symptomized impending crisis loomed as chronic ills by the end of World War I. And the image of a "City of Opportunity" was changing in some neighborhoods to that of a city of tragedy and failure.[2]

Nearly thirty years before the World-War-1 migration of blacks, Newark began to face problems linked to its growth as an indus-

From *Urban New Jersey since 1870*, edited by William C. Wright. Trenton, N.J., 1974. 10–45. Reprinted by permission of New Jersey Historical Commission.

trial city. While there were many sources of instability, the most important between 1890 and 1920 was the limitation of space—Newark was unable to house its working-class residents. The population rose 128 percent during this period, and by World War I there were simply too many people for the relatively small usable land area. Nearly 18 percent of the city's land area was uninhabitable marshland in the Ninth, Tenth and Twelfth Wards.[3] Worse, the city could not absorb areas outside its corporate limits commensurate with its rising population. The upshot, as the City Plan Commission noted in 1915, was that the number of available dwellings for workers declined and the city's middle class fled to suburban areas:

> This conclusion must be modified in view of the facts, above stated, to the effect that the residential possibilities of Newark have nearly reached their limit. Cities normally expand in area in proportion to increase in population. Newark has not so expanded for many years. While there has been an increase in the number of persons actively engaged in business in Newark, an increasing number of these persons have made their homes in suburbs.[4]

Moreover, a private survey of housing gave an equally gloomy prospect of city development. In this case, however, regional planning for Newark and peripheral towns was urged as a possible solution to the growing crisis in living space and housing.

> It will be utterly impossible for Newark to house its working population in individual homes unless the city and all of its contiguous [sic] suburbs within Essex County at least, can be treated as a single political unit in the preparation of street, district, block, and lot plans form . . . Considerable economy in the planning of city and suburbs as well as in the administration of all city institutions and of private business, could be affected if the suburbs could be incorporated in political Newark.[5]

The housing shortage reached a critical level with World War I. During the war an estimated 50,000 to 100,000 new residents sought employment in the numerous war-related industries. The city boasted full employment and could have put thousands more to work, yet these workers and their families faced an already tight housing market. In 1919, the city commission, in a desperate act to meet the housing shortage, allocated funds to erect a tent colony for the hundreds evicted from their dwellings as well as those who simply had no place to live.[6]

Working-class families faced grim alternatives—either to submit to exploitation in the city or leave, only to be replaced by others in search of lodging. Many had to submit to rent profiteering and overcrowding.[7] Mayor Charles P. Gillen, in his 1918 Annual Report, declared housing Newark's central problem and attacked extensive rent profiteering.[8] Other public officials had similar reactions. State Assemblyman Henry G. Hershfield, as the governor's representative to the Newark Board of Commissioners, labeled the housing situation "intolerable."[9]

Such conditions during and immediately after the war sparked the first calls for public housing. One spokesman who saw the housing need as a "cause celebre" was Dr. W. G. Hanrahan, a representative of the Newark Tenants' League and the Essex County Rent Payers' Association. In April 1920, Hanrahan urged that the Board of Commissioners arrange a referendum to float a bond for one million dollars "to build neat, substantial, low-priced homes for our people, as far as possible on city property or acquired property."[10] But the call for public housing by civic-minded activists like Hanrahan would not find acceptance until the late 1930s, when the federal government made such schemes financially feasible for Newark. The commissioners did not adopt the plan in 1920, and the acute housing problems only worsened. To be sure, the city had grown accustomed to weathering crises simply by ignoring them and avoiding fundamental changes in municipal policy. In spite of the adoption of zoning in 1920, for example, housing availability, conditions, and residential planning during the following thirty years showed little improvement. Early housing policy was designed to ameliorate immediate emergencies. In 1920 the city responded to the problems by allocating funds to erect additional tents.[11]

Newark's population growth between 1890 and 1920 not only aggravated the shortage of housing, but also burdened city services and the city treasury. By 1916, the city's bonded debt had increased enough that the tax rate rose. The *Newark News* warned early in 1916 that "the assessments on real estate have nearly reached the actual value of the property," and that "in some instances owners would be glad to sell for even less than the amount for which they are assessed."[12] Moreover, between 1916 and 1919 the per capita cost of government increased three times as much as it had between 1910 and 1916—a result of the dramatic population rise during the First World War. City expenses from 1916 to 1919 rose faster than the population, while the tax rate showed a marked increase.[13]

Some observers saw such problems as housing shortages, rising city costs, and the rising tax rate as symptomatic of major ills in the Newark community. In 1916, the City Plan Commission, easily the most discerning of Newark's municipal agencies, made a wide-ranging prognosis for urban recovery. The body's recommendations—to establish a zoning plan, to adopt a general plan for the future development of cities in northern New Jersey, and to create a central body to put the plan into effect— dramatized the beleaguered condition of Newark. Interestingly enough, the commission viewed population congestion as the major problem in Newark's housing.[14] Newark's proximity to New York was cited as an underlying problem too. In 1913, the commission noted "the large number of New York commuters who sleep in Newark, but think only in terms of the city of their business." New York City served to "pull upon the time and attention of men doing business in Newark," the commission continued; it was "always in sight across the meadows and . . . always making enticing appeals to the attention."[15] Preoccupation with New York, it was claimed, diminished civic endeavors and thinned the ranks of reformers in Newark.

Though in 1920 Newark was beset by housing and financial problems as well as what might be called a crisis in identity, it still attracted thousands of new residents. Of those who suffered from conditions in the beleaguered city, no group was so hopelessly trapped and victimized as the blacks. This was caused as much by the impact of white racism on the blacks who settled in Newark as by the fact that black numbers rose along with the city's many problems during and after World War I. Blacks faced two severe problems: the hostility of white resi-

Table 1
Percentage of Blacks in the Newark Population, 1870–1940

Year	Total Population	Number of Blacks	% of the Total Population
1870	105,059	1,789	1.7
1880	136,508	3,311	2.4
1890	181,830	4,141	2.2
1900	246,070	6,694	2.7
1910	347,469	9,475	2.7
1920	414,524	6,977	4.0
1930	442,337	38,800	8.8
1940	429,760	45,760	10.7

dents and the demeaning conditions that increasingly characterized Newark life.

Although it was not until World War I that blacks and the problems associated with their growing numbers caused any discernible reaction in the city, the race has a long history in Newark (Table I). Through the first half of the nineteenth century blacks numbered fewer than 2,000. After the Civil War black residency grew steadily; however, Newark had a large immigrant labor force which made the city unattractive to many potential black migrants.[16] Racial discrimination in the city's labor unions and industries also served to stave off large-scale migration.[17] By 1900 Newark contained only 6,694 blacks, who lived in small clusters close to white working-class residents. Indeed, except for a small predominantly black enclave near the business section, blacks lived in relative anonymity in predominantly white neighborhoods.[18]

Dispersed as they were between 1900 and World War I, blacks seemed of little threat to the whites; the period had a superficial racial tolerance, and some of the older black residents even felt that life was congenial.[19] Blacks and working-class whites frequently lived on the same streets, shopped in the same stores, and sent their children to the same schools. In 1909 the Baxter School, founded in 1828 for black students, was closed after the Board of Education concluded that separate schools were unnecessary.[20] During this period there were few publicized incidents of racial violence or other overt displays of animosity toward black Newarkers.

Some blacks, according to William M. Ashby, executive secretary of the Negro Welfare League during the First World War, established profitable businesses supported in part by whites. C. M. Brown was called "Chicken Brown" in reference to his thriving poultry stand at Newark's Center Market. Mary and Frank Anderson operated a restaurant and hotel patronized mainly by white firemen and policemen. Jacob Little ran a tea and coffee concern which conducted business with whites throughout Essex County. John S. Pinkman, John Booth, and Fletcher and Sons conducted profitable moving and storage businesses. The business group also included black caterers—Joe Wright, Grant Reeves, and Emmett Thomas—and a small professional group of doctors, teachers, lawyers, and undertakers.[21]

But while some of the old black Newarkers point to the success of a few blacks as evidence of race progress, it is clear that for the masses life was difficult. For most, Newark was not a "City of Opportunity," despite the boasts of the leading businessmen and industrialists. Discrimination made blacks economically and politically inferior to whites. Between 1890 and 1910 they were largely concentrated in the lowest-paying occupations, those tending to stigmatize them as socially inferior. Some 64.2 percent of the black men in the city in 1890 worked as unskilled laborers, servants, draymen, and livery stable keepers. Black women, too, were relegated to the low-paying, unskilled occupations—88.3 percent labored as laundresses and servants; of the 640 women in these two occupational groupings, 442 were servants.[22] By 1910 there was little discernible improvement. Black laborers, deliverymen, janitors, porters, servants, waiters, and teamsters constituted 53.4 percent of the black male work force, while 79.9 percent of the employed black women were laundresses and servants.[23]

Blacks also faced discrimination from their white working-class counterparts, making it more difficult for them to move into well-paid jobs. Labor unions in the city, as elsewhere in the state, practiced discrimination against black workers. The constitution and bylaws of the Newark Theatrical Mechanics' Association restricted its membership to "any white male person of good character, in sound health at the time of application."[24] A canvass by the Bureau of Statistics of Labor and Industries found that of the twenty-two labor organizations canvassed in 1903, only six were open to blacks.[25] Moreover, the tendency of blacks to work as domestics and as common laborers made the possibility of union protection even more remote. And although blacks worked in some of the city's factories, they were found largely in jobs which trade unions virtually ignored. William M. Ashby notes that only a few blacks employed in Newark's construction industry were members of the Hod Carriers Union.[26]

Socially and politically, too, the premigration black community was relegated to a subservient position. There is little indication that blacks were permitted to participate in Newark's social and political life. White newspapers seldom carried news concerning the general black population or individual Negro citizens. When they made the headlines, it was usually in reference to an alleged crime.[27] Within the city government blacks wielded little individual or collective influence. The early black politicos operated on such a small scale that many of the local people contemptuously called them "little peanut politicians."[28]

A 1916 issue of *The Newarker*, a magazine on local civic life published by the city museum, provides a rare and revealing glimpse of the white population's attitude toward black Newarkers. As the city prepared to celebrate its 250th anniversary, the Afro-American community was portrayed in clearly derogatory terms based on the old happy-slave stereotypes.

> There are a goodly number of worthy colored folk in Newark. They probably wish to participate in our celebration. Mr. Albert C. Fletcher, of the Schools and Philanthropy Committee, has shown the right spirit by undertaking to organize a group of 250 jubilee singers.
>
> With such a mellifluous lot of musical colored folk and a car load of watahmilyuns, the firmament over Newark will be crowded with angels on the nights when they vocally jubilate. There is nothing so wonderfully fascinating to well-attuned ears as a colored chorus, a large group of jubilee singers from the pine-tanged South.[29]

It is important to note that William H. Maxwell, a leading Negro in Newark, blasted the implications and racial stereotypes found in the article. The phrase "to participate in our celebration," claimed Maxwell, "dares to place the colored people entirely on the outside, begging to get in." And the image of crowds of musical blacks in a "car load of watahmilyuns," who would provide entertainment in the city's otherwise all-white celebration, brought the observation that "already too many white men . . . have the habit of associating the negro [sic] with watermelon and chicken and this kind of tactics," though these have "ever been bitterly despised by the negro [sic]." Indeed, the printing of such a prejudicial article, remarked Maxwell, was "transferring into written words that which thousands of others . . . [were] thinking."[30]

But although many whites in the city, as William H. Maxwell observed, thought of blacks as comic figures during the early part of the twentieth century, they did so only when the black community was small and dispersed; proving little threat to the white population. After 1916 the black population grew, and the problems associated with the people's poverty, culture and skin color concentrated in a distinct ghetto. From then on blacks were seldom portrayed in comic terms. Increasingly they were associated with neighborhood decay, crime, vice and disease. They were frequently seen as undesirables in the city. As these feelings deepened during the 1920s most blacks, particularly the newcomers, faced white residential segregation, an unsympathetic city government, and even some hostility from the old black residents.[31]

The intensification of racial tensions after 1916 resulted at first from the migration of blacks during World War I; however, it stemmed, too, from the general decline of living conditions in Newark between World Wars I and II. Between 1915 and 1920 the number of blacks in Newark increased by 80.6 percent—from 9,400 to 16,977. These years marked a major shift of blacks from the southeastern United States to the urban North. New Jersey's role in the drama was major, for its industrial landscape, and the social and political opportunity migrants hoped to find there, made the state a desirable area for settlement. Moreover, with European immigration virtually choked off by the war, the state's industrial interests actively encouraged the migration of blacks to cities such as Newark. Munitions plants, brickyards, wire factories, and other war-related firms—many for the first time—considered blacks a source of labor.[32] As the leading industrial center, Newark brought more blacks within its boundaries than any other city in New Jersey. An undetermined but apparently large number labored at the Flockhart Foundry, Coe's Steel Company, Carnegie Steel Company, Benjamin Atha Steel Company, and Worthington Pump Company. Considerable black employment was also found in the city's leather factories and at Swift's Packing Company in adjacent Harrison.[33] For black men particularly the war marked a major change in working conditions, if not an end to the discrimination that kept them in unskilled jobs. In contrast to their earlier entrapment within domestic occupations, by 1920 over one-half (55.8 percent) of the black male laborers were employed in the manufacturing and mechanical industries.[34]

Although blacks faced employment discrimination, housing discrimination was a more vexing problem during the war. Housing was hard to come by for the black newcomers and was generally substandard. Most of the residential areas outside the central city were virtually closed to blacks. Helen Pendleton, a white social worker in Newark, observed that after the migration began "the signs To Let and For Rent in the part of the city where small houses and flats were available were changed to 'For Sale,' and a recent advertisement for rooms, inserted by Negroes, brought only two replies, neither of them from Newark."[35]

The newcomers inherited deteriorating tenement districts built in the late nineteenth century. They were "forced into finding lodgings in basements and in the worst parts of [the] city." In contrast to New York's Harlem, which had been a prosperous middle-class area before its black influx, Newark greeted its black migrants with ghetto conditions just as it had greeted immigrants with adverse circumstances at the turn of the century. In 1916 the *Newark News* described the infamous Third Ward: "There are many sleeping rooms in the Third Ward into which the sun never looks, whither the air enters only by way of damp, narrow shafts, some of them not more than five feet wide."[36]

The Negro Welfare League, an interracial group started in 1917, held a similar view. Most of the dwellings in the Third Ward, according to the league, were poorly heated and of considerable age, and a substantial proportion of them lacked lighting facilities, inside toilets, and running water.[37]

Black families were easy prey for white landlords who demanded that poor blacks pay more rent than their white counterparts. Again, the observations of Helen Pendleton reveal the conditions. In 1919 she wrote:

> I know a family just arrived from the lower part of Alabama—man and wife and seven children (they almost all have seven children)—living in three rooms, the central room perfectly dark, and for that they have to pay fourteen dollars a month. The family who moved out of there were white people and they paid nine dollars. The landlady downstairs said quite explicitly that she charged these people fourteen dollars because they were colored.[38]

Land values in the Third Ward, for example, had remained stationary between 1873 and 1914. It was an unsightly area, according to the *Newark News*, since its development had been "unrestricted, haphazard, muddled, ignorant and irresponsible ... —the jumbling of stores, tenements, factories and stables."[39] Yet in spite of its many problems, thousands of newcomers settled in the Third Ward during the war. For the blacks, settlement was particularly difficult: their families were often too large for the available housing since poverty forced blacks to take on boarders to help meet rent payments. By any standards the housing for blacks was "terrible," according to one old Newarker.[40]

With inadequate living facilities in the densely populated central city, health conditions for blacks could only deteriorate during the war. In 1919, the death rate for blacks was 26 per 1,000 persons, twice that of Newark's whites. Pneumonia and tuberculosis ranked as the principal causes of death for blacks.[41] The Third Ward, which contained the greatest concentration of blacks, was notorious for its disease and death. Along with the Fourteenth Ward it led the city in cases of diphtheria; it ranked first in epidemic meningitis, erysipelas, influenza, and tuberculosis, and second in typhoid fever, gonorrhea and syphilis.[42] Black infant mortality was highest in the city in 1917.[43] Poor health among blacks resulted not only from poor housing but also from racial policies excluding blacks from many hospitals as well as inadequate medical service in black areas. In 1920 there were only eleven black doctors, eight black nurses, and one social service agency assisting blacks. Most were virtually unprotected against the ravages of sickness that characterized the war years.

The newcomers also faced suspicion from members of their own race. Indeed, some of the older black residents viewed the racial transformation during the war with considerable alarm. "Send the damn Niggers back down to Georgia where he [sic] came from. He doesn't know how to act," was one expression of contempt, according to William M. Ashby. Another black Newarker who remembers the period revealed his lingering bias to the author when he said that the blacks coming from the South during the war were "common" and "didn't know how to act" once they reached the city.[44]

Little organized effort was made by the established Newark blacks to assist in the adjustment of the migrants until the biracial Negro Welfare League was organized in 1917. However, throughout the war its work among the burgeoning black community could never keep pace with the social ills most people faced daily. Although some black churches assisted the migrants with shelter, food, and spiritual uplift, their efforts touched only a small portion of the growing population.

The resentment of resident blacks toward the influx of thousands of their southern brethren resulted from fear over the future image of blacks in the eyes of whites. These blacks, many of whom had managed to cast off the stigma of alleged rural backwardness, had known some measure of racial tolerance before 1917. Their small numbers and virtual isolation throughout the late nineteenth and early twentieth centuries had helped sustain mutual disregard between whites and blacks. And they had found it easy to claim marginal progress, since few blacks in the city were frustrated by prejudice, discrimination and exploitation in employment and housing. The migration, however, ended the old race relations and shattered illusions of group progress.

Indeed, the massive social problems associated with the settlement of southern blacks stigmatized the majority of blacks as untutored and powerless ghetto dwellers. When the war ended the contours of Newark's black community had been virtually set.

Equally important, the migration had an impact on the entire city. Not only did it strain the housing market, but it caused city services to decline even further, especially in the neglected black areas. Newark's dilemma overwhelmed the city when its political leadership failed to heed the warnings of enlightened urban planners, social workers, and civic leaders. The decline, which had had its beginnings before the war, was quickening and deepening, though Newark glistened to outsiders as an illusory "promised land."

Newark's Enduring Black Ghetto, 1920–1940

Between the wars, from 1920 to 1940 life for most blacks in Newark continued to be difficult. Blacks still found many jobs out of reach even when their intelligence and experience qualified them. Politically, years between the wars marked a rising influence of race politicians and voters; blacks, however, were largely unable to use the political system to improve their conditions in Newark substantially. During the period, too, black housing scarcely improved; rather, as more blacks entered the city—between 1920 and 1940 their numbers rose from 16,977 to 45,760—they were forced to settle in the worst neighborhoods, those being abandoned by poor and working-class white immigrant groups. The continuation of such conditions during the period was important for it meant that there was little safety or power in numbers. The ghetto, in short, endured along with many of Newark's fundamental problems noted earlier in the paper.

Not only was migration considerably larger after 1920 than before, it also brought a more industrialized working force into the city. In contrast to the earlier migrants, who constituted a shifting rural proletariat, the post-1920 migrants often originated in the urban South. Hundreds of them, according to contemporaries of the period, had previously worked in textile firms and factories as unskilled and semiskilled laborers. Some, it has been observed, had even worked as skilled laborers.[45] While it is difficult to measure the extent to which the newcomers brought industrial experience with them, the Fifteenth United States Census reveals that the Negro worker and his working conditions improved between 1920 and 1930. Some of that improvement resulted from the influx of more highly skilled laborers: over half of the black males were employed in manufacturing and mechanical industries in 1930. Most were still relegated to jobs as laborers, but in contrast to conditions prevailing in 1920, many had moved into semiskilled and even skilled occupations. By 1930 a surprisingly large number of black men worked as mechanics, painters, carpenters, and helpers in building construction. Blacks made inroads into truck and tractor driving and virtually dominated the longshoremen and stevedore occupations. While improvements were admittedly modest beside those of white workers, they symbolized real vitality among the black working class during the 1920s. Most of the improvements were probably enjoyed by blacks who had entered the city before 1920, but since there were not many of those, a considerable number of the successful workers must have arrived after 1920. Working conditions among black women also improved during the 1920s. Most continued to work in the domestic employments, but some were moving into industrial work.[46] Despite a decrease in factory work during the early depression years black women continued to hold jobs in the cigar and tobacco factories and the clothing industries.

Another distinguishing feature of the migration was the greater prevalence of professionals among Negroes. Although their numbers were small, they acted as a vanguard in most race protests and activities during the 1930s and 1940s. The increase of professionals during the 1920s was possibly attributable to two factors: first, many professionals, especially ministers, had to leave the South because their constituencies had declined thanks to the northern exodus;[47] second, many, particularly physicians and dentists, came because Newark's growing black population had few black practitioners during the first two decades of the twentieth century.[48] The existence of a ghetto, in short, virtually guaranteed a black physician, dentist, or lawyer a successful practice. The number of black male professionals doubled in Newark between 1920 and 1930. The number of black female professionals also doubled particularly because teachers and nurses increased drastically. In the trade and clerical occupations as well, black employment increased between 1920 and 1930. By 1930, the city contained over 300 black insurance and real estate agents.[49]

The modest advances of black industrial workers and professionals during the 1920s, however, were crushed by the Great Depression of the 1930s. Even before the beginning of the new decade, the prospects for black workers grew dim. After the stockmarket crash in 1929 workers throughout New Jersey faced cutbacks in employment. By early 1932, an estimated 400,000 persons in the state were out of work; approximately one-third of the state's total population was either unemployed or "affected" by the general unemployment by 1934.[50]

In Newark, the state's largest city, the depression caused acute hardships. In 1931, an estimated 60,000 persons, representing 30.1 percent of the working population in 1930, were unemployed.[51] The total number out of work, however, was probably higher since many transients were uncounted and unassisted. "Do we know how many female unfortunates are covering the streets of Newark and wanting a sandwich and a night's lodging?" queried one resident at a meeting of the Board of Commissioners in 1932. "If we were living in the Third Ward," he said, "we would see."[52] Scores of unemployed men wandered through Newark's shopping district, seeking refuge inside the doorways of department stores or, on hot summer nights, resting on park benches. In the Hill District, according to the *Newark Evening News*, conditions were darker than in the darkest days of Imperial Russia.[53] Thousands of families hit by unemployment sought assistance, raising the total number of caseloads in private and public relief agencies between 1929 and 1935 to over 20,000 relief and family cases.

The black community suffered from the depression more than any of the city's other ethnic groups. As in other American cities, blacks were generally the first to experience unemployment and the last to find work when state and federal relief agencies created jobs in the city. Although blacks constituted 8.8 percent of Newark's population in 1930, they represented 17.7 percent of the city's unemployed in 1932.[54] In 1930, 20.3 percent of the blacks in the city were unemployed, while for whites unemployment was much less, at 11.3 percent.[55]

One reason employment problems were so severe was that blacks were commonly relegated to unskilled jobs.[56] Black concentration in domestic and personal employment also intensified black unemployment, particularly among the women, since those workers were quickly discharged from their jobs after 1929; Eugene Kinckle Jones, the Industrial and Field Secretary of the National Urban League, commented in 1932 that it was increasingly difficult to place domestic workers in Newark.[57] Moreover, the black worker often had less seniority on the job than the white worker. The Interracial Committee found the median length of residence of blacks in Newark to be ten years, compared to approximately twenty-three years for whites.[58]

The color line was also a factor. Many whites considered the black man a burden on the city, and this feeling intensified as economic recovery became more remote. Blacks were excluded from most labor unions: the Interracial Committee's study in 1932 revealed that the forty-one labor unions surveyed contained only 3.3 percent black representation, or 268 of a total membership of 18,019.[59] The Commission on the Condition of the Urban Colored Population made similar findings in 1938: 131 locals with a total membership of 87,480 contained only 3,195 black workers or 3.7 percent of the total membership.[60] The only exception was the Congress of Industrial Organizations, which actively sought black members after the mid-1930s.[61] Moreover, the large-scale unemployment of black workers made union organizing among them untenable. In the early 1920s the predominantly black Hod Carriers Union, Local 609, boasted over 800 race members, but by 1930 its members had dwindled to 253.[62]

Denied union participation and industrial employment, the black worker saw his fortunes continue to diminish through the 1930s. Indeed many firms in Newark and throughout New Jersey refused to hire blacks even as menial laborers. Harold Lett, executive secretary of the Urban League between 1934 and 1945, recently made such an observation in recounting his 1930 study of black labor conditions in New Jersey:

> We discovered that of these 300 and some thousand employees, only 3¹/₂% were Black workers in any capacity, 55% of those 1,870 some employers didn't have a single Black worker in any capacity, not even menial, not even floor sweepers. More than a half of them didn't have a single Negro worker and felt completely justified in so doing. So this meant, then, when you broke down the statistics in making a final report, that the Black who then was 5¹/₂% of the population of the state, was 3¹/₂% of the gainfully employed. But he was 25% of the relief load. And white folks were yelling their heads off because there were so many Blacks on relief.[63]

By 1940, though employment was generally improving in Newark, conditions for blacks continued to lag. Black males, for example, constituted 9.1 percent of the total male working force in 1930 but declined to 7.1 percent by 1940. Employment for black females also declined from 13.4 percent in 1930 to 10.5 percent in 1940. White employment, compared to that of the blacks, rose during the decade. Between 1930 and 1940, white male representation in the work force increased from 90.3 percent to 92.6 percent, while that of white females rose from 86.5 percent to 90 percent. Despite an increase in the proportion of black males in the industrial and mechanical trades, by 1940 over half were still employed as laborers. In both unskilled and skilled industrial occupations black males lost ground between 1930 and 1940. Similarly, professional males decreased in number during the period, particularly ministers, whose ranks declined by nearly 50 percent by 1940. The number of blacks employed in the trades also declined during the depression years. For black women the 1930s brought many setbacks in industrial employment. Declining prospects in laundry work forced 60 percent of black female workers into domestic employment, by 1940. Their labor, as Harold Lett and Eugene Kinckle Jones have observed, was generally exploited, often temporary, and basically unrewarding. Despite a modest increase in some nondomestic jobs, black women had made little progress in employment since 1930.[64]

The prevalence of black unemployment during the 1930s forced many to seek relief in Newark's private and public relief agencies. Unfortunately, however, they faced many barriers to equality with the white unemployed. Explicitly or through unspoken policy many of the private relief agencies in Newark limited assistance to blacks or, in some cases, fully denied them aid. For example, the Salvation Army and the Goodwill Mission, the two largest lodging houses in the city, refused to lodge black destitutes, and the local Red Cross chapter refused assistance to families—going so far as to deny them flour.[65] Some private agencies which refused to assist blacks claimed that assistance would attract more black reliefers to the beleaguered city.[66]

Among the agencies that did not exclude blacks from their services, limited financial resources undermined effective relief. Such groups included the Newark Female Charitable Society, the Social Service Bureau, the Church Mission of Help, the Travelers' Aid Society, and the New Jersey Urban League. None of these agencies could afford more than marginal and temporary relief to the black unemployed. Most of them were not relief groups in any case, but, rather, social service organizations seldom able to dispense food, clothing, and heating fuel. Given their bureaucratic and financial limitations many private agencies could not substantially lessen the hardships brought by the depression. In 1932, the New Jersey Emergency Relief Administration observed:

> A great many of those now engaged in actual emergency relief work experience a difficult mental adjustment due to the fact that an organized effort for emergency relief discovers a considerable amount that is not the result of unemployment, to which little attention may have been paid hitherto. At first touch it looks like an emergency relief problem; in fact, though it requires relief, it is a permanent problem.[67]

Along with the problems caused by the depression, the full emergence of the Third Ward as a predominantly black slum area marked the interwar years. Life in that centrally located area had long been harsh, but as more blacks entered, living conditions became appalling. Popularly known as the Hill District, the Third Ward became one of the most densely populated communities of its size in the United States between 1917 and 1940. It was also one of the most chronically unhealthy.[68]

Furthermore it gained notoriety as a wide-open section. Despite its somber image of collective race failure, many referred to it as the "Roaring Third." During the 1930s several small bars and clubs opened in dubious tribute to the area's social energy, and its residents witnessed the rise of prostitution, gambling, numbers, and even scattered evidences of opium usage.[69] Although some whites profited from the Hill District's infamy, which attracted scores of white men in search of a good time, most white residents of Newark were probably afraid to travel through the area.

Fear of the blacks seemed most pronounced among the remaining whites in the central city. When, for example, Prudential Insurance Company sought to build a housing project for Hill District blacks, one old Jewish resident spoke for many white residents still trapped in the Third Ward when he addressed the Newark Board of Commissioners in opposition to the plan:

> Honorable Mayor and all Commissioners. I got my experience when I lived thirty-six years in the Third Ward. Ten years ago or twelve ago when we used to live, and all the good people were living with us and our children were able to pass the streets. Now since a few years ago we could [sic] not pass the streets. About ten, eleven o'clock, everybody has got to be in the house. Now

they move away—all the good people move away and all our Third Ward goes to pieces. We cannot do nothing; all our children we cannot do nothing. . . .[70]

If it was thought that "all the good people" were moving away from the Hill District, it is not difficult to see why the blacks, many of whom were recent arrivals in Newark, were seen so negatively by the white working class. For the older white residents still living in the central city the blacks appeared as intruders, yet there was little they could do to stop further influx. Whites in the better neighborhoods of the northern and southern areas of the city sought to prevent black entry into their communities. Although absolute race exclusion was difficult in Newark because blacks had traditionally lived throughout the city, white real estate agents and property owners successfully kept most blacks out of the areas peripheral to the central city. By 1940, 63.4 percent of Newark's total black population was concentrated within sixteen of the city's ninety-eight census tracts, an area roughly bordered by Orange Street to the north, Avon Avenue to the south, High Street to the east, and Bergen Street to the west. Whites continued to live in this area during the interwar years; however, their total numbers declined as many left for better conditions in the peripheral areas of Newark or in the suburbs. As Kenneth T. Jackson has observed, the white working-class residents could generally leave blighted conditions as their fortunes rose. Blacks, however, were trapped in the ghetto by their weaker economic status and the discrimination of many whites in other areas of the city.[71]

Restricted to the oldest sections of the city, the blacks continued to inherit areas that immigrant groups had escaped. From these areas spread the blight which would later characterize much of Newark in the 1950s and 1960s. While Newark's precarious development during the late nineteenth century caused ghetto development by forcing together tenements and factories in the central city, it took a later generation of political leaders to rationalize many conditions that might have been improved. Further study of the city commission's role in planning Newark's growth is needed; however, some tentative observations can be made concerning the impact of its zoning ordinances during the interwar period. The sources examined thus far suggest that Newark's first zoning ordinances in 1920 and the revisions in 1930 helped to frustrate residential development in much of the central city. And rather than containing poor housing conditions that had long plagued areas such as the Third Ward, the extravagant use of commercial zoning implicit in the ordinances intensified decline throughout the central city.

In 1920 nearly all of the heavily-populated Third Ward was zoned as a business district despite the commercial decline of the area during the early twentieth century. Noncommercial construction, or needed housing, was effectively blocked. At the same time the Third Ward's chaotically mixed noncommercial dwellings—frame tenements, two- and three-family houses, and single family dwellings—were allowed to stand alongside the area's garages, factories and stores.[72] Moreover, the 1920 ordinances divided Newark into five districts with strict controls on housing standards, lot size and the number of families that could be housed in a given area. The Third Ward was zoned as a "B district," effectively rationalizing the smallness of its rear yards, side yards, inner courts, outer courts and building areas. As a "B district," too, the Third Ward was distinguished by the high admissible population density—140 families per acre of land. A revision of the city's zoning ordinance in 1930 brought little change in the Third Ward; it continued to be designated as a commercial area.[73]

Although Newark's first zoning ordinances in 1920 were enacted long after the Hill District's decline began, it is possible that they contributed to the substandard conditions that characterized life throughout the interwar years. One condition was the mixing of residential dwellings with manufacturing and commercial structures. "Commercial and industrial uses scattered throughout residential areas," the Newark Planning Board noted in 1946, "often are a major cause of blight and always are detrimental to the neighborhood. It will be extremely difficult to rehabilitate these areas so long as the old stores or factories remain." In most areas of the Hill property owners were usually "unwilling to develop their property for some form of residential use," many fearing that a business might be established nearby.[74]

Consequently, the inner city remained chronically underhoused between 1920 and 1940. A housing boom in Newark during the 1920s brought little solace to Newarkers living in the Hill. "There is very little improvement that has taken place in the past thirty years as I remember that section," remarked an old resident of the Hill in 1930.[75] Seven years later, a Health Department study which labeled the entire Hill District as a blighted area gave that view substantial credibility. During the 1930s the demolition of housing outweighed new private construction in the expanding black slum.[76] By 1940 a major report of the Central Planning Board, which ironically repeated recommendations made by another agency at work prior to World War I, noted that most dwellings in the Hill needed major repairs and lacked private baths, toilets, and even running water. The board's report, coming over twenty years after the city's first zoning ordinances, included the recommendation that the central area of Newark be rezoned to encourage housing construction.[77]

An examination of the city commissioners' deliberation over the zoning ordinances of 1920 and 1930 failed to shed much light on their motivations. Typically, that body couched its sentiments in calls for civic improvement and in political bombast. Still, one conclusion can be drawn from the disproportionate use of commercial and industrial zoning the city fathers displayed in 1920 and 1930: it appears that the commissioners desired to protect areas clearly residential from industrial or commercial intrusion while accommodating the business interests that had investments in the central sections of Newark, such as the Hill District, the Ironbound section, and other areas with a mixture of residential, industrial and commercial dwellings. Racial motivation behind municipal policies such as zoning in American cities still needs more study. In Newark, blacks had no input into the 1920 or 1930 zoning plans, and they demonstrated no discernible understanding of the importance of local zoning. In short, zoning was not an issue. Black leaders focused their interests on ending the discriminatory policies of city agencies rather than on the inner workings of city government. This made it possible for white business and political interests to implement policies that maintained substandard conditions in black communities.

Living conditions improved during the World War II boom, enabling some blacks to improve their standard of living modestly. For some, the war brought housing relief in the form of publicly subsidized dwellings for war workers and low-income residents.[78] Considerably fewer managed to move into the peripheral areas of Newark where the housing and surrounding environment made a family's existence easier than life in the ghetto.

On other fronts, too, there was slight improvement during the war: segregation gradually ended in many of Newark's downtown theaters and stores, while middle-class blacks and white liberals formed several successful interracial organizations. The oldest group of this type, the Urban League, formed in Newark in 1917, continued to attract some of the city's most influential reformers, clergymen and professionals.[79]

Black fortunes also rose politically; their votes gained patronage positions and secured the appointment of two blacks, Harold Lett, of the league, and the Reverend William Hayes, pastor of Bethany Baptist Church, to the Newark Housing Authority. Moreover, public agencies that had traditionally ignored the blacks displayed increasing sensitivity to the problems posed by discrimination and poverty.[80]

But if World War II marked some improvement in the economic and political status of black people, life in Newark continued to victimize most of their numbers. The housing reforms, the rising political involvement, and the end of remaining vestiges of Jim Crow eradicated none of the many harsh realities. Those changes, despite their importance, were largely superficial and benefited a relatively small number of blacks.

Housing, to be sure, continued to be black Newark's major problem. White discrimination in the better neighborhoods caused some of the hardships, but certainly Newark's general housing conditions made matters worse for the growing black population. In 1945, the Central Planning Board observed that the deterioration of housing facilities containing 22.2 percent of the population "had become so serious . . . that relatively large areas needed to be demolished and entirely rebuilt." Intensifying the problem, between 1929 and 1944 only 6,571 dwellings were constructed in Newark, compared with a total of 25,999 between 1921 and 1928. About a third of the dwellings in the later years were in public housing projects. Approximately 68 percent of the city's housing had been built prior to 1920; 27.6 percent had been constructed in 1899 or earlier. As in earlier years, Newark's housing problems affected blacks more adversely than other ethnic groups. One-half of the black population, according to the board, lived in "unhealthful or unwholesome quarters."[81]

The 1940s also marked the continued exodus of industries and middle-class homeowners. Aging manufacturing firms chose to modernize or expand in new locations, outside of Newark, where there was "a more favorable tax situation, where land was cheap and where there was less congestion."[82] The industrial decline of the city after the war diminished city revenue and dimmed the prospects of black workers. Property-owning families left the city for some of the same reasons that forced industries into other areas. Their exodus, however, was incomplete since many of them continued to work in Newark. As a result, the city's large rent-paying population and the smaller group of homeowners who paid property taxes suffered from the narrowing tax base and the declining city services that nonresidents used but did not adequately help to pay for.[83]

Newark faced other problems during and after World War II which are examined in my dissertation. For poor blacks especially, the years 1940–47 contained both hope and despair. After the war boom, hope waned in many families. While it is difficult to assess the mood of the masses of blacks living in the ghetto, an angry protest in 1943 by one of their numbers who called himself "A Voice of the Black Race" might be instructive. His comments, which came in the wake of the arrest of seven Allah Temple of Islam members for draft evasion, revealed the frustrations of the ghetto and, too, the fear that life in black Newark would not improve:

> And I'm sure after all the suffering the black race took from the devastatable [*sic*] whites, there is a lack of interest in every black soldiers heart, even though he is sent off to war, on how this war turns out; For he knows that the whites will not tolerate him being in the same boat as they are. He knows if he ever returned, Jim Crow, discrimination and segregation will be waiting for him as before. The 7 black men saw it in the nick of time. They would rather sit in jail than to go and fight for the white man's benefit. They know that the white man's prejudice is unbreakable.[84]

Notes

The author wishes to acknowledge the criticisms and encouragement of Professor Seth M. Scheiner of Rutgers University in the preparation of the manuscript. Special thanks are also extended to the New Jersey Historical Commission for its research grant and to the staff of the New Jersey Room, Newark Public Library. Other persons who have encouraged the author and provided helpful observations on the history of blacks in Newark include Professors Bruce Cohen of Worcester State College, Elliot Rosen of Rutgers University, Mrs. Vera McMillon of Newark, Mr. George Thompson of Newark, Mr. William M. Ashby of Newark, Mr. Fred Martin of Jersey City, and Ms. Cozetta Williams of East Orange, and Harold Lett of Newark (Dec. 1974).

1. Samuel H. Popper, "Newark, New Jersey, 1870–1910: Chapters in the Evolution of an American Metropolis" (Ph.D. diss., New York University, 1952), pp. 14, 51.

2. Blake McKelvey, *The Urbanization of America, 1860–1915* (New Brunswick: Rutgers University Press, 1963); *Newark Evening News*, February 29, 1916.

3. City Plan Commission, *Comprehensive Plan of Newark* (Newark: City Plan Commission, 1915), p. xx; Central Planning Board, *A Preliminary Report on Land Use for Newark, N.J.* (Newark: Central Planning Board, 1945), p. 7.

4. City Plan Commission, *Comprehensive Plan*, p. xxii.

5. E. P. Goodrich and George B. Ford, *Housing Report to the City Plan Commission*, Newark, N.J. (Newark: Plum Press, 1913), p. 57.

6. Board of Commissioners, *Minutes of Meetings of the Board of Commissioners of Newark, N.J. . . .*, 1919 (Newark: Essex Press, 1919), p. 38. (Hereafter cited as *Minutes*.)

7. For a view of the housing crisis in Newark during the war and the official response, see: *Minutes, 1916–1920*; and Board of Commissioners, *Annual Reports, 1916–1920* (Newark: Essex Press, 1916–1920). (Hereafter cited as *Annual Reports*.)

8. *Minutes, 1918*, pp. 23–25.

9. *Minutes, 1920*, pp. 5–6.

10. Ibid., p. 4.

11. Ibid., pp. 22–24.

12. *Newark Evening News*, January 3, 1916.

13. Bureau of Municipal Research, New York, *Introduction and Explanatory Excerpts From a Survey of the Government, Finances and Administration of the City of Newark, N.J...* (Newark: n.p., 1919), p. 8.

14. *Newark Evening News*, January 12, 1916.

15. City Plan Commission, *City Planning for Newark* (Newark: City Plan Commission, 1913), p. xxvii.

16. *Newark Evening News*, May 16, 1966.

17. Popper, "Newark, New Jersey, 1870–1910," p. 143.

18. William M. Ashby, who was executive secretary of the Negro Welfare League (renamed the New Jersey Urban League in 1920) during World War I, observes that "Blacks were scattered in large and small patches all over the oldest part of the city," except in the Forest Hill, Roseville, Vailsburg, and Woodside sections. The Lyons Farms section, now known as Weequachic, was virtually undeveloped as a residential area. See William M. Ashby, "Reflection on the Life of Negroes in Newark, 1910–1916" (Address delivered to the Frontier Club, February 16, 1972), available at the Newark Public Library.

19. Marcus Cooke, private interview with the author, Montclair, December 7, 1971.

20. Marion Thompson Wright, "Mr. Baxter's School," *Proceedings of the New Jersey Historical Society* 59, no.1 (January 1941): 116–33.

21. Ashby, "Reflections," pp. 8–9.

22. U.S., Bureau of the Census, *Eleventh Census of the United States, Population: 1890* (Washington, D.C.: U.S. Government Printing Office, 1895), 1:698.

23. U.S., Bureau of the Census, *Thirteenth Census of the United States, Population: 1910* (Washington, D.C.: U.S. Government Printing Office, 1914), 4:583.

24. *Constitution and By-laws of the Newark Theatrical Mechanics Association Lodge No. 28, 1895*, (Newark: Advertiser Printing House, 1895).

25. Bureau of Statistics of Labor and Industries of New Jersey, *Twenty-Sixth Annual Report* (Somerville: Unionist-Gazette Printing House, 1904), pp. 210–11.

26. Ashby, "Reflections," p. 6.

27. *Newark Evening News*, 1900–1917, *passim*.

28. Ashby, "Reflections," p. 17.

29. *Newarker* 1, no. 3 (January 1916): 55.

30. *Newark Evening News*, January 11, 1916.

31. *Minutes*, September, 1930, pp. 82–83; October, 1930, pp. 18–22. In an address at the Robert Treat Hotel in 1928 Thomas Puryear, the executive secretary of the New Jersey Urban League, displayed at least some antipathy toward migrant blacks when he claimed to a predominantly white audience that "The vast majority of the migrant Negroes within our gates are of the unstable, detached, drifting element of the population from which they came" (*Newark Evening News*, September 25, 1928).

32. Lucy Millburn, et al., "Historical Summary: The Interracial Movement in Newark," mimeographed (Newark: Newark Interracial Committee, 1945), p. 2; Emmett J. Scott, *Negro Migration During the War* (New York: Oxford University Press, 1920), pp. 56–57.

33. Ashby, "Reflections," p. 6.

34. U.S., Bureau of the Census, *Fourteenth Census of the United States, Population—Occupations: 1920* (Washington, D.C.: U.S. Government Printing Office, 1923), 4:1179–81.

35. Helen Pendleton, "Cotton Pickers in Northern Cities," *Survey*, February 17, 1917, p. 570.

36. *Newark Evening News*, February 2, 1916.

37. Negro Welfare League, "Report by the Friendly Visitors Committee," Papers of the Negro Welfare League, March 27, 1917, New Jersey Urban League, Newark.

38. New Jersey Conference of Charities and Correction, *Proceedings of the Sixteenth Annual Meeting* (Rahway: New Jersey Reformatory Print, n.d.), pp. 166–67.

39. *Newark Evening News*, February 4, 1916.

40. William M. Ashby, private interview with the author, June 19, 1972.

41. *Annual Reports*, 1919, p. 216.

42. Ibid., pp. 240–41.

43. *Annual Reports*, 1917, p. 295.

44. William M. Ashby, private interview with the author, June 19, 1972.

45. Harold Lett, private interview with the author, Newark, December 1973; Interracial Committee of the New Jersey Conference of Social Work, and the New Jersey Department of Institutions and Agencies, *New Jersey's Twentieth Citizen: The Negro* (n.p., 1932), pp. 8–9; Alma Burlington, interview with Ciro Scalera, Newark, tape in Oral History Files of the author, Department of

History, Rutgers University, Newark; Egerton Elliott Hall, *The Negro Wage Earner of New Jersey* . . . (New Brunswick: Rutgers University School of Education, 1935), pp. 27, 47–48.

46. U.S. Bureau of the Census, *Fifteenth Census of the United States, Population: 1930* (Washington, D.C.: U.S. Government Printing Office, 1933), 4:1036–39.

47. L. C. Florant, "Negro Migration 1860–1940," (Revised draft of a memorandum prepared for the Carnegie Corporation's Study of the Negro in America), pp. 71–72, Schomburg Collection, New York Public Library, New York City, N.Y.

48. William M. Ashby, private interview with the author, Newark, June, 1972.

49. *Fifteenth Census of the United States, Population: 1930*, 4:1036–39.

50. State of New Jersey Emergency Relief Administration, *Unemployment and Relief Conditions in New Jersey* (Trenton: n.p., 1932), p. 13; State of New Jersey Emergency Relief Administration, *Third Annual Report* . . . (n.p., 1934), p. 5.

51. Department of Public Welfare, *Annual Report* (Newark: Department of Public Welfare, 1931), unpaged.

52. *Minutes*, April, 1932, p. 33.

53. Ibid.

54. New Jersey State Temporary Commission on the Condition of the Urban Colored Population, *Report* (Trenton: Temporary Commission on the Condition of the Urban Colored Population, 1938), p. 79.

55. Ibid.; *Fifteenth Census of the United States, Population: 1930*, 4:1036–39.

56. Douglas H. MacNeil, *Seven Years of Unemployment Relief in New Jersey, 1930–1936* (Washington, D.C.: Social Service Research Council, 1938), p. 129.

57. New Jersey Urban League, "Minutes of the Executive Committee," January 12, 1932, Papers of the New Jersey Urban League, Urban League of Essex County, Newark.

58. Interracial Committee, New Jersey Department of Institutions and Agencies, New Jersey Conference of Social Work, *Negro in New Jersey, Community Report XIX* (Newark: n.p., 1932), p. 5.

59. Ibid., p. 26.

60. New Jersey State Temporary Commission on the Condition of the Urban Colored Population, *Report*, p. 33.

61. Harold Lett, private interview with the author, December, 1973.

62. Interracial Committee, *Negro in New Jersey*, p. 28.

63. Harold Lett, private interview, March 30, 1973, unpublished interview, Newark Public Library, p. 4.

64. U.S. Bureau of the Census, *Fifteenth Census of the United States, Population: 1930*, 4:1036–39; *Sixteenth Census of the United States, Population: 1940* (Washington, D.C.: U.S. Government Printing Office. 1943), 4:205–6, 209.

65. Interracial Committee, *Negro in New Jersey*, pp. 48, 49; "Minutes of the Annual Meeting," February 9, 1932, New Jersey Urban League, Urban League of Essex County, Newark.

66. *Newark Evening News*, October 28, 1930.

67. New Jersey Emergency Relief Administration, *Unemployment and Relief*

Conditions in New Jersey, p. 13.

68. Beatrice A. Myers, and Ira De A. Reid, "The Toll of Tuberculosis Among Negroes in New Jersey," *Opportunity* 10 (1932): 279–82.

69. Interracial Committee, *Negro in New Jersey*, p. 32; Essex County Crime Conference, "The Reasons Behind The Negro Delinquency Rate," October 25, 1935, Harold Lett Papers, Newark Public Library, Newark; *Annual Report of the Department of Public Welfare* (Newark: Essex Press, 1946), pp. 1–2; Curtis Lucas, *Third Ward Newark* (New York: Ziff-Davis, 1946), chaps. 1–3.

70. *Minutes*, October 15, 1930, p. 5.

71. Kenneth T. and Barbara B. Jackson, "The Black Experience in Newark: The Growth of the Ghetto, 1870–1970," in *New Jersey Since 1860: New Findings and Interpretations*, ed. William C. Wright (Trenton: New Jersey Historical Commission, 1972), pp. 51–53.

72. *Official Map of the City of Newark and Vicinity, Essex County, Building Zones, 1920*, (Newark: n.p., n.d.); *Building Zone Ordinance of the City of Newark, N.J., December 31, 1919*, (n.p., n.d.), pp. 3–7.

73. *Building Zone Ordinance*, p. 14; *Zoning Ordinance of the City of Newark, N.J., January 8, 1930* (n.p., n.d.); *Map of the City of Newark, 1940* (Newark: n.p., n.d.).

74. In 1946 the Central Planning Board observed: "The present ordinance is badly out of scale in respect to existing zoning. At the time the original regulations were adopted, Newark was a mature city and had almost reached its maximum growth. Previous uncontrolled development had resulted in widespread scattering of stores, shops, and industries and in some parts of the city practically every corner had one or more commercial enterprises of one kind or another. In an effort to recognize these previously established commercial areas and to avoid the creation of as many non-conforming uses as possible, the framers of the early ordinances were extremely liberal in setting aside commercial districts. The frontage along many of the north and south streets was classified for business use and in some parts of the City, notably in the First, Third, and Eighth Wards, large areas were set aside for that purpose. As a result of these actions much more area is zoned for business than ever will develop for that purpose" (Central Planning Board, *A Preliminary Report on Zoning For Newark, N.J.* [Newark: Central Planning Board, 1946], pp. 5–6).

75. *Minutes*, September 17, 1930, p. 80.

76. Department of Health, "The Negro in Newark: Correlation of Areas of Negro Concentration With Blighted Housing Areas," mimeographed (Newark: Department of Health, 1937).

77. Newark Housing Authority, *Survey of Housing Conditions in Newark, N.J.* (Newark: Newark Housing Authority, 1940), p. 3.

78. Housing Authority of the City of Newark, *Public Housing in Newark* (Newark: n.p., 1944), p. 4.

79. New Jersey Urban League Papers, 1940–50, Urban League of Essex County, Newark; Membership Lists of the New Jersey Urban League, ca. 1930–50, available from the author.

80. *Newark Evening News*, March 30, 1942; Department of Public Welfare, *Annual Report of the Department of Public Welfare* (Newark: Essex Press, 1943),

pp. 1–2; *Newark Evening News*, April 24, June 21, 1945.

81. Central Planning Board, *A Preliminary Report on Housing Conditions and Policy for Newark, New Jersey* (Newark: n.p., 1945), p. 4.

82. Central Planning Board, *The Master Plan for the Development of the City of Newark, N.J.* (Newark: Central Planning Board, 1947), p. 11.

83. Eugene Bonds, "The Financial Administration of Newark, N.J." (New York University, Graduate Division for Public Services, 1943), p. 1. For another view of the impact of middle-class exodus see *Annual Meeting of the General Assembly, December 13, 1933*, (Newark: Welfare Federation, n.d.), p. 4.

84. *New Jersey Herald News*, January 30, 1943.

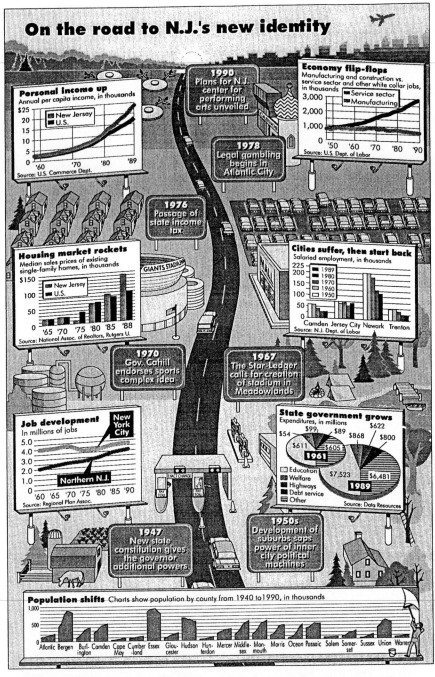

On the road to N.J.'s new identity

Personal income up
Annual per capita income, in thousands
- New Jersey
- U.S.
$25, 20, 15, 10, 5, 0 — '60 '70 '80 '89
Source: U.S. Commerce Dept.

1990
Plans for N.J. center for performing arts unveiled

Economy flip-flops
Manufacturing and construction vs. service sector and other white collar jobs, in thousands
- Service sector
- Manufacturing
3,000, 2,000, 1,000, 0 — '50 '60 '70 '80 '90
Source: U.S. Dept. of Labor

1978
Legal gambling begins in Atlantic City

1976
Passage of state income tax

Housing market rockets
Median sales prices of existing single-family homes, in thousands
- New Jersey
- U.S.
$150, 100, 50, 0 — '65 '70 '75 '80 '85 '88
Source: National Assoc. of Realtors, Rutgers U.

GIANTS STADIUM

Cities suffer, then start back
Salaried employment, in thousands
- 1989
- 1980
- 1970
- 1960
- 1950
225, 200, 150, 100, 50, 0 — Camden Jersey City Newark Trenton
Source: N.J. Dept. of Labor

1970
Gov. Cahill endorses sports complex idea

1967
The Star-Ledger calls for creation of stadium in Meadowlands

Job development
In millions of jobs
New York City
5.0, 4.0, 3.0, 2.0, 1.0 — Northern N.J.
'60 '65 '70 '75 '80 '85 '90
Source: Regional Plan Assoc.

EXACT CHANGE

State government grows
Expenditures, in millions
$622, $54, $99, $89, $868, $800, $611, $605
1961
Education, Welfare, Highways, Debt service, Other
$7,523, $6,481
1989
Source: Data Resources

1947
New state constitution gives the governor additional powers

1950s
Development of suburbs saps power of inner city political machines

Population shifts Charts show population by county from 1940 to 1990, in thousands
1,000, 500, 0 — Atlantic Bergen Burlington Camden Cape May Cumberland Essex Gloucester Hudson Hunterdon Mercer Middlesex Monmouth Morris Ocean Passaic Salem Somerset Sussex Union Warren

1985 surveys found New Jerseyans more positive about their state than about their municipality or neighborhood, a marked reversal from earlier trends. The Newark Star-Ledger *graphically depicted its notion of the modern roots of change in the state in this April 7, 1991, illustration. Drawing by Frank Cecala; courtesy* Newark Star-Ledger.

17

In the nineteenth century German scholars developed two different explanation for historical events. The first has been referred to as the "great man" theory, the view that individuals, particularly outstanding men, have had a direct effect on the past. Without Alexander the Great, Napoleon, or George Washington, the world would have been a different place. The second argued that impersonal "forces" (such as, for example, capitalism and control over the means of production) determine the path mankind has followed. Biography, as some of the preceding essays have shown, has been influenced by both sets of ideas: it either envisions its subjects as people who move societies forward or as people who exemplify their times.

Similarly, Gerald Pomper's concluding chapter from *The Political State of New Jersey* (1986) can be considered from these two perspectives. Pomper claimed that New Jersey has undergone numerous profound alterations since 1965 for two main reasons. First, the structure of the government was significantly modified by the Constitution of 1947 and subsequent revisions to the document in 1966. These changes, which gave increased power to the governor and a more active role to the courts, triggered in turn a series of other developments. Second, voters acted independently and political candidates ran on their own initiative; parties correspondingly played a less determining role. But most important, Pomper has argued, particular individuals played critical roles in changing the state. Specific judges and governors stood out as leaders; what they did and said made a difference.

Did changes in the structure of state government or the rise to power of new and talented leaders have a demonstrably greater effect on New Jersey's recent history? Could the two factors have worked together? Before 1947 New Jersey's constitutions of 1776 and 1844 created weak governors; few who held that office stand out with the exceptions of William Livingston, who served during the American Revolution, and Woodrow Wilson, who went on to become president. But since the 1947 constitution, a number of prominent governors have emerged, such as Richard Hughes, Brendan Byrne, and Thomas Kean.

Exactly what are some of the changes that have occurred in New Jersey over the past quarter-century? Has the state's sense of identity become clearer? Has the environment become cleaner? And how has the relationship between local and state governments, the tax system, and educational facilities changed?

Pomper has emphasized institutional and individual leaders as significant in the process of change, but he has also cited the importance of "new patterns of culture" and economic development. Cultural changes, according to Pomper, include a reduction of party loyalty and a related increase of independent voters, the use of new campaign techniques, and the proliferation of interest groups willing to hire lobbyists and march on Trenton, all of which has greatly altered how politicians operate in New Jersey. And the state's economy has turned increasingly from industry to service jobs and from urban locales to the suburbs and the countryside beyond. At one time the state assisted business by building roads and identifying suitable locations. Now it is concerned with controlling pollution, fostering new technology, and providing an educated workforce, actions that do not always immediately benefit existing businesses. In what other ways has the role of the state government changed to meet and cope with new economic developments?

New Jersey's "identity crisis" may not have disappeared entirely, its ethnic and racial diversity may occasionally cause problems, its aging population may make the "generation gap" more pronounced, and increasing economic differences (the separation of rich and poor) may have geographic dimensions (suburb and city). In addition, political power is diffused among levels of government and between the governor, the legislature, the courts, and interest groups. What, aside from strong leaders, might alleviate these problems?

This last article was written by a political scientist. Historians avoid dealing with the present, preferring some perspective on events. Does what happened in the last few years make a difference for the future? What type of governor has James Florio been? Was Pomper's optimism justified? From a longer, historical perspective, how, in the end, has New Jersey's past brought it to its present, and what actions does its past suggest for its future?

Suggested Readings

Laccetti, Silvio R., ed. *New Jersey Profiles in Public Policy.* Palisades Park, N.J., 1990.

Mappen, Mark. "The Best and the Worst Governors." In *Jerseyana: The Underside of New Jersey History.* New Brunswick, N.J., 1992. 222–31.

Stellhorn, Paul A., and Michael J. Birkner, eds. *The Governors of New Jersey, 1664–1974: Biographical Essays.* Trenton, N.J., 1982.

Studies by the Eagleton Institute at Rutgers University and articles in the *Newark Star Ledger, Trenton Times,* the Sunday New Jersey section of the *New York Times, New Jersey Monthly* Magazine, and *New Jersey Reporter* provide perspective on the state's recent history.

◆ ◆ ◆ ◆ ◆ ◆

The Political State of New Jersey: Conclusion

Gerald M. Pomper

When Governor Richard Hughes sought reelection in 1965, New Jersey was an unimpressive state. To visitors, its most prominent feature was the turnpike, which took them past the foul pig farms of Secaucus, the smoking refineries of Elizabeth, and the empty rural stretches below Camden. To residents, the state government was but a distant presence. Trenton gave little to its constituents by way of services or funds, but then it also asked little by way of taxes or political participation.

To recall New Jersey only two decades ago is to remember what was absent rather than to regret what has been lost. Consider the simple use of leisure. In 1965, Newark's crowded residents did not spend summer weekends at Round Valley, because the dam and recreation area were still undeveloped. No fans cheered major league athletic teams in meadowlands that provided only a corridor for travelers en route to watch the Yankees or Giants or Knicks or Rangers. Ocean swimmers either would find beaches on the New Jersey shore closed to nonresidents or they would have to pay significant fees to enjoy the sand and surf. Nature lovers could wander through the primitive Pinelands, but no state controls existed to prevent the eventual loss of this rich botanical life and these quiet rivers to suburban sprawl. Atlantic

City was little more than a museum, its street names reminding visitors of Monopoly games, and its annual Miss America contest a monument to the eroding model of female triviality.

In political life as well, the state was more of a geographical description than a civic commonwealth. To paraphrase Gertrude Stein, in New Jersey there was no "there" there. The sacrosanct principle of home rule left communities largely free to determine the degree of their commitment to public education, to compete for industrial development, to use zoning ordinances to exclude new residents with "undesirable" incomes or color, to foul their neighbors' water and air. Citizens were regularly reminded of their local interests by high property taxes, but the state's limited role was disguised by a revenue system that asked individuals to make only indirect contributions to the state when they bought gasoline or liquor or cigarettes. Altogether, in 1965, the state spent only $182 for governmental services for each New Jerseyan.

Politicians themselves literally stayed at home. Public careers were founded on strong county parties whose power was reinforced by strong voter loyalties to their locally dominant Republican or Democratic organizations. Legislators came to Trenton usually only once a week and concluded their business quickly enough to spend their nights at home. They left Trenton governmentally stunted, without significant legislative staff, without long-term leaders, and with only a limited executive bureaucracy.

How different is New Jersey in 1986, as Governor Thomas Kean begins his second term. In seeking recreation, New Jerseyans now camp in the mountains; swim at the shore; crowd the Meadowlands' stadium, racetrack, and Byrne arena; walk through the Pinelands reserve; and gamble at Atlantic City casinos. These new opportunities did not just happen; they have come through a series of concerted state actions. Reversing the historic deference to localism, the government in Trenton, with the approval of the state's voters, created regional authorities and enacted legislation to promote a vision of the more general interest.

The same assertion of a state interest, rather than a local interest, is evident in many other areas of public policy as well. The historic decision of the state supreme court in *Robinson v. Cahill* revived the long-dormant issue of the state's responsibility to provide a "thorough and efficient" education for every child regardless of the wealth of his or her community. Though implementation of improved educational opportunity has trailed behind principle, the result still has been the state's assumption of a large share of the public schools' costs.

Similarly in economic development, decisions are still made principally by private interests, but these actions are now supplemented and occasionally guided by state efforts to promote the conversion of New Jersey to a center for high technology. Housing patterns are no longer determined only by the wishes of builders and the wishes of municipalities: a state concern for lower-income families also must be heeded. Moreover, New Jersey has learned the basic environmental lesson that even its small portion of the earth must be considered as an interdependent ecological system. Upriver communities can no longer discharge their wastes upon downriver shores, and upwind cities can no longer pollute the lungs of their downwind neighbors. Undergirding all of these new policy directions is a revised financial foundation. With each paycheck and each purchase New Jerseyans are instructed that the state government exists and now is responsible for half of their total nonfederal tax bill.

The Emergence of State Politics

New Jersey has become a state indeed. Although one of the original members of the Union, there is some truth in the observation that New Jersey did not emerge as a full political entity until the last few decades, and that it might even be considered one of the youngest states in the nation. To be a state means more than having a formal government that issues regulations and more than being represented by a star and a stripe in the national flag. Full statehood also requires the mutual involvement of the citizens and the government: the citizens must be interested in and aware of the activities of their public officials and the government should be concerned about and responsive to popular needs. In this sense, New Jersey is only now reaching political maturity.

The process, however, is not complete. Garden Staters do not yet evidence the state pride or state consciousness of Texans or Iowans; Trenton is still less of a going governmental enterprise than Sacramento or Albany; and most legislators still commute no more than twice a week to the capital. New Jersey is a state of contrasts and ambiguities that evidence its transition from past passivity to modern activity. Moreover, there is no assured destination as New Jersey moves through this transition. The possibilities include a reversion to past patterns, or new fragmentation into different groupings, or further strengthening of the state's new cohesion. Whatever happens in the future, however, will depend at least partly on the factors that have recently changed the character of the state, factors such as changing institutions, new patterns of politics and culture, economic development, and fiscal innovations, as well as the significant influence of individual leaders.

Formal Institutions

Formal governmental institutions do not completely control the realities of politics. They do, however, channel the political process and provide boundaries for what it is possible to achieve. By adopting a new constitution in 1947, New Jersey greatly enlarged these possibilities and provided opportunities for creative leadership.

The new state charter strengthened gubernatorial powers, although no paper document could create the necessary human qualities for real leadership. It permitted two four-year terms (instead of the previous limit of a single three-year tenure), thus facilitating a longer-range view from the executive office. The constitution further enhanced the power of the executive by consolidating the bureaucratic agencies and placing them under the direct control of the governor; by giving the chief executive strong financial powers to prepare the state budget and to delete any specific appropriation; and by arming the governor with the political clout inherent in the conditional veto over legislation.

These bones of a new state constitution, however, still required the muscle and brains of real persons before they could move. Sometimes governors would be content simply to administer the apparatus and to enjoy the pale spotlight that inevitably illuminated the only state official elected by all of New Jersey's voters. Yet all found it necessary to respond in some way to the new expectations for leadership that the 1947 charter created.

In the judiciary the effect of constitutional change was even more apparent. The new constitution eliminated overlapping and competitive jurisdictions and consolidated the legal system under a single hierarchy. Immediately the state supreme court established itself as a leader among the appellate benches of the nation. The court improved legal administration itself and made criminal law. Then it turned to basic policy questions, focusing public and legislative attention on the quality of education, the environment, and housing opportunities. Here again, individual leadership was critical. While the modern state charter provided opportunities for judicial impact, the justices themselves had to make the most of them.

The legislature was the institution least affected by the new structure of government. This is because, when it established the 1947 constitutional convention, the legislature provided multiple defenses against any alteration of its own most treasured feature—representation by one senator for each of the twenty-one counties. County equality had been the norm since the nineteenth century, when a rural New Jersey was divided along north-south lines. In the twentieth century, even as the state became more urban and suburban and a variety of social and ethnic differences created divisions among its residents, the old equal county representation remained, preserving the power of the rural counties in the legislature. Institutional change was limited to increasing the term of legislators and making their election more coincident with that of the governor. By refusing to change its representational base, and by neglecting to alter internal procedures, the legislature remained the least modern branch of the state government and the most severely malapportioned in the nation. Its archaic features consequently hamstrung the modernization of state policy for a long time.

Despite the legislature's reluctance, however, it too eventually changed under the U.S. Supreme Court's mandate of representation on the basis of one person, one vote. In 1966, a new and limited constitutional convention completed the renovation of state government. Counties no longer had direct political representation in Trenton. Instead, legislators in both senate and assembly had to be elected from legislative districts of equal population.

The effects of this change were not immediately obvious, for many Trenton veterans continued to win election in the new districts. With their replacement, however, older customs of the legislature began to pass. Senators and assembly members were less prone to see themselves as the emissaries of their county parties. Acting more as individuals, they might concern themselves only with local interests, but they also learned that they could not gain their ends without considering those of other constituencies as well. The legislature became more professional and more institutionalized. Committee specialization made the members more expert, more aggressive, and more involved in the general problems of the state. Leadership no longer rotated automatically, allowing strong personalities to develop experience and accumulate chips for trading. Staff was hired, providing continuity and expertise in policy-making. And the legislators, sometimes surprisingly and always haltingly, found themselves capable of dealing with major public issues.

The New Politics

Aided by these new institutional structures, new patterns of politics also developed in New Jersey and furthered the emergence of the state as a distinct political entity. The changing character of the political parties is illustrative. Earlier, party organizations had been isolated and largely self-sufficient county baronies, engaged with government only when necessary for their own ends, but largely able to fend for themselves. Frank Hague, Democratic boss of Hudson County, or Frank Farley, Republican boss of Atlantic County, ruled communities that were economically viable and politically secure against competition by the opposition party. Patronage jobs were wanted and plentiful; legislators served at the sufferance of the boss; and governors waited in line for nomination to a weak office.

This political situation has changed considerably. The county and local governments now need state assistance, not neglect. Party organizations need the help of state leaders and even of the state party apparatus to raise funds, to develop campaigns, and to defend policy positions. Patronage still exists but the opportunities at the local levels are limited, while the best-paying and most influential political appointments are controlled by the state executive. Nominees for the governorship are no longer beholden to county leaders. Able to raise their own funds, either privately or through public financing, and able to appeal directly to the voters through the media, they have less need to win approval from county organizations. Instead, county organizations seek to clutch at the short coattails of popular politicians, such as Bill Bradley or Tom Kean. Even legislative candidates, now running in districts that do not follow county lines, have less reason to heed the directions of any would-be political boss.

The source of these political changes is to be found in the behavior of the voters, who are more independent and less loyal to their traditional parties than formerly. The national trend to party independence has been not only evident but exaggerated in New Jersey. Until recently, only half of the state's electorate would spontaneously declare itself committed to the Republicans or Democrats, in contrast to at least three-fifths of the electorate in the entire United States. The Garden State appears to have the right social conditions to breed independence—suburban communities and high transiency. Furthermore, without statewide newspapers or television stations voters also lack the consistent cues and arguments that promote long-term loyalties.

The weakening of county organizations and the loosening of party loyalties have provided new opportunities for politicians with different—and sometimes broader—outlooks. Indeed, changed politics has required that politicians adapt to new circumstances. Strong local parties, when they existed, assured candidates a solid base of support, but also exerted a degree of discipline on these candidates through their control of nominations. When the parties weakened, political aspirants were freed from the discipline, but they had to rely more on their own resources. If voters will no longer respond to the call for party loyalty, then office seekers must invoke personal loyalties. If local canvassing no longer effectively mobilizes the electorate, then media advertisements, direct mail, and candidate-centered strategies may do the trick. If the party's coffers are empty, election funds can be obtained from individual contributors and from the proliferating political action committees. These new political techniques already dominate statewide elections and many races for Congress, and are likely soon to affect even the state legislature.

In this altered environment, the party organizations, in their own self-interest, will further the trend toward statewide polities. A more volatile electorate requires greater campaign effort and greater campaign spending, beyond the resources available locally. This increased cost of election encourages local party units to raise and spend funds more centrally. As new campaigning techniques become more prevalent, the parties will seek economies of scale in the use of polls, media advertising, and direct mail solicitation.

Similarly, the popularity of a particular gubernatorial candidate will now affect outcomes in races for freeholder or mayor. The new residents of Leisure Village, for instance, may know nothing about Monroe Township's politics, but their votes may well be influenced by a Brendan Byrne or a Tom Kean, who is responsible for old-age assistance programs. Such appeals give local candidates and organizations a selfish reason to be more concerned about the qualifications and policies of persons at the head of the ticket.

Gubernatorial nominations evidence the party organizations' changed relationship to statewide politics. In the past, these nominations were decided by bargaining among powerful county leaders and only ratified later in primary elections. This tight control was destroyed in the 1970s, when individualist campaigning—aided by state funding—led to open contests, prolific spending, party splits, and even to challenges to incumbent governors, such as Cahill and Byrne.

Today parties are taking at least halting steps towards creating mechanisms to live in the more open environment of gubernatorial nominations. Proposed amendments to the election finance law would decrease potential candidates' access to public funding, and thus limit the number of aspirants. In 1985 Republicans rallied without dissent behind the reelection candidacy of Governor Kean. Democrats still had a primary contest, but party leaders were able to discourage some possible aspirants and to limit competition to three significant contenders. Efforts are also under way to develop a system of party endorsements for statewide candidates through pre-primary conventions. With a broad popular base, such conventions might provide a new means of uniting the parties.

Interest groups also affect New Jersey's shifting politics. Certainly the presence and influence of these groups in Trenton is not new—railroads have lobbied for profitable concessions, teachers have pressed for collective bargaining powers, and businesses have urged low corporate taxation. Nor is there anything novel in the self-interested concerns of these groups. What is new about interest groups in New Jersey is their scope, their methods, and, to some extent, their increased statewide focus. There are more groups represented in Trenton, occupying more buildings on State Street, making more demands, and providing more grist for the legislative and executive mills than there used to be. As recently as 10 years ago, only 165 lobbyists, representing 175 organizations, had officially registered with the state attorney general. By 1985 the numbers had grown to 450 lobbyists working on behalf of nearly 900 organizations.[1] In a mutual interaction, the greater activities of the state stimulate more group efforts, and the increased activities of the groups provide more work for state government.

Not only are there more groups, but they have a wider range

of interests as well. Economic and business interests predominate, but there also are associations to promote the needs of the handicapped, to permit or to prohibit the use of bear traps in state forests, to provide aid to cities, to advance the demands of dental associations or professors. As more and more varied interests become involved, lobbying methods become more diverse. Groups no longer confine themselves to lobbying legislators in the corridors of the State House, but now also attempt to use the resources of numbers and money. The legislature frequently endures mass lobbying efforts or mass pilgrimages to Trenton, as large groups converge on the capital to press their demands. Many interests have formed political action committees to collect funds that are contributed to the election campaigns of friendly legislators. Public participation in politics now extends beyond voting to include active electoral mobilization and financial contributions. Even though the contending interests are concerned with relatively narrow objectives, these activities teach New Jerseyans that they have a personal stake in Trenton.

Some groups focus more directly than others on state concerns. There are not only such established associations as the New Jersey Chamber of Commerce, the state AFL-CIO, and the League of Women Voters, but also temporary alliances between various groups and prominent individuals. They all seek changes in a broad range of policies, often through public referenda on bond issues or constitutional amendments. Efforts of this kind have urged state government to broaden the tax base, increase spending on public and higher education, and develop the Green Acres conservation program. These activities promote the growing state awareness by New Jersey's residents.

The Emergence of New Jersey

As New Jersey's politics has changed, so has its political culture. For the most part, the underlying culture of a community such as a state is more fundamental than the decisions of its transient public officials. Reflecting the state's traditions, politicians in New Jersey have exemplified an individualist culture in which professional specialists pursue particular interests.[2] But cultures can be changed, usually by external occurrences, but also sometimes from the internal promptings of politicians.

Political Culture

Political culture includes at least three aspects: identification, expectations, and support.[3] New Jersey has been changing in all three respects. There is a greater sense of identity with the state as a political entity. More activity is expected of the people in Trenton. While New Jerseyans remain skeptical of the honesty and competence of their government officials, they seem to be offering more positive support in recent years.

In a remarkably short period of eight years, according to surveys taken between 1977 and 1985, New Jersey has overcome its feelings of inferiority. Four out of five residents now find the Garden State a good or excellent place to live. This level of satisfaction is not unique in the United States, but New Jerseyans at least are no longer *less* satisfied than those living in the rest of the country. That fact is itself remarkable in a state where residence has sometimes drawn the scorn once accorded the vice-presidency: "It isn't a crime exactly. You can't be sent to jail for it, but it's a kind of a disgrace. It's like writing anonymous letters."[4]

The improved self-image of New Jersey parallels a happier view of its state government. Both the governor and the legislature are now evaluated more positively by citizens than in the past. Moreover citizens now give a higher rating to the state than to either their own municipalities or their particular neighborhoods. Previously, the local areas were preferred.[5]

External or nonpolitical factors partially explain this change of attitude. The advent of major league sports, the development of tourism and casino gambling, and economic development have all contributed to the state's enhanced self-image. Yet, being nonpolitical in nature, these causes cannot fully explain political effects. Even winning sports teams (and New Jersey lacks champions) are not necessarily sources of civic satisfaction. Gambling successes and good jobs provide private rewards, but do not in themselves produce public gratification.

Rather an explanation for the marked alteration in New Jersey's political culture must be sought in an understanding of changing political activity. The state has reason to be proud of its leadership in various areas of public policy. Long before environmental protection became a national concern, New Jersey was taking action to control air pollution. It has gone on to protect the other critical resources of seashore and water. In the Pinelands Act the state reserved a fifth of its entire area from unrestricted development, a planning innovation unmatched by any other industrial state. When the national government was reducing its commitment to education, the state drastically altered its tax structure and attempted (although not yet successfully) to equalize schooling for all children. In electoral politics, New Jersey has pioneered in the public financing of election campaigns and in techniques such as postcard registration to increase voter participation.

Through such actions, New Jersey's political leaders have done more than just reflect the state's culture; they have also helped to transform it. In the process they have been civic educators, teaching the state's people that they do have a collective identity and a responsibility to the polity beyond their individual needs and particular interests. A succession of governors from Hughes to Byrne to Kean have taught the need for state programs in transportation, education, and environmental protection. Legislators such as Assembly Speaker William Hamilton assumed the responsibility for restructuring the state's tax system and then went back to their constituents and justified the state's new role. Appointed administrators, aided by unidentified but thoughtful civil servants, have developed new policy goals and techniques. Chief justices such as Arthur Vanderbilt and Joseph Weintraub instructed the electorate in the elements of legal and social justice. These and other leaders have altered the political culture, and the community life, of New Jersey.

Economic and Fiscal Change

Paralleling these political changes have been developments in the state's private and public economy. Policy actions depend ultimately on the resources generated by nongovernmental production of goods and services. State governments can neither create money nor borrow beyond their means. Government, however, can affect the uses and distribution of the state's economic resources—and it has done so in New Jersey.

The dominant feature of the state's economic development over the last four decades has been the shift of jobs and wealth out of the cities and into the suburbs and rural areas. The principal lines of communication are no longer the railroads that link Trenton and Newark, but the interstate highways that bring new offices to Morris County and new residents to Monmouth County, as well as the computer and satellite networks that free industry from fixed geographical locations.

This dispersion of industry has stimulated state action in both urban and other areas. The Newark riots of 1967 were only the most dramatic manifestation of the cities' loss of jobs, declining schools, and shrinking tax base. The decline of urban prosperity created needs that could only be met by state or federal action. The state government responded by promoting economic development in the cities, providing direct revenue aid, and even by paying some of the salaries of local firefighters. While these measures have not halted urban decline, they have made the existence of Trenton far more visible and important in these localities and in the lives of their citizens.

In the more prosperous areas economic change has also promoted state involvement, although for different reasons. The state has been active in creating the infrastructure for growth. At first, New Jersey's government was largely concerned with providing physical facilities, such as highways, or aiding businesses in finding suitable locations. A broader role has developed more recently. The state is now concerned as well with providing the human resources and the social conditions required for economic development—conditions such as education, technical research facilities, and recreation. It is also attending to the consequences of development, especially pollution and toxic wastes.

Inherently, these are state rather than local activities. High-speed highways are not limited by municipal and county boundaries. As industry extends along these highways, Trenton must promote regional planning, regulation, and fiscal equity. Similarly, only the state can control the ill effects of chemical dumps or provide the large funding and the large population base required for advanced technology research centers and outstanding higher education.

Economic development and its political response also affect the consciousness of New Jersey's citizens. New Jersey is no longer a state typified by the bedroom suburban commuter whose work and lifestyle is centered in New York or Philadelphia. The overwhelming proportion of residents both live and work within the state, and they are joined by increasing numbers who commute into New Jersey. As she drives to work along Interstate 80, the programmer from Leonia sees not only her local streets, but parts of her state. As he looks for housing, the transferred worker has new choices made available by real estate development guided by state policy. As increased state funding improves educational opportunities as well as the visibility of Rutgers, more high school graduates attend their own state university. Through hundreds of experiences like these, New Jerseyans develop more awareness—and perhaps more pride—in the commonwealth.

Certainly, the new fiscal system promotes a greater state awareness. Taxes are important not only for the revenues they raise, but also because they teach taxpayers about the relative size and differing roles of various levels of government. As the property tax declines in its relative impact, less attention need be given to the local governments and school districts; as sales and income taxes increase, state government must be given more heed.

This state's residents are surely no more eager than other Americans to pay taxes. Yet, even as many sister states imposed spending limitations on government, New Jersey adopted an income tax and then raised both the sales and the new income levies. As the nation debates federal tax revision, it may well find a model in New Jersey, which has a simple income tax including mildly progressive rates and virtually no loopholes. These fiscal changes were made politically feasible by the imposition of budget caps, which promised relief from local taxes and from rising government expenditures at all levels.

The use of the caps illustrates the changed focus of government in New Jersey. The law makes the state government appear both prudent and generous. School districts and municipalities are held to small percentage increases in their spending, and both are subject to strict supervision by state agencies. Trenton's spending, on the other hand, had been statutorily limited only by the growth of the state's economic base. This restraint was so inefficacious, however, that it lapsed without controversy. The state is now legally unrestricted in its spending increases, even as it maintains restraints on the lower levels of government.

The state also generously distributes property tax rebates. While these checks have sometimes been timed to aid the governor's personal standing, their greater significance is that they contrast a benefit received from the state with a cost imposed by the locality. They reinforce the lesson that New Jerseyans have been learning for twenty years—state government is important.

Fragmentation and Uncertainty

New Jersey's recent state activism is not a certain harbinger of future innovation. Indeed, for all of the changes that have taken place, the future of the state is still uncertain. Even with new revenue sources and the assumption of new responsibilities, New Jersey's state government spends only an average amount of money for each citizen and still ranks below the national norm in expenditures on some vital functions including education. Similarly, even as they display new state pride, citizens have but overcome past feelings of inferiority; they are yet to be convinced of the superiority of life in the Garden State. The glass of state achievement is just half full; it is also half empty.

Change is a rule of life for a state as much as for individuals. New Jersey now seeks to resolve its collective identity crisis, and thereby shows the contrasts and strains that inevitably accompany such periods of transition. The state may revert to past political patterns, to institutional incohesion, citizen cynicism, functional failures. But the state may also continue its recent movement toward self-confidence and achievement. The future will depend on leadership and on the ability and effort of politicians to chart policies and to convince the public.

These leaders still face obstacles. Fragmentation persists as a major characteristic of New Jersey politics, as it does in American government generally. In fact, some recent developments have increased the divisions in the state, making it even more difficult to achieve coherent public policies. These divisions are evident both in the social structure and the formal institutions of the state.

Ethnic pluralism, for instance, has been characteristic of New Jersey from the days of the first Dutch and Swedish settlers. That pluralism has resisted the homogenization of the "melting pot" and is likely to complicate political action. Political ingenuity will be needed to build coalitions among past powers such as the Irish, the Italian-Americans (now the largest population group in the state) and other emerging factions.

Blacks have become a visible and self-conscious force also, especially within the Democratic party. Governing many of the state's larger cities and mobilizing an enlarged electorate, they demonstrated their growing importance in the impressive votes gained by Kenneth Gibson in the 1981 and 1985 gubernatorial primaries. Bloc voting by blacks, however, can complicate the necessary building of coalitions either within the Democratic party or with Republicans. Hispanics are another significant ethnic group, but their impact has been limited by competition with blacks. Moreover, Hispanics are not always united, since there are considerable political differences between, for example,

Cubans and Puerto Ricans.

New Jersey also has a growing generation gap. This state has a large older population and is second only to Florida overall in the median age. At the same time, the state and its high-technology industries are attracting more young people, particularly professionals. Age differences can lead to policy differences. Senior citizens will be more enthusiastic about the allocation of casino revenues for aid to the elderly, while Yuppies will be more favorable toward educational spending. The interests of these groups will sometimes clash directly as in the recent outlawing of mandatory retirement.

Economic differences among groups, however, are likely to remain the most fundamental, and could become significantly magnified. As the economy changes, the social division grows between the cities—poor, aging, and based on declining manufacturing—and the suburbs—wealthy, developing, and based on expanding technology. Of course, class differences have always existed in New Jersey, but in large cities these classes at least saw one another on the streets and in the schools. The new economy separates classes along geographical lines. The same highways that keep traffic moving around the state also allow travelers to avoid the unpleasant sights of urban decay. The same computers that make the home an office, isolate the office worker and insulate the citizen from an awareness of others and of their common lives.

Political institutions are meant to bridge these differences between ethnic groups, generations, geographical areas, and social classes. New Jersey has begun to develop such unifying mechanisms, but barriers remain strong and perhaps invulnerable. Thus, the tradition of home rule even when subordinated continues to influence state politics. The number of children decreases, but 611 school districts maintain their independence, even if some are no more than paper constituencies. The spread of industry along highway networks calls for regional planning, but municipalities continue to compete for the best ratables while avoiding the housing development envisaged by the *Mount Laurel* decision.

Crisis has sometimes forced action. The most obvious example is the change in the fiscal and school systems which followed the decision in *Robinson v. Cahill*. Though the legislature had enacted a new school law in 1975, the lawmakers could not agree on funding it. As Richard Hughes, then Chief Justice remembered, "They dilly-dallied along, and they postponed and postponed." Finally, they faced both the demands of the governor and the pressure of school closure by the courts. Then, but only then, "the Legislature realized they were in real trouble, and they passed an income tax 10 days later."[6] New Jersey's state government cannot be considered effective if it is able to act only in such dire circumstances.

Paradoxically, as the separate institutions of New Jersey's government become stronger, there may be a decline in the overall effectiveness of the state. To some extent, the dynamism of New Jersey under the new constitution resulted from a practical weakness in the theoretical system of the checks and balances. The governor's considerable authority was not matched by an equally strong legislature. Therefore, his control over the budget and final authority over legislation through the conditional veto was not threatened by a vigorous opposition on the other side of the State House. The judiciary, too, could innovate because it could eventually persuade or push the legislature into following its lead in new policy directions such as school finance and land use. Moreover, the executive and judicial branches were sometimes allied against threats to their autonomy from the legislature, as in disputes over the governor's appointive power or bureaucratic regulation.

As the legislature has modernized, it has developed the power to balance more effectively the actions of the governor and the judiciary. In the long run, this change increases the prospect for effective statewide policy. In the short run, however, the legislators' proper concern for their own districts and their favorite interests can retard coherent policy-making. In responding to *Mount Laurel*, for example, the common reaction has been to seek local relief of the burden of low-cost housing, not to formulate a broad and effective policy. In dealing with the budget deficit of 1982 and the budget surplus of 1985 alike, most legislators have been more prone to defend pet appropriations than to look toward a long-range fiscal plan for the state. This emphasis on immediate needs is matched by the executive's effort to dominate policy disputes.

The inherent localism of the legislature and its inevitable clashes with the separate executive branch are reinforced by underlying tendencies in electoral politics. Candidate-centered campaigns provide few incentives for cooperation among legislators and build no bridges across the formal institutional divisions. The present changed and centrifugal environment of politics rather encourages independence by officeholders and intervention by interest groups. With parties still weak, political action committees become more important. Their role is most obviously illustrated in campaign finance, where the PACs' share of spending rose from 17 percent of all legislative contributions in 1979 to 24 percent in 1981 and then to 39 percent in 1983.

Increased spending in elections is the most visible manifestation of the growth of interest groups in the state and is itself a testament to the new power of state government. The direct effect of their activity, however, is a further fracturing of power as each group seeks its particular goals. Broad visions of the public interest arise only accidentally from the clashes of these groups. Achieving such vision is made more difficult in the absence of effective statewide media, which are unlikely to appear in the foreseeable future.

Dispersal of power results as well, ironically, from New Jersey's policy innovations like the campaign finance law. This legislation has made party nominations more open and campaigning more honest. Yet, at the same time, it has restricted the parties, which are the major potential agent for coherent government, in the choice of their most visible leader, the candidate for governor. The law's limits on expenditures have also promoted a reliance on media campaigning. This trend may result in more telegenic candidates, but it may also lessen the chances of electing chief executives who can effectively build support for their policy goals.

The state has also been creative in finding novel devices to raise funds and promote policy goals, devices such as lotteries, casino gambling, and regional authorities. Each of these techniques, however, builds its own rigidity into the state budget or removes an area of policy from direct political control. The long-term danger is that too many sources of revenue will be reserved for too many favored functions and that too many decisions will be made by autonomous authorities. Inevitably, there will be limits to what the state can do and how much its citizens will pay. At that point the state government may find itself confined in bonds of its own making.

New Jersey's Future

New Jersey now gets much from its state government and demands much. The state's future problem may be that its citizens will expect more than either Trenton or any state agency can deliver. In the past state politics was less significant, but it was also easier to manage. Today, being more important, state politics is more difficult to control and direct.

In the past, there were relatively few active players in the game of New Jersey politics and government. Limited policy initiatives could be undertaken if there was agreement among the state's few leaders—the governor, major corporate executives, and the most powerful county bosses. Now, there are more initiatives but also more players. Mass media observe state government more carefully; party discipline is more difficult to achieve; and many interests must be consulted and conciliated. The politics of small groups has been replaced by the politics of participation, and this is more complicated and often more frustrating, even if it may also be more significant.

Leadership remains the key factor. It was not inevitable that New Jersey would recognize its problems with education, the environment, and economic development[7] or that it would increase its taxation in order to attempt solutions. No provision of the constitution compelled Richard Hughes to broaden the tax base or William Cahill to foster medical education or Brendan Byrne to preserve open space or Thomas Kean to upgrade the public schools. These and other actions followed from visions and choices deliberately made by these governors and by other political leaders.

Different choices will confront different leaders in the coming years. As the federal government restricts its activities, New Jersey and her sister states will be facing new needs and additional demands. An aging population requires more expensive health care, and a more complex society requires innovative education. A slack economy worsens social distress, just as a booming economy worsens environmental dangers and housing shortages. Citizens will continue to debate the equity of taxation, to invoke governmental power in their own interests, and to define their common identity.

Public officials, whether hesitant or eager, inevitably will shape New Jersey's future. They may respond creatively and achieve long-term successes. They will certainly make errors, produce unexpected consequences, and sometimes delay until crises impend. They will surely need to be people different from their predecessors. They will need to develop skills in media presentation and public presentation and rely less on techniques of individual negotiation and personal persuasion.

One element, however, will remain constant. In New Jersey as elsewhere successful politics will require leaders who have both "passion and perspective," who understand that "man would not have attained the possible unless time and again he had reached out for the impossible."[8] At times, New Jersey has had such leaders; it will need more in the future.

Notes

1. The earlier figures are from Philip Burch, "Interest Groups," in *Politics in New Jersey*, Alan Rosenthal and John Blydenburgh, eds., (New Brunswick: Rutgers University, Eagleton Institute of Politics, 1975), 83. The recent figures are from the Attorney-General's Office of Legislative Information (1985).

2. Daniel Elazar, *American Federalism: A View from the States*, 2nd ed. (New York: Crowell, 1972), 84–126.

3. Alan Rosenthal, "On Analyzing States," in *The Political Life of the American States*, Alan Rosenthal and Maureen Moakley, eds. (New York: Praeger, 1984), 13–17.

4. Finley Peter Dunne, *The World of Mr. Dooley*, Louis Filler, ed. (New York: Collier Books, 1962), 50.

5. The data are summarized in Figures 1.2 and 1.3 and Tables 1.1 and 1.2 [not included]. See also the discussion by Matthew Kauffman, "New Jersey Looks at Itself," *New Jersey Reporter*, 14 (March 1985): 13–17.

6. Virginia D. Sederis, "Mr. Hughes Remembers," *New Jersey Reporter*, 14 (April 1985): 17.

7. Stephen A. Salmore and Barbara Salmore, *Candidates, Parties and Campaigns: Electoral Politics in America* (Washington: Congressional Quarterly Press, 1985), 201.

8. Max Weber, *Politics as a Vocation* (Philadelphia: Fortress Press, 1965; originally published in 1919), 55.

Index

Printed in the United States
23954LVS00006BB/70-84

9 780813 532677